# The Workers' State

**Pitt Series in Russian and East European Studies**

Jonathan Harris, Editor

# The Workers' State

## INDUSTRIAL LABOR AND THE MAKING OF SOCIALIST HUNGARY, 1944–1958

**Mark Pittaway**

University of Pittsburgh Press

Published by the University of Pittsburgh Press, Pittsburgh, Pa., 15260
Copyright © 2012, University of Pittsburgh Press
Manufactured in the United States of America
Printed on acid-free paper

10 9 8 7 6 5 4 3 2 1

Library of Congress Cataloging-in-Publication Data

Pittaway, Mark, 1939–2000.
 The workers' state : industrial labor and the making of socialist Hungary, 1944–1958 / Mark
Pittaway.
    p. cm. — (Pitt series in Russian and East European studies)
 Includes bibliographical references and index.
 ISBN 978-0-8229-4420-1 (hardcover : alk. paper)
 1. Working class—Hungary—History—20th century. 2. Labor—Hungary—History—20th
century. 3. Hungary—Social conditions—1945–1989. 4. Hungary—Social policy. I. Title.
 HD8420.5.P58 2012

 305.5'620943909045—dc23                                            2012022369

# Contents

# Foreword
## Nigel Swain

MARK PITTAWAY DIED at the tragically young age of thirty-nine not long after he had submitted the manuscript for this book to the University of Pittsburgh Press. He first discussed the project with me in the summer of 1992, and, as his friend and former teacher, I undertook to act as his literary executor and charged myself with the task of seeing this book and any other completed manuscripts through to publication.

Although the original insights behind *The Workers' State* began to coalesce twenty years ago, Mark's vision matured in the intervening years. While keeping his focus on labor within a socialist economy, he developed an interest in legitimacy and the process by which regimes establish and maintain their legitimacy. His scholarship broke new ground in establishing convincingly that Hungarian workers, even at the highpoint of Stalinism in the 1950s, were not the undifferentiated mass of totalitarian theory. The working class was stratified along (at least) age and gender lines and, equally important, able to secure victories over management in its day-to-day workplace struggles. All of these original insights remain in the book, but they are now located within the wider context of strategies adopted by the regime to establish legitimacy in the face of working-class expectations. In order to do this, Mark took the story both back in time to 1944 and the end of the war and forward in time to cover both 1956 and post-1956 consolidation. In this expanded vision, we see how the regime established legitimacy, haltingly; how it maintained it tentatively; and how it lost it entirely in 1956, before compromising with a rather different kind of legitimacy.

This book represented for Mark his final word on the Hungarian working class. His focus at the time of his death had switched to producing a monograph from his wide-ranging research project "Making the Cold War Border: Dividing Europe between Austria and Hungary, 1938–1960" (the Borders Project). In this project he examined how the ethnically divided communities in the border regions survived World War II, how the Holocaust was implemented there, and how very different new cold war political orders were established; he sought, that is, to revisit cold war history from a social historical perspective. That project remains unfinished; its book can never be written, although an article from it did appear posthumously in *Past and Present* in May 2012. Nevertheless, many of the materials that he collected for the Borders Project and for this book are held at the Department of Central and East European Studies at the University of Glasgow and available for scholars. Mark's extensive collection of books in Hungarian, together with books in German relating to the Borders Project, is located in Glasgow University's library.

All who have been involved in the publication of this book would agree, I think, that Mark submitted a very clean manuscript. There was very little for me to do. The book went through the standard peer review process, and the two anonymous readers made a very small number of suggestions, which I have tried to address. In doing so, I have restructured and very slightly amended the text in one respect but have made no cuts of substance. I was guided throughout by my knowledge of Mark's wishes or my interpretation of them in the light of his other writings.

I am sure that if Mark had seen the book through to publication himself, he would have added a preface or acknowledged in some other format his gratitude to the many people who have helped him over the years. But the manuscript as submitted to the press contained no such text. I know Mark would have wanted to thank his family (parents Janet and Trevor, sister Karen, brother Neil) for their nurture and support. But I cannot begin to second-guess who else he might have thanked and who perhaps might have been singled out for special mention. A recurrent theme in all of the tributes that were paid to Mark in obituaries and other forums was his generosity as a scholar. He was always open and willing to share his knowledge with others. That openness, I think, worked both ways. He had a voracious appetite for knowledge. He gave of his own freely, and he was equally open to how other people's findings could complement, supplement, or modify his own. He had a vision of a new history of Eastern Europe, one to which he, together with a large community of like-minded scholars, would contribute. I think in Mark's memory it would not be inappropriate for me to thank all those who met with him and discussed, argued, and debated with him at conferences, workshops, and seminars; in coffee houses, *Kneipen, sörözők,* and pubs—all those who helped him develop his historical understanding and mature into the fine scholar that he became before his life was cruelly cut short.

For myself I would like to thank Peter Kracht and Amberle Sherman of the University of Pittsburgh Press for their care, consideration, and understanding in bringing Mark's most important work to the reading public and Eszter Bartha and Sándor Horváth in Hungary and Zsuzsanna Varga in Glasgow for their help checking references.

Nigel Swain
Liverpool
February 2012

# The Workers' State

# Introduction

ON 30 APRIL 1958, while on trial for his life for his role as the president of the Újpest Revolutionary Committee during the turbulent events of October and November 1956, Pál Kósa was asked to explain the sources of his "dissatisfaction" with the social and political order in Hungary during the early 1950s.[1] He responded, as someone "who had always worked with my hands, with my wife working as well, we and our two children often found ourselves in difficult situations." He continued: "I never had the opportunity to express my opinions about the mistakes. . . . In the factory I participated in mass meetings, but they always discussed production, rarely social issues."[2] Despite the attempts of the political department of the Budapest police and the prosecutors to prove that his role in the events was motivated by "counterrevolutionary" ideas, Kósa had been far from unsympathetic either to socialism or to the regime. During the late 1940s, while working as a joiner in one of the largest of Újpest's textile factories, he had joined the Hungarian Communist Party (Magyar Kommunista Párt, or MKP), eventually leaving the shop floor to become a propagandist paid by the Újpest Party Committee in 1947. "At that time," recounted Kósa during a police interview following his arrest in November 1956,

"I spent a lot of time among the workers and I had a good knowledge of the mistakes that were committed during the building of the people's democracy." These he blamed for the creation of a dictatorship over the workers in which "those in leadership positions separated themselves from the masses, and paid more attention to their own welfare, than to solving practical problems. . . . They ran roughshod over internal democracy in the party and in the end could not explain . . . why the state security services arrested many in the party and on factory committees."[3]

Expelled from the party with the consolidation of outright socialist dictatorship in 1948, he spent the early 1950s as a skilled worker and then as an artisan. Propelled by the crowd in October 1956 to a leadership role, he used his authority as a working-class former communist disillusioned with the regime to found the local revolutionary committee in industrial Újpest.[4] Arrested and imprisoned in November 1956 after the arrival of Soviet troops, then indicted for his role in the revolution, he was tried, convicted, and eventually executed in the summer of 1959.[5] While he had been placed at the forefront of the local events of the revolution by the working-class crowd, by the time of his trial and execution, many of the same workers had begun to forget the political goals they had supported in 1956. So silent were they about political demands that party officials were able to write in February 1958 that "in general workers are satisfied with the work of the party and the government," a conclusion that reflected the growing focus by workers on exclusively material issues.[6]

## Legitimacy and the Socialist State

In the months and years that followed the suppression of the 1956 Revolution, representatives of the reconstituted ruling party—the Hungarian Socialist Workers' Party (Magyar Szocialista Munkáspárt, or MSzMP)—were deeply worried by their relationship with industrial workers. In early 1957, party officials commented with dismay that among the thousands who left the western county of Győr-Moson-Sopron for Austria, there were many "workers from traditional working-class families."[7] With the regime's consolidation, party officials underplayed the role and extent of worker participation in the revolution, arguing that the majority simply remained "passive" in the face of "counterrevolutionary" mobilization, but they were worried by the shallowness of their support in industrial communities. They explained this by maintaining that, before 1956, "the working class was primarily disappointed in the party leadership and did not see the party as the true representative of their class."[8] As a result of this concern, the MSzMP placed "improving the relationship between the party and the working masses" and "further increasing the living standards of the working class" at the heart of its program.[9]

While such concern among the apparatus was in part motivated by the desire to buy off the substantial discontent among workers that had been clearly visible during the revolution, it had much deeper roots.[10] The notion of Hungary's postwar state as the natural representative of the country's working class was fundamental to the sense of purpose of many of its leaders; this was apparent in their shock at the breadth of worker participation in the revolution, as many recognized that "the mistakes that were committed, oppositional elements in the factories, the remnants of right-wing social democracy, revisionism, and the spread of nationalist ideology ensured that during the counterrevolution considerable sections of the workforce, especially young workers, took up arms against the people's democracy."[11] The sense of shock, the centrality of the notion of being the representative of the working class to the self-image of the regime, and its desire to repair its shattered links to industrial workers shift focus to consideration of the nature of Hungary's postwar state, the extent and nature of its embeddedness in society, and the sharply contested nature of its legitimacy.

Most analysis of the postwar Hungarian state, and by extension the socialist regimes that came to power at the same time in Hungary's Central and Eastern European neighbors, has assumed not merely the autonomy of the state from society but also its effective dominance over it. State socialism, especially its early phase, has often been interpreted as a period of overbearing restriction in which social actors were subordinated to overriding attempts by the state to direct social process.[12] Increasingly, however, historical research has expanded our awareness of how social actors were able to place limits on and thus to circumscribe state action. This shift in focus from the exploration of the extent of state power toward consideration of the limits of dictatorship has tended to qualify, rather than to challenge directly, notions of state dominance. Furthermore, it has avoided the issue of what was specifically socialist about socialist states and how they were embedded in the societies that they ruled.[13]

Discussion of the socialist state has often concentrated on its despotic nature. It has either focused on the state security agencies and the pervasiveness of political surveillance and repression or, alternatively, on the power exercised by state agencies to deploy considerable coercion and force to effect social transformation. It also assumes—in contrast to much recent writing about states—that the socialist state was a monolithic entity. This work has drawn attention to the state's dual nature. On the one hand, states consist of a concert of institutions that are social actors in their own right, populated by different groups and pursuing agendas that can be both complementary and contradictory. On the other hand, these institutions enter the social realm projecting an appearance of both unity and of being above society. This appearance, or state effect, is produced through the projection of a myth of the state as a unified whole.[14] This state effect is fundamental, for it shapes and is also shaped by what Michael Mann has termed the "infrastructural" power of the state—namely its ability to enforce its will on an everyday level, through the mobilization of certain social groups to populate its institutions and thus assert its authority.[15] The production of the state effect and the acquisition by the state of infrastructural power is connected too to the issue of legitimacy. This emerged in especially stark form in a state like postwar Hungary, where the concert of state institutions was radically remade by the traumas of war, occupation, and regime change, in a context in which many of the forces that had enabled the production of a state effect prior to 1945 were destroyed and replaced by a new political project that sought to recast the authority and legitimacy of the Hungarian state on an entirely new basis.

At first sight, the issue of legitimacy seems to be a strange one to raise in the context of the postwar Central and East European socialist state. Socialist regimes could not be regarded as legitimate if measured by the most common criteria for judging the legitimacy of a political regime—that a regime conformed to given legal and social rules, if those rules could be justified in terms of the belief systems of both the dominant and subordinate, and then, if the subordinate consented to the exercise of power.[16] But the concept of legitimacy, when applied in this sense, appears both descriptive and static; as such, it has little potential for interrogating historically the social roots of the socialist state. There is much, therefore, to be gained from a more historically contingent definition of legitimacy, as a state of affairs in which a given regime's claim to rule met with a sufficient degree of acceptance to ensure that it was able to acquire the necessary degree of "infrastructural" power to rule on a day-to-day basis and thus appear as a coherent, unified actor ruling above the rest of society. According to this historically contingent reconceptualization of the concept, legitimacy has always been a fluid and contested state, defined by the relationship between a given regime's construction of its own claim to legitimacy and the constellation of values and cultural and political identities among those it attempted to rule. The legitimacy of a given regime was thus often claimed, established, contested, and undermined, "as a dynamic reality which existed in the critical space between the rulers and the ruled."[17] Furthermore, because of its centrality to the acquisition of "infrastructural" power by any given state and to the generation of the myth of the state as a unified and coherent actor, the achievement of a sufficient degree of legitimacy among enough of the ruled has been a central aspect of state formation.

Within the everyday practice of socialist regimes, repression and legitimacy were linked closely. Certain legitimacies enabled regimes to pursue policies of severe repression against some of those they ruled. Yet these legitimacies also placed hidden limits on the ability of a state to rule through repression, for it could not deploy violence in ways that undermined the regime's legitimacy, as this, in turn, undermined the regime. This observation is of relevance to Hungary, for acceptance of the socialist state among many though not a majority of the ruled in the Hungarian case suggests that for certain social groups it possessed a degree of legitimacy. Although such groups could see the state as legitimate, even if at the same time the members of such groups were simultaneously victims of state coercion, the paradox of the socialist state followed from the fact that, at least in Hungary, perceptions of its legitimacy among the social groups that supported it were never shared by the majority who opposed it. As far as many Hungarians were concerned, socialist rule did not depend merely on forms of coercion that could coexist with perceptions of its legitimacy but also on naked force and the fear of force. Among these groups, this reinforced the perception of the state as illegitimate. This led the state, in turn, to use repression increasingly as a strategy of government as it came to believe that it faced politically motivated "enemies." This reliance on repression blinded the state to the way in which its infrastructural power was embedded socially. As discontent spread to groups that had been prepared to offer conditional support to the early socialist state, Hungary's rulers responded with force, thus laying the foundations of an outright crisis of the regime.[18]

Using the prism of legitimacy to examine how the infrastructural power of the socialist state was embedded socially in the changing circumstances of the fourteen years between 1944 and 1958 shows not only how legitimacy was always sharply contested but also how it was established and then eroded under different sets of circumstances. The political actors who played leading roles in the process of post-war state formation sought to construct their legitimacy with reference to the social by seeking to define their state-building project as a means of transforming class relations within Hungarian society. As early as 1943, Hungarian communists who would later play a central role in postwar state building laid the ideological foundations of their later claim to political legitimacy; Mátyás Rákosi argued that the state they sought to build would be a "democracy" committed more to reversing class-based inequalities than any notions based on the rule of law or representative government. In rural areas, he argued, "the acid test of the new democracy is the land question. He who does not want land given to the peasants, who wants to retain the system of great estates, is an enemy of Hungarian democracy." In industrial areas, "the basic demand of Hungarian democracy is the immediate abolition of any obstacle to the full economic and political realization of the power of the working class."[19]

With the formation of the new state in late 1944 and early 1945, the MKP and its allies believed that they had liberated Hungary from not only the Nazi-affiliated Arrow Cross Party but also twenty-five years of what they labeled "tyranny," "fascism," and "reaction" that had followed the defeat of the Soviet Republic in 1919.[20] In agriculture, they argued that "liberation" and the consequent "land reform opened a new era in the development of the country."[21] In addition, one "inescapable condition" of the consolidation of the "new" state was the improvement of "the situation of the working class."[22] While in keeping with the rhetoric of the "popular front" the MKP and the Left insisted that they stood for the creation of a "national unity" above classes, much of its rhetoric—of leaders and rank-and-file alike—assumed that industrial workers formed the social cornerstone of the left-wing democracy.[23] This meant that they were expected to develop a "new" working-class consciousness. This amounted to a demand that workers take responsibility, under the leadership of the MKP, for the reconstruction of the country.[24] Workers would exercise "discipline" and "restraint" in the pursuit of the reconstruction effort; in the words of one senior MKP ideologist, they should "abandon the kind of behavior that big capital expects of them."[25]

Calls for restraint and moderation from the MKP's leadership underlined one of the central contradictions at the heart of the party's class-based construction of the legitimacy of its project. In order to demonstrate "that the Communist Party is a workers' party" and that its subject, and that of the state it was building, was the "working class," workers had to support party policies actively in the workplace and community.[26] This brought the party and workers into conflict as early as 1945, with waves of unofficial strikes sparked by the consequences of hyperinflation.[27] The contradiction at the heart of the emergent state's claim to a class-based legitimacy was that its policies often clashed with the aspirations, cultures, and political identities of "actually existing" industrial workers. Although this contradiction emerged as early as the summer of 1945, it became more serious during the years that followed. In part, this had to do with Hungarian communism's increasing emphasis on its claim to rule primarily on behalf of the working class. With its election defeat in November 1945, its earlier emphasis on the cross-class dimensions of "national unity" became subordinated to a conception of the nation in which the industrial working class was placed at center stage. Increasingly, social groups such as smallholders were defined as too culturally "backward," too much under the influence of notions of hierarchy and organized religion to be central to the Left's claim to legitimacy.[28] Such perceptions led many in the MKP leadership to argue that, in the "democracy," "only one class could assume the leading role, namely the working class."[29] These sentiments became stronger as overt dictatorship was constructed during 1948 and 1949, as the MKP effectively took over Hungary's Social Democratic Party (Magyarországi Szociáldemokrata Párt, or MSzDP) in June 1948 to become the Hungarian Workers' Party (Magyar Dolgozók Pártja, or MDP). Rákosi himself, when introducing the constitution of the new socialist state to parliament in 1949, commented that while industrial workers' "consciousness has begun to change, because the country is theirs, they build it for themselves," but among "the peasantry, progress is slower."[30]

With the creation of overt dictatorship, the goals of the MDP shifted from building a "democracy" to the "construction of socialism." With the central goal of the "construction of socialism" being "the speeding up of the industrialization of Hungary, in the first place the development of heavy industry and machine manufacture," the regime promoted a vision of socialist industrial modernity.[31] It combined this goal with a rhetorical celebration of productive labor, especially the labor of the male skilled workers in the heavy industrial sectors that were identified as being at the forefront of the "construction of socialism."[32] At the same time, the opening of the "new Communist working class" to social groups outside the industrial work-force was promoted as one of the means through which a genuinely socialist society would be born. In the words of one party secretary, taking work on the construction site for which he was responsible would form the means by which "fearful, pas-sive, insecure village laborers" would "be transformed into class-conscious, fighting workers."[33] While productive manual labor in industry was celebrated and taking work in industry was proclaimed as a gateway to full citizenship in the emerging socialist state, Hungary's rulers sought to create a new "Communist working class" from the collective of actually existing industrial workers who would be capable of acting as the subject of their vision of revolutionary transformation. Consequently, they defined much of preexisting cultural practice in workplaces as part of the "damaging legacy of capitalism in the thinking of workers"; they sought through the introduction of labor competition, new wage systems, and management struc-tures to create workers who were aware that "from one day to the next that we have to produce more."[34] Furthermore, they were "responsible for the fate of their country, for the victory of socialist construction."[35]

The socialist industrialization drives of the early 1950s brought out in especially stark form the contradictions that lay at the root of the socialist state's claim to legitimacy. The regime failed to create its new "Communist working class" as state socialist economic institutions allowed class identities to reproduce themselves among workers, and those identities were situated as antagonistic to the socialist state. This problem was exacerbated by the extreme conditions the implementa-tion of the first five-year plan created. The intensification of labor, the reductions in wage levels, and the severe material shortages that resulted from the socialist industrialization drive created a gulf between workers and the socialist state that represented the root of a deep crisis of legitimacy for the regime. As discontent and social protest built up, the state responded with repression. Meanwhile, it papered over its legitimacy deficit by arguing that those protesting did not identify with their new "Communist working class" and that their protest was therefore illegitimate. Labor mobility and absenteeism were blamed on rural, agricultural elements who did not wish to accept assimilation into the socialist industrial pro-letariat.[36] Skilled worker opposition was frequently attributed to the machinations of "right-wing Social Democrats," who sought to undermine "socialist construc-tion" for political reasons, or worker opposition was blamed on "enemy elements" more generally.[37] While such a process of attribution intensified the legitimacy gap in industrial communities, it contributed to the development of a "common sense" among the apparatus, embodied in internal reports and discussion of the situa-tion on the industrial front right up until the outbreak of the 1956 Revolution. This "common sense" rested on an illusion that as much as resistance was the work of a

politically motivated minority, the majority supported the regime and thus understood "unpopular measures." As late as the imposition of production or "norm"
increases—which were effectively state-mandated wage cuts—in the heavy engineering sector in late spring 1955, which provoked massive discontent on factory
floors, officials of the National Council of Trade Unions (Szakszervezetek Országos
Tanácsa, or SzOT) prefixed their descriptions of unrest with the astonishing statement that "most of the workers understand the need for norm revision."[38]

## Contingent State Legitimacy in Context

The contradictory policies pursued by Hungary's Soviet occupiers suggest that
they had little in the way of a coherent plan for the country's future in early 1945.
While the country's smashed economy and devastated agricultural sector were bled
dry to support the material demands of continued conflict and the troops stationed
in the country, the Soviets pursued policies of retribution through an insistence on
reparation, radically antifascist political justice, the semilegal deportation of thousands of male civilians, and the expulsion of ethnic German minorities.[39] Formal
retribution was bolstered by semiofficial violence against people and property by
the occupying forces, who often instituted waves of terror characterized by rape,
looting, and random murder. The cumulative effect of such practices on a population who had been warned that the Soviets were mortal enemies in a war of national
survival ran counter to the occupiers' policies that aimed to create a legitimate, yet
pliant, political order.[40]

That pliant political order was not, at least at the turn of 1945, an overt socialist
dictatorship; Soviet intervention in Hungarian politics was limited, and the postwar government rested on a multiparty system based on the principles of a "popular
front," whose rule would be legitimized through free elections. While the MKP was
"first-among-equals" in the postwar multiparty coalition government and enjoyed
a key role in the security services of the new state, "dictatorship of the proletariat"
was firmly off the agenda.[41] This policy of limited Soviet intervention clashed, however, with the more radical goals of the MKP itself, which dreamed of revolutionary
transformation. Its leaders built their organization and base of support in preparation for an eventual "dictatorship of the proletariat" and saw initial Soviet moderation as a tactical and, above all, a temporary step—so much so that, at times,
they had to be restrained by the Soviets.[42] The radicalism of the MKP was even
greater at its grassroots. Many of the Communists it recruited in late 1944 and early
1945, motivated by the memory of the Soviet Republic of 1919 and expectations of
wholesale revolution, found the moderation of the party leadership and the Soviet
occupying forces difficult to understand. Some engaged in their own spontaneous
acts of revolutionary violence.[43] Although such voices could be cowed by party discipline, the MKP was driven by the radicalism of much of its natural working-class

constituency—a radicalism often fueled by frustration that the MKP and the unions it dominated in 1945 had failed "to defend the interests of the workers."[44]

This constellation of forces was partially the product of but also coexisted with the political dynamics of a deeply polarized society, one sharply divided and traumatized by the human tragedy of World War II. The 1930s had witnessed a turn in the nature of the country's interwar authoritarian regime, presided over by the regent, Admiral Miklós Horthy. It gradually marched through Hungary's institutions of representatives of radical-right groups, which had played a central role in the defeat of the Soviet Republic in 1919.[45] By the end of the decade, Hungary's governing elite, albeit under pressure from the growing influence of Nazi Germany abroad and domestic national socialist mobilization at home, was committed to the reshaping of the country as a "national Christian" society, which entailed, among other things, increasingly radical anti-Semitic measures and aggressive territorial revision. This resulted in a political culture characterized by the hegemony of an association between the "Christian" and the "national"; a deeply antisocialist climate in which the labor movement was stigmatized as unpatriotic; hardening divisions between Jews, along with other perceived "outsiders," and the rest of the population; and the mobilization by the state of the population behind the goals of territorial revision.[46] Furthermore, this political culture drove the complex process by which Hungary became entangled in World War II on the side of Nazi Germany by the second half of 1941.[47] Hungary's involvement in Hitler's war against the Soviet Union—justified internally as a struggle between "civilization" and "Bolshevism"—was deeply traumatic and marked first by military and, consequently, human catastrophe on the eastern front in early 1943 and then continual reverses, mounting casualties, and the specter of eventual Soviet occupation of the country itself.[48] An ever more brutal conflict was presented by the state and interpreted by the population as a struggle to ensure "the survival of the Hungarian people in the terrible storm of the war."[49] With a political elite increasingly split between those who sought a way out of the conflict through rapprochement with the allies and those who advocated unequivocal support for Nazi Germany, the population became ever more fearful and polarized. Economic hardship and air attacks on urban centers met with national socialist agitation. Social tensions mixed with both popular and official anti-Semitism to further harden the divides between Jewish Hungarians and the rest of the population. Meanwhile, increasingly despotic policies toward the working-class and rural poor, necessitated by the dynamics of Hungary's war economy, combined with the growing specter of defeat and anger at mounting casualties to produce left-wing mobilization.[50]

Germany forced a resolution of the political conflict within the elite over continuing the war when it invaded in March 1944, and it represented a new stage in Hungary's involvement. Germany's most ardent Hungarian sympathizers among the governing elite were brought to power. Political opposition was repressed severely, while, most significantly, occupation enabled the deportation of the majority of the Jewish population. Between mid-May and the end of July, more than 430,000 Jews—in actions that took place throughout the country, save the city of Budapest—were deported, of whom the overwhelming majority were murdered.[51] The growing proximity of the front drove renewed political conflict that culminated in the German-supported Arrow Cross coup, which brought Hungary's radical national socialists to power in October. With the Red Army marching across Hungary, the country's fascist rulers intensified their drives against remaining Jews and initiated party-directed campaigns of murder against political opponents, both real and perceived. As the east of the country was occupied by the Soviets and the remainder became the theater of a bloody conflict, the Arrow Cross implemented plans to evacuate the country's bomb-damaged industry and its starving urban population to Germany. By early 1945, with Arrow Cross–ruled Hungary restricted to a portion of the west of the country, residents were hungry and cold and lived in considerable fear—both of their immediate rulers and their German patrons, as well as their likely Soviet "liberators."[52]

The combination of the actions of Soviet troops, the radicalism of the social base of the MKP and the Left more generally, the legacy of polarization and fear left by Hungary's experience of war, genocide, multiple occupation, and the parlous state of the shattered economy generated a climate deeply unfavorable to the consolidation of "popular-front" rule in 1945. The creation of the "popular-front" regime was accompanied by a widespread belief that the end of the war was only temporary and that renewed military conflict between the victors would bring further political upheaval.[53] Postwar Hungary was not only deeply tense; it was also a state in which there was no majority for either the MKP's or the Red Army's state-building project. The MKP and its left-wing allies proved unable to win support beyond the substantial but restricted ranks of industrial workers, the rural poor, and the smaller group of left-wing intellectuals. Most of the rural majority, those who attended church, and the urban middle class rallied behind a more conservative vision of a parliamentary state that protected private property, defended the family, and asserted Hungary's national independence from the Soviet occupier. In the first postwar national elections, in November 1945, the Independent Smallholders' Party (Független Kisgazdapárt, or FKgP) appealed successfully to this political constituency in order to win a substantial majority of votes, thus ensuring that the MKP's vision of the postwar state could not be legitimated through democratic means. Trapped by the rejection of its vision by a conservative majority and by its own desire for outright social transformation, the fear among many of its activists and supporters of a return of the prewar regime, and their frustration with the party's moderation, the MKP responded by intensifying political polarization. Defining its enemies as "reactionaries," mobilizing its supporters, using its control over the police and emergent security forces, and drawing in Soviet support, it progressively destroyed the FKgP as an organization capable of realizing the aspirations of the majority during 1946 and 1947 as part of its bid to reverse the results of the 1945 elections and assert its vision of the postwar state.[54]

The MKP's success in imposing its vision of the postwar state, cemented by the rigged parliamentary elections of August 1947, was one that occurred in a society characterized by considerable political polarization and where its legitimacy was deeply contested. Supporters of a more conservative vision of the country's future, despite their numerical weight in society, were excluded from any political influence. This state-building project depended for its legitimacy on social groups like industrial workers and the rural poor, who were socially excluded yet politically central. This dependence created a dynamic of radicalization that interacted with the international pressures created by the onset of the cold war to shape the social bases of an emerging dictatorship. By late 1947, with the breakdown of the wartime alliance internationally and the defeat of its political enemies at home, the MKP was able to press ahead with the construction of dictatorship, swallowing its MSzDP allies to form the MDP in June 1948 and dispensing with all other parties during 1949.[55]

The debt of the emergent dictatorship to the practice of Soviet Stalinism was quickly visible in its institutions and its practice; the last years of the 1940s witnessed a substantial expansion of the state security apparatus and its scope for repression and surveillance. At the same time, the state divided Hungarian society into its allies and "enemies of socialism," as the state attributed social tensions and everyday protest to political malcontents and blamed "western, imperialist agitation" in the cold war climate for domestic political conflict. This message was underlined by a series of show trials, beginning with that of László Rajk, a Communist Party member who served as minister of the interior for much of the "popular-front" period. The trials were designed to spread the message that "enemies" could be found everywhere. Yet when "enemies" were identified outside the ranks of the MDP, it was clear that the practices of the emergent dictatorship represented an adaptation of Stalinist techniques to the polarized climate of postwar Hungary. Individuals, organizations, and social groups that had sustained political cultures antagonistic to the MKP in the "popular-front" years were targeted. Those with close personal connections to the political institutions or security services of Hungary's interwar regime faced particularly intense persecution. The churches, especially the Catholic Church, were subjected to outright attack, as their leaders, clergy, and believers were stigmatized as part of what the regime termed the "clerical reaction."[56] This was tied to an "intensification of the class struggle" as the regime implemented policies of radical nationalization and a redistribution of wealth toward working-class wage earners. In agriculture, it entailed the spread of methods of class-based taxation that underpinned the attempts of the state to organize the rural poor into agricultural collectives.[57]

Consequently, large sections of society saw the dictatorship as an attack on their very way of life. This was particularly marked in conservative, rural Hungary, where attacks on both religious belief and landownership through the collectivization drive placed the state and its representatives on a collision course with the moral economies of village communities.[58] Yet the regime's relationship with those in whose name it claimed to rule was also tense. Representatives of the regime claimed, as did the MDP's secretary, Mátyás Rákosi, in 1949, that they were the political representatives of the "worker-peasant alliance" and that, as a consequence of their actions, "the vast majority of the proletariat, exploited by the capitalists[,] has turned into the working class serving the construction of socialism."[59] This required that industrial workers and the rural poor outwardly demonstrate their support for the goals of the regime. These goals, however, clashed sharply with both the cultures and aspirations of the rural poor in agriculture, as well as the expectations of those living in industrial communities across the country. This contradiction was brought to the fore by the forced industrialization drives mandated by the regime in the first five-year plan, begun in 1950, and the ever more intense collectivization drives combined with the compulsory requisitioning of agricultural produce to feed the industrial centers. These measures created a climate of material penury that left the regime bereft of any real legitimacy among those it claimed as its supporters by 1952. To ensure compliance with its goals, the regime fell back on the repressive apparatus it had established in the late 1940s—a strategy that risked the explosion of the social tensions into an open crisis for the socialist regime.[60]

The catalyst for the open crisis was the decision of the MDP's Soviet patrons to rein in Rákosi following the death of Stalin in 1953, through the appointment in June of Imre Nagy, a reformer, as prime minister. Relaxation in the cultural, industrial, and agricultural spheres followed; the power of the repressive apparatus was curtailed as political prisoners were freed.[61] Yet the attempts at reform were botched. The economy continued its slide into shortage-induced chaos, which combined with tensions between urban workers and those in agriculture, exacerbated by Nagy's relaxation of pressure on rural dwellers, to produce discontent.[62] This situation was used by opponents of reform who rallied around Rákosi, who retained his power base as secretary of the MDP, initiating a power struggle within the elite, which finally removed Nagy in 1955. The turn away from reform produced a growing revolt within the party and among left-wing intellectuals, who were unprepared to tolerate the abandonment of reform, given impetus by the moves toward de-Stalinization initiated by Nikita Khrushchev during 1956, which served to weaken Rákosi and his allies at the head of the MDP.[63] Yet, outside the party, with renewed collectivization drives provoking open revolt in rural areas and forced industrialization leading to new attacks on working-class living standards, which met with considerable protest from a workforce less willing to be cowed than during the early 1950s, the regime faced outright crisis by mid-1956.[64]

Given the almost complete lack of legitimacy enjoyed by the regime, it was unsurprising that the convergence of mounting social tension produced by halting reform, followed by restriction, a power struggle in the party that led to Rákosi being replaced by his economic policy mastermind Ernő Gerő, pressure from the Soviet Union for de-Stalinization, and demands from left-wing intellectuals for outright democratization produced a revolution in October 1956. The speed with which the institutions of the state collapsed, the breadth of popular mobilization, and the rapid transfer of the locus of political legitimacy to the revolutionary crowd were testimony to the depth of popular anger and the desire for change. When the Soviets intervened on 4 November to install János Kádár and his "Revolutionary Workers' and Peasants' Government," it seemed that the creation of a stable, socialist political order would be all but impossible; it was an impression underpinned by the scale of the antigovernment strike, the sporadic armed resistance, and the flight of tens of thousands from the country.[65] Yet the defeat of the revolution and the swift consolidation of the Kádár regime in the years immediately following 1956 laid the foundations for stable socialist rule over the course of the following three decades. This stability was not merely the product of the suppression of the revolution and the campaign of judicial retribution that followed it. Retribution was often selective, directed at specific, prominent targets, and was as much about affirming the official myth of 1956 as a "counterrevolution" as it was about ensuring stability.[66] The defeat of the revolution produced an enforced peace within Hungarian society; among opponents of socialist dictatorship, defeat and the lack of Western intervention led to a climate of resignation and acceptance that ensured their selective incorporation into the political system during the 1960s.[67] Yet among other groups, especially among industrial workers and to some extent among the rural poor, Kádár's consolidation rested on a different social base. While there remained an awareness that the regime was a government imposed by the armies of foreign power, it was able to generate a degree of popularity and acceptance in the late 1950s on the grounds that it distanced itself from the practice of the early 1950s by seeking improvement in the standards of living of its constituency and through a greater rhetorical privileging of industrial workers.[68]

## Real and Imagined Working-Class Identities

Faced with mobilization among industrial workers during the 1956 Revolution, many officials in the MSzMP after its suppression interpreted that workers' protest through Stalinist lenses and concluded that the workforce had been so "infected" with alien elements and so influenced by the politically motivated that its "working class," envisaged as the collective subject of socialist transformation in 1950, had all but ceased to exist. For Lajos Kelemen, first secretary of the MSzMP in the industrial Budapest district of Kőbánya, the revolution proved that the time had come to accept that "part of the working class simply doesn't agree with us. They just do not accept this system." This view had deep roots, for "there were twenty-five years of Horthy fascism, which corrupted a large section of the working class politically and morally." Prior to the onset of socialism, he argued, many skilled workers "were particularly well paid; now they are not rewarded as highly, and therefore stand against us." Socialist industrialization, instead of creating "a new Communist working class," had, according to Kelemen, created a situation in which "there are large numbers of the de-classed, who are now found in our factories."[69]

The national party leadership was never prepared to go so far as Kelemen and instead maintained a variant of the myth that the disappearance of active support for the system during the revolution was from the impact of the activities of the "Rákosi-Gerő clique" on the morale of a basically loyal working class.[70] The policy of the MSzMP was based on the notion of addressing the justified grievances of industrial workers, and, by paying close attention to them, it assumed a basic unity of interest between the party and those within the working class it regarded as being its most "class-conscious members." It asserted that workers automatically "recognized and appreciated the benefits of socialist society."[71] It also suggested that they were fully aware and grateful to the state because "the workers in general live much better, and much more securely[,] than they did in the Horthy era."[72] Yet the tension between official evaluations and the pessimism of an observer like Kelemen was revealing of the way in which the MSzMP replaced the MDP's project of transforming workers into a "new Communist working class" with a claim to rule in the name of a "working class" as it existed within the Hungarian social imaginary.

This imagined "working class" rested on notions that presented certain actually existing industrial workers as representative of the workforce as a whole. These belonged to the skilled, urban elite centered predominantly in the industrial suburbs that surrounded Budapest or to the most industrial of provincial centers in which heavy industry was concentrated, among whom socialist trade union and other labor movement activism had been concentrated prior to the onset of socialism.[73] While this imagined "working class" was conceived as a unified social body, industrial workers' identities and attitudes had been, even prior to the advent of socialist dictatorship, highly diverse. The uneven pattern of Hungarian industrialization, shaped by its peripheral capitalism, had created an industrial workforce that was highly segregated spatially.[74] The industrial districts of Budapest itself, together with the working-class towns that lay adjacent to the capital and several larger industrial cities, for example Győr, formed predominantly industrial communities on the eve of World War II. In these areas, relatively large factories in light and heavy industry alike were embedded in industrial districts together with smaller, often artisan-owned and run industrial enterprises that shaped one particular kind of working-class community.[75] Yet equally important were the industrial company towns, like Ózd or Salgótarján, relatively isolated from other major urban centers and dependent on either a single industry or an enterprise, where most workers lived in housing at the company-run colony, while a minority commuted from their rural hinterlands. Claustrophobic, relatively isolated, and characterized by both overbearing management control and poor housing, such communities tended to be breeding grounds for class tension.[76] While large numbers of industrial workers commuted from rural areas, rural Hungary itself was also the location of significant industrial communities. These varied from those located around establishments like sawmills or brick factories, which had been mainstays of the earliest phases of Hungarian industrialization, to more substantial enterprises like the most isolated coal mines or southwestern Hungary's oil industry, which began production in the late 1930s.[77]

Cutting across the distinctions and identities generated in different kinds of industrial community were those produced by hierarchical gradations between workers. Dominant discourses of working-class culture placed a skilled elite at the apex of a set of hierarchies that also played a considerable role in shaping workers' identities. These notions had material roots, tied to the limited supply of highly skilled industrial labor, their preferential position in wage bargaining, and the division of labor in many industrial enterprises. Yet these material factors interacted with a bundle of cultural practices and notions in which discourses of gender, generation, and the rural-urban divide were embedded. Highly skilled workers, and their attributes of mastery of machinery, trade, and dexterity, were frequently labeled as masculine. Notions of "respectability" were tied to discourses of gender both within and beyond the workplace. Such notions were used to exclude female workers from access to jobs that were defined as both highly skilled and remunerated.[78] Discourses of generation were embedded in rites of passage in industrial workplaces, into institutions such as apprenticeship and into prevalent cultures of seniority.[79] Discourses of the urban and rural were deeply embedded within workers' cultures and interacted with the position of rural commuters within the divisions of labor of many factories to segregate rural dwellers in peripheral positions within the labor process.[80]

While patterns of settlement interacted with cultural notions of hierarchy and other distinctions such as sector-based occupational cultures and identities that related to religious observance to produce a complex spectrum of worker identities, the formation of political identities reinforced divisions that socialist state formation was forced to negotiate. Socialist political identities had considerable influence on industrial workers; during Hungary's early industrialization, the country had imported its skilled workers from other parts of the Austrian-Hungarian monarchy and its Central European neighbors, bringing the ideas of the developing European labor movement to new industrial centers. The development of friendly societies, trade unions, and socialist political activism culminated in the formation of the social democratic MSzDP in 1890. The growth in the organization and militancy of the labor movement quickly brought it into conflict with the liberal, dualist state, driving further radicalization, which culminated in working-class mobilization that led first to democratic revolution and then to the foundation of the brief Soviet Republic in 1919.[81] The defeat of revolution left Hungarian socialism marginalized and split, between a "legal" social democratic MSzDP, which sought an accommodation with the hostile interwar regime, and an "illegal" Communist tradition, driven underground and motivated by the memory of the Soviet Republic.[82] With the Soviet Republic and by extension socialism's "internationalism" blamed for Hungary's losses of territory in the Treaty of Trianon, socialist politics were branded as unpatriotic within hegemonic discourses of national identity. In the 1930s, this led the country's ruling parties to make limited incursions into industrial communities, winning support, albeit highly restricted, among small segments of the workforce.[83] Hegemonic discourses of antisocialism and nationalism combined with social radicalism and popular anti-Semitism to produce a more populist, working-class fascism, which generated considerable support for Hungary's national socialists in industrial communities at the end of the 1930s.[84]

The plural nature of workers' identities interacted within different industrial communities to produce cultures that were far more diverse than the discourses of political actors allowed, especially with regard to the various parties implicated in Hungary's postwar state-building project. Patterns of conflict, consent, and accommodation to the various stages of the MKP and its successors' state-building project varied considerably across different industrial communities and groups within the workforce. In considering the relationship between industrial workers and socialist state formation in postwar Hungary, therefore, due attention must be paid to the differing nature of the experience across a range of industrial communities at the local level. It is for this reason that this book concentrates on the experience of state formation in three distinct industrial communities in Hungary; while none provides the scope for a fully comprehensive account of what occurred in working-class Hungary between 1944 and 1958, they are representative of certain kinds of communities, and a comparison among all three allows for generalization.

## Introducing the Case Studies

This book draws its evidence from three very different industrial communities. Újpest, an administratively independent city in the industrial suburbs of greater Budapest prior to 1950 and, since then, the fourth district of the Hungarian capital, lies on the eastern bank of the Danube in northern Pest. Tatabánya, a predominantly heavy industrial city formed in 1947 as the result of a merger of four villages fifty-five kilometers west of Budapest, is the second case study. The third is made up of the cluster of villages in the Letenye district of Zala County, in the far southwest of the country, where economic structures were transformed by the discovery of oil in 1937. All three industrial communities were different in terms of their patterns of industrialization, occupational structures and cultures, local identities, and political outlooks.

Újpest's formation, industrialization, and growth were closely tied to the industrialization of Pest from the early nineteenth century. Originally part of the manor of the Károlyi family, the land that constitutes modern Újpest was parceled out by the landowner and offered for rent in 1831. The largely vineyard-cultivating tenants were joined over the following decade by several industrial entrepreneurs attracted by the closeness of the area to commercial Pest. Later arrivals were artisans, many from the Czech lands and Austria, who initiated the first wave of industrial development. With the completion of Hungary's first railway line between Pest and Vác in 1846 and the proximity of the Danube, Újpest grew; it had a population of only 12 in 1832 but of 6,722 by 1870.[85] The following thirty-five years saw Újpest's transformation into a major industrial center; the late nineteenth century saw an extension of leather working and the furniture industry, large textile plants that had consolidated by 1887 into the Magyar Pamutipar cotton factory, a more diverse machine-manufacturing sector, and an electrical goods industry, fronted by the United Incandescent Lamp and Electrical Company, founded in 1896.[86] By 1910, it had a population of 55,197, of whom 35,909, or 65.1 percent, were economically dependent on industrial employment. Consequently, it was a center of the emergent socialist labor movement and a site of considerable strike activity during the first decade of the century.[87] The strength of the local labor movement made the town a center of support for the revolutionary upheavals at the end of World War I and during the brief Soviet Republic, and it ensured that a strong and militant socialist subculture persisted in many of the town's factories into the 1920s.[88]

With the spread of the textile industry in the town, by 1930 twelve textile plants operated locally, joined by further light industrial enterprises. With other sectors hit by the depression, the predominance of light industry was reinforced.[89] On the eve of Hungary's entry into World War II in 1941, Újpest remained a predominantly working-class town; of a population of 76,000, 46,334 were dependent on industrial employment.[90] With the turn of national policy toward increasingly institutionalized anti-Semitism, the large Jewish population—10,882, according to the 1941 census—was placed under greater pressure.[91] Újpest had not been immune from the mobilization of the working class by national socialist parties at the end of the 1930s; indeed, the Arrow Cross won 43.44 percent of the vote in the city in 1939, easily outpolling both the MSzDP and the conservative governing parties.[92] Yet Újpest's relative autonomy as a county borough and the rootedness of notions of civic independence in local identities from both neighboring Budapest and the surrounding Pest County insulated it to some extent from the full consequences of national trends. Following the restoration of local administration in 1922, a cross-class left-of-center alliance of liberals and the MSzDP kept control of the city council throughout the interwar years and, pursuing policies of public works, limited housing improvement, and modest social reform, were able to repel the attempts of the right-wing governing parties at the national level to dislodge them, right down to World War II.[93]

While Újpest was a working-class town with considerable municipal autonomy that pursued left-of-center policies of social reform and was part of a major conurbation, the villages that later made up Tatabánya had an entirely different character. Its story as a community began in 1896, when geologists working for the Hungarian General Coal Mining Company (Magyar Általános Kőszénbánya Rt., or MÁK Rt.) discovered large coal deposits on the estate of the Eszterházy family close to the multiethnic villages of Alsógalla, Felsőgalla, and Bánhida, only six hundred meters from the Budapest-to-Vienna railway line. Given its good transport links and the ongoing process of industrialization across Austria-Hungary, the mine expanded quickly, meeting the rising demand for coal from the Austrian capital.[94] The growth of the mines transformed patterns of population and settlement; in the 1880s, the three villages where mining began were small multiethnic communities. Two, Alsógalla and Felsőgalla, were populated largely by German speakers, while the other, Bánhida, had a Slovak majority population. The combined populations of the three communities increased from 3,255 in 1880 to 9,657 in 1900; their ethnic composition also changed. Most of the new labor attracted to the mines was Magyar speaking, but the population retained its multiethnic nature.[95] While issues of ethnicity represented an undercurrent in the formation of working-class identity, more important was the role that MÁK's policies played. Most "key" workers were settled in company housing known as "colonies," which the employers used as a tool of discipline and supervision over the core of the workforce. These colonies formed the basis of the settlement of Tatabánya; by 1941, Tatabánya itself had a population of 7,312, while industrialized Bánhida's was 11,763, Felsőgalla's 17,110, and Alsógalla's 1,770.[96]

Despite the fact that around a third of all mine workers were rural commuters by the mid-twentieth century and that there were other substantial industrial establishments in the Tatabánya area—two major power plants, a cement factory, an aluminum smelter, and a quarry—coal mining and thus the culture of the mining colony played a central role in the determination of local identity. In 1941, of the 37,955 people who lived in the four communities that later formed Tatabánya, 19,024 were economically dependent on employment in mining; only 10,687 had employment in industry or construction.[97] The lack of independent city government above the level of the four villages gave large local employers, especially those that provided company housing in the colonies—most significantly, MÁK Rt.—extensive power over the lives of their workers. In MÁK Rt.'s colonies, access to housing and social benefits was determined by status-based lines of demarcation, often referred to by workers as the "caste system," which reinforced hierarchies of class and rigidly separated workers, office staff, engineers, and managers. Workers reacted strongly against this "caste system," and it became one of the significant points of reference in the construction of identities among Tatabánya's miners.[98]

Given the claustrophobic nature and the culture of status-based distinction in the mining "colonies," as well as the misery for those urban workers who were excluded, the district became fertile ground for the growth of a militant labor movement. In 1919, Tatabánya was a stronghold of the Soviet Republic; its suppression locally was violent, with gendarmes shooting at demonstrating mine workers. The consolidation of the interwar regime was accompanied by a restoration of the power of MÁK Rt. over the mining community. During the interwar years, there existed a widespread subculture of protest that most frequently manifested itself in "go-slow" or wildcat strikes that occasionally erupted into more serious unrest, including the bitter and unsuccessful ten-week miners' strike in 1925. The moderate MSzDP proved unable to represent this militancy adequately, and it rapidly lost support among the local workers, some of whom turned to "illegal" Communist activity.[99] The discrediting of the legal labor movement and the obstacles to Communist political activity combined with the radical mood to produce space for Arrow Cross mobilization in the district in the late 1930s. In the 1939 parliamentary elections, the Arrow Cross took 38.98 percent and the MSzDP 11.47 percent in the Tatabánya parliamentary constituency, while national socialist activity led the district to become a center of the Arrow Cross–incited miners' strike in 1940.[100]

While Újpest and Tatabánya were very different kinds of industrial communities on the eve of World War II, the villages in the south of Zala County, between Letenye and Lenti, that formed the site of the oil fields were hardly industrial communities at all. When the social observer Róbert Páldy visited the region in 1938, he found isolation along the border with Yugoslavia where "the area was almost half forest and the population live, practically speaking, almost exclusively from tilling the land in tiny hamlets." He recorded that "most of the population are without any spiritual or physical support in the closed villages," an isolation reinforced by the distance of the railway, the expense of the bus services, and the poor roads; it was a place where "rainy weather" cut off some of the villages entirely from the outside world.[101] The transformation of the region came with the discovery of oil at Budafapuszta, near Bázakerretye, in 1937 by the European Gas and Electric Company, a subsidiary of Standard Oil. The find led to the creation of a substantial drilling operation supervised by a new subsidiary company—the Hungarian-American Oil Industry Public Company (Magyar Amerikai Olajipari Részvénytársaság, or MAORT) in June 1938. With the discovery of further substantial oil and gas deposits close to the villages of Kútfej, Lovászi, and Tormafölde, MAORT's operations expanded with a new drilling plant, which started production at Lovászi in December 1940. After extraction began at nearby Pusztaszentlászló in 1942, the region became a site of significant oil production, just four years after the start of oil drilling.[102] In this poverty-stricken, isolated agricultural region, labor was not hard to recruit; MAORT was flooded with applicants, even from the families of landholders attracted by the promise of relatively high wages and income security. Although the skilled work, so crucial to the labor process in oil drilling, was initially performed by foreign workers, with locals taking the unskilled positions, MAORT quickly sought to shape a local workforce. It did this by insisting that its skilled foreign drilling masters train local skilled workers. The company also sought to use its position of power in the local labor market to insist on strict work discipline, and it imposed a one-year probation period on all its recruits. As early as 1940, local residents made up 94.6 percent of all manual workers.[103]

Before oil production was taken over by the state after the United States entered World War II in 1941, MAORT had created a distinctive culture among the oil workers. The American owners insisted on a flattening of cultural distinctions between the white-collar employees and the manual workers, something almost unheard of in status-obsessed Hungary, and the model of workplace cooperation that was created even attracted comment in the postwar years.[104] This practice was reinforced by the high pay, status, and skill levels of many of the manual workers; 75.87 percent of the company's 4,202 manual workers were skilled workers in 1943.[105] Yet the practice was also a product of the creation of a distinctive rural working-class culture among oil workers. In a poor, agricultural region, many saw working in the oil industry as a chance to gain a degree of financial security and prosperity not guaranteed by meager smallholdings, allotments, or gardens, yet the arrangement also allowed most oil workers to retain land and their families to acquire wealth to support their small-scale agricultural activities or their subsistence plots. Men went to work in the oil industry, leaving women to manage agricultural activity. With few workers living in the company housing adjacent to the plants and many commuting from neighboring villages, employment in the oil industry was an extension of a rural, conservative, smallholder culture.[106] This culture, combined with high pay and a strong company-based identity that transcended many of the divisions of status at the plants, created a climate in which the labor movement was unable to make any inroads, something that was ruefully noted by representatives of the MKP in the postwar period.[107] Yet in their own ways, all three industrial communities posed challenges for Hungary's postwar would-be state builders in the decade and a half that followed the end of World War II.

The first of this book's eight chapters concentrates on the beginnings of postwar state formation in Hungary's industrial communities. Against the background of the military victory of the Soviet Union and the Red Army occupation of Hungarian territory at the end of World War II, the MKP and its allies worked to build a state that was able to effect radical and lasting social transformation. They argued that the end of the war had brought a "liberation," which enabled the reshaping of the Hungarian state and nation around industrial workers and the rural poor. Yet, as this notion of "liberation" became the founding myth of the new postwar state, it failed to secure the legitimacy of the MKP's state-building project in industrial communities. War and the regime change that followed were experienced as a period of trauma, fear, and penury by workers. Consequently, only certain sections of the industrial workforce constituted a reliable social base for this state-building project, and these groups often demanded more radical and immediate change than the party was prepared to offer. This precarious position was underlined when the MKP attempted to legitimate its state-building project through elections in autumn 1945, which resulted in defeat by the most conservative of the legal antifascist parties.

Electoral defeat led to a withdrawal of trust among the MKP's working-class supporters amid the mobilizing Right and penury induced by hyperinflation, forcing the Left to shift to a strategy that rested on intensifying the political polarization of Hungarian society. This allowed the MKP to reconstruct its own legitimacy among left-wing workers by presenting itself as their best defender against the threat of "reaction." Chapter 2 explores the MKP's construction and limits, arguing that the organization was rooted specifically in those local working-class cultures, where left-wing political identities were most deeply embedded. Support for the political goals of the Left did not, however, translate into unconditional support for the productivist policies of the MKP in the workplace; patterns of support and opposition were instead bought through a series of informal bargains at the local level, where responses were often rooted in the everyday cultural practices of the communities concerned. The scope of these bargains was circumscribed politically; right-wing workers found themselves less able to buy in, while their opposition in production met with repression. As popular-front politics were undermined by the atmosphere of polarization and the MKP's politics of confrontation, the limited postwar democracy broke down, and the victorious Communists constructed an overt socialist dictatorship.

In this situation, the partial and uneven legitimacy established by the MKP in 1946 and 1947 evolved; no longer able to so credibly deploy the threat of "reaction" as a tool to mobilize workers, Hungary's "new" rulers built support by offering tangible material improvement or the promise of future improvement to their supporters. As chapter 3 shows, this stored up problems for the regime as support among workers was bought at the price of the subversion of labor policies that prepared the ground for economic planning in the future. The new state's stance toward areas that opposed it, characterized by escalating repression, anticipated its response to widespread discontent when it emerged later.

The newly merged MDP in 1948 had little intention of respecting the social dynamics that had enabled the creation of socialist dictatorship. It instead sought to forge from the actually existing industrial workforce a new "Communist working class" that would act as the collective subject of its project to transform Hungary into a socialist society. Chapter 4 analyzes the outright failure of this project of transformation, as it foundered on its failure to persuade workers to identify with this new "working class." This problem of identification rested on both the persistence of preexisting identities among workers and a deeper reproduction of class identities enabled by the subjective experience of implementing economic planning in workplaces. Planning rested on commodified, fragmented labor, while the state's attempts to industrialize brought wage cuts, increased work intensity, and provoked protest, which in turn brought repression.

Meanwhile, this cold war industrialization drive forced an expansion in the workforce, the impact of which is considered in chapter 5. Hierarchies based on gender, generation, or rural-versus-urban dynamics within the workplace were challenged as the state combined the introduction of new groups to industrial labor with its program of creating a new "working class," while many of the "new" workers themselves were deeply antagonistic to the regime. Furthermore, their integration into production, dictated by increasing bottlenecks and shortages that combined with discontent to produce chaos in mines, at factories, and on construction sites, generated endemic informal bargaining between lower management and workers, in which hierarchies were reproduced and a discontented elite within the workforce pushed "new" workers to an alienated periphery.

The industrialization drive of the early 1950s was not merely accompanied by failed transformation in workplaces but also produced penury, which was exacerbated by severe shortages of basic goods. By 1953, the regime had lost all legitimacy, which forced the party leadership, under Soviet pressure, to make limited changes in personnel and policy that initiated a three-year power struggle. Chapter 6 concentrates on this retreat, which brought the regime no respite as political dynamics in industrial communities crystallized. These were dynamics that had been shaped by the conflicts through which class identities had been reproduced through the contradictions between the regime's attempts to constitute actually existing industrial workers as a new "Communist working class" and workers' everyday experiences of alienation in both workplace and community. Thus, the stage was set for the revolution that erupted in October 1956 and revealed the regime's crisis of legitimacy by demonstrating the lie that the actually existing industrial workforce was in any sense the subject of the regime's political project. Instead, as chapter 7 shows, worker participation in the revolution brought the submerged social conflicts that had characterized the early 1950s out into the open in the public realm.

As chapter 7 also shows, alongside the emphatic anti-Stalinism and the flowering of democratic patriotism during the revolution, the events of October and November 1956 were marked by political ambiguity about goals and the revelation that political attitudes, cultures, and divisions from the late 1940s had been reproduced in the 1950s. After the Soviet intervention in November, the newly installed Kádár regime was able to play on these phenomena in order to win support in some industrial communities for its argument that, in fact, a "counterrevolution" had occurred in autumn 1956. The consolidation of the Kádár regime among industrial workers, as chapter 8 shows, was as much about winning acceptance for its myth of 1956 as "counterrevolution" by meeting many of the social and economic demands advanced during the revolution, while closing the door firmly on its political goals. Thus, paradoxically, while the events of the revolution underlined the absolute lack of legitimacy of the regime by the autumn of 1956, its social and political defeat proved fundamental to the consolidation of a socialism whose hegemony, while not uncontested, was nevertheless considerable. This was because of a further paradox in that the consolidation and thus the strength of the regime rested on radically moderating its goal of transforming workers and coming to accept that the working class as it "actually existed" was the subject of its rule.

# 1

# The Limits of Liberation
## March 1944–November 1945

IN MID-SEPTEMBER 1945, as workers' wages were reduced to nothing by rapidly accelerating hyperinflation, officials of the Textile Workers' Union defended to a furious membership in Újpest the rates enshrined in the agreement they had negotiated collectively with the state and employers. The mass meeting exploded at the comments of one official, who argued that "those who dare to say that living standards today are not even half those of 1939, who maintain that they are starving[,] are liars, who can only be motivated by bad intentions." As the speakers lost control of the mass meeting completely, István Ács, a leading Communist on the factory committee of the Domestic Cotton Weaving Factory (Hazai Pamutszövőgyár, or HPS), who was presiding, attempted to calm the situation. Ács, although a prominent local activist in the MKP whose views were known to be more radical than the official line advanced by the party leadership, was a divisive figure, and his intervention transformed the disorder from one motivated by economic matters into a demonstration against the policies of the MKP. He was shouted down by one section of the crowd, who referred to him as an "Arrow Crossist"; when he attempted to persuade the crowd to sing the "Internationale," many responded angrily, rejecting the political culture of the "new" state that the labor movement was building: "Is that part of the collective agreement too? Why shouldn't we sing the *himnusz* [Hungarian national anthem]?" As a large section of the crowd attempted to turn the meeting into an anti-Communist demonstration, it split along political lines, with the Communists and many of the workers from Ács's own HPS rallying behind the speakers. The anti-Communists attacked the stage and violence erupted. In the melee that ensued, one female worker was taken to hospital, and the pitched battle stopped only when the police intervened.[1]

While the degeneration of the mass meeting into a riot was primarily the product of the insensitive comments of one union official, the events in Újpest were indicative of the social and political tensions that gripped industrial communities in Hungary as the Left attempted to construct the institutions of a "new" state in the aftermath of war. Only some workers saw the events of 1944 and 1945 as being ones of "liberation," for they were marked by violence, fear, penury, and chronic insecurity—a situation that generated profound anger in industrial communities. That anger, as the division of the Újpest meeting shows, did not generate a unified political reaction; instead, the political attribution of blame for the desperate situation of Hungarian workers at the end of World War II reflected deep-seated political polarization. Just under three weeks after the riot, on 7 October 1945, municipal elections were held in the Hungarian capital and the urban communities adjacent to it, including Újpest. The results shocked the workers' parties. In Budapest, they resulted in an outright victory for the FKgP, while in heavily working-class Újpest, in contrast to all expectations, the workers' parties managed to secure only the narrowest of majorities on the municipal council (table 1). Behind the results lay marked political differences among workers; many argued that the desperate economic situation would "improve when the Smallholders take power." The fury of such workers was directed at the country's Soviet occupiers, who they blamed for their insecurity and the poor economic situation—"the Hungarian people produce in vain, when the Russians take it all away from us"—while others maintained that "there is no bread because the Communists are in charge." Even among the majority who remained loyal to the Left and accused many working-class FKgP supporters of "attacking their own class," workers were deeply discontented and thus focused on the poor material situation.[2]

The focus of many workers on material issues and deep-seated political polarization during late 1944 and much of 1945 contrasted with the official vision of the period as one of "liberation." This contrast was significant, for the notion of 1945 as a "liberation" that was promoted by the Left in the immediate postwar period assumed the status of the founding myth of the popular-front regime and, later, of Hungary's socialist state. When Újpest's own memorial to the Soviet soldiers who fell while driving out the Germans in January 1945 was unveiled in May 1947 in the presence of both the local elite and Hungary's president, Zoltán Tildy, László Pesta,

TABLE 1. Results of the municipal elections in Budapest and Újpest, 7 October 1945

| Party | Budapest | | | Újpest | | |
|---|---|---|---|---|---|---|
| | Votes | Percentage (%) of the vote | Seats on the municipal council | Votes | Percentage (%) of the vote | Seats on the municipal council |
| Dolgozók Egységfrontja (Workers' Unity Front)[a] | 249,711 | 42.76 | 103 | 19,223 | 51.94 | 41 |
| FKgP | 295,187 | 50.54 | 121 | 16,530 | 44.66 | 36 |
| Nemzeti Parasztpárt (National Peasants' Party, or NPP) | 11,741 | 2.01 | 5 | 799 | 2.16 | 2 |
| Polgári Demokrata Párt (Civic Democratic Party, or PDP) | 22,392 | 3.83 | 9 | 457 | 1.24 | 1 |
| Magyar Radikális Párt (Hungarian Radical Party, or MRP) | 5,013 | 0.86 | 2 | 0 | 0 | 0 |
| TOTAL | 584,044 | 100 | 240 | 37,009 | 100 | 80 |

*Source:* Adapted from PtSzL, A Magyarországi Szociáldemokrata Párt iratai (Papers of Hungary's Social Democratic Party, hereafter I.283f.)17/85ö.e., 45; Sándor Balogh, *Választások Magyarországon 1945: a fővárosi törvényhatósági és nemzetgyűlési választások* (Budapest: Kossuth Könyvkiadó, 1984), 109.

[a] An electoral alliance of the MKP and MSzDP.

though a senior member of the local FKgP, a figure associated with local Left, gave the speech of dedication. He maintained that, during the "liberation," the "great Soviet people had offered their hand in friendship, and offered the possibility for the Hungarian people to find themselves and to build their lives in circumstances of freedom, to clear away the rubble, and begin their next, new thousand years."[3] Ernő Gerő, speaking at the beginning of April 1945 at an MKP meeting held to celebrate the "liberation" of Tatabánya a little more than a week earlier, argued that "just now the Red Army has liberated the last of Hungarian territory from the German–Arrow Cross fascists. Unfortunately, we did not liberate ourselves, we fought on the side of fascist Germany; Hungary was the country that fought on the side of Hitler until the end, and the consequence is that our country is in ruins." He continued: "When the Soviet government saw that the Hungarian people were short of everything, they gave help and credits to the new Hungarian national government. We did not yet merit that help, we have to prove that we are not fascists, but democrats."[4]

The attempts of those such as Gerő and later, at a more local level, Pesta, to shape the meaning of the events of 1944 and 1945 became fundamental to the postwar regime's attempts to construct its legitimacy. At "liberation," the actions of the Red Army, it was argued, had transformed the position of industrial workers within Hungarian national life. As far as one trade union leader in Tatabánya was concerned in February 1946, "while during the war it was big capital that did everything to boost war production, today the situation has turned around. Today it is the workers who know that producing more is the only way to put the country back in order." Because of the links made between the "liberation" myth presented by the Left and its claim to rule on behalf of the workers, the actual working-class experience, as well as their response to Hungary's war-induced regime change, set the stage for the relationship between the state and industrial workers well into the period of the socialist dictatorship.[5]

The combination of a focus on immediate material concerns with intense political polarization, so visible in Újpest in autumn 1945, was typical of working-class responses across the country to the end of World War II. The experience of life under the German occupation and then the Arrow Cross, combined with that of becoming a theater of intense military conflict, and subsequent Soviet occupation generated considerable insecurity. This produced a deep-seated desire for a protective state that would restore order. Material penury, induced by the policies of both German and Soviet occupiers, led to a desire for state action that would provide economic stability and greater social justice. The Hungarian state in 1945 was incapable of delivering either, creating a legitimacy vacuum that reproduced intense political divisions. While the left-wing majority of urban, industrial workers blamed the Germans and Arrow Cross for Hungary's plight, saw in the country's left-wing rulers a guarantee that the interwar regime and those responsible for the war would not return, and hoped that the Left's rule would bring greater social justice, this view was not shared by more conservative Hungarians. They saw a left-wing regime supported by the Soviet Union as fundamentally incompatible with their national identity and refused to accept the "new" state, which they regarded as an affront to national independence and a threat to the country's survival. So deep seated was the political division between them that they associated themselves with different communities and blamed very different political, military, and social actors for the insecurity that gripped postwar Hungary.

This division was reflected in the differences in response seen in each of the three case studies presented here. In all three, workers felt the need for greater security—both physical and material—as a result of the way in which the war ended in their communities. Yet the kinds of political future that their populations wanted and popular responses to the weaknesses of Hungary's postwar state varied considerably. In the oil fields of southern Zala, with no traditions of labor movement activity whatsoever, aspirations focused on a restoration of order and stability within village communities. The principal threat to oil workers at the national level was seen as the Red Army, which insisted that MAORT produce for them by way of reparations and refused to compensate the workforce by granting them access to adequate supplies of food and goods, and, at the local level, the Soviet troops, who had engaged in widespread rape, violence, and theft against the rural population.

These factors reinforced preexisting conservative political identities and created a climate that was profoundly hostile to the MKP. In Tatabánya, however, marked by considerable militancy in the interwar years, the MKP won substantial support among working-class residents. This support derived from a widespread desire for more egalitarian social relations in workplaces and the community, a desire that stemmed from class tension generated in the interwar years by the power of large employers over local life. This basic support paradoxically coexisted with intense frustration at the moderation of the local MKP leadership, fueled by the general failure of state builders either to master the desperate economic situation or bring about immediately tangible social change at the local level. Újpest presented a more complex picture of a divided workforce. During World War II, activism rested on an overwhelming desire to protect the local community from the ravages of conflict. Yet the circumstances in which the war ended led to a situation in which Újpest's new rulers could not present themselves unequivocally as protectors of the community because of their association with the Red Army and their failure to master the desperate economic situation. This created polarization; while a majority supported the Left, this support was concentrated disproportionately among the skilled male elite, who had provided the backbone of the socialist labor movement. Others were only prepared to support more conservative positions.

## Újpest in the Eye of the Storm

In the aftermath of the fighting, the Újpest branch of the MKP announced that it had saved the city. "The storm of history," it claimed, "galloped over Újpest. It did not, in general, destroy to the extent that it did elsewhere: Újpest did not share the fate of Budapest. The Arrow Cross were not able to murder the same number of innocent people that they did elsewhere. The Germans and their stooges could not blow up the large factories, the water works, the power plants, the electrified railways, the roads, and the houses here. Újpest was saved by the Újpest Resistance Movement. A majority of participants in this movement were Communists."[6] This claim, however, was based on a selective remembering of events from the period of the German occupation onward. In concentrating on the representation of the armed struggle of a relatively small number of local Communists, it omitted mention of the traumas of the deportation of the city's Jewish population, the random violence of Arrow Cross rule in the city, and then the climate of fear that accompanied the Soviet occupation and the early phases of the building of the new state locally.

For those brought to power at the national level by the German invasion in March 1944, Újpest was a symbol of all they sought to change in order to reverse the course of the war. The city's identity was defined by its large Jewish population, its substantial labor movement, its traditions of municipal autonomy and progressive politics, and its resistance as a community to the "national Christian" policies of governments throughout the interwar years. This identity shaped an image of the city as enemy territory in the minds of Hungary's "new" rulers in 1944, and consequently the authorities sought to reshape local society; the mayor, Pál Hess, elected as the result of pressure by the radical-right county-level authorities on the city council in 1943, chose the route of collaboration. The city's labor movement was banned, and the headquarters of the local Social Democrats and the trade unions were taken over and transferred to the official labor organization—the National Work Center (Nemzeti Munkaközpont, or NMK).[7] The socialist labor movement was driven underground, as the NMK sought—largely unsuccessfully—to supplant it in the factories.[8] The despotic policies to subordinate workforces to local managements in the interests of maintaining war production since the early 1940s intensified.[9] The growing frequency and severity of air attacks on Újpest, combined with the raw materials shortages caused by war-based production, increased fear among workers and residents.[10]

The most radical consequence of the German occupation was the implementation of the "final solution" in the city. Within weeks of the German occupation, in early April 1944, the collaborationist government ordered the concentration of Jewish populations in ghettos and the confiscation of their property.[11] In the large local Jewish community, the implementation of ghettoization was a visible process, as an estimated fourteen thousand people were crowded into a small number of streets midway between the city center and the major industrial district alongside the Danube, as well as into the city's football stadium, in late May.[12] The implementation of the government's anti-Jewish measures during the period between ghettoization and the deportation of Jews from the city in the first three days of July was not only visible but also marked by considerable brutality and theft, both by German soldiers and by the local organizations charged with aiding deportation.[13] The implementation of the "final solution" met with a variety of reactions in the city. At one extreme, it was supported by the members of the extreme right-wing parties, many involved in local institutions, and those who benefited from the chaotic distribution of Jewish property, especially housing.[14] At the other extreme, enterprises like the United Incandescent Lamp and Electrical Factory took a range of official and unofficial steps to protect their Jewish engineers from the authorities, who at one stage sent the gendarmerie into the factory to remove its Jewish employees.[15]

The most common popular response to the deportations, which only seventeen hundred local Jews survived, was one of passivity, which was underpinned by a sense of fear and shame.[16] It left a long-term legacy of trauma and unease; it also destroyed one of the local foundations of the "progressive" nature of the local political culture, which had allowed the city to withstand the pressures of the rightward shift in the 1930s, by murdering many of those who had shaped a progressive, left-leaning middle-class milieu. In many of the factories, where the attempts of owners and managers to protect their Jewish employees had been either unsuccessful or nonexistent, the deportations had an immediate impact on relations in production. In the Chinoin Pharmaceuticals Factory, the drafting of many engineers and white-collar staff into labor battalions and the deportations of others left entrenched in management a group who were loyal to the pro-German government and, later, to the Arrow Cross regime.[17]

This dynamic of fear and polarization was given further impetus by the dramatic events of 15 October 1944. Within hours of Horthy announcing Hungary's withdrawal from the war, he was overthrown by the German occupation forces, who replaced him with Ferenc Szálasi and the Arrow Cross. With Soviet troops advancing across eastern Hungary toward the capital, the new regime revived the attempts—hindered by Horthy—to wipe out the Jewish population that remained in Budapest, initiated a wave of terror against its known opponents, and bolstered the German army's scorched-earth policy by dismantling plants and evacuating them—together with the population—westward.[18] In Újpest, the new regime was actively terroristic. The face of the local Arrow Cross comprised the armed party activists, given powers equivalent to those of the regular police. They gained considerable notoriety for arbitrary violence, torture, and murder, directed especially against Jews who remained, political opponents, and even those they suspected of avoiding the general call-up into the army as the Soviets approached.[19] This violence was combined with the implementation of scorched-earth policies through which enterprises were dismantled and their raw materials and machinery transported west to Germany while their workforces were forced to fight as part of the collapsing Hungarian army.[20]

The terroristic nature of local Arrow Cross rule, perceptions of its deeper illegitimacy, the imminence of the arrival of the Red Army, and the fact that the Arrow Cross policies and those of the Germans were seen as endangering the very conditions of existence for the local community produced a fragmentation of state authority and widespread resistance. The source of resistance was diverse, ranging politically from army officers who refused to accept Szálasi to the city's Communist partisans. The resistance itself also took different forms, from attempts to protect Jews, to the prevention of machinery being transported westward; from the passive resistance of doctors in the local hospital against attempts to remove patients and medicines, to the armed actions of the Communists against the Arrow Cross and the Germans.[21] What unified the fragmented resistance was a desire to protect the local community. It was a desire founded partially on a strong sense of local identity in Újpest but based also on the sense of threat that German and Arrow Cross policies posed to the well-being of the local population. Another contributing factor was a sense that the scorched-earth policies would destroy the economic foundations of the community's existence by dynamiting its infrastructure and dismantling its factories. Even the Communist "partisans" subscribed to this agenda of the protection of the community, refusing to join the Red Army directly in order to, in the words of their commander, László Földes, ensure that "our small force can achieve great results in saving this city."[22]

As Budapest was surrounded, air raids became constant in Újpest and were quickly supplemented by artillery attack. The population took refuge in their cellars, and workers sought safety in the shelters of their factories.[23] With food supplies disrupted, the population went "hungry."[24] With the city under siege, the Communist partisans became increasingly bold, turning the streets into a battleground contested between themselves, the Arrow Cross, and retreating Germans. In the days before the arrival of the Soviets, as the authority of the regime collapsed, they were able to take control of the former headquarters of the Social Democrats, free forty-eight prisoners from the local headquarters of the Arrow Cross, and then destroy the building the day before Red Army troops arrived.[25] As a consequence, when the Germans were driven out of Újpest on 10 January 1945, there was a strong local Communist organization able to fill the political vacuum in the city and represent the provisional government, which then ruled from the provincial city of Debrecen in anticipation of the fall of Budapest. The Red Army occupied the local court buildings to set up a city command that remained for three years after 1945.[26] Backed by the Red Army, the local MKP reorganized the Újpest city police force, creating the impression, in contradiction of the party's "popular-front" line at the national level, that the Communists aimed to take power immediately.[27] "Before the liberation," remembered local MSzDP activist Jenő Pál Nagy, "we believed that only the Communist Party would be allowed"; he recounted his sense of surprise when told by the local MKP leadership that "on the contrary, the Social Democratic Party remains, and others also."[28] Tension between political parties, fueled by suspicion of the local MKP's intentions, ignited arguments over the representation of parties on the city's "national committee"—the major local organ of public administration—and the unelected city council it appointed, which held office until the October elections.[29]

The chief difficulties that the "new" state faced with the local population related only in small part to suspicion of the MKP's intentions but stemmed mostly from the people's experience during the first few months following the end of World War II. Public sentiments were influenced by the failure of state institutions to master the desperate economic situation and the close relationship between local institutions and an unpopular Red Army. Újpest's population not only had been severely affected by the physical reality of war, as well as the fear that the events of 1944 generated, but also faced a deep-seated material crisis. Prior to the events of autumn 1944, workers had experienced a prolonged period of food shortages and declines in real incomes; in 1944, real wages in the United Lighting and Electrical Factory for the skilled stood at only 55 percent of their 1914 level.[30] Added to this was the impact of armed conflict; when the population fled to their cellars and the food supply ran out, doctors estimated that local residents all lost 15 to 20 percent of their body weight during the period of siege, leaving a legacy of both short- and long-term physical weakness, as well as vulnerability to illness.[31] The need of a physically weakened and hungry population to survive led them to emerge from their cellars after the end of the fighting, despite the fear of disorder and disease.[32] Survivors wondered "what will happen now. . . . The main question for most workers wasn't the wage, or earnings, but whether there would be work itself"; for others, the way was opened to the black market and the "possibilities for speculation."[33] Crime offered another possibility, generating a situation in which labor movement activists attempting to restart production demanded the "restoration of total security, for both persons and property."[34]

Újpest's new left-wing rulers sought support by combating the disorder through the organizing of a reformed local police force.[35] However, the behavior of Soviet troops toward civilians fatally undermined the new rulers' attempts to seek support. Due to the close operational links between the Red Army and the organizers of the "new" state, the troops' behavior deeply corroded the "new" state's legitimacy. Almost immediately after the occupation of the city on 10 January came "the second wave [of Red Amy troops]. . . . Then, the period of fear came. They stole, they raped."[36] While crime against property heightened fear and insecurity, rape left a legacy of trauma, for both victims and bystanders. Despite the public silence shaped by taboo, rape played an important role in generating a popular sense of Hungarian victimization at the hands of a foreign conqueror; it later became central to the reproduction of anti-Communist political identities.[37] The precise extent of the rapes committed by the occupying troops proved impossible to estimate, but it was nevertheless widespread.[38] The threat of such violence engendered considerable fear among working-class women.[39]

To rape was added the fact that Soviet troops rounded up considerable numbers of local male civilians as prisoners of war in the immediate aftermath of its occupation of Újpest; some twenty months later, in September 1946, the newspaper of the local FKgP carried the names of seventy-six men who had been rounded up on the city's streets in early 1945, then interned in Hungary and Romania, and finally taken forcibly to the Soviet Union. Given that the newspaper's figures were based on information about the residents of one Romanian transit camp for two months in summer 1945, the total numbers deported from Újpest in this way almost certainly ran well into the hundreds.[40] The deportations had a semilegal basis; a Red Army order issued in December 1944 forced the Interior Ministry of the new Hungarian government to prepare a list of those with German names so that they could be rounded up to perform forced labor for the war effort, though in practice the Red Army used this tactic as cover to take civilians at random as prisoners of war.[41] The managers of the Chinoin Pharmaceuticals Factory complained in March 1945 that "large numbers of our skilled workers have been taken away because of their German names"; aware that not all of them had been interned simply to support the war effort, it asserted that some had "been sent to Gödöllő," the first of the transit camps for those bound for captivity in the Soviet Union.[42] János Sztankovits, the future United Lighting and Electrical Factory Stakhanovite—the category of outstanding worker copied from practice in the Soviet Union—was one of those detained by Red Army troops on the Újpest streets and "taken to a place where there were already several hundred," before being taken to the Gödöllő camp and a series of others in Hungary and Romania. After several months without adequate supplies of food, he was deported to the Soviet Union.[43] As a result of the widespread deportations, being taken away for "a little work" became a popular euphemism for being detained arbitrarily and indefinitely by the occupiers.[44]

The fear generated by the rounding up and deportation of male civilians deeply corroded the legitimacy of institutions like the local police, and the contradictions between two aspects of the police role in early 1945 exacerbated the climate of fear. The first relevant aspect was their roundup and internment of former Arrow Cross members and those who had supported the actions of the regime after March 1944.[45] Internees were held in local camps; Újpest's had more than one hundred inmates two months after the Germans retreated.[46] The internees were deployed to clear rubble or perform other forms of labor in the interests of the immediate reconstruction of the community.[47] At the same time, however, the government and the Red Army charged local authorities in the chaotic postwar climate with ensuring that *all* citizens of working age were mobilized to clear war damage and prepare the way for the reconstruction of the country.[48] Many residents confused the attempts of the police in Újpest to organize reconstruction efforts with both their own retributive drives and the rounding up and imprisonment of male civilians by the occupying forces.[49]

For those who had been active in or had supported the local labor movement, fear and hunger were tinged with hope; the arrival of the Red Army and the painful destruction of "national Christian" Hungary created the space for a country more socially just than prior to 1944. Pál Pánczel, secretary of the MKP cell in the United Incandescent Lamp and Electrical Factory, remembered the strength of common purpose among the skilled workers who had been members of the labor movement in the prewar years, a sentiment that transcended institutional divisions between them: "even where they were not in the same organization, they supported our efforts with all their strength."[50] The local Communist leadership built its institutional power in the factories by mobilizing local networks of skilled workers, often transcending patterns of party affiliation. Jenő Pál Nagy, despite his status as an MSzDP activist, was asked by the city's Communist leadership to "go to" his factory and "restore order."[51] Likewise, the initial task of local activists in the textile workers' union was to "assist in restarting production with our full strength."[52]

When activists arrived in their factories, they organized the manual workers and remaining members of management to begin the clearing of rubble and to prepare for production. In the absence of clear management structures, the activists established factory committees to coordinate the early reconstruction efforts. Their role was regulated by a directive of the provisional government as early as February 1945.[53] However, these actions were in reality highly localized responses by labor movement activists, skilled workers, and some engineers to factory circumstances.[54] Some of these activists proved difficult to control, as they adopted a more militant stance toward factory owners and managers than the more moderate official line of the state and left-wing parties allowed. The most radical was the entirely Communist factory committee set up in the HPS under the auspices of István Ács. This committee demanded the immediate socialization of the factory and refused to admit its owners to the site. Thus, reconstruction was mired in a bitter dispute in which the owners withheld operating capital from the plant until the militants in the factory committee recognized their ownership. This, in turn, hindered production and especially deliveries to the Red Army, a situation that led to the army's intervention in order to enforce a settlement, which restrained the factory committee.[55]

The vast majority of the factory committees, however, were too preoccupied with the extent of the material crisis that faced their factories and their workers to seek immediate revolutionary transformation. The condition of factory infrastructure was poor overall, and attempts to clear war damage were hindered by further natural catastrophe, most notably when the ice-covered Danube burst its banks in February 1945, flooding many of the large factories in the industrial district adjacent to the river, disrupting production, and leaving behind considerable damage.[56] Often the legacy of destruction and the lack of resources to repair anything beyond what was essential to current production had considerable effect. The inability of the factory committee or management to repair the roofs in the shoe-making plant of the Wolfner Leather and Shoe Factory led to a situation throughout 1945 in which any rainy weather made it impossible "to put many machines to work," "materials were ruined," and "workers were permanently rained on."[57] Factory committees not only faced the challenge of restarting production with a severe lack of resources but also were forced to meet the needs of a hungry and discontented workforce in circumstances of almost complete economic breakdown. By March 1945, workers in the Magyar Pamutipar had lacked regular food supplies for several months as markets remained empty; the factory was still unable to guarantee its workers a lunchtime meal each day and could distribute only small quantities of meat and oil each week.[58]

While some factories were able to secure food for their workforces through barter with rural producers, this source was uneven and insufficient.[59] In the first six months following the end of the war, they were dependent on the Red Army for securing food, their orders, and raw materials. Hungary's ceasefire agreement, concluded in January 1945, compelled the country to allow its industrial plant to be used for the Soviet war effort against Germany.[60] Given the shattered economy, the promise of military production represented a lifeline for many of Újpest's factories, as the Red Army named military commanders for several of the most significant industrial plants in the city. Demand from the Soviet military for cotton fabric meant that the local sites of the Magyar Pamutipar worked under Red Army command until June 1945.[61] Likewise, their need for boots ensured that of a total of seventeen local leather factories that had existed in 1944, nine had restarted production by early April 1945.[62] In a climate of scarcity of raw materials and work, serving the needs of the Red Army guaranteed particular factories the ability to employ workers and produce goods continuously. In a situation marked by generalized food shortages, it also gave factory committees limited possibilities to bargain with the Red Army to ensure that most of their workers were fed.[63]

Yet the consequences of Soviet military supervision for workers' jobs were far from benign; in one plant, the United Incandescent Lamp and Electrical Factory, they were catastrophic. Hungary's ceasefire agreement allowed the Soviet Union to exact reparations for the country's participation in World War II by dismantling industrial plant and shipping it east.[64] The United factory, in view of its leading role in the manufacture of lighting and radio components and its record of technical innovation, was thus targeted. The Soviets dismantled the factory between March and mid-May 1945; only 4 percent of the machinery remained in place, while 75 percent of all raw materials were taken.[65] The factory employed approximately five thousand persons in late 1944; by May 1945, when the Red Army left, it could guarantee work to only about four hundred.[66] Although the factory committee organized the workers to defend the factory against the attempts of the Red Army to dismantle it, these efforts were unsuccessful. The workforce was faced with the task of reconstructing a factory damaged by not only war but also the policies of new occupiers.[67] The consequences of the dismantling of the factory for the legitimacy of the MKP were considerable. The "embittered" feeling of many workers toward the Soviets reflected on the MKP in the factory.[68] It also prevented the MKP from gaining a hegemonic position within the factory even as the factory recovered from being dismantled.[69]

Not all large plants were deemed essential to the war effort and thus given a Soviet military commander in early 1945. This meant that many factories were simply unable to restart production. While small and medium-sized establishments were disproportionately affected, some large factories also experienced this problem. In the Chinoin Pharmaceuticals Factory, central to the production of medicines, the Red Army confiscated the plant's raw materials, its motor vehicles, and its horses, leaving it without orders and thus forcing management and the factory committee to plead with the provisional government for the resources to restart production.[70] While such behavior on the part of the occupation authorities undermined the ability of the local and national left-wing state to present themselves unequivocally as agents of reconstruction and thus as protectors of the material needs of the local community, the parlous state of the economy produced deep-seated social divisions. In a climate of generalized food shortages and material crisis, an industrial job became valued because it guaranteed a degree of preferential access to basic means of subsistence. Even as the Soviet military withdrew from direct management of local factories in summer 1945 and production increased, total levels of industrial employment recovered relatively slowly, and many smaller plants were simply unable to restart production. Where they did, production continued to be mired in stoppages caused by the severe lack of capital, raw materials, and coal.[71] By the end of 1945, the number of workers employed in industry stood at only 65 percent of the April 1943 level.[72]

Those excluded from industrial employment were forced to take desperate measures in order to survive. Locally organized campaigns to repair bridges and clear the railway lines, officially heralded by the left-wing parties as "shock work," were often masked opportunities to provide casual employment to the local poor, who received little more than a hot meal for their labor.[73] The desperate situation of many created a crime wave as those with access to money, clothes, or foodstuffs gained through industrial employment were frequently the victims of violent theft. The city's railway station became a hotspot of crime against property and persons as armed gangs pilfered wagons and attacked commuters for food. Many left Újpest for rural areas not only because of endemic crime but also to gain access to food by trading their labor to agricultural producers or to barter their possessions to survive. Their empty flats in Újpest became targets for break-ins.[74] Crime, endemic shortages, and the chaotic condition of the local economy allowed a black market to mushroom throughout the summer months, and industrial enterprises, workers, and agricultural producers were implicated. In September 1945, six hundred pairs of boots were taken without authorization from the Wolfner Leather and Shoe Factory, ostensibly for sale on the black market. At the same time, the factory's construction workers—charged with rebuilding the factory—spent regular work hours repairing the villa of the plant's chief engineer in the Buda hills to supplement their meager incomes.[75]

Black market activity fed, and was in turn fed by, accelerating hyperinflation, which fatally undermined the new state's reconstruction effort from summer 1945 and thus its claim to meeting popular demands for greater material security. War, German occupation, and then the demands of the Soviets for reparation bled the Hungarian economy dry, while economic devastation, the disorganization of agriculture, and the need of the bankrupt Hungarian state to print money combined to ignite hyperinflation.[76] In summer 1945, working-class anger grew in Újpest at the fact "that for months we have been able to tell that there is a problem with prices and goods. On one day fruit disappears from the market, on another day, potatoes, onions, or other products, so they can reappear several hours later at double the original price."[77] Throughout the spring and summer, factory meetings were dominated by worker complaints that "wages are not in proportion to prices."[78] The situation worsened throughout the late summer and early autumn as prices spiraled out of control and the attempts of local authorities to regulate the sellers were met with traders withdrawing goods from the local market, in turn leading to the periodic disappearance of bread, flour, potatoes, and vegetables from the marketplace.[79] As the value of wages was reduced to practically nothing, the attempts of the government to link remuneration to a recovery in production levels, mooted over the summer, became irrelevant.[80] Unions, factory committees, and management, under pressure from discontented workers, raised wages; in the Magyar Pamutipar over the course of eleven weeks in summer 1945, the wages of skilled and semi-skilled workers more than doubled and unskilled workers' wages trebled.[81] This, in turn, further fueled hyperinflation, and by the time of the November elections, the authorities had tacitly admitted they were powerless to stop it. As the unions and government admitted that the severe devaluation of wages was undermining the reconstruction effort, in a panic measure they abandoned their attempts to hold down wages, instead insisting they keep pace with prices.[82]

Yet these compensatory wage increases simply fueled hyperinflation. This in turn created a reservoir of frustration; workers feared a winter without "fat or fuel."[83] Perceptions of the marginalization of workers in the face of endemic speculation were reinforced by cases like that of one elderly woman, killed by the collapse of a wall as she gathered wood to exchange on the market for vegetables from which to prepare broth for her starving lodgers.[84] The sense that the state was failing to protect the material interests of workers ignited protest both inside and beyond the walls of the factories. In the United Incandescent Lamp and Electrical Factory, militancy among the workers grew throughout the autumn. By early December, shop stewards admitted they simply had no control over a series of wildcat strikes as groups of workers demanded that they be paid in the lamps the factory produced, so they could exchange the items on the black market.[85] An increased propensity to direct action was marked among the working-class women who shopped in the Újpest market; when potatoes were suddenly unavailable in late October, conflict erupted between shoppers and local sellers, which led to the shoppers demanding an audience with the mayor. He underlined the perception that the authorities were powerless to deal with the situation by proclaiming to the demonstrators that "God himself lacks the power to bring potatoes to Újpest!"[86]

The inability of the state at either the national or local level to meet the material needs of the population not only provided the backdrop to the poor performance of the left-wing parties in the elections of autumn 1945 but also undermined the authority of the state. Popular responses to its crumbling authority reflected the underlying political polarization of local society. Many on the Right blamed the poor food supply situation and hyperinflation on "the need to supply the Red Army."[87] Among the more socialist-inclined majority of Újpest workers, much of the blame for the poor economic situation was laid at the door of "speculators," who wished to enrich themselves at the expense of those who lived on their income from work alone. Many complained bitterly that workers were asked to bear the burden of reconstruction while others reaped the benefits. According to one textile worker speaking at a mass meeting held at the beginning of December, "Workers are at least as hungry for much of the time as they always were, if not hungrier. . . . The factory owners have done much better. Today we always agree to restraint, to being cold, to walking around in rags, and to hunger. They always find a way out."[88] The growing sense of exclusion reignited the demands of many for the pursuit of more radical policies that had been ruled out by the MKP leadership and their allies in the popular-front government at the beginning of the year. Among labor movement activists, there were growing calls for greater socialization: for one United Incandescent Lamp and Electrical Factory Communist, "the means of production remain in the hands of the capitalists. It would be good if not only the mines were nationalized, but the large factories too."[89] This mood of radicalization and growing polarization shaped not only the background to the November 1945 elections in the town but also the period immediately thereafter.

## Pushing the Limits of "Liberation" in Tatabánya

In Tatabánya, open rebellion against the "moderate" stance of the MKP leadership erupted several months before the November elections, in the summer of 1945. Protest was sparked at the end of July by a delay in the payment of wages, caused by delays in transferring money from the headquarters of MÁK Rt. to Tatabánya. The failure to pay wages was met by a spontaneous and comprehensive work stoppage, which spread rapidly across the local coal mines. The local MKP attempted to persuade the miners to return to work, arguing that "every minute that work stops in the mine today lengthens our suffering." These appeals fell on deaf ears; even the membership of the local MKP proved impervious to them.[90] The leadership instead had to address a range of grievances—that they had failed to nationalize the mines immediately, had allowed "former Arrow Crossists, who had acted as spies for the mine owners," to return to work, and had reinstated whole swaths of the former management despite the opposition of the miners. This reinstated management, as far as workers were concerned, undermined the unions and refused outright to pay the wages negotiated in the collective agreement for the coal-mining sector signed a month previously.[91] This agreement had been seen as a pact for reconstruction, one through which goods and better wages would be provided in exchange for increases in production. Through this pact, miners had hoped, their desperate material situation would be alleviated. They saw the local MKP as mistakenly protecting an unpopular management whose members were sabotaging attempts to create a more socially just Hungary.[92]

The nature of the explosion of frustration in Tatabánya underlined the difference in local political dynamics relative to those present in Újpest. Tatabánya was a very different kind of industrial community, and both the local experience of the death of "national Christian" Hungary and reactions to the events of the war shaped these dynamics. Fundamental to these dynamics was what happened among coal miners, the dominant occupational group in the district. As World War II progressed, the considerable support for the Arrow Cross that had existed in the mining colonies receded. It was replaced with a growing left-wing militancy brought on by wartime inflation, food supply problems, and despotism in the workplace—stimulated by the fact that the mines and power plants worked under military command. Throughout 1943, membership in the MSzDP-affiliated Mineworkers' Union increased, while those who shared the underground Communist subculture that had been present in the mining colonies grew in confidence and in organization.[93] Increased class tension was superimposed onto political polarization between workers and white-collar staff as the military situation became more critical; in 1943, one miner complained bitterly about management to a journalist from the local church newspaper: "they say we are unpatriotic . . . they say that, who don't know anything about patriotism, nor the living conditions of workers."[94] At the same time, managers lamented the fact that many fell under the influence of "parties," which they accused of destroying the paternalistic aspects of the mining colony, viewed as a microcosm of an idealized Hungarian "national community."[95]

These dynamics of class-based and political polarization provided the backdrop to the local events that followed the German invasion in March 1944. As in many other industrial communities where there had been substantial Arrow Cross support earlier in the decade, it revived and energized local national socialist organizations, which preempted the local authorities by attacking well-known labor movement activists and trade union property, before they were themselves restrained by the pro-German government. The labor movement was driven underground, thus bringing activists who escaped imprisonment into closer contact with illegal Communist groups who had, by the summer, organized a district-wide structure.[96] Unlike in Újpest, measures to deport the Jews were of less significance in the Tatabánya area. According to the 1941 census, only 344 Jews lived in the four local settlements.[97] The city itself did not have a recognized Jewish quarter.[98] Tatabánya experienced the occupation regime primarily as an intensification of repression against the local workforce. That repression had support from white-collar staff who had been disturbed by increased labor activism prior to March. Tension festered, provoked by perceptions of the occupation's illegitimacy, fury at falling real wages, and poor working conditions, as well as the approach of the Red Army. Despite draconian sanctions, this tension was so endemic that it made it impossible for management to maintain work discipline in many mines and factories.[99] According to one manager in summer 1944, "The workforce reacts like a seismograph to every political shift. The collapse of our production can be traced directly back to the events of last year on the eastern front, and then the arrival of the Germans earlier this year."[100] This climate, in turn, fed Communist activism that sparked an intensified police presence and waves of arrests across the district in late summer and early autumn.[101]

Given the rising tensions, the Arrow Cross coup in October 1944 produced a fragmentation of state authority similar in nature to that found in Újpest, if more stark in degree. While the hardcore armed party activists were often violent, they faced widespread noncooperation, not merely in the workplace but also in the broader community, even among the military.[102] The local experience of Szálasi's regime was associated with the three-month period when the Tatabánya district lay on the front line between the Germans and the insurgent Red Army. As part of the plan to encircle Budapest, the Red Army broke across the Danube south of the capital at the beginning of December and drove northwest, reaching the Tatabánya area just before Christmas.[103] The arrival of the Red Army in the district on Christmas Eve took the local authorities—and the German occupiers—by surprise. A disorganized attempt to dismantle the local aluminum smelter and transport it west, to prevent it falling into Soviet hands, was frustrated by the resistance of the workforce, determined to preserve the factory where they worked.[104] In the mines, many engineers and other white-collar staff decided to flee in the face of the Soviet advance. In anticipation of a prolonged period of chaos, management "distributed three months' food, and three months' pay." In the climate of panic, not all workers turned up to be paid.[105]

The Soviets overran the mining communities of Felsőgalla and Alsógalla, but not Bánhida, on 26 December. Red Army occupation lasted only a month, and the front line ran through the urban area. As in the rest of the country, the population experienced widespread rape, theft, and violence from their occupiers.[106] News of this behavior was carried west, leading those who had fled to advocate "revenge" against the Soviets and their supporters.[107] Locally, however, it did not have the calamitous long-term effect on the legitimacy of the Left's state-building project that it had in Újpest. This was because it was overshadowed by the behavior of the Germans and the Arrow Cross after the district was retaken on 26 January. One major focus of Arrow Cross efforts was to ensure that all those not employed where they were essential to the war effort, including teenagers enlisted in the *levente* (the army cadets' association), were called up into the army and sent west. The numbers conscripted from the district and the neighboring villages were substantial, ensuring that in the postwar years many local families waited for the return of their members from the western prisoner-of-war camps, as well as from Soviet ones.[108] These measures provoked both resistance and considerable fear. Open resistance was met with the arbitrary violence of Arrow Cross activists; in one incident in March, nine-teen people who avoided the call-up were summarily executed.[109] Many simply hid, while others formed so-called community "self-defense" units that existed only on paper yet entitled them to a pass that exempted them from the call-up. While this was effective as a strategy for avoiding conscription and transfer west, it left those pursuing it vulnerable to eventual arrest by the Red Army and subsequent deporta-tion to the Soviet Union.[110] The Germans and Arrow Cross were also determined to pursue their economic "scorched-earth" policy by removing plant infrastructure in anticipation of their eventual retreat. These attempts were largely frustrated by the scale of widespread passive resistance. The workers hid "spare parts for the machin-ery and irreplaceable materials" from the Germans, who were intent on stripping the mines of everything necessary for production.[111] In Tatabánya and Bánhida, management dissuaded German troops from leveling the strategically important power plants, arguing that, should the Germans retake the plants, they would need to restart electricity generation immediately.[112]

When, after three months on the front line, all four of the Tatabánya settlements were finally occupied by the Soviets on 20 and 21 March 1945, the end of the war was met with considerable relief. In contrast to the December occupation, the situation stabilized quickly, with Red Army troops moving quickly to secure the mines and the two power plants.[113] The power vacuum left by the retreating Germans was filled by the district leadership of the MKP, a tightly knit group of Communist miners. Largely veterans of the Soviet Republic and the illegal labor movement, some of them had worked either in France or Belgium, or in the Soviet Union immediately after the defeat of 1919. This group had formed the illegal organization that had been spreading Communist propaganda among mine workers since March 1944, and they had avoided both arrest by the gendarmerie and unwanted attention from Arrow Cross activists.[114] This district leadership gained a key position during the first occupation of Tatabánya in January 1945 when, in contravention of the popular-front agreements at national level, the local leadership of the MSzDP argued against the legalization of the MKP. This stance outraged left-wing Social Democrats, who strengthened the local MKP by cooperating with its leadership directly, thus going over the heads of their own leaders. This allowed the MKP to found a five-member workers' council to begin the process of organizing the mines and thus individual workers' councils in each of the pits, bypassing the MSzDP.[115] Although the MKP's attempts to found a new state locally were suspended by German reoccupation at the end of January, they were resumed almost seamlessly in March. By early May, one observer from party headquarters was so concerned about the degree of MKP control of the newly organized local police that he described them as a "party police force."[116] This effective monopolization of the state and the anti-Communist stance of the local MSzDP leadership set the stage for later political tension.

The power of the local MKP leadership was contested from within the organizing party as well as from outside it. Considerable support during the period of illegality translated into a large mass base—the MKP had 2,524 members across the four settlements by autumn 1945.[117] It also meant that there had been more than one illegal Communist organization in the area prior to March 1945; some refused to accept the authority of the local, official leadership and began to agitate against it, demanding in summer 1945 that it resign.[118] Opposition to the local leadership centered on the figure of Teofild Sándor, a local baker who had founded an illegal communist organization in one section of the mining colony as early as 1938. In 1945, he was able to rely on a base to found a party cell in his local neighborhood. Increasingly disillusioned with the moderate line of the MKP at the local and national levels and furious at corruption in the police and their willingness to back management in the mines, Sándor became a rallying point as early as summer 1945 for those who demanded a more radical stance from the local MKP.[119]

Behind this unusual political constellation in which leaders of the district MKP were squeezed by actors committed rhetorically to socialist transformation to both their right and left was an almost unanimous expectation that the end of the war would bring radical change. Workers were unprepared to tolerate a situation in which prewar social relations continued. As early as May, stokers in Power Plant No. 1 reacted with fury to MÁK Rt.'s continued failure to pay them. They complained that "everyone crowded into their shelters when the Russians advanced on us, but we did our duty at work. When land mines exploded on the roofs of the power plant, . . . we had to go from one boiler to the next. As a result of their heroism, three of our colleagues lost their lives." Despite their deeds, "it never occurred to anyone in management to thank us, nor to think we were worthy of praise. On top of all this, they decided that we owed the company money. They really hurried to collect it."[120] In meeting the expectations revealed by complaints like this one, and with the continuing atmosphere of class tension, the local MKP faced a number of interrelated challenges. The first was to restart production in the mines, the associated factories, and the power plants; the second was to deal with endemic shortages of both money and food; the third was to contain the radicalism of many workers and their anger against a management that had collaborated actively with the country's wartime regimes. Restarting production was, in some ways, the least of the problems faced. Throughout the three months when Tatabánya had been a theater of conflict, coal production had continued, interrupted only by occasional stoppages. During the final battle for the city in mid-March, the cableways to transport coal were damaged and the power lines were downed. Most damage was caused by a nine-day power cut, which began on 17 March.[121] The loss of power put the pumps out of action, thus flooding the mines, some of which were completely submerged. The first priority of the five-member workers' council was to prepare the mines for production.[122] The miners who went in to make the necessary preparations "worked for nothing, free of charge, at the price of considerable exertion to create the conditions for starting work."[123] Material damage had been sustained by other industrial plants—the cement factories and the aluminum smelter—by the fighting, aerial bombardment, and the theft of raw materials and machinery by retreating Germans.[124] The machinery necessary to restart production was repaired in a highly improvised manner, by sending workers to cannibalize war-damaged vehicles for spare parts, which were then adapted to repair machinery.[125] Yet little could be done without electricity, which meant that reconstruction of local power plants had to take priority. At Bánhida's plant, "the boilers and the machinery had huge problems . . . there was no fuel for the machines, gasoline, or oil. Getting fuel caused huge problems, the workers went everywhere, . . . one can say on foot, to get all the things they needed, to begin production."[126] Destroyed power lines hindered power supply not only to the mines but also to Budapest, which the district's plants also supplied.[127] The downed power lines that connected Bánhida to the capital were rebuilt by a fifteen-member youth brigade who worked voluntarily "in rain, wind, and negotiated minefields, just to see reconstruction begin."[128]

This restoration was achieved in a desperate economic situation, one in which workers labored not only without pay but also without adequate sources of food. While the minority of workers who owned their own land failed to turn up to work in the immediate aftermath of war, those workers who were left had little access to food. "The overwhelming majority of miners," reported the management in March 1945, "are . . . those who live in the settlements built near the mines, where there are hardly any sources of food other than the depots maintained by the mine."[129] They admitted that "for as long as our workers cannot buy sufficient food at prices they can afford from their wages, there will not be the required peace in Tatabánya. This situation will adversely affect the ability of our plants to produce."[130] Local agricultural production had first been devastated by war damage and theft by German and then Soviet troops.[131] Agriculture then suffered further with the improvised "wild expulsions" of ethnic German farmers from the villages in Tatabánya's rural hinterland in the wake of the arrival of Soviet troops and the repopulation of villages with "settlers."[132] Finally, the chaotic local implementation of the land reform also played a part in making food locally scarce throughout 1945.[133] MÁK Rt's own attempts to procure food for its miners by bartering coal with agricultural producers in the Great Plain were less than successful. On the company's own admission, its efforts were undermined by corruption within the mine management, while the amounts secured were insufficient; the distribution of food was accompanied by "nervousness and discontent."[134] Consequently, individual workplaces, the workers' parties, and the unions attempted to organize barter with local producers; in August 1945, however, the local MKP found that smallholders were willing to hand over beans only in exchange for large quantities of construction materials.[135]

In this climate, the reinstatement of unpopular managers who had fled in 1944 provoked particular resentment. Through the spring, strong pressure from miners hindered the reinstatement of many unpopular engineers and managers, forcing the national leadership of the MKP to demand that its local organization throw its weight behind the reinstatement of all white-collar staff essential to production.[136] The gradual reduction in the space for workers to prevent the reinstatement of unpopular white-collar staff occurred in tandem with drives by mine management, supported by the MKP leadership, to extend working hours and tighten work discipline.[137] Increasing tension as summer approached, fueled by the persistently catastrophic food supply situation, provided the background to open rebellion in the mines in July 1945. The district leadership of the MKP responded by demanding that workers follow the party's productivist line, blamed political opponents for stirring up discontent, and demanded sacrifice from workers in the interest of future social transformation. It argued that behind the strikes and protests lay an attempt by "the reaction of the past" to blame "the Communist Party for its old sins."[138] Yet a senior local Communist recognized that "many workers are disappointed in their leaders, but I am convinced that we will succeed in abolishing the capitalist system, and that in this the Hungarian working class stands on the side of the Soviet Union."[139]

Although the MKP as an institution maintained considerable support in the district, workers bitterly criticized the moderation of the local leadership. Behind the political tension lay enormous discontent, fueled by a material crisis for workers—one that was especially apparent in the mines—that compromised reconstruction efforts. The strikes of the summer were ridden out, while management attempted to defuse material discontent through a series of informal compromises disguised as labor competition and shock work initiatives that enabled workers to receive limited payment in kind—though generally in footwear or clothing, rather than food.[140] The reception of these campaigns demonstrated the degree of mistrust among workers; miners refused to join them until they could be shown that the promised goods had actually arrived.[141] The discontent that bred the strikes continued to rumble, while the food situation worsened. A poor harvest meant that workers were unable to obtain fruit to make jam for the winter months.[142] Intensifying hyperinflation in autumn 1945 meant that, for miners, "it was absolutely impossible to buy any food with money in the [neighboring] villages."[143] With the food depots attached to the mines unable to provide even subsistence levels of food and with money rendered effectively worthless, workers labored for local smallholders in exchange for food.[144] Workers laboring in the fields rather than in the mines and factories combined with physical enfeeblement from months without adequate food to endanger production. By October 1945, a combination of sickness and widespread "black" or black-market work by miners in neighboring villages meant that on any given day 30 percent of the workforce was absent.[145] Absenteeism depended heavily on the food that could be distributed to workers from the mines' depots and stores. By October, supplies of potatoes and vegetables ran out, causing to miners "to run to the villages for potatoes" instead of turning up for work.[146] Of those who did, in one pit, angry miners "agreed to descend, but as a protest worked less."[147] Attempts to buy off discontent through special shifts for which miners would be paid in clothing or footwear became so frequent that production levels were maintained only on such shifts.[148] The utter inability of either the state or employers to guarantee local workers the basic means of subsistence led to their almost complete loss of authority in production.

Paradoxically, however, the local MKP's utter inability to pursue reconstruction, given the depth of material crisis and the resulting discontent, coexisted with overwhelming support among workers, especially coal miners' support for communism in Tatabánya. As the November elections approached, miners regarded it as axiomatic that the MKP was "the miners' party." Consequently, the MKP appeared socially exclusive and as having little to say to other industrial workers or to smallholders.[149] This paradox rested on the unusual local political constellation. Crucial also was the fact that many miners differentiated between the promise of social transformation the MKP represented and the unpopular policies implemented by the district leadership. Furthermore, only two workers' parties were organized in the district, and the MSzDP was a distinct political minority. It was discredited among a majority of workers by its moderation in the interwar years and its relatively right-wing stance.[150] Discontent among miners was expressed politically as a series of demands for more radical action than the local MKP leaders were prepared to countenance. These demands were taken up politically, following the open rebellion in July 1945, by the rank-and-file of the MKP itself, which blamed the district rather than the national leadership for following an overly moderate line. Demands that the "local leadership resign" were heard from the summer of 1945, while protesters demanded that Teofild Sándor "form a new leadership."[151] While neither the local nor the national MKP leadership was prepared to tolerate the existence of alternative centers of power, the radicalism of many workers locally and their discontent provided the basis for the MKP to mobilize them behind their political goals as politics polarized following the 1945 elections.

## The Production of Alienation in Southern Zala

Within days of the Red Army driving the Germans out of the oil fields of southern Zala in April 1945, MAORT's factory committee began to shape the local, company-based variant of the "liberation" myth. "The oil fields were all finally liberated on 3 April!" it announced. "Blown-up wells, burning storage depots, plundered warehouses, burned-down offices and houses, and paralyzed machinery marked out the route taken by the retreating German troops. Our employees arrived at the site only two hours later, led by the Red Army; at their head was an expert, Dr. Simon Papp, the chief geologist, who guided them in overcoming the greatest difficulties." It continued: "since then the tons of oil both produced and transported has risen day by day, so that the refineries have been able to work more, and thus, the belief has grown within us that by extracting this treasure from Hungarian soil we are contributing considerably to the reconstruction of our ruined country."[152] Unlike official rhetoric heard in much of the rest of industrial Hungary at the time, this statement spoke little of the "liberation" of workers that came with the military end of World War II; it simply credited the Red Army with having enabled the restoration of the pre-1944 structures of management, which would in turn enable work to restart and thus return the company and the country to normality.

The space for this company-based adaptation of the "liberation" myth in the Zala oil fields was made possible by the strength of company-based identities among the workforce and the utter lack of a local labor movement. The deeply conservative political culture of the villages that surrounded the drilling sites ensured that neither any variant of the "liberation" myth nor the program of the MKP had much resonance in the immediate postwar years. For most of the interwar years, the region had remained politically loyal to the conservative ruling parties, a pattern broken in 1939 when poor landholders used the introduction of the secret ballot to vote for National Socialist candidates.[153] The approach of war was experienced as a period of achieving Hungarian national goals at the local level. The oil fields lay on the country's Treaty of Trianon border with Yugoslavia; tensions generated by Yugoslavia's attempts to implement land reform, to the detriment of Magyar populations just across the border in what had been a previously unified region, affected local opinion, providing the basis of support for policies of territorial revision. With the dismemberment of Yugoslavia in April 1941, Hungarian reoccupation of the Prekmurje region of Slovenia that bordered the oil fields was greeted approvingly.[154] Yet, as the war intensified, locals experienced subsequent years as ones of disruption and grief; greater numbers of friends and relatives fought and died at the front, the requisitioning of agricultural produce intensified, and prices increased.[155]

MAORT itself was placed under state supervision, and the representatives of its American owners left the country when the United States entered the war in December 1941. Wartime measures, however, did not represent a very radical break, as the company's Hungarian management remained in place.[156] With rapidly increasing production in the recently discovered oil fields in Zala, this natural resource became of central strategic importance to both Hungary and Germany. Under state supervision, the company was forced, largely against its will, into producing oil from the new fields at a rate that their geologists believed would compromise future production, largely to satisfy Germany's wartime demand for oil.[157] Although the company lost its autonomy in determining the pace of production, it was able to continue company-based paternalism by extending social policy measures to protect its permanent staff from the erosion of their living standards under inflationary conditions and to support the families of those who fought on the front.[158] The war, at least prior to the German invasion, was seen as physically distant, a perception manifest locally through the employment of Jewish labor service battalions at sites such as Lovászi, as well as the rapid pace of production.[159] The period following the German invasion saw greater pressure to further increase production.[160] The oil fields then became targets for air attack. Thirteen oil field workers were killed when Bázakerretye was bombed in July, and seventeen more died in an attack in October.[161] Arrow Cross rule represented a further intensification of existing trends rather than a decisive break with them; the strategic importance of MAORT as a supplier of oil to German troops was reinforced. Berlin, desperate to retain control over the oil produced in southwestern Hungary, intervened to prevent the Arrow Cross and its own army from dismantling the plants and carrying them west, ensuring that oil was produced continuously until the end of March 1945, days before the Soviets arrived.[162]

The way in which the war ended, and the first weeks that followed its end, had a decisive effect on how the postwar regime came to be seen and came to play a central role in reinforcing a conservative, anticommunist political culture. The oil fields were among the last communities in Hungary where the Soviets drove out the Germans at the beginning of April 1945. What ensued was a period of intense disorder and fear as the new local authorities dissolved the gendarmerie, without, in rural areas, replacing them with an adequate local police force.[163] At the heart of the crime wave that followed the end of the war were soldiers of the Red Army; over the course of the spring and summer of 1945, Soviet troops engaged in a wave of theft, rape, and murder that terrified rural communities.[164] Widespread rape had deeply traumatic effects; the chief notary in the neighboring town of Lenti referred to the "shame" that accompanied the substantial numbers of pregnancies in the villages.[165] To the deep-seated trauma was added the fact that many young men from southern Zala villages were rounded up and deported to the Soviet Union as prisoners of war. These factors led many to see the end of the war as a generalized attack on the whole fabric of family and community life perpetrated by the country's new occupiers.[166] Given the association of the local MKP with the Soviets, it found itself in an "unsustainable situation" because of the simmering fear and fury directed against the Red Army, which fueled anticommunism.[167] Anti-Sovietism and anticommunism were also driven by the view that the end of the war represented a period of vulnerability for Magyars, thus fueling a sense of national victimization underpinned not only by the behavior of the Red Army but also by news of severe retribution against Magyars who lived just over the border in Prekmurje, following its reincorporation into Yugoslavia.[168]

It was in this climate, and with little participation from political representatives of the new state in Budapest, that oil production restarted after a two-week break. Oil was of central strategic importance to the Red Army, just as it had been to the Germans, and under the terms of the ceasefire agreement, MAORT, an enterprise that had functioned as part of the war economy, was placed under Soviet military control. The management of the company together with its nominated Soviet commanders had made preparations for a speedy start to production once the Germans had been driven out of southern Zala. Within a week of the arrival of the Soviets, the first oil well was reopened in the Lovászi field, and over the course of the next few weeks, production restarted all across the region, reaching 80 percent of the 1944 level by June 1945.[169] The relationship between the Soviets, plant management, and skilled workers was, however, strained. Soviet commanders demanded that high quantities of oil be mined. The plant's employees believed that the levels of production demanded would compromise long-term oil production at the wells. Overproduction led to the release of large quantities of gas into the atmosphere. This was a problem not merely because substantial quantities of natural gas would go to waste; because of the geology of both the Bázakerretye and Lovászi fields, the pressure of underground natural gas was used to force oil to the surface. By allowing large quantities of natural gas to escape because of the rate of production, pressure was reduced overall, thus endangering future oil production, a fact that not only concerned managers but also bred resentment among all employees, reinforcing a sense of exploitation of workers by the plant's Soviet overseers.[170] This situation was exacerbated by the politics of food provision. With the complete collapse of markets and transportation, resentment grew among the workforce during the late spring and early summer 1945 because the Soviets took the oil and gas the workers produced without supplying them adequate food in return, further fueling the anti-Soviet anger.[171] Direct military control ended in July 1945, though the oil wells continued to produce oil for the Soviets as part of Hungarian war reparations, even after MAORT was formally handed back to its American shareholders in November 1945.[172]

Throughout 1945, however, production, food distribution, and the political organization of the plant were hindered by a number of factors. Workers had to operate machinery that was often in a poor state of repair; as far as members of management were concerned, "drilling . . . equipment and machinery . . . were for the most part imported from the United States. The materials we were compelled to import from Germany during the first years of the war were not of the quality required, and in the second half of the war there was no possibility to secure any machinery at all." This was blamed for a "growing number of continual, severe breakdowns," which led the highly skilled workforce to cooperate closely with engineers to find improvised solutions to problems in production.[173] The stress on local autonomy and improvisation was strengthened by the geographical isolation of sites at Bázakerettye, Lovászi, and Pusztaszentlászló and exacerbated by the catastrophic lack of functioning vehicles in the oil fields. Company managers complained that "the roads are poor, there is no railway line, and we have an old fleet of vehicles that is just inadequate to keeping our plants' production to [their] wartime level[s], and

ensuring that around 14,000 people are fed."[174] The combined demands for cooperation and adaptation in production caused by the poor state of machinery, the
enforced decentralization brought about by the lack of transport infrastructure,
and the need to improvise to feed workers led to the foundation of the first factory
committees at the drilling plants in late April 1945.[175]

Despite the early development of plant-level factory committees, the organizing of oil field labor came from outside, shaped by the legal requirement that
MAORT have one factory committee to supervise its operation. This was based on
one MAORT plant committee in the neighboring town of Nagykanizsa, where the
company maintained machine plants to service the oil fields. This plant's committee, filled largely with MSzDP activists, formed the core of a central factory committee for the MAORT, set up on the initiative of the national trade union council
and headed by János Dombay—a prominent local Social Democrat and member
of parliament. The role of this committee was to integrate the local factory committees into the emergent national industrial relations systems, and each MAORT
plant was allowed to have two representatives.[176] Its attempts to integrate what had
traditionally been high wages for MAORT workers into the standardized systems
of payment established through national, sector-wide collective agreements made
the cross-enterprise committee deeply unpopular.[177] Furthermore, in the climate
of high inflation, the committee's attempts to standardize payment in kind for
all company sites were opposed by workers locally and proved utterly ineffective.[178] Neither of the two workers' parties was able to properly organize the rural
oil fields, due to the conservative culture there, yet the MSzDP, given its position
of hegemony on the factory committee and its close links to managers and engineers, had a marked advantage. Even the MSzDP, however, found that its ability to
recruit members among oil workers did not translate into votes in the November
1945 elections.[179] Given the conservative political culture of southern Zala, the simmering anti-Soviet anger among the population and the integration of its rival, the
MSzDP, into the company-based culture of the oil fields, and its consequent powers of patronage, the MKP found it very difficult to make any inroads. By the end
of August, it had only 49 members at Bázakerretye, where 1,086 manual workers
were employed; 18 members out of 860 workers at Lovászi; and 11 of 280 workers at
Pusztaszentlászló.[180]

The intermeshing of the working-class culture of the oil fields with the rural,
agrarian culture of the villages in which they were situated was a further factor
that allowed conservative political identities to reproduce themselves. In early 1946,
only 19.5 percent of workers at Lovászi and 18.7 percent at Bázakerretye lived in
company housing, close to the plant sites. Of Lovászi's and Bázakerretye's oil workers, 76 percent and 64.2 percent, respectively, lived "in the neighboring villages in
their own houses."[181] The culture of maintaining a family smallholding while family
members were also working in the drilling plants—a feature of the Zala oil fields

from the beginning of their development—was strengthened in 1945 by the impact of land reform. In the administrative district in which the oil fields were located, 10.9 percent of the total population received land from the distribution process.[182] In Bázakerretye, small amounts of land went to some landless oil workers, while a significant number of those who already had plots were assigned additional lands that increased the size of their holdings.[183]

The fluidity of the boundaries between agriculture and industry also shaped patterns of conflict in the oil fields, and these were especially evident in reactions to hyperinflation and food shortages in the second half of 1945. In August, as the value of wages was eroded severely, the central factory committee recorded considerable "dissatisfaction with wage levels" among the workforce.[184] As food became increasingly difficult to obtain, management was forced to admit that they "couldn't get hold of enough . . . so that everybody could receive some, therefore it is impossible to distribute it equally."[185] Faced with absolute shortages of food and poor transportation, the factory committees at individual plants were left to their own devices. The Bázakerretye committee had managed to obtain agreement to withhold a limited amount of the oil and gas it produced so that it could exchange this for food in the neighboring villages. It also agreed to connect houses in some villages to the gas supply in exchange for foodstuffs. The engagement of the factory committee in local barter relations allowed it to alleviate the dreadful material crisis faced by its workers.[186] Other plants were both less well organized and less able to replicate Bázakerretye's success, and some complained bitterly at the preferential situation of that area's workers, demanding "a just distribution" of food obtained among all MAORT workers.[187] At Lovászi, the distribution of food did not begin until December 1945, with workers receiving three kilos of flour, four kilos of meat, and four kilos of bacon for the month.[188]

The miserable conditions of many oil workers produced a huge "black" economy, as workers who were able used company resources to earn supplementary incomes to survive. This was marked among groups like the drivers, who were prepared to transport paying passengers in total contravention of company regulations.[189] Among the rural, smallholding workforce, many simply absented themselves to engage in agricultural work either on their own smallholding or on others' smallholdings in return for food. Given the desperate economic situation, neither management nor factory committees had effective sanctions, except to exclude those workers from the company-based distribution of foodstuffs, which were consequently reserved for the relatively skilled, best-paid minority who lived in company housing.[190] Given that many rural workers had taken jobs on the assumption that regular incomes from the plant would make their agricultural smallholdings viable, the ongoing conditions in which wages were devalued and agricultural goods scarce meant that attempts to enforce work discipline were utterly ineffective.

In late 1945, workers who did regularly show up to work would attempt to conserve their energy for alternative work in agriculture—"people don't do any serious work on most of the sites," one frustrated representative reported to the factory committee.[191] Production levels were maintained despite the passive resistance of a rural workforce, who were forced to engage in a local shadow economy in order to survive; an atmosphere of tremendous tension resulted from the material situation.[192] Because of the lack of a labor movement tradition, the conservatism of most workers on the sites, and the investment many had in agricultural activities in circumstances of economic involution, this tension did not lead to open protest. Instead, in the November 1945 parliamentary elections, it underpinned, along with widespread popular anti-Sovietism and anticommunism, a substantial vote for the FKgP in the villages that made up the oil fields.

# 2    Struggles for Legitimacy
### November 1945–August 1947

THE NOVEMBER 1945 parliamentary elections, and those held a month earlier for local authorities in Greater Budapest, represented a watershed in Hungary's process of postwar state building. The MKP and its allies presented them as a referendum on the new regime and a chance to strike a blow at its opponents. On the eve of polling in Budapest, Ernő Gerő wrote that "the Hungarian people will decide whether they are prepared to tolerate for any longer sabotage by reactionaries camouflaged as democrats or whether they will create order with a firm hand in the interests of Hungarian democracy."[1] While the municipal elections represented a warning, the completeness of the rejection of the MKP and its vision of the postwar state was revealed by results of the November parliamentary elections (table 2). While the MKP was shocked by its narrow third-place finish in the popular vote, it did succeed in winning the second largest number of seats; furthermore, the Left together commanded more than 40 percent of the vote. Nevertheless, almost 60 percent of the vote had gone to a party that advocated taking postwar state building in a very different direction to that envisaged by the MKP.

The geography and sociology of the election result reflected the patterns of

TABLE 2. Overall national results of parliamentary elections, 4 November 1945

| Party | Votes | Percentage of the vote | Parliamentary seats won |
|-------|-------|------------------------|-------------------------|
| FKgP | 2,697,508 | 57.03 | 245 |
| MSzDP | 823,314 | 17.41 | 69 |
| MKP | 802,122 | 16.95 | 70 |
| NPP | 325,284 | 6.87 | 23 |
| PDP | 76,424 | 1.62 | 2 |
| MRP | 5,762 | 0.12 | 0 |

*Source:* Adapted from Sándor Balogh, *Választások Magyarországon 1945: a fővárosi törvényhatósági és nemzetgyűlési választások* (Budapest: Kossuth Könyvkiadó, 1984), 147, 161.

popular response to Hungary's war-induced regime change. Outside of the radical counties of Hungary's far southeast, with their traditions of agrarian socialism, the FKgP won the rural communities and small towns where a majority of Hungarians lived. Its dominance across the conservative west of the country, where it averaged more than two-thirds of the vote, was considerable, and it polled relatively poorly in urban centers with significant industrial populations.[2] As in the Zala oil fields, where it won decisively (table 3), the FKgP victory rested on the reproduction of Hungary's dominant conservative political cultures, a process aided by the experience of Soviet occupation, the spread of a propertied "smallholder" identity made possible by land reform, and cultural antagonism toward the Left and especially toward communism.[3] What was remarkable about the results in the villages surrounding the largest oil plants was that, while they reflected the preferences of Hungary's rural majority, they were strikingly out of character with the results in other industrial communities. Aside from settlements like Bázakerretye, where significant company housing meant that there was a large landless, working-class population and that the workers' parties were therefore able to win a majority of the vote, what was most marked was the irrelevance of industrial employment to political preferences in southern Zala, as a consequence of the agrarian culture of the oil fields.

Most industrial communities voted for the Left. In the majority of them—cities like Győr, Miskolc, and Pécs—as well as in the industrial towns around Budapest, including Újpest (table 4), the MKP fell behind the MSzDP in the local vote. The existence of an alternative socialist party, which had an infrastructure that had functioned in the interwar years, disadvantaged the Communists, ensuring that most left-wing votes went to the Social Democrats.[4] The support won by the MKP was concentrated in areas with a radical tradition and that had been scarcely touched by the legal labor movement in the interwar years; it did particularly well in the closed communities of industrial company towns, where class tension and pres-

TABLE 3. Results of the parliamentary elections in the Letenye district of Zala County, 4 November 1945

| Settlement | FKgP | | MSzDP | | MKP | | NPP | | PDP | |
|---|---|---|---|---|---|---|---|---|---|---|
| | Votes | % of the vote | Votes | % of the vote | Votes | % of the vote | Votes | % of the vote | Votes | % of the vote |
| Bánokszentgyörgy | 386 | 53.91 | 137 | 19.13 | 45 | 6.28 | 124 | 19.55 | 8 | 1.12 |
| Bázakerretye | 225 | 44.29 | 207 | 40.75 | 67 | 13.19 | 2 | 0.39 | 7 | 1.38 |
| Becsehely | 1,338 | 91.95 | 46 | 3.71 | 7 | 0.48 | 49 | 3.37 | 7 | 0.48 |
| Borsfa | 559 | 89.73 | 52 | 8.35 | 5 | 0.80 | 5 | 0.80 | 2 | 0.32 |
| Bucsuta | 303 | 85.11 | 12 | 3.37 | 6 | 1.69 | 34 | 9.55 | 1 | 0.28 |
| Csörnyeföld | 446 | 79.08 | 83 | 14.72 | 31 | 5.50 | 1 | 0.18 | 3 | 0.53 |
| Dobri | 465 | 96.29 | 13 | 3.02 | 2 | 0.46 | 1 | 0.23 | 0 | 0 |
| Kerkaszentkirály | 241 | 82.82 | 19 | 6.19 | 35 | 8.59 | 6 | 2.06 | 1 | 0.34 |
| Kerkateskánd | 276 | 92.31 | 16 | 5.35 | 3 | 1.00 | 3 | 1.00 | 1 | 0.33 |
| Kiscsehi | 258 | 94.16 | 3 | 1.09 | 7 | 2.55 | 5 | 1.82 | 1 | 0.36 |
| Kistolmács | 161 | 64.92 | 38 | 15.32 | 41 | 16.53 | 6 | 2.42 | 2 | 0.80 |
| Kútfej | 383 | 75.10 | 96 | 18.82 | 31 | 6.08 | 0 | 0 | 0 | 0 |
| Letenye | 1,644 | 73.16 | 206 | 9.17 | 235 | 10.46 | 153 | 6.81 | 6 | 0.40 |
| Lispeszentadorján | 453 | 88.65 | 35 | 6.85 | 18 | 3.52 | 5 | 0.98 | 0 | 0 |
| Lovászi | 357 | 80.95 | 69 | 15.65 | 12 | 2.72 | 3 | 0.68 | 0 | 0 |
| Maróc | 182 | 80.18 | 11 | 4.85 | 12 | 5.29 | 19 | 8.37 | 3 | 1.32 |
| Molnári | 248 | 46.10 | 170 | 31.60 | 118 | 21.93 | 1 | 0.19 | 1 | 0.19 |
| Murarátka | 202 | 57.71 | 77 | 22.00 | 4 | 1.14 | 63 | 18.86 | 1 | 0.29 |
| Muraszemenye | 582 | 69.95 | 162 | 19.47 | 54 | 6.49 | 29 | 3.49 | 5 | 0.60 |
| Oltárc | 471 | 87.22 | 33 | 6.11 | 5 | 0.93 | 28 | 5.19 | 3 | 0.56 |
| Petrivente | 169 | 51.37 | 107 | 32.52 | 25 | 7.60 | 16 | 7.90 | 2 | 0.61 |
| Pusztamagyaród | 532 | 80.36 | 41 | 6.19 | 29 | 4.38 | 57 | 8.61 | 3 | 0.45 |
| Semjénháza | 431 | 62.61 | 105 | 23.65 | 10 | 2.25 | 56 | 10.36 | 5 | 1.13 |
| Szécsisziget | 206 | 92.38 | 10 | 4.48 | 7 | 3.14 | 0 | 0 | 0 | 0 |
| Szentliszló | 131 | 41.72 | 63 | 20.06 | 86 | 27.39 | 33 | 10.51 | 1 | 0.32 |
| Szentmargitfalva | 120 | 41.67 | 158 | 54.86 | 3 | 1.04 | 2 | 0.69 | 5 | 1.74 |
| Tormaföldе | 479 | 90.06 | 32 | 6.00 | 17 | 3.19 | 4 | 0.75 | 0 | 0 |
| Tornyiszentmiklós | 494 | 87.61 | 35 | 5.16 | 18 | 2.65 | 26 | 3.83 | 5 | 0.74 |
| Tótszentmárton | 358 | 64.62 | 112 | 21.12 | 34 | 6.14 | 31 | 5.60 | 4 | 0.72 |
| Tótszerdahely | 357 | 39.49 | 328 | 36.17 | 178 | 19.69 | 38 | 4.20 | 1 | 0.44 |
| Valkonya | 144 | 81.82 | 28 | 15.91 | 2 | 1.13 | 1 | 0.57 | 1 | 0.57 |
| Várfölde | 227 | 79.93 | 26 | 9.15 | 15 | 5.28 | 12 | 4.22 | 4 | 1.40 |
| Zajk | 193 | 79.75 | 19 | 7.85 | 11 | 4.55 | 19 | 7.85 | 0 | 0 |

Source: Adapted from Zala Megyei Levéltár, XXXV.38f.1945/31ö.e., 16; and Csaba Káli, "Az 1945. évi nemzetgyűlési választások Zalában," in Zalai történeti tanulmányok, ed. Csaba Káli (Zalaegerszeg: Zala Megyei Levéltár, 1997), 328–29.

TABLE 4. Results of parliamentary elections in Újpest, 4 November 1945

| Party | Votes | Percentage of the vote |
|-------|-------|------------------------|
| FKgP | 15,537 | 42.13 |
| MSzDP | 11,508 | 31.20 |
| MKP | 8,568 | 23.23 |
| NPP | 596 | 1.62 |
| PDP | 549 | 1.49 |
| MRP | 122 | 0.33 |

*Source:* Adapted from László Hubai, "Az országgyűlési választások Újpesten, 1920–1947," in *Dokumentumok Újpest történetéhez, 1840–1949,* ed. András Sipos (Budapest: Budapest Főváros Levéltára, 2001), 423.

sure for radical change were at their greatest—settlements like Ózd, Salgótarján, and the four villages that later made up Tatabánya (table 5).[5]

The MKP reacted to its defeat by abandoning any pretense that its vision of the postwar state could be legitimated through democratic means; instead, it maintained that the election's center-right victors were, in fact, enemies of democracy. Aided by the considerable suspicion of the FKgP and fear of a return of "reaction" among the leaders and supporters of its allies, especially the MSzDP, the MKP secured a leading role on the left through tactical aggression by polarizing politics into a struggle between an FKgP it painted as "reactionary" and the workers' parties. As Mátyás Rákosi argued in 1946, "As a consequence of the unconstrained havoc caused by the functioning of reactionaries inside the Smallholders' Party, the majority of the party stands passionately against the socialist workers' parties and, at one and the same time, directly and clearly has come under the influence of the cartels, the banks and big capital."[6] By using political polarization as a tool, the MKP was able to assert its leadership over the rest of the Left, despite its poor electoral performance, and thus mobilize Hungary's substantial left-wing minority against the FKgP. Furthermore, the central role that the MKP had played in the early phases of postwar state building during 1945, as well as its continued presence in government given the insistence of the occupying forces on a continued "popular-front" coalition despite the FKgP's clear victory, allowed it to acquire power over state institutions—especially through the security services—out of all proportion to its electoral support. It sought to use this power, in tandem with its strategy of mobilization, to destroy the political coalition on which the FKgP's 1945 victory rested by driving its right and center out of the party, and thus the government. This strategy reached its culmination in the first of half of 1947 with the discovery of the "conspiracy against the Republic," through which the MKP succeeded in forcing the FKgP prime minister, Ferenc Nagy, into exile.[7] The wholesale destruction of the FKgP's parliamentary majority paved the way for new elections in August 1947, which cemented the MKP's control over the popular-front government.

TABLE 5. Results of parliamentary elections in Alsógalla, Bánhida, Felsőgalla, and Tatabánya, 4 November 1945

| Settlement | MKP | | MSzDP | | FKgP | | NPP | | PDP | |
|---|---|---|---|---|---|---|---|---|---|---|
| | Votes | % of the vote | Votes | % of the vote | Votes | % of the vote | Votes | % of the vote | Votes | % of the vote |
| Alsógalla | 176 | 20.90 | 474 | 56.29 | 172 | 20.43 | 10 | 1.19 | 10 | 1.19 |
| Bánhida | 3,814 | 56.01 | 2,113 | 31.33 | 769 | 11.29 | 56 | 0.68 | 57 | 0.69 |
| Felsőgalla | 4,877 | 59.65 | 2,607 | 31.89 | 692 | 8.46 | 0 | 0 | 0 | 0 |
| Tatabánya | 1,880 | 51.76 | 1,470 | 40.47 | 240 | 6.61 | 22 | 0.58 | 20 | 0.58 |
| TOTAL | 10,747 | 55.23 | 6,664 | 34.25 | 1,873 | 9.63 | 88 | 0.45 | 87 | 0.44 |

Source: Adapted from Politikatörténeti és Szakszervezeti Levéltár, A Magyar Kommunista Párt iratai, I.274f.16/109ö.e., 193.

The MKP's use of undemocratic tactics was, however, seen as legitimate by many industrial workers, especially in the kinds of closed, industrial communities where the party had won most of its support in the 1945 elections. Indeed, among Tatabánya's miners, Ferenc Nagy's removal in May 1947 was greeted with considerable approval.[8] This approval was the product of the social dynamics that underpinned the MKP's campaign of mobilization that followed the 1945 election in most industrial communities. The results crystallized the frustration that had been building with what was seen as the overly moderate line of the MKP and the workers' parties. The victory of the FKgP focused this frustration, generating the impression that attempts to build a more socially just Hungary would founder on the occupation of power by the center Right. This produced polarization, which allowed the MKP to construct legitimacy among left-wing workers; this successful effort to present its legitimacy rested on generating a perception of the party as their best defender against the threat of "reaction." When it moved to unify the left-wing parties with the formation of the Left-Wing Bloc in early 1946 and called for demonstrations against what it represented as the persistence of "reaction" in the FKgP, these efforts met with broad support in industrial areas. According to the local MSzDP, approximately thirty thousand workers from Újpest joined a demonstration to support the aims of the Left-Wing Bloc in Budapest in March 1946.[9]

The MKP's ability to mobilize left-wing workers against "reaction" was, however, conditional on it finding ways of politically managing considerable working-class discontent. In the first half of 1946, as hyperinflation continued to accelerate out of control, the material crisis of many workers intensified. The MKP blamed hyperinflation on "speculators," whom it linked politically to the "reaction," bringing it some political gains. This stance offered no meaningful relief to workers, and often its attempts to target "speculators" spiraled into violence that escaped its control. Furthermore, it continued to frustrate reconstruction as near-starvation conditions and the need to participate in a black-market economy to survive made rebuilding the industrial infrastructure nigh on impossible. In August 1946, the popular-front government was forced to implement a stabilization package that involved the abolition of one currency, the *pengő*, and its replacement with a new means of payment, the *forint*. While this move did stop hyperinflation in its tracks, it did not eliminate high prices, more limited inflation, or persistent problems of the supply of goods to industrial areas. Furthermore, it resulted in huge increases in unemployment, and this, combined with continuing endemic poverty in industrial areas, produced deep discontent with the material situation. In workplaces, it generated attempts to tie remuneration tightly to production levels, and to economic policy priorities; the reshaping of labor policy to support reconstruction often challenged workers' expectations and ignited protest.

Late 1946 and 1947 were thus characterized by considerable tension and frequent explosions of working-class protest, which the MKP and its allies were forced to contain. This process of containment rested on the channeling of working-class anger against inflation and poverty into avenues for blaming these problems on the activities of "speculators," selective repression, and the toleration of a series of informal compromises in workplaces that undercut the aims of some of the labor policies that they were supposed to implement. In so doing, the conditional and incomplete legitimacy that was established by the MKP among most workers in 1946 and 1947 set the scene for the labor policies later promulgated by the socialist regime. Yet the scope of this containment was limited by political polarization; the MKP was only tolerant of compromises at the local level that bolstered its support. With workers who adopted right-wing political identities and utterly opposed the "new" state, it was more than prepared to resort to repression.

The repressive stance of the MKP was most marked in the Zala oil fields. The Communists reacted to their dreadful results there by defining the area as hostile territory—they blamed US ownership and the political conservatism of oil workers for their failure to win support. Thus, they sought to extend their control and influence—a project that met with little success; in attacking MAORT, they further reinforced their own isolation. The wage policies they advocated to support stabilization exacerbated this situation, for they eroded the relatively high wages of MAORT's workers compared to the wage levels that had been in place prior to 1944, thus reinforcing the alienation of oil workers from the postwar state. In Újpest, the situation differed, for groups of workers reacted differently to state policies according to the political identities they adopted and to their own factory circumstances. While the majority supported socialist transformation and were thus receptive to mobilization, protest rumbled over wage policies in workplaces, superimposed on tension caused by the MKP and MSzDP battling each other for hegemony in the factories. Among such workers, discontent in the workplace was mitigated through informal compromise—a route closed to the right-wing minority, who were dealt with more despotically. In Tatabánya, support for the MKP remained remarkably constant between November 1945 and August 1947. This support rested on established working-class identities, which provided the local underpinning for the MKP's politics of polarization. Yet, paradoxically, it also coexisted with tremendous discontent and frustration that challenged the policies of the popular-front government.

## The Grassroots of Postwar Communism in Tatabánya

In a short period of time after the end of the war, Hungary witnessed the Left's defeat in the parliamentary elections, the growing signs of assertiveness from the right of the FKgP (despite the party leadership's consent to continued coalition), the nationalization of the mines, and the creation of a republic.[10] These factors combined with working-class anger at the desperate economic situation to produce overwhelming demands for a harder line from the MKP. This crisis was fueled at the local level by the persistent failure of MÁK Rt. to pay its employees on time during the autumn and winter months.[11] Consequently, the workers' demands of the MKP became increasingly radical and violent, prefiguring the Communists' aggressive stance toward opponents and providing the social underpinning for aggressive MKP tactics. Workers demanded that the local party use its power to employ the repressive apparatus against local employers—a sign of the workers' spent patience with the politics of coalition, and of conciliation. "The miners demand," one local trade union official told a mass meeting of the district's MKP membership in January 1946, "that their old rights must remain. The employers must guarantee their wages paid in foodstuffs, and if they don't fulfill this," then management "should be interned for five to ten years."[12]

The violence of such demands was in large part a product of the desperate material situation, for over the course of the winter, hyperinflation, and consequently the state of penury in the district, had reached crisis proportions. In late 1945, the national trade union council established a "living minimum"—a very basic poverty line, which allowed them to document the deterioration of working-class living standards nationwide. By mid-January 1946, average working-class wages covered only 16.57 percent of this living minimum.[13] Because of the almost total nonavailability of foodstuffs, even this calculation failed to capture the true nature of the misery faced in industrial areas in general and the Tatabánya district in particular. For the whole of the first half of 1946, workers in the area were "simply unable to buy food with their wages, because we are located in an industrial district . . . where tens of thousands are forced to barter for food."[14] Consequently, the management's loss of authority in the mines had turned into outright collapse by the turn of 1946; one observer noted that the labor situation was so bad that "no one was prepared to apply for underground work." The value of coal to workers as a means of exchange for scarce food, particularly in view of the irregular payment of wages, meant that many underground miners were prepared to resort to violence to prevent its trans-port to purchasers; according to one observer, "armed miners decide who should be given coal." Given the complete lack of trust in management's willingness to pay them and uncertainty about the future of the country, miners rejected demands that they work harder in the interests of reconstruction outright: "we . . . already provide the capital with huge quantities of electricity, and they want coal as well?"[15]

As production levels fell from summer 1945 onward as a consequence of the impact of hyperinflation on the labor situation in the mines countrywide, the econ-omy suffered from growing paralysis as coal supplies to key industrial sectors and transport dried up.[16] In the aftermath of election defeat, the MKP shifted tactics to win support from miners by blaming private mine owners for the economic crisis, arguing that they were speculating from illegal coal sales while pleading a lack of resources from which to pay or feed their workforces.[17] The MKP skillfully used the crisis to force their reluctant coalition partners, especially the FKgP, to accept nationalization of enterprises engaging directly in coal production. In addition, prior to the nationalization, the MKP also won support for placing coal production under direct state supervision, a measure implemented on New Year's Day 1946.[18] The campaign for nationalization involved Rákosi himself addressing Tatabánya's miners to enlist their open support for the MKP's position in December 1945.[19] This effort was aided by the ambiguous stance of the Ministry of Industry, controlled by the MKP's major local rivals—the MSzDP—toward nationalization.[20] They were thus able to retain their control of factory committees in the mines during elections in February 1946.[21]

While the MKP was able to obtain the votes of a majority of mineworkers in the factory committee elections by blaming private ownership of the mines and the employers for miners' and the country's problems, this support was by no means unconditional. The MKP used its power over state institutions and the unions to revive the productivist, pro-reconstruction economic policies that had foundered with spiraling hyperinflation the previous summer. First, the MKP moved to miti-gate the effects of hyperinflation by increasing centrally mandated payment in kind for workers with large families. In addition, it linked wages to rising production, just as it had the previous summer—this time, however, it linked payment by results to payment in kind, forcing employers to pay their workers in food and clothing; where this was not possible, it linked workers' monetary wages to the prices of foodstuffs of predetermined calorie values in order to protect working-class liv-ing standards.[22] It bears mention, however, that given the utter worthlessness of money in Tatabánya, workers were simply not prepared to accept anything other than wages paid in kind.[23] Underground-face miners in Tatabánya were given pro-duction targets, or norms, to reach, established at a decentralized level by their immediate supervisors working in consultation with union officials and the coal hewers themselves. Achievement of a certain percentage of the target triggered the payment of premiums. Other workers were given an hourly wage, with a premium supplement if the pit in which they worked hit its production target.[24] This was combined with a campaign of mobilization, launched by the district at the instigation of the national leadership of the MKP and termed the "battle for coal" (*széncsata*). The MKP, speaking in the name of the Tatabánya miners, called on their workmates countrywide to raise production levels in the interest of reconstruction.[25]

Superficially, the "battle for coal" both echoed the small-scale labor competitions of late 1945 and anticipated those organized on a larger scale over the coming years. Local party activists demanded that the names of the miners who exceeded their production targets be publicized as part of an attempt to demonstrate that the campaign "was launched for them."[26] The reception of the "battle for coal" among mineworkers rested on the complex dynamics of their attitudes to the "new" state, especially the MKP. Arguments that promised future social transformation, particularly a transformation of the enterprise, did win support among the workforce; claims that with "nationalization the role of the workforce within the enterprise will be transformed," as the state would then be "not only an employer but the guarantor of workers' rights," did win consent for increased production.[27] Arguments that stressed the importance of "more production" for an improvement in the material situation, which had miners complaining that "we walk around in rags and don't have sufficient food," also played a role in mobilization.[28] To this was tied the promise of a final end to inflation with the introduction of a stable currency, the forint, in August 1946, which, propagandists argued, required "higher coal production" in order to guarantee its success.[29] While the miners proved receptive to such calls, they also, paradoxically, remained deeply distrustful; they demanded guarantees in exchange for working more. "The workers are mistrustful of the norms, they want guarantees [that they will be paid]," reported one MKP official. Miners demanded that union officials, rather than the direct managers of production, set the production norms and, as a confidence-building measure, pressured both party and union to demand that premiums be paid retroactively, as the price of accepting the pact for reconstruction offered them.[30] Behind this distrust was not merely the experience of the failure of a similar pact for reconstruction offered to them the previous year but also the fear of a return of the interwar political order, which both bound the majority of the miners to the MKP and also, paradoxically, fed their distrust. Management, the MKP, and local authorities put to work almost 140 persons interned for their support either for the Arrow Cross or the old regime in the mines, and 60 of them were given positions—in view of their training—as skilled coal hewers in order to mitigate the labor shortage.[31] The claims of some of these workers that "the gendarmerie will take charge again, because the current situation is not stable" both reminded miners of the fragility of the political order in view of the election results and was deeply corrosive of morale.[32]

As the "battle for coal" became central to the MKP's attempts to present itself as the guarantor of reconstruction, it became clear that attempts to persuade miners to increase production were dependent on improvement in their material situation. As one local official pointed out, "Victory in the battle for coal will be achieved if, and only if, miners receive all the support the government can give."[33] Just as with the open rebellions against the moderate policies of the MKP in June 1945, what threatened the success of the "battle for coal" was management's continued inability to pay the wages mandated by the state. Original plans to organize Sunday shifts during which 25 percent of the coal mined was retained by those participating came to nothing.[34] As the state's measures to protect miners from high inflation went into effect at the beginning of 1946, the factory committee was aware almost immediately that mine managers ignored them by "underpaying" the workforce.[35] Anger built as MÁK Rt. failed to pay workers in kind in full, instead opting to pay them in increasingly worthless cash during the first two months of 1946.[36] This failure threatened to sabotage the "battle for coal" as miners responded by refusing to accept payment in cash and threatened strike action until all their wages were paid in food and other goods.[37] Such conflict was defused through state pressure on the mines, which ensured that production premiums were paid in coal, which the miners could then exchange for goods on the black market.[38]

While tensions persisted throughout the spring because the mine depots also began experiencing shortages of foodstuffs, which contributed to a state of "permanent nervousness" in the mining community, the material situation of mineworkers was mitigated considerably by the fact that the authorities gave the mines top priority when distributing food as the result of pressure from the MKP and their strategic importance to the national economy. In the local power plants, workers, unions, and managers alike experienced the misery of food shortages and complained bitterly about the preferential treatment of mining enterprises in the distribution of food.[39] This preferential position allowed the mines to recruit large numbers of unskilled and semiskilled laborers to work underground across the Tatabánya field, while between December 1945 and June 1946 the number of skilled coal hewers— leaders of the brigades that cut the coal—remained remarkably stable, increasing from 1,886 to 2,119, and the numbers of cart men, who provided the manual labor that moved the coal, rose from 1,037 to 2,033.[40] By agreeing to labor in the mines, such workers gained access to foodstuffs and other goods in kind for themselves and family members that they would not have otherwise received.[41] It also created a labor reserve, which management, with the cooperation of the factory committee and use of the campaignlike atmosphere of the "battle for coal," were able to deploy flexibly across established lines of demarcation and skill at the coal face to raise production.[42]

Production increased during the first half of 1946, largely as a result of the hiring of additional workers, in circumstances in which much machinery remained in an unusable state.[43] It was also aided by a relative stabilization of the material crisis faced by mineworkers, though the extent of this relative stabilization ought not to be exaggerated, given persistent problems with the payment of wages either in money or in kind and marked antimanagement sentiment.[44] Following the eventual nationalization of the mines in May 1946 but not of the nonmining enterprises owned by MÁK Rt., their subsequent incorporation into the Hungarian State Coal Mining Company (Magyar Állami Szénbányák Rt., or MÁSz Rt.), the promise of a better life to be brought by a more stable currency, and the stirring of class hatred through campaigns directed at "speculators," many in the district were prepared to trust in the MKP's vision of the future even if they were at present angry and frustrated.[45] This anger and frustration was politicized in highly particular ways due to the unusual local political constellation that had arisen a year previously. The district party leadership's loss of authority led to a willingness among some grassroots Communists to express their discontent through direct action. Given that many were armed, some had been prepared to use violence to ensure that coal was supplied only if miners received food or clothes in exchange. As a consequence of the spread of violent sentiments among miners in a desperate material situation, some were prepared to engage in acts of terrorism. In summer 1946, the mining colony was hit by a wave of incidents in which armed activists attempted to shoot those in management positions or those responsible for the distribution of food. The MKP leadership and the local police linked these incidents to Teofil Sándor, known for his advocacy of violent direct action against those he saw as representatives of the "reaction." Arrested and tried for one of the attacks, Sándor received a sentence of three months' imprisonment for his apparent involvement. Protest in the mines and a petition for his release resulted in his freedom, though the MKP district leadership expelled him from the party.[46]

Violent direct action was one extreme manifestation of frustration with the policies of the MKP locally. Left-wing frustration existed together with anti-Communist sentiment among a minority of residents. They expressed their mistrust of the promises that the "battle for coal" and other productivist policies represented as open political opposition. One constant rumor that accompanied attempts to increase coal production during the first half of 1946 was that "of every five hundred wagons of coal, three hundred are bound for Ukraine."[47] Anti-Communist sentiment was especially strong among ethnic minority groups; given the multiethnic nature of the four villages and some of the outlying rural communities from which local workers commuted, this was a central issue. During early 1946, the centrally mandated expulsions of ethnic Germans were under way, while a future "exchange of populations," in which ethnic Slovaks would be forced out of Hungary and replaced by ethnic Magyars from Slovakia, was anticipated.[48] Among ethnic Germans, the fear of deportation fueled anticommunism, despite the fact that miners were often exempted because of their importance to the economy.[49] Within the Slovak population in Bánhida, there were wild rumors to the effect that

"15,000 agricultural workers, 8,000 industrial workers, including miners, eight engineers, and the Bánhida priest" would be expelled, and substantial fear and discontent resulted.[50] Because the MKP was the leading political force in the district and essentially controlled the police, the local trade union, and its associated factory committees, the MSzDP became the rallying point for the anticommunist minority, in direct contrast to the national leadership's policy of close cooperation with the Communists. The late spring and early summer period was marked by disputes between the MKP and MSzDP over the control of the local branch of the Mineworkers' Union, and the conflicts culminated in an election in which most leadership positions were won by MKP candidates.[51]

Political tension was recast and the nature of material discontent was altered substantially by the introduction of the forint in August 1946. The launch of the new currency was accompanied by a tightening of economic policy as state revenues were increased, spending was cut back, and price controls were introduced in the interest of securing price stability, while state influence over the economy was extended. Under the influence of the Left, especially the MKP, productivist policies that stressed state-led national reconstruction became more prominent.[52] These policies informed a renewed drive to link wages to output across industry, mining, and construction, enforced through new collective agreements that abolished much payment in kind, replacing it with cash wages combined with a system of rationing for basic goods and foodstuffs. Enterprises were forced to establish production targets for all workers, and these were based on historical company records and generally set at 75 percent of the production level in 1938–39. Workers were well rewarded for making their target; bonuses for fulfillment were heavily progressive.[53] In the mines, especially among the underground workers, these principles were carefully adapted to specific labor processes and linked all wages to coal production. In order to ensure realistic incentives for increasing production, bonuses were paid when only half of the production target was reached, ensuring that wages rose rapidly. These policies enabled wage levels to recover considerably in the year that followed the currency reform, even if they did so from a very low base. This pattern was replicated in both Tatabánya's mines and its industrial enterprises.[54]

While currency reform did eliminate hyperinflation and the specific material crisis that resulted, it did not wipe out the deep-seated material discontent, poverty, and insecurity among workers locally but merely recast the problems. Many of the sources of material discontent that had formed the basis for the construction of class identities in the district during the interwar years were reproduced when the material crisis induced by hyperinflation diminished. Fury at dreadful housing conditions in the mining colonies proved especially potent, as already poor conditions had been exacerbated by war shortages and war damage. The company housing established by MÁK Rt. between 1896 and 1906 was often poorly built; according to the local newspaper, "small houses were crowded onto small plots of land, without gardens and roads of the necessary size." In late 1946, 25,188 people lived in 6,844 apartments in the mining colonies of the district. One visitor in 1947 noted that "as a result of the fact that there are in general three or four children in one family and that newly married couples live with their parents, the flats are overcrowded[;] often between eight and ten people live in one room." So great was the overcrowding that, with the closure of the local internment camp, miners were accommodated in its barracks.[55]

The persistence of poor housing conditions and low incomes, despite rising wages, made local workers feel there was a lack of positive change. This sense of stagnation provided a frame through which local class identities reproduced themselves and were articulated through material frustration. The complaint of one stoker on the mining railway, András Pancsics, expressed this frustration well. Although "he always worked hard, he was unable to feed and clothe his family adequately from his low wages, let alone buy the necessary furniture."[56] Such feelings drove fury over high prices, which, despite wage increases, remained too high for many, and shopkeepers and market vendors frequently received blame for the situation. One miner's wife complained in 1946 that she "could not buy shoes and clothes for her children. These prices are terrible, and furthermore, we cannot be sure we will get anything during the winter."[57] In a climate of persistent food shortages, high prices, and poverty, many women in the mining communities kept land allotments, often more than a kilometer from where they lived, to provide themselves with some opportunity for self-provision.[58] Alongside persistent poverty, despite rising wages, currency reform, and the economic policies designed to counteract the problem, there came a wave of layoffs that was especially marked in the industrial enterprises surrounding the mines and in small-scale industry, creating a visible problem of unemployment by the end of 1946.[59] The rationing system for the provision of goods introduced with the forint in August 1946 was linked to and administered through the place of work of the head of the household.[60] Without access to the preferential food distribution that industrial employment provided and faced with recourse to an almost nonexistent safety net, the newly unemployed boosted the ranks of the local poor.[61] The growth of a large group without access to employment, generalized low wages, and relative shortages meant that the black market and organized crime—often violent organized crime—though far less prevalent than in the period of hyperinflation, persisted, contributing further to the climate of insecurity.[62]

The mines were not immune from the pressures toward layoffs, although skilled workers were relatively protected. The number of skilled coal hewers in Tatabánya's mines increased from 2,119 to 2,228 in the last six months of 1946, while the impact of job cuts among the underground workers fell disproportionately on the manual workers who cleared the coal; their numbers fell from 2,033 to 1,635 over the same period.[63] Layoffs in the mines reflected the impact of economic policies to support stabilization, which set prices for coal at an artificially low level in order to have cheap energy to support reconstruction in other sectors, which meant that MÁSz Rt. produced coal at a loss and was forced, in turn, to drive down production costs as the collective agreements mandated increases in wages.[64] Almost from the moment of stabilization, management sought to increase production with less labor and to better utilize the labor it employed.[65] These pressures became increasingly overt; when the three-year plan was announced to miners in January 1947, management and the local party stressed the need for "cheap production," which meant cutting the use of raw materials like wood, raising production per worker, and, in the long term, increasing mechanization.[66] In the short term, this productivity drive led to poor working conditions; in Tatabánya's Síkvölgyi Pit, little of the machinery functioned in late 1946. Increases in production were achieved only through exceptional physical effort and relaxations in the safety regulations, which led to serious accidents.[67] This was accompanied by an increasingly punitive stance on the part of management as the proportion of shifts missed was reduced from 23.5 percent in September 1946 to 12.9 percent in January 1947.[68] These drives were matched by the introduction of severe punishments for infractions on the job—measures that provoked fury because they were meted out to manual workers, while engineers, mine management, and other white-collar staff were exempt.[69]

Anger at the continuities in management personnel and culture further fed reproduced class identities in the mines. Miners demanded the democratization of management, justifying their call by arguing that "after the liberation the miners started production with their heroism and sacrifice at work, and met the challenge of the battle for coal in the middle of the misery of the inflationary period. From those periods one can find many examples of miners who are capable of management and leadership. They should be given their place in the management of the state coal mining company and in the pits themselves."[70] In practice, while the central state demanded reductions in administrative and management personnel through the implementation of the so-called B-List policy, which involved using criteria of political loyalty to the "new" state to reduce white-collar staff, these layoffs were implemented unevenly in the mines because management cited the importance of their expertise to production. This generated fury among miners, who accused the leadership of their union and the MKP of protecting senior management and "oppressing workers."[71] Anger at continuities in management often combined with poverty to feed cynicism; in late 1946, the opinion that "democracy is good for the bosses, they can buy everything," was one that articulated the simmering discontent of many.[72]

Antimanagement sentiment was reflected in discontent at the system of payment in the mines. The tying of wages to performance, though this policy brought about increases in incomes, offended the moral economy of many miners. Collective agreements introduced with the forint aimed to standardize wages in the mines nationwide; job rates were harmonized, while the production targets given to miners could be adjusted in certain circumstances to take into account conditions in particular pits. During hyperinflation, mine managers had conceded a role for miners, especially the skilled coal hewers, in the establishment of their own work targets; with stabilization, in the interests of standardization, management assumed sole responsibility for setting production quotas.[73] The exclusion of the skilled workers from processes that impacted their wages caused bitter resentment, and many took this as a sign of the betrayal of the promise of the "new" democracy, leading them to demand the restoration of their role.[74] Although at a formal level, this effort was never successful, the informal renegotiation of wages did reappear, forming a safety valve for much of the discontent that built up among the workers. Payment by results among underground workers resulted in a huge differentiation in earnings among those who worked at the coal face; some of the variation was due to differences in work performance, but often the cause was inappropriate production targets. In August 1946, the average earnings of a coal hewer on a shift in the Tatabánya area were 15.81 forints; the lowest earning hewer took home 8.92 forints per shift, while the highest earner pocketed 28.47 forints.[75] Mineworkers with the lowest earnings responded with fury, arguing that the office workers had simply established production targets without examining the actual conditions in which workers had to produce.[76] Unpopular managers, often insecure in their positions because of state policies like the B-Lists, found themselves under overwhelming pressure to raise wages informally.[77] The cumulative effect was considerable informal subversion of the entire wage system, so that direct managers of production appeased angry miners, which in turn led to large increases in wages. In August 1947, mine management estimated that it should be paying an average of 16.18 forints per shift to each coal hewer; in practice, it paid 20.29 forints.[78]

The opportunities to bargain informally were considerable and were not confined to the mines; those in other local industrial enterprises also had such opportunities.[79] Their extent should not, however, be overestimated because these opportunities tended to be confined to the skilled, and in the mines, this meant the coal hewers and those who worked directly at the coal face. Furthermore, they rested on restricted, decentralized, and informal countervailing power. Large-scale open protest over state policies was less successful. The increasing use of cash wages meant cutting back on payment in kind, including allowances of coal paid to workers. In a climate characterized by the continued existence of a black market, any move to cut this allowance was bitterly opposed by miners.[80] When the policy to cut payments in kind was implemented, the result was a strike, which quickly spread across the Tatabánya mines on 4 December 1946 and had stopped all production by the morning shift on the following day.[81] The strike was spontaneous, culminating in a huge and angry mass meeting of an estimated five thousand miners in the district's sporting stadium. Speakers expressed their frustration with inflation, low living standards, and the continuing power of management. The strike split local union activists, and many ordinary MKP members participated, though it collapsed quickly; having expressed their anger, many returned to work within twenty-four hours of having stopped.[82]

The issue of cutting coal allowances had triggered an explosion of frustration with what many felt was a lack of meaningful social change locally. The MKP leadership, both nationally and locally, attributed the explosion of protest to the machinations of politically motivated "troublemakers," and it responded with selective repression. The MKP officials believed that "Arrow Crossists who had returned from the west were the loudest," while the local MSzDP "talked demagogically." Others sought to prove, with limited results, that Teofild Sándor, despite his expulsion from the party, and his allies had incited the strike. Although they lacked any real proof, the MKP, in deciding that Sándor was a "troublemaker," used its control over the police to remove him from the Tatabánya district, destroying his potential to become a rallying point for those in the MKP who were disappointed with its policies. In blaming political malcontents, however, the MKP completely misunderstood the nature of the strike as a simple expression of frustration over the persistence of managerial hierarchies and poor material conditions. After all, many of the strikers were the MKP's natural supporters.[83]

Despite its opposition to the strike, the MKP paradoxically remained the only party capable of giving credible political expression to the frustration through which class-based cultural identities were reproduced in the district. In part, this local success was based on the MKP's national strategy of polarizing politics between itself and the FKgP; much discontent in Tatabánya was tied to the fact that many workers believed too many concessions were being made to those who had supported antilabor policies under the interwar regime. Because many workers perceived the FKgP as the natural representative of such groups, the MKP's militant and antidemocratic conduct was greeted approvingly by many locally.[84] This approval rested on the MKP constructing its legitimacy as protector of working-class interests against a "reaction" that consisted not only of national political actors but also those who locally were seen as threatening the material well-being of workers. In August 1946, the MKP's organization of activists began to comb local markets to identify "speculators" who raised prices and thus could be reported to the economic branch of the local police.[85] These activists were also prepared to be a vociferous mouthpiece for antimanagement sentiment. While, in practice, the implementation of the B-Lists was uneven, the MKP presented itself as an enthusiastic advocate of a wholesale purge of unpopular managers, thus channeling working-class anger. As unemployment rose, MKP rhetoric stressed that "it was unthinkable that the worker, who yesterday selflessly built the factory, today should just be dumped from his machine into the street. . . . But on the other hand it is undoubtedly essential to get rid of the unnecessary directors and managers, who earn under various headings twenty to thirty times that which is earned by a skilled worker."[86] The Communist-controlled local newspaper framed the issue of the B-Lists in the following terms: "In our opinion it is not the capitalists but the Hungarian people who are rebuilding this country. We will implement the B-Lists not against the workers but against former exploiters and now unnecessary managers. Hungarian economic life needs to be freed of these hyenas."[87]

Although the MKP's only significant local opponents, the MSzDP, attempted to profit from working-class discontent by seeking to blame the MKP, its efforts were less than credible. Not only did the MSzDP's past count against it, but by spring 1947, it had become too associated with mine management. Despite the fact that workers made up 3,012 of its 5,543 declared members in the district in June 1947, the MSzDP was disproportionately strong among unpopular mine managers. Furthermore, it was common knowledge in the mining colonies that MÁSz Rt.'s central management and administration was dominated by MSzDP members, thus ensuring that they were closely associated with unpopular management decisions, making it impossible for them to effectively exploit discontent.[88] Yet, while the MKP maintained its hegemony in the Tatabánya district and destroyed the FKgP at the national level, aided by the impact of the climate of national polarization in the particular circumstances of the mining colonies locally, it was unable to extend the support it had gained in 1945. The climate of fear among ethnic Germans and, to a lesser extent, Slovaks, alienated from the postwar state by the MKP's policies of forced expulsion, and the persistent resistance of the anti-Communist minority, some of whom had supported the Arrow Cross in the 1930s, presented real barriers to the MKP in seeking to expand its support locally.[89] This was why, in the August 1947 elections, which followed the effective destruction of the FKgP as a national party, the MKP's result in Tatabánya was little better than it had been in 1945 (table 6).

## Strengthening the Left and Competing for Hegemony in Újpest

In Újpest, the 1945 elections resulted in a majority for the workers' parties, but unlike in Tatabánya, the MKP was forced into a clear third-place finish, behind not only the FKgP but also the MSzDP. By August 1947, the workers' parties had extended their total share of the vote and diminished the impact of the Right, which was split between a multitude of conservative parties that had not contested the 1945 elections. The drop in the Right's share of the vote was due more to the manipulation of the voter lists, which led to the removal of 10.3 percent of all adults—the 10.3 percent most likely to support conservative positions—than it was to actual changes in political affiliation. Within the Left, however, the 1947 results represented a significant narrowing of the difference between the MKP and MSzDP when compared to 1945, although the MKP had good reason to be disappointed that it had not overtaken its Social Democrat rivals (table 7).[90]

TABLE 6. Results of the parliamentary elections in Alsógalla, Bánhida, Felsőgalla, and Tatabánya, 31 August 1947

| Party | Alsógalla | Bánhida | Felsőgalla | Tatabánya | Total |
|---|---|---|---|---|---|
| MKP (Votes) | 284 | 4,419 | 5,572 | 2,308 | 12,583 |
| MKP (%) | 41.27 | 55.48 | 60.00 | 53.81 | 56.61 |
| MSzDP (Votes) | 311 | 2,680 | 3,153 | 1,657 | 7,801 |
| MSzDP (%) | 45.20 | 33.65 | 33.95 | 38.63 | 35.09 |
| Keresztény Női Tábor (Christian Women's Camp, or KNT) (Votes) | 46 | 289 | 200 | 190 | 725 |
| KNT (%) | 6.69 | 3.63 | 2.15 | 4.43 | 3.26 |
| FKgP (Votes) | 33 | 284 | 161 | 62 | 540 |
| FKgP (%) | 4.80 | 3.57 | 1.73 | 1.47 | 2.43 |
| Független Magyar Demokrata Párt (Independent Hungarian Democratic Party, or FMDP) (Votes) | 7 | 166 | 69 | 39 | 281 |
| FMDP (%) | 1.02 | 2.08 | 0.74 | 0.91 | 1.26 |
| NPP (Votes) | 2 | 76 | 104 | 16 | 198 |
| NPP (%) | 0.29 | 0.95 | 1.12 | 0.37 | 0.89 |
| MRP (Votes) | 5 | 34 | 16 | 11 | 66 |
| MRP (%) | 0.73 | 0.43 | 0.17 | 0.26 | 0.30 |
| PDP (Votes) | 0 | 17 | 12 | 6 | 35 |
| PDP (%) | 0 | 0.21 | 0.14 | 0.12 | 0.16 |

Source: Adapted from, "Kimutatás a megyénkben leadott szavazatokról," *Szabad Esztergom*, 7 September 1947, 2–3.

Despite its hegemonic role within the local state, the MKP's weaker position in the factories reflected the fact that many left-wing workers supported the MSzDP, largely on the basis of persistent labor movement traditions from the interwar years. Many of the networks of skilled workers mobilized by the MKP leadership in mid-1945 to establish factory committees were populated by those who later joined the MSzDP; with the exception of the leather-working and textile sectors, the Social Democrats gained an early advantage over their Communist rivals in recruiting members.[91] When the memberships of factory committees were formalized in late winter 1946, the two workers' parties attempted to enforce the principle of "parity" on their local factory cells; in practice, this meant that workers voted for a single list based on a factory-level agreement between the two parties. In the sixty factories large enough to have a factory committee, 127 MSzDP members were elected, as opposed to 148 who were members of the MKP. In some plants, workers objected to the lack of a real election or local agreement was absent. In these cases, the elections

TABLE 7. Results of the parliamentary elections in Újpest, 31 August 1947

| Party | Votes | % of the vote |
|---|---|---|
| MSzDP | 13,200 | 30.93 |
| MKP | 12,033 | 28.20 |
| Magyar Függetlenségi Párt (Hungarian Independence Party, or MFP) | 10,381 | 24.33 |
| FKgP | 2,318 | 5.43 |
| FMDP | 1,376 | 3.22 |
| Demokrata Néppárt (Democratic People's Party, or DNP) | 1,207 | 2.83 |
| KNT | 648 | 1.52 |
| PDP | 563 | 1.32 |
| NPP | 532 | 1.25 |
| MRP | 415 | 0.9 |

*Source:* Adapted from László Hubai, "Az országgyűlési választások Újpesten, 1920–1947," in *Dokumentumok Újpest történetéhez, 1840–1949*, ed. András Sipos (Budapest: Budapest Főváros Levéltára, 2001), 423.

were contested; in sectors locally where significant numbers of committee elections were contested, the results revealed the MSzDP was slightly ahead, with the MKP close behind. In heavy engineering, Social Democrat candidates won 52.43 percent in contested elections, with the Communists polling only 46.49. Even in textiles, where the MKP was better entrenched, its candidates polled only 48.37 percent in elections to contested committees, compared to 49.49 for candidates of the MSzDP.[92]

These results challenged the MKP's perceptions of its own role as the natural representative of the working class and architect of the postwar regime, at both the national and local levels. In the aftermath of the 1945 elections, it saw itself as the natural leader of those within the coalition who opposed FKgP hegemony. Aware of its weakness in certain industrial areas like Újpest, it sought after the election to "consolidate and expand with all our strength what is presently a small camp [of Communists] within the industrial working class."[93] Despite its continued open commitment to popular-front coalition and to working-class unity in the face of a "reaction" it claimed had embedded itself within the FKgP, the MKP was profoundly suspicious of the Social Democrats. The Communists saw "working-class unity" in part as fighting against "the underground struggle of right-wing Social Democrats against the Communist Party, the front of working-class unity, and the whole of the Hungarian democracy."[94] This was a particular issue in Újpest because the local MKP blamed the "right-wing agitation" of its Social Democratic rivals for its failure to secure a hegemonic position on local factory committees in early 1946. Among the factory-level defeats that had most infuriated the local MKP was that in the United Incandescent Lamp and Electrical Factory, where the dismantling of the factory by the Red Army a year previously had created a markedly anti-Communist climate. This was exacerbated, the local MKP leadership argued, by MSzDP agitators who mobilized support by accusing the MKP of supporting rape and deportation by the occupying authorities in 1945.[95]

While the bitterness of the struggle between the MKP and MSzDP over hegemony in the factories was a recurring issue within working-class politics in Újpest in 1946 and 1947, the Left, especially the Communists, faced more immediate problems in early 1946 that were not dissimilar to those in Tatabánya. The results of the November 1945 election and endemic hyperinflation generated a local crisis of confidence for the Left; the local Social Democrat factory organizer, Oszkár Sümegi, complained that "after the elections a climate of dismay took hold in the factories, in part a consequence of the election results, but . . . also a result of the further deterioration of the general economic situation."[96] Even among the loyal Communist minority in the United Incandescent Lamp and Electrical Factory, MKP organizers in early 1946 noted deep disappointment. "These workers had real trust in our party," they stated, "and are now demanding that we finally take some strong, indeed drastic measures."[97]

This political climate rested on class identities that were reproduced through intense frustration with the lack of positive change brought about since the end of World War II; left-wing workers argued that "reconstruction looks like a process in which the capitalists save their property, and they can accumulate their capital through our work."[98] The coal shortages generated by the persistent labor problems in mining areas had a severe impact on some factories in Újpest; in the Wolfner Leather and Shoe Factory, production was brought to a complete halt by the shortages of coal, leaving 1,312 persons without work for the first two months of 1946.[99] The food supply situation was not as desperate as that in Tatabánya, as some food was available at the local market, though often only through barter, rather than cash, while local factories were able to pay their workers in foodstuffs most of the time, under the calorie-linked wage agreement.[100] Nevertheless, high inflation still generated misery and extreme anger among local workers; in the Magyar Pamutipar, while the wages of weaving machine operators by the end of March were 280.8 times greater than they had been in January, and when adjusted to take into account the calorie-linked wage system were 595.1 times higher, the rate of price increases was even greater.[101]

The failure of wages to keep pace with prices stimulated protest on shop floors across the city; the situation generated by inflation was so tense that small mistakes in the payment of wages in the United Incandescent Lamp and Electrical Factory sparked spontaneous work stoppages that spread rapidly across the factory.[102] Most of this anger was directed outside of production, toward actors who were seen to be "profiteering" at the expense of workers. In March 1946, workers in the Domestic Cotton Weaving Factory (HPS) accused market traders of raising their prices in response to newspaper reports of higher wages, producing a situation in which "workers do not see the benefit of their higher wages."[103] Fury against market traders led to wild rumors about the origins of meat sold at the city's market; the most unpopular vendors were accused of selling human flesh to local consumers.[104] Such hysteria was fueled by a climate in which workers often felt that "the hyenas among the speculators compete to use the situation to shortchange the workers."[105]

Often market vendors were seen as part of a large black market in which workers felt forced to participate. Many also believed it was organized to ensure that excessive profits could be reaped from their misery. The theft of goods such as fuel or even raw materials from local factories by impoverished workers was endemic.[106] While in most cases this pilferage was for their own gain, the greatest profits from black-market activity were obtained by local business operators in an environment in which goods were scarce.[107] This was the tip of the iceberg of a huge local "black" economy, the existence of which was enabled by the industrial structure of Újpest, where prior to the war large factories had coexisted with many workshops and smaller enterprises. At the end of the 1930s, thirty-two hundred artisans had employed six thousand people in the city; by 1946, small-scale industry was threatened with "final eradication," as a result of severe shortages of raw materials.[108] For many artisans, participation in the black market was essential to securing materials and thus to survival. Sometimes accessing the black market involved the subcontracting of work to skilled workers employed in large factories; they would be able to steal raw materials and use factory machinery to earn supplementary incomes or obtain goods through payment in kind.[109]

Among the socialist-inclined majority of Újpesters there remained considerable outward support for the workers' parties, despite material frustration; on May Day 1946, at the height of hyperinflation, the MKP and MSzDP were jointly able to mobilize twenty-five thousand people for their local demonstration.[110] Despite intense party rivalry at the factory level, many of the left-wing majority found it difficult to distinguish between the two parties, as both argued that they represented the promise of socialist transformation. Although some Social Democrat activists attempted to appeal to the substantial anti-Communist minority, their official rhetoric at the local level was often indistinguishable from that of the MKP; the MSzDP's local newspaper was prepared to go as far as justifying the Red Army's dismantling of the United Incandescent Lamp and Electrical Factory by maintaining that it was the price to be paid for "Ukraine, for the villainy of the Horthyites, and the Szálasites."[111] At times, so great was the degree of agreement between the two parties that many expected them to merge into one. This impression made it difficult for both parties to win support from the other among the socialist-inclined majority, and it often led MSzDP activists to use anticommunist appeals to attract those who were more conservative.[112] Members of these groups were not especially receptive, and they became increasingly restive during hyperinflation. The loud expression of antisocialist opinions, especially in the context of wildcat strikes, and the appearance of right-wing graffiti led to the direct intervention of the MKP-dominated local police in the Magyar Pamutipar in April 1946.[113] What made this simmering discontent dangerous to the local state and the workers' parties was that, although they were able to maintain considerable outward support among the left-wing majority, these expressions were largely formalistic. Behind them lay a climate of weariness and resignation, as a "consequence of the general financial and economic collapse."[114]

To some extent, as in Tatabánya, economic stabilization and the elimination of hyperinflation represented a turning point. It was welcomed as consumption was transformed; prior to August 1946, the state of the Újpest market indicated how "total war" had brought "total misery." Afterward, proclaimed one local newspaper, not only "black marketers" and "speculators" shopped at the market but also "proletarian women got and are getting their groceries."[115] Yet, as in Tatabánya, while goods reappeared and incomes increased as a consequence of the wage measures implemented in factories, dominant class identities reproduced themselves through material complaint about standards of living, which many felt to be too low. As a consequence of the disruption caused by hyperinflation, workers were especially sensitive to problems with the supply of goods or to the slightest price increases. Instances in the autumn with goods supply, especially when "soap and sugar disappeared" from local markets, provoked fury, while increases in prices provoked demands of the state "to stop exporting eggs." Discontent and anger against black-market activity that continued into the post-stabilization period persisted.[116] Behind this lay an instrumental and materialistic climate in which workers, irrespective of political affiliation, placed primary importance on material issues. Many workers "openly say that they are not very interested in politics, merely their wages and what they can buy with them."[117]

The memory of hyperinflation contributed to this attitude, as did continuing poor living conditions and poverty in the city during 1946 and 1947. Living standards for many workers, especially the unskilled, remained persistently low. As Viktor Danyó, an unskilled worker in the Wolfner Leather and Shoe Factory, commented, "I maintain a family of five from a weekly wage of sixty forints. I don't own a decent set of clothes. I go to party meetings and to church in the same torn pullover."[118] Alongside material poverty, there was a serious problem of poor housing in the city, especially among those who lived in the tenements associated with the largest factories, where the dire economic conditions and war damage generated a crisis situation. Much of the workers' housing stock had degenerated into "slums," which, according to the local FKgP, had been cited as examples "of the worst misery" and had appeared in police reports as places where "the crime situation was far from the best."[119] In one typical tenement, described by a reporter as "a prisonlike slum," the working-class residents complained in 1947 that, "when it is time to pay the rents, the landlord turns up; when repairs are needed, he doesn't." In another tenement, one with more than one hundred residents, locals complained "that there was no working toilet"; furthermore, "all of the water pipes were leaking, and as a result the walls were permanently damp."[120]

Anger at poor living conditions was overshadowed by the huge increases in unemployment that stabilization brought about; as in Tatabánya, new economic policy brought about a wave of layoffs in workshops and small-scale industry. Although large plants expanded their workforces, these new jobs were invariably insufficient to prevent the emergence of unemployment as a major local issue. Local Social Democrat factory organizers spoke of "mass unemployment" as a consequence of "major redundancies" emerging in the city as early as October 1946, while the local authorities were forced to discuss makeshift public works and the introduction of rudimentary welfare measures to support those who had lost jobs.[121] Workers were infuriated by the emergence of mass unemployment and were not placated by the existence of limited unemployment benefits, public works, or other welfare measures. Those who worked in the city's Istvántelki railway yards bluntly told MKP activists that "it isn't unemployment benefits that we need but work itself."[122]

With the deteriorating situation in the local labor market, many suspected that the MKP was prepared to use mass unemployment in its battle to beat back the MSzDP in the factories. The branch-level trade unions had been given monopoly control over the exchange of labor by the first postwar government, effectively allowing the party that controlled a union to secure jobs for its supporters in those factories taking on workers. In Újpest, the MKP controlled the labor exchange offices of the leather workers', joinery workers and furniture makers', textile workers', and chemical workers' unions. These they used shamelessly as a means of recruiting new members, thus expanding their base in the city's light industrial factories.[123] Even within factories, the MKP frequently used reductions in staff, either mandated through the B-Lists or for ostensibly economic reasons, to ensure that MSzDP members were targeted to tighten its control within plants. In the United Incandescent Lamp and Electrical Factory, one semiskilled worker faced the plant's disciplinary committee for advising an assistant in the plant's day-care center to leave the MSzDP for the MKP in order to avoid redundancy in May 1947. "Join the Communist Party," she is alleged to have said, adding, "These layoffs are happening because the Communist Party is in a minority on the factory committee. If you join the Communists, you even have a chance of a better job."[124] In the Communist-dominated HPS textile factory, the Social Democrat–controlled Metalworkers' Union secured the appointment of one Ferenc Prontvay as a maintenance fitter in the plant in November 1946. Prontvay was subjected to a campaign of harassment, directed by his shop steward, that aimed to force him to join the MKP. After he refused, the factory committee and the plant director summoned him to be warned that his work was inadequate. Within three days of this meeting, he was dismissed.[125]

The politicization of employment reflected bitter battles for control of the factory committees across the city between the Communists and Social Democrats, as the MKP deployed a variety of questionable tactics—from the manipulation of elections to campaigns that aimed at the dismissal of MSzDP activists—in order to achieve greater control.[126] These tactics, and Social Democrat responses, led to sporadic political disputes; the most spectacular occurred in the HPS, where István Ács had presided over an entirely Communist factory committee in 1945. In the 1947 factory committee elections, though the MKP retained the presidency of the committee, the MSzDP won a relative majority; consequently, politics at the factory level became polarized into a series of bitter campaigns in which the MSzDP sought to break the MKP by offering material advancement to workers who joined the Social Democrats. The local MKP, working through the factory branch of the Textile Workers' Union, which it controlled, responded in kind, placing undue pressure on groups of workers to join the party. The director of personnel and social affairs, Gábor Havas, an MSzDP member, intervened, arguing that "Social Democrats in the HPS were oppressed" as result of the actions of the MKP, a measure that prompted the MKP to intervene to secure his removal, maintaining that he was "seriously damaging working-class unity" in the plant.[127] The use of such tactics as part of the politicization of life in the factories not only led to bitter disputes but also, when combined with the materialistic aspirations of the workforce, could result in endemic clientelism, which bordered on open corruption. In the United Incandescent Lamp and Electrical Factory, one member of the factory committee nominated by the MKP was said in 1947 to accept "gifts" from the rural, female workers who sorted glass components, so that "they could keep their jobs and earn good money."[128]

Clientelism, as well as broader patterns of protest and bargaining within factories, occurred against the backdrop of a deep-seated political divide among workers—between the left-wing majority, concentrated among the male skilled elite, and a substantial, conservative minority made up disproportionately of women, who worked in semiskilled positions in the city's light industrial establishments.[129] Among left-wing workers, despite the bitterness of the rivalry between activists from the MKP and the MSzDP, many of their supporters regarded them as largely indistinguishable. This perception enabled many left-wing workers to participate in joint demonstrations held to support the second anniversary of Újpest's "liberation" and the first anniversary of the proclamation of the republic, in January 1947.[130] Reproduced class identities, however, fed a situation in which the nature of this support was conditional. Workers grumbled at what they saw as continuing "inflation" and the persistence of antilabor practices on the part of local employers; they demanded

a more radical stance from the workers' parties and rewarded local factory branches that adopted an aggressive stance toward management.[131] This relationship, not
dissimilar to that which existed more generally in Tatabánya, served as the basis
for the MKP's successful mobilization of left-wing workers behind its attempts to
destroy the FKgP as a leading political force. When the Communists unveiled the
"conspiracy against the republic" in early 1947, in which they linked a conservative
secret society to FKgP leaders and a plot to exclude the Communists from government after the conclusion of Hungary's peace treaty, workers responded. Many were
mobilized, joining demonstrations and the MKP in greater numbers, because they
saw the Communists as effective protectors of workers against those forces they
believed would return Hungary to the antilabor practices of the interwar years.[132]

Among those local workers who supported more conservative positions, reproduced class identities did not feed demands for a more radical stance from the
workers' parties but did contribute to outright distrust of the whole of the emergent postwar political order. In the spinning and weaving shops of the city's textile
factories, the left-wing parties often had no meaningful presence at all, as labor
movement activism tended to be concentrated among the skilled male maintenance
staff and the masters.[133] The women who operated the machines in plants like the
Újpest Yarn Factory demanded political activists tell them "when prisoners of war
will be brought home," a statement that highlighted anti-Soviet opinion. They also
expressed their material discontent: "why can't the democracy make it possible for
women not to work?" Furthermore, they differed markedly from left-wing workers
in terms of who should bear the blame for their material situation, complaining that
"all the Jews live well, none of them work," and exclaiming that "the leaders of the
unions and the Communists all live well from the money that we have to pay out
in membership fees."[134] One issue of particular importance, which interacted with
popular religious sentiment among working-class women in the textile factories,
was that of free time on Sunday. While Sunday work was not the rule, in some factories managers found themselves under pressure to introduce Sunday shifts, which
were resisted strongly by female machine operators, often forcing management to
make the shifts voluntary. The desire of such workers to protect their Sunday spread
to direct action among workers on Saturday night shifts; the city's textile factories
were hit by a wave of wildcat strikes in February 1947 instigated by female workers
who complained that, "if they worked Saturday night, they could not spend Sunday
with their families."[135]

Patterns of political affiliation not only influenced patterns of protest but also—
together with other factors, most significantly the nature of the labor process in
particular plants—helped shape the space available for workers to bargain informally and thus subvert the standardized, payment-by-results wage systems that
were introduced through the collective agreements as part of the 1946 stabilization
package. Just as in the mines, the performance-based wage systems offended the

moral economies of most workers, irrespective of their gender or the sector in which they worked.[136] Workers often suspected that the payment systems introduced were attempts to increase the intensity of work, and they thus sought to secure optimum wage levels by regulating their pace of work and demanding higher wages. In the BÁMERT Mining Machinery Factory (a contraction of Bányagépek és Mechanikai Szállítóberendezések Gyára RT, or Mining Machinery and Mechanical Transport Installations Factory plc), skilled workers regulated their performance as close to 120 percent of their production target as possible; the very highest hourly earnings were consistently only 17 percent more than the average during early 1947.[137] While workers consistently attempt to regulate their own pace of work, only certain groups were able to employ this strategy successfully. In textile plants, among the machine operators, a climate that hindered rate busting formed a central part of dominant shop-floor culture. In June 1947, in the spinning shops of the Magyar Pamutipar, workers placed considerable informal pressure on their workmates not to produce in excess of an informally established rate; one operator who broke the informally agreed rate was physically assaulted for doing so. In view of the factory committee–controlled disciplinary panel's alienation from the labor movement, it officially regarded such behavior as "sabotage."[138] Where workers were more closely bound to the labor movement and often more skilled, this culture was tacitly tolerated. The machine shop of the United Incandescent Lamp and Electrical Factory was a center of labor movement activity in the plant; it was also a part of the plant where informal attempts to control job rates were endemic. The future Stakhanovite József Kiszlinger recounted that when he first arrived in the factory in 1947, his attempts to increase his earnings by maintaining a faster pace met with a wave of hostility from his workmates. One member of the factory committee backed them, warning Kiszlinger, "[You] should look after yourself, I really recommend it. Don't stand out too much." He was eventually driven out by a work culture that was underpinned by the union and both workers' parties in the plant.[139]

## On the Periphery in Southern Zala

As with those of Újpest's workers who were unable to rely on the shop-floor power of the labor movement to subvert unpopular centrally mandated wage policies, Zala's oil workers were frustrated by the situation in which post-stabilization wage policies had placed them. Throughout 1946 and 1947, workers' wages declined, creating considerable anger. As far as the management and the American oil company owners were concerned, this ire was due to changes that they had not desired— they made clear that the decline had occurred as a result of the state forcing them to link wages to production. They maintained that they wished to maintain the prewar system of high hourly wages, with which, they argued, "we managed to achieve production records with Zala peasants that stand with the best in the world."[140] Word of the owners' position filtered through to the drilling plants. Workers themselves complained to local representatives of the workers' parties about central regulation of wages, arguing that "the American owners would increase wages" if only the government, the unions, and the left-wing parties would give them a free hand.[141]

The politics of wages at the drilling plants formed part of a battle for control over Hungary's oil industry. The Left's defeat in southern Zala in the November 1945 elections and the MKP's subordinate position on local factory committees fed the Communists' instinctive suspicion of MAORT. It regarded the company as nothing more than "a well-organized American fifth column." As early as January 1946, it saw MAORT as "enemy" territory; as far as the nation's Communist activists were concerned, MAORT's engineers had "driven the workers day and night under the German occupation to achieve peak production of oil." They considered its white-collar staff to consist of "friends of fascism and other reactionary elements." The company had attempted to spread the "myth" among its workforce that only American democracy was "true democracy" by constituting them as an overpaid "aristocracy of labor."[142] Their sense of the MAORT as enemy territory fed their paranoia that the company was working to subvert the "new" Hungarian state's economic goals by hindering the production of oil. Some Communist officials who visited the plants believed in the existence of "an illegal organization inside the MAORT whose goal is the conscious sabotage of production." Although the MKP recognized the need to broaden its highly restricted support among oil workers, its paranoia about the company conditioned its behavior to such an extent that its actions often reinforced local working-class suspicion of the Communists and their intentions.[143]

The small number of local MKP activists had a more realistic appreciation of the reasons for the dreadful performance of the party in the oil fields, attributing it to the strength of company-based identities, the impact of land reform on a propertied, semi-agricultural workforce, and the influence of the Catholic Church, with its anti-Communist stance, on the rural population.[144] With no base in the oil fields at all—only 150 oil workers in the area were paying dues to the MKP in May 1946—the party found it difficult to attack the MSzDP, which was well entrenched on MAORT's central factory committee, as well as most of the individual committees at the oil field plants.[145] The dominance of anti-Communism was so strong that most workers at Lovászi in May 1946 believed that war was imminent and that, after it, "the English would take over the running of the factory, and then fire all those who were members of the workers' parties."[146] Given their dire material situation in the climate of hyperinflation, most workers were not interested in politics. Even for the families of oil workers entitled to goods in kind from the company's warehouses in the town of Nagykanizsa, the situation in the first half of 1946 was desperate: "the housewives of MAORT workers queued from dawn to midday in front of the warehouse so that they could get their quarterly entitlement of one hundred and fifty grams of meat."[147] At the rural drilling plants, the situation was worse; at Lovászi, cash was worthless and bread was the only good whose supply could be regularly guaranteed. Flour, oil, meat, bacon, and eggs had arrived only occasionally since the beginning of the year. While manual workers had been supplied secondhand clothing through the Mineworkers' Union, 25 percent of workers could not work because of shortages of adequate footwear.[148] In order to alleviate this situation, some drilling plants set up their own workshops for the repair of clothes and shoes.[149] More unofficial forms of coping emerged among landless workers, as some stole oil, with the tacit agreement of union officials and engineers, in order to participate in the local black market and thus feed their families.[150] Many workers who held land were to some extent able to protect themselves from the impact of severe material penury; however, their contact with the state, through the system of compulsory requisitioning of agricultural produce to feed both the industrial centers and the Soviet troops stationed in the country, generated huge discontent. Smallholders were rarely self-sufficient in anything like all of the agricultural products they needed and bitterly resented compulsory deliveries; they argued that the state forced them to sell "a kilo of fat for 40 pengős, and in general a cow for 12,000 pengős. At the same time workers pay millions for a kilo of fat and just as much for meat." Consequently, they demanded to know "who is filling their pockets."[151] Most smallholders who took work in the oil fields farmed on the very edges of subsistence; for them, compulsory deliveries represented a threat to their livelihoods. There were many who were forced to hand over to the state the only cows they owned, despite the fact that they used the animals not only for milk but as the sole source of power on their plots.[152]

While stabilization did serve to end the immediate material crisis for oil workers, it brought outcomes that were profoundly unpopular.[153] This was in part a consequence of the gradual decrease in oil production. As MAORT continued to produce for reparations during 1946, both Hungary's Soviet occupiers and its government demanded increased production. As natural gas escaped, pressure in the oil wells was reduced, and by summer 1946, the production of oil was falling. MAORT's owners and managers—citing the long-term interests of the company—planned cuts in overall production. With the extension of state control over the economy that stabilization implied, and the linking of labor and wage policy to overall production levels set by the state, this climate created a difficult situation.[154] In the interest of economic stabilization, the company was ordered to implement the B-Lists against its white-collar workers, but in view of the centrality of many of them to production and the impact of falling oil production, the B-List implementation spread to include substantial numbers of manual workers.[155] The company moved to act on these B-List demands by "sending" workers "back to agriculture."[156] With the task of implementation placed in the hands of the factory committee, which was dominated by members of the landless minority of workers who supported the workers' parties, mainly the MSzDP, it argued that "only those who have property, their own house, land, a pension, or some other kind of income would be placed on the B-List [i.e., the list for dismissal]."[157] Workers, however, were furious. As one factory committee member commented, "It is impossible to make the workers understand the situation. There is a general view that the company is full of administration. Then they get an explanation of the B-Lists that states it is not possible to fire white-collar workers, because we need them!"[158]

It was not only the threat of "misery and unemployment" posed by staff reductions that generated discontent. Another factor was the impact of post-stabilization wage policy on the company's workers, a situation that reinforced workers' alienation from the "new" state. Along with other workplaces covered by the Mineworkers' Union collective agreement, both unions and the state insisted on the introduction of a progressive payment-by-results system for each worker. Furthermore, the collective agreement tied MAORT to national wage rates, which, in the opinion of the company, guaranteed a standard of living for its workers amounting to only half that of the 1939 level.[159] These changes represented a culture shift for MAORT, whose management believed that "it was only possible to achieve good results in production . . . with well-paid staff, who demand a high standard of living, alongside good technical support for production, the necessary supervision, attention to each individual worker, and proper selection."[160] Furthermore, given the nature of production at the drilling sites, it was difficult to introduce individualized performance-based wages. Through effective negotiation, MAORT was able to opt out of the sector-wide collective agreement for mining in August 1946, though they had to link all wages to a notional production norm for each enterprise. Thus, while individual work targets were not established, wages at each drilling plant were tied to the amount of oil it produced.[161]

This reprieve was only temporary, for pressure built on both the company and the factory committee to introduce a more individualized system of payment by results at the drilling plants. That pressure finally culminated in a directive from Hungary's Supreme Economic Council (Gazdasági Főtanács)—the major organ responsible for directing the country's three-year plan and effectively under the control of the MKP—on 30 June 1947 that it do so, as part of a state demand for greater "rationalization" within privately run enterprises.[162] Prior to this instruction, however, wages had been declining across the plant as they had been rising across the rest of the economy. "While some companies where workers have payment by results," complained the company in 1947, "have seen average production target fulfillment of 160 to 180 percent, our company's staff have seen" the equivalent of only "60 to 80 percent fulfillment."[163] This was a consequence of management's moves to rationalize production and to reverse what they saw as irresponsible overproduction at the behest of first the Germans and then the Red Army, which they saw as endangering the long-term future of the oil fields. In 1947, production dropped by

20 percent in the Bázakerretye fields, by 13 percent at Lovászi, and by 14.5 percent at Pusztaszentlászló.[164]

Low wage levels, which were felt to be lower than in the early war years, were a major source of anger among workers at the drilling plants. One landless Lovászi drilling master, Károly Feny, who lived in company housing, expressed his discontent to MKP agitators in June 1947, saying that he earned "between 610 and 630 forints per month, plus a production premium, which depends on how much oil has been produced. . . . From this they take away 190 to 250 forints for rent and for gas."[165] Many workers refused to blame the company, given the strength of company-based identities, and instead blamed the state and the unions for unfairly holding down their wages; this perception fed nostalgia for the pre-1945 era, even among the landless minority more prepared to support the workers' parties.[166] Among such workers, a major source of discontent was the housing situation close to the plant sites at Bázakerretye and Lovászi. Company housing for workers at Bázakerretye had been badly damaged by bombing, and housing was also in short supply at the other oil fields, forcing some workers to pay high prices to lodge with local families. As elsewhere, workers without access to their own sources of food believed themselves to be the victims of high prices.[167] This housing problem was, however, frequently attributed to continued Soviet occupation or the consequences of the "lost war, if it was not blamed on the Communist Party."[168] Among those with land, working-class complaints about housing or high prices did not affect them as directly as they did the landless, but there was still substantial discontent, notably over the levels of agricultural taxation and compulsory deliveries, which was often seen as an "imposition" by the left-wing state in Budapest, and its Soviet backers, that undermined the ability of smallholders, especially the poorest, to maintain their plots.[169] The impact of such measures fed a culture of anti-Soviet and anti-Communist complaint; the issue of the return of prisoners of war from the Soviet Union, and their treatment locally as they began to trickle back to the villages in 1947, was an especially sensitive one for the Left.[170] Furthermore, the rural communities surrounding the oil fields were full of the rumor of an imminent war that would remove the Red Army from Hungary. Given the strong influence of the Catholic Church over rural workers with land, as well as the Church's uncompromisingly conservative stance in Hungary, it provided the vehicle for expressions of anti-Communism. During its "missionary weeks" in Zala in March 1947, church members held demonstrations in the two largest towns; in Zalaegerszeg, twelve thousand persons participated in a demonstration, in a remarkable show of strength.[171]

The MKP made little progress in extending its base among workers at the drilling sites. It used issues such as poor housing and the relative unpopularity of white-collar staff, especially during the waves of redundancies that accompanied the implementation of the B-Lists in August 1946, to broaden its base and increase its influence on factory committees.[172] Despite sporadic local successes on some sites for

TABLE 8. Results of the parliamentary elections in the Letenye district of Zala County, 31 August 1947

| Settlement | DNP | | MKP | | MSZDP | |
|---|---|---|---|---|---|---|
| | Votes | % of the vote | Votes | % of the vote | Votes | % of the vot |
| Bánokszentgyörgy | 392 | 62.82 | 49 | 7.85 | 95 | 15.22 |
| Bázakerretye | 287 | 43.88 | 109 | 16.66 | 219 | 33.49 |
| Becsehely | 840 | 74.66 | 40 | 3.55 | 97 | 8.62 |
| Borsfa | 254 | 57.59 | 21 | 4.76 | 104 | 23.58 |
| Bucsuta | 155 | 53.63 | 39 | 13.49 | 34 | 11.76 |
| Csörnyeföld | 227 | 55.50 | 43 | 10.51 | 71 | 17.34 |
| Dobri | 316 | 84.27 | 1 | 0.27 | 25 | 6.67 |
| Kerkaszentkirály | 151 | 51.36 | 88 | 29.93 | 12 | 4.08 |
| Kerkateskánd | 107 | 54.59 | 13 | 6.63 | 19 | 9.69 |
| Kiscsehi | 203 | 75.46 | 11 | 4.09 | 29 | 10.78 |
| Kistolmács | 31 | 12.97 | 65 | 27.20 | 56 | 23.43 |
| Kútfej | 186 | 47.69 | 55 | 14.10 | 122 | 31.28 |
| Letenye | 796 | 37.42 | 339 | 15.94 | 252 | 11.85 |
| Lispeszentadorján | 357 | 73.91 | 18 | 3.73 | 62 | 12.84 |
| Lovászi | 356 | 70.36 | 41 | 8.10 | 62 | 12.25 |
| Maróc | 116 | 57.71 | 12 | 5.97 | 45 | 22.39 |
| Molnári | 231 | 48.84 | 188 | 39.75 | 12 | 2.5 |
| Murarátka | 215 | 71.19 | 22 | 7.28 | 17 | 5.6 |
| Muraszemenye | 301 | 37.02 | 110 | 13.53 | 112 | 13.78 |
| Oltárc | 254 | 63.18 | 90 | 22.39 | 14 | 3.4 |
| Petrivente | 43 | 22.40 | 54 | 28.13 | 25 | 13.0 |
| Pusztamagyaród | 352 | 64.35 | 42 | 7.68 | 50 | 9.1 |
| Semjénháza | 105 | 57.38 | 8 | 4.37 | 12 | 6.5 |
| Szécsisziget | 45 | 20.93 | 9 | 4.19 | 56 | 26.0 |
| Szentliszló | 88 | 30.45 | 133 | 46.02 | 35 | 12.1 |
| Szentmargitfalva | 84 | 30.55 | 37 | 13.45 | 72 | 26.1 |
| Tormafölde | 274 | 56.15 | 16 | 3.28 | 60 | 12.3 |
| Tornyiszentmiklós | 361 | 52.90 | 60 | 8.78 | 56 | 8.2 |
| Tótszentmárton | 183 | 48.54 | 109 | 28.91 | 29 | 7.6 |
| Tótszerdahely | 242 | 43.06 | 151 | 26.86 | 65 | 11.5 |
| Valkonya | 97 | 60.25 | 7 | 4.39 | 24 | 14.9 |
| Várfölde | 192 | 69.57 | 22 | 7.97 | 20 | 7.2 |
| Zajk | 99 | 38.08 | 29 | 11.15 | 48 | 18.4 |

*Source:* Adapted from ZML, Zala Vármegye Törvényhatósági Bizottsága Központi Választmányanak iratai (Papers of the Central Executive of the Zala County Local Authority Committee, hereafter IV.403f.), 1d., Jegyzőkönyv Letenyei járásban a választás eredményéről, kelt Letenye, 1947. évi szeptember hó 1. napján.

| FKgP | | NPP | | MRP | | FMDP | | PDP | |
|---|---|---|---|---|---|---|---|---|---|
| Votes | % of the vote | Votes | %of the vote | Votes | % of the vote | Votes | % of the vote | Votes | % of the vote |
| 27 | 4.33 | 44 | 7.05 | 15 | 2.40 | 2 | 0.33 | 0 | 0 |
| 4 | 0.61 | 3 | 0.46 | 28 | 4.28 | 2 | 0.31 | 2 | 0.31 |
| 22 | 1.95 | 71 | 6.31 | 45 | 4.00 | 6 | 0.53 | 4 | 0.38 |
| 30 | 6.80 | 8 | 1.81 | 19 | 4.31 | 3 | 0.68 | 2 | 0.47 |
| 6 | 2.08 | 35 | 12.11 | 13 | 4.50 | 6 | 2.08 | 1 | 0.35 |
| 33 | 8.07 | 10 | 2.44 | 24 | 5.87 | 1 | 0.67 | 0 | 0 |
| 18 | 4.80 | 2 | 0.53 | 10 | 2.67 | 3 | 0.79 | 0 | 0 |
| 20 | 6.80 | 7 | 2.38 | 12 | 4.08 | 4 | 1.37 | 0 | 0 |
| 22 | 11.22 | 14 | 7.14 | 14 | 7.14 | 7 | 3.59 | 0 | 0 |
| 7 | 2.60 | 0 | 0 | 15 | 5.58 | 4 | 1.49 | 0 | 0 |
| 5 | 27.20 | 19 | 7.95 | 2 | 0.84 | 1 | 0.41 | 0 | 0 |
| 2 | 3.08 | 4 | 1.03 | 7 | 1.79 | 4 | 1.03 | 0 | 0 |
| 8 | 27.64 | 74 | 3.48 | 59 | 2.77 | 13 | 0.61 | 6 | 0.29 |
| 4 | 0.83 | 15 | 3.11 | 25 | 5.18 | 2 | 0.40 | 0 | 0 |
| 4 | 4.74 | 7 | 1.38 | 10 | 1.98 | 6 | 1.19 | 0 | 0 |
| 5 | 2.49 | 14 | 6.97 | 9 | 4.47 | 0 | 0 | 0 | 0 |
| 4 | 0.84 | 1 | 0.21 | 32 | 6.77 | 1 | 0.21 | 4 | 0.84 |
| 0 | 3.31 | 25 | 8.28 | 10 | 3.31 | 3 | 1.00 | 0 | 0 |
| 6 | 19.19 | 93 | 11.44 | 31 | 3.81 | 4 | 0.49 | 6 | 0.74 |
| 7 | 1.74 | 5 | 1.24 | 29 | 7.21 | 3 | 0.76 | 0 | 0 |
| 5 | 2.60 | 57 | 29.69 | 8 | 4.16 | 0 | 0 | 0 | 0 |
| 0 | 5.48 | 46 | 8.41 | 21 | 3.84 | 6 | 1.10 | 0 | 0 |
| 5 | 2.73 | 36 | 19.67 | 9 | 4.92 | 7 | 3.83 | 1 | 0.54 |
| 1 | 37.67 | 20 | 9.30 | 4 | 1.86 | 0 | 0 | 0 | 0 |
| 1 | 0.03 | 19 | 6.57 | 13 | 4.82 | 0 | 0 | 0 | 0 |
| 1 | 22.18 | 6 | 2.18 | 14 | 5.09 | 1 | 0.37 | 0 | 0 |
| 2 | 18.85 | 38 | 7.79 | 5 | 1.02 | 2 | 0.41 | 1 | 0.2 |
| 5 | 12.45 | 57 | 8.35 | 51 | 7.47 | 8 | 1.17 | 5 | 0.68 |
| 7 | 1.86 | 30 | 7.96 | 17 | 4.50 | 1 | 0.27 | 1 | 0.27 |
| 2 | 3.91 | 41 | 7.30 | 39 | 6.94 | 2 | 0.36 | 0 | 0 |
| 4 | 2.48 | 25 | 15.53 | 4 | 2.44 | 0 | 0 | 0 | 0 |
| 5 | 1.81 | 20 | 7.25 | 16 | 5.82 | 1 | 0.33 | 0 | 0 |
| 2 | 20.00 | 20 | 7.69 | 9 | 3.46 | 2 | 0.77 | 1 | 0.39 |

limited periods, as in Bázakerettye in early 1946, the party faced a local MSzDP that was firmly entrenched. The MSzDP had organized the plants with infrastructural support provided by the Social Democrat officials in the National Council of Trade Unions, and it also enjoyed a good working relationship with MAORT managers, who were able to develop a mutually beneficial modus vivendi.[173] The local MSzDP, aware that it was recruiting among workers who were more conservative than its own membership, was not averse to using the promise of political protection as an inducement to join the party; in early 1947, the MSzDP told prospective members that in the near future one thousand oil workers would lose their jobs and that the party would ensure that no Social Democrat would be found among them.[174] At Lovászi in April 1947, an MKP county-level organizer blamed the employers' support for the MSzDP and the agrarian culture of many workers for the fact that of the almost one thousand workers on the site, only thirty were Communists.[175] This climate further underlay the dreadful performance of both workers' parties in the oil fields in the August 1947 election, when the southern part of Zala voted overwhelmingly for the Right (table 8).

The persistence of the oil field workers' rebuffing of MKP overtures contributed to its taking an increasingly radical stance toward the MAORT and reinforced the party's suspicion of the company's owners, its management, and its workers. The Hungarian state and its Supreme Economic Council, controlled by the MKP, sought increased production of oil to support the goals of the three-year plan and increasingly argued that "American capital" was hindering the reconstruction of the country's oil refineries by starving them of crude oil to refine.[176] This stance placed the state on a collision course with the company, which was interested more in a long-term rationalization of production in their Zala fields; MAORT was reducing the amount of oil mined to recover from what it regarded as excessive wartime production. An increasingly bitter dispute resulted, with economic planning bodies insisting on ever greater control over production levels, wages, and costs on the site, while MAORT's American owners and its Hungarian management attempted to preserve room for manuever.[177] The struggle between the state and the company for control became increasingly bitter, as the MKP, frustrated at its lack of control and influence over a company it regarded as an "American fifth column," became ever more shrill, accusing the firm's management of direct "sabotage" of the economy.[178] This set the stage for how overt socialist dictatorship would be built in the oil fields, as the MKP and, from June 1948, its successor, the MDP, became progressively more despotic in their attempts to assert control, in the absence of any meaningful support among oil workers.

# 3 The Social Roots of Dictatorship
## August 1947–August 1949

IN SPRING 1949, one female factory committee member in Újpest's Chinoin Pharmaceuticals Factory told party agitators of the changes that had occurred in the pattern of shop-floor politics over the previous two years. Prior to "fusion," when the MKP swallowed the MSzDP to create the MDP in June 1948, she remembered "real hatred" between the working-class members of the two parties. In the factory canteen, there were "two or even three camps" who sat separately: "On one side the Communists sat, on the other the right-wing Social Democrats, and there was an uninterested side too. If the Communists announced a mass meeting, then the Right, as far as they could, kept everyone away." Almost nine months after the party fusion, this image of a factory whose workforce was split by overpoliticization was replaced by one in which all were unified around work and material improvement: "now one can see the impact of agreement in production." Politics, as far as this factory activist was concerned, had been replaced with work.[1] Her view of the replacement of tension with harmony, as the result of the creation of an overt socialist dictatorship from a fractious "popular-front" regime, was the idealized view of a party activist, often contradicted by many of her comrades and colleagues, who complained that behind the superficial peace there remained tension: "There are still many reactionaries. The people listen to us, but they are neither willing to make any sacrifices nor take on any party work."[2]

Almost immediately following its victory in deeply flawed, albeit competitive elections, in August 1947, the MKP, responding to both the changing international situation and its precarious hold on many of Hungary's formal political institutions, began to build overt socialist dictatorship (table 9). It drove conservative opposition parties out of parliament, consolidating its control over the Left by swallowing the MSzDP, ensuring that no Social Democrats whom local MKP organs saw as being right wing could make it into the new, unified party—the MDP. Over the course of spring 1948, the shift from limited pluralism to overt dictatorship was accompanied by a transition from the mixed economy of the "popular-front" era to a full-fledged socialist economic order, underpinned by radical nationalization of large enterprises; between March 1948, when the decision was made to launch a fatal blow at the private sector, and November of that year, 780 companies were taken into public ownership.[3] Mátyás Rákosi himself celebrated this, arguing that industrial workers "worked for the capitalist factory owner no longer, but for the flowering of their own people"; as a sign of this change, "where it has been possible, we have placed old, experienced, trustworthy industrial workers who have clear command of their skill, at the head of the nationalized factories."[4] As part of this shift, the emergent regime demanded that industrial workers accept incorporation into a new "Communist working class" able to construct socialism as a consequence of changed mentalities toward labor: "the goal of the people's democracy is to replace the uninterested wage slave, with the kind of worker[s] who fully [understand] the social importance of what they produce and consequently [see] constant improvement in quality and raised quantity as second nature."[5] This social revolution was not confined to industry but was also directed at the far more hostile ground of Hungary's rural communities, where a majority of the population lived.

Throughout the popular-front era, the MKP had emphasized its militant defense of private property in agriculture; often the Left had presented itself as the defender of the land of poor smallholders against a "reaction" who, they contended, wished to remove it from them.[6] From summer 1948, the regime advocated an end to individual landholding and began a series of drives to force smallholders into agricultural collectives; for Ernő Gerő, this meant "taking steps to create large-scale agricultural enterprises based on cooperatives that involve the collective holding of property in the villages."[7]

This attack on private property represented a marked escalation of the political polarization of Hungarian society. Most rural communities had been bastions of support for political conservatism, and attacks on the very institution of small-scale farming represented a move that underlined the despotic nature of the new political order as far as rural residents were concerned. The state stepped up its attacks

TABLE 9. Overall national results of parliamentary elections, 31 August 1947

| Party | Votes | % of the vote | Parliamentary seats won |
|---|---|---|---|
| MKP | 1,113,050 | 22.27 | 100 |
| DNP | 820,453 | 16.41 | 60 |
| FKgP | 769,763 | 15.40 | 68 |
| MSzDP | 744,641 | 14.90 | 67 |
| MFP | 670,547 | 13.42 | 49 |
| NPP | 415,465 | 8.31 | 36 |
| FMDP | 260,420 | 5.21 | 18 |
| MRP | 84,169 | 1.68 | 6 |
| KNT | 69,536 | 1.39 | 4 |
| PDP | 50,294 | 1.01 | 3 |

*Source:* Adapted from Sándor Balogh, *Parlamenti és pártharcok magyarországon, 1945–1947* (Budapest: Kossuth Könyvkiadó, 1975), 525.

on religion, especially the Catholic Church, both a cornerstone of society in many villages and a rallying point for political conservatives; church schools were nationalized in the teeth of bitter opposition—occasionally violent opposition—from the hierarchy, parish priests, and parents alike.[8] The protest these measures generated was met with an intensification of repression. Hungary's internal security forces were renamed and reorganized, becoming the Államvédelmi Hatóság (State Security Agency, or ÁVH) in late 1948. While the agency employed several thousand at the time of its creation, by early 1950 it provided work to twenty-eight thousand persons.[9] The state was more than prepared to use its expanded apparatus of repression against prominent opponents; its arrest of Hungary's Catholic primate, József Cardinal Mindszenty, and his subsequent trial on charges of conspiracy against the state in 1949, demonstrated the state's attitude toward vocal political opponents.

Polarization within Hungary and the pressure of the international situation outside, especially the impact of neighboring Yugoslavia's break with the Soviet Union, produced paranoia among the elite as the MDP leadership sought to secure its rule.[10] Soon after fusion, the MDP began measures to purge its membership of "opportunistic" elements; 170,000 persons, or just under one in five of all members in 1948, were expelled.[11] The message that activism in the labor movement did not exempt anyone from the attentions of the socialist state's repressive apparatus was reinforced in 1949 by the arrest, trial, and execution of László Rajk, the Communist interior minister between 1946 and 1948, on trumped-up charges that he conspired with Belgrade to destroy Hungary's people's democracy. As the state swallowed independent institutions, Hungary's remaining legal parties were incorporated into the Hungarian Independence People's Front (Magyar Függetlenségi Népfront, or MFNF) as part of the preparations for single-list elections in May 1949. Institutions like the trade unions were not exempt and fell victim to the attempts of the new state to enforce labor policy in order to ensure the smooth introduction of centralized economic planning in workplaces. The unions were reformed, expected to abandon their concentration on the struggle for "higher wages, and the improvement of working conditions," and instead focus on the education of "class-conscious constructors of socialism."[12]

Despite the repressive nature of the state, the regime was seen by most left-wing workers as legitimate. Indeed, after 1956, much of the party leadership saw 1948 and 1949 as a transitional moment when the party enjoyed the trust of the working class prior to the onset of the excesses of the "Rákosi-Gerő clique."[13] After the 1947 elections, the legitimacy established by the MKP among left-wing workers, resting on the assertion that they were their best defenders against the machinations of "reaction," evolved. In autumn and winter 1947, workers facing persistent unemployment and high prices remained as frustrated with what they saw as the lack of social transformation as they had been in the first half of the year. During 1948, by offering left-wing workers the promise of the "construction of socialism," the regime offered a clear vision of a future of social transformation. By nationalizing on a large scale and promoting labor movement activists off the factory floor into administration and management, they were seen as presenting the promise of the clear change such workers had demanded since 1945. Furthermore, much of the increasing scope of repression, especially that directed against political conservatives such as groups like agricultural smallholders and churches, had many convinced that to succeed, socialist transformation would still have to be defended against "the reaction." When directed against those within the party, repression was either ignored or it generated considerable confusion.

This vision of the MKP's legitimacy was restricted to the left-wing majority of workers; the construction of a dictatorship increased political polarization within the working class, as the rural, the religious, or the simply politically antagonistic became convinced that the regime was on the way to becoming a bloody, short-lived dictatorship, like that of Béla Kun, who had held office briefly thirty years earlier. In this polarized climate, the legitimacy that the regime gained was highly conditional. Real incomes rose throughout 1948 and 1949, while the party promised that "socialist construction" would bring "an increase in the living standards of our people, guaranteed by industrialization and the reorganization of agriculture."[14] Furthermore, there was an inherent clash between the aspirations of workers and the goals of the regime, in so far as they sought to remake workers as class-conscious soldiers of socialist construction through various measures (e.g., payment-by-result wage systems and labor competition) that were generalized and intensified throughout 1948 in preparation for central planning. In workplaces, this inherent clash was often papered over through the politics of informal compromise on the job. Labor competition was generalized in March 1948 when the National Labor Competition was launched in association with the development of brigades and competition between them. It was intended to act as a means through which the relationship of workers to their labor would be transformed, but workers saw it in strictly instrumental terms.[15] Labor competition thus became mired in practices of localized informal bargaining at the point of production, dependent crucially on the ability of lower-level management to guarantee workers increased earnings, or preferential treatment, for its success. Paradoxically, attempts to transform production became bogged down in the practices policy makers sought to eliminate, practices that enabled the regime to build its legitimacy among left-wing workers but at an economic cost that threatened its longer term desire to industrialize the country—a situation that would form the basis of a crisis of legitimacy for the regime during the first half of the 1950s.

In Tatabánya, the tensions created by the need of the new regime to generate a semblance of legitimacy for itself, as well as the importance of raising coal production in order to lay the foundations of future industrialization, caused the contradictions of this situation to emerge in especially stark form as early as summer 1949. The promise of tangible socialist transformation and the benefits it would bring workers in the not-too-distant future were sufficient to prevent an open crisis of legitimacy for the new socialist regime, for the moment. In Újpest, the construction of dictatorship was marked by considerable social polarization between the left-wing majority—who welcomed the creation of the dictatorship—and the right-wing minority, who were bitter opponents of the new political order. Consolidation of the new regime was based on a settlement with the left-wing majority that promised real material improvement. Yet this settlement was based on a series of highly localized informal compromises that subverted the regime's labor policies, while they both generated and exacerbated bottlenecks within the economy that would become endemic later. While in both of these cases the breakdown of support for the regime lay in the future, this was not the case in the Zala oil fields, where the construction of dictatorship was accompanied by an intensification of the state's confrontation with the company and its workforce. MAORT was nationalized as its managers were put on trial for "sabotage" of the economy; at the same time, the villages around which the oil fields were located were centers of opposition to the policies the socialist state imposed on agriculture and the churches. Furthermore, the oil fields lay on the border with Yugoslavia—thus, they were subject to considerable political control, while the ÁVH became a major presence in local life. As the state implemented its wage policies and labor competition, which were subverted by informal compromises, oil workers and their neighbors were deeply discontented and awaited the "liberation" of Hungary as a result of war with the Western powers.

## A Revolution from Outside in Southern Zala

In February 1949, Pál Székely, the director of MAORT who had been appointed by the state after the company had been removed from American control and placed under Hungarian administration, proclaimed that as a consequence "of being taken into state administration . . . the spirit at MAORT has changed," for workers increasingly understood the need to support socialist construction.[16] Such proclamations were directly challenged by party officials observing that, at the drilling plants, their control over an alienated workforce was little greater in the second half of 1949 than it had been under a very different situation two years previously. At Lovászi, Miklós Lüllik, the factory party secretary, complained that "we see serious mistakes with work discipline. They stem from the fact that the workers are just not sufficiently class conscious. They just do not understand that their individual work performance and that of the collective are closely connected. . . . Without individual responsibility we cannot work well. . . . As a plant next to the national border, we have to place even greater weight on the issue of vigilance."[17]

The lack of consent regarding state policies in the workplace that Lüllik observed at Lovászi was more generally felt across the oil fields and was a legacy of popular reaction to the construction of dictatorship that had begun two years previously in the aftermath of the elections. While the villages in the region of the oil fields—with the exception of Bázakerretye—voted overwhelmingly for the center-right Demokrata Néppárt (Democratic People's Party, or DNP), their vote paradoxically strengthened the resolve of the MKP. This was because the MKP's Social Democrat rivals inside the oil plants had failed to win the votes of all their members, the majority of whom cast their ballots for the parties of the Right. In Bázakerettye itself, where the MSzDP recorded 430 members, it obtained only 219 votes, as opposed to the MKP, which received 109 votes, though it had only 70 members there.[18] Echoing justified complaints nationally that the MKP had won the elections through recourse to fraud, local Social Democrats complained that the voting results demonstrated massive cheating by the Communists. Despite this, the Social Democrats were deeply shocked by their performance and attempted to recover ground by blaming the Communists for price increases that hit the county immediately following the election.[19]

In Budapest, the MKP drove home the advantage it had won in the elections by excluding their right-wing opponents from the political arena outright, using questionable legal means. It then began its takeover of the MSzDP by proclaiming its intention of merging the two workers' parties under its leadership.[20] The drive for greater political control occurred as economic conditions worsened, with southern Zala experiencing a combination of increasing unemployment, high prices, and food shortages. Party officials recorded a climate in which "the days go by, inflation increases, speculation spreads," as the MKP simply concentrated on political power.[21] Among the relatively left-wing minority without land, workers "wait to see deeds [from the government], and they don't see them. They always can be heard to say that promises made before the election just remain promises."[22] Outside this relatively small group, antagonism was far stronger. As far as the majority was concerned, the MKP's drive for greater political control exacerbated their anger, sometimes expressed in "a wave of anti-Semitism."[23] The police and party activists recorded that many village residents believed "the current 'democratic' government of Hungary is simply giving the country up to the Russians, just as a few years ago the then rulers gave us to Hitler."[24] The considerable political tension resulted in endemic rumors; gasoline shortages were taken as a sign "that we are on the threshold of war."[25] In some villages, panic was generated by the rumor that all males older than seventeen and younger than forty-seven would be conscripted, while elsewhere it was believed that "in Austria the Communist Party has been banned and they are killing Communists, something that will be happening here soon." The climate of tension was further exacerbated by high levels of agricultural taxation, combined with shortages of seed, and a consequent struggle to survive among those with the smallest plots.[26]

It was in precisely this climate of tension in autumn 1947 that MAORT management implemented individualized systems of payment by results across the drilling sites. The system chosen was one introduced during the autumn of 1947 and based on the measuring of work against a series of performance indicators (*mutatószám*), a system designed for situations in which the performance of workers could not be measured directly. Work performance was calculated by translating the work done into numerical values via complex calculations in which factors such as working time, the amount produced, the value of what was produced, and the extent of waste could be taken into account, depending on the labor process. This score would then determine the final total payment level.[27] Implementation was gradual and slow; by early December 1947, only 50 percent of workers on the drilling sites were working according to payment by results, a situation that made these workers' wages 30 percent higher than those who remained on the old system, generating pressure on management to introduce the system in more areas of the plants.[28] At the same time, the new wage system implied marked changes in the relationships between engineers, the direct managers of production, and the workers. Those in charge of the direction of production assumed a more immediate responsibility for work performance, which gave them more direct power to determine an individual's level of payment. In addition, these decisions were subjected to a further layer of bureaucratic supervision and calculation. Furthermore, wages were linked to national expectations of production, this in a period of declining oil production. While state organs, working with the trade unions, were prepared to make minor concessions to buy off discontent, the introduction of the new wage system contributed to a wave of hostility toward the new MKP heads of MAORT at the end of 1947.[29]

Persistent political problems and a desire for greater control over production led the MKP to launch a bid to oust the Social Democrats from their position on the company's factory committees, as part of its preparations for the "fusion" of the two parties during the first half of 1948. At Bázakerretye, while the number of members in the MKP's factory organization hovered at around one hundred in the seven months following the election, the MSzDP suffered from the fact that it enjoyed little positive support among its own membership, given that a substantial portion of them supported more conservative political positions. Thus, it was vulnerable to an aggressive campaign launched by the national Communist leadership against "right-wing Social Democrats" in early 1948 and the growing national pressure toward "fusion," which both limited the MSzDP's freedom for maneuver and led many of its anti-Communist members to resign in disgust.[30] This vigorous campaign peaked in March 1948, when the MKP used the absence of key MSzDP activists from the plants to attend a party conference called to decide on its "fusion" with the Communists in order to take control of the MAORT central factory committee and the individual factory committees below it. In order to do this, the MKP called a mass meeting of working-class activists drawn from its membership and the left wing of the MSzDP from the oil fields in Nagykanizsa, during which, in the name of the workers, they demanded the removal of twenty-six members from the plants' committees.[31]

While this effective putsch prepared the way for the "fusion" of the two parties and the foundation of the MDP in the oil fields in June 1948, it also eased the way for the introduction of party-initiated campaigns that aimed to restructure the institutions of production in preparation for the creation of a planned economy. Wages based on the principles of payment by results were dovetailed with labor competition campaigns that mobilized workers to produce more. March 1948 saw the launch of the first national campaigns to replace sporadic "labor competitions" in those workplaces where the MKP was strong with a national competition, one that aimed to mobilize all workers behind goals of increased production.[32] MAORT's drilling plants were in a special situation; nationally, the MKP had linked the introduction of national competition campaigns to the wave of nationalizations that occurred in the same month as the launch of the competition. Workers had to prove that "the country is theirs, they are building it for themselves." Yet MAORT remained in American ownership; while labor competition was introduced only in May 1948 in the oil fields, officials stressed that it was to prepare for nationalization in the future, through supporting a drive to rationalize production that would lay the foundations for its insertion into the planned economy.[33] The party called on its members to "set an example for all the workers" in order to achieve this goal.[34] Despite this effort, the organization of the labor competition in the oil fields was slow, something the party attributed to its weakness and the geographical remoteness of the drilling plants. The party even accommodated workers' skepticism, making its case for the labor competition in early June 1948 through an appeal to the "individual profit" that workers might gain from participation.[35] The profoundly instrumental attitudes among workers resulted in a situation in which lower-level management and a weak party accommodated demands for low production targets. As a result, workers on the drilling platforms pocketed rising wages, while production fell throughout the second half of 1948—attracting the ire of national representatives of the regime, which was determined to tighten its control over the oil fields.[36]

Behind this need to appease the workforce lay a considerable gulf between oil workers and a weak party. Throughout spring and summer 1948, a "tense climate" existed in the MAORT oil plants—a product of the ever greater sense of threat felt in anticommunist regions like southern Zala, as overt socialist dictatorship was built. Tension in the region was generated and intensified by three sets of measures that interacted with each other. The first measures were those connected to the regime's anticlerical policies and their impact in communities where the Catholic Church was a dominant local actor. The second were those brought by the regime's overt attacks on private landholding and its attempts to launch agricultural collectivization, while the third were those connected to the closure and militarization of the border with Yugoslavia, following Tito's split with Stalin in June 1948.[37]

Relations between the Communists and the Catholic Church in southern Zala had been poor throughout the postwar period. As the MDP was created, the new regime's moves to nationalize church schools worsened relations even further. In Zala's rural communities, many believed that those who supported the state's measures would be banned from "burying their dead" and "christening their children," as many priests attempted to organize a rearguard action against nationalization measures taken in this climate of intensifying state pressure.[38] While the Catholic Church was forced to accept nationalization of its schools, it continued to put pressure on the emerging dictatorship. In September, Cardinal Mindszenty's visit to the county seat, Zalaegerszeg, resulted in as many as twenty-five thousand supporters descending on the city; the demonstration was accompanied across the county by anti-Communist rumor, which proclaimed that Mindszenty would "arrive at the head of British troops, and that plainclothes British and American troops would protect" him.[39] The state was unprepared to tolerate the emergence of the Catholic Church as a focal point of opposition, so Mindszenty was arrested in December 1948. This arrest was greeted with shock, though reaction to it in the oil fields was tempered, for many reckoned that if the socialist dictatorship was sufficiently secure to arrest Hungary's Catholic primate, then it was more than capable of repressing those who supported him. In order to demonstrate loyalty to the regime, Lovászi's parish priest distanced himself from Mindszenty's vocal anti-Communism in the wake of the arrest, while those oil workers who lived in the villages and attended church were unprepared to discuss openly either the arrest or the subsequent trial.[40]

Growing fear of the emergent dictatorship in southern Zala's rural communities was stimulated by the parallel launch of the new regime's attack on private agricultural landholding and its advocacy of agricultural collectivization. In the Letenye district, in which the drilling plants were located, of a total population of 32,972 in 1949, 24,063 were dependent economically on agriculture, and of these, 19,699 were tied to small landholdings of between one and ten holds or kh.[41] Only 18.3 percent of the population were classified as industrial workers, and of these, many owned land.[42] From August 1948, the state began the organization of agricultural cooperatives. This move was underpinned by large increases in the compulsory deliveries of agricultural products that the state demanded smallholders make, as well as hikes in other forms of taxation. These were in turn accompanied by open discrimination against wealthier landholders, who were defined by the state as kulaks and subjected to harsher taxation. While compulsory deliveries were sharply progressive and linked to the size of property, poorer smallholders often found them difficult to meet.[43] Poorer smallholdings were found overwhelmingly in the villages near the oil drilling plants in 1949 (table 10). The immediate turn toward policies of high taxation and collectivization was not unexpected, especially to the more anti-Communist individuals among the rural population, but the new policies generated fury and persistent fear that locals would be forced into the new collective farms. Among those with vineyards, many believed that, by autumn 1948, owners would be denied access, their property would be placed under police guard, and the state would bring in workers to harvest the crop. Many openly attempted to refuse to deliver agricultural produce to the authorities and met with direct repression. Opposition to agrarian policy, especially collectivization, mixed with popular antagonism toward the anticlerical stance of the state motivated many to use Mindszenty's September 1948 visit to Zalaegerszeg as an opportunity to demonstrate against the emergent dictatorship.[44]

The extent of popular Catholic opposition and tension generated by collectivization necessitated a marked increase in the scope of repression. The ÁVH became increasingly active in southern Zala.[45] The repression and the resulting tension were further exacerbated by the increasingly strained relationship between Hungary and Yugoslavia. The oil fields of Hungary were along the border with Yugoslavia, which had been expelled from the COMINFORM in June 1948. The second half of 1948 saw a progressive militarization of the border, which culminated in its effective closure in 1950. Further measures were taken in 1949, which witnessed the erection of a border fence, the construction of watchtowers, and the clearance of all land within five hundred meters of the border. In 1949 and 1950, a minefield was laid. With the transfer of the border guard from the army to the ÁVH in 1949 and the stationing of a division of border guard troops adjacent to the drilling plant at Lovászi, the area in which the oil fields were located became increasingly militarized.[46] This was accompanied by increasing state supervision of the southern Zala population; freedom of movement in and out of a defined area extending some fifteen to twenty

TABLE 10. Agricultural landholding by size of farm in the Letenye district of Zala
County, 1949

| Size of farm (holds) | Number of farms | % of total farms |
|---|---|---|
| 0–1 | 2,182 | 33.25 |
| 1–3 | 1,578 | 24.05 |
| 3–5 | 781 | 11.90 |
| 5–10 | 1,199 | 18.27 |
| 10–15 | 544 | 8.29 |
| 15–20 | 189 | 2.88 |
| 20–25 | 48 | 0.73 |
| 25–35 | 27 | 0.41 |
| 35–50 | 9 | 0.14 |
| 50–100 | 5 | 0.08 |
| TOTAL | 6,562 | 100 |

Source: Adapted from Központi Statisztikai Hivatal, 1949: évi népszámlálás 3. részletes mezőgazdasági
eredmények (Budapest: Állami Nyomda, 1950), 324–25.

kilometers from the border was restricted in 1949, and residents of this border zone
needed a permit to live there and a pass to enter. Both the Lovászi and Bázakerettye
oil fields were located in this zone.[47] In villages adjacent to the border, many felt
deeply ambivalent about the Soviet-Yugoslav conflict. Remembering the retribu-
tions directed against relatives in Prekmurje after its reincorporation into Yugoslavia in 1945, many were receptive to the state's anti-Tito message. On the other
hand, the state's suspicion of the border region's Slovene- and Croatian-speaking
minorities, its anticlerical and antismallholder policies, and the deployment of large
numbers of border guards had by summer 1949 created a situation in which "people
are scared, they don't dare to state their opinions in front of strangers."[48]

The emergent dictatorship's politics of repression and confrontation in southern
Zala were matched by its drive to tighten state control over MAORT. In August 1948,
the authorities in Budapest and the ÁVH launched a series of arrests of MAORT
managers, including the former chief geologist, Simon Papp, on trumped-up
charges of sabotage of the national economy. The state publicly released the details
of the charges the following month, ostensibly to justify measures that placed the
company under state supervision, a situation that lasted until its full nationalization
at the end of 1949.[49] When MAORT was taken under state supervision, the news
was greeted with an explosion of rumors about imminent war in southern Zala;
villagers and oil workers alleged that unknown aircraft had "photographed" the
drilling plants.[50] Within the plant, the supervisors, headed by the regime's appoin-
tee as director, Pál Székely, sought to boost oil production so that MAORT could
meet the targets the state had laid down in the three-year plan.[51] The accusations of
"sabotage," made against senior management in Budapest, were used at the drilling

plants to intimidate workers and engineers to drive up production. Objections to driving up production because of the geology of the fields and the poor condition of much of the machinery had little influence on the representatives of the regime who had assumed responsibility for production. They believed that MAORT had invested in "the education of an aristocracy of labor" and not "in the renewal of equipment."[52]

The proclamation of "sabotage," established through the show trial of MAORT's management, acted as a license to those constructing Hungary's dictatorship to engage in the micromanagement of production. By the beginning of 1949, local party activists at the Bázakerretye site had investigated every production stoppage and machine breakdown in order to establish individual responsibility.[53] This micromanagement, which led local party activists to criminalize certain production practices as "sabotage," intimidated many engineers, foremen, and drilling masters who maintained a public attitude of "indifference" toward the party on site in an attempt to conceal deeper patterns of fear and resentment.[54] This was especially so where activists, obsessed with maintaining continuous production, questioned the judgments of skilled drilling masters they distrusted.[55] Intimidation of some was combined with an attempt to consolidate the regime's control over the plants, as "workers' directors" were assigned to the heads of each of the plants. These functionaries, who, like Károly Papp, were brought in from the Greater Budapest industrial district of Csepel to head the Lovászi plant, came from a milieu more supportive of the new regime than southern Zala. Labor competition, which had hitherto been little more than a drive to arrange a means for higher wages, was relaunched as a tool to shape working practices. Lovászi party organs admitted in November 1948 that labor competition had hitherto existed "only on paper." Management brought in assistance from Budapest to ensure its proper introduction, in view of the regime's continuing weakness locally.[56] The drives to tighten control over production coincided with the national state's moves in January 1949 to bring trade unions under tighter party control and to transform them from bodies that represented workers into organs with specific responsibilities to mobilize workers for production and supervise company-based social and cultural policy.[57] In line with state policy, union branches at the oil wells were transferred from the Mineworkers' Union to the Chemical Workers' Union. Local leaderships were selected on the basis of a single list, prepared by the party committees at the plants, rubber-stamped by the county union bureaucracy, and then imposed on the membership.[58]

The transformation of the local unions reopened discontent over wage levels; the oil field plants fell under the collective agreements of the Chemical Workers' Union, rather than those of the Mineworkers' Union, thus denying oil workers the privileged wage rates of miners.[59] Given national wage policies, this locked oil workers into wage rates that made permanent the postwar erosion of their income relative to that of other workers.[60] In addition, the new local unions implemented centrally mandated policies of wage restriction; almost the first thing the new unions did was drive through increases in the production targets, thus holding back wage increases.[61] The discontent this move generated remained under the surface, as workers maintained a public, though tense, silence over such matters.[62] Behind their silence lay considerable fear, generated by the visible presence of the ÁVH on the drilling sites. The security services were desperate to find evidence of apparent sabotage and willing to place pressure on party activists to seek it out, especially at Lovászi, where the proximity of the border made local security personnel deeply paranoid.[63]

While simmering discontent was being held in check through the generation of a climate of intimidation and fear, the implementation of policies to transform working practices was failing to transform production. Although there was in theory an elaborate cross-enterprise labor competition that aimed to mobilize work brigades and individuals for exceptional achievement in production, in practice, attempts by the new management to force increases in overall production levels meant that the competition rarely had any meaning for those working at the drilling sites.[64] The forcible ramping up of production coexisted with familiar phenomena; the pressure on drilling masters to maintain continuous production at all costs resulted in endemic machine breakdowns and an epidemic of industrial accidents, which in turn led to production stoppages.[65] The overexploitation of the fields caused—as it had prior to production cuts in 1947—the large-scale escape of natural gas into the atmosphere, thus compromising future production.[66] Many oil workers, aware of the link between current overproduction and future production, as well as being distrustful of Hungary's new rulers, believed that "the Communists always speak of increased production but are prepared to put it in danger in the interests of maintaining their own power." Many argued that, before long, "serious decreases in production will occur," in view of the overexploitation of the fields.[67]

While the new regime nominally controlled the MAORT drilling plants by late spring 1949, it had failed to either transform production or build a secure base for itself among workers. In June 1949, the Letenye district party committee reported despairingly that "the manual workers are not sufficiently class conscious to apply the principle of vigilance in production. . . . In MAORT, they regard the whole thing almost as if it were still American property."[68] Behind this apparent lack of "class-conscious" behavior lay huge distrust of the regime, fed by the climate of fear and repression that had accompanied the construction of dictatorship in the region and a set of workplaces naturally hostile to it. While that climate of fear prevented open protest, it did not stop that distrust manifesting itself through widespread rumor both about the intentions of the regime and its likely future. In advance of the single-list parliamentary elections in May 1949, which ended any semblance of political pluralism, workers argued that the regime would continue the measures it had begun by taking over unions and would "abolish collective agreements."[69]

Others maintained that, "if the Communists win, then workers won't get their wages in money anymore, but in vouchers; with them, they will be able to buy only the goods that the government allows."[70] This position underlay a refusal among MAORT workers to believe official promises of improved living standards in the future; as far as one was concerned, "only illiterate Communists will benefit from the increase in living standards."[71] This atmosphere of outright antagonism would dog the regime as it persisted with its revolution in production across the oil fields.

## The Contested Construction of Dictatorship in Újpest

On 14 November 1947, management in the Wolfner Leather and Shoe Factory, supported by the plant's MKP cell, implemented changes to payment practices in the facility. Prior to that date, workers had received "two envelopes" every Friday; the first contained their wages as stipulated by the collective agreements; the second, a local unofficial payment, compensated workers for poor fulfillment of their production norms. On this particular Friday in November, workers received only the first envelope. Although the trade union and the shop stewards had been informed of the change, in one workshop, workers laid down their tools for three hours. When workers returned to work on Monday, discontent spread quickly among those in the leather-cutting workshops, and a strike spread rapidly across the factory, disrupting production for most of the rest of the day.[72] The strike in the Wolfner plant was not an isolated incident. Just as in Zala County, autumn 1947 was period of simmering material discontent, which bubbled up into a series of short-lived work stoppages across the city's light industrial plants. Yet the MKP attributed the wave of protest not to material circumstances but to the presence of "right-wing Social Democrats" in the factories and the weaknesses of its own organizations on the shop floor, thus highlighting the need for greater political control within industrial production.[73]

Tightening control involved the use of highly repressive practices, including direct police intervention, to destroy the Újpest MSzDP prior to fusion with the MKP.[74] Even in factories with strong MSzDP traditions, such as the United Incandescent Lamp and Electrical Factory, the destruction of the Social Democrats was used as a means of tightening control over the trade unions and factory committees. With nationalization in March 1948 and the reorganization of factory management that followed, the plant-level union was rationalized as shop stewards were subordinated formally to a union executive authority that consisted of a secretary and officers for "wages," "production," "social policy," and "education."[75] The reorganization of the union and the destruction of the MSzDP had been accompanied by attacks against labor movement activists like Jenő Pál Nagy, who had been asked by the city MKP leadership three years previously to organize the factory in the aftermath of World War II and who played a key role in reconstruction after the plant was dismantled by the Red Army. The local MKP leadership harassed these activists simply because of their continued membership in the MSzDP and their advocacy of a unionism independent of the state. They, and the model of labor movement activism they represented, was labeled redundant given the state's emphasis on the "construction of socialism"; they were accused of "not wanting that the Hungarian people, the United Incandescent Lamp and Electrics' own workers, raise their living standards progressively by means of their own labor."[76]

While the MKP's drive for greater control in the Zala oil fields was almost entirely the result of pressure from above, in Újpest the construction of dictatorship was aided by the active participation of the left-wing majority of the city's workers. The Social Democrats were not merely broken through pressure from the police and a ruthless local MKP leadership that stood behind them. The party also imploded. In the period prior to the August 1947 elections, both the MKP and the MSzDP were committed to Hungary's socialist transformation; despite their bitter rivalry for the control of many factories, the actual differences between the two parties were unclear to most workers. Following the elections, as it became clear that the MKP would lead the socialist transformation of Hungary, rather than an MSzDP many had joined as a consequence of a tradition that stretched back into the interwar years, it was easy for most left-wing workers to transfer their formal allegiance. As early as November 1947, the MSzDP Újpest factory organizer, Oszkár Sümegi, noted that "disinterest" toward the party was driving noticeable decreases in membership, which he blamed on a sense that the Social Democrats were simply being overshadowed by the MKP.[77] By February 1948, as it became clear that "fusion" was inevitable, rank-and-file Social Democrats jumped en masse to the MKP; in that month, 35 percent of the membership in the Pannonia Furrier Factory and 60 percent of the membership in the United Incandescent Lamp and Electrical Factory left to join the Communists.[78] While intimidation played a role in persuading a limited number of white-collar members and trade union activists to jump ship, the mass character of the party's implosion was a sign of a desire among left-wing workers for a unified workers' party. In the Magyar Pamutipar, local MKP organizers talked of "fusion" from below in the factory after eight hundred Social Democrats in the plant defected in the first three weeks of February, leaving the factory's Social Democrats with so few activists that they were unable to elect leaders.[79]

The climate that had generated the implosion of the MSzDP in Újpest was experienced by left-wing workers regardless of party affiliation, and it led them to accept the emergent dictatorship as the fulfillment of their wish, expressed since 1945, for a state committed to greater social justice. This sense was especially strong among rank-and-file labor movement activists. One shop steward in the United Incandescent Lamp and Electrical Factory proclaimed on the eve of nationalization, "Socialism is the future, and with it the issues of capitalist supply and demand will disappear. There has been no change over the years in the management of the factory. . . . The workers do not trust the management as a whole. . . . We need a workers' director immediately."[80] The combination of growing institutional control by the MKP and, then, after June 1948, the MDP, with the enthusiasm of left-wing workers for what seemed like socialist transformation, accompanied the beginnings of the state's drive to transform production. Workers, partly motivated by this spirit, and also by their rising earnings, were prepared to argue that "labor competition should have been introduced a long time ago."[81]

Despite achieving considerable support for the emergent dictatorship among the left-wing majority of workers in Újpest during 1948, the MDP remained deeply frustrated at both its lack of control in production and the persistence of certain forms of work culture that it had sought to eliminate by nationalization and the elimination of the MSzDP. In the United Incandescent Lamp and Electrical Factory's machine shop—a stronghold of male skilled workers and a center of labor movement activism that had been the social base of the MSzDP in the plant—the informal regulation of performance relative to production quotas, and thus the control of earnings, had survived six months of attempts to put labor competition into place instead. Shop stewards, linked closely to particular categories of workers, supervised the pace of work and thus the earnings claimed; the shop's turners were regulated to ensure that no one appeared to make more than 135 percent of the norm, in order to protect workers against a possible speed-up of production.[82] Despite the extension of state control over the unions and the purges of the MDP's membership, the emergent state faced considerable resistance in Újpest's factories when it attempted to boost labor productivity by raising production targets in February 1949.[83] In the Mauthner Leather Factory, workers complained that their new norms were "too high" and that, if the norms were not lowered, they "would quit." The norm increases resulted in an "atmosphere of discontent among the workers," which, in view of greater political control, did not result in wildcat strikes. Instead, foremen were successfully placed under pressure by groups of skilled workers to fake workers' timesheets by illegally adding work remunerated on the basis of fixed hourly wages, in order to raise their wages.[84] Paradoxically, partially suppressed protest and considerable political control coexisted with more generalized support for the regime. Workers both appreciated an improvement in their own material situations and approved of "class war" politics, as they believed "those groups who live most easily will disappear in the near future" as a result of the regime's policies.[85]

As the dictatorship was constructed locally during 1948 and the first half of 1949, support for it was not universal, especially given the persistence of deep-seated cultural division among Újpest workers that had underpinned political identities over the previous few years. In plants like the United Incandescent Lamp and Electrical Factory, the nature of political division was especially visible. Among the skilled male elite, as early as the proclamation of the program of the MDP in June 1948, there was considerable support for socialist transformation. Among the semiskilled female majority, opinions were more mixed. Many of these workers were religious, which made them instinctively more skeptical of the "new" state, given its drive to nationalize church schools and the bitter opposition of the Church.[86] Among the large number of rural commuters who worked in the city, there was considerable distrust of the state. Such distrust had been stimulated by the beginnings of the agricultural collectivization drive, which led to a culture of rumor about the impact of punitive agricultural taxation on their livelihoods. Thus, the rumors that began among rural workers spread on the city's shop floors.[87]

Given that Újpest was an urban community, agrarian discontent rumbled in the background; the same could not be said of issues of religion, which were especially central for workers who came from particular parts of the city. While church attendance among the residents of the tenements and neighborhoods surrounding the city center was negligible, this was not true of the outlying neighborhoods, like Megyer, where the local priest, Lajos Márk, proved to be an implacable opponent of the regime's anticlerical policies.[88] Although the state blamed Márk for the fact that the nationalization of the local school generated considerable discontent in the neighborhood, Megyer had a very different character compared to much of the rest of Újpest—one that was more rural, given its location on the periphery of the city, more agrarian, given the substantial numbers who had benefited from land reform in 1945, and one that was dominated by a Catholic political culture.[89] As large numbers of residents took employment in the city's factories, they took their antagonism toward the state's anticlerical policies into industrial establishments. Anti-Communist graffiti that appeared in the United Incandescent Lamp and Electrical Factory in June 1948, in support of the Church's position on the nationalization of church schools, was attributed to Megyer residents furious at the regime's anticlerical policies.[90] Megyer's exceptionality within Újpest meant that anti-Communist, pro-religious activism had little opportunity to spread to other city neighborhoods. The highly restricted base of support for politically conservative positions in the city was underlined by popular reaction to the arrest of Mindszenty in December 1948. As in Zala, many of those who adopted anti-Communist positions were shocked at the arrest, which was quickly followed by the detention of Megyer's priest.[91] Often their reactions were tinged with anti-Semitism directed against the MDP leadership; many saw in Mindszenty's arrest and the purges of party members a concerted attempt to ensure that "Christians would be expelled" from the party, "but not Jews." Such opinions were minority ones, as distrust of the Church among the left-wing majority ensured little popular support for Mindszenty; indeed, so great was anticlerical feeling among the left-wing majority, there were cases of workers being assaulted by workmates for carrying copies of Új Ember (meaning "new person")— the Catholic newspaper—to work as a mark of protest against state policies.[92]

Distrust of the Church and generalized support for socialist transformation did not translate into unconditional trust of the regime among the left-wing majority, however. Memories of the war, fear of political instability, and distrust of the Soviet

Union, especially of the Red Army, were easy to awake. In the Magyar Pamutipar in January 1949, shortly before the Mindszenty trial got under way, a rumor took hold that, in preparation for the trial, "all hotels, canteens, and bigger buildings would be occupied by Soviet troops who will arrive in the next few days." Others stated that the troops would then use Hungary as a base "to launch war against Yugo-slavia."[93] Furthermore, though the majority of workers were prepared to believe party accusations when directed against Mindszenty, in part because they associ-ated the Catholic Church with an interwar regime they feared might return, they showed almost complete incomprehension when the state security services were unleashed against leading members of the party during 1949. When László Rajk's arrest became public in the summer, left-wing workers in the United Incandescent Lamp and Electrical Factory found the accusations "very difficult to believe" and, as a consequence, preferred to "speak little of them."[94]

The conditional nature of the support of left-wing workers for the regime was a product of the fact that, with the liquidation of obviously right-wing parties, left-wing workers were more impatient to see real material improvement after the pri-vations of previous years. This sentiment underpinned workers' responses to the announcement of the industrialization drive that was the centerpiece of the first five-year plan, in April 1949.[95] Many workers asked party activists, "Why does our pay remain so low? Why are we throwing money at heavy industry?"[96] Although local incomes and living standards had improved substantially since 1947, as they had across the country as a whole, class identity as a source of frustration over rela-tive poverty, so characteristic of the period that immediately followed the introduc-tion of the forint, persisted even into better economic times.[97] One activist, who popularized the first five-year plan on the boundary of Újpest, where it met the industrial Budapest suburb of Angyalföld, commented that the "working-class neighborhood" in which she lived was "difficult territory. The poorer the people, the more difficult the agitation is, because they only see exclusion; they are dif-ficult to convince of what they have gained."[98] From 1947, the local state promised to tackle dreadful housing conditions for those living in Újpest's slums and to allevi-ate chronic problems of severe poverty and homelessness.[99] Poverty was in retreat, especially severe poverty, as a result of huge decreases in unemployment during 1948. By mid-1949, there were shortages of skilled labor, which led to the pursuit of more punitive policies toward beggars and the homeless on the streets of Újpest.[100] Official propaganda that popularized the first five-year plan dominated the local press during spring and summer 1949; it aimed to build on the economic improve-ment of the previous two years while defusing persistent discontent at the poverty of many residents by promising concrete material improvements in the near future. It pointed to the limited construction of housing for workers in the city in order to argue that it had already ended "twenty years" of neglect in housing for workers, and it promised even greater investment for apartment construction in programs of generalized modernization of the urban infrastructure.[101]

Class identity persisted within the city's industrial workplaces, too; resentment at the privileges of other social groups underpinned a suspicion of management and white-collar staff, which came to the surface when the state attempted to transform workplaces in ways that challenged established working practices and occupational identities. In the United Incandescent Lamp and Electrical Factory, workers were deeply suspicious of the beginnings of National Labor Competition in 1948, arguing that it was manipulated so that "engineers would gain extra pay."[102] While such suspicions were not wholly borne out, the complaint was revealing of how the politics of labor competition in Újpest's factories encapsulated the ways in which the state's construction of its legitimacy clashed with its productivist intentions to create highly specific social dynamics on shop floors across the city.

In some workplaces, labor competition was nothing new. By the time the National Labor Competition program was announced, a number of local enterprises had participated in events they called labor competitions since 1945. These were at their most highly developed in plants in the textile sector. In the Magyar Pamutipar, competition was introduced in the second half of 1947 as a means of breaking the considerable pressure on individual workers, especially in the spinning shops, not to exceed the informally agreed rate.[103] Two interconnected competitions took place in the spinning shop; the first was between different work groups, defined by their position within the labor process in the shop, who would gain a prize as group. In addition to this, individual performance would also be rewarded. By introducing parallel group and individual competitions, shop management aimed to break antagonism toward high individual performance in reaching production targets by rewarding the groups of which such workers were part.[104] Both management and workers were pleased with the result of their experiment in the spinning shop; production was 5.8 percent above target for the period the competition ran, while thirty-two thousand forints in prize money had been distributed to workers over and above their wages, both to individuals and members of groups. However, the consent of workers was secured only through the making of additional payments for participation; those who failed to win prizes were compensated with semilegal payments by management: "They get the total value of their overfulfillment in their pay packets. Not even those who play professional sports get as much."[105] Consent from workers to drive up their production had been achieved only by paying exceptional wage rates to workers; undeterred, management moved to introduce a slightly modified version of the competition to other shops.[106]

The way in which the Magyar Pamutipar's labor competition became mired in informal bargaining, as consent could be secured only by guaranteeing everyone, including the "losers," increased earnings, characterized the introduction of

National Labor Competition in the city. Within public discourse, competition and participation within it was intended by the regime as a demonstration that workers understood the need to change their attitudes toward labor so that they could be held up as an example to others. According to the Textile Workers' Union newspaper, those who had been rewarded for exceptional performance in the first national labor competition were "those workers who recognized that they worked in the service of the welfare of the whole nation and had earned the respect of the entire nation."[107] These examples of exceptional production were created at the factory level as managers, unions, and party organizations were carefully monitored against set production targets that stipulated throughout 1948 the proportions that were to participate. Furthermore, state organs demanded that their local officials organize workers into socialist brigades—groups of workers organized around a specific task in production. They were then expected to link the activities of such groups to concrete activities in production in order that the performance of both the workers and those organizing the campaigns could be measured.[108]

During 1948, while enterprises at the national level were assessed in competition against a standardized set of criteria based on production, productivity, and good work discipline, the translation of these criteria to factory-level reality tended to be highly uneven. In the United Incandescent Lamp and Electrical Factory, management and the party organized the labor competition by distributing concrete tasks central to production to sections of the plant and demanding they be completed ahead of time.[109] These practices continued with the beginning of the organization of socialist brigades in the factory, which were given key responsibilities in the completion of some of these tasks.[110] In the city's textile factories, much depended on the degree to which management and local activists took seriously the need to organize labor competition. Where it functioned, the competition adopted highly decentralized forms as workers were directed to conduct specific tasks that were about removing obstacles to greater and better quality production. The concern with the quality of the finished product in textiles necessitated the introduction of factory-specific forms of labor competition in some plants; in the Magyar Pamutipar, while the workers were exhorted to increase production in spinning shops, their foremen were rewarded on the basis of the quality of overall production.[111]

The key, however, to ensuring that a skeptical and materially focused workforce mobilized behind these tasks was material reward itself. On the eve of the introduction of National Labor Competition in Újpest, propagandists were issued guidance on how to deal with workers who were suspicious of participation on the grounds that it would be used as a new form of exploitation. These guidelines instructed propagandists to draw workers' attention to the profit they could gain from participation: "first, you will earn more; second, with higher production, you will reduce the prices of basic goods; third, if you achieve exceptional results, you'll get a substantial special payout yourself, or for your group."[112] Given the naked appeal to popular demands for increased living standards, it was hardly surprising that the mobilization of workers behind labor competition was predicated on its ability to guarantee higher wages. In the United Incandescent Lamp and Electrical Factory, it was "higher wages" and the promise of them that guaranteed working-class support for competition.[113] Equally important, delays in the payment of promised rewards undermined support for it; in the Budavidék and Újpest Wool Spinning and Weaving Factory, activists blamed the overly bureaucratic regulations on the payment of prize money for delays in those payments and the resulting discontent.[114] Exceptional material payments were often tied to being decorated with the status of "outstanding worker" (*élmunkás*). In the Magyar Pamutipar, two spinning machine operators, Erzsébet Suhai and Magda Fábián, sought to win outstanding worker status by beating the production performance of a preexisting outstanding worker in the neighboring HPS plant. When they did so, but were refused the status and therefore any special payment, they declined to join the labor competition, denouncing it as a political fix.[115]

In many workplaces, especially those where semiskilled labor was predominant, the link between labor competition and increased wages brought about changes in workers' behavior. In the Magyar Pamutipar's weaving shop, the number and length of visits to the toilets during shifts fell markedly during April 1948, as workers focused on increasing their earnings.[116] This focus on increased earnings, however, generated forms of behavior that were not as welcome from the productivist standpoint of the state. As the competition became better established during the summer and autumn of 1948, many managers noticed that workers' focus on "innovations" to increase their earnings led to a neglect of the quality of production.[117] The speedup of production, and the increases in scrap production, placed severe pressure on the provision of raw materials, especially in light industrial sectors, where supplies had already been disrupted by the onset of the cold war and the circumstances of nationalization. Work stoppages were the result, and they prevented workers from earning and thus provoked tension between them and technical staff.[118] In such circumstances, under pressure from workers desperate to make enough to survive, lower-level managers were placed under pressure to turn a blind eye to production of poor quality, leading to greater scrap production.[119]

The institutionalization of labor competition through a tacit settlement whereby authorities at a local level bought a skeptical workforce with the promise of higher earnings cemented the legitimacy of the regime among left-wing workers, who saw labor competition as a reform that addressed their material discontent. This settlement, however, undercut the state's attempts to prepare for centralized economic planning. By the end of 1948, policy makers in Budapest grew concerned at increasing production costs, which they blamed on "lax" production targets on factory floors.[120] Their attempts to restore order by tightening production targets in January and February 1949 were bitterly unpopular on factory floors in Újpest, but they did not destroy the legitimacy of the regime among its working-class supporters.[121] This was because of the strength of the agreements through which labor competition had been implemented locally; mobilized through labor competition to restore earnings levels in the factories, the agreements frustrated the regime's productivity drive.[122]

## The Contradictions of Socialist Construction in Tatabánya

By the spring of 1949 in Tatabánya, just as in Újpest, labor competition had become predicated on patterns of workplace bargaining. However, this activity took on a very different form in the mines—the local area's major employer—because of the insurmountable constraints to raising wages. The mines operated a wood yard responsible for preparing the timbers to shore up the walls and roof; the work was physically strenuous, and the workers were underpaid relative to their privileged underground workmates. The workers often made up their wages by performing high levels of overtime, which was remunerated with special premiums.[123] Because of the focus of economic plans on headline coal production, socialist labor competition did not arrive in the wood yard until the formation of the first brigade in February 1949. While this brigade promised to improve productivity and production, it demanded of the mines' central competition committee that the production targets of workers in the yard be "reduced, because it is impossible to feed and clothe ourselves from our earnings, to the degree that the hard physical labor [in the wood yard] demands."[124]

The use of the institutions of labor competition as a means of seeking material improvement occurred against a background in which poverty, though less than in 1947, remained endemic. Poor housing, especially in the mining enterprise colonies, persisted from the immediate postwar years; throughout 1949, within the 5,258 flats the company had at its disposal, an average of 3.2 persons lived in each room. Furthermore, in 255 of the apartments, there were more than 7 people crowded in each room. More than 60 percent of the mines' workers lived in these colonies, and this situation affected the ability of the mines to retain labor. With the onset of the three-year plan, unemployment dried up during 1948 and 1949, creating severe shortages of skilled male labor; however, while rural dwellers and those whose housing lay outside the colonies were attracted by miners' wages, opportunities to leave Tatabánya for work in areas with better housing also increased.[125] As a result, there was increasing labor turnover; of the 5,572 underground workers employed in the mines in 1949, 1,672 left the company during the year, while among aboveground workers, 1,165 of 2,201 workers departed. Although these workers were replaced, turnover of this level disrupted production.[126] Yet the discontent driving the high turnover coexisted with a strongly Communist political culture in Tatabánya that bolstered support for the regime but sometimes ran counter to its intentions. Following the disappearance of the MSzDP in 1948, its newspaper, *Népszava* (meaning "the people's voice") was taken over by the trade unions, which launched campaigns to boost subscriptions among workers during 1949. Tatabánya miners were deeply hostile to such campaigns because of the newspaper's previous associations with the Social Democrats. Many workers associated it with the figure of Károly Peyer, the anti-Communist MSzDP leader during the interwar years, and many miners believed he had betrayed them. Propagandists had to explain that "fascists don't write for *Népszava* anymore."[127]

The combination of substantial material discontent with a strong Communist political identity being shared by the majority of Tatabánya workers had been present in 1947. As one working-class MKP voter, Béla Bria, explained after the August 1947 election, "I expected a Communist victory because I knew that the working class is convinced that the Hungarian Communist Party has done more than the others for the workers." But he warned that "now, after the elections, there will be even more work for the Communists. . . . My own situation is currently really difficult. I earn 280 to 300 forints a month. Now we pay a monthly fee of 120 forints for our basic food, and sorting out our household needs from the rest is a real problem for my wife. I hope this doesn't go on for much longer and [that] Communist victory will bring us improvement."[128] In the short run, however, the MKP found such expectations impossible to meet. In late September, the mining colony was hit by potato shortages, which workers blamed on the inability of the government to tackle "speculation." One miner's wife complained that one "Friday morning I wanted to buy two kilos of potatoes for lunch, but they weren't to be found anywhere. On Saturday I could get three kilos, but only at one forint twenty fillérs per kilo [the official price in the company shop was only fifty-eight fillérs]. I was forced to buy them for this price, because, if I hadn't, someone else would, and I wouldn't have anything to cook. There wasn't a single potato in any other shop or in the market. This has been the situation since Saturday."[129] This "potato crisis" lifted the lid on a well of discontent over high prices and low incomes; one miner noted, "We are five in our family, and when I bring home my money, my wife doesn't know how we'll make ends meet. . . . With these high prices, my pay doesn't even cover the cost of food." Such discontent generated demands that the government take urgent action against "speculators."[130] Persistent shortages of potatoes led the local trade union to send a delegation to the Ministry of Industry in Budapest; anger was such that, when the delegation returned and reported that it had received a verbal promise of potatoes but not an order documented in writing, miners refused to begin their morning shift on 10 October in Pit No. XIV. When the pit factory committee president, Barnabás Varga, repeatedly called on the miners to start work, the meeting became radicalized; miners who defended the strike as "justified" and called for potatoes to be delivered immediately, at the beginning of the stoppage, increasingly demanded to know why the MKP protected "Jewish" traders.[131]

After the end of the "potato crisis," persistent anger directed at "speculators"

took increasingly anti-Semitic forms, a phenomenon that was testimony to an erosion in the authority of the MKP among those who had supported it. MKP activists complained that "inflation" created a climate of "insecurity," which allowed
"rumors of war" to circulate and ultimately erode their control in the mines.[132]
Workers passionately "attacked the government for not doing anything" about the
situation, yet blamed "Jewish shopkeepers" for speculation.[133] The erosion of the
authority of the MKP among its core working-class constituency culminated in
open rebellion in the mines at the beginning of 1948. While persistent food shortages and high prices fed the climate of tension, the focus of the uproar was the collective agreement for workers in mining for 1948. The publication of the agreement,
due in November 1947, was delayed into 1948. Miners distrusted their union and saw
the MKP as "weak" in the face of the management of the state-run mines. The non-
appearance of the agreement exacerbated their discontent: "opinion is divided, they
don't know what it will contain, but they are already speculating that they will have
to pay five forints for their flats and that there will be no help with their rents."[134]
When the collective agreement was finally published at the end of January 1948,
these fears proved to be well founded. Underpaid workers in aboveground positions
were forced to pay rents for company housing that had previously been free, though
their underground colleagues continued to be exempt, a situation that intensified
discontent over the miserable living conditions in the fifty-year old colony. Affected
workers announced that "we will not accept having to pay rents for our flats, and we
strongly protest this!"[135]

Discontent among aboveground workers over rents became mixed with anger
at some of the wage provisions of the agreement among underground workers. The
focus of this anger was a provision introduced, at the insistence of the government,
to all of the 1948 collective agreements in order to ensure the spread of production
targets calculated according to "scientific" methods. This provision stipulated that
where such production targets were not in force, all should be set at the level of average production during September and October 1947.[136] The announcement of these
measures led to two of the three shifts in Pit No. XIV—the location of the work stoppage during the "potato crisis"—striking on 15 January; the miners refused to work
toward the targets the agreement introduced. The strike on this occasion failed to
spread, and miners reluctantly resolved to return to work on the condition that the
union leadership fully explain the agreement to the workers.[137] The tense peace in Pit
No. XIV did not last long, however. On the morning of 6 February, miners walked
out at nine o'clock. At the beginning of the afternoon shift, at two o'clock, they were
joined by workers from a further eight pits and several of the aboveground plants.[138]
The wages issue acted as a catalyst that lifted the lid on a more generalized wave of
grievances; attempts by the mine managers to settle the strikes locally and informally through a relaxing of the production targets foundered on the militancy of
younger workers, leading management to decide that "their demands simply can-

not be met."[139] After hearing that national officials were to hold talks with their local counterparts, the most militant of the strikers descended on the local trade union headquarters and prevented the visitors from entering the building.[140]

The following day, the strike spread further while the strikers gathered in a disorganized show of strength in the Tatabánya stadium. When the MKP leadership addressed the crowd, demanded they returned to work, and threatened MKP members present with expulsion, those present responded furiously, calling on the party leaders "not to bring party politics into this."[141] The strikers were infuriated at the attitude of the MKP, which had chosen to confront them. By the afternoon, the Interior Ministry had ordered representatives of the state security agency to Tatabánya, in order to identify and detain the strike's ringleaders.[142] The Communists and party members in the union leadership warned the strikers that they would not negotiate with them until the strike ended; the strikers who dominated a trade union mass meeting elected a leadership made up of members of both workers' parties. This strike committee demanded that the collective agreement be rewritten, that wages be linked to prices, that company apartments be rent free, that payments in coal be increased, and that a pay supplement be introduced for older workers. The miners returned to work on the grounds that the strike committee should be allowed to negotiate a lasting settlement. This tacit agreement was never honored by management.[143]

While the state security agencies arrested many they identified as troublemakers, the MKP expelled those of its members who served on the strike committee.[144] It refused to accept fully that the strike had been a result of mounting material frustration and instead blamed "right-wing Social Democrats" and "fascists."[145] The national leadership moved not only against the MSzDP but also against the Tatabánya leadership and the central factory committee of the mines, whose weakness it blamed for its loss of control.[146] Yet, paradoxically, its drive for control following the strike was successful because the MKP began to address, in its own way, many of the grievances that lay behind the strike. The MKP recovered the initiative it had lost in the autumn by renewing the "struggle against reaction" in late winter 1948, blaming "capitalist elements" for persistent low living standards locally, as socialist transformation moved onto the party's national agenda. The MKP met with considerable approval when it attacked shopkeepers for having "profiteered" against shoppers; it attacked those who gave "loans" to workers at weekly rates of interest of sixty forints—thus using class-based rhetoric to channel anti-Semitic sentiment.[147]

The MKP's local campaign during the first half of 1948 dovetailed with the process of socialist transformation in the city, which raised expectations of positive change. Those companies outside the mines were nationalized.[148] Nationalization played a central role in re-cementing Communist influence in Tatabánya, because it came so soon after the four villages that made up the district were unified to create a city administration.[149] With the integration of the mines and other local plants into the state sector, the new city played a central role in the construction of an emergent socialist society, given the central role of its mines and power plants as providers of energy for industry nationwide. This significance was especially marked in the power plants, where Tatabánya's central role was stressed as the provider of power that would support the regime's plans to bring electricity and lighting to all villages and that would support the development of industry. The managing director of Power Plant No. 1, Pál Kovács, told his workforce that lack of electrification was "a central problem of socialism." As a consequence of the fact that "in recent years no new power plants have been built in Hungary," the sector was in urgent need of new investment. The first of these new investments in expansion "would be carried out in Tatabánya."[150] As far as Kovács's equivalent in the city's mines was concerned, after the war, "industrial enterprises would never have restarted without the nourishment of coal"; therefore, the targets in the economic plan underlined the mines' centrality in creating a "pleasanter, happier, socialist Hungary."[151]

The rhetoric of planning thus imagined Tatabánya as being at the center of the state's program of socialist construction, and its overwhelmingly working-class population was placed at the heart of this program, given its role in delivering the goals of the plan. In early 1949, the new city had 40,221 inhabitants, of whom 33,843 were dependent on manual industrial employment for their livelihoods.[152] Thus, Tatabánya's new civic identity stressed its role as a home for workers who were placed at the heart of the state's productivist program. For a community that had been treated as marginal, its placement at the forefront of "socialist construction" generated expectations of social improvement, especially of the city's housing conditions. The state had already begun to build new housing, though in extremely limited quantities; local authorities planned the construction of 129 flats between 1947 and 1949, and they promised "Central Europe's most modern workers' housing."[153] While this investment had only a marginal effect on conditions in the city, it raised expectations. Faced with the announcement of new investment in local industry, workers and their representatives realized that "new workers are also necessary" and that they would need somewhere to live; in the power plant, the factory committee president assured workers that those who "will have responsible jobs, need to move to near the power plant." Thus, increased production was expected to lead to major investment to solve the housing crisis locally.[154]

While the promise of positive change was not greeted approvingly by all, the degree to which socialist transformation was contested in Tatabánya was far less than in the rest of the country. The overwhelming majority of the local population, including some among church congregations, sympathized with the state's anticlerical measures. Mindful of this fact, all but one of the local priests refused to condemn the nationalization of church schools in spring 1948, and some publicly supported the regime in "settling relations between the democracy and the Church."[155] Virulent anticlericalism was strong among Communist supporters and activists and was stirred by the climate of tension between the Church and state nationally. At times, the anticlericalism expressed was so crude that the party took steps to restrain its activists.[156] The beginnings of agricultural collectivization had a marginal impact on all but restricted neighborhoods of the city itself, given its overwhelmingly working-class character. Only 3.1 percent of the total population lived in households that owned a farm, and, of these farms, 63.8 percent were quite small, occupying less than three holds.[157] Outside the city, in neighboring villages like Vértesszőllős, from which many miners commuted to jobs in the city, the regime's agricultural policies were a greater source of social tension. Of the population of 1,725 in 1949, 67.36 percent were dependent on manual employment, mainly in neighboring Tatabánya, while 23.01 percent made their livelihoods on farms owned by a household member.[158] Just as in the city, the overwhelming majority of these farms were tiny—67.6 percent were of three holds or less.[159] In this socially divided community, while many smallholders complained of penal levels of taxation, this attitude met with little sympathy from the working-class majority, especially at times of food shortage, such as during a shortage of flour in the local shop in May 1949. Miners' wives complained bitterly that "things are going really well for the peasants, when miners' wages are falling because they've increased the production targets."[160]

While established class identities could be mobilized in villages such as Vértesszőllős to blunt opposition to the regime's agrarian policies or could underlie the local appeal of the regime's rhetoric of "socialist construction" in Tatabánya, they also shaped ambivalence about the concrete attempts of the state to transform production. In industrial establishments, like the aluminum smelter, the cement factory, and the power plants nationalized in spring 1948, attitudes toward labor competition, payment-by-results wages, and labor policy were shaped by the instrumental and skeptical attitudes so visible in Újpest. In the cement plant and the quarry, the attempts to restrict wages through the 1948 collective agreement had not produced a strike but had led to widespread passive resistance, in which workers held up production to such an extent that the slowdown endangered their ability to fulfill three-year plans. Relaxations in production targets disguised by labor competition resulted.[161] During the norm revision in February 1949, when production targets were increased, a wave of class resentment was unleashed, which activists and management had to defuse through the labor competition as workers in the aluminum smelter demanded to know "how great will the increases in norms be for the white-collar staff?"[162] The attempts to separate the aluminum smelters' workers from the Mineworkers' Union, and the relatively high wage rates in the latter's collective agreement, provoked a petition among the workers opposing the regime's reorganization of the union.[163] The use of competition to paper over this discontent and reward core workers, at the expense of low-paid rural commuters, defused much open discontent, while those on the periphery responded through recourse to absenteeism.[164]

The regime had far greater difficulties in the mines, because the opportunities to secure consent for labor competition by raising wages were not present. Thus, its attempts to transform production became ensnared in patterns of informal bargaining in ways different than those used elsewhere in the economy and that preempted patterns of conflict that emerged across industry during the early 1950s. Performance-based wages did not rise substantially in the mines; miners' real wages in Tatabánya in spring 1948 were little more than they had been after stabilization in late summer 1946.[165] After the campaigns to revise production targets in early 1949, even nominal wages were lower in the mines than they had been the previous spring; furthermore, the differentials between the skilled coal hewers and other workers had been eroded by the operation of the wage system. While skilled coal hewers had earned an average of 34.45 forints per shift in June 1948, they took home 32.81 forints in February 1949. For underground workers as a whole, nominal wages fell less, from 29.42 to 28.82 forints, while aboveground workers' wages fell marginally, from 19.67 to 19.03.[166] Such figures were striking for three reasons. The first was because the state sought to protect the high earnings of coal hewers, relative to other workers in mining, and of skilled workers in other industrial sectors. Second, although such figures were affected by short-term factors like the 1949 revision of production targets, they were far out of line with the rest of the economy, where increases in production targets arrested continuous wage increases, rather than slashed nominal wages.[167] The third reason is that the mines were not at all immune to the endemic informal subversion of officially prescribed wage determination processes that plagued other sectors.[168]

Because of the linking of wages to production targets laid out in the plan—especially for underground workers at the coal face—stagnant wages were closely linked to the inability of the Tatabánya mines to increase their production as much as other industrial sectors. Engineers from the headquarters of the state mining company reported in November 1948 that "Tatabánya's golden age is over." In the fifty-two years of mining there, half of the coal had been extracted; what remained was deep, geographically distant from the earliest mines, and dangerous to mine given the underground lakes that lay adjacent to many of the coal faces.[169] Thus, as plan targets for the mines were raised gradually so that the demand for coal from an expanding industrial sector could be satisfied, these problems became ever more apparent. Pit No. XII was required to raise its production of coal gradually throughout 1949, yet most of its coal faces were exhausted, forcing mine management to extend the fifteen kilometers of tunnels that made up the pit in order to open new faces—a challenge that, in the temporary absence of funds to invest in modernizing underground transportation, required stretching existing manpower. This forced the introduction of Sunday shifts to complete maintenance over a huge area, with a stretched workforce who, during the week, could not all be guaranteed workplaces that allowed them to hit their production targets and, thus, their expected wage given the payment-by-results system.[170] The tensions generated by shortages of workplaces at the face where it was possible to produce coal, and groups at the face who were paid according to the coal they produced, generated a stream of complaints from miners who produced coal in one week and then the next had to work with rock—from which they earned nothing.[171]

There was little room to increase production through labor competition given the physical constraints, while the success of those individuals who participated was predicated on access to places at the face where they could produce coal and thus be able to compete. Competition was organized in its early phases by young Communist activists. In Pit No. XIV, brigade number 202 was formed in January 1948—the beginning of National Labor Competition in the mines—under the leadership of one coal hewer, Pál Koós. Relying on excellent connections to unions, the party, and management—one of the brigade's members was Barnabás Varga, the Communist factory committee president during the "potato crisis"—the brigade was able to clear obstacles to its own achievement, becoming the second-highest producing brigade in the country.[172] This practice was not restricted to Pit No. XIV, as party and union officials received rewards for labor competition participation across the Tatabánya mines, which led miners to denounce labor competition as a means by which Communists reserved for themselves the best positions at coal faces.[173]

While labor competition never ceased to be a vehicle for advancing the interests of party activists in informal bargaining over the best places to work at the coal face, complaints forced the opening of such opportunities to other groups. In so doing, however, hierarchies of generation and social origin within the mine were reproduced in ways that anticipated broader processes throughout industry at later dates. The older, more skilled and experienced workers were able to argue that they were intrinsically "the best workers," deploying discourses that supported dominant work hierarchies to secure a monopoly over the best workplaces in competition and resisting attempts to force them to rotate workplaces. The losers in this process were frequently commuters from rural areas and the young.[174] This produced different reactions from those cast to the periphery. Rural workers reacted by turning their backs on competition; they refused to speak to the deputies who managed production, and they left their workplaces promptly at the end of the shift, leaving carts in the way of those who took over from them.[175] Youth, however, reacted to their marginal position by attempting to appropriate the discourse of labor competition to improve their own access to good places to work, especially during 1949, as it became obvious that labor competition had not solved problems in production. As the state began its "revolution in production," youth played an important role in subverting generational hierarchies in mines.[176]

In early summer 1949, this "revolution in production" remained just around the corner. Given the problems of production, especially in the mines, some phenomena in Tatabánya anticipated problems that would emerge nationwide a year later, when the state clamped down on rising wages and thus shattered the material base of its own legitimacy. Although simmering discontent, even in Tatabánya, was channeled through the politics of bargaining within labor competition and manifested itself in rising labor turnover, the promise of the results of "socialist construction" and a sense that "class war" policies were moving in the right direction were sufficient to ensure that, in 1949, the city's Communist political culture remained strong.

# 4

# Revolution in Production
## August 1949–January 1951

THE NEW REGIME was blind to the highly conditional and uneven nature of the legitimacy it had established for itself by summer 1949. It also was not content with the mere consolidation of its authority but sought a wholesale transformation of the relations between the state and its worker-citizens, and of the nature of the work itself. The nature of the links it sought to forge between state formation, the economy, and the everyday experience of labor was most clearly embodied in its new factories, designed to concentrate manufacturing in sectors previously dominated by small-scale production. Újpest's Danube Shoe Factory was one such project, created as a separate enterprise in 1949 out of a division of the Wolfner Leather and Shoe Factory. Three years later, it had become the largest factory in the sector countrywide, producing 2,513,000 pairs of shoes annually and employing 2,513 persons.[1] The growth of both production and the workforce was the product of the state's policy of profilization, which accompanied the introduction of the first five-year plan, through which production of a given product was concentrated in one plant as much as possible, to enable effective supervision.[2] Shoe production in Újpest prior to 1948 was concentrated in a dense network of factories and workshops—an industrial district characterized by a multitude of small-scale enterprises that relied on handicraft methods of production.[3] As shoemaking factories and workshops were nationalized in December 1949, they were closed and their workers redirected to the Danube Shoe Factory.[4] These workers were expected to radically change their working practices, for the new factory was based on principles of mechanization, together with specialization and vertical integration, splitting the individual tasks involved in making shoes into their component parts and reintegrating them by organizing work around a series of conveyor belts, thus ensuring a continuous workflow through the new factory. The reorganization of production shaped a labor process visible to factory management and central planners, enabling them to calculate work targets, and thus remuneration, scientifically and to control quality.[5]

The combination of concentration, specialization, supervision, and scientific management that was embedded in the design of new plants like the Danube Shoe Factory was intended to create a labor process that supported an accumulation regime that had been in the making since August 1946. This regime rested on the bureaucratic coordination of production and consumption, through which the socialist state mobilized resources centrally to achieve economic development and distribute products and services to citizens.[6] The aims of this accumulation regime were embedded institutionally in the content of socialist citizenship and its interaction with the practice of centralized economic planning, which specified the benefits and obligations of the socialist citizen in relation to production and consumption. The constitution of the People's Republic of Hungary, formally established in August 1949, stated that "the basis of the social order of the Hungarian People's Republic is work." All citizens of the new state had an obligation "to work according to their ability" in order to participate in "the construction of socialism." In assessing the particular obligation of each citizen, "the Hungarian People's Republic attempts to realize the socialist principle 'from each according to their ability, to each according to their need.'" This obligation to work amounted to the participation of each citizen in the economic life of the country, which was "determined by the state people's economic plan."[7]

Participation in socialist labor was central to the emergent state's vision of citizenship. The social and economic benefits of this citizenship were enjoyed by citizens as members of the "working people"; as far as Hungary's 1951 Labor Code, which further institutionalized the principles enshrined in the 1949 constitution, was concerned, "According to the principle of socialist distribution, everyone participates according to their capabilities in socially necessary labor and everyone receives a share of the results of social production according to the quantity and quality of their labor."[8] In keeping with this principle, the identity of citizens as workers was fixed in personal identification documentation through "new" work books introduced in 1950 that linked individuals to their place of employment, codified their skill levels, and acted as means through which worker-citizens could access a range of other state institutions.[9] The institutional embedding of the obligations of socialist worker-citizens through centralized economic planning had direct implications for the organization of labor in enterprises themselves. Planners always intended the formal object of the plan to be the individual producer; workers were supposed to have their own individual first five-year plans. The logic of breaking down plan targets to every worker shaped labor policy, the wage relation, and the campaigns of mobilization in every workplace in the country.[10]

This did not mean that all workers actually had their own individual plans; such attempts foundered frequently on the complexity of the task of creating devolved targets for an extended period.[11] However, the logic that national performance in production was the sum total of the individual performances of all who contributed to the socialist economy shaped policy overtly from summer 1949. The regime stressed individual, rather than collective, labor competition and was seeking to reshape the principal institution through which workers were mobilized for production.[12] When individual competition emerged as the dominant form of competition, it was conceived by planners and policy makers as a means by which workers could be directed to raise not only production quantities but also quality and through which the workplace and relations within it could be reorganized to serve the goals of socialist construction.[13] Pressure to introduce Stakhanovite socialist competition began in late autumn 1949, focusing in particular on a "Stalin shift" to celebrate Stalin's seventieth birthday on 21 December 1949.

Socialist competition was combined with attempts to remake the wage relation by tying systems of payment by results both to individual performance and to the goals laid down in the plan. This was to be done through a shift toward the *darabbér*, or piece-rate system, in most industrial workplaces in 1950. Workers were paid according to the difficulty and skill level of the work they performed at a given time, rather than a set wage according to their job description.[14] Furthermore, the workers received the rate for their work only if they met 100 percent of their norm, or production target; underfulfillment and overfulfillment of that norm was remunerated in strict proportion to performance. The aim of this system was to pay workers strictly according to their overall contribution to the fulfillment of plan targets. To this end, the state attempted, with uneven success, to intensify its attempts to ensure that norms were calculated according to approved "scientific" principles, in order to prevent them from becoming subject to on-the-job bargaining between the worker and the direct supervisor.[15]

The attempt to introduce a factory regime based on mobilization behind the plan confronted the conditional bases of the socialist state's legitimacy among its supporters, and the contradictions were papered over through informal compromise during late 1949 and early 1950, much as they had been during the previous eighteen months.[16] As the state concentrated more investment in priority sectors, it was increasingly unprepared to pay the price for endemic informal compromise on the job, expressed in a rate of wage growth higher than the increase in the value of total production.[17] Just as the state was forced to construct its legitimacy in a climate of political polarization internally, its stress on industrial expansion was also a product of the closely related process of polarization internationally with the deterioration of relations between the great powers as a consequence of the onset of the cold war in Europe. The belief of both Moscow and Budapest that confrontation in Central Europe would ignite open military conflict led economic planners to place emphasis on the rapid development of armaments and machine manufacture so that both the domestic socialist regime and the Soviet Union would be prepared for war.[18] This had several consequences. Resources were diverted from boosting living standards because food shortages resulted from the state's attempts to transform agriculture in the teeth of bitter opposition from rural producers. Campaigns were introduced to force workers to give a significant portion of their cash income to the state, such as the "plan loans" campaign in 1949 and the "peace loans" in 1950. Real wages in industry were slashed through huge increases in production targets in August 1950; as a consequence, the total wage bill for heavy industry fell by 13.5 and for light industry, by 11.4 percent in that month alone.[19] Furthermore, the concentration of resources on the expansion of armaments and machine manufacture disrupted relationships between industrial sectors. For reasons discussed in the previous chapter in relation to Tatabánya, the production of coal, and therefore all energy, fell behind that planned for priority sectors. Sectors that produced primary products, like steel manufacture, were relatively underdeveloped; raising production levels to those needed required huge new investment in plant. This occurred at a time when the three-year plan had already transformed the labor market, replacing unemployment with labor shortages. Meanwhile, priority sectors consumed a disproportionate share of the resources available in the interests of achieving the plan targets at all costs. These factors combined to shape severe shortages of raw materials and labor in industrial sectors, which led to a rhythm of production characterized by frequent stoppages. Because of the tying of wages to performance against plan targets, endemic shortages generated widespread wage insecurity at precisely the time that the state slashed real wage levels.[20]

Workers responded in two ways. First, the importance of informal bargaining as a means of preserving a degree of control over remuneration at the point of production was reinforced. Second, it smashed much of the legitimacy the regime had gained during 1948 and 1949 among left-wing workers, as its measures provoked considerable protest. The regime in turn responded with repression. This, in itself, was nothing new. As seen in the reactions of those building the dictatorship when open protest erupted among Tatabánya's miners or in the dictatorship's general response to its lack of support in and control over southern Zala's oil fields, they had been prepared since 1945 to see resistance as a sign of the activity of "enemy" elements. Repression had, however, been used only selectively. This changed during late 1949 and 1950. The unification of work and citizenship encouraged more widespread recourse to repressive measures as small-scale resistance to wage and labor policy was politicized as "enemy" activity. Consequently, the "revolution in production" saw the creeping use of repressive measures to coerce workers. When repression was used against left-wing workers during summer and autumn 1950, it represented a turning point, for it crystallized the legitimacy gap that opened up in industrial communities as a consequence of the regime's labor policies.

The case studies differed in the extent to which the "revolution in production" and the extension of repression that followed it represented a turning point. In southern Zala, where the state had already escalated repression at the oil drilling sites during 1948, the events of late 1949 and 1950 represented a continuation of existing trends, rather than a decisive break with them. Because of the tensions imposed by the mines' failure to meet their targets, by summer 1949 many in Tatabánya felt the impact of the strains of mobilization on their working conditions and their earnings. They had remained supportive of the regime because of the promise of material improvement and radical social change. It was this promise that disappeared during the "revolution in production," which was accompanied by the reemergence of chronic shortages of food in the city, increasing chaos in production, and greater intervention by the ÁVH in both the workplace and the community. These conditions shattered the legitimacy of the regime. In Újpest, individual labor competition spread rapidly during autumn 1949 in the factories, yet its implementation rested on an extension of the methods used to promulgate labor competition during the previous year. That implementation was predicated on the program's ability to guarantee increased earnings for those who participated. This formula was utterly destroyed by the norm revision in August 1950—so much so that, in some sectors, individual labor competition all but collapsed. By the end of the year, a workforce alienated from the state sought protection from the income insecurity engendered by the spread of shortages through refocused informal bargaining.

## From Workplace Transformation to the Politics of Confrontation in Újpest

In March 1950, prior to the liquidation of the Újpest Shoe Factory as an independent enterprise and its subsequent incorporation into the Danube Shoe Factory, planners brought the factory into line with the rest of the sector by introducing wages calculated according to individual performance. It did so at a time when the state, concerned over wage increases elsewhere, was determined to make no concessions to their informal negotiation. Given disorganized production and poor raw material provision, the first wage payments were greeted with fury among the workers; one was hauled before the plant's disciplinary committee for attempting to organize a meeting to force the time-and-motion staff, imported from the Danube Shoe Factory to calculate production targets, out of the factory. Justifying this move, for which he was dismissed, he maintained that "in the last week I took home only 85 forints, a tiny amount when one considers I have a family. . . . We didn't want to organize politically, many in the factory were just furious that we earned so little; we felt that something was seriously wrong, perhaps that the norm wasn't established properly."[21] Management took a hard line against even individual acts of protest, which elsewhere would have led to relaxations in work norms. Another worker's norm was established at "1,600 pairs, which I just couldn't meet under any circumstances. My pay was very low. When I complained, they said my machine was bad." After the foremen refused to switch her to another machine, she proclaimed that she "couldn't work for this amount of money." Without the promise of a different machine, she demanded a change in her work norm. When this was not forthcoming, she warned that "I'm not coming to work until my norm is sorted out." Management fired her.[22]

Although the Újpest Shoe Factory was not typical in the degree of breakdown in the relationship between the state and workers in spring 1950—the local ÁVH noticed the plant's workers were overrepresented among those who criticized the regime on the crowded trams before the beginnings of shifts—in other respects it both demonstrated the state's attitude to established patterns of working-class culture and anticipated reactions that would become more generalized over the coming summer.[23] The state began to challenge established patterns of working-class culture seven months prior to its enforced change of the wage systems in the Újpest Shoe Factory. In the Hungarian capital and the industrial communities that were eventually incorporated into it in 1950, Budapest's party organs paid close attention to reforming production. They argued in late summer 1949 for "the decisive importance of productivity," advocating "a labor competition resting on a broad base," the most advanced form of which was "individual competition."[24] As party organs publicly sought to mobilize their activists in the factories, the industrial branch ministries placed hidden pressure on management to pay attention to productivity and the organization of labor. The Ministry of Light Industry—responsible for Újpest's textile, leather, shoe, and fur factories—demanded in summer 1949 that its efforts in the last months of the three-year plan focus on preparations for the first five-year plan that would succeed it in January 1950. To this end, it called on managers to ensure that plan fulfillment on paper rested only on real increases in overall production; it called for plan targets to be given to each "workshop and machine" to ensure that workers worked—where possible to an individual plan—and demanded that managers develop "the closest working relationship" with the trade unions under "the direction of the party."[25]

As with the National Labor Competition, introduced in Újpest during the previous year, local party and union activists, as well as managers, adapted their mobilization of workers behind individual competition to local factory circumstances. In the United Incandescent Lamp and Electrical Factory, the party argued that, up to August 1949, "the innovators and brigades have gained certain good results," but in some workshops, "very old working practices" predominated. These were not workshops where semiskilled workers had been subordinated to payment-by-results wages calculated according to "scientific" methods already but where informal bargaining over job rates was endemic; in the machine shop, shortages of labor and "old working practices" meant the workshop was "absolutely over-loaded," generating shortages and stoppages elsewhere.[26] As a consequence, the skilled workers in the shop were targeted by the campaign.[27] Despite official claims of the "spontaneity" of labor competition, the factory party organization handled the campaign from above. Its networks of activists were mobilized to persuade and coerce workers into making pledges to improve their individual performance, while party members were expected to lead the pledges in order to set an example to their more reluctant workmates.[28]

Among semiskilled workers, individual labor competition was marked by pledges to increase rates of norm fulfillment and for workers to supervise production on more than one machine at once. In the machine shop, however, it began with the formation of a brigade, the so-called "Produce More" brigade that promised to blaze the trail for new production methods.[29] A focus on the leading members of the "Produce More" brigade is revealing as to the challenge they posed to the dominant culture of on-the-job control. The workers were not only party members but to some extent were excluded from the informal networks that allowed most of the skilled workers to control their remuneration. Their leader, József Kiszlinger, a twenty-five-year-old turner at the beginning of the campaign, was a party member who had been driven out by his workmates two years previously for seeking to "bust rates." When he returned in August 1948, little had changed; "there was a consensus among the workers: 'we won't go above this level.'" Anyone who went over the informally agreed 120 or 130 percent was regarded with anger because "they were busting the rate."[30] At the core of the brigade were like-minded young workers in their twenties who had either trained outside the factory or had arrived in their current jobs only recently. Among those who would later become Stakhanovites were János Lutz and his friend, Ferenc Szlovak, both of them young workers committed to breaking established shop-floor culture.[31]

The use of labor competition to bust rates was deeply unpopular in the machine shop; discontent was exacerbated by statements of members of the brigade that they intended to teach their "less developed" workmates new production methods.[32] Those who had been decorated as "outstanding workers" the previous year led the active opposition: "the outstanding workers are threatening those who want to radically increase their production."[33] Open opposition was accompanied by rumor that production targets would increase and wages fall if the shop joined the labor competition en masse.[34] As autumn wore on, the authorities in the factory shifted from merely promoting individual competition and began supplementing it with a drive to introduce the Stakhanovite movement, especially in the machine shop. To ensure that some workers were decorated as Stakhanovites, officials identified and promoted a small number of individual workers who "would know beforehand the results they would achieve."[35] Production on the shop floor was reorganized around certain preselected individuals who worked closely with the foremen and factory administration to ensure they had a regular supply of materials. Ferenc Szlovak achieved his exceptional performance as a result of the "permanent attention of the foreman and wage calculator." Many workers dismissed his results as "not based on any kind of reality."[36] National authorities urged local activists to defuse such opposition through "political work."[37] This was rooted in a two-track strategy that the party pursued in the machine shop. The first track was to ensure that all workers, not just those selected as Stakhanovites, benefited materially from the reorganization of the shop; the local party saw it as important that "those workers who only make 120 percent don't lose heart; they can get better results too."[38]

The second way was to select as Stakhanovites workers who opposed the regime; this was achieved through a mixture of persuasion and coercion. János Sztankovits was one such worker. Older than the younger workers of the "Produce More" brigade, he was thirty-two in 1949, had also been a member of the MSzDP in the interwar years, and distrusted the Communists. In 1945, he was detained by Soviet troops on the streets of Újpest and deported to the Soviet Union. He worked in a Moscow machine factory until 1948 and was decorated as a Stakhanovite in view of his abilities as a trained skilled worker in the disorganized postwar Soviet economy. Upon his return home, he went back to work in the United Incandescent Lamp and Electrical Factory. Urged to join individual labor competition by party agitators in late 1949, he turned on them: "I . . . told him where Stalin could stick his shift, I worked for him for three years for free, I wasn't even given proper clothes, I was freed and why should I work for him again?" These comments brought Sztankovits into immediate contact with local representatives of state security agency. The head of the workshop advised him to "'try and make the best of it so that they can at least see that you're not part of the enemy.' On that basis I decided to show them that I knew how to work."[39] With assistance from management and methods learned by coping with Soviet machinery in Moscow, Sztankovits began exceeding norms on the milling machines.[40] His workmates retorted that he should "go back to the Soviet Union, if you like it so much there."[41] Another such case was that of Ignác Pióker, who became the factory's best-known Stakhanovite. He had come to Újpest in the 1920s as a refugee from his native Transylvania and was employed in the plant as a planer, a job that was not regarded as skilled, and was thus relatively poorly paid in the machine shop.[42] In the postwar years, Pióker persuaded shop management that he was worthy of skilled-worker status. He gained a special fixed hourly rate—rather than one dependent on his production results—in recognition of the quality of his work. During autumn 1949, however, pressure was exerted on the hourly rate workers to be paid according to performance and join individual labor competition. Pióker refused, arguing that "the quality of my work will be lost."[43] Economic pressure proved more successful than agitation, given that the twenty hourly paid skilled workers who remained at the beginning of the competition earned 3 percent less monthly than the very weakest skilled workers paid according to their results.[44] The party's eventual persuasion of Pióker to exchange his hourly wage rate for the status of Stakhanovite was clearly designed to undermine dominant patterns of shop-floor culture—an example of the "political work" necessary to create the Stakhanovite movement.[45]

The attack on the culture of the skilled in the United Incandescent Lamp and Electrical Factory represented both the translation of national goals through the more local priorities of activists and the dynamics of resistance to the regime's labor policies at the point of production. This was also true of other factories and resulted in different dynamics of mobilization. In the textile plants, the pressures that drove the introduction of individual competition related to concern over plan fulfillment. While not so central to the regime's productivist policies as machine manufacture, textile plants were expected to increase their production gradually, but this was to be done with little or no new investment.[46] At one and the same time, machinery in Újpest textile plants was old, supplies of raw materials were being disrupted both by the circumstances of their nationalization and the economic consequences of deteriorating superpower relations, and labor shortages developed because of wages that were low relative to other sectors as unemployment disappeared. As a result, plan fulfillment had become problematic by summer 1949.[47] Given demands to complete their three-year plans by the end of the year, formidable problems relating to labor shortages, management, and the party, and only uneven support by the local union, the intensity of production increased during the autumn.[48]

This attempt to increase production was marked by more continuity with practice prior to the summer of 1949 than had occurred in the United Incandescent Lamp and Electrical Factory. The focus on increasing production fulfillment and the earnings of semiskilled machine operators through the competition continued; what was new was a greater focus on persuading and coercing individual workers to operate a greater number of machines simultaneously. By mid-November 1949, propagandists in the Magyar Pamutipar persuaded the best workers across the plant to employ "new" work methods to shift from operating seven machines each simultaneously to ten. They did so by demonstrating that those who had made the switch earned more money in five days on the new system than they had in six on the old.[49] Many of those workers who increased the number of machines they operated met with a hostile wall of silence because most workers felt threatened by the increased intensity of work and believed they would not share in the prosperity brought by increased individual competition, especially given the limits to increased production that were revealed by the technical condition of the machinery and the provision of raw materials to the plant.[50] These problems expressed themselves as frequent shortages of raw materials for those left out of competition, as the spinning shops were often hard pressed to fulfill their plan, which led to severe shortages in the weaving shops. The poor quality of production in the spinning shops at times translated into work stoppages in the weaving shops.[51] Consequently, workers argued that, "if they work on more machines, positions will be cut; there won't be enough work for everyone."[52]

The tensions exploded when management and the party announced how they wished to organize production for the Stalin shift, which was the campaign to commemorate the seventieth birthday of the Soviet leader that would culminate with the afternoon shift across the country on 21 December.[53] The party announced that a number of machine operators would work on twenty machines simultaneously— each one would be given preferential access to raw materials and attention from the maintenance staff, and each would also have two unskilled workers to assist them. They would become Stakhanovites. In the spinning shop, this announcement produced "mass hysteria," as workers threatened to "beat any woman on the afternoon shift who operates twenty machines."[54] While the hostility of some toward those who achieved exceptional production fulfillment by working twenty machines persisted during and after the Stalin shift, it was defused during December by running the shift as a campaign in which management and the party aimed to ensure that all workers, not just those selected as Stakhanovites, received some material benefit. Between the end of November 1949 and January 1950, the proportion of workers in the Magyar Pamutipar engaged in individual competition rose from 64.6 to 78.6 percent. This generated substantial increases in earnings for most workers, as the authorities ensured regular supplies of raw materials during the campaign and relaxed quality controls to ensure production targets were hit.[55]

This strategy generated support for the campaign but masked the deeper patterns of unease; in the HPS, for the Stalin shift itself on the afternoon of 21 December 1949, "by a quarter to two the workers had arrived en masse, so that they wouldn't even miss by a minute the start of their shift at two. At two o'clock work began. Our workers perhaps have never worked as enthusiastically as on that day."[56] This pattern was not confined to the HPS. In the United Incandescent Lamp and Electrical Factory, the Stalin shift, as far as one local newspaper was concerned, heralded the arrival of "the spirit of socialist competition" in the plant, as workers were successfully mobilized behind competition as their incomes, not just those of workers selected as Stakhanovites, rose.[57] The Stalin shift itself was a resounding success for the party in the plant; according to the factory newspaper, the shift was marked by "the good organization of production," while "the tool room worked like never before."[58]

Yet the generation of workers' acquiescence in the launch of the Stakhanovite movement rested on far from stable foundations, because increased earnings had been bought through unprecedented efforts to mobilize raw materials and labor in the interests of completing the three-year plan, and those efforts were not sustainable. With the end of the campaign for the Stalin shift, many of the special measures introduced by managements to aid Stakhanovites were removed; in BÁMERT in January 1950, new Stakhanovites "spent several half-days searching out raw materials, tools, or the relevant technical specifications."[59] Many of those organizing the campaign in factories had believed it to be temporary—an attempt to speed up production to meet end-of-year plan targets and not an attempt to transform production permanently.[60] In low-priority sectors such as textiles, which had been plagued by poor provision of raw materials in mid-1949, shortages and consequent work stoppages reemerged with a vengeance in early 1950.[61] In the Wolfner Leather Factory, the Stalin shift had been possible only because of an expansion of overtime to ensure that production targets could be met after raw materials, which had been in short supply, arrived.[62]

The disappearance of the campaignlike atmosphere of the last weeks of 1949, the reemergence of patterns of discontinuous work caused by spreading problems of raw material shortages, as well as the need to protect the performance levels of Stakhanovites in view of political pressure, led to discontent. Other workers isolated Stakhanovites in their workplaces and threatened them; the Mauthner Leather Factory's first Stakhanovite was bluntly asked by one workmate, "Are you crazy? You work so much that you'll just break down and you'll see that everyone else will spread the rumor about you that you just cheat."[63] Discontent rarely took the form of open protest, but in some sectors, especially textiles, it led many machine operators in Magyar Pamutipar's spinning and weaving shops to quit, generating absolute shortages of labor that threatened continuous production by March 1950.[64] In factories where production was dependent on skilled workers, in short supply, such discontent was papered over through intensified informal bargaining over the production targets. In the BÁMERT by early spring 1950, the sporadic supply of raw materials meant that "the workers stand idle for hours and weeks at a time as they don't have any work, or when work arrives, it all comes together." Such conditions had to be turned around quickly, creating a situation in which there was "a lot of scrap production." Foremen ran "around for raw materials, technical specifications, or work and don't have time to really organize and supervise the work." In this environment, production targets became the subject of bargaining between skilled workers and foremen: "in the smithing shop the time-and-motion man calculated a time of fifty-five minutes for one piece of work, but when the workers complained that they couldn't do it in the time, then it was revised to 180 minutes, and the workers made 110 percent [of regular pay for exceeding their norms]."[65] Sometimes, as among skilled workers like tool makers in the United Incandescent Lamp and Electrical Factory, this strategy spread to the toleration of claims for wages for work that was not really completed except on paper.[66] The dynamics of shop-floor bargaining as lower management tried to protect Stakhanovites, channel discontent, and manage the consequences of discontinuous production in a climate of generalized labor shortages appeased workers and created a situation in which wages remained substantially higher during the first half of 1950 than they had been a year earlier.[67]

As the campaigns surrounding the Stalin shift resulted in an evolution of informal structures of workplace bargaining in a climate of discontinuous production that proved resistant to state control, the intention of the state to mobilize all workers to steadily increase their production foundered. Behind this failure, however, the regime saw in the increase of individual competitors a way of preparing the ground for individualized remuneration. In plants like the Chinoin Pharmaceuticals Factory, where the nature of production presented insurmountable obstacles to driving up the quantities produced, management paid special attention to the importance of individual, scientifically calculated production norms to a local labor competition that concentrated in late 1949 on reducing the quantity of raw material used in production.[68] In those plants that had been in the vanguard of the Stalin shift, the party pressed forward with campaigns to individualize wages in line with the focus of labor competition over the previous six months. In the Magyar Pamutipar, the factory newspaper argued that no worker should receive rewards for the work of another and thus that "group norms," paid to a minority of workers, should disappear, to be replaced by individual work targets for all that would in turn aid individual competition.[69] In the HPS—despite the high performances of some individuals—the office in charge of production targets refused to pay the full wages due to exceptionally performing workers and instead paid the members of the group to which they belonged an equal share of that group's performance in January 1950. This move generated fury from both the new Stakhanovites and from the party, which instead insisted on fully individualized performance-based wages.[70]

The drives for individualization prepared the way for the introduction of darabbér in most of Újpest's factories in spring 1950. The system was presented as one in which workers would be able to see a direct link between their work and their pay; in order to mobilize workers behind the plan, factory authorities regarded it as important that "every worker can supervise their own work . . . and that they can calculate the wages they will be paid, immediately upon completing their work."[71] With the introduction of the darabbér, every job was placed into a category determined according to a judgment by planners as to the skill level necessary to complete it; this determined the rate for the job. Workers and jobs were matched by placing workers into skill categories that corresponded to those by which jobs were classified; while a worker could take jobs lower than their own skill category, they could not take those classified at a higher level. Workers were also given a norm, or production target, for this job, and 100 percent fulfillment would trigger the payment of the full rate.[72] While the regime had sought to introduce the system for all workers and all work between March and May 1950, the progress of the introduction of darabbér was often painfully slow, as enterprises found it difficult to support the classification of all work or design the technical norms that were supposed to accompany them. Those from whom flexible work across skill categories was required, such as maintenance fitters in the United Incandescent Lamp and Electrical Factory, could not be easily transferred to darabbér. In mid-June, approximately sixteen hundred workers in the plant worked according to the new system, twelve hundred had their performance calculated through indirect methods based on several performance indicators, and almost four hundred were still paid according to the old system.[73]

In those parts of the plant where the darabbér was introduced, workers refused to accept the argument that it would make the link between production and earnings transparent; female semiskilled workers, on hearing they would be paid according to the new system, complained that "they would not be able to earn good money."[74] The introduction of darabbér had almost no effect on earnings, for established patterns of shop-floor bargaining, which aimed to maintain workers' earnings and thus protect them from the ever more discontinuous rhythms of production as shortages and work stoppages became more widespread, adjusted to the new system. As foremen in the United Incandescent Lamp and Electrical Factory implemented the darabbér, they were careful to ensure that work was classified in a way that reflected their expectations of what certain individuals should earn, in complete contravention of the regulations.[75] The cumulative effect of entrenched informal bargaining subverted the regime's politics of productivity; during the first months of 1950, production fell back from the levels of the Stalin shift, stabilizing by April. Earnings stubbornly refused to fall.[76]

In view of its need to finance industrialization, the regime became more impatient with this situation. It decided on a major clampdown after sporadic campaigns against "fraud" in relation to norms and wages, through which it sought to criminalize workplace bargaining, proved relatively ineffective.[77] Individual wage rates were raised during July and August 1950, but this move concealed drastic centrally mandated hikes in production targets that were designed to "close the damaging difference between the wage system . . . and the production fulfillments achieved in the labor competition."[78] The "increase in basic wages and the revision of the norms" in July and August 1950 represented a central turning point in the relationship between industrial workers and the socialist state because it destroyed the regime's conditional legitimacy among the left-wing majority of industrial workers. The major reasons for this were the sharp reductions in wages and increases in work intensity brought by the new production targets. Nationwide, the cuts in nominal wages were substantial; they fell by 14.3 percent in heavy industry, 12.5 percent in light industry, and 19.4 percent in construction in August 1950—the first month that wages calculated according to the new production norms were paid.[79] Yet another crucial factor was that the state, determined to ensure that the impact of the higher production targets would not be blunted by shop-floor pressure, as earlier campaigns had been, was prepared to use repression to drive the norm increases through.

In the United Incandescent Lamp and Electrical Factory, following the announcement of the new norms, open opposition was dealt with severely. Two workers were fired for agitating against the new production targets in August 1950, while a further four were handed over to representatives of the state security agency for combining "agitation" with rumor mongering about the effects of the rise in targets on workers' incomes at a time of reemerging shortages of basic goods.[80] This tough line ensured that open opposition was sporadic, as intimidation ensured that discontent would generate no open protest. The attempts of warehouse workers to organize an impromptu strike by refusing to load trucks quickly collapsed under the weight of intimidation.[81] Yet, while repression did stifle protest, it fueled a silent fury among left-wing workers, who felt betrayed by their state. Their fury expressed itself in certain forms of protest that the state was less able to deal with effectively through recourse to repression. For example, some workers protested by canceling subscriptions to official publications; across only one part of the factory, subscriptions to the national party newspaper *Szabad Nép* (meaning "free people") fell from 125 to 90, while those to the factory newspaper fell from 700 to 120 within the space of two weeks following the announcement of the norm increases.[82]

The collapse in the legitimacy of the regime among those who had been its supporters was underlined when, in September 1950, the authorities demanded that workers offer up at least one month's wages as an annual contribution to their "peace loan" campaign. This demand brought to the surface the workers' anger at the sharp reductions in real wages. One skilled worker and party member in the Mauthner Leather Factory was blunt; he maintained that "he would gladly agitate in favor of giving a loan and in favor of peace, for he loves his homeland and hates war, but he is not able to pledge a *fillér,* because of his financial situation. . . . He stressed, that even if they expelled him from the party, he would still not be able to pledge anything."[83] In the Magyar Pamutipar, one electrician accused party agitators of "stealing money from people's pockets," while a machine operator, when told that the loan was necessary to defend the country in the event of the superpower confrontation over Korea spreading into Europe, bluntly retorted that the Americans were not the aggressors in eastern Asia.[84] In the United Incandescent Lamp and Electrical Factory, even the star Stakhanovites, Ignác Pióker and József Kiszlinger, were only prepared to "lend" substantially less than their income for a single month.[85]

Pióker's and Kiszlinger's respective failure to cooperate fully with state-directed mobilization was a product of the fact that the increases in production targets had affected their own ability to earn a living. Pióker had achieved 358 percent of the old production targets in May 1950, 317 percent in June, and 305 percent in July; over the first ten weeks of the new norms, he reached an average of 169.4 percent of his target. The drop in Kiszlinger's overall performance was lower—197 percent in July, to an average of 166.8 percent over the first ten weeks of the new targets.[86] Workers in the Tánsics Leather Factory greeted the failure of their Stakhanovites to make the new norms as a sign that their earlier "feats" in production had been achieved through "fraud."[87] Stakhanovites found themselves isolated and unpopular in their workplaces and frequently blamed for the increases in production targets. In order to head off this unpopularity, some Stakhanovites voiced public opposition to elements of the drive to increase work norms; in the Magyar Pamutipar spinning shop, machine operators accused one Stakhanovite of setting the pace for the norms to which others had to work. After some weeks of pressure and threats, she went to the office in charge of production targets and demanded that the officials "come down to the factory and prove that the norm was established on the basis of the performance of an average worker, and not on her performance as a Stakhanovite."[88]

This was difficult to prove because the intensity of work necessary to meet the new norms set for the semiskilled operators in the spinning and weaving shops was particularly high, a situation that was exacerbated by their lack of countervailing power, relative to other workers, to bargain their norms down. Because Stakhanovism had been based on the multimachine movement in the Magyar Pamutipar, those who operated a small number of machines were forced to operate more simply in order to survive; large numbers of workers who could not make their norms operating two spinning machines simultaneously had to start operating four in order to earn the same amount.[89] This arrangement sped up the pace of work, while the strain on machinery produced more breakdowns and raw material shortages, and poor quality resulted in frequent stoppages and discontinuous production; by November 1950, 57.8 percent of workers in the Magyar Pamutipar and 47.5 percent in the neighboring HPS failed to achieve 100 percent of their production targets.[90] Squeezed between their own need to survive in an environment characterized by increasingly disorganized production, their unpopularity on the shop floor, and a lack of interest from management, Stakhanovites were rare, and Stakhanovism barely existed, except on paper, in the Magyar Pamutipar by the end of 1950.[91]

In the United Incandescent Lamp and Electrical Factory, management retained its commitment to Stakhanovism, which it saw as a tool to ensure some control over production. In view of its unpopularity following the tightening of production norms, it would never again become the means for mobilizing workers to increase their production that it had been in December 1949.[92] While total production in the plant in the second half of 1950 was substantially higher than in the previous year, raw material shortages began to disrupt production seriously, as the newer norms were introduced. The machine shop ran out of ball bearings and screws, which could not be supplied due to problems elsewhere in the economy, generating a pattern of discontinuous work.[93] Increasingly discontinuous rhythms of production, characterized by stoppages and rushes as raw materials arrived, and the constant pressure to make do, combined with high production norms, led workers to cut corners in the manufacture of components. When transferred to the radio assembly plant, some 10 percent of the components went unused, creating further problems of supply that, in turn, meant that workers on the assembly lines could not meet their norms.[94] Together with discontinuous production, factory management noticed problems in recruiting skilled labor, especially to jobs where there were nationwide supply shortages.[95] In certain areas of the factory, these factors, combined with the atmosphere of simmering discontent, led to the reemergence of local, informal bargaining over the setting of production norms as time-and-motion staff came under growing pressure from foremen to relax norms for certain skilled workers.[96] The beginnings of such bargaining in a new context heralded changes that would become widespread as discontented workers sought protection from insecure earnings by exploiting informal relationships at the point of production, fatally undermining the regime's attempts to mobilize workers behind the plan.

## The Death of Popular Communism in Tatabánya

On 30 December 1950, at twenty past eleven in the evening, a huge underground explosion shook Pit No. XII. Ninety-five miners had descended not long before to begin the night shift; at the moment of the explosion, "miners on the afternoon shift had hardly returned home. In the lamp room the night shift were preparing the afternoon shift workers' lamps for the following afternoon."[97] The night shift across the city stopped at the news of the explosion, and the relatives of those underground rushed to the pithead for news. As morning approached, the devastating scale of the disaster became clear; the emergency staff had succeeded in saving only 14 of the 95 underground workers. Eighty-one were dead. Seventy-three of the dead had a total of 188 dependents.[98] Given the scale of the tragedy, the authorities were keen to establish responsibility. Within hours of the explosion, members of the local ÁVH had descended with the emergency medical staff, only to be thrown out by one mining engineer for "hindering" the work of the emergency services.[99] Rákosi in Budapest closely involved himself in the progress of the investigation.[100] Within weeks, charges had been brought against another mine engineer, the deputy director of the pit, and a deputy for gross negligence leading to loss of life, for which all three were convicted and imprisoned. The Budapest prosecutor's office asserted that all three were "representatives of the Horthy system, who haven't changed in the least in the six years since the liberation. The heroic attitude to work of the Hungarian working class has not affected them, they still hate the working class, and they do not value workers' lives."[101]

The state's attempt to blame "enemy" elements for the disaster—although typical of the Stalinist political culture that had been established by the end of

1950—failed to convince miners. The explosion crystallized a marked withdrawal of support among miners for mobilization in the workplace. During 1950, the growing intensification of labor and drives to increase production had exacerbated the chaos in the mines and generated "gloom."[102] Many were painfully aware that conditions in the mines led to an increase in the overall rate of accidents and risked a serious disaster. Within two weeks of the explosion, an electrical fault caused an underground fire in Pit No. VI; although no miner was injured or killed, it caused serious disruption of production for several weeks.[103] The insecurity created by both incidents led to wild rumors circulating in the mining community about further accidents; according to one rumor, three miners had burned alive in a fire in Pit No. XIV, while in another the cableways outside the Síkvölgyi Pit were rumored to have snapped under the weight of the coal they carried, apparently killing two cartmen standing underneath. Miners blamed the regime's attempts to raise production for the explosion: "on the workers' trains, in the shops, and right across Tatabánya they are saying the cause of the explosion was the labor competition." Miners' wives instructed their husbands as they left for work: "after this, look after yourself; work more slowly; don't join the labor competition, so that at least you have a chance of coming out of the mine alive."[104]

The mood of the first days of 1951 contrasted starkly with that of summer 1949, when the regime had secured its legitimacy among workers in Tatabánya by offering them the promise of socialist transformation. Despite the existence then of severe material difficulty for many, attitudes to labor competition revealed the existence of an implicit contract—one that had vanished eighteen months later—through which workers were prepared to change working practices in order to build a new society, one in which their material difficulties would be solved. The nature of this bargain was visible at the ceremony held on the final day of August 1949 to decorate new outstanding workers in the Tatabánya power plant. Both the plant director and the secretary of its trade union exhorted those gathered to change their work methods to achieve the goals of the first five-year plan and thus guarantee higher productivity. Within the context of the meeting, both new and old outstanding workers replied, accepting the need for better work but also demanding that it be embedded in a contract through which the material grievances of power plant workers would be addressed. One worker, Lajos Csányi, welcomed his colleagues into "the family of outstanding workers." He called on all workers to improve their work methods but argued for generalized wage increases in return and improvements in the supply of goods to Tatabánya. He argued that "it is unacceptable that we here can only buy green pepper for 1 forint, 80 fillérs, when in Budapest it costs just 80 fillérs."[105] Within a year it would be impossible for any workers, even Stakhanovites, to use a public meeting to demand changes in wage levels, or in living conditions, in exchange for improved production.

As in Újpest, this shift was a consequence of the regime's desire to transform production from summer 1949 onward, in both of the new city's industrial establishments but most importantly in its mines. During the autumn, the authorities focused labor competition both on the completion of the three-year plan in the city's mines and on preparations for the increases in production that would be demanded by the first five-year plan from the beginning of 1950.[106] Yet, due to the nature of the labor process in coal mining, labor competition did not focus on individual competition to the same degree as in other sectors; in December 1949, the trade union reported that, while 1,586 brigades functioned in the city's pits, there were only 203 individual competitors, from a total manual workforce of 9,820.[107] Where "individual competitors" worked, they were used to promote "Stakhanovite-inspired" work methods within the mine; workers' apparent innovations in the labor process were used to increase production.[108] This focus was not merely a product of the specific labor process underground but also of the way in which the tightening labor market worked to limit recruitment. In 1949, Tatabánya's workforce was smaller than the level planned, with labor shortages occurring as younger workers left the city in search of jobs in areas with better housing conditions.[109] Consequently, management, in order to meet its 1950 plan, prepared to increase productivity through a rationalization of labor and increased mechanization.[110] Mine mechanization in Hungary prior to World War II had been uneven, however, and progress during the late 1940s in building functioning drilling, loading, and transportation machinery was slow, hampered by the crisislike conditions under which mining engineers had to work, including the economic situation, a severe lack of foreign capital to buy imported machinery or components, the cold war, and shortages of raw materials.[111] Throughout 1949, the investment plans for installing mining machinery were underfulfilled as a result of late deliveries, breakdowns, and the slow, bureaucratic procedures for the approval of new investment.[112]

Therefore, labor competition focused on the rationalization of production, through changing labor practices. The 1949 collective agreements attempted to standardize wages paid according to results in the mines and to individualize wages within brigades by regulating the rates payable to workers for different tasks at the coal face.[113] Furthermore, mine management kept control over wage costs far more effectively than in other sectors by ensuring that work norms remained tight.[114] Authorities called for mine engineers to maintain the necessary conditions for miners to fulfill production targets, which effectively became a license for many to blame the poor work of engineers for problems in production. Consequently, by the turn of 1950, when four of Tatabánya's pits were surveyed, all of their engineers participated in labor competition, while only 54.25 percent of the total workforce were so engaged.[115] While engineers were forced to guarantee the conditions for a new kind of "Stakhanovite" labor competition, working-class activists in both the party and the youth wing of the trade unions played a central role in providing the star competitors to introduce new methods.

Young miners had appropriated the discourse of labor competition in early 1949 to improve their position within informal networks of bargaining. In this they were aided by the local branch of the Trade Union Young Workers' and Apprentices' Movement (Szakszervezeti Ifjúmunkás- és Tanoncmozgalom, or SzIT), which had promoted labor competition among the young since 1948.[116] Over the summer, youth brigades secured good places to work in relatively mechanized parts of the mines by promising to raise their production, with one youth brigade in Pit No. IX producing an additional five carts for every twenty-four hours they worked.[117] János Varga, leader of a youth brigade and an SzIT activist, joined competition to compete with "Communists" who already "were leading in production. . . . Why should I do less well than them? I wanted to produce more, I wanted to keep up with the other Communists, while at that time I was getting married and needed the money."[118] Given labor shortages and an aging workforce—the average age of a coal hewer had been 39.2 years in 1935, rising to 41.8 years in 1949; that of an assistant hewer had risen since 1935 from 28 to 30.4 years, while that of a cartman had increased from 22.6 to 26.7 in 1949—management placed a premium on youth, which increased the relative bargaining power of the SzIT company branch.[119] Consequently, young SzIT activists were placed at the forefront of the Stalin shift campaign in the Tatabánya mines.[120]

As János Varga noted, the other group comprised the working-class party activists, who took up the challenge of driving up production through "new" work methods, relying on political connections to gain the requisite access to a good place to work at the coal face. In Pit No. XIV, brigade number 219, led by Barnabás Varga—the former mine factory committee chairman and former member of prize-winning brigade number 202, which had led labor competition in the first half of 1948—became the centerpiece of official mobilization in autumn 1949. The brigade was a tightly knit group of nine workers committed to transforming production. One of the young cartmen in the brigade, András Tajkov, as a representative of his pit in enterprise-wide production meetings, constantly challenged the engineers over their opposition to installing loading machinery close to the coal face.[121] With the onset of the campaign for the Stalin shift, the brigade began to rationalize its production; it worked, with the cooperation of managers and engineers, to ensure that those involved in preparing the coal face descended before the rest of the shift, while their colleagues changed, so they could begin work as the previous shift left. They reworked roles within the brigade to ensure that they worked with optimum efficiency during the shift and, furthermore, ensured a sufficient supply of carts to transport the coal, which acted as the basis for a system through which Tajkov, with the assistance of engineers, was able to change the rails that carried the carts to ensure a continuous supply.[122] With these methods—and the support of management—the brigade continuously increased its production well into 1950.[123]

The brigade's boosting of production attracted the ire of many fellow min-

ers. One coal hewer openly criticized Varga: "The high percentages have gone to
Barnabás Varga's head! It's not enough for him to make two hundred percent; he
wants to appear in *Szabad Nép* every day." Others commented, "Whoever has got
bored of life should try working according to Varga's methods."[124] This opposition
was encouraged not only by the challenge the brigade posed to traditional working
practices in the mines, or by the fact that the brigade owed its preferential position
in production to the fact its members were party activists, but also by the material
profit its members gained. As poor housing and food supply problems persisted,
Varga proclaimed in early 1950 that "the democracy has given us a healthy, beautiful flat. From my earnings we furnished it, bought valuable pictures, and a radio,
and I've bought my wife a fur coat."[125] Yet, because of the geological condition of
the mines and the shortage of relatively good workplaces, only a minority of miners
could ever have the opportunity to work effectively or safely according to Varga's
methods. In contrast to other sectors, therefore, the campaigns leading to the Stalin shift had a marginal effect on overall earnings in mining, merely exacerbating
inequalities between brigades depending on their ability to secure an appropriate
work station that was in a relatively mechanized area of the mines. In Pit No. XV, in
December 1949, the average earnings of those workers responsible for mining coal
at the face—including the 30 percent supplement for underground work—varied
from 55.9 forints per shift for members of the best performing brigade to only 25.18
forints for the weakest performers.[126]

In early 1950, the patterns of informal bargaining around places to work at the
face seemed almost unchanged by the introduction of Stakhanovism as older, male
skilled workers were able to monopolize the best positions. In Pit No. VII, which
was close to the mining colony and, although an old mine, one where the potential
for earnings was still relatively good in 1950, workers trained as skilled coal hewers
made up 89 percent of all underground workers paid in payment-by-results wages,
while in the more disorganized Pit No. XVII such workers made up only 51.7 percent of those paid according to such wage systems.[127] This situation was exacerbated
by the fact that skilled workers were often prepared to form brigades only with
friends, neighbors, or kin; this pattern aided the reproduction of hierarchies within
the mine workforce. By April 1950, András Tajkov, Barnabás Varga's cartman, had
himself graduated as a coal hewer and a month later became a Stakhanovite; he
thus led his own brigade. Tajkov himself admitted that his brigade was built on the
basis of ties of kin, neighborhood, and friendship, as this guaranteed the "common
spirit" necessary for work underground at the coal face.[128]

The socially exclusive dimensions of informal bargaining around workplaces
reinforced the peripheral positions of other groups. This was especially the case with
the 17.8 percent of the workforce who lived in villages and commuted to Tatabánya
on a daily basis. Most of these workers owned small plots of land and worked in the
mines to provide financial relief during the winter months.[129] With the emergence of

labor shortages in 1949, management offered many of these miners permanent positions; some, especially in harvest periods, were unwilling to accept their side of the bargain and absented themselves—with or without permission—to work on their plots or those of their neighbors.[130] Absenteeism seriously disrupted the work of the brigades to which these commuters were allocated; one mixed brigade's second shift could not be allocated work on twenty occasions during the third quarter of 1950, while its third shift could not produce on seven occasions because none of its village-dwelling coal hewers turned up for work. This, in turn, made older workers who lived within the city more determined to preserve the socially exclusive character of their brigades and their favorable position in informal bargaining.[131] The peripheral position of commuters reinforced their alienation, making them more likely to be absent from the mine to work on their household's smallholding. This situation was not merely marked in mining but also on the city's construction site and in its cement works. For workers who were also heads of households with land, "the land comes first, and only after that the factory."[132] The socially exclusive nature of bargaining also limited the authorities' attempts to alleviate labor shortages by employing women in positions in the mines that had been traditionally filled by men. Throughout 1950 to October, the number of women working in Tatabánya's mines had risen to 1,082—an increase of 11.5 percent. Despite attempts to break down hierarchy, only a limited number had been given positions in key areas of underground work; only ten had become cartmen, working with a brigade at the coal face. Despite employing rhetoric that stressed gender equality, management admitted that most women were employed in more traditionally feminized aboveground positions to free men for work underground. This relative failure preempted the outcome of campaigns in the broader economy to open up male-dominated jobs to women over the coming years.[133]

Given the overwhelming dominance of the mines in the local economy, the Stalin shift and the Stakhanovite movement in other workplaces were all but invisible in the local press. This was also due to the fact that many of the city's workplaces were in sectors in which the nature of competition did not easily allow individual workers to celebrate meteoric rises in the fulfillment of their production norms. In the city's power plants, for example, competition was designed to ensure that the boilers ran and power was produced on the basis of ever lower coal consumption.[134] Despite the achievement of some apparently exceptional results in the building of new flats and other infrastructure necessary to turn Tatabánya into a new, "socialist" city, the construction site was plagued by chronic disorganization and a discontented workforce of largely rural origin.[135] The mines faced the challenge of constantly increasing plan targets throughout 1950, and although they were successful in meeting their targets for coal production in all but one month during the year, this was achieved only in those pits where the uneven process of mechanization was well advanced. Elsewhere it led to ever more chaotic production.[136] The shortage of good workplaces at the face was exacerbated by labor shortages, which forced maintenance to be undertaken only when needed, which in turn, led to the introduction of Sunday shifts and overtime so that the mine could achieve its plan targets and miners could meet their norms.[137] In Pit No. VI, which suffered from persistent flooding, the need to replace rotten timbers, with only low numbers of maintenance staff available, meant that there were "as many workers doing maintenance as work[ing] at the face" in summer 1950.[138] Absolute shortages of wood generated production stoppages.[139] New machinery frequently malfunctioned, while older machinery installed to transport coal from the face was simply incapable of coping with the ever increasing intensity of production.[140]

Growing chaos, combined with a tense political climate, generated not so much in Tatabánya itself but by collectivization and attacks on the Church in its rural hinterland and by the general politicization of production, led the ÁVH to assume a more overt presence in workplaces. In April 1950, a party member in Pit No. XV was disciplined for warning those of his workmates wishing to express their discontent openly that they should "beware" of one worker, "because he is an informer."[141] Given the spread of supervision over the expression of political opinions, workers tended to say what they thought only among friends; a trade union official noticed that workers were reluctant to express opinions "in front of officials, or representatives of public bodies."[142] The regime, deploying the rhetoric of Stalinism, labeled disorganized production, or the failure to reach plan targets, as "sabotage"; when the construction of a new State Department Store for the city fell behind schedule in April 1950 and investigations revealed chaos at the construction site, the local newspaper maintained that its management had fallen into "the hands of the enemy."[143] This led managements across the city, frightened that they themselves would be targeted, to involve the ÁVH in matters that previously would have been dealt with by internal disciplinary procedures. This was illustrated by a case in the Cement Factory, when the cableway operator failed to apply the brakes at the end of his shift. As a consequence, the cableway moved of its own accord, causing fifteen carts to smash into each other. The management called in the ÁVH, suspecting "sabotage," though the officers they sent to investigate concluded the matter was not sufficiently serious to be anything other than an internal disciplinary matter.[144]

This set the stage for the implementation of the norm revision in July and August 1950. In Tatabánya, just as in Újpest, repression was used to crush open opposition, as officials were instructed to simply call in the ÁVH.[145] Nevertheless, neither repression nor the threat of repression failed to prevent some sporadic explosions of anger. In Tatabánya's mines, where labor competition had not led to the kinds of generalized increases in wages visible in the rest of the economy, average hourly wages still fell by 6 percent as a result of the changes to the norms.[146] In Pit No. XI, two Stakhanovite coal hewers, having just received their wage packets in late July

1950, arrived at a production meeting and led a mass walkout of the workers present to protest at the impact of the norm revision on their wages.[147] Workers more often reacted with silent fury. In Power Plant No. 1, the workers listened to the announcement of norm revision in complete and deliberate silence.[148]

The regime's legitimacy among Tatabánya's left-wing workers was shattered not only by wage cuts and the suppression of protest against them but also by chaos in production, especially in the mines, and a mounting crisis in the supply of food to the city. These factors together destroyed the popular base for the regime that had been built by offering the promise of socialist transformation during 1948 and 1949. The city's food supply was dependent on local agriculture and the ability of the authorities to enforce compulsory deliveries of agricultural produce in circumstances of near civil war in the countryside over the regime's collectivization drive. Consequently, by the end of September 1950, meat was available only in some stores in the city, on one day every week. Even by informally rationing potatoes to five kilograms per week per family, the local council realized it did not have sufficient access to supplies to guarantee regular availability throughout the winter—a situation alleviated only by special deliveries organized in Budapest.[149] As the situation unfolded over the autumn, chronic shortages of bread, flour, and sugar led shoppers in Tatabánya to queue in front of empty shops to demand instant deliveries, provoking the authorities to use agitators and the police to send them home.[150]

By late 1950, the social base of the popular communism established in Tatabánya had collapsed, as the regime was seen to have turned against working-class aspirations for higher standards of living and to have backed unpopular measures in the workplace with repression. Food shortages and growing chaos in workplaces convinced many that instead of bringing material improvement, the regime had betrayed them. While in 1949 an implicit contract through which workers would change their work methods and raise their production in exchange for a higher standard of living was visible in production meetings, working-class fury was palpable as agitators tried to persuade them to sign up to grant "peace loans" to the state in autumn 1949. Most refused to say what they thought, but some hinted at it when asked to pledge money; in Pit No. VI, one miner told agitators that "he wouldn't say anything, because, if he did, there would be trouble."[151] In the machine shop at Újtelep, when asked to pledge money for the "peace loan," two skilled workers turned on the agitators, expressing what many felt but were unprepared to express in public. "Under the old system," they said, "I could buy one set of work clothes with one day's wages, now I have to work for a week before I can afford a set."[152] While party activists labeled the two workers "right-wing social democrats," in practice they had given voice to the root of the collapse of the legitimacy of the regime in the city, for despite having voted for the Communists, many no longer believed the system they had built offered the material improvement they sought.

## Producing Oil on the Borders of Stalinist Hungary in Southern Zala

After the conclusion of the "peace loan" campaign in autumn 1950, the regime turned to focus on what it regarded as worsening work discipline, and it targeted those workers who lived in rural areas and owned land. It labeled these workers *kétlaki*—an ideological construct that emphasized the way, in so far as Hungary's socialist state builders were concerned, such workers occupied a dual and contradictory position within class relations: one as an industrial worker and the other as a propertied, agricultural smallholder.[153] Rákosi himself initiated the party's campaign against them, arguing that "these workers during the harvest go absent from their factories and disrupt the rhythm of production. At the same time, because of their work in the factory they don't pay enough attention to their land, which shows itself in their production. These kétlaki workers simultaneously disrupt industrial and agricultural production."[154] The party's campaign was designed to persuade such workers to choose between industry and agriculture, and it promoted the former by suggesting they offer their agricultural land to the state. This was a nationwide campaign and was organized in Tatabánya's mines and construction sites in the final months of 1950.[155] Given that in the Zala oil fields employment was embedded in a rural culture of small-scale landholding, the antikétlaki campaign had considerably more impact. Propagandists at Bázakerettye could not target all of the 60 percent of workers who came from a household with land.[156] They thus limited themselves to persuading two hundred named individuals to surrender their land. An examination of the social composition of these individuals was revealing of the ways in which agricultural and industrial labor were enmeshed in the oil fields. Of the two hundred, 92.5 percent owned plots of less than three holds in size, while exactly 30 percent owned less than one hold of land. Oil workers were committed to small-scale individual landholding; a mere 6.5 percent held land as members of agricultural cooperatives. Furthermore, while among the two hundred there was only one white-collar member of staff and a single drilling master, the kétlaki identified by the propagandists were broadly representative of the manual workforce; there was no observable correlation between skill, pay levels, and the size of property owned.[157]

The degree to which oil workers were embedded in the agrarian culture of the rural region in which they lived was revealing of the way in which the regime's pressure on the border communities of southern Zala shaped oil workers' reactions to the regime more than did its labor policies. By late 1949, its policies of class-based taxation of rural producers and the linked policy of organizing smallholders into agricultural collectives decisively shaped patterns of everyday life in the region's communities. Agricultural collectives were marginal, as most individual smallholders remained stubbornly attached to their land; in the Letenye district surrounding the oil fields, agricultural cooperative groups—the first stage on the way to creating agricultural producer cooperatives—had been founded in only seven of the thirty-three villages by the turn of 1950.[158] They covered only 5 percent of all agricultural land in the villages where they had been set up, and they constituted a mere 2.08 percent of the district's land.[159] As in the country as a whole, only the very poorest of smallholders were prepared to join cooperatives.[160] Furthermore, production was often disorganized because either the members or the cooperatives themselves lacked resources, while the machine tractor stations, set up by the state to provide machinery and support, functioned poorly.[161]

Consequently, activists faced considerable challenges when they attempted to persuade any other than the rural poor to join cooperatives; in one district, agitators noted that "members only have 1 or 2 holds of property. Even those poor peasants who have between 4 and 5 holds and 8 holds do not want to join the cooperatives."[162] Behind this reluctance lay deep-seated class resentment, as many felt a regime they had opposed was stealing their land to transfer it to those on the margins of village life, thus infringing the moral economies of rural communities. This was confirmed for the propertied by the sight of cooperative members who had "to learn to read and write" in order to understand how they would be paid.[163] The informal networks of social control, based on neighbors, kin, the Church, and popular religious belief were deployed to police the propertied, in order to prevent them from submitting to party pressure and agreeing to join cooperatives. In Becsehely, local believers spread the rumor that "those who join the cooperatives will be damned."[164] The climate of tension caused by the founding of cooperatives frequently erupted into open violence; in Zalamerenye, persons unknown opened fire on cooperative members working in the fields, while within days the local party secretary received an anonymous letter warning him to "leave politics, or there will be trouble."[165]

The tense climate in the villages, generated by collectivization, fed and was fed by penal levels of agricultural taxation, most notably for those classified as kulaks, but which were also being sharply increased during 1949 and 1950 for all categories of landowner. Worker-peasants in MAORT complained bitterly of the weight of agricultural taxation, which "they were not able to pay," and compulsory deliveries, as well as the strictness with which they were collected.[166] Pressure also increased through campaigns to "consolidate" the landholdings of new cooperatives. This meant that land farmed individually was confiscated so that new cooperatives could operate across a unified area; the smallholders whose land was taken away were compensated, usually with poorer quality land at the edge of the village.[167] When these campaigns began in villages near the oil fields in 1949, they brought to the surface the tensions surrounding the organization of early cooperatives. Some smallholders complained bitterly that those "affected by consolidation will lose their right to private property" and that those outside cooperatives would only "receive worse land than they had before."[168] One MAORT worker-peasant protested at having to exchange his smallholding for another by turning up on the property of the village cooperative to cut one of its best meadows for hay. He expressed his contempt for the cooperative members who chased him off, simply shouting back, "I shit on the cooperative!"[169] Combined with such anger was a fear, heightened by campaigns such as consolidation and the nationalization of small-scale enterprises in December 1949, that their land would be simply expropriated, and their way of life would be lost. Such fears were exacerbated by widely held opinions that "kulaks shouldn't be bothered to work their land, because they will have it taken away in the next year"—something that many believed would be extended to other landholders.[170]

Another major factor that determined the relationship between the regime and its institutions on the one hand and the local population on the other was the proximity of Yugoslavia. Despite tension along the border and the security measures introduced to control it, Yugoslav citizens with agricultural land in Hungary were still allowed to cross to work it at the end of 1949. These so-called dual property owners (*kettősbirtokosok*) were able to convince Hungarian smallholders that, despite the collectivization drives, the situation in Hungary was better than on the other side of the border.[171] Yugoslavia was in the throes of its own collectivization campaign, and, by 1949, the countryside was marked by tension and widespread violence that was at least as severe as that in Hungary.[172] Hungarian smallholders, themselves concerned with their own sharply rising taxes and compulsory deliveries, were convinced that what friends and relatives were expected to deliver and pay was much higher.[173] Yet political tension between the two countries destabilized the state locally because of the fear of war. Hungarian authorities intercepted letters warning of imminent conflict that Lendava residents had sent to relatives who worked over the border at MAORT.[174] A combination of the construction of permanent watchtowers by the Hungarian border guard and military exercises along the border in February 1950 produced panic among residents. Others told agitators seeking to persuade smallholders to join cooperatives that they were wasting their time, for "spring will bring change."[175]

The ÁVH closed the border in spring 1950. In part, this was the final stage in a process of militarization that had been under way since 1948. Yet it occurred against the backdrop of the Yugoslavs establishing an oil drilling site in spring 1950, which raised fears that the Yugoslavs were seeking to "steal" oil from the Lovászi field.[176] Furthermore, the process of militarization was combined with the deportation of "unreliable elements" from the region close to the border; it began with the deportation of members of religious orders in early June 1950.[177] Given the association of popular Catholicism with anticommunism, and especially resistance to collectivization in southern Zala, these deportations provoked fury and raised fears that generated near hysteria. Around Nagykanizsa, some warned that "after the priests they will round up the children and the kulaks, and bring Russians to take their places."[178] This was followed two weeks later by more generalized deportations from villages within the *határövezet* (border zone) itself. Deportees were rounded up at dawn on 23 June, which generated hysterical reactions in the villages next to the oil fields. In Semjénháza, one female resident awoke the entire village with the news— false as it turned out—that "they were taking away the priest." Even officials in the MAORT party refused to support the deportations, on the grounds that the reaction would weaken their authority among workers further, while one kulak reacted by maintaining "the fate that awaits us, is that of the Jews in '44."[179]

Agricultural collectivization and policies toward the border region immeasurably strengthened perceptions of the socialist state as dictatorial and terroristic among oil workers. Growing paranoia among the local ÁVH about the proximity of Yugoslavia changed their view of MAORT. They no longer mistrusted it because of the legacy of American ownership but came to regard it and its workforce as vulnerable to "Yugoslav influence." In June 1950, the local ÁVH commander in Nagykanizsa recommended that the subunits of the department, which ran the organization's network of agents who specialized in the detection of spying and sabotage, pay special attention to the oil fields. While its past as an American company and the political unreliability of its workforce were relevant, the most important factor for the ÁVH was that, "before and after the liberation, the residents of border villages maintained close contacts with Yugoslavia." At Lovászi, "it is beyond doubt that very many Yugoslav citizens, or persons with connections to Yugoslavs, gained employment," while at Bázakerretye, "there are also persons with connections to Yugoslavs." This justified the organization of a network of agents to root out "spying" and "sabotage."[180]

This paranoia, together with the power of the ÁVH, as well as the local population's utter distrust of them, produced fear and tension. At Lovászi, where the situation was especially strained because of the number of ÁVH officers stationed there, violent incidents broke out between them and oil workers in 1950. In May, a dispute between two serving ÁVH officers and workers drinking after their shift in the Lovászi works's canteen turned to violence after one officer referred to one of the workers involved in the dispute as "that shitty peasant." At this, the workers attempted to evict the officers from the canteen, and a fight broke out.[181] In October in the village of Lovászi, a dispute between a young worker and an ÁVH officer over a local girl led to serious violence between state security officers and some of village's young men. News that, as a consequence of the violence, two young men had "disappeared" led many residents to complain that "they hardly dared sleep in their beds at night."[182] While the local party in the MAORT did not generate fear and tension to quite the same extent as local representatives of the ÁVH, it was seen by oil workers as a leading representative of a hostile regime. Furthermore, its distrust of MAORT, its managers, and many of its engineers had not disappeared with nationalization.[183] The mutual distrust of party and workers for each other produced a situation in which the party was seen as interventionist, arbitrary, and dictatorial. In one incident, which provoked complaint from the management, the party secretary at Bázakerettye, Elek Horváth—himself a former drilling master at the Lovászi plant—visited a drilling site in December 1950. Unhappy with the speed at which they were working, he began to shout at them, to ask them "what is the use of them drilling so quickly, if no oil comes out of the hole they're making. Their work isn't worth anything, because 'we are interested in oil.'" The work group slacked their pace, defending themselves by pointing out that the party secretary had "told them off" for drilling so fast.[184]

The complete breakdown in relations between oil workers and the socialist state influenced the attempts of the regime to reshape production in 1949 and 1950. The broken relations were also affected by shifts in policy toward oil production, as the authorities in Budapest, following MAORT's nationalization, became aware of the real limits to raising the production of oil over the course of the first five-year plan. Zoltán Vas, president of the National Planning Authority (Országos Tervhivatal, or OT), warned in 1949 that "all we will achieve if we continue with slash-and-burn production is that major problems will surface during the fourth year of the five-year plan, in the form of shortages of crude oil." Economic planners thus envisaged a gradual decrease in production at Bázakerretye and Lovászi from 1950; increased production would come from new fields, and the weight of investment was concentrated on research to locate them.[185] In this context, there was little economic need to change the nature of labor competition on the site; the competition launched in March 1949 focused already on the completion of the three-year plan and preparations for the first five-year plan.[186] The Stalin shift at the oil wells therefore was less about driving up total production and more about demonstrating participation in the national campaign, while workers were mobilized—as they had been from the first labor competitions in the plants in 1948—with the promise of increased incomes. While much was made in the factory-level press about introduction of "Stakhanovite" methods at drilling sites, both in the immediate aftermath of the Stalin shift and into 1950, such claims lacked real substance.[187] While, at Bázakerettye, the plant made its target for production of crude oil by 102.19 percent during the Stalin shift, the average fulfillment of norms by the workforce was 144.2 percent; thus, the campaign raised earnings without increasing total production proportionately.[188]

The abolition of MAORT, and its replacement with five companies in January 1950, reorganized the administration of oil production but barely affected realities at the drilling sites.[189] While the drilling plants participated in the periodic labor competition campaigns launched by the state in Budapest, their engagement with these campaigns was highly formalized and based more on steps to reduce the costs of production, through efficiency gains, than attempts to increase production per se.[190] Behind the façade of a highly formalized labor competition, oil production became increasingly disorganized and discontinuous during 1950. In part, this was a product of the burdens imposed by "slash-and-burn" production; 1950 was the peak year of production at both Bázakerettye and Lovászi, and the strains of attempting to operate wells continuously at peak production were felt constantly, through stoppages in production and damage to machinery.[191] It was also a consequence of the impact of shortages and discontinuous production across the rest of the economy on the drilling plants. The declining quality of machinery and equipment delivered to the drilling plants, and sometimes its nondelivery, led to attempts to maintain production through recourse to improvised solutions, sometimes with catastrophic results. In one of the worst incidents, the Bázakerettye drilling plant expanded its network of pipes for the transportation of gas and oil around the plant during 1949 and 1950. Because of raw material shortages, some of the new parts of the network had to be built with poor-quality pipe that had been left over in the plant's stores. As a consequence, when the new network was put to work, some of the new piping broke under the pressure, causing a serious fifteen-day production stoppage at Bázakerettye's gasoline plant.[192]

As in the rest of the economy, it was in an environment characterized by increasingly discontinuous and disorganized production that the authorities implemented the "increase in basic wages and the revision of the norms" at the drilling plants in summer 1950. Workers' reactions were not especially different from those elsewhere. Across the drilling plants, many workers maintained that the regime had betrayed its promises and that the revision of the norms represented a shift toward the exploitation of workers. Some maintained that the wage system was simply a "capitalist" piece-work system in all but name. Another maintained that "it isn't the person that matters, they just value the work."[193] The storage tank staff maintained that "the former system was better" and that ÁVH officers present on the site were no better than "work-avoiding scoundrels."[194] What was, however, very different in the Zala oil fields was the significance and political context of the wage reductions. In Újpest, they represented a very clear turning point, destroying relations between workers and the regime, while in Tatabánya, they allowed a more gradual loss of trust in the promise of socialist transformation and material improvement to crystallize; in Zala, they confirmed existing perceptions. Given collectivization, the overbearing presence of the ÁVH in daily life, and mutual political suspicion going back to 1945, norm revision merely confirmed for most oil workers that they lived under an exploitative, oppressive, and illegitimate regime. What was new was that they shared this perception with those who had supported socialist transformation two years previously. This remained unchanged right up to 1956.

# 5

# Expanding Workforces, Reproducing Traditions
## January 1951–June 1953

ALTHOUGH THE LEGITIMACY gap between workers and the state that formed the backdrop to the 1956 Revolution had opened up more than six years earlier, the workforce the regime then confronted was substantially different from the one whose culture it sought to transform in 1949 and 1950. When government statisticians surveyed twenty enterprises at the beginning of 1954, they discovered that only 62.8 percent of the approximately 93,000 industrial workers they questioned had worked in industry five years previously.[1] The shift they picked up was a result of the substantial expansion of the industrial workforce that occurred between 1950 and 1953; at the end of the period, the numbers working in industry and construction were one and one-half times the figure from three years previously (table 11). The state had sought this expansion of the workforce. When the first five-year plan was passed into law in 1949, it mandated the creation of 480,000 extra jobs in industry by 1954. When the regime raised plan targets dramatically in early 1951, the party called for industrial employment to expand by a further 170,000 over the original 1949 target.[2]

TABLE 11. Number of workers in industry and construction by sector, 1949–1953

| Sector | 1949 | 1950 | 1951 | 1952 | 1953 |
|---|---|---|---|---|---|
| Heavy industry | | | | | |
| Mining | 67,048 | 71,027 | 75,600 | 81,602 | 93,547 |
| Steel production | 32,106 | 35,956 | 41,160 | 39,736 | 44,914 |
| Machine manufacture | 66,069 | 68,935 | 83,936 | 94,877 | 104,653 |
| Power goods production | 10,284 | 13,789 | 16,274 | 18,723 | 17,971 |
| Low-power electrical goods production | 10,092 | 11,222 | 13,929 | 13,657 | 15,082 |
| Precision engineering | 1,572 | 3,422 | 5,951 | 7,698 | 9,694 |
| Mass production | 12,956 | 16,985 | 23,898 | 26,304 | 27,009 |
| Transport repair yards | 16,430 | 17,140 | 16,035 | 16,846 | 19,105 |
| Electrical production | 3,583 | 4,970 | 5,353 | 6,124 | 7,372 |
| Construction material production | 22,538 | 31,805 | 34,978 | 38,216 | 46,408 |
| Chemicals | 15,745 | 13,314 | 14,580 | 18,202 | 19,273 |
| Rubber production | 3,017 | 2,623 | 2,837 | - | - |
| Total | 261,440 | 291,188 | 334,531 | 361,985 | 405,028 |
| Light industry (excluding food processing) | | | | | |
| Wood processing | 10,965 | 12,610 | 15,049 | 15,968 | 17,737 |
| Paper manufacture | 5,217 | 4,887 | 4,661 | 4,502 | 5,064 |
| Printing | 10,066 | 10,891 | 9,386 | 8,390 | 7,770 |
| Textiles | 67,529 | 73,644 | 78,912 | 81,939 | 79,496 |
| Leather and fur products | 3,945 | 4,133 | 3,759 | 3,881 | 4,136 |
| Clothing | 10,278 | 15,799 | 21,562 | 24,692 | 26,626 |
| Total | 108,000 | 121,964 | 133,339 | 139,372 | 140,829 |
| Food processing | 43,150 | 43,580 | 46,181 | 52,049 | 62,628 |
| Total for all industries (excluding construction) | 412,590 | 456,732 | 514,051 | 554,024[a] | 616,544[a] |
| Ministry-owned construction | - | 121,888 | 150,566 | 195,681[b] | 194,827[b] |
| Local construction | - | - | 32,058 | | |

Source: Adapted from four volumes prepared and published by Központi Statisztikai Hivatal: Statisztikai évkönyv 1950 (Budapest, 1951), 13; Statisztikai évkönyv 1951 (Budapest, 1952), 21, 131; Statisztikai évkönyv 1952 (Budapest, 1953), 22, 118; and Statisztikai évkönyv 1953 (Budapest, 1954), 27, 90.
[a] These figures include so-called local industry, which was left out of the sector-based figures.
[b] This figure represents the total for both ministry- and locally owned construction; no breakdown is available for either 1952 or 1953.

The expansion of the industrial workforce was motivated by the circumstances in which the first five-year plan was implemented, and that expansion formed a central cornerstone of the state's project of social transformation. By tying the obligations of citizenship to labor, the state defined work for the benefit of society as being central; according to the 1951 Labor Code, in a capitalist society, "the majority are forced into exploitative labor without legal obligation. . . . In socialist society, the means of production are owned by society. On the basis of the social ownership of the means of production, the economic, political, and legal order of socialism excludes the possibility that one person may live without working on the basis of the detriment to another. From this, it follows that persons who wish to share in the benefits of what society produces can do so only if they participate in the work of society."[3] While legal texts like the Labor Code emphasized work in the socialist sector as an obligation, the integration of previously marginal groups into socialist labor, especially into industrial labor, was seen as a condition of their participation in, and a benefit of, socialist society. In this spirit, one author argued in 1951 that only by securing "the broadest integration of women into every branch of production" would the promise of socialism in eliminating gender inequalities be realized.[4] The boundaries between arguments for policies that expanded the labor force on the grounds of its centrality to the regime's project of social transformation and those that rested on technocratic justifications were fluid at best. From 1950, attempts to mobilize the rural poor and women within the household for industrial labor were justified through the specific goals of meeting the employment targets laid down in the plan.[5]

The blurring of ideological and technocratic justifications ensured, just as with policy toward labor competition and wages, that the expansion of the workforce would mesh with policies that aimed to shape the regime's new "Communist working class" and to replace the established cultures of industrial workers, especially those that rested on presocialist notions of skill. The position of a skilled worker was embedded in discourses of generation and seniority in that, prior to 1950, to achieve the status of skilled worker required a prolonged period of apprenticeship under a master.[6] With the first five-year plan, this system was abolished and replaced by a standardized training system based on formal schools linked to workplaces.[7] Hierarchies of skill and generation were further challenged in late 1951, when, under orders from the OT, worried by mounting labor shortage, special crash training programs were introduced to train unskilled and semiskilled workers for skilled positions.[8] The state not only broke the power of skilled workers over training through the apprenticeship system but also challenged the gendered hierarchies through which many high-paying, skilled positions had been labeled as masculine as part of a bid to open such jobs to women. Planners did this by setting quotas for the number of women to be employed by sector and skill level. Although in traditionally male-dominated skilled occupations in heavy industry these quotas were never met, they represented a substantial challenge to preexisting patterns of hierarchy.[9] Cutting across all these measures, the state attempted to reduce "the gap between town and country" and solve the labor shortage problem through massive programs of labor recruitment in rural areas. It hoped to transform village dwellers into urban workers, further challenging hierarchies between urban and rural workers in the factories.[10]

Older skilled workers refused to accept many of the newcomers as their equals, so much so that the party's theoretical journal criticized skilled miners for their "skill-based chauvinism, the way they look down on new workers who have come straight from the village and on female workers."[11] Their refusal to accept the regime's measures to create a new "Communist working class," of which they too would be a part, fed and was fed by the deepening crisis of legitimacy. During 1951 and 1952, the regime persevered with productivity drives seeking to use labor competition to intensify the pace of work and tighten production norms—most dramatically in 1952, as shortages and unrealistic plan targets destabilized production. Looking back on shop-floor relations in the early 1950s, a skilled worker who fled in 1956 later told American-sponsored interviewers that "we were relentlessly driven to work more and more—this terrible competition in work we were forced into. We always heard, 'You did it in only ten minutes; the other fellow in seven.' . . . The winners were announced, and it was also announced how much higher pay they received. But, after a few weeks, they rearranged the wages. People worked themselves to death, and they quit doing good quality work."[12] Another remembered that, "after the readjustment of norms, the workers would be embittered for weeks."[13] Outside the factories, within the sphere of consumption, the regime bred tension by forcing the population to bear the costs of the industrialization drive; in December 1951, the government imposed serious reductions in working-class real incomes when the abolition of rationing was combined with huge hikes in official prices, which were only partially covered by compensatory wage increases.[14] Between 1951 and 1953, workers' real wages fell sharply, sinking to 84.4 percent of their 1949 value by 1952.[15] Even these figures understated the true extent of the hardship experienced in industrial communities, given that most experienced severe shortages of foodstuffs and basic goods as a crisis in agriculture—generated by the economic climate in the countryside as a result of high taxation and the collectivization drive—affected urban centers.[16] Approximately two hundred thousand workers who took industrial employment between 1949 and 1953 were refugees from the material hardship and repression that accompanied the collectivization drives. Their discontent was generated by the twin impact of labor and agricultural policy.[17]

The enormous tensions in industrial communities were held in check by widespread repression. The threat of repression was underlined when, in 1951, the state began putting prisoners to work in mines and at construction sites alongside paid workers.[18] While repression did prevent explosions of open protest, a discontented workforce was able to use the labor shortage to articulate its material discontent by quitting jobs or merely being absent, which reached epidemic proportions.[19] To suppress discontent, in 1952 the authorities made it a criminal offense to quit a job or be absent from one without authorization, but these measures failed to reduce the incidence of either phenomenon. In the first year of the passage of the law, enterprises proved unwilling to use it.[20] Given the breadth of the legitimacy gap between the regime and workers, and the chaos in production, class identities among workers reproduced themselves in the form of political antagonism toward the regime, while established occupational, gender, and generational identities were deployed, preventing any meaningful identification of actual industrial workers with the state-promoted subjectivity of the new "Communist working class."[21] Informal bargaining over the norms or access to scarce work persisted throughout the early 1950s. This practice was strengthened by purges of foremen, introduced in the interest of securing greater control over production, which in practice resulted in the promotion of huge numbers of skilled workers more prepared to make concessions to former workmates than their predecessors had been.[22] Consequently, older skilled workers continued to sit at the apex of a hierarchy similar to that which existed when the regime had begun its transformation of working-class culture. In three factories in the capital in October 1953, skilled workers with between six and ten years' experience earned 149 percent of what workers who had worked in the plants for only a year took home.[23] Women, the young, and those from rural areas continued to occupy peripheral positions within the workforce.[24]

The three case studies here show how this process of the reproduction of tradition occurred and thus how the attempt to forge a new "Communist working class" failed. Újpest's factories show how traditional hierarchies between the skilled and others adapted to the conditions of the early socialist economy, demonstrating remarkable continuities between patterns of stratification and culture based on sector, skill, generation, social origin, and gender, and those that had existed during the late 1940s. In this regard, Tatabánya was similar, though to certain traditional hierarchies new ones were added, given the extent of the change in the local workforce, because of the way poor living conditions generated especially severe labor shortages. With the employment of prisoners in the mines, hierarchies were established between the free and the captive, while a workforce of rural origin, housed for long periods in temporary hostel accommodations, created a new group on the periphery of the local workforce. Southern Zala was in some respects typical of many of the rural counties whose workers lived in hostel accommodation in the urban centers during the 1950s. The regime attempted to recruit rural dwellers for work in industry, and the dynamics of that recruitment process depended on popular responses to its agricultural policies. Yet the presence of oil fields, and the discovery of one new one during the period, meant that the regime was dependent on a discontented rural population to staff the drilling sites it established in the region.

## Agricultural Labor, Industrial Employment, and the Workforce Expansion in Southern Zala

At the beginning of 1951, the state realized that it would need 160,000 new workers in order to meet its targets for industrial employment over the course of the coming year, as it faced worsening labor shortages in industry and construction. The government launched a campaign of mobilization targeted in large part at "workers freed from agriculture" by the collectivization drive to provide new workers for the expanding industrial centers.[25] Its numerical targets were broken down by county; embedded within them was an assumption that the poor agrarian counties of the Great Plain and those adjacent to the western border—including Zala— would provide the labor for those regions marked for industrialization.[26] In so far as these border districts were concerned, mobilization for geographically remote industrial employment was not solely about transferring workers from agriculture to industry; it was also about ensuring their progressive depopulation on grounds of national security.[27]

In view of the fear of the state that reigned in Zala's border districts by early 1951, campaigns to mobilize labor were met with the hysteria that had greeted deportations from the same villages less than a year previously. In Bánokszentgyörgy, labor recruiters called a mass meeting of village residents in February 1951. Local army officers volunteered to support the recruitment effort, and their appearance immediately prior to the meeting proved counterproductive. Residents who witnessed their arrival refused to leave their homes because "the army is here and they will take" residents "away."[28] Pursuing the recruiters through the villages adjacent to the oil fields was a wave of rumor that the true purpose of the campaign was to take residents away "to Siberia, to Korea, and to other places for forced labor."[29] Consequently, these campaigns proved utterly unsuccessful. Recruiters managed to sign up only 6.7 percent of their target of 3,660 new workers from Zala in February and March 1951.[30] The April target was lower, at 2,210, yet the recruiters achieved only 9.6 percent.[31] The recruiters followed hard on the heels of the extension of rationing at the beginning of January, through which the state attempted to respond to the food shortages of late 1950.[32] This effort proved utterly ineffective. Infrequent supplies of food and goods to village shops combined with a lack of trust in the promises of local authorities to produce waves of "buying up certain essential goods" like "soap and matches" at the time the recruiters arrived. This in turn was taken as a sign that war was imminent, a view apparently supported for many by news of the situation in Korea. In Bucsuszentlászló, "they are waiting for the English," while in Zalaszentmihály, "they await the American aggressors."[33]

Panic and rumor that destabilized the state locally was based on insecurity and fear felt by residents, and this feeling was especially acute close to the border. Rumors among oil workers of the imminent deportation of substantial numbers of border region residents resurfaced continually.[34] When the regime began deporting a new round of "class enemies" from border villages in June 1952, their attempts met with silent demonstrations of support for the deportees by residents in Letenye, Bánokszentgyörgy, Kerkaszentkirály, and Tornyiszentmiklós. The participants in silent demonstrations believed that deportation was not merely about removing "class enemies" but was also a policy of progressively depopulating border villages, and they argued that in due course even "honest workers" would face removal.[35] These fears were exacerbated by their daily experience of dealing with members of the ÁVH responsible for the protection of oil fields. Tension and violence between those stationed to protect production at the drilling sites and workers remained such a problem at Lovászi that a local ÁVH commander admitted in 1952 that "the workers believe wrongly that the ÁVH exists only to maltreat them."[36] This perception was a result of the violent treatment of workers by state security officers; in one of the worst incidents, in July 1951, a dispute between a plainclothes ÁVH officer and an oil worker outside a pub in Dobri led to the worker receiving such a severe beating that his head was split open. The beating was witnessed by many oil workers.[37]

Fundamental to social relations in southern Zala, however, was the impact of the regime's agricultural policies. While they depleted trust in the regime and frustrated early labor recruitment campaigns, they also generated the poverty that, paradoxically, allowed subsequent attempts to mobilize labor for industry to succeed. The years 1951 and 1952 were at the peak of the pressure that the socialist state placed on agricultural producers, both through taxation and compulsory deliveries and in efforts to get them into agricultural cooperatives. For a modest landholding of eight holds in western Hungary, the burden of tax alone was, "under normal circumstances, . . . 250 forints per month, but in many cases rose to 300 forints" if farmers failed to make their compulsory deliveries.[38] For smallholders in Felsőrajk, compulsory deliveries to the state "represented the most serious problem" for those who "farmed individually." The quantity of produce that needed to be delivered, the low prices the state paid for it, and the methods through which produce was collected provoked considerable resentment. The local council's collectors "did not take into account" whether a harvest had been good or bad. "An official supervisor" was present at threshing, even when it was done by hand in a smallholder's own yard. If the quantity recorded by the supervisor was "not delivered within three days, then" the farmer was "prosecuted and all their produce confiscated."[39] The linking of compulsory deliveries to the size of a landholding and the heavily progressive nature of the requisition meant that "up to 8 holds, compulsory deliveries could, with real difficulties, be met somehow; for properties above 8 holds the burden of compulsory deliveries was just unbearable."[40]

The impact of compulsory deliveries and "class war" policies resulted in substantial social leveling in villages during the early 1950s. Nationally, of the 104,000 farms classified as owned by kulaks in 1949, some 63,300 were classified thus on the basis that they were greater than 25 holds in size. By the beginning of 1951, 16,800 of these farms had vanished or had fallen below this threshold.[41] These leveling tendencies were reflected across Zala. While in the economic year 1948–49 there had been 1,152 kulaks countywide, only 885 remained in summer 1952.[42] In Felsőrajk, wealthy farmers "in general kept the extent of their property at eight holds, and simply gave away the rest."[43] While in Felsőrajk this meant that the property was incorporated into the local state farm, elsewhere it resulted in a strengthening of local agricultural cooperatives. Coerced donations of land from the wealthy, combined with the severe pressure of compulsory deliveries on the poorest smallholders who struggled, aided the organization of cooperatives. At the end of 1950, the various forms of agricultural cooperatives covered 24,613 holds of land and had 6,020 members countywide; a year later they held 44,053 holds and had 10,184 members.[44]

Despite the expansion of agricultural cooperatives, many villagers remained resolutely opposed to joining collectives. Often their justifications repeated the prejudices that those joining were those who were unable or unwilling to work for themselves. One oil worker refused to consider joining because "it has happened several times that factory workers harvested" for the cooperative, while their "workers decided to take a four-hour lunch break."[45] Such impressions were heightened by the disorganization of many of the cooperatives and the problems of remuneration, generated by the fact that members were paid every six months a share of the cooperative's profits, calculated according to the measured work units they had contributed. Given their chronic lack of capital, the low morale of their workers, severe disorganization, and the hostility of the village around them, the incomes they could guarantee their members were meager. In one cooperative, a member complained "he could not buy cigarettes" from the money he had been paid.[46] In another cooperative, members chose to focus on the private plots they had given over to viticulture, because of miserable incomes earned cultivating the grain grown on the cooperatively farmed land. Consequently, the harvest collapsed into chaos.[47]

In communities like Felsőrajk, structured by notions of status and property, the cumulative effect of the regime's agrarian policies was to create a subjective perception of equality among members of the local community—an equality characterized by poverty and privation: "now the people are the same . . . all of the differences based on property have been washed away." The silent fury of many at the regime was expressed in support for the Catholic Church, which residents saw as the only, albeit limited vehicle, for the expression of opposition; as one resident remembered, "A picture of Primate Cardinal Mindszenty can be found on the walls of many peasant houses."[48] This silent fury was a product of the fact that the regime's agrarian policies had brought penury to rural communities; in 1950, the average real income of the agricultural population stood at 85.1 percent of that of workers and employees; despite the cuts in real wages experienced by those who lived "from wages and salaries" during the early 1950s, the agrarian population fared far worse— by 1952, their real incomes stood at only 61.7 percent of the level of workers and employees.[49] Reductions in real incomes because of compulsory deliveries hit village populations hard, for many smallholders and cooperative members were far from self-sufficient in terms of what they produced. The climate of privation resulted in rural families not being able to buy "footwear and clothing" easily. Furthermore, in Felsőrajk, "there was hardly a house in the village where one had a week's supply of flour and fat."[50]

For those who lived purely from agriculture in the village, the "only way of earning money" was to take any produce left over after compulsory deliveries and try to sell it at the Nagykanizsa market. Many resorted to this course of action, for the amount the state paid them for what they were forced to deliver often did not cover the costs of production, let alone meet their living expenses. The difficulty with this was that to trade, a smallholder needed to ensure that their compulsory deliveries were in order, for the management of the market "checked strictly" the book of each seller in which the obligations and deliveries of each smallholder with a permit for the market were recorded, before allowing them to trade.[51] In order to maximize the produce a smallholder could take to market, many of them attempted to cheat compulsory deliveries through a range of strategies, which included bribing the officials "who took in the produce," "watering down the milk" they delivered, and hiding grain.[52] These strategies met with uneven success, and the burden of compulsory deliveries meant that smallholders went to market less often; in Felsőrajk, "they only go to market if they have something to sell."[53] It was the dreadful economic situation and the need of the rural population for cash that progressively eroded their resistance to drives to recruit labor for industry. This was combined with a depoliticization of recruitment efforts, as many of the construction enterprises that were given the right to sign up workers from Zala's villages turned down the help of local party organs and began recruiting on their own terms. Despite this, rural dwellers were relatively reluctant to take work at distant construction sites, and when they did, they often returned home after seeing the poor working and living conditions. Those who took work at the Tatabánya construction site came home as a result of the "damp, broken flats" where male workers were housed. Others went to work at the regime's showpiece construction site at Dunapentele-Sztálinváros and returned complaining that "they had been given work where it was impossible to earn any money."[54]

Rural dwellers were keener to take work closer to home, and locally, industrial employment expanded as a consequence of the first five-year plan. While Zala was on the periphery of the regime's project of constructing socialism, it nevertheless benefited from some of the investment in new industrial plant. The county's two major towns—Zalaegerszeg and Nagykanizsa—were both marked for industrial development. The former gained a major clothing factory and, as a result of the oil fields, a refinery by the mid-1950s.[55] While the clothing factory attracted a predominantly rural, female workforce during the early years of its operation, in terms of gender composition it was exceptional.[56] New workplaces were staffed either by the male head of the household or the sons, while women were left to manage the family farm in their home village. As a consequence of the spread of a worker-peasant identity in the villages and the impact of the regime's agrarian policies, "the women have never worked as much as they do now. No one employs anyone else in the village because there aren't applicants, and it's impossible to accept them anyway. Women have to leave the housework to work in the fields."[57]

The oil fields were a significant source of employment for smallholders seeking paid work outside agriculture. While oil production at Bázakerettye and Lovászi fell gradually from 1950 onward, the decision of the state to invest in research paid off when a major new field was discovered at Nagylengyel, north of the existing drilling plants on the fringes of Zalaegerszeg, in 1951. By 1953, the new field produced 378,000 metric tons, or slightly more than 46 percent of all oil produced in the county. The discovery of the Nagylengyel field increased the level of state investment locally and generated more jobs.[58] Employment increased, however, even at the plants where production fell; at Bázakerettye, total employment rose from 826 to 1,116 over the course of 1951. While the reorganization of the enterprises and the burden of administering oil production in a planned economy led to an explosion in administrative staff—their numbers rose from 36 to 103 during the year—manual employment also increased, from 681 to 828.[59] These increases were a product of the padding of workforces, which was a management response to pressures generated by the operation of the broader economy in the oil fields. Overall labor shortages, the need to hit strict plan targets when production fluctuated significantly, and shortages of tools and materials produced an uncertain climate that encouraged plants to create a labor reserve, which could be deployed flexibly to ensure that targets could be met.[60]

These increases drove a restratification of the workforce, as rural male youth were employed in greater numbers in manual labor positions at the drilling sites. The proportion of employees under the age of twenty-six at Zala's drilling sites rose from 23.8 percent to 29.6 percent between January and August 1951.[61] Among these were a large number who came from households with individual agricultural landholdings; of this group at the older drilling sites, 57.1 percent were the children of an individual smallholder in 1952. The sons of landholders came from households with slightly larger farms than those workers who owned a smallholding in their own right; only 26.34 percent had parents with fewer than three holds of land, compared with 36.9 percent of workers who held the land themselves. Therefore, the expansion of the workforce modified a preexisting worker-peasant culture rather than overturned it.[62] A more radical break was visible at Nagylengyel, where household strategies for coping with the regime's agricultural policies drove the children of relatively prosperous farmers to take work at the drilling site. Of those workers at the rapidly developing site in 1952, only 10.41 percent held any land in their own right, and even some of those were also sons of smallholders. Parental smallhold-ings were also larger among the Nagylengyel workforce than at "older" drilling sites—none were less than three holds in size, and a majority—52.8 percent—were between five and ten holds.[63]

The changing composition of the workforce encouraged the party, unions, and management at the oil fields to renew and extend their offensives against *kétlaki* workers. The regime attempted to persuade workers that not just they but their parents as well should give up their land. Furthermore, they included not only con-ventional agricultural landholdings but also small vineyards in the categories of property they expected workers to give up.[64] The regime blamed the rural culture of new oil workers for their failure to accept the "work discipline" of older workers at the drilling sites.[65] Often officials were deeply paranoid about the impact of opposi-tion to the regime's agrarian and anticlerical policies in villages on the attitudes of workers in production.[66] Yet their attempts to persuade workers with land that their welfare was better secured by choosing to become a fully waged industrial worker without land met with limited success, especially among workers who were sons of agricultural landholders.[67] Young workers often took their families' opposition to agricultural collectivization into production; those from villages where resistance to the founding of collectives was most stubborn were often the ones most pre-pared to oppose agitators vocally at the oil wells.[68] Attempts to collect money during peace loan campaigns from the family members of kétlaki workers provoked fury, as workers themselves refused to pledge anything while their relatives "locked their doors" in the face of agitators who tried to collect door to door.[69]

Attempts to turn kétlaki into landless proletarians failed not only because such workers had taken jobs at the drilling sites in order to preserve the economic inde-pendence of their families as propertied smallholders in the face of attacks by the state but also because their jobs alone did not deliver real material security. As in the rest of the economy, workers' wages were tied as much as possible to individual performance. During the early 1950s, policy makers sought to ensure the adoption of piece-rate wages in as many different sectors of the drilling sites as possible, abol-ishing the previous system of performance indicator–based wages during 1951 and 1952.[70] The extent of the regime's effort was indicated by the situation at Bázakeret-tye in May 1953: 91.1 percent of the plant's workers were paid according to piece-rate wages, 6.6 percent received a fixed hourly wage, and 2.3 percent were paid according to the premium system. Managers implemented piece-rate wages to avoid bargain-ing over the norms; 51 percent of those paid according to piece rates worked on "sci-entifically" established norms. Although all workers fulfilled their norms by at least 100 percent, the system opened up inequalities based on measurable performance in the plant. While the bottom 35.4 percent of workers paid on piece rates fulfilled their norms by less than 110 percent, 24.4 made them by more than 120 percent.[71]

Wage insecurity was generated by the interaction of performance-based wages and disorganized production. Throughout 1951 and 1952, oil drilling suffered from shortages of raw materials and equipment, which were blamed for failures to meet plan targets. At Bázakerettye, supplies of oxygen and calcium carbide failed to turn up in September 1951, leading to stoppages of work in the machine shop. At newly drilled wells, tubing ran out, leading to failures to install pumping equipment. The plant was forced to wait 117 hours for the tubes to be delivered to enable oil production to continue.[72] The resulting fluctuations in workers' wages increased tension. When workers' earnings were hit by production difficulties, a tide of complaints often arose about the shortcomings of engineers, who were accused of not "paying attention to the working masses."[73] In order to deal with the situation, managers developed informal wage agreements with the skilled workers who were essential to production, but these separate arrangements compromised company wage budgets.[74]

These patterns of bargaining were structured by notions of hierarchy that were as endemic at the drilling sites as in other sectors. They provided the basis for conflict between workers as the workforce was expanded. For "older" skilled workers at Lovászi, it seemed by early 1953 that the environment created by MAORT more than ten years previously had disappeared. They complained that "they did not earn and it was not enough to live from." Not only had the high wages of an earlier era disappeared, but the crash training courses designed to turn the unskilled laborers recently arrived from local farms into skilled workers threatened their status. "Older" workers complained that "unskilled workers with only one or two years of employment can't be sent to school to become drilling masters, because they just don't have the necessary experience, and after they've finished school they won't be able to pull their weight."[75] Notions of hierarchy were not confined to "older" skilled workers where dominant discourses of gender were concerned. The work culture of the oil fields was deeply masculine. Consequently, attempts to mobilize women for industrial work provoked huge resistance from the men at the drilling sites. As in much of the rest of the economy, campaigns by the state to recruit women to jobs traditionally performed by men had been implemented at the drilling sites. In January 1951, of 925 manual workers employed at southern Zala's Oil Research and Deep Drilling Enterprise, 35 were women; by August, there were 158 female workers from a total of 1,225.[76] Men did not accept that women should be employed in certain positions. Inciting particular controversy was the employment of female workers as truck drivers at the drilling sites, which often led management to make concessions to male protest.[77] In March 1953, at Bázakerettye, management fired 4 of the 5 women working as truck drivers. Prior to their dismissal, they complained of outright intimidation from male colleagues. Management refused to protect them and instead appeased male protest. After they "had done 35 to 40 hours' overtime," the company refused to pay them "a single hour's overtime; instead they recorded them as having been off work."[78]

While some of the kétlaki were discriminated against individually, especially as the graduates of crash training programs, they were not disadvantaged as worker-peasants. The basis of their integration into the workforce not only frustrated the attempts of the authorities to persuade them to surrender their land but also underlined the utter failure of the regime to transform southern Zala's oil workers into members of the new "Communist working class." Despite first increasing the scope of rationing, then abolishing it outright at the end of 1951, the regime was still dealing with persistent shortages of food and basic goods during the early part of the decade—a situation that hit the landless, even those without allotments, especially hard.[79] Because of this, the kétlaki were often in favorable positions in their workplaces, given their location in a household economy that gave them more access to scarce or expensive foodstuffs than their landless counterparts; they also benefited from their ability to supply foodstuffs to landless workmates. In certain circumstances, managers were prepared to authorize absenteeism at harvest time, and the ability of the kétlaki to supply limited foodstuffs could provide a basis for their integration into informal bargaining. Given their value in this regard and the insecurity of factory earnings, they carefully regulated their pace of work in the factory to ensure sufficient energy and time for work on the family landholding.[80]

While generalized penury provided a material background to the reproduction of a rural working-class culture, the decreases in overall living standards, endemic shortages of basic goods, and the chaos in production generated mounting discontent that culminated in a climate of growing, if submerged, revolt by early 1953. It was triggered by a two-month bread shortage in the villages surrounded by the oil fields in spring 1953, and for many residents, this was the last straw after two and a half years of falling living standards. One resident in Semjénháza turned party agitators supporting the collection of compulsory deliveries away, saying that "instead they should be bringing bread."[81] In response to the party's attempts to mobilize residents in Páka for single-list parliamentary elections, locals threatened not to vote unless the state "gave the workers more bread."[82] At the oil drilling sites, workers confronted demands that they work harder and better with the blunt response that "the plan could not be fulfilled without flour and bread."[83] This situation was dangerous for the regime not only because it crystallized huge material frustration that had built since 1950 but also because it coincided with the death of Stalin, which awakened hopes of political change in a region that had never accepted the legitimacy of the socialist state. Rumors began to circulate that upheaval in Moscow was imminent and that it would in turn bring change in Hungary. One such rumor was spread by a worker who "had heard on American radio" that "many are seeking to replace Comrade Stalin, including the head of the Soviet security services, who has several armed divisions ready." The wave of rumors that the Soviet Union was about to collapse as a result of infighting and that Hungary would follow in its wake spread through the oil fields.[84] The deep-seated material frustration, desire for change, and the hope generated by events beyond Hungary's borders in spring 1953 heralded and anticipated the mounting crisis that would engulf the regime over the following three years.

## Struggling with a Permanent Labor Shortage in Tatabánya

Frustration with a desperate material situation expressed itself not only in increased tension but also by a desire to leave Hungary. By the first half of 1953, the border guard was worried by considerable activity along the boundary with Austria. It had grown steadily throughout the decade and was dominated by the "escape" of "class enemies" from the country.[85] One escapee who crossed the border in early summer 1953, Jenő, had worked a year previously for low wages at a construction site in the western border town of Kőszeg before going to a meeting led by labor recruiters "to hear what they have to say" about coal mining. Deciding that "it could not possibly be worse than the construction site," he enlisted as a miner in Tatabánya. Faced with low pay, the pace of mining work, and dormitory accommodation, which he shared with thirty-two others, he left mining, initially for a job in a local cinema, and then escaped to Austria.[86] Jenő's experience in early 1953 was not unique; the first half of the year was marked by a crisis in food supply to the city during which mineworkers' families "could not always get bread, or fat." Another new recruit to the mines "often saw people queuing in front of the shops. I heard comments from miners' wives that if things didn't get better, they wouldn't allow their husbands, or their children, into the pit." As a single thirty-three-year-old, frustrated by the penury he observed, he escaped the country with three workmates.[87]

While escape from Hungary was an extreme reaction to material penury, frustration with dreadful living conditions thoroughly undermined the state's attempts to plug labor shortages in both mining and construction in Tatabánya through recruitment campaigns. Problems of labor shortages in the city's mines—already serious in 1950—grew steadily worse, reaching crisis proportions in early 1951.[88] The local authorities sought to resolve these problems by investing in housing, though, given both the scale of the task of upgrading urban infrastructure and the lack of resources available, their plans could never meet the demand.[89] The problems of securing relatively small numbers of construction workers to complete these apartments proved intractable.[90] In part, this was because of the scale of construction in Tatabánya, where the demands of socialism's dream of social transformation interacted with the pragmatic demands of industrialization. Only a city since 1947,

Tatabánya was an industrial sprawl that stretched across thirteen kilometers and was underpinned by infrastructure that was inadequate. The reality of Tatabánya's urban fabric, its strategic position at the heart of the country's largest coal field, and the regime's desire to create a state organized around socialist labor led planners to demand the transformation of Tatabánya, as the only "large mineworkers' city," into a genuinely socialist urban space.[91] With the reorganization of local government in 1950, Tatabánya assumed the role of the seat of Komárom County, creating a demand for accommodation for an army of public administrators. In seeking to meet these demands, planners concentrated on shaping a new settlement—the new Tatabánya—that could serve as a city center for the whole conurbation. This step had the effect of diverting scarce raw materials and labor from the construction of residential flats from 1950 on.[92]

The enormous demand for labor generated by mining, the expansion of the city's power plant, and the transformation of Tatabánya into a massive construction site could only be met by recruiting the rural poor. The limits to possible labor recruitment from villages in Tatabánya's hinterland were revealed by the summer of 1951. In these villages, there was already a culture of kétlaki seasonal employment; these potential workers' awareness of local labor market conditions meant that they were uninterested in construction, given that the wages paid were lower than those in the mines. They prioritized work on their own smallholdings; in Tarján, villagers promised recruiters in summer 1951 that "once threshing was over, they would come and work in the mine."[93] In the distant counties in the Great Plain region, labor recruitment for Tatabánya foundered on tension generated by the regime's agrarian policies. Some, especially from those villages where there was a tradition of taking jobs in construction that reached back to the prewar years, were prepared to do so.[94] Employment in mining, however, proved an especially hard sell. Hostility toward mine work was so generalized that in Biharugra the local council leader refused to allow recruiters into his village, arguing that "no one will leave here to die in the mines."[95] As in Zala, the mounting state-generated crisis of subsistence in agriculture blunted opposition to recruitment across the east of the country throughout 1951. This resulted in large numbers of young males, between twenty and thirty-five years of age, from households that belonged either to agricultural cooperatives or had small landholdings, mainly from counties in the north of the Great Plain, taking work in Tatabánya by the end of the year.[96]

In many of the villages from which new labor recruits came, the hostile attitude toward taking work in mining meant that many "new" recruits' first experience of work in Tatabánya was at the city's construction site. It was only after working locally that they became aware of the higher wages in mining and consequently left the site for the pits.[97] Construction in the city was characterized by chaos and marked by the consequences of unrealistic plans, absolute shortages of raw material, and an inexperienced and overwhelmed management.[98] The consequences of chaos forged simmering discontent among the workforce, which destroyed the authority of management in production. When management failed to pay new recruits the two-hundred-forint fee they had been promised for signing their contracts, the affected workers refused to start work until the money turned up.[99] Workers expressed their fury at discontinuous production and insecure wages by rejecting assigned work unless they could secure in advance the wage rate they demanded from site supervisors.[100]

The chaos in construction was in part produced by shortages that resulted from a crisis in the enterprises that supplied them. Although construction in Tatabánya was fortunate in that the city had both a quarry and a large cement plant, these too suffered from the regime's operation of the economy. In order to support the expansion of construction, the Cement Factory's plan targets were hiked during 1951, and to hit these targets the state planned the modernization of the plant. Given the endemic nature of shortage and the prioritization of machine manufacture and armaments, cement production was a low priority for planners, and investments in new capacity were simply not completed on time.[101] This, combined with the failure of the quarry to fulfill its increased production targets, resulted in the nondelivery of raw materials and bitter squabbles between the two workplaces over the shortages and production stoppages that resulted. Given wages that were low relative to coal mining, the plant suffered from an acute labor shortage.[102]

Attempts to solve the problems of labor shortages and turnover were hindered by appalling working conditions. During 1952, such conditions fueled enormous discontent, which culminated in a dispute over the failure of management to install ventilation to remove dust from the cement furnaces, and it led both the workforce and the trade union to accuse the managing director of "being uninterested in workers' complaints."[103] As in other establishments, the spread of discontinuous production and insecure wages produced informal bargaining that reproduced hierarchies within the workforce. These conflicts were exacerbated by the attempts of the authorities to mobilize peripheral groups, such as those from rural areas, youth, and women in order to deal with labor shortages. In early 1953, female workers who loaded the lime kilns complained that, despite performing labor that was no easier physically than that expected of everyone else, the best of their number had been denied the status of Stakhanovite as a result of the trade unions' willingness to appease the hostility of male skilled workers toward their presence in the plant.[104] During 1951, of the 862 workers who had taken work in plant as a result of labor recruitment campaigns in the villages, 787 had left within a year, many complaining of poor conditions in the plant and work from which it was impossible to make a living.[105]

The construction site, cement factory, and other enterprises in Tatabánya were subordinate to the coal mines, which dominated the local economy. In order to meet the rapidly increasing demand for energy from expanding sectors of the economy, the first five-year plan for mining envisaged an increase in total coal production of 55.2 percent. In 1951, this figure was revised upward to 142 percent for the same five-year period. The plans that were received by the Tatabánya mines demanded sharply increased production, and planners in Budapest continually raised the production targets.[106] These increased targets intensified the problems experienced during 1950, transforming them into an outright crisis of production over the following two years. During the first half of 1951, the mines achieved only 89 percent of their target in the production plan.[107] Because of labor turnover, the numbers employed, especially underground, remained stagnant.[108] Consequently, as the crisis in production grew, the amount of coal mined per worker fell from 54 metric quintals of coal per worker per month in 1950, to 49 metric quintals during 1951.[109] The factory regime that had developed underground since 1948, based on informal bargaining between work groups around access to scarce places at the face, was further consolidated.[110] The consequence was to increase inequalities of earnings between groups of workers based on their formal performance against production norms; in December 1951, in those pits managed by the Lower Tatabánya Mining Enterprise, 25.6 percent of workers paid according to piece rates fulfilled their norms by less than 79.9 percent; 17.6 percent fulfilled theirs by between 80 and 89.9 percent, and a further 18.8 percent reached 90 and 99.9 percent. At the extreme, 9.8 percent of workers overfulfilled their norms by between 20 and 49.9 percent, and 3.5 percent made 150 to 199.9 percent of their target.[111]

While patterns of hierarchy determined the opportunities for work groups to successfully maintain their wage levels through informal bargaining, just as they had in 1950, the large influx of "new" workers modified preexisting patterns of hierarchy. Notions of experience were crucial to this process; of the 1,201 workers taken on by the Lower Tatabánya Mining Enterprise during the last five months of 1951, 75.2 percent had no previous experience of mining.[112] For much of this inexperienced group of "new" workers, working for the first time in the coal mines was a profoundly alienating experience. While they found themselves at the bottom of the hierarchies that structured workplace bargaining, they took anticommunism from their home villages into the mines. Stakhanovites, who manipulated their political connections in order to secure good places to work or other kinds of advantage, provoked particular anger. One "new" worker regarded them as "Stakhanovite swindlers," who earned good money at the expense of their workmates.[113] Another found himself working for András Tajkov's brigade: "I saw how much easier it was for him, because we brought him everything. . . . It infuriated me that I did the work and he took the money and praise."[114] Fury at the way Stakhanovites exploited hierarchies of bargaining within mines was shared by more established mineworkers, who regarded as reprehensible the shameless tactics of those, like Tajkov, who demanded they should "always be first" in production.[115]

Anger at Stakhanovism united workers, but other manifestations of hierarchy deeply divided them. In the battle for the scarce places at the coal face, experience and established notions of skill could be deployed by urban, "older" workers against the "new" workers on the grounds of experience. This provided the material background to the furious response from established mineworkers to the introduction of "new" recruits to the mines on a significant scale during 1951. The impression that the authorities would use these recruits to break patterns of hierarchy was strengthened by the extensive efforts the trade union invested in inducting "new" miners into work at the coal face.[116] The opening of crash training programs that would enable the recruits to become skilled coal hewers in record time especially offended the elite; established miners "did not regard it as just, that someone could become a coal hewer after only one year." Most had "had to work for six to eight years under a master, and it would be impossible to turn new workers into good skilled workers in any other way."[117] Such sentiments and a view that "new" miners threatened the preferential positions of the established miners led to open conflict, which was often so intense that the local newspaper criticized "old" coal hewers for their treatment of new recruits: "they don't teach them, or explain the work to them, but instead employ the most brutal methods."[118] What this ambiguous phrase often meant in practice was illustrated by one incident in Pit No. VIII, when "one new worker asked an older worker for help, and from this an argument developed that resulted in the head of the new worker being split open" as a result of a blow from "a mining lamp."[119]

Although this hostility abated, it did so only as a consequence of the crystallization of the hierarchy in structured informal bargaining, in which notions of experience were used to justify management placing new recruits at the bottom of hierarchical relations in the mines. One senior party official complained, "In many places, they don't give 'new' workers an adequate place to work. Furthermore, it often happens that they hang around with no work."[120] Patterns of discontinuous work and poor conditions combined with the complexity of the performance-based wages to produce both insecurity of earnings and a powerful sense of the injustice of wages, which many "new" workers saw as being based solely on relations of bargaining within mines, rather than on work itself. They saw these relations as being biased against them; one named the mine in which he worked as "the Pit of the *fillérs*, because they don't count the production of the many smallholders and kulaks who work as miners there" when determining wages.[121] Increasingly, "new" workers began to watch the techniques used by their more experienced workmates to protest when they were placed in jobs from which they could not earn sufficient income. One common technique was employed one night in November 1951 in Pit No. XI by two coal hewers, József Podmanik and Elek Hock. Three hours into their shift, "seeing that in their new workplace there were considerable difficulties and they couldn't keep up their earlier pace of production," they laid down tools and walked off the job.[122] These forms of protest, termed "work indiscipline," were emulated by "new" workers in an attempt to improve their bargaining positions. This generated an epidemic of absenteeism as "new" miners stayed away from work, rather than accept their allocated workplaces. In Pit No. XI in April 1951, a production stoppage caused by an hour-and-a-half long power outage acted as the catalyst for discontent that had built over the unequal distribution of good workplaces. Forty-one walked off the job; all but four were "new" recruits to the mine.[123]

Managers dealt with such incidents by treating them as infringements of the Labor Code, devolving their authority to punish workers who failed to turn up for part or all of their shifts to so-called workers' or social courts in the mines.[124] Attempts to deploy the disciplinary code were widespread but largely ineffective. While some workers were prepared to intimidate the working-class party activists who judged the work discipline infringements, it was not this that undermined courts' sanctions. When they realized that their attempts to bargain would be met with repression, "new" workers simply quit. In the Lower Tatabánya Mining Enterprise during the last five months of 1951, while 1,201 new workers had been taken on, 966 quit the enterprise. Excluding those whose departure was due to either death or incapacity, 50.1 percent left without even giving notice—in outright contravention of labor law, while a further 6.6 percent were fired for disciplinary offenses.[125] As virtually all new recruits lived in the city, at a distance from their families, in overcrowded, dirty, uncomfortable hostel accommodations riddled with petty crime, the proportion of the mines' workforce living in such hostels had risen from 5.1 percent in 1950 to 30 percent by 1953, but once such workers became convinced that there were few opportunities to earn money in mining, there was little to keep them in Tatabánya. The failure of the mines to retain "new" labor reached catastrophic proportions during the first half of 1952; of the 1,786 recruited in 1951, 1,406 had left by April 1952, and of the 785 who had joined the company in the first three months of the year, 615 had left by mid-April.[126]

Despite the difficulties in finding all workers places at the coal face from which they could easily make their production targets, labor shortages were a serious problem for mine management because of the rhythms of production in the pits. The first three weeks of a month were characterized by low production. As the deadline for meeting the monthly plan target neared, management attempted to reach it by employing "a scorched-earth policy in production. In the last ten days of the month, most of the labor was directed to the coal face, they neglected maintenance, and this damaged their chance of making the plan" later.[127] High turnover limited the ability of mine managements to do even this; by spring 1952, a number of mines had fallen short of their targets because they did not have the labor to mobilize and "storm" their plan.[128] Tatabánya's mines were far from unique, as the whole economy was gripped by labor shortages exacerbated by job mobility and absenteeism. The national state was anxious to crack down and demanded that enterprises treat sudden quitting and unauthorized absenteeism as "offenses against the plan," which would carry punishment of up to five years' imprisonment.[129] While management in Tatabánya was prepared to use the tool of criminal prosecution in several exceptional cases, especially to discipline absentees during summer 1952, it had little long-term effect. Lower management became reluctant to take action because use of the criminal law by managers led to an increased propensity among workers to use violence in order to intimidate supervisors. This issue was underlined when police chose to take no action after an incident in which one worker who had been disciplined for sleeping on the job attacked the supervisor who had found him while the latter took a Sunday walk with his wife and son.[130]

Faced with a growing crisis of labor supply exacerbated by chronic turnover, in June 1952, managers began deploying prison labor in the mines to alleviate shortages.[131] Prisoners had also been present at the city construction site and in the quarry since the previous year.[132] By February 1953, when 405 prisoners worked in the mines, management admitted that plan fulfillment depended on their use. Although they were paid the same wage rates as their free workmates, they were forced to work toward higher production targets and were placed in those parts of the mines regarded as highly dangerous and thus especially difficult to earn good money in, thus replacing labor at the bottom of the informal hierarchies of the mines, positions that were proving increasingly difficult to fill.[133] One former forced laborer who was put to work in Pit No. XIV in 1953 remembered that "the political prisoners were often concentrated in the most dangerous places," where miners were at risk of drowning because of the proximity of underground lakes to the coal faces.[134] By early 1953, prisoners and free miners were often employed together; given the simmering discontent among ordinary miners, this had serious consequences for morale among forced laborers. While prison guards were employed to keep the two categories of miner from fraternizing, these attempts often proved futile; free miners sympathized openly with prisoners.[135] Given that both groups worked according to the same wage systems, when production was disrupted, they made common cause in bombarding supervisors with complaints.[136]

The open sympathy for prisoners was a symptom of the lack of legitimacy of the regime among all free miners. Discontinuous work, an increasing pressure to produce, and a rocketing accident rate combined with perceptions of severe poverty to generate enormous opposition to the socialist state; miners complained that the "wages are tiny, they can't live on them."[137] These sentiments were not confined to the miners but were shared by all of the city's workers. When the regime attempted to increase productivity and cut wage costs through norm revision in spring 1952, their measures provoked a wave of complaint about wage levels all across the city. In the Bánhida Power Plant, workers complained that norm revision would cost them "200 forints per month," and, as a protest, they withheld payment of their union dues, leading to a 20 percent decrease in receipts.[138] Low wages were, however, only one factor fueling working-class discontent, for Tatabánya suffered from severe shortages of food and basic goods throughout the early 1950s. During 1951, local authorities in the city were unable to guarantee sufficient deliveries of meat to be able to supply miners their rations. "Older miners only rarely are able to have bacon, or any other cut of meat, with the bread they take to work," complained the trade union.[139] Absolute shortages were exacerbated by poor quality, especially of bread. In the city bakery in 1952, sawdust, pieces of wood, and stones found their way into bread.[140] Consequently, miners "wanted to eat homemade bread, as the factory-made bread was of appalling quality," and they demanded that the authorities make flour and yeast available in the stores.[141] Given the poor quality of goods, the price increases that accompanied the abolition of rationing in December 1951 provoked protest, as working-class shoppers jammed the counters of shops, demanding that sellers justify the differences between old and new prices.[142] While price increases further reduced working-class real incomes, they failed to solve the problems of supply. By early 1953, the situation was worse than ever. Endemic shortages of flour provoked complaints that staff in the state stores reserved the scarce supplies that did turn up for friends, relatives, or for those prepared to make under-the-counter payments to them.[143]

In addition to chronic poverty and shortages of consumer goods, housing conditions in the city deteriorated; by June 1953, as many as fifteen hundred families were without housing. While most of the "new" recruits were crowded into inadequate hostel accommodations, conditions in the mining communities were worse than ever. Given endemic shortages of construction materials and labor, the company that maintained the colony flats for the mineworkers was incapable of keeping them in a good state of repair, and they crumbled further. The scale of the crisis management was underlined when parts of the mining colony were flooded by polluted water.[144] While new flats were completed in the city and the vast majority of them were distributed to manual workers who only had to pay low rents, the rate of construction fell far behind demand.[145] Furthermore, life in Tatabánya's new town had the quality of living at a disorganized construction site. One new resident, András Preizler, complained in July 1953 that fresh vegetables only rarely appeared in the local shop; the running water and electricity to the new flats were frequently cut off, while the new town was so distant from the mines and other settlements that residents were entirely dependent on a public bus service that was overcrowded and unreliable.[146] By late spring 1953, just as in southern Zala, the well of material frustration in Tatabánya had reached crisis proportions, as chaos, shortages, and poverty shaped the contours of everyday life in the city.

## Reproducing Hierarchies in the Diversified District of Újpest

In early 1953, Budapest's evening newspaper stated that, "a few years ago, when standing on the banks of the Danube at the border of Újpest, the visitor was confronted by a view typical of the 'outskirts.'" The article maintained that the construction of monumental public housing, where the district's main street, the Árpád Street, met northern Pest's major industrial artery—the Vác Road—had transformed this view. The completion of this project heralded greater future investment that would propel the transformation of Újpest from run-down industrial suburb to a district of the capital of socialist Hungary.[147] Just as in Tatabánya, the construction of new apartment buildings failed to keep pace with demand, as the existing housing stock deteriorated. Typical of the dire housing situation of many skilled workers was that of János Varró, a "serial innovator, who had been promoted as" trade union "production officer because of his good trade union and party work" in the Újpest Leather Factory, where he had worked since 1949. From his monthly salary of seven hundred forints in May 1951, he paid two hundred forints to rent one room, which he shared with his pregnant wife and young daughter.[148] Attempts to deploy "class war" policies to alleviate the situation were ineffective; between May and July 1951, the regime deported 12,704 "class enemies" from Budapest.[149] Of the flats vacated by the deported, 1,200 were distributed among the employees of the fifty-four largest industrial enterprises in the capital. Another 122 flats went to workers from Újpest plants, barely denting the housing shortage. Furthermore, few of the recipients could afford the rents for their new flats; in Magyar Pamutipar, 7 of every 8 recipients refused their allocated flats on these grounds.[150] Pressure on housing was further intensified by an influx of young workers: "in Budapest there are many 19-, or 20- to 23-year-olds who come from the countryside and have no work, and no flat." Faced with a lack of housing, "they spend the nights on park benches or in the twenty-four-hour grocery stores."[151] The inability of Újpest factories to provide new housing for their "new" workers contributed to significant turnover.[152]

While the completion of a tiny number of showpiece housing projects contrasted with the misery experienced by most Újpest residents, a similarly surreal situation characterized the supply of goods to the district. In order to emphasize promises that the incorporation of the city into Budapest in 1950 would bring material improvement, the state prioritized the construction of a large, three-floor State Department Store in the center of Újpest. Completed in 1952, it apparently heralded the arrival of an era of mass consumption at the capital's industrial periphery.[153] In reality, for many consumers, the State Department Store goods were too expensive, and the networks of local shops many used to buy basic goods and foodstuffs remained crowded and old-fashioned throughout the decade.[154] While the capital was better provisioned than were provincial industrial centers, shortages of food and goods and discontinuous supply severely affected Újpest. In early 1953, workers on the morning shift in the Újpest Thread Factory complained bitterly of having to rise at four in the morning on weekdays to be sure of being able to buy meat, before the start of their shift at six. If they waited until after work, daily supplies had already been sold.[155] Furthermore, there was also underlying discontent about the declining quality of clothes and shoes. The issue of shoes was sensitive in Újpest, for the Danube Shoe Factory in the district was the country's largest shoe producer.[156]

Lack of control over the quality of production was endemic in the shoe factory. As early as May 1951, high-quality production in the vertically integrated plant was hindered at every stage. Production plans were imprecise. Leather was poorly cut and then passed on down the production line without question. Those stitching the shoes then worked to production plans that bore little relation to those used by the leather cutters. In order to control production to the smallest degree, shoes for left and right feet were made on different production lines, working with no reference to each other, resulting in a situation where almost no pair precisely matched. Faced with so many shoes of such poor quality, where different kinds and colors of leather were used in the same pairs, quality controllers were encouraged to turn a blind eye in order to ensure that the plant met its production targets.[157] Workers too were interested in ensuring that quality control was weak, as virtually all were paid according to piece-rate wages; during 1951, 83.6 percent of hours worked were remunerated in this way. Many of the weaker workers were under substantial pressure to speed up; the proportion of workers who failed to make their norms each month hovered around 20 percent throughout the year.[158] Just as workers were financially accountable for production, the plant had to cope with severe and increasing problems of shortages of raw materials, especially leather. The Danube Shoe Factory's production increased dramatically, as did the number of workers it employed, rising from 1,227 in July 1951 to a peak of 2,032 in September 1952.[159] Its major supplying enterprise, the Tánsics Leather Factory, which had originally been the Wolfner plant, of which the Danube Shoe Factory had once been part, faced severe problems of plan fulfillment. It could not source adequate supplies of leather to process, and it also suffered a labor shortage, which meant that the total numbers of workers the plant employed actually fell—from 564 in February 1951 to 540 a year later—when they should have risen.[160]

By summer 1952, the disruption of production due to infrequent deliveries of leather reached crisis proportions; stoppages of work caused by raw material shortages caused a sharp drop in the proportion of working hours paid according to performance. Increasing disruption led this proportion to drop to 70.6 percent in July 1952, and while it bottomed out, the proportion of hours worked according to piece rates during the year was only 78.7—almost 5 percent lower than a year previously.[161] Earnings became increasingly dependent on informal bargaining rather than actual production, and groups of workers decreased their production in order to guarantee more favorable work targets. Because of the vertical integration of the shops in the plant and a work flow in which raw materials arrived in the shop charged with preparation, then were handed over to be cut, stitched, and finished along a conveyor, those shops that dealt with raw materials first were in a favorable position to bargain up wages. In October 1952, the average monthly earnings per worker in the preparation shop stood at 883.90 forints, against an overall factory average of 760.54 forints. Yet the degree to which successful bargaining was not merely dependent on the formal position of a given shop within the relations of production was illustrated by the gender distribution of earnings in the preparation shop. Of all workers across the factory in October 1952, 60.1 percent were female, a proportion that fell to 43.1 percent in the preparation shop. Average male earnings in the shop were 1,030.49 forints during the month, compared to 708.12 among the women. All of the top 10 percent of earners in the shop were men.[162]

A minority of these male skilled workers had been employed in the district's smaller shoe factories in the late 1940s, but the majority were former independent craftsmen. Their concentration in the Danube Shoe Factory was a consequence of the decimation of privately owned small businesses as a result of radical nationalization; by the early 1950s, a negligible number of small workshops and two privately owned shoe factories employing a total of forty-six persons survived in the district.[163] Many of those regarded work in large socialist factories as poor compensation for the loss of their previous livelihood. One, who later escaped to the West, recounted that, "in 1945, . . . I decided to go into business for myself. I rented a small shop and began to manufacture children's shoes, which could be manufactured out of waste material and textile material. . . . In 1948, my permission of trade was revoked and I had to close down. Then I became a partner in a shoe store in Budapest that I was able to maintain for two years. In 1950, the store was taken over by the state and I was left without any money. There was nothing else to do but to apply for a job" in the Danube Shoe Factory.[164] Another, forced out of private trade in 1947, regarded the "material situation" of workers in the plant after nationalization as "desperate."[165] The skilled had little but contempt for the Taylorized labor process in which their skill and expertise had no place: "We received the model from the central office. Then we started to manufacture it without any experimentation. The old workers like myself tried to explain to the foreman, sometimes even to the production manager, that the model was no good. However, our voice did not count."[166] As production became more unpredictable as a consequence of the discontinuous provision of raw materials, as pressure on the factory increased because of the poor quality of its output, and as some skilled workers were promoted to foremen, the skilled gained greater ability to bargain down their norms.[167]

The reassertion of the cultural capital of older male skilled workers in the circumstances of disorganized production drove a reproduction of hierarchies that embedded themselves in bargaining. The skilled argued that they were superior to other workers. Sometimes their arguments were profoundly gendered. Recounting the nature of shop-floor relations in the early 1950s, one skilled worker argued that some of the urban "girls . . . did not stick to their job. They came and left after a few weeks." He maintained that the young women who came from rural areas, who made up the majority of the workforce, "were rather awkward with their hands."

The defense of the preferential position of older male skilled workers was not directed only at women or those who came from rural areas; younger skilled workers
were also frequently condemned because of the way crash training courses left them
ill equipped for work in the plant. "They wanted to educate a skilled worker during the course of six months. In our case we had to spend years and years in this
business till we learned it," he recounted. "In one case, the friend of the local party
secretary got a job as a cutter because of the money. Such a fellow wasted a lot of
material and created many problems in production."[168] The ways in which opinions
like these became hegemonic, shared by skilled workers, foremen, and production
managers, and came to structure informal bargaining was illustrated by the case of
the number 302 production line. Mean monthly earnings there in October 1952—at
655.70 forints—were well below the factory average and below those of the other
lines, which all produced similar products.[169] It received worse raw materials than
the others. Its plan fulfillment was consistently poor. Management dumped inexperienced workers there. One trade union official told party investigators that, "across
the factory, this production line is nicknamed 'the agricultural cooperative line.' In
part the workers use this term because of the large number of workers from rural
areas who are on it, and also because of the number of beginners."[170]

These patterns of hierarchy and the ways in which they structured responses to
the expansion of the workforce manifested themselves differently in the district's
factories. As the state increased the labor supply, mobilizing the young, women
from within the household, and those from rural areas to take work in industry
in Budapest, Újpest's plants offered new workers different possibilities for earning
income. These were dependent on the interaction of state wage policies and the
potential for earning against performance-based wages given the different positions
of factories within the economy. Újpest's large plants covered by the Metalworkers'
Union collective agreement—the United Incandescent Lamp and Electrical Factory and the BÁMERT factory, renamed the Duclos Mining Machinery Factory in
1952—had an advantage in recruiting labor, especially male labor, because of their
high wage rates. Perceptions of the United Incandescent Lamp and Electrical Factory in the local community as a good employer ensured that, with approximately
forty-five hundred workers during 1951, it did not suffer from an absolute shortage
of workers.[171] Local residents "always inquire whether we are taking on workers. The
work in the factory is light, the earnings pretty high, and this attracts people."[172]
The plant enjoyed a favorable position in the planned economy due to its centrality
in the production of radio components and specialty electrical goods. Yet it was
far from immune to the discontinuous production that affected earnings, which
destabilized the factory's ability to retain labor.[173]

The Duclos Mining Machinery Factory employed 1,119 workers by the beginning
of 1953.[174] Production in the factory was determined by the pace of expansion dictated by the first five-year plan, which mandated year-on-year production increases

of 50 percent between 1950 and 1954, underpinned by a major construction program that expanded and modernized the plant.[175] This expansion program suffered from shortages of construction materials, forcing the plant to strive for its plan targets without sufficient space to produce the requisite goods during 1952; this cut workers' earnings, for they "simply cannot get the kind of percentage that they could in a more comfortable place."[176] The impact of delayed expansion of the plant combined with the impact of the norm revision meant that the proportion of the workforce who failed to make 100 percent of their norms peaked at 20.9 percent in July 1952. Given the importance of the manufacture of mining machinery to the economy, the enterprise used a relatively strong bargaining position to ensure that the authorities prioritized the expansion of the plant. It was also able to place pressure on its supplying enterprises to deliver raw materials and components that enabled it to limit production stoppages caused by raw material shortages. Consequently, the number of working hours paid according to piece rates rose from 58 percent in June 1952, to 65.9 percent a year later, as average norm fulfillment rose from 119 to 149 percent, while the proportion of those failing to make their norms fell to 8.8 percent.[177]

The Chinoin Pharmaceuticals Factory was covered by the Chemical Workers' Union agreement, which guaranteed lower wage rates than the Metalworkers' Union agreement did. A flagship plant of the country's pharmaceuticals sector, Chinoin was marked for substantial expansion; its total number of workers increased from 1,295 in September 1951 to 1,580 by November the following year.[178] In order to meet its production targets, it required substantial modernization; given that planning authorities had prioritized other sectors, management complained throughout 1951 that the investments it needed to make its plan had not been approved. When they were, the machinery they needed, including special equipment imported from East Germany, did not arrive on time, creating discontinuous production, which was also exacerbated by unreliable deliveries of raw materials.[179] This, combined with the subjection of most workers in the plant to piece-rate wages, contributed to 20.9 percent of the plant's workers failing to meet their norms in the aftermath of the norm revision in June 1952.[180] Measures taken by the state to complete the refitting of the plant and improve raw material supplies to the factory led to higher plan and norm fulfillment by the end of the year.[181]

This pattern of gradual stabilization of the conditions of production was not marked in the light industrial establishments, which included furniture manufacture, textiles, leather working, and the fur trades, which accounted for the overwhelming majority of the district's forty-two plants and employed most of its workers.[182] All were in low-priority sectors, and as key plants in machine manufacture swallowed a disproportionate share of resources, investment necessary to raise production to meet plan targets in light industry was neglected. New plants like the Danube Shoe Factory were exceptional; more typical was the district's largest textile plant, the Magyar Pamutipar, where the strain placed on aging machinery hindered production.[183] While in high-priority sectors the extent of production stoppages caused by poor raw materials provision stabilized during 1952, in light industry the situation worsened. Discontinuous production caused the percentage of hours worked according to piece rates across the district's five largest light industrial plants to fall from 84.3 percent in February 1952 to 76.3 percent by November.[184] Wage rates across light industry were substantially lower than in other sectors.[185] This contributed to high labor mobility, as maintenance workers in light industry sought skilled jobs in local heavy engineering plants, while the semiskilled female workforce could move to similar positions in higher paying plants like Chinoin or the United Incandescent Lamp and Electrical Factory, where conditions were better.[186] Despite huge increases in the numbers employed in all large plants, as mandated by planners, the actual number of workers in the district's five largest light industrial plants rose slightly over the twelve months following November 1951, from 7,685 to 7,970. When the substantially new Danube Shoe Factory was excluded from the figures, the numbers employed in the four largest established light industrial plants in the district fell from 6,340 to 5,994 over the same period.[187]

In this context, attempts in the heavy engineering plants, especially the United Incandescent Lamp and Electrical Factory, and the Duclos, to train new skilled workers were where the implementation of state labor policies was the most focused. In the United Incandescent Lamp and Electrical Factory, in line with state policies, traditional apprenticeship systems were abolished, as trainees were placed together in a dedicated space "on the fourth floor of a five-story building."[188] By September 1951, 390 trainees were enlisted. In keeping with the state's attempts to break gendered patterns of hierarchy by enlisting women to train for skilled positions that had been the exclusive province of men, 110 of the trainees were female, including 43 of the 128 training to be precision instrument makers, the most highly paid manual job in the plant. A majority of those in the crash courses designed to retrain semiskilled workers for skilled positions—126 of 186—were women.[189] As in the rest of the economy, newly trained workers were looked down on by older skilled workers, as they were given positions in those parts of the plants that were strongholds of the male skilled elite, like the machine shop. Established skilled workers "did not want to accept" new trainees as skilled workers and so pushed them to the periphery within the shop. In 1952, this caused "disagreements between the old and the young" over rights of access to high-paid work. Unable to progress in the machine shop, one young female re-trainee "wanted to escape to Austria," citing her poor earnings relative to the earnings of others as the reason.[190] In late 1952, a female miller, Emma Szabó, sick of not being given work that would allow her to earn a good income within the shop, attempted to raise her earnings by submitting fraudulent time sheets.[191]

Notions of hierarchy and concerns over the quality of much of the "new" labor fed hierarchical relations of bargaining. According to one skilled worker, "There are trainees who have absolutely no interest in the skill that they train for. It would be better to send them elsewhere, because all they do is destroy work discipline."[192] A climate of insecure earnings, generated by a combination of payment according to piece rates and discontinuous production, encouraged established workers throughout the factory to defend their positions when faced with more recently arrived workers who demanded the same opportunities to earn. One new worker who arrived in the special lamp division of the plant in 1951 found her requests for better work met with hostility from established workers and supervisors: "why have they put someone here who still doesn't know how to do any work, when we have people already who understand what they have to do?"[193] In shops dominated by skilled workers, the solidarity between foremen and established skilled workers, which was often based on the fact that the foremen had begun their careers as skilled workers themselves, ensured collusion that denied the newly trained, both male and female, access to well-paying work. In the factory's vacuum technology division in May 1953, "the informal selection of work has still not disappeared. As a consequence of this, the large, long batches are given to the key workers, and for this reason young, promising workers are just not able to develop."[194]

The ways in which access to preferential work depended on hierarchies that were based on gender, generation, and social origin were illustrated by the experience of one young iron turner in the Duclos Mining Machinery Factory. This individual was put to work on "a Milano type turner's lathe. This was a bigger machine. . . . In spite of my youth I got this assignment because I was a good worker." In the shop, "bigger machines, say, horizontal lathes, planes, grinding machines, and cog milling machines, were operated by workers" of "forty to fifty" years of age, despite the fact that "most of the iron turners were teenagers who graduated as apprentices in the factory." Generation was not the only hierarchical relationship that structured access to work on the best machines; of the excluded majority, "sixty percent . . . were peasant boys from the countryside," and "among the iron tuners were women, about three or four percent."[195] Those younger skilled workers allocated the worst machinery complained of neglect by their immediate production supervisors, who concerned themselves with the "core" of the workforce. One day in November 1952, a female turner named Margit Ambrus stopped work because of problems with the technical specification to which she worked. It took her four hours to gain the attention of the foreman, who preferred to give his attention to other workers, so for four hours she was unable to work—or earn—at all.[196] The peripheral position of younger or less skilled workers produced resistance, as they developed their own informal bargaining strategies to secure a desired rate of pay for their work. At varying times, this involved producing scrap when a high norm was given for a job or simply using "unauthorized methods," which threatened to destroy the machinery, in the interest of making their rate.[197]

The frustration of the regime's attempts to overturn traditional hierarchies in terms of access to the highest paid skilled positions in metalworking in the district was paralleled by the way in which hierarchy stratified factory workforces. This was especially marked in terms of the persistence of the gendered stratification of workforces within and between factories. In the United Incandescent Lamp and Electrical Factory in 1952, approximately 55 percent of workers were women. "This proportion was not even across different workshops," cautioned the party committee, adding that "there are very few women in the machine and tool shops. . . . The vast majority of female workers are semiskilled machine operators."[198] In textiles, the opening of employment opportunities in other sectors interacted with hierarchy and gendered notions of appropriate work to reinforce the feminization of work across the sector. In the Magyar Pamutipar, by far the largest textile plant in the district, women made up 63.6 percent of the workforce in December 1950; by November 1952, they were 68.1 percent.[199]

Just as in the Danube Shoe Factory, hierarchies operated across light industry, even in the textile plants. This was most obvious in the way that gendered hierarchies infused the advantages that predominantly male maintenance staff had in bargaining around their norms compared to the semiskilled machine operators, most of whom were female, in both spinning and weaving shops. The relative autonomy of maintenance staff and management's dependence on them to maintain the pace of production when most machinery was old and broke down frequently gave them considerable countervailing power to bargain down their norms and secure higher earnings.[200] This route was not open to the female machine operators, who instead faced pressure to work harder and faster and had few means of resisting.[201] During the Congress Labor competition campaign in 1951, the machine operators protested that "it just isn't possible to maintain this tempo. . . . It's a miracle that the workers manage it."[202] Despite many workers' lack of countervailing power over their norms or their pace of work, hierarchy was far from irrelevant to bargaining in spinning and weaving shops. The multimachine movement was hegemonic, and, given the demands placed on management to mobilize the workers who operated most machines for frequent labor competition campaigns, they were able to guarantee for themselves those machines that were in the best working order, as well as the best supplies of raw materials. In the weaving shop of the Magyar Pamutipar in 1951, a gulf opened up between those working on eight machines at once and those operating sixteen, because the former received poor quality cotton that frequently broke, hampering their ability to earn. One young worker complained that "there are materials of variable quality. The good quality ones are taken by the 'good' workers. . . . It's easy to work well when you have good materials."[203] Hierarchies of generation and of urban-rural origin played a role in the definition of "good" workers, given the shortages of both smoothly functioning machinery and high-quality raw material. Rural commuters were often excluded from good positions in the factory. They responded by claiming to be sick so they could work on their family landholdings, which reinforced perceptions that they were poor workers. "It was clear to everybody," reported the Magyar Pamutipar's factory newspaper, "that as Rózsa Hamál's 'illness' didn't prevent her tending her beans at home, she could come into the factory to complete her work."[204] The young were placed on machines from which they could only produce scrap, and they responded by walking off the job, consequently finding themselves branded as "poor" workers.[205]

While machine operators in textiles had less countervailing power over their pace of work and earnings than did workers in other sectors, the combination of payment-by-results wages and discontinuous production led all workers, including the skilled elite in heavy engineering, to feel that they had to work harder for less reward. One young skilled worker in the Duclos Mining Machinery Factory complained that "one year after I started my job" in "the factory, . . . the norms, meaning the time to complete products, were reduced by 30 to 40 percent on . . . average." The sense of constantly having to work more for less, the housing crisis in the district, and the dire shortages of food and basic goods generated material frustration, which then assumed meanings that were increasingly politicized. In these circumstances, the attempts of the regime to use cold war rhetoric to mobilize workers proved counterproductive, as they began to make unfavorable comparisons between their own standards of living and the conditions they believed were enjoyed by workers in the West. The same Duclos worker remembered that "we discussed . . . that in America people have to work less and they still have a better life."[206] The growing perception of this difference was spread by the practice of listening to Hungarian-language radio broadcasts from sources such as the Voice of Free Hungary, which spread in industrial communities like Újpest during 1952 and early 1953.[207] With the death of Stalin and the turbulent events of spring 1953 in some of Hungary's immediate neighbors, the ways in which mounting material frustration became politicized threatened to erupt into open working-class rebellion against the regime. When the regime in East Berlin raised work norms across industry in June 1953, open popular protest spread across the German Democratic Republic, and news of these events had an electrifying effect on shop floors across Budapest.[208] The regime in Hungary, however, would defuse this particular crisis in the short term; however, it would do so in a way that exacerbated the deeper crisis of legitimacy for the regime and paved the way for the 1956 Revolution.

# 6    Dynamics of Reform and Retreat
### June 1953–February 1956

EVEN BEFORE THE explosion of popular protest across the German Democratic Republic in June 1953, Moscow was concerned about the climate of mounting tension across Central and Eastern Europe that followed the death of Stalin. Worried about the possible political impact of the worsening material crisis in Hungary, the post-Stalin Soviet leadership summoned the leaders of the Hungarian party to Moscow in mid-June to demand that Mátyás Rákosi relinquish some of the power that had been concentrated in his hands, that Imre Nagy, excluded from party leadership because of differences with Rákosi over the pace of collectivization, be made prime minister, and that pressure on living standards and repression both be relaxed to relieve political tension.[1] Following these demands, the MDP's Central Committee criticized the policies pursued since 1948, arguing that, over the previous five years, "a cliquelike leadership broke with the masses" and relied excessively on considerable repression against the population, leading to considerable injustice and a distorted economic policy.[2] Imre Nagy, as the new prime minister, announced the changes necessary to correct these "errors" to parliament and the Hungarian public at the beginning of July. Signaling a shift in economic and social policy, he proclaimed that "before the country we must say openly that the goals of the increased five-year plans were in many respects beyond our means, their realization placed too great a strain on our resources, they hindered increasing the material basis of our welfare; indeed, they caused a reduction in our standard of living in recent times."[3]

As this "New Course" was implemented, the government appeased workers' discontent by tacitly relaxing some of the more draconian measures taken to maintain "work discipline," and it boosted living standards through a dual strategy of reducing the prices of consumer goods and increasing wages.[4] The attempt of the regime to buy its way out of its crisis of legitimacy among industrial workers foundered on economic realities. The industrialization drive had created a series of relationships among enterprises that generated structural problems of shortage, which proved resistant to state attempts to redirect the economy. This was brought home as early as autumn 1953, when the long-term failure of the state to expand electrical generation capacity at the same rate as industrial production expanded combined with unseasonably cold weather to produce power outages and electricity rationing that persisted into 1954.[5] Furthermore, economic growth during the early 1950s was based on extensive mobilization of resources, including labor, while attempts to use that labor more intensively were frustrated, thus depressing the overall growth in labor productivity per worker in industry.[6] The relaxation of repression and concessions made in the workplace further reduced management control over labor, leading to an epidemic of turnover in 1954, while wage hikes raised the overall cost of production as workers pocketed wage increases and beat down their production norms.[7] As the state cut investment in high-priority heavy industrial projects to pay for its social measures, the economy stalled under the impact of these structural pressures. Even with the abandonment of key projects, the annual plan for 1954 was only fulfilled to 95.8 percent.[8]

The unraveling of the regime's project of socialist transformation during 1954 was profoundly alarming for many of those who held key positions within state institutions or at the heads of large enterprises and who had been promoted as a result of party activism from the shop floor at the end of the 1940s. Ambrus Borovszky, the director of the regime's flagship Stalin Steel Works, which faced huge cuts in investment as a consequence of the New Course, confronted Nagy at the opening of one division of the factory: "He explained that we don't need industry here, … but we are a peasant state, we need to live from the work of peasants."[9] Party officials in villages, who had often acted as the bulwark of an unpopular regime by implementing its agrarian policies, found aspects of the relaxation of the collectivization drive bewildering. As Nagy's government relaxed pressure on agricultural producers, especially members of agricultural cooperatives, it launched an uneven liberalization of the rules for leaving collectives—a step that produced a wave of attempts to depart, threatening their survival. Between 1953 and 1955, the proportion of land farmed by individual landholders rose from 42.9 to 48.5 percent, while that farmed by agricultural cooperatives fell from 33.7 to 23.7 percent.[10] Consequently, many party officials believed that their attempts to defend socialism locally were undermined by leaders nationally.[11] Furthermore, as pressure was relaxed on agricultural producers and surviving artisans and as shortages persisted, social differentiation grew between those who worked in the private sector and those who lived from wages. In both 1954 and 1955, the real incomes of individual landholders grew at a faster rate than those of industrial workers.[12] In Budapest in 1954, party officials were alarmed by the numbers of skilled workers who had gained artisans' permits and set up small workshops where their incomes were some three to four times higher than they had been receiving in the factories.[13]

The belief of much of the party apparatus that New Course policies threatened socialism allowed those in the leadership, especially Rákosi, who had never accepted his demotion in June 1953, to fight a rearguard action against Nagy. During 1954, creeping administrative restrictions chipped away at the concessions granted to individual smallholders, cooperative members who sought to leave, and industrial workers who moved from job to job. These restrictive measures gathered force, taking the form of an explicit political attack on Nagy; he was removed as prime minister and excluded from all party functions in April 1955 as punishment for pursuing a "right-wing, antiparty line."[14] The attack led to polarization within party ranks rather than any consolidation of Rákosi's authority. The freeing of large numbers of prisoners and internees after June 1953 highlighted the extraordinary degree of repression, the ubiquity of show trials, and the abuse of power in the internal security services during the early part of the decade.[15] Many intellectuals sympathetic to socialist transformation in the late 1940s had enjoyed the relative cultural freedom of the post-1953 period and were determined to criticize both the abuses of power by Rákosi and his allies and the widespread material misery. This group, and those sections of the party membership who sympathized with its members, were not prepared to tolerate any reversal of the measures announced by Nagy and became ever more vocal in their criticism of the leadership.[16]

The attempts of the new prime minister, András Hegedüs, to press ahead with a modified version of "socialist construction" confronted the continuing crisis of legitimacy of the regime. Given the temporary relaxation of pressure on both agrarian and industrial communities, the population was unprepared to tolerate any turn away from policies that improved living standards and threatened to reintroduce practices abandoned in June 1953. Therefore, the policy shift introduced in spring 1955 provoked a collapse in the authority of the regime that intensified open rebellion across the country. This was especially marked in agriculture, where the state attempted to reverse many of the concessions granted less than two years earlier and to renew collectivization. A year later, many cooperatives created since the dismissal of Nagy, often through the deployment of violence by the authorities against reluctant smallholders, were in a state of "collapse rather than at the stage of the beginning of collective labor."[17] Reactions to the new government's attempts to tighten its control over production and to increase productivity by raising norms and slashing wages were similar. They played a central role in igniting a climate of rebellion in factories and mines and at construction sites, setting the scene for the events of 1956 in industrial communities.[18]

Workers' reactions to New Course policies were complex. The regime failed to gain credit for the increases in living standards, for many workers believed that the changes were a product of fear of "a Revolution like that in the GDR" among the leadership in the summer of 1953. As real incomes increased—workers' real wages were 7.1 percent higher in 1955 than in 1949, more than making up for the decreases since 1950—the enormous hunger for material improvement after an extended period of privation sharpened rather than abated. Urban workers especially were profoundly resentful of the gains made by the agrarian population and those of their workmates who had access to land as a consequence of the New Course. This was in part because of visible and growing social differentiation, but it was also due to the fact that many workers did not feel they were benefiting from increasing prosperity. The situations of some groups of workers, especially those in cities with large families, remained desperate, while large numbers were still unable to afford basic items like clothes.[19] This was in part because of the ways in which the New Course reinforced informal control over remuneration at the point of production and the power of the hierarchies within the workforce upon which it rested. Consequently, the male skilled elite benefited disproportionately from the increases in wages, and while worker-peasants were able to compensate for their peripheral positions in the workplace because of the permissive climate toward agriculture, this was not true of other groups, like women and the young, whose peripheral positions were reinforced. Thus, the increases in living standards between 1953 and 1955 bought the regime some breathing space but did not solve the crisis of legitimacy in industrial communities. At the same time, growing and evident divisions within the elite, as well as generalized cynicism over a seemingly ever-changing political line, weakened the state's authority. This set the stage for the outright unraveling of its authority and an open crisis when it turned toward modified socialist industrialization during the second half of 1955.

Újpest's highly differentiated industrial workforce experienced the crystallization of hierarchy in its factories and the power of the skilled male elite on its shop floors. Considerable working-class discontent was driven by—and drove—a crisis in production that undermined support for central planning. All workers remained dissatisfied materially, and, as the state's authority crumbled in late 1955, skilled workers in particular envisaged an imminent end to socialist rule. In Zala's oil fields, which expanded as a result of the rapid growth of the Nagylengyel field and the opening of the Zalaegerszeg refinery, the attitudes of workers toward the regime were as much affected by the temporary reduction and then increase in tension in the rural communities that surrounded the drilling sites as they were a consequence of changes in agrarian policies. The worker-peasant workforce, focused on household needs and seeing labor in the oil fields as an imposition by an illegitimate regime, developed attitudes that were instrumental in getting them to work at the drilling sites but, in turn, undermined managerial authority. The relaxation of plan targets and large wage increases in the mines in Tatabánya brought relief to miners without solving the material problems of other workers or those on the peripheries of workforces in the pits. Furthermore, given a lack of employment opportunities for women and little access to incomes from agriculture, workers in the city saw themselves as losers from the process of social differentiation that the New Course introduced. Consequently, when the regime clamped down on wage increases in all of the city's workplaces—the mines included—these measures were greeted with outright fury.

## Privatization, Shortages, and Frustration in Tatabánya

The first sign of the New Course in Tatabánya was the opening up of a limited public space to discuss some of the sources of the material discontent that had built with the regime, after more than three years during which the state had resorted to repression to shut down all public discussion of the issue. In the Cement Factory, within ten days of the announcement of a new government program, the factory newspaper broke its silence to articulate discontent with poor working conditions in the plant. It demanded that management "fulfill the simple requests of the workers" for improvements and that nonmanual staff abandon their attitude of "indifference" toward the welfare of those who worked in manual positions in the plant.[20] In the mines, management, party, and union responded by reviving the procedures for negotiating working conditions and social policy in the enterprise-level collective agreement, a process largely ignored during the early 1950s. To this end, miners were invited to comment on the fulfillment of the collective agreement for the third quarter of 1953. Officials were consequently bombarded with a whole string of complaints. Drivers on the mine railway complained that, even with a skill, they still earned 87 *fillérs* less per hour than a semiskilled worker without equivalent training. In Pit No. XI, one worker argued that accidents were caused by the inadequacy of miners' lamps. Younger workers condemned those who ran workers' hostels, blaming them for the lack of running water and the poor conditions.[21]

The opportunities for expressing discontent continued to be controlled closely, and open expressions of political dissent were repressed. Despite the opening of space for criticism that had been entirely absent prior to summer 1953, miners distrusted the regime utterly. Among their complaints was that the implementation of the government "program" had no credibility.[22] This attitude was most pronounced among "new" workers who had arrived from rural areas. After Nagy's announcement that there would be more assistance to agriculture and that collectives could be disbanded, "miners of smallholder origin . . . went to the mine offices en masse, to demand their work-books, so they could go home to their land." The authorities sought to stem the tide of those who wished to leave by denying them permission—some responded by quitting without authorization. Other young workers "stayed at their hostels and stayed away from work for days" as a protest.[23] The cumulative impact of this protest, combined with the freeing of a significant number of the prisoners employed in the mines as a consequence of the government program, produced a major problem of labor turnover. In August and September 1953, 2,522 workers left the mines, compared with a total of 3,706 for the first seven months of the year, creating an absolute labor shortage that led to a deep-seated crisis in production.[24]

While mine managers complained that chaos in the mines was due to the government abolishing many of the penalties, especially the right to fine for work discipline infringements, the state solved the crisis temporarily by implementing wage increases at the end of 1953. It granted miners a 16 percent raise over their October wages, to go into effect 1 December; in Tatabánya, the average monthly wages of coal-face workers rose from 1,369 to 1,907 forints as a result of the measure.[25] Consequently, at the end of the year, the raised wages allowed the mines to recruit the labor necessary to reach the plan targets, but production costs exploded spectacularly, and output per worker fell.[26] The New Course saw large wage increases across the city, in the power plants, aluminum smelter, and the cement factory and quarry, as well as the construction sites, as national measures to increase real incomes were introduced.[27] Wage increases formed the basis of a shift in the way the regime presented itself and its policies. While, prior to June 1953, it had promoted Hungary's industrialization in order to secure the "construction of socialism," its emphasis over the autumn stressed increasing workers' welfare by bolstering consumption.[28] To strengthen this emphasis on a more consumerist socialism, the regime lowered the prices of eight hundred different consumer goods and introduced measures to improve supplies of bread, flour, and sugar.[29] In Tatabánya, the regime argued that its price reductions were a means of increasing the value of workers' wages, thus raising incentives to work and allowing miners to achieve levels of comfort of which they had previously only been able to dream. As a consequence, maintained the local newspaper, "carpets have arrived in the homes of our miners. But, so has furniture."[30]

Reactions to a more consumerist socialism among Tatabánya workers were complex. The shift in emphasis failed to deliver any positive support for the regime, largely because of the breach of trust that its policies since 1950 represented, plus the inability to deliver on its promises. But the change did represent a real shift from the previous climate of penury and plan-based mobilization. Furthermore, it addressed a popular hunger for material improvement, bolstering trends toward social privatization generated by popular experiences of the socialist economy that, in turn, underpinned the regime's retreat from policies of further social transformation. These trends were at their most visible in working-class attitudes toward the home and especially in the popularity of limited schemes that offered support for construction of private homes. The housing crisis in Tatabánya had been an explosive issue since the late 1940s, and it continued to bubble in the 1950s. In 1954, of the permanent population of the city, 4.4 percent lived in only one room; 62.4 percent lived in a flat consisting of only a single room and a kitchen. Only 52.7 percent of the city's flats and houses had running water, and a mere 8 percent had an inside toilet. Despite nearly five years of construction, the state's apartment construction program had had only a slight impact on conditions in the city by 1954; only 7.7 percent of the local housing stock had been constructed since the end of World War II.[31] Because of their focus on conditions for the city's permanent residents, these statistics were silent on conditions in the workers' hostels, where 30 percent of the mines' total workforce and half of young miners lived in 1953.[32]

As the New Course was announced, and the minority who had gained new flats struggled with life in the middle of a disorganized construction site, the local newspaper celebrated the beginnings of settlement in a new part of the city, the "garden suburb" (kértváros). Eleven houses with "red brick walls and new roofs" had been completed. They were privately owned family dwellings, and their new owner-occupiers expressed their gratitude to the socialist state for having been given the opportunity to own their own homes for the first time. One housewife told a newspaper that "we have been married eighteen years, but before the liberation we simply couldn't think that we would ever own our house. Before, the radio or new kitchen furniture was simply an unachievable goal for us. And now, I own my own house."[33] Tatabánya's private houses were part of a national scheme of subsidized construction opened only to coal miners in 1952 as part of the state's attempts to solve labor shortages. The program was conceived originally as a means of making life in mining towns attractive to those who had come from rural areas by allowing them villagelike family housing, and propaganda focused on the experiences of those residents who were recent migrants to Tatabánya.[34] Contrary to these expectations, however, it was the skilled male urban elite of the mines' workforce who were the most likely to take advantage of the scheme. Of the 434 manual workers who joined the scheme between 1952 and 1955, 313 were highly paid underground face workers, and only 72 "new" recruits to the mines signed up for their own houses.[35]

The reactions of workers, and of officials, at other workplaces demonstrated the appeal of private family housing to urban workers in the city as the garden suburb expanded. In the Cement Factory, ties of kin to miners meant that some workers in 1954 "had already built family houses with their sons. These comrades have already developed so many plans for themselves that the desire has awakened in [the rest of] us to have the same possibilities."[36] The interest the scheme generated among workers in the Bánhida Power Plant led managers to see advantages in allowing its own staff to participate. "The workers will better care for their own house" than for state property, they argued. Furthermore, "work discipline will be improved if the loan for building the house is linked to their workplace. The building of private houses therefore will create a stable workforce."[37] The popularity of the scheme and the demands for its extension were produced partly by the increase in incomes after June 1953 and by the desire for a comfortable home, given the persistence of the dire housing situation. The slow pace of construction of new flats for rent and the problems of poor quality construction and housing shortages for new residents in new Tatabánya also played a role.[38] Yet these factors, in themselves, do not explain this popularity sufficiently, for the garden suburb itself suffered from similar disorganization as a consequence of the operation of the economy. The first houses were built with such poor-quality material that "the roofs of almost all of the completed houses collapsed under the weight of the snow, because the roof frames were so weak."[39] As late as November 1953, the new houses had not been connected to either electricity or water supplies, thus requiring residents to use two wells, while in the absence of any paved road connecting the garden suburb to the rest of the town, drivers refused to take their buses to the suburb in rainy weather.[40]

Despite these problems, the popularity of private houses rested on the opportunity they offered for a degree of autonomy from the operation of the shortage economy. Each house came with a plot of land, which most miners sought to use for self-provisioning. A major complaint of new residents was that "no hen house or pig sty was built, and people had to build them afterward," for "if someone had their own house, they wanted to at least keep a couple of chickens and raise a pig."[41] Even propagandists celebrated the degree to which miners were able use their land for self-provisioning. The local newspaper commented that, in one garden, "potatoes, vegetables, and other things will be growing shortly" to feed the miner's family that lived in the house.[42] Among workers in the cement plant, it was hearing about the plans of homeowners to "conjure fruit from their gardens" that was one factor in fueling demands that the scheme be extended to them.[43] The misery many endured as a consequence of severe shortages of food and basic goods increased the attractiveness of self-provisioning, for it gave the residents a hedge against the unpredictability of deliveries to state stores across the city.[44] Despite measures taken to improve the supply of goods, deliveries of meat and fresh vegetables to state stores proved unreliable, sometimes forcing working-class customers to pay higher prices to buy direct from producers in the "free markets."[45]

The relaxation of state control over agricultural producers taking goods to market led to increases in the incomes of the wealthier among them, and these increases were greater than those of miners and other industrial workers—a phenomenon that both provoked deep-seated class resentment and legitimized the focus of workers on self-sufficiency, or shadow economic activity outside their main job. One visible sign of this was the way in which the cash incomes and consumption of commuters seemed to outstrip those of other workers. In 1954, clerks in the Tatabánya branch of the National Savings Bank (Országos Takarék Pénztár, or OTP) noticed that young worker-peasants became less dependent on their wages, which would be left in their accounts for months on end, as they lived from their families' agricultural activities. After a reasonable amount had been accumulated, it would be spent on consumer goods or on a luxury item such as a motorcycle.[46] The feeling among urban workers, many of whom were among the elite in mines and factories, that they were being left behind those who had supplementary incomes from outside their formal workplace was strengthened by the low ratio of wage earners to dependents in Tatabánya relative to the national average. This was due to the industrial structure of the city, in which there were fewer employment opportunities for women than in most other industrial communities.[47]

Although these processes strengthened an ideal of social privatization, they contributed to a sense of mounting frustration among most workers, who could not easily provide for themselves, participate in agriculture, or escape the dire housing situation in the city, which meant that the regime gained little credit for the increases in wage levels. Average workers' monthly wages in the Tatabánya mines, at 1,602 forints in 1955, were substantially higher than two years earlier, when they had been just 1,289 forints, while those in the cement works had risen from 967 to 1,147 forints over the same period.[48] The relief of absolute material poverty had changed the structure of consumption across the county of which Tatabánya was a part—in 1953 food made up 56.5 percent of all sales in the county's shops, a proportion that had fallen to 47 percent by the first quarter of 1955.[49] Despite this, there was anger that the incomes of other groups rose faster than those of urban workers, and frustration persisted at the disorganization of supply and the poor quality of many of the goods offered by the state sector. Consumers complained that there was no choice when it came to buying clothes, as distributors dumped endless runs of the same designs in identical colors in the state stores.[50] The city's furniture vendors received only a small proportion of what they had ordered from suppliers as a consequence of the disorganization of the economy. A typical complaint came from one miner's family: "We would like some kitchen furniture; we've been after it for months. If a couple of pieces turn up, they get snapped up in minutes. We're always too late."[51]

The sense that workers in the urban core, especially those employed in the mines, were losing out in terms of visible social differentiation was sharpened by the persistence of poor working conditions. Promises of improvements foundered on disorganized production and a casual lack of concern over safety, which led conditions to deteriorate in 1954. During the second quarter, there was one fatal accident each month in the mines, while a total of 1,922 workers were injured due to industrial accidents during the first half of the year.[52] Consequently, skilled miners believed that they were not valued as human beings by the regime, a situation that mirrored the one that had formed the basis for their radicalism against a different regime a decade previously. This sentiment was articulated in a conversation in one pit between a "new" worker from a village adjacent to the border with Austria and a skilled, urban miner in 1954. The "new" worker was asked where he came from; when his older workmate realized that he came from close to the border, he replied, "If I was in your place I wouldn't stay here for a minute; I'd go to the West, where at least you are valued for as long as you can work; here you are just treated like a dog to whom they occasionally throw a bone so you don't starve."[53]

While urban, older skilled miners were deeply cynical about the regime's post-1953 focus on improved living standards, New Course policies further strengthened their position relative to urban workers at other workplaces in the city. The mines' position in the local economy was strengthened by the impact of cuts in investment at the construction site to pay for wage increases elsewhere, forcing the construction management to "rationalize" and lay off workers during 1954.[54] This exacerbated problems of turnover among those who remained, as workers responded to the running down of their enterprises by quitting for higher paying jobs in the mines, returning to agriculture, or working in the burgeoning private construction sector, thus reinforcing the crisis of production at the construction site.[55] Manual employment at the county's state-run construction sites—of which by far the largest was Tatabánya's—stood at 2,489 in 1955, compared with the 3,665 that had been employed two years previously.[56] The cement works and aluminum smelter also recorded net job losses during the period; the power plants steadily increased their numbers of employees, while the employment of manual workers in the mines rose from 12,915 at the beginning of the New Course to 14,136 by 1955.[57]

Furthermore, the wage increases for miners served to reinforce prior practices of informal bargaining that reflected hierarchy, guaranteeing greater reward to those with the access to the best places to work at the face. Superficially, the December 1953 wage increases seemed to have increased the wages of low-paid surface workers relative to underground face workers.[58] All workers, however, were paid according to their performance, and the existence of percentage wage supplements for those underground meant that when they performed above their norm, their wages increased disproportionately. One senior manager in the Tatabánya mines explained: "If someone produced 20 percent more, because they wanted to earn . . . they actually got 40 percent more in wages."[59] While even weaker workers pocketed wage increases—one coal hewer who consistently performed below his norm saw his monthly wage rise from 1,565 forints in March 1953 to 2,014 by January 1954— high performers could increase their earnings spectacularly. Béla Prekob worked at the front as a hewer and was regarded as "a really good worker" by the trade union. Between March 1953 and January 1954, he increased his norm fulfillment rate modestly, from 114 to 130 percent. The effect on his monthly income was enormous—it rose from 1,822 to 3,297 forints.[60] Given the physical state of the mines—and despite the overall reductions in plan targets—good performance against the norm required continuous access to good places to work at the face, which could not be guaranteed to everyone. Where the physical state of the mine did not permit this, management often manipulated the norms it gave to its "key" workers in order to help them guarantee their earnings.[61]

Because of the increased differentiation of earnings, the stakes involved in successful informal bargaining were raised, increasing tension sharply. In one incident, a fight broke out between two coal hewers in January 1954 over access to a work site where the "technical conditions" for production "were present"; the incident resulted in the dismissal of one of two workers.[62] Hierarchy was used by "older" workers and their groups to justify preferential access to good work sites, while younger workers and those from rural areas complained that they were dumped in the worst spots, with no help or support.[63] Peripheral workers continued to protest by refusing to accept assignments where they felt they would be unable to make enough money; in some pits, management responded with an effective "lockout" of such workers. In December 1954, the director of Pit No. XII admitted to a policy of not allowing these workers into the mine for the next "two to three days."[64] This discontent produced a resurgence of labor turnover, as large numbers of "new" workers, especially those with connections to agriculture, quit the mines. Relaxation of state pressure on agriculture made this an attractive option, and during the second quarter of 1954, the numbers quitting reached 2,048, at a time when the mines took on only 1,471 new workers. This, in turn, produced an absolute labor shortage across the city's mines, which hindered efforts to fulfill the plan.[65] The reemergence of labor shortages, temporarily eliminated in the first weeks following the wage rise in December 1953, resulted in increasingly chaotic production from spring 1954. Because the highest wages were gained from work at the face and because there was a general shortage of workers, management neglected mine maintenance and transportation. The impact of this neglect led in turn to production stoppages at the face.[66]

Labor shortages were exacerbated by growing restrictions on the use of prison labor in the mines—a consequence of government policies that reduced the numbers of those imprisoned for political offenses. Government measures markedly reduced the numbers of forced laborers working in four pits in the city, including a number who had been given the opportunity to train as skilled workers during late 1953 and early 1954.[67] While the use of prisoners continued on a smaller scale and they were supplemented by military conscripts in the mines to alleviate the labor shortage, the situation deteriorated further. Attempts to control absenteeism and prevent workers from quitting proved ineffective.[68] The pressure on the mines to meet production targets without sufficient labor remained, despite the fact that the geological situation of the mines meant that extracting the coal was far from easy. To ensure production continued during the week, Sundays were reserved for "overtime" shifts, during which maintenance work was done. Every month, each worker took on average five shifts—or forty hours—above their normal contract of employment; by late 1954, many workers had not had "a day off work for months."[69] The consequence of this was that, even when adjusted for higher employment levels, the rate of industrial accidents in the mines was significantly higher in 1954 than it had been in 1938.[70]

Faced with its loss of control over production, falling productivity, and escalating wage costs, the regime was more concerned with the amount it was paying miners in wages than about the conditions in which they worked. The regime reformed the wage system in February 1955, anticipating the policy changes that would be implemented two months later, when Nagy was removed. The changes involved increasing the wage rates for preparation of the coal face and for some skilled maintenance work, while reducing those of the brigades that mined the coal. At the same time, management standardized norms, linking them closely to production targets, and introduced a layer of bureaucratic supervision for the approval of norms, to prevent them from becoming an object of bargaining at the point of production.[71] Planners estimated that the changes would lead to an average 5 percent cut in basic levels of pay, before the application of the underground workers' premium, for those who achieved results in production equivalent to those paid under the previous system. Given improved production—the trust fulfilled its plan by 103.1 percent in February 1955, the first month wages were paid according to the new system—preparatory and maintenance staff received small pay increases, while the average wages of all other groups fell slightly.[72]

The tightening of wage policy was not confined to the mines. With the Hegedüs government stressing modified "socialist construction" following Nagy's removal in April 1955, the state tightened production norms in other sectors as well, especially heavy engineering.[73] This meant wage cuts in some of the city's other factories, especially the Duclos Mining Machinery Factory, in order to curb wage growth during the spring and early summer. The responses of workers echoed their reaction to the larger norm increases of nearly five years previously, though they were much bolder this time, warning their union officials openly that "if their wages fall, they will not pay their union dues" as a protest.[74] The shift toward more policies of income restriction, while less radical than in 1950, was a highly dangerous step for the regime for several reasons. First, the New Course both stimulated aspirations for material improvement and heightened frustration with the failure of the state to deliver. Second, for a state that claimed to rule on behalf of workers, the New Course years saw an opening of visible social differentiation that many believed was to their detriment; at a time when many expected the state to improve the position of the urban working class relative to other groups, it attacked their incomes. Third, memories of the utter privation of the early 1950s were fresh, and, consequently, workers were not prepared to see a reversal of the all-too-limited material improvements they had seen since 1953. For these reasons, the shift of 1955 created an outright political crisis of authority for the regime. This was illustrated by events during the campaign to persuade workers to pledge a portion of their incomes to the state's annual peace loan campaign in autumn 1955. Across the city, miners made it clear that they would be prepared to pledge money to the campaign only if they were given opportunities to earn more money. Faced with a near unanimity of feeling, managers and party activists appeased miners, promising as many of them as they could better work sites. When it quickly became clear these promises could not be met, fury resulted.[75]

## Paying the Price of Political Illegitimacy in Southern Zala

The tightening of production norms that followed the end of the New Course in southern Zala in summer 1955 met with little open protest, but there was, however, widespread, fragmented, passive resistance. At the Nagylengyel drilling plant, the low-level frustration of production by workers angry at the impact of state wage policies on their incomes led one party official to comment that "wage changes have hit the workers, but that doesn't excuse the fact that they are not doing their jobs." So bad was the situation that he argued in favor of mass dismissals, for "we just can't put a supervisor alongside each and every one of them."[76] The frustration of management and party authority by low-level sabotage, undisciplined behavior, and neglect on the site was not a phenomenon peculiar to the post–April 1955 political climate. It reflected the way in which a worker-peasant workforce, deeply hostile to the socialist state, had developed a highly instrumental attitude to socialist labor in general and, more concretely, toward work at the oil wells. This instrumental relationship had crystallized in response to the relaxation of pressure on rural communities that followed the announcement of the New Course. While it had weakened the authority of the state and its representatives in southern Zala, it produced an enforced stalemate because what most local residents had hoped Imre Nagy's appointment heralded was the beginning of the end of socialism itself—a hope that had been frustrated, at least for the time being, by the end of summer 1953.

The announcement of the new government program lifted the lid on a well of expectations that the collapse of the socialist state was imminent, a situation that had been building since Stalin's death. The sense of mounting political crisis was sharpened by the dire food shortage in the oil fields—a situation that failed to improve throughout the summer, with workers at Lovászi complaining that they had not seen white bread in the local shops for months.[77] Nagy's announcement of policy changes encouraged those who had previously remained silent to hope that outright revolution was imminent. One argued that "the Soviet Union has recalled its ambassador, and at any moment power will change hands; they've already blown up factories in many places." Others called for more radical change than that promised by the government, making demands that they would have scarcely dared express before: "the new government's job is to break with the Soviet Union; up until now we've been like a sponge, and it's simply no longer possible to squeeze anything more out of us."[78] In the border villages, the rumor spread that "the party has been abolished."[79] While the amnesty granted by the new government to political prisoners did not allow many of those deported from the border regions during 1950 and 1952 to return home, relatives of the deported expected to see their loved ones back in their home villages. One farmer's wife believed the "radio had said that everyone interned would come back home, including those who had been deported, and [she] noted that among them were her daughter and son-in-law." A local kulak, Sándor Csiszár, argued that "the situation has turned . . . the deported will be able to come back, and they will be in charge again."[80]

The sense that revolutionary political change was imminent had the strongest effect on the border region's deeply unpopular agricultural cooperatives. In Kerkaszentkirály, members determined to dissolve their cooperative, arguing that they would have to give the land back to those who had been deported when they returned. Within days of the new government's announcement, in Miháld cooperative members held a mass meeting in which they decided they were "returning to farming individually." The expectations of radical political change led to abortive efforts among individual landholders to organize a tax strike and boycott compulsory deliveries, arguing that the "regulation" governing such matters "had been scrapped, and there would be a huge change soon."[81] Despite attempts by the authorities to stem the tide of those wishing to leave, during the second half of 1953, the proportion of Zala's agricultural land farmed by cooperatives fell from 19 to 14.4 percent, as members left to farm individually.[82] The crisis of authority of the state, as well as the pressures toward the collapse of socialist agriculture, eroded patterns of everyday consent within the labor process in the oil fields. The worker-peasant workforce expressed discontent with the working conditions within the plants and at the reluctance of local authorities to dissolve collectives and return agricultural land to them. Emboldened by the promise of relaxation, the workers' protest grew in a climate in which they believed that "now we can do what want, no one can punish us now!"[83]

The climate that dominated the week following the announcement of the new government program was one of generalized disorientation among the authorities in southern Zala, confronted as they were by a deep-seated legitimacy deficit. This slide in confidence was arrested by a speech Rákosi gave in Budapest on 11 July. In it, he specified the limits of the changes the party leadership envisaged: "we must challenge those who destroy discipline with undiminished vigor," while "we will not tolerate agitation against cooperatives, just as we will not tolerate agitation against our socialist construction."[84] This formed the basis of a gradual counterattack in which the party and security agencies in southern Zala deployed repression selectively against those among the population who were most radical in opposing the village-level political authority of the state. Given the deep-seated opposition to agricultural cooperatives, this pushback was insufficient to prevent the collapse of many of them; however, summer 1953 was characterized by a bitter struggle, with the party and the authorities on the one side and many cooperative members on the other, to stem the tide of those abandoning collective agriculture. As the party excluded those it believed were the "ringleaders" of agitation from cooperatives, those who attempted to organize their dissolution discreetly collected signatures for the necessary petitions, away from the eyes of the authorities.[85] These activities were accompanied by the firing of those oil drilling plant workers who were believed to be playing a central role in undermining "discipline"—especially when they could also be accused of "agitating" against cooperatives in their home villages.[86] While this repressive counterattack did dispel the illusion that the socialist regime was about to crumble from above, when combined with the promise of reform represented by Imre Nagy's original declaration, it generated confusion and tension. The reaction of István Gergó, a cooperative member in Kútfej next to the Lovászi plant, was indicative; he maintained that "we have been deceived, because they say first that we can leave the cooperative; then they say we can't." For others responding to the continuing situation of dire shortages in local shops, "they are making us promises in vain, because there isn't anything at all."[87] The simmering tension and resentment directed against the authorities, combined with the expectations generated by Nagy's reform program and generalized frustration, exploded sporadically during summer 1953. The worst explosion of tension occurred during a soccer match between Lovászi's plant team and that of the Zalaegerszeg branch of the border guard, part of the ÁVH, in early August. The match was tense, and, during the second half, an early lead taken by the border guard team was clawed black, and the oil workers took the lead. One of the border guard team players then scored a goal as the result of a clear hand ball. When the referee upheld the goal, the furious spectators invaded the pitch, physically attacking not only the referee but also the border guard team, shouting that the ÁVH were "all a bunch of scoundrels." As the violence escalated out of control, the match had to be abandoned fourteen minutes before the final whistle was to be blown.[88]

Tension between the population in general, oil workers in particular, and the ÁVH, which was the most obvious symbol of the repressive and illegitimate nature of the state, did not diminish over the period of the New Course but instead festered. The ongoing tension manifested itself in occasional confrontations between members of the ÁVH and the oil workers at Lovászi, which sometimes became violent. In the worst incident, in spring 1954, the plant's party secretary was badly beaten by ÁVH officers after the former intervened in a dispute between them and one of the plant's engineers while they were drinking in the drilling plant's club.[89] The

ÁVH was left relatively isolated by the climate of the New Course, for party organizations in the drilling plants responded to the new environment by balancing selective repression with a willingness to recognize their "errors." The Bázakerettye party organization maintained that, since 1948, it had achieved considerable results, but the price it had paid for its achievements was that "a really hard struggle had to be waged against the various enemy elements, the right-wing Social Democrats and members of the Dombay clique that appeared in our factory." This struggle had, the group argued, necessitated a centralization of power that had led to, in an appropriation of the language of national party decisions that criticized Rákosi, "a lack of collective leadership." This created a "cult of personality" around factory party leaders that had, in turn, generated abuses of power that enraged workers; one party committee member "demanded in the restaurant that they give him wine, on days when it was not available to the workers." The situation also created a climate, argued the party, in which workers' opinions were treated with a casual contempt by the authorities in the plant. This had led to the neglect of the "collective agreement" and deteriorating working conditions.[90]

While the "self-criticism" of the party at the drilling plants created a greater willingness on the part of the organization to respond to workers' criticisms, its economic measures left most oil workers, especially the landless, unimpressed. The factory party exhorted workers to increase production in autumn 1953 by arguing that "the living standards of the workers in our homeland as it builds socialism are increasing at an ever greater rate. . . . The fruits of well-performed work are making our lives ever happier." Thus, "plan fulfillment" in the future was the basis for a "further increase in our standard of living."[91] Oil workers were more than prepared to respond by maintaining that they had seen no improvement in their standard of living. When the state reduced prices of basic foodstuffs, bread again disappeared from the shops in the villages near the oil wells. The difficulties were not simply restricted to bread; "at miners' day at Bázakerettye the Zala County retail department showed that they really had smoked bacon and salami. But afterward, it vanished again, and if some does turn up (often just salami), there is so little that it runs out within hours."[92] To the persistent shortages of food were added complaints about low cash wages, poor facilities at work, housing shortages, and a lack of transport to workers' home villages.[93] Despite attempts to increase wages in late 1953, many workers, especially the landless, felt that their living conditions had improved little, if at all. Throughout 1954, workers at the drilling sites complained bitterly that no one in power was listening to their complaints.[94] As late as 1955, male skilled workers fitting the network of pipes that traversed the drilling sites complained that "they were always outside in the rain and the mud" but taking home only nine hundred forints per month—well below the industrial average—while the plant's female manual workers earned more.[95]

The complaints of the landless minority at the drilling sites reflected the ways in which the relaxation of the New Course years affected social differentiation both within and outside a predominantly rural workforce, most of whom had connections to agriculture. In the two years following Nagy's announcement, living standards across Zala rose substantially, as did overall consumption levels.[96] In a predominantly rural county like Zala, much of this increase in living standards was generated by the package of tax reductions and reductions in compulsory deliveries for the rural population, including members of agricultural cooperatives, that were phased in during late 1953 and early 1954.[97] These tax reductions brought relative differentiation among rural producers in that poorer smallholders and "the not inconsiderable number of members of cooperatives that do not work well" failed to benefit. This was because they produced for subsistence, so they could not "use favorable sales prices" for their produce to increase their cash incomes.[98] For most of the individual farmers in Felsőrajk, therefore, "the New Course led to a small increase in the purchasing power of the village population." The slow easing of economic problems meant that there were "many more" animals in the village "than before 1953" by 1955. Furthermore, it meant that "there was no significant improvement in clothing, but, once more, everyone again had clothes for special occasions."[99] The spread of industrial employment, which had been accepted as a matter of survival during the early 1950s, became a means of social improvement during the middle of the decade, as incomes from wages remained a significant proportion of total household income in rural communities. Nationally, by 1952, wages accounted for 10.9 percent of the total income of agricultural households, as a consequence of members of smallholders' families taking industrial jobs; despite the more favorable climate for agricultural production in the mid-1950s, this share did not decline in any significant way—it was 10.3 percent in 1954.[100]

Worker-peasants benefited visibly and disproportionately from both the reduction in agricultural taxation and the increases in wages, and they were thus able to play a central role in increasing consumption across the county. The extent of this new consumption was visible in the home loans made to prospective private house builders by the OTP across Zala during the first half of 1954. While 6.96 percent of these loans were made to individuals with senior positions in the local or state party bureaucracy, what was most noticeable was the range of manual, working-class occupations among most of the borrowers. In an overwhelmingly agrarian county, only 26.11 percent of borrowers were individual smallholders, cooperative members, or agricultural laborers, and a further 15.28 percent had a nonmanual occupation. Furthermore, the majority of workers borrowing were rural; only 19.1 percent of borrowers lived in Nagykanizsa or Zalaegerszeg, the two largest area towns, and, among those, white-collar house builders were disproportionately represented. Of all Zala's home loans, 19.75 percent were given to oil workers, and 83.88 percent of these were rural, worker-peasant commuters.[101] The favorable position of worker-peasants relative to the landless was visible in relations toward official consumption. The landless were overly dependent for their food on a network of state stores, of which there were very few in the villages surrounding the oil plants. Those that did exist often had poor supplies, as the local authorities directed food to the stores in the county's large towns.[102] At the same time, worker-peasants were often able to provide for themselves from smallholdings, thus mitigating their dependence on state-run commerce for food. Given the gradual increase in housing construction and the desire for the modernization of the existing housing stock in villages, made possible by the rise in worker-peasant living standards, demand for a range of goods, from ovens to electrical wiring, nails, and simple tools, formed much of the basis for overall growth in sales in state shops between 1953 and 1955.[103]

Such goods were frequently in short supply in local shops—a fact that provided the material background to an epidemic of workplace theft in the county's industrial enterprises—including its oil plants—in 1954 and 1955. This wave of petty crime was revealing of the markedly instrumental attitudes that those from agricultural households had toward the socialist enterprises that employed them. At Bázakerettye, an epidemic of theft across the site in September 1954 in which "valuable materials disappear from the" pipe fitters' "workshop and its neighborhood" had led the party to ask the ÁVH to watch everyone, both those working on the night shift and those approaching the area of the shop after dark. Frequently, the material that disappeared was copper pipe, in high demand in neighboring villages.[104] Metal of all kinds and tools disappeared; in November 1954, supplies of copper plate vanished from Zalaegerszeg's oil refinery and asphalt factory, and officials believed the stolen materials would eventually make their way out of the factory gate to be used in a burgeoning rural shadow economy.[105] Sometimes workers were caught in the act of stealing; at Lovászi in late spring 1955, twelve bags of cement vanished, of which six were found in the possession of one rural worker.[106]

The growing importance of the shadow economy formed only part of the explanation for the attitudes of worker-peasants toward socialist labor, as theft was only one of the most extreme ways in which it was manifested. Labor in industry was embedded in strategies that supported the household economy. Furthermore, it was associated with the attacks on hegemonic rural mentalities that the collectivization campaigns represented and, politically, with an illegitimate regime. All of these factors combined to shape the attitudes toward labor at the drilling sites. Industrial work was seen as firmly subordinate to household needs, an imposition dictated by necessity rather than a means of material advancement welcomed by workers themselves. In the Zalaegerszeg Oil Refinery, worker-peasants demanded long periods of unpaid leave because they wanted "to build a house," and they expected to receive it. Managers often complained that worker-peasants limited their output in the factory in order to conserve energy for work in the home after the end of their shift. Often these management complaints were expressed pejoratively as they "sleep at night" on the job "because they are working in the day at home and by the time they get to the factory are tired out, and they want to recover by relaxing in the factory."[107] The actual limiting of output by worker-peasants was often only slightly less blatant; at Nagylengyel, such workers were often accused of leaving work early and telling their supervisors that "today we have already done enough."[108] At the same time, worker-peasants considered themselves entitled to a given wage level and responded furiously when they failed to receive expected wages. In appeasing this fury, lower-level management at places like Nagylengyel, which had an almost entirely new, rural workforce, disregarded official systems of payment almost entirely. This crude form of informal bargaining, conditioned by the attitudes of a worker-peasant workforce, created a situation in which wages rose relentlessly, and to a greater extent than did production.[109]

Much of the bargaining power that worker-peasants were able to exert lay in the material realities of production. The amount of oil mined at Nagylengyel continued to rise, but the expanding production was hampered by persistent shortages of equipment, spare parts, and raw materials because of the general disorganization of the economy. Discontinuous production led company management to maintain a labor reserve, which could be mobilized when equipment arrived or was in working order. This practice in turn led to labor shortages at moments of peak production, during which management paid progressive bonuses to oil workers, which then led to sharp increases in wage expenditure that were not proportionate to the amount of oil produced.[110] At the other two drilling enterprises, at Bázakerettye and Lovászi, in contrast to the new site at Nagylengyel, total oil production fell sharply in 1954 and 1955. Similar pressures generated by disorganized production and labor shortage led to a situation in which, as production fell, expenditure on wages increased.[111] Just as at Nagylengyel, the New Course years witnessed the crystallization of an instrumental attitude among largely worker-peasant workforces toward socialist industrial employment connected to an outright loss in managerial authority at the point of production. By early 1954 at Bázakerettye, the members of brigades had developed an elaborate informal system of shift swapping in order to assist workers who wished to work on their household plot or smallholding—a system that simply bypassed the bureaucratic requirement of management approval. Those responsible for setting norms were frequently assaulted physically by workers who sought to maintain their job rates. When faced with the threat of management sanction, they responded by quitting. Foremen found themselves having to negotiate production on a day-by-day basis with a workforce that simply refused to accept the legitimacy or authority of the factory management.[112]

While in Tatabánya the growing social differentiation of the New Course era played a role in fueling frustration among urban miners with a lack of real improvement, in southern Zala, the hopes awakened by Nagy's announcement of an imminent end to the dictatorship and its agrarian policies never materialized. Although the living standards of worker-peasant households improved, a tense stalemate emerged as workers developed highly instrumental attitudes toward socialist labor. While the rearguard action of the party and security agencies had prevented the open collapse of the regime in 1953, the superficial impression of social peace concealed deeper tensions, the consequences of which, for the regime in Budapest, were visible only in falling labor productivity in the oil fields. Likewise, the shift in policy that followed Nagy's replacement by Hegedüs in April 1955 produced no open explosion but strained the tense stalemate of the New Course years toward the breaking point. The most immediate effect of the change was felt in the regime's attempts to renew its collectivization campaigns and in a revival of its drive against the presence of *kétlaki* at the drilling sites. Party organizations in the oil fields proposed to "explain to those workers" with land "that it is only large-scale agriculture that can . . . meet the increased demands of socialist industry."[113] Its drives against worker-peasants in the oil fields were dovetailed with a collectivization drive that rested on little other than intimidation and violence against local smallholders. This effort met with considerable passive resistance, stimulated by the fact that it was conducted by a state whose authority was crumbling. Consequently, its campaigns failed to undermine the dual worker-peasant existence but did generate enormous tensions, which surfaced only as the regime crumbled during 1956.[114] The attempts of the state to raise productivity levels and reduce wage costs by abolishing piecework in August 1955 for workers in the brigades that produced oil directly and tying wages explicitly to a premium that depended on plan fulfillment had similar effects. These measures provoked sporadic protests, particularly as the new payment policies coincided with the 1955 peace loan campaigns. Although quiet was restored, these sporadic outbursts of protest were especially prevalent among worker-peasants, who refused to see why they should pledge money against both their agricultural and industrial incomes when one was being hit through renewed collectivization drives and the other through norm revision. Such protest was a sign of the way in which the policies of the Hegedüs government were increasing political tension in southern Zala.[115]

## Blocked Reform and Crumbling Authority in Újpest

In mid-June 1955, when factory management announced that the centrally mandated revision of the norms would soon be implemented in the United Incandescent Lamp and Electrical Factory, it provoked a storm of protest. Workers asserted that "continuous work was not guaranteed for them, and that therefore they don't earn enough, but after the norm revision—precisely because continuous work is not guaranteed—they will earn even less."[116] Factory-level reactions anticipated the mounting political crisis. Many in the plant noticed that, with the signing of the Austrian State Treaty, the country's neutrality was guaranteed and the Red Army had to leave the country, something the plant workers believed signaled imminent political change in Hungary. Dezső Mekis, one of the norm setters who faced daily expressions of anger over the revision of the production targets, was dismissed for telling workers that their wage reductions were only temporary, for events on the other side of the western border signaled that, "in Hungary, elections will be held under United Nations supervision, and we will then be able to have a policy of neutrality like Austria."[117] The impression, however, that the world beyond Hungary's borders was changing contrasted with the everyday experience of factory life in which the centrally determined 1955 campaign represented merely an acceleration of trends already visible to workers for a year.

During summer 1954, after a year of wage increases across the factory, its parent ministry, responsible for steel and machine manufacture, demanded that management reduce production costs and tighten control over the poor quality of output. In response, management introduced into two shops a system of work norms and wages that were differentiated according to the overall quality of output and were established on the basis of "scientific" principles. As the new systems were brought in, average hourly wages fell by 2 percent in the affected shops, as they rose by a similar amount across the whole enterprise.[118] As managers attempted to roll out a wage system based on the new principles throughout the factory during the autumn, they introduced norm revision by stealth, forbidding "general revisions of the norms" and demanding instead that shop managers target "ostentatiously lax norms," while "strictly implementing the rules on the recording of scrap."[119] The concern with quality was even less new elsewhere in Újpest, which had an economic structure more diversified than that of Tatabánya and southern Zala, where the economy depended largely on mining and the production of energy. This new system of production control preceded the announcement of the New Course, for the declining quality of finished products and the accumulation of scrap had reached crisis proportions by early 1953. So poor was the quality of production for export that foreign buyers returned more than 30 percent of goods purchased; indeed, an incredible 45 percent of shoes for export were rejected, severely affecting Hungary's foreign earnings and increasing its debt burden.[120]

The consumerist conception of socialism implicit in the New Course was also used to place exceptional stress on the overall quality of production, and it allowed for public discussion of the shortcomings of the produce of socialist enterprises. The United Incandescent Lamp and Electrical Factory was held to account in March 1954 by a presenter on Hungarian Radio who had bought a 40-watt lightbulb that had blown within seconds of his lamp being switched on. Speaking on the air in the "name of the customers," he accused someone "of taking from my pocket 10 forints and 90 fillérs, which I worked for. I do not know who the guilty person was. I ask the bulb in vain, it lies dead in my trash can and it is what it is: dead, but it could have lived for another year. It could have lit up in the evening, but it doesn't; it was made so that it didn't create light, only anger."[121] In Újpest's State Department Store, those responsible for selling shoes were deluged with complaints. One shop assistant recorded an incident in which a "customer asked for children's shoes, but said she didn't want any from the Danube Shoe Factory." When asked why, the customer replied "because I know how bad they are." When asked where she worked, "it emerged that it was in the Danube Shoe Factory, perhaps even on line number 301, and probably she is the person producing useless shoes, and that is how she knows how bad they are."[122] The assumption that poor quality could be traced to individual workers was embedded in policy makers' responses to the problem, so they attempted to make each worker financially accountable for the quality of their individual production. In the Danube Shoe Factory, while workers in shops with persistently poor production had been subject to small shop-wide wage penalties since 1952, the introduction of the New Course coincided with the attempt to make workers directly accountable for the quality of their production through their wages. All work was divided into three categories, the first being work that met all of the requirements in terms of quality and for which a worker would receive full pay. For second-category work, they would only receive 85 percent of the regular rate, and for third-category work, only 75 percent. This was combined with incentives for all workers in a shop by means of a premium that all workers would receive if the shop met quality targets.[123]

Attempts to improve the quality of production by making workers individually accountable for their output through the wage system were fatally flawed and met with huge resistance. In the Danube Shoe Factory, skilled workers responded to the introduction of the quality-based wage system by quitting because "the piece rates we pay are just not acceptable," forcing management in turn to relax norms in order to retain workers.[124] While problems of quality were related to the responses of some workers to payment systems in factories, they were also closely linked to the impact of the operation of the economy on the labor process, especially of the production rhythms encouraged by the impact of economic planning on shop floors and their interaction with shortages and infrequent deliveries. The strains that had arisen in factories during 1952 and early 1953 reached crisis proportions during the latter half of 1953, especially in light industrial sectors, as a consequence of those sectors' peripheral position relative to the planning apparatus and because of interenterprise bargaining. As the crisis in coal production resulted in a lack of coal and the crisis of electricity generation triggered constant power cuts, the resulting shortages of energy severely disrupted industrial production in Újpest during autumn 1953 and winter 1954. Outages, as well as rationing of electricity, severely restricted regular production.[125] Raw material supply was also in crisis; by the end of 1953, the Danube Shoe Factory could be guaranteed only three-quarters of the leather necessary to meet its plan targets.[126]

In addition to generating further chaos in production, the New Course created a climate in which workers were quick to respond to fluctuations in earnings by simply quitting. This response was a product of the interaction of several factors. First, the raising of expectations followed by the frustration of those expectations, just as had occurred in Tatabánya, generated huge anger. The principal difference between Újpest and the mining town was that, in the former, workers' expectations were frustrated almost as quickly as they were raised. Within factories this was a product of the rapidly growing chaos in production. It was also exacerbated, however, by the failure of the authorities to address local demands adequately in so far as they related to consumption. The announcement of the government program had led to the expression of some open discontent, especially over collectivization among rural workers but more generally over a lack of political democracy. Within days, under the impact of selective repression, the open expression of such discontent had subsided, to be replaced with a sense of expectation: "We will happily continue to work, if everything that Imre Nagy has promised is delivered."[127] By the time the government introduced its price cuts, workers were disappointed, complaining that the goods most important to them, like fat and flour, had not been included in the process. Low-paid workers in light industry complained that price cuts ignored them and favored other workers because "only the prices of the more expensive goods have fallen."[128]

Generalized discontent interacted with the greater countervailing power given by the New Course to some workers to shape a dynamic of labor mobility. This was especially marked among Újpest's worker-peasants, who benefited disproportionately from the increase in agricultural incomes.[129] In contrast to southern Zala, where opportunities to benefit from the greater ability to sell produce were limited, most of Újpest's worker-peasants commuted from Pest County, where much agriculture had long been oriented to supplying the markets of Budapest's outer industrial districts.[130] Within such villages, the relaxation of controls in 1953 provided opportunities for both farmers and local craftsmen, ensuring that collective agriculture was restricted to "those who had nothing," "widows," and those "who didn't have either a horse or a cow."[131] Given this environment, which was exacerbated by the strains of commuting on overcrowded, uncomfortable, and unreliable public transport, many from worker-peasant households who took jobs in industry during the early 1950s actively sought to return to agriculture.[132] One typical example was László Kibik, who worked in the boiler room at the HPS. He left his job "without permission" in July 1953, in the wake of the new government program. When challenged as to why, he explained that "his father has 15 holds of land, and he wants to help him with the harvest." Management commented acerbically that he "had worked for two years at the enterprise and had not taken leave during the harvest period in either year."[133]

The relaxation of pressure on private commerce and industry created a similar environment that increased the countervailing power of many skilled workers. With the announcement of the government program, skilled workers in the Tánsics

Leather Factory saw "leaving factory work, to go and get a trade permit," as an option more attractive than working in a socialist enterprise.[134] While the legal private sector had been decimated by radical nationalization, a culture of suppressed private economic activity had persisted through the early 1950s among some groups of skilled workers. Artisans who survived nationalization and faced discrimination in access to raw materials subcontracted jobs to skilled workers, who fulfilled the contracts by moonlighting and used factory facilities and equipment in doing so. In the early hours of 17 June 1951, the United Incandescent Lamp and Electrical Factory's security staff interrupted one foreman, seven mechanics, two painters, a fitter, a carpenter, and two unskilled workers using factory materials and machinery to complete "private" work for one local entrepreneur.[135] Other former artisans took skilled positions in the state sector while maintaining private and illegal economic activities within the bounds of their households. One skilled worker in the Danube Shoe Factory supported his wife's business of making watch straps, which at first operated legally but continued even after the state revoked her license. He "worked in the factory from 6 a.m. to 2:30 p.m. then came home, took . . . dinner and sat down to cut 10 to 12 watch" straps. He stated that "they were sewn together by my wife on the same night and next day she delivered them to the different storekeepers."[136] The relaxation of control in 1953 drove sharp increases in the number of artisans, as many skilled workers left state-run industry; the number of artisans nationally stood at 48,300 in March 1953, on the eve of the New Course, and had risen to 78,745 by the end of 1954.[137] The pull created by the relaxation of pressure on the private sector drew skilled workers from plants like the Danube Shoe Factory, which had sucked labor from small-scale industry as it had been nationalized. Management complained that "there are countless examples of outstanding skilled workers, even in some cases Stakhanovites, who are quitting without authorization or behaving in an undisciplined manner, in order to leave the enterprise for small-scale industry, or a cooperative, or a new trade."[138]

The expansion of the private sector was only one factor shaping the reactions of skilled workers. In turn, together with other factors, that expansion gave labor mobility a specific intersectoral dynamic.[139] The differential pay rates between sectors had affected the composition of factory workforces in the early 1950s; this was exacerbated under New Course conditions. The pull of higher wages in other sectors, as well as "easier work" in factories like the Chinoin and the United Incandescent Lamp and Electrical Factory, caused particular problems for Újpest's light industrial plants, especially its large textile factories.[140] While the departure of skilled workers formed part of the context of a labor shortage crisis in light industrial enterprises across the district, it was especially pronounced among the large numbers of semiskilled workers who made up the bulk of those working in these sectors. Light industrial plants, and especially textile plants, had coped with their problems of labor turnover prior to June 1953 by recruiting women from rural areas to take jobs as machine operators. Although official propaganda celebrated their incorporation into the labor force as a sign of the upward social mobility brought about by socialist industrialization, this rhetoric concealed the bleak realities of life on the industrial fringes of the capital for young women of rural origin. In the Magyar Pamutipar, "many girls live as room renters—there are many trainees among them who earn 400 to 450 forints a month and have to pay 200 forints for their room, or just for a bed. Lots of them say that they will leave the enterprise and go home."[141] While younger machine operators from rural areas were at the very bottom of hierarchies in Újpest's textile plants, discontent with working and living conditions among all semiskilled workers was marked. Urban workers too suffered from dire housing conditions and complained that "there are many married couples who have lived for years as room renters and have applied many times to the council," while new flats went to "military, state and party officials."[142] At the same time, low-paid workers believed their incomes were being squeezed by high prices; urban workers demanded to know "why peasants can buy pianos, motorcycles, and other goods that cost a lot of money."[143] Discontent and poor living conditions drove not only labor mobility but also a search for supplementary incomes, thus fueling absenteeism. One machine operator frequently skipped work to "go to the countryside, as her 'new occupation' is to trade fat and red paprika."[144]

These factors exacerbated endemic labor shortages across light industry, and these problems reached crisis proportions during 1954. In the weaving shops of the HPS, 16 percent of all of the machines stood idle by June 1954 because of a lack of workers to operate them. This situation had progressively worsened; in January, only 150 machines were left unattended on any one of the three shifts, but by June the number stood at 333.[145] In attempting to cope with the consequences of labor shortages, management had become locked in a vicious circle. Requests for paid holidays were refused, while management instructed workers to operate an ever larger number of machines simultaneously, creating a situation in which many worked close to the limits of their physical capacity.[146] High-intensity work combined with the inexperience of the workers who could be recruited exacerbated the problems with the quality of finished production, while discontent manifested itself in what party activists termed "carelessness" and an "absence of a sense of responsibility" in work.[147] Working conditions remained poor. The dust, heat, and noise in the machine shops of the Magyar Pamutipar lay behind a significant problem of absenteeism due to sickness and the failure of "new" workers to become accustomed to factory life.[148] All of these factors in turn interacted to reproduce the problems of labor mobility, as workers, faced with ever deteriorating working conditions and higher work intensity, quit their jobs.[149] This vicious circle, reproduced in other light industrial sectors, lay behind the futility of attempting to raise the quality of production through a reliance on quality-related, performance-based payment systems, as workers responded to being made financially accountable for what they saw as problems not of their making by complaining and/or quitting.[150]

Despite their ineffectiveness, quality-based payment systems rested on a discourse that sought to explain the poor quality of much production by pointing to a general decline in the quality of labor. In his speech to the third congress of the MDP in May 1954, Ernő Gerő proclaimed, "In earlier times numerous products of Hungarian industry were famous worldwide due to their excellent quality. Hungarian turners, Hungarian fitters, cabinet makers, and any number of other specialists were famous in many countries." After implicitly drawing conclusions about the links between the quality of labor prior to the advent of socialism and the quality of their products, he told the congress that "we have to achieve a state where the products of our industry are more beautiful, better, longer-lasting, and cheaper than the products of capitalist Hungary."[151] While Gerő drew the link implicitly, Újpest's factory press was much less subtle. The Danube Shoe Factory's newspaper argued in 1953 that "for a long time now there has been an error in quality work. We have not produced shoes of sufficient quality either for export or for the home market, which would allow us to be proud of our factory's products." The key to turning this situation around, it maintained, lay in "good and class-conscious workers, who by complying with social supervision help in the creation of good quality."[152] Yet, in addition to the question of "class consciousness" in production, there lay differences in skill level; in assessing the poor response of maintenance staff to machine breakdown in the plant, the factory newspaper noted that "maintenance staff are not equal, they do not all have the same command of their skill."[153] In the United Incandescent Lamp and Electrical Factory in October 1954, when seventy cogs had to be classified as "scrap," the factory press blamed a "recently qualified young skilled worker" and his inexperience for the debacle.[154]

The growing use of such arguments by representatives of the state extended a space in which the arguments deployed by the older, male elite of skilled workers, especially in elite sectors such as heavy engineering, were given a legitimacy that they had not received prior to 1953. Younger skilled workers increasingly faced open discrimination that was embedded in the official practices of management. In the Duclos Mining Machinery Factory, one such worker regarded the attention quality inspectors paid to the output of younger, less-experienced workers as a means by which management created "additional unpaid work in the piece-rate system."[155] In the United Incandescent Lamp and Electrical Factory, in 1954, management introduced a system by which "workers with an insufficient command of their skill" were identified by their foremen. When they were due to work on the afternoon shift, such workers had to report for compulsory "theoretical training" that preceded the beginning of the shift.[156] Formalized patterns of discrimination helped to crystallize reproduced hierarchies of generation and skill in the town's heavy engineering plants. Labor shortages and workers' discontent, though less pronounced in the heavy industry than in local light industry, combined with the chaos that dominated production to drive an erosion of managerial control over remuneration. The factory party secretary in the Duclos plant conceded in 1955 that "we have allowed the illegal relaxation of norms; furthermore, we have ourselves backed promises to change the norms."[157] This strengthened the ability of groups of "key" workers—normally, older, more skilled workers—to secure an expected rate of pay from foremen and lower-level management. The United Incandescent Lamp and Electrical Factory's toolmakers sat at the apex of relations of hierarchy among workers in the factory. Even after the state-backed attempts to restore managerial authority in the plant in summer 1955, they had extended and preserved a considerable degree of informal power over their pace of work and remuneration. "The workers," complained one official, "choose their work, they don't want to take on work outside what they are used to. . . . They won't do work in the lowest wage categories."[158] Younger skilled workers were unable to choose the nature of their work or to bargain their norms down or their rates of pay up. In the Duclos Mining Machinery Factory in 1954, many younger skilled workers believed that "only category six work was good work and the only good norm was one that could be overfulfilled by 170 percent." Consequently, when faced with higher production norms, younger workers responded by producing "an endless amount of scrap."[159]

While everyday relations in the factories during the mid-1950s allowed hierarchies that had been reproduced during the early part of the decade to crystallize, production was increasingly immune either to the attempts of the state to control it or to managerial authority. By the end of 1955, despite the shift in economic policy earlier that year, the cumulative effect of chaotic production and the failure of Hungarian industry to deliver promised exports had led to an accumulation of state debt that in turn forced the authorities to reduce their imports of raw materials, provoking an even deeper crisis in production.[160] Just as the mounting crisis led economic planners and the reemerging discipline of economics to blame the overcentralization of the planning system and the lack of enterprise autonomy, those working in enterprises blamed the structures of economic planning and mismanagement for their poor performance. Even the Budapest Party Committee admitted in 1954 that the United Incandescent Lamp and Electrical Factory, a world market leader during the 1930s, had "fallen behind the most developed industrial countries" in terms of its "development and its product range."[161] The plant's employees were blunter: "In the years before the war the United Incandescent Lamp and Electrical Factory . . . was the only plant in Hungary that could compete with the Americans. . . . As a consequence of socialist reorganization . . . the quality of its products fell, just like those of the other reorganized enterprises."[162] The perception of many skilled workers that their role in production had been devalued by the centralization and bureaucracy that characterized planning shaped a working-class version of this critique. This view lay behind the incredulity expressed by many workers by the end of 1955 at news of Hungary's "growing foreign indebtedness," and it led many to be more openly critical of the party. The frustration with persistently poor standards of living led skilled workers to call for more independent organs to represent their interests within the plant. They often attempted to situate the local trade union organization in opposition to the party. Skilled workers encouraged the trade union to become independent of the party and to oppose factory management more directly. One argued that "the trade union was only thing that represented the interests of the working people; where there have been results since 1945, they have only been thanks to the trade union."[163]

The willingness of many of the skilled male elite to blame the bureaucratic control of production for the poor performance of the economy, combined with their submerged demands for a more formal structure for representing their interests at the factory level, anticipated the climate that allowed for the creation of workers' councils during the 1956 Revolution, less than a year away. At the same time, signs of the crumbling political authority of the regime were already visible during 1955 on Újpest's shop floors, especially in those workplaces where the male skilled elite were predominant. While the government in Budapest attempted to turn toward a policy of increased economic and political restriction during the second half of 1955, the signs of thaw in the outside world did not go unnoticed, a phenomenon stimulated by the popularity of listening to foreign radio broadcasts. By the turn of 1956, in the United Incandescent Lamp and Electrical Factory "the news broadcast by Radio Free Europe, the BBC, and the Voice of America was the most important daily topic of conversation in the factory."[164] Workers believed that the re-arming of Germany and the Austrian State Treaty proved that "the Soviet Union pursued a policy of concessions, and the only reason for this is that the United States is in a position of strength."[165] From this belief grew the hope that the changing balance of power internationally would create the conditions for domestic political change; in Újpest, many workers "believed in" the rumor of "an apparent agreement between [Soviet leader Nikita] Khrushchev and [British prime minister Anthony] Eden to turn Hungary into a neutral and independent state, on the Austrian model."[166] The prevalence of such views at the end of December 1955 anticipated the outright revolution that would occur ten months later. The climate that had given rise to them—persistent discontent, a deepening economic crisis, a regime intent on renewed restriction after a brief period of ineffective reform, and the thawing of the international climate—provided the stage on which the drama of 1956 was enacted. It was, however, unexpected events in Moscow in February 1956 that provided the spark that ignited the crisis which engulfed the Hungarian regime.

# 7

# The Process of Revolution
## February–November 1956

WHEN THE TEXT of Nikita Khrushchev's denunciation of Stalin's "crimes" to a closed session of the Twentieth Congress of the Communist Party of the Soviet Union in February 1956 was leaked to the world's press within days, Western radio stations broadcast the news directly to the Hungarian public. Given Mátyás Rákosi's self-presentation as "Stalin's best pupil," the disquiet about Hungary's own political trials after Nagy instituted partial amnesties, the ideological chasm that had opened in the party, and the already crumbling authority of the regime, the news of the speech and its content initiated the collapse of the regime from above. At first, the panic-stricken party attempted to deny that the speech had been made; the party was forced to retract the denial. Its impact on the MDP was dramatic. Party members demanded answers from their leaders during mass meetings held to discuss Khrushchev's speech and its implications: "Stalin led the party for thirty years, how can it be that his mistakes have been discovered now?" "What is the current situation in Hungary with the cult of personality? Was Rajk wrong?" "I own a copy of Stalin's complete works and have read them all. What do I do with them now?"[1] More dramatically, it gave a powerful sanction to the stubborn criticism of

Rákosi within the party and among its intellectuals—especially writers and journalists—who were unreconciled to the reversal of the New Course that had taken place in April 1955.

At the same time, the international context undermined the authority of Rákosi and his allies. The successful negotiation of the Austrian State Treaty and the consequent withdrawal of Soviet troops from the eastern part of the country awakened hopes that similar concessions could, in the right circumstances, be wrenched from Moscow by Hungary. The shifts in Soviet policy brought a reconciliation between Moscow and Belgrade, one that had explosive political consequences for Budapest. Many of Rákosi's opponents within the MDP saw in Yugoslavia a model of a more democratic form of socialism. Furthermore, the process of reconciliation undermined Rákosi, not only because of Tito's distrust of the Hungarian leader but also because it reopened the issue of the trial of László Rajk, executed after a show trial six and a half years previously for allegedly conspiring with Belgrade and the West to destroy the socialist order.[2] At the same time, Hungary was not the only country within the Soviet bloc that was characterized by a severe ongoing crisis of legitimacy. The drama of de-Stalinization in Poland was the most visible manifestation of crisis across the region. When, in June 1956, a protest over wages in Poznań turned into violent rebellion against the state and it was brutally crushed by troops, many in Hungary, despite the distorted reports in official media, drew parallels between their situation and that of Poland.[3]

By the beginning of summer, the interaction of these factors had produced a situation in which a regime bereft of authority clung to power in the face of widespread popular dissent. Intellectual demands for outright democratization were now publicly expressed in the context of debates within the Petőfi Circle (a debating club that had been established in the spirit of the New Course within the official Communist youth organization), while university students, a group regarded as privileged and previously close to the regime, loudly joined the demands for a truly democratic socialism.[4] In a misguided attempt to defuse the crisis, Moscow intervened in July to ensure that Rákosi was replaced by Ernő Gerő—a step that brought the regime nothing, for Gerő was as compromised a political figure as Rákosi, while the way in which the switch occurred underlined the MDP's dependence on Moscow. By late summer, the party apparatus in the capital was in a state of "panic," while the reburial of László Rajk at the beginning of October increased the confidence of those demanding outright democratization. One such intellectual, Tamás Aczél, remembered that "it was then that we realized, that everybody realized, that this wasn't just an affair of a few Communist intellectuals but that everyone felt as strongly, the same way, against the regime."[5] The crumbling of the authority of the regime was occurring in step with the culmination of political upheaval in Poland that brought Władysław Gomułka to power despite opposition from hardliners in the Polish party and despite the doubts of the Soviet leadership. This situation led the Hungarian students to become bolder; appropriating the language of democratic patriotism and the cultural memory of 1848, they too pushed for change, demanding the outright democratization of Hungary's government and the reassertion of its independence from Moscow. As part of this campaign, they organized a demonstration on 23 October in support of their demands, and it triggered a series of events across Budapest that evening. Those events transformed the situation, as the demonstrators became a revolutionary crowd that spoke in the name of all Hungarians and demanded the overthrow of the system. The use of violence by defenders of the regime against these crowds transformed the situation into a moment of outright revolution.

Over the following days, as the events in Budapest were replicated nationwide, political power shifted from the party and regime to the revolutionary crowd. In cities across the country, the crowd, organized through initially peaceful demonstrations, assumed the role of representative of the "will of the people."[6] Crowds played a central role in the "cleansing" of public space through the theatrical removal of monuments and artifacts associated with either the Red Army or the socialist regime.[7] The frequent incidents in which representatives of either the army or state security services fired on initially nonviolent crowds after 23 October both radicalized the revolution and highlighted the illegitimacy of the regime. Such acts of violence against revolutionary crowds bolstered their claim to act in the name of the people as a whole.[8] Workers played a central role in the demonstrations in urban centers all across the country and were overrepresented among the dead and injured when crowds were fired upon; of those killed when the state security agencies fired on demonstrators in Mosonmagyaróvár on 26 October, workers were 65.15 percent.[9] Crowds, often predominantly populated by workers, smashed the control of intellectuals and students over the course of the 1956 Revolution, radicalizing it and broadening it. These crowds' deeper significance lay in their role as revolutionary subjects, which brought the regime's crisis of legitimacy that had festered since 1950 out of the factories and industrial districts and into the heart of the public sphere. The transfer of authority from democratic socialist intellectuals and students to the crowd surprised and shocked many of those who had supported radical democratization; as far as one prominent intellectual was concerned, "the idea of an uprising never entered our minds."[10] Crowds were often a public demonstration of the refusal of workers to allow the regime to speak on behalf of them; this circumstance fatally undermined the attempts by a stunned and powerless party leadership to repair its authority during the last days of October through a "turn to the working class."[11] At the same time, the public demonstration of the emptiness of the regime's claim to legitimacy opened the floodgates to the radicalization of the revolution and to representatives of political traditions that resolutely opposed the socialist regime.

The importance to the revolution of the overturning of the regime's claim to legitimacy as the representative of the working class embedded itself in its political language. The ubiquity of the "workers' council" as revolutionary organ was testimony to this, as was the way in which the political languages of democratic patriotism sat together with appeals to the workers; one pamphlet on 31 October addressed its audience as "Hungarians, Workers, Fellow Citizens!"[12] While it played a decisive role as a motivating force in shaping events, the notion of a united, predominantly working-class crowd as revolutionary subject was a myth produced by the ways in which it occupied public space and was resisted by the regime and by the means by which it asserted itself.[13] Although the revolutionary crowd appeared as the unified embodiment of the will of the nation, the crowds were far from homogeneous, either politically or socially. The patterns of disunity between different groups of workers in social conflict in the years preceding 1956 reproduced themselves at the outbreak of the revolution. For this reason, the skilled and unskilled, women and men, rural and urban, propertied and landless played different roles within the revolution, for beyond their demand for change they had different priorities and, indeed, different visions of the country. Outright political division produced dynamics of radicalization in different localities, driving forward the revolution until the realities of the situation were again transformed by the second Soviet intervention, after 4 November.

At the local level, the process of revolution was tightly connected to social conflicts in the period that immediately preceded its outbreak. In Zala's oil fields, a largely worker-peasant workforce wanted an end to collectivization in agriculture yet had been beaten back by selective repression and had developed a strictly instrumental attitude toward their work at the oil wells. Tension over renewed collectivization and anger generated by low wages at the oil wells in an anti-Communist region made southern Zala ripe for revolution. The events in Budapest produced both an outburst of anger locally and a complete and rapid transfer of power. In Tatabánya, the militancy of younger workers in the mines and key workers like the city's bus drivers—fundamental to bringing miners to work in the geographically dispersed new city—initiated the revolution locally. Communist officials were driven out of power but did not disappear completely. While most miners supported the strike, their willingness to return to work once the Nagy government accepted the political demands of the revolution suggested that this majority did not wish to take the revolution in the same direction as the anti-Communist radicals. In Újpest, the events of late October and early November were more complex and contradictory. Given the proximity of Újpest to Budapest, the struggle between intellectuals and the regime had a direct and immediate impact on workers locally. In many factories, skilled workers, management, and even the party supported radical de-Stalinization. These groups provided the base for workers' councils, which were determined to protect enterprises and production as the strike began in response to the violence in Budapest on 23–24 October. The strikers formed the local working-class crowd who elected their own revolutionary committee. The crowd radicalized, provoking a struggle between them and those in the factories, who remained more moderate—a split that characterized the local revolution down to 4 November.

## The Dual Revolution in Újpest

On 23 October, as the students prepared to march through the capital and the regime dithered over whether to permit or ban the demonstration, political upheaval was felt in the way that it had been throughout the year in Újpest's factories. In the morning, the students' demands, expressed as "sixteen points" encompassing demands for national independence and radical democratization, were circulated among the workers of the United Incandescent Lamp and Electrical Factory, where they had "a considerable impact."[14] Student activists turned up at the gates of the Chinoin Pharmaceuticals Factory, and a representative was allowed to address a mass meeting of workers: "A university student spoke and read out their demands expressed as a series of points. . . . Some of the points were met with enthusiastic applause."[15] Responses to the student-led protest on 23 October revealed the cracks in the regime's authority, as young workers, who had maintained a silent distance from the debates surrounding reform over the course of the year, left their afternoon shift to head for the city in the early evening to join the growing protests.[16] Their older workmates who had participated in open factory-level debate over the future of the country were more restrained. In the Chinoin plant, they responded positively to an appeal by the factory's director urging workers to "await the view of the party regarding the demonstration."[17]

The crisis in the regime that unfolded following the news of Khrushchev's denunciation of Stalin's crimes in February 1956 had been visible to all workers; however, different groups had different responses, with the skilled workers most likely to criticize the practice of socialist rule openly and to engage with the project of intellectuals for a fully democratized socialist order within bodies like the Petőfi Circle. Most workers reacted to the broadcast of the contents of the "secret speech" criticizing Stalin by maintaining that "not everything is in order in Moscow, and it is likely that important things will happen in the near future." They were at the same time aware of the possibility of violent repression if they expressed their discontent too openly and believed "it is cleverer to listen and wait for events."[18] Party members, however, were furious at the manner in which the speech became public, especially as it took the party almost four weeks to admit to its members that Stalin had been criticized. One activist exclaimed in frustration that the workers "say that you didn't know anything, Radio Free Europe already broadcast it ages ago."[19] Party members on shop floors were forced to respond to the question that "if during the last twenty years there was no collective leadership . . . and Stalin suppressed collective leadership, why was it that this issue was not raised while he was alive?"[20] Such questions were a form of implicit taunting of activists, given their role in supporting the policies of a regime that, in the eyes of many, could be criticized in similar ways. This situation led party members to appropriate the language of Khrushchev's denunciation of Stalin's "cult of personality" and to adapt it to express their criticisms of tensions locally. One party member in the Chinoin factory used the meeting called to discuss the Twentieth Congress in Moscow to attack factory management: "The cult of personality could be seen in this factory among the upper- and middle-ranking economic cadres. It has happened more than once that the workers did not dare to criticize or to make concrete proposals because they were scared of management."[21]

While at the end of March, public criticism of the regime from within party ranks was muted, it gathered speed, spurred on by the continuing depth of discontent in factories and the boldness of reform-minded Communist intellectuals outside. The meetings of the Petőfi Circle had a marked effect in radicalizing opinion, especially given that many younger engineers from Újpest factories participated in its meetings.[22] During June, the demands articulated publicly within the meetings became more radical, with calls for rehabilitation of Rajk and for the resignations of Rákosi and Gerő. During the circle's debate on the press held the day before violent protest shook Poznań, participants demanded freedom of the press and a transformation of the political system.[23] Party leaders in Újpest reacted hysterically to the demands expressed openly within the Petőfi Circle debates, calling on the national leadership to intervene to prevent them from being used by "enemy elements."[24] The state of siege felt by those who wished to defend the regime was in part a consequence of reactions to events in Poznań. Workers in the United Incandescent Lamp and Electrical Factory regarded events in Poland as a wake-up call to the regime: "The reason riots broke out in Poznań was not because of the enemy and foreign spies, but because twelve years after the end of the war living standards remained low. . . . The People's Democracies are equal on the political level, but economically Hungary and Poland are the most underdeveloped, and in the two countries living standards are the lowest."[25] Furthermore, the spirit of rebellion encompassed party members, as demands for political change were linked to demands for the removal of unpopular economic measures.[26]

While worker discontent generally remained steady throughout the country, especially as the impact of Hungary's increasing foreign debt was felt on shop floors as the state cut back on purchases of raw materials, that of party members and the skilled elite was channeled by the promise of radical political reform within the factories. As part of an attempt to overcome the sense of drift in economic policy since 1954, the regime drew up draft principles for a second five-year plan that it made public in April 1956.[27] In an attempt to win support, the regime opened the principles for public debate among workers, thus creating a space, used mostly by the skilled male elite, where they could express their grievances with the existing material situation and institutions and demand change.[28] In the Duclos Mining Machinery Factory, workers attacked the "stupid wage system and price policy" for disrupting production and causing "the end of the month rush" to meet plan targets.[29] Criticism extended to spheres of everyday life outside the factory gates; a female machine operator in the Újpest Yarn Factory demanded that checks be established on the "seventy-year-old doctors" in the local hospital who were "not trusted by the workers." Her workmate wanted "drains to be placed on the streets so that polluted water doesn't flow into the yards of houses."[30] Often suggestions touched on both agrarian and industrial policy: "Listen to the peasants, don't decide from above what is planted on what land. . . . In the interests of improving agricultural production, take notice of those who work on the land."[31]

The open climate of discussion within factories, combined with limited experiments in economic decentralization in some of the district's light industrial plants, created a new factory-level political constellation. The Danube Shoe Factory was permitted to experiment with a "new planning system" from the beginning of the second quarter until the end of the year. While the factory remained subject to an indicative plan, it was to be dependent for its income entirely on the number of shoes it sold and was encouraged to control its costs and thus make a profit.[32] With its emphasis on decentralization to the enterprise level and its reduction in centralized bureaucratic control, the "new planning system" was compatible with the prescriptions of those who had sharply criticized centralized economic planning in the context of the Petőfi Circle's two-part debate on the principles of the second five-year plan.[33] Linked to the reform movement, experiments in decentralization opened the way to the more direct involvement of workers in the decision-making processes. By July, both the de-Stalinizing party and the official trade unions were themselves committed to the direct participation of workers' representatives in the affairs of their enterprise.[34] Skilled workers were especially vocal in calling for more direct participation in factory affairs, particularly as they sought to avoid a situation in which the decentralization of responsibility to the enterprise produced a dictatorship of management. Likewise, they remained distrustful of the ability of official bodies such as the party and unions to offer them any more than a sham de-Stalinization, in which the form of industrial democracy substituted for its reality. This fear lay behind the brutal comments of one skilled shoemaker in a letter to the factory newspaper in the Danube Shoe Factory: "In the period following the liberation, old, committed trade unionists were promoted to become managers. We should say clearly that later these comrades became detached from the workers, they became one-sided and didn't speak up sufficiently for the interests of the workers. . . . New people filled the trade and leaders were co-opted, not elected. . . . Union leaders regarded anyone who stood up for their interests as the enemy, and dealt with them accordingly."[35] Others criticized the way in which unions had become nothing more than tools of the management; as far as one fitter in the Duclos Mining Machinery Factory was concerned, "it is useless complaining to the party and factory committee because they can't do anything. What happens here is basically what the director says."[36]

As autumn 1956 arrived, there existed an embryonic political constellation that rested on the skilled elite, some in factory-level trade union and party organizations, as well as managers that supported a de-Stalinized socialist order based on extensive enterprise autonomy, with the strong, independent representation of workers within the workplace. By October 1956, some skilled workers took advantage of this new atmosphere and used their factory newspaper to demand direct participation in management at both the shop and factory levels.[37] While this embryonic political constellation provided the basis for some of the early workers' councils that emerged in the heat of revolution, prior to its outbreak the more generalized discontent of the vast majority of workers was more immediately visible. This rested in part on growing economic frustration but also on a number of other political themes—especially a growing sense that the time was ripe for Hungary's rulers to assert their independence from Moscow. In this context, while Rákosi's removal had been welcomed, the manner of his removal further discredited the regime because it emphasized the dependence of the MDP on Moscow, while Gerő was seen as insufficiently distinct from his predecessor.[38] Given the MDP's collapsing authority, the factory-level party organizations capitulated to workers' demands and distanced themselves from the national leadership. In August, in the Duclos Mining Machinery Factory, the factory party committee demanded that "the rights of the workers be secured" in disputes with management and that workers were right "to demand a just wage system."[39] The growing thaw in relations with Yugoslavia, the reburial of László Rajk on 6 October, the retention of power by Gerő despite being discredited by his Stalinist past, and the lack of any clear leadership from the regime pushed the situation to a crisis point. This crisis in turn culminated in the events of 23 October, when the regime, faced with an open challenge on the capital's streets, at first hesitated and then allowed the demonstration. The denunciation of the demonstrators as "counterrevolutionaries" by Ernő Gerő in his radio broadcast, the consequent gathering of crowds in front of national radio headquarters, which were then fired on, followed by the news of the intervention of Red Army troops, provided the context for the transformation of the situation into one of outright revolution.

It was Újpest's young workers who were drawn to the initial demonstrations. This group—urban, yet isolated from dominant relations in power in their workplaces—played a central role in radicalizing those demonstrations and then in spreading disturbances back to the industrial suburbs. One second-year industrial apprentice who was working in the United Incandescent Lamp and Electrical Factory on 23 October "heard that there was a demonstration in Budapest in Stalin

Square." Immediately catching the tram and trolleybus into central Pest, he was forced to get off some way short of the square because "the crowd was so big that the trolleybuses stood in a jam and everyone went on foot."[40] Often youth participation in the early stages of the 1956 Revolution resembled lower-level and less political forms of youth disorder in industrial communities. One group of young men, on hearing of the demonstration, determined to go to the hostel for local student nurses and "take the girls off to the demonstration" in Budapest. Once they discovered that the director of hostel had locked the inhabitants in, they began to shout "Russians go home! Rákosi to the gallows!" until the police arrived.[41] For those who reached the crowds in the center of the capital, then experienced the initial violence of the domestic security agencies and, by the early hours of 24 October, the first wave of Soviet troops called in by the regime to assist in the restoration of order, participation transformed their role rapidly. The second-year industrial apprentice from the United Incandescent Lamp and Electrical Factory found himself going with a group from the demonstration to demand that Hungarian Radio read the students' "sixteen points," and he was thus part of the crowd fired on by representatives of the state security agency. He joined one group of young workers who decided to arm themselves by demanding the weapons that were stored in factories for civil defense purposes. During the early hours of 24 October, in a repetition of scenes that occurred in industrial districts across the capital, the young workers walked up the Vác Road—which connected the city center to Újpest—and raided the factories that lined their route, seeking out small arms. Factories, however, were not undefended, as the regime had trained porters and security staff, in anticipation of a possible war, to resort to force to defend their factories.[42] In one factory, therefore, they found that "the porter on the door was already armed with a machine gun."[43] Violence between armed young workers and factory security guards had spread to Újpest as workers reported for the morning shift. At the gate of the United Incandescent Lamp and Electrical Factory, one worker was injured when he and others walked into the middle of a gun battle between an armed band in search of weapons and factory security staff determined to prevent them from getting through the gate.[44]

The morning shift in the plant was unable to ignore the impact of violent political conflict, for they had witnessed it at the gate of their factory. As the morning progressed, the full impact of the events of the previous night and the ongoing conflict around them between armed bands and Soviet troops was felt on the shop floor. Fury grew, and a sense of the transformed nature of the political situation led the authority of the regime within the plant to implode, even though the security staff had been able to hold off those who sought to bring the revolution in through the factory gates. One-third of the workers, influenced by the news of violence, had failed to report for work, but, in the middle of the morning shift, workers in the tool workshop and in the vacuum plant—the strongest supporters of outright democratization in the plant before 23 October—stopped work to organize a mass meeting of the two-thirds of the workforce present. They decided to launch a strike and remove the red star from above the factory gate.[45] Once a strike in support of radical political change and the withdrawal of Soviet troops had begun, most workers left the factory for the streets. As news of the work stoppage at the United Incandescent Lamp and Electrical Factory spread, its workers were joined by those of other Újpest plants. They formed a large spontaneous demonstration that grew over the course of several hours; there "were many people in front of the State Department Store, and leaflets were distributed from a black car. They shouted and told me that we were all on strike."[46] The crowd destroyed the Soviet war memorial; the more radical of the demonstrators turned on the local police station, yet a majority remained at the site of the war memorial, and, as a result of local activists addressing the crowd, they chose a body of people to represent them and thus take over public administration. The crowd thus delegated a local "revolutionary committee" through chaotic acclamation, rather than election as such.[47] The disorganization and political ambiguity that were inherent in the "election" of Újpest's revolutionary committee were visible in how skilled artisan and one-time MKP official Pál Kósa was chosen to lead it. Kósa, on hearing the news of the strike and the destruction of the Soviet war memorial, headed out to the demonstration simply to see what was happening. While there, he was recognized within the crowd: "One person, who didn't like me, told the crowd that I was a party functionary, I should be treated like the other vagabonds, and my place was hanging from a lamppost. At that time I was well known in Újpest, and many people opposed this person's opinion." This authority, based on personal popularity, despite his prior political history, enabled him, by addressing the crowd, to assume a leading role as the group split between radicals and moderates. Through a chaotic process of debate, it selected the "Revolutionary Committee" and gave Kósa the job of formulating its political demands.[48]

While the territorial revolutionary committee's legitimacy was rooted in the crowd, which itself was split between moderates and radicals, the events of 24 October separated it from events in the factories. With the departure of most workers for the streets, factory party organizations tried to maintain control over the workplaces by organizing the election of workers' councils, in the absence of most of the workers, in order to ensure that only "trustworthy people would be elected."[49] In some factories, these attempts were successful; in the Gheorgiu-Dej Shipyards, on the southern fringes of Újpest, the plant's party organization used its workers' council as cover to prevent local revolutionary activists empowered by the territorial revolutionary committee from gaining access to the site until the very end of October.[50] However, similar attempts by the factory party leadership at the United Incandescent Lamp and Electrical Factory were not successful. A coalition of skilled workers and engineers took control, among them those who had used the factory newspaper before 23 October to demand direct participation in management. In the forty-eight hours that followed the election of the United Incandescent Lamp and Electrical Factory workers' council, it remade the institutions of the factory. One production director was removed, as was the managing director, who was replaced with the president of the worker's council. It abolished the Personnel Department, which under Rákosi had been used as the representative of both the party and the ÁVH. It also announced that the strike would be maintained and full wages would be paid, while low-paid workers would be given a 15 percent wage increase and other workers, 10 percent. It introduced more fundamental reforms of factory administration, beginning with administrative decentralization and the elimination of bureaucracy, an overhaul of the payment-by-results wage system, and a call for the establishment of a seventy-one-member general workers' council and shop workers' councils under it.[51] The skilled worker majority whose thinking dominated the changes instituted by the workers' council made their philosophy and distrust of centralization clear at a meeting of all the councils in Újpest on 29 October: "the mistakes of recent years show that we have to build from below, we have to solve problems using our own strength." Yet they also underlined their distrust of the radicalism of those who supported bodies like the territorial revolutionary committee in Újpest, which drew their legitimacy from the crowd, given their own political commitment to democratic transformation of the socialist system, rather than its overthrow: "it seems that the power that has been paid for with the blood of our young people is falling into the hands of different, fractious elements."[52]

The skilled elite that dominated most of the early workers' councils built on the calls for factory democracy that preceded the revolution, forcing radical transformation of management structures and working conditions. But politically, they tended to be more moderate than much of the crowd. This stance, coupled with the knowledge that many Communists continued to participate in workers' councils, brought them into conflict with the revolutionary crowd and its delegated representatives. Distrust deteriorated into conflict; on 29 October, a false statement on national radio that fifteen hundred workers had reported for work at the United Incandescent Lamp and Electrical Factory provoked demonstrations against the workers' council, whom they accused of sabotaging the revolution, despite the fact that the workers' council stated clearly that the factory "will not restart work until Soviet troops leave the country."[53] The failure to pay wages to strikers at the neighboring Duclos Mining Machinery Factory provoked demonstrations at the factory gates, as the most radical of the workers blamed those on the workers' council "who did not represent the workers' interests" for this failure and demanded the council be purged of Communists.[54] The growing radicalization of the crowd, and the consolidation of authority by the territorial revolutionary committee, restricted the room for maneuver of many of the workers' councils, especially those with weaker leadership. The local revolutionary committee decided—against the will of many of the workers' councils, especially that of the United Incandescent Lamp and

Electrical Factory—that all the districts' workers' councils were "provisional" and that "persons who had been functionaries could not be elected."[55] While the United Incandescent Lamp and Electrical Factory's workers' council managed to preserve its independence from the Újpest Revolutionary Committee and its distinct political line, most of the district's workers' councils succumbed to the radicalization of the revolution during the very final days of October.[56]

This assertion by the crowd—and the territorial revolutionary committee that spoke in its name—of its authority over the moderate workers' councils was a product of the radicalization of the revolution that dominated the last days of October and the first days of November. With the myth that the regime in any sense spoke in the name of the working class shattered, combined with the tremendous anger and suspicion directed at representatives of the state security agencies, the regime's authority was swept away, opening the door to two linked political processes. The first was the reappearance of political opinions and cultures driven underground during the first years of socialist dictatorship. The second was the increasing violence deployed by activists in the name of the revolution, with measures including actively purging those they saw as enemies of their revolution. Indicative of this was the way in which, after anti-Communist activists took control of the Chinoin Pharmaceuticals Factory workers' council, they sought to cleanse the factory of all Communist influence. They first banned the reestablished Communist Party—the MSzMP—from founding a workplace cell but agreed that the recently restarted FKgP could organize the factory's workforce. Then, they hauled the plant's director before them and demanded he renounce his belief in communism as a condition of his continued employment. When he refused, he was summarily dismissed.[57] This radicalization of the revolution increased the confidence of the most militant of its younger working-class activists, who saw it as giving them a license to lead the process of purging in the name of the revolution. This was visible in the role that young activists who were connected to the crowd and the Újpest Revolutionary Committee assumed in removing "Communists" from the Danube Shoe Factory's workers' council on 31 October. The crowd contained some workers from the plant who complained loudly that "the workers' council was in the hands of the Communist director." In response, four armed young workers, led by the son of one factory employee, decided they would storm the factory by force and "arrest" the director, as part of a process through which the workers' council would be purged.[58]

The director "arrested," Antal Koós, refused to flee from the four armed men who sought to purge the factory's workers' council. As some of the activists removed the weapons from the factory and persuaded anti-Communist workers to elect a new workers' council, Koós was imprisoned in the cellar of the Újpest council house along with other "Communists" rounded up by young working-class activists operating in the name of the Újpest Revolutionary Committee.[59] Few prominent local supporters of the regime were prepared to face retribution at either the hands of a radicalizing crowd or the various groups operating in the name of revolution-ary organs. Feeling increasingly under threat within the sharply radicalizing anti-Communist climate, many opted to leave the district for places where they would be less easily recognized. The president of Újpest's local council, the figurehead of the regime in the district, left her flat at seven in the morning on 29 October, spent two hours in the council buildings with the revolutionary committee, and then left the district—under the protection of the party organization and its security organs. Her daughter and younger sister, who remained at the flat, were warned by party officials to leave it for their own safety, right on the eve of the second Soviet interven-tion, on 3 November.[60] Although given the apparent victory of the revolution during the first three days of November, this sequence of events seemed of minor impor-tance; the disappearance of substantial sections of the regime's local and factory-based apparatus, as a consequence of the fear of being subjected to retribution in the name of the revolution, would prove crucial after the military victory of the Red Army in Budapest and the overthrow of Imre Nagy's revolutionary government on 4 November. The restored regime would thus have a network of local activists that it could mobilize to begin the painful task of reconstructing its shattered authority.

## An Uncertain Transfer of Power in Tatabánya

While, in Újpest, supporters of the regime went underground, in Tatabánya they were able to maintain a greater public presence even after the regime in Buda-pest collapsed and as they lost the control of the streets in the mining city. The party organization in Pit No. XI was able to claim, after the suppression of the revolution, that "its political work never stopped, despite the counterrevolution." It maintained control of the mine for a full two days after mass demonstrations erupted in Tatabánya on 26 October and relinquished power only after four hun-dred demonstrators forced their way into the mine to elect a workers' council. Even then, the factory party organization attempted to get its candidates elected to the council, despite demands from the more radical workers that they wanted "a work-ers' council without Communists."[61] The election was characterized by ugly scenes as radicals warned that they would "wipe out the Communists" and drove out the party's activists by telling them "they should be in the forced labor camp."[62] After preventing the election of any Communists, the workers' council locked the room occupied by the party and trade union. Yet, despite their formal disappearance, a hard core of party activists continued to meet and attempted to agitate against the more radical members of the workers' council in the mine.[63]

While supporters of the regime persisted in acting as a group throughout the 1956 Revolution, the upsurge of protest that began in Tatabánya on 26 October came relatively late—three days after the beginning of the revolution in the capi-tal. Events in Budapest had an impact among certain groups of the workforce—

especially among forced laborers and the sizable number of young workers who lived in hostels. As the students in the capital prepared for their demonstration, protest broke out among prisoners in the forced labor camp attached to Pit No. XVIII of the Tatabánya Coal Mining Trust, located in the neighboring town of Oroszlány. Observing the accelerating collapse of the regime, the prisoners concluded by mid-October that "they wouldn't be shut inside for much longer." As news of events in Budapest filtered through to the mine, at noon on 23 October the prisoners attempted to overpower the guards at the mine entrance and break out. The factory guard was able to restore order only by firing on the prisoners, killing three.[64] In the early hours of 24 October, following the night of fighting in Budapest, one truck full of armed young workers from the capital arrived in the city to recruit supporters and spread the strike. At Pit No. VI, their attempts to picket the mine for the morning shift met with "indifference" from most of those reporting for work and a strong response from the local police, who took them into custody.[65] The atmosphere in the city, especially among the young, was tense because they wanted to fight alongside those in Budapest resisting the first Soviet intervention. Indeed, some of the more radical "already on the 24th . . . caught buses to Pest and participated in the battles against Soviet tanks."[66]

Despite the dynamics of labor turnover and hierarchical bargaining, by 1956, young, hostel-dwelling workers had become a permanent part of the workforce in the mines and some of the other industrial enterprises, even though their older workmates still had more perquisites. This in part was because of the intractability of the labor situation in the mines, which, compared to the early years of the decade, by 1956 served to enhance the bargaining position of single, young males willing to remain in employment in the city, thus forcing management to promote them to an extent.[67] The degree to which those who had left agriculture to join the industrial workforce as "new" workers in the early 1950s had become an integral part of the workforce by the middle of the decade, if they stayed on the job, was shown by a survey of coal hewers in Tatabánya in the immediate aftermath of the 1956 Revolution. While 35 percent had worked in the mines for ten years or more, 39.2 percent had taken work in the pits between 1947 and 1954, mostly during the labor recruitment drives of the early 1950s.[68] The housing problems for many of these workers remained unsolved in view of the persistent housing shortage. A widespread practice of renting rooms or just beds had grown up, with some residents able to demand up to three hundred forints a month from prospective room renters. One two-room flat in the city was shared by a seven-member family and eight others who simply rented a bed. Most, however, lived in the workers' hostels.[69] Within the hostels, a strongly masculine youth culture had developed, one shaped by poor living conditions and the antagonism toward the regime brought by the young from their home villages and adapted to the environment of Tatabánya. One hostel resident passed the time in the city by walking "to the cinema. If I had enough money

I went into the cinema, but most of the time I didn't have enough for a ticket," or he read "forbidden paperback westerns" that were originally published in the 1930s and 1940s. Faced with the boredom of hostel life, those living there built up a sense of solidarity: "the residents would not have betrayed their neighbors." Often they spent their spare time listening to Western radio stations, "if they could find the station." Listening to Western radio formed a ritual of initiation into the hostel community: "The guys watched each other to see how they all reacted to the things they heard, how they behaved. To those who had just arrived, we warned them that if they told anybody, we would cause them problems."[70] By the mid-1950s, this masculine youth culture, which embraced both younger, permanent skilled workers and apprentices alike, generated an undercurrent of violent disorder, often fueled by alcohol abuse. The limited number of venues serving alcohol in the city contributed to overcrowding, while "hourly fights" broke out around liquor stores. Older workers complained that the young would disrupt film screenings at the theater when they disliked the film shown.[71]

However, this youth culture in the city only underpinned political activism after the outbreak of the revolution across the nation. Among other groups of workers, with the partial exception of worker-peasant commuters angered by collectivization, the process of de-Stalinization in Tatabánya, in complete contrast to the experience in Újpest, met with little visible response.[72] The management, trade union, and party elite failed to take national policy shifts seriously. When the "second" first five-year plan was opened up to debate in the Tatabánya Coal Mining Trust in May 1956, there was little meaningful participation in the discussion by miners. The "contributions" to the "debate" from the floor were carefully stage-managed, with only mine managers making recommendations.[73] While enterprise-level officials and shop stewards welcomed shifts to increase the independence of factory committees and give workers greater rights of participation in the affairs of their factory, they expressed skepticism as to whether it would ever be realized, for "many times there are constant breaches of law from the higher state leaders; it is common that there are measures that say they have to involve the trade union, but they still leave them out."[74] The casual contempt of many managers and low-level party officials for reforms in the city was demonstrated by the ways in which they ignored changes to labor competition. As part of attempts to decentralize the formal responsibility for production—away from the planning ministries and toward individual enterprises—the state reshaped labor competition to make it more decentralized and flexible in April 1956. It abolished the title "Stakhanovite," replacing it with the label "exceptional worker." The state also deemphasized quantity of production against the plan and introduced a broader range of measures of "exceptionality."[75] In the Tatabánya Cement Factory, management had manipulated Stakhanovism before the changes in order to reward its core workers; despite the official changes, it continued its policy of rewarding workers by proclaiming them "Stakhanovites."[76]

The frustration of de-Stalinization not only fed but was also a product of urban workers' deep disillusionment, which rested on the severe credibility deficit for the regime. After the cuts in wages implemented during 1955, the local party revived its rhetorical stress on a consumerist model of socialism throughout 1956. By August, the local party sought to cast its appeal to the population in terms of its ability to supply consumer goods to the "working people" of the city. As part of a summer campaign to raise coal production, mine management promised that it would secure between 100 and 120 washing machines, to be given to the workers who performed best in the competition. Meanwhile, the local State Department Store promised that "a Czechoslovak bicycle and homemade washing machines" would arrive in the store, as would "portable radios."[77] The credibility of such consumerist appeals had been undermined by the wage cutting of the previous year and the impact of mounting economic difficulties on workers' pay throughout 1956. In the Bánhida Power Plant, for example, workers' remuneration was structured in such a way as to create an incentive for them to save coal. This incentive did not take into account the quality of the coal provided to the plant; lower quality coal forced stokers to use more of it to keep the generators going. As a consequence, monthly pay in April 1956 fell by an average of almost two hundred forints per worker, generating fury.[78] In the mines in June 1956, 53.7 percent of workers took home between one thousand and two thousand forints per month, which placed their wages at just above the industry average.[79] Because of the lack of employment opportunities for women in Tatabánya, household incomes were well below the national average, generating demand for the creation of substantial light industrial employment locally to relieve poverty.[80] In addition, frustration at the shortages of goods in the state retail sector, particularly of bread and fresh meat, persisted.[81] The existence of a huge, semirural shadow economy around the town contributed to a sense among urban workers that they were, despite the proclamations of the authorities to the contrary, being left behind other social groups.[82]

On the eve of the 1956 Revolution, there was widespread disillusion with the regime in the city. Characteristics of this political disillusion included marked tension among hostel-dwelling youth and worker-peasant commuters and a more general crisis of credibility for the regime among urban workers that was rooted in material frustration. Discontent, however, remained largely submerged. Tension over the housing shortage did surface during early summer 1956. One young couple decided to solve their own problems by moving in with a local widow. When they were evicted by the widow's son-in-law, who had never agreed to the arrangement, the couple decided, as a protest over their eviction and housing shortage, to construct a makeshift wooden shelter in the local cemetery. As a result, angry rumor spread through the city; some said that "a family has voluntarily moved to the cemetery," while others maintained that "someone forged papers that told them they had to use violence to force the miner's family to live in the cemetery." As a consequence of the storm of rumor and anger, the local council was forced to intervene to find the couple somewhere to live.[83] Groups other than workers were slow to mobilize politically. Despite intellectual mobilization in the capital, Tatabánya's own local intelligentsia gathered for the first time on the evening of 23 October as the demonstration in Budapest turned to violence; many believed they were only present to debate the "correct" relationship locally between the party and schoolteachers.[84]

During the first days of the revolution, as news of the armed clashes and the crisis of political authority in the capital filtered through to Tatabánya, the climate in the mining city was tense. Given their geographical distance from the theater of armed conflict, Tatabánya residents waited for events to unfold, as the official county press proclaimed that, in the face of the crisis, "production is uninterrupted countywide."[85] The probability that open protest would be repressed was underlined by expressions of determination from the party that "we will defend the people's power."[86] The spark that ignited the local revolution was provided by one key group of workers—the city's bus drivers. Their power was based on the geography of the city—an urban sprawl—in which the mines and other workplaces were geographically dispersed at considerable distance from where their workers lived. The network of city buses provided the only way for many workers to reach either the shopping and administrative areas in new Tatabánya or their workplaces. The transportation network suffered from labor shortages and severe underinvestment; its buses were in a poor state of repair, and when spare parts were needed, the fleet was at the mercy of the operation of the economy. Furious passengers complained of lateness, overcrowding, and frequent cancellations, while the drivers themselves worked long hours for low pay and often faced travelers' anger over poor service.[87] On the morning of Friday, 26 October, some of the bus drivers, along with their supervisors, decided to found a workers' council at the city's depot. Replicating events elsewhere in the country, they removed the red star from the front of the building, issued a series of demands, and called on drivers reporting for work to strike.[88] By lunchtime, all of the city's bus drivers had joined the strike, thus making it impossible for many of those working the afternoon shift in the city's mines and factories to get to work.[89]

The launch of the bus drivers' strike was the catalyst that opened the door to mobilization among young workers. Apprentices arriving at the Mining Technical School on the morning of 26 October refused to attend their classes and instead prepared to demonstrate with some of the striking bus drivers.[90] During the late morning and lunchtime, demonstrations were made up of relatively small groups of younger workers. The group of demonstrators that passed the city's hospital at lunchtime was "seventy to eighty strong" and made up of bus drivers and mine apprentices. "At their center a dark young woman carried a national flag, they sang the *himnusz* [Hungarian national anthem], and shouted that 'Hungarians belong with us' and carried on."[91] Their appearance as a small number of demonstrators was misleading, a product of the fact that Tatabánya had no real city center and that potential supporters of the demonstrations were dispersed geographically. One local journalist recorded that "everywhere the people were out on the street. They gathered in groups to discuss the revolutionary events. By the State [Department Store] a larger group gathered. Some of them had cut out the red star from the flag."[92] As the various groups of demonstrators approached workplaces and various government buildings, they gathered strength. When one group arrived at the entrance to the offices of the Tatabánya Materials' Supply Enterprise, they shouted "Russians go home!" and "demanded that the company management take down the five-pointed red star from the building. A worker I didn't know took it down right in front of me." After witnessing the removal of the red star, many workers inside the building walked off the job to join the crowd: "after the crowd of demonstrators sang the *himnusz,* it departed and continued its march."[93]

As the crowds grew in strength and size, they radicalized over the course of the afternoon and sought to take control of key institutions across the city. Because of the crowds' geographic dispersion throughout the city, this process was characterized by considerable confusion, as separate sections of the crowd had different goals. Some workers from Power Plant No. 1 headed for their place of work to take it over and confronted a factory guard unit that the party had organized to defend the plant from the demonstrators. The revolutionaries were able to overpower and disarm them, set up a provisional workers' council, and distribute weapons among themselves before joining the demonstrations elsewhere across the city.[94] As some of the demonstrators gathered around the county party headquarters in new Tatabánya acquired arms, the more militant younger workers went in search of more, forcing their way into the city police station, demanding that any political prisoners in custody be freed, and removing weapons. The police, anxious to avoid violence, cooperated fully with the demonstrators.[95] Others stormed the local radio station—the Mineworkers' Radio, which broadcast across the city through a network of speakers fixed to electricity and telegraph poles—during the late afternoon.[96] At around the same time, sections of the crowd turned on the county party committee headquarters, which they took, forcing senior officials to leave hurriedly through the back entrance. Over the course of the evening, protestors overran the camp where forced laborers working in the mines lived. The protesters freed the prisoners, while demonstrators took weapons from the county's state security headquarters and the barracks of the local army officer training school.[97]

Two evenings previously, Hungarian National Radio had been able to claim the support of Tatabánya's miners for the state's attempts to suppress the revolution in Budapest: "The Tatabánya and Oroszlány miners learned to their fury about the fascist provocation. In many factories they have formed a workers' guard to maintain order and discipline."[98] On the evening of 26 October, the pretense that the party could depend on the workers to defend its power even locally was now in tatters. Yet the revolution itself lacked leadership and was simply the product of a spontaneous, decentralized crowd, lacking any overall political coordination. During the late evening of 26 October, those occupying the Mineworkers' Radio, fearful of the radicalism of some of the young workers in the crowd and worried by the power vacuum in the city, decided to organize the election of a revolutionary council the following day.[99] The local party, despite their loss of the county party headquarters to the crowd during the late afternoon, saw in this new revolutionary council an opportunity to influence and moderate the course of the local revolution. On the following morning, the county party leadership made clear its support "in the exceptionally serious, difficult situation" for the creation of the "Provisional Workers' and Soldiers' Council." The first task of this new organ, it argued, would be "to create public order" by "collecting the weapons from unauthorized and irresponsible elements."[100]

An attempt to elect members to this Provisional Workers' and Soldiers' Council took place in a mass meeting at Tatabánya's People's House. The effort was thrown into confusion, however, and meeting participants finally resolved not to elect a full council in the absence of the formation of workers' councils in the factories, electing a provisional steering committee instead.[101] What had disturbed the process of election was class tension. Most of those who filled the steering committee places were local professionals who had been assumed to be the leaders of the local revolution by virtue of the fact that they had been invited to attend a meeting of the city's intelligentsia on 23 October. That meeting was, according to popular myth, called to create a local version of the Petőfi Circle, even though the reality of the meeting was far less politically unambiguous than such rumor suggested.[102] Workers present at the meeting were unprepared to allow "professionals" to constitute a revolutionary council, and the election was delayed after the intervention of a coal hewer who called on his fellow workers "not to allow ourselves to be played games with, because from where I'm standing, lawyers, doctors, and teachers want to take over the running of the city."[103] The professionals, who formed the core of the steering committee and played key roles after a full council was elected the following day, were themselves divided, between moderates, who wished to stabilize the situation locally in cooperation with the party only if it was wholeheartedly committed to reform, and radicals, led by the young teacher, György Mazalin, who believed that the revolution demanded the outright overthrow of the existing system. The radicals were strengthened on the one hand by the presence of large numbers of armed, young workers on the streets.[104] On the other hand, the local party, which remained in existence and in contact with the council, never accepted the authority of the new revolutionary organs and believed it had the right to "consider" and "accept" or to "reject" their demands. Mine managers were deeply suspicious of this revolutionary council.[105]

Management faced a collapse of its authority, however, as the more radical revolutionary activists, supported by many armed young workers, organized workers' councils during the last days of October. They were organized against the backdrop of a strike that was the product of both public transport ceasing to function and outrage at the violence perpetrated by Soviet troops and the security services against demonstrators nationwide.[106] It was in this climate that the provisional steering committee of the Tatabánya Workers' and Soldiers' Council sought to ensure the election of workers' councils to assume the functions of management in the factories.[107] With radicals in the crowd and close to the revolutionary council aware of the continued presence of the party in the factories, they determined to use the elections of workers' councils as a means of purging their workplaces of the party.[108] Thus, elections to the workers' councils degenerated into a battle between those loyal to the old regime and more radical younger workers. Amid the chaotic circumstances of the elections in many of the pits and factories, as in the case of Pit No. XI, the force of numbers could be used to influence the course of meetings, which were open mass meetings of the workers present. The demand of the radicals that "we will not tolerate paid functionaries among us," combined with their force of numbers, was sufficient in most workplaces to ensure that radicals prevailed.[109]

While most urban workers solidly supported the strike throughout late October, they were more moderate than the younger radicals and proved willing to support the line proposed by the relatively moderate majority of the Tatabánya Workers' and Soldiers' Council. As a condition for ending the strike, the council demanded that Imre Nagy's government in Budapest meet sixteen demands, which included a mix of political demands for the withdrawal of Soviet troops and a democratic government based on principles of national independence, as well as demands of more direct interest to workers such as the abolition of the norms and labor competition in the city's factories and mines.[110] The issuing of demands was sufficient to mobilize workers in key positions to return to work in order to maintain some production. This was especially critical in the mines, where pump operators were needed to prevent the pits from flooding and maintenance staff worked to ensure that the mines were ready for production. On the Monday morning following the issuing of the demands, "the mines were already busier," as a slow but steady stream of coal-face workers returned to the mines. In the absence of a reply to the council's demands from the government, those miners made clear that they were prepared to regulate their pace of work, so that only just enough coal would be produced to ensure the functioning of the power plants and emergency services in the city.[111] The shift in the stance of the government over the course of the following week, with the promise of outright democratization and eventually Hungarian neutrality, was sufficient to convince urban workers to abandon the strike, when the Komárom County Revolutionary Workers' and Soldiers' Council announced that the demands of the revolution had been met. The return to work in the mines began on the afternoon of Friday, 2 November, and spread to all of the city's workplaces on Saturday morning.[112]

During the course of the strike, the atmosphere among urban miners in their colonies had been relatively calm. The most marked sign of protest outside the factories, and away from the crowds, was the spontaneous occupation of empty flats by families determined to use the collapse in the authority of the state to solve their housing problems, before such flats could be distributed to others. There were 297 flats in the city illegally occupied in this way—testimony to both the level of frustration with the housing shortage and the illegitimacy of the official flat distribution system; all of the families who took direct action were without adequate accommodation.[113] Even as miners returned to work on 3 November, their numbers were well down compared to the numbers reporting for their shifts on 25 October.[114] While large numbers of working-class youth had joined the demonstrations, those who had come recently from the eastern part of the country and who were effectively long-distance commuters returned to their home villages, ransacking the hostels as they left.[115] While long-distance commuters melted away, in areas where there was substantial commuting from villages to industrial establishments on a daily basis the revolution in Tatabánya stimulated upheavals in its rural hinterland. In Várgesztes, all but 6 of the 97 households had members working outside agriculture in 1956, virtually all in mining. News of revolutionary events in neighboring Oroszlány and Tatabánya, brought by commuters, led to the overthrow of the local council and its replacement by a national committee elected by demonstrators.[116] In Tatabánya's hinterland, issues of agricultural landownership figured prominently, together with demands for Soviet withdrawal and generalized anticommunism. Worker-peasants were as likely to join the anticollectivization revolt as were other village dwellers; in Vértesszőllős, demonstrators demanded the breakup of the local collective farm and the return of land to its previous owners.[117]

## The Worker-Peasants' Revolution in Southern Zala

Just as in Tatabánya's rural hinterland, in southern Zala worker-peasants at the oil wells played a central role in spreading the revolution from the county's urban centers to the villages. The process of revolution in the oil fields began on Thursday, 25 October, in the Transdanubian Oil Industry Machine Factory in Nagykanizsa— the nearest large town to the drilling sites—when workers put down their tools in protest at the first Soviet intervention and took to the streets proclaiming their support for the students in Budapest, the withdrawal of Soviet troops, the introduction of a multiparty system, the removal of Communists from leading positions, withdrawal from the Warsaw Pact, and a democratic government.[118] On their march through the town, they were joined by other workers; in a pattern similar to events in the rest of the country, younger workers among the demonstrators removed the five-pointed stars from public buildings.[119] This group converged on the town's memorial to their Soviet "liberators" in 1945, where one speaker told the crowd that "the time has come to destroy that abominable symbol that has stood here for twelve years. We have been waiting twelve years for this!"[120] In response, a group of young workers, led by a twenty-six-year-old pipefitter from the local construction enterprise, demolished the memorial by placing a chain around it and using a truck to pull it down.[121]

The following morning, those workers who commuted by bus from Nagykanizsa to Bázakerettye brought the news to the drilling plant of the demonstration and destruction of the Soviet memorial the previous evening. As the news spread across the site, work stopped and oil workers congregated in front of the machine shop. Someone had acquired several national flags, and the gathering became a demonstration. By the time it reached the site office, up to two hundred workers had joined.[122] At the site office, where management, the party, and the union were located, the crowd grew increasingly loud and angry. It demanded that office workers commit their demands for democratization to paper and that party and union officials join their protest. While one section of the crowd occupied the offices, emptying the enterprises' personnel files and burning them, most continued their march from the site into Bázakerettye village.[123] The crowd, joined in a vain attempt to calm the situation by one official from the district party committee present at Bázakerettye, headed for the Soviet war memorial in the center of the village. With the help of two tractors from the oil wells, in a reenactment of events in Nagykanizsa the previous night, they demolished the memorial. They then removed the five-pointed star from the front of the cultural center and headed for the police station and the local ÁVH barracks.[124]

Among those sections of the crowd that had remained at the site office were a number of worker-peasant commuters from neighboring villages. They determined to spread the news of events in Bázakerettye deeper into the oil fields' rural hinterland. Commandeering the trucks parked in front of the offices, they decorated them with flags and drove them to neighboring villages. Their intention upon arrival was to gather a crowd and proclaim that "demonstrations have begun in Bázakerettye, and all the pictures of Rákosi and Stalin need to be burned, along with the red flags."[125] On arriving in the village of Várfölde, Bázakerettye worker-peasants residing there organized an impromptu demonstration under the slogan "Down with the Communists, down with the agricultural producer cooperatives, down with the council!" The demonstration was directed in the first instance at the local council, responsible for the collection of taxes from smallholders and the management of compulsory deliveries. Demonstrators, interested in the local tax and compulsory delivery records, forced their way into the council archive. They removed and burned the red flags that lay within. The boiling of pent-up anger was directed against those who were responsible for implementing the regime's agrarian policies in the villages, as local officials were threatened with violence, some were told to leave, and the windows of their houses were broken. Even as a national committee was elected, politics in the village over the next few days related to the legacy of the regime's agricultural policies, as a bitter struggle raged between the formerly propertied and the propertyless over the future of the local agricultural producer cooperatives.[126]

The explosion of anger in villages like Várfölde was testimony to the way in which the ripples of the upheavals in Budapest acted as a spark that caused an already tense situation to transform itself into rural revolution. The collapse in the authority of the state in the county had been visible at the beginning of the year— a product of the attempt after the shift in April 1955 to renew the collectivization drive. Across the county, those forced through intimidation to join new agricultural cooperatives, created so that local party organs could meet centrally imposed targets, refused to cooperate and adapt to the new structures. During spring and summer 1956, officials recorded that, in twenty-two new cooperatives, members refused to work the fields in common outright, while these "strikes" spread to a further twenty villages countywide, where party-based campaigns had sought to eliminate individual landholding entirely since mid-1955.[127] The attempts of local authorities to increase the amounts of produce smallholders had to deliver met with tremendous resistance as, by June 1956, almost three and half times as many smallholders were reported to be behind with their compulsory deliveries than was the case a year previously.[128] Political tension in villages led to a number of incidents of physical violence between farmers and party activists, including one incident in which a former local party secretary was seriously beaten. Activists seeking to organize cooperatives found themselves beaten back by a wave of intimidation when they attempted to enter hostile villages.[129]

By early spring 1956, party activists at the oil wells had come to regard as futile the efforts to persuade worker-peasants to surrender their land as part of the collectivization campaign. This was because, as far as those at Bázakerettye were concerned, "workers are forced to work in agriculture, because they simply don't earn enough in the factory to cover their living costs, especially if they have a large family."[130] This was a symptom of a deeper crisis at the oil fields, caused by the effects of the state's introduction of a new wage system in August 1955. Monthly salaries among oil drilling brigades had been well below the industrial average during the New Course era, but the changes of 1955 exacerbated the problem. Average monthly wages among the oil production brigades at Bázakerettye had stood at 1,140 forints for the first seven months of 1955. Given the workings of the system of premium-related payments through which most oil workers and the fact that the plant barely fulfilled its plan over the winter of 1955–56, average wages fell to 990 forints during the first quarter of 1956.[131] At Nagylengyel, they remained stagnant—the average monthly wage for workers stood at 1,107 forints during the first quarter of 1956.[132]

The patience of workers wore thin: "they won't turn up for meetings, events, or seminars, they say that they'd rather go home and work, because they don't even earn above the poverty line in the plant." This sentiment combined with the passive resistance that had been present during 1955. "If the workers make mistakes," stated one manager, "they refer to family and material problems and that they are inattentive for this reason."[133]

This deep-seated material discontent was dangerous because the impact of the political upheavals that accompanied de-Stalinization was felt in the oil fields, just as it was across the county. It was partly a product of the Twentieth Congress of the Communist Party in Moscow and the debates in the Petőfi Circle in Budapest that led workers in distant Zala to raise questions about Rákosi's responsibility for the show trials of the early 1950s, which contributed to the crumbling of the state's authority locally.[134] The gradual thaw in relations with Yugoslavia assumed concrete form with the gradual relaxation of control over the border, as the *határövezet* (border zone), introduced in 1949 to prevent movement from the rest of the country to villages close to the border, was abolished in March.[135] The removal of the *határsáv* (border strip), which had prevented residents from entering a zone of five hundred meters from the border, followed a month later, while plans were laid for dismantling the barbed wire and minefields that separated the two countries over the summer.[136] As a consequence, ÁVH units along the border with Yugoslavia were instructed to improve their relations with the local population by offering direct assistance to local agricultural cooperatives and maintaining close contacts with residents.[137] At Lovászi, where relations between the local population and the border guard had been especially poor, this brought about notable and radical change. The contradictions that were felt between the regime's agrarian policies and material frustration among oil workers and the signs of visible thaw in relation to Yugoslavia, as well as the passionate debates over de-Stalinization, produced radicalization among workers and disorientation among party members. Few accepted Rákosi's legitimacy, and throughout the spring, open criticism of his "cult of personality" was heard at the sites.[138]

This confluence of factors produced an explosion of political protest among party members at Lovászi in August 1956, more than two months before the outbreak of the revolution. It focused on the figure of the plant director, Károly Papp, imported by the regime when the oil wells were nationalized in 1948. Papp had become notorious for bullying workers and cursing them to their faces. Complaints had festered about his use of factory property for personal purposes, especially a limousine bought by the enterprise. Activists connected his behaviors to those of Stalin and Rákosi, as they accused Papp of shaping a "cult of personality" around himself. This concern was heightened by the attempts of the state to devolve more authority to management as part of economic reform, something many workers regarded with horror given Papp's personality, what they regarded as his contempt for "collective agreements," and his willingness to give bonuses to managers and withhold them from workers.[139] Furious complaint against Papp acted as a focus among workers for more general material and political discontent. Attempts to defuse discontent over wages by promising an increase from July 1956 foundered on the complexity of calculating wages, resulting in a situation in which expectations were raised but monthly pay increased only slightly, if at all.[140] Anger at "poor wages," broken promises, and a decision by the OTP (National Savings Bank) to turn down applications for loans from all but nine of those who wished to build houses provoked angry demands for "firm leadership on a more democratic basis" in place of the dictatorship of the current director.[141] The change in the climate was pronounced; when the factory party committee attempted to stem the protests by removing those it regarded as "troublemakers," the district party insisted instead that the "justified complaints" of its activists be addressed properly and that the director be "punished" so that he became "more accessible to the workers and that he pays more attention to resolving workers' complaints."[142]

The upheavals of August influenced the course of events when the revolution spread to Lovászi on 26 October. The events began when skilled workers in the machine shop decided to organize a demonstration; they raided the House of Culture for national flags and handed them out among the workers. They headed for the local ÁVH barracks, and many of the border guard troops there, in keeping with the radical changes in their relations with the population that had characterized relaxation along the Yugoslav border, decided to join the demonstrating workers.[143] While some of the demonstrators pushed on to the adjacent village of Kútfej, workers converged on the local restaurant and removed the statue of Stalin. Then they moved on to the House of Culture, where the crowd elected a workers' council of twenty-two and an executive committee of ten to take over the running of the enterprise. Their eleven demands included national independence, the cleansing of the country's leadership of "Stalinists," and democratization. They also made clear that "we will continue production, but we will not give a drop of oil to Soviet tanks," and they called on the Soviet Union to repatriate all remaining prisoners of war.[144] On hearing of the election of the workers' council, Károly Papp, on the pretext that his wife had fallen ill at home in Nagykanizsa, sought to leave the site using the company limousine. Radicals in the crowd, motivated by complaints that he had used the car as his personal property, blocked his way and demanded that he depart the site on foot and surrender his pistol. It was only after the intervention of more moderate elements that a settlement was reached; Papp would be allowed to use the car only if he accepted that two workers accompany him to ensure its safe and immediate return.[145]

The conduct of the crowd toward Papp reflected a number of factors that shaped revolutionary politics in the oil fields. The first, familiar from other contexts, was division between moderates and radicals over the degree to which Communists were to be removed from factory life. The second and closely related process was the degree of reaction to those who, like Papp, had arrived in the fields after nationalization and the MAORT trial that had accompanied the creation of socialist dictatorship eight years previously. Divisions between radicals, concentrated among the skilled oil drillers and engineers, and workers' council members covering the rest of the plant at Lovászi led to the drilling section electing a workers' council that remained autonomous from the plant's council for just over a day, in order to remove several unpopular Communists, including the section director and the most zealous of the staff responsible for calculating work norms.[146] At Bázakerettye, the factory director faced persistent demands that he resign, given that he had been formally a member of the ÁVH, even though he maintained he had joined under pressure from above. Despite these demands and his own attempts to resign because he believed his position was untenable, he remained in his post until 3 November.[147]

The strength of company identities in the oil fields led to representatives of the individual plant workers' councils convening in Nagykanizsa on 30 October to set up a "Central Workers' Council" for the entire oil field. In steps that evoked memories of the Central Factory Committee that had supervised MAORT between 1945 and 1948, it assumed responsibility for coordinating production and ensuring that the wage levels and benefits for oil workers were the same across all sites.[148] At the more local level, and especially at Bázakerettye and Lovászi, the workers' council was preoccupied with reorganizing the factories' security staff and realizing the demands of workers that they continue to produce but withhold oil until they received reassurance that it would not be used to fuel Soviet tanks. Given the problems of storage and the damage that could be done to long-term production as a consequence of any short-term stoppage, both councils had to coordinate a gradual and partial shutdown of their wells within each plant.[149] On wage questions, the two councils remained moderate, refusing to change the existing wage rates within the plant and shifting their practice only when, at the end of October, the new Central Workers' Council demanded that no premiums be paid to those demoted from administrative positions to manual ones because of their political pasts under Rákosi and that the lowest paid workers receive a special bonus.[150] This moderate line was related to the fact that the workers' council rested largely on those landless workers who continued to work, while more radical, anti-Communist worker-peasants returned to their home villages in order to overturn the local apparatus, agricultural cooperatives, and agrarian policies.[151] The closeness of these workers' councils to landless workers was reflected in their denunciation of local farmers for responding to the revolution by increasing the prices workers had to pay for basic foodstuffs.[152]

Because of the absence of a local landless workforce of any significance and the greater degree of integration of Nagylengyel's workforce with the local property owners involved in agriculture, the workers' council in that town and the political context in which it operated were entirely different. News filtered through to Nagylengyel on 26 October that workers' councils had been elected at Bázakerettye and Lovászi, and union officials sympathetic to the revolution demanded that the factory committee president convene a mass meeting to elect a council at Nagylengyel. The committee president attempted to delay calling the mass meeting, and the dissident activists began the task of organizing an election for the following day.[153] As rebel activists began organizing their meeting, twelve kilometers away in the county town of Zalaegerszeg, residents, led by pupils from one local grammar school and some of the city's workers, took to the streets. The protests turned violent when demonstrators were fired upon in front of the county party headquarters—two were killed instantly, a further four were seriously injured. As anger mounted, county party officials, realizing that neither the Red Army troops stationed in the county nor the regime in Budapest could offer them support, determined to flee.[154] Given the numbers of workers who commuted to Zalaegerszeg from neighboring villages, the violence in the county town led to explosions of anger outside it. In Lickóvadamos, three kilometers from Nagylengyel, an angry crowd marched through the village that evening, demanding "Rákosi to the gallows! Nothing else for Gerő!"[155]

The mass meeting at Nagylengyel took place in a climate in which long-term anger among the worker-peasant workforce over the renewed collectivization drive was sharpened by fury at the violence used against demonstrators in Zalaegerszeg the previous day. The factory committee president made the mistake of opening the mass meeting by addressing those present as "comrades." Some in the crowd responded by shouting, "What do you mean 'comrades'? Your time is up!"[156] It rapidly became clear to the angry crowd that factory management and the trade union leadership had decided in advance who they wished to be elected to the new workers' council and wanted the crowd to endorse their list through a show of hands. The mood became ugly as the attempts by management to control the meeting were drowned out by a chant that "the Stalinists' time is up, it is time to rid ourselves of them." Taking control of the meeting, the crowd secured the election of its own candidates. The meeting became increasingly radical, replacing the heads of the labor and personnel departments, as well as the factory committee president. There were loud demands to fire all those who set production norms.[157] While the new workers' council coordinated with those at Bázakerettye and Lovászi on the issue of maintaining production and proved more moderate than the crowd that elected it, it took a markedly more radical stance than those at other drilling sites, seizing the factory's personnel papers with the intention of examining them carefully as part of a drive to root out those who had acted against workers from the factory. While it fired neither those who set norms nor Communists en masse—indeed it praised the factory party secretary, despite his own public declaration of support for the party before the workers' council—it resolved to determine through an assessment of their past behavior whether they should stay at the plant.[158]

Many of the crowd came from worker-peasant households, lived in the neighboring villages, and wanted to take the revolution home. When they did so, as in Várfölde, worker-peasants targeted the local party and council officials who had implemented the regime's agrarian policies. One thirty-year-old unskilled worker returned home to Lickóvadamos after the election of the workers' council. Together with five others, all of whom worked at Nagylengyel or in Zalaegerszeg factories, they determined to hunt down and drive the party secretary from the village. Discovering him drinking wine with the village council leader, a number of the group beat him unconscious before they were restrained by the others.[159] In Dömefölde, a revolutionary crowd that largely consisted of oil workers was determined to destroy the agricultural taxation and compulsory delivery records held by the village council. One member of the crowd demanded that the council secretary and party secretary help them gain access to the council building and to the location where papers were stored under lock and key. In an increasingly threatening atmosphere, the secretaries handed over the materials before fleeing. Once the demonstrators had collected the papers together, they burned the lot the following day.[160] In keeping with the anger of rural crowds at the regime's agrarian policies, agricultural producer cooperatives that did not collapse outright were also targets of the initial revolutionary wave in villages around the oil fields. In Becsehely, the revolutionary crowd, with the participation of some oil workers, forced its way into the offices of one of the local agricultural producer cooperatives, where they destroyed its license to operate, as well as socialist realist paintings depicting strikes by agricultural laborers.[161] These violent explosions of anger were testimony to the deep-seated illegitimacy of the regime in the villages and the festering fury that had been generated by its challenge to established property and social relations. Becsehely was typical of many of southern Zala's villages in that revolutionary violence lasted for only a day and subsided after the swift transfer of power to a local revolutionary committee that resolved to dissolve agricultural cooperatives and return the land to the original owners.[162] By the end of October, at both the oil drilling plants and in the villages around them, power had been transferred to new revolutionary organs, and the state security services and the party seemed to have been smashed. This appearance was deceptive, however, for after the second Soviet intervention, which began on 4 November, and the military and political defeat of the revolution, Hungary's socialist state would successfully be reconstructed.

# 8 The Foundations of Consolidation
## November 1956–June 1958

ON THE EVENING of 1 November 1956, the revolution appeared to have triumphed, as the MDP had dissolved itself, to be refounded as the MSzMP (Hungarian Socialist Workers' Party), and Imre Nagy had declared Hungary neutral. Yet in Moscow, the Soviet leadership had decided that Hungary's revolution now threatened its own hegemony across the eastern half of Europe and that Nagy was both unable and unwilling to resolve the crisis in the country to Moscow's satisfaction. The Soviet ambassador to Hungary, Yuri Andropov, persuaded János Kádár, the new head of the MSzMP, to fly to Moscow in secret from the military airfield at Tököl, south of Budapest.[1] For both the Soviet leadership and many former Communist officials, the growing radicalism of the revolution was deeply disturbing. Conservative parties, openly to the right of those allowed during the popular-front period, were founded.[2] Cardinal Mindszenty, freed by revolutionary action, spoke on national radio.[3] Most disturbing for the Soviet and Communist leaders was the revolutionary violence, of which the most notorious incident was the aftermath of the bloody siege of the Budapest Party Committee building in Republic Square on 30 October, when, after the occupation of the building, those who had besieged it, enraged with the loss of life of many of their number, lynched twenty-three of its occupants.[4] Many of those who remained loyal to the former regime consequently came to constitute a domestic base of support for the attempt by Moscow to destroy the revolution.[5]

The Red Army struck back on the morning of 4 November, overthrowing Imre Nagy and putting in place a "Revolutionary Workers' and Peasants' Government" under János Kádár. Street battles raged for up to seven days in some of the working-class districts of the capital, and approximately 16,700 were injured and 2,502 died—overwhelmingly young workers under thirty years of age.[6] While the Soviets crushed armed resistance quickly, workers responded with a general strike, which the Kádár government attempted to break by offering the carrot of wage increases and the stick of repression. On the initiative of the Újpest Revolutionary Committee, the Central Greater Budapest Workers' Council was formed in the United Incandescent Lamp and Electrical Factory to negotiate with the new government. While the workers called off the general strike on 17 November, relations between the workers' council and workers and the state remained tense, punctuated by frequent stoppages of work. By early December, it had become clear that agreement between Kádár and the Central Greater Budapest Workers' Council was impossible, for the council had become a focus for militant opposition to the regime. The latter reacted by rounding up revolutionary activists, to which the workers' council responded with a renewed general strike call, which in turn led to the arrest of the leaders of the Central Greater Budapest Workers' Council and its suppression.[7]

While the atmosphere, especially in industrial areas of the capital, was tense, with strikes and open demonstrations as late as January 1957, the unity and determination of workers to protest subsided as early as the second half of November 1956.[8] As the leaders of the Central Greater Budapest Workers' Council were taken into custody, workers were increasingly divided on the wisdom of striking, and, consequently, by mid-December 1956, in most of the country the will to strike had collapsed outright.[9] While the targeted use of repression was central to breaking the strike, it often proved to be counterproductive, for news of arrests only provoked more explosions of protest.[10] Three further factors strengthened targeted repression. The first of these was the flight of many from Hungary; between 4 November 1956 and the end of May 1957, 182,438 persons left the country. Official estimates suggested that 63.5 percent of those were industrial workers, while the predominance of the young among refugees suggests that young workers, who had played key roles in radicalizing the revolution, were overrepresented.[11] The second two factors were economic. As the regime strengthened, it grew able to prevent enterprises from paying striking workers. As the end of 1956 neared, the economic effects of the revolution and the continued strike were felt through the spread of shortages, especially of coal.[12] The regime used the growing threat of unemployment provoked by shortages as an effective means of coercing reluctant strikers to return to work.[13]

By the turn of 1957, although the Kádár regime had smashed the revolution, it was clear that it could not pacify Hungarian society unless it successfully constructed a semblance of legitimacy for itself. This was an especially challenging task given the Kádár regime's status as a government installed by the army of a foreign power and the polarization between a small minority who defended the regime and the overwhelming majority. While the MSzMP's organizational strength was built from below during early 1957, it was constructed on the ruins of the discredited MDP. It had far fewer members than its predecessor; the concentration of its membership in the capital and its considerable strength among the officials who staffed the state apparatus pointed to a party based on the most hard-line of the supporters of the socialist regime.[14] At the same time, the residual anger that the events of 1956 had produced, even among urban workers, manifested itself in a willingness to support institutions and express opinions associated with opposition to socialism. Consequently, church attendance grew in popularity in industrial districts in the capital throughout 1957; according to one official, "there hasn't been such attendance for years."[15] In the postrevolutionary climate, there was a marked revival in the public expression of anti-Communist opinions in factories and industrial districts. Many argued bitterly about the ways in which Hungary's post–World War I losses of territory, especially of Transylvania, had been maintained by Soviet troops after 1945. Anti-Semitic opinions were frequently expressed to bring into question the notions that Hungary's rulers represented workers: "we could put together some statistics to see how many Jews actually do any manual work."[16]

The restored regime sought to bridge this gulf by differentiating itself from both Imre Nagy and the revolutionary movement and those, like Rákosi and Gerő, whom it had attacked. It maintained that it defended the socialist system against a "counterrevolution," driven by an internal "reaction" supported by the Western powers, that sought to use the situation in Hungary to restore a capitalist system. The myth of "counterrevolution" was manufactured through a concrete propaganda effort in which the events of 1956, at both the local and national levels, were distorted and re-presented to the population through special publications, of which the most significant were the national "white books" and their local equivalents, as well as the press.[17] The practice of judicial retribution was tied explicitly to the manufacture of this myth through a series of political trials that, unlike those of the Rákosi years, concentrated on actual events but sought to place them in the mythical context of the regime's official view of 1956 as a "counterrevolution."[18] It balanced this, however, with an emphatic anti-Stalinism in that it blamed the leadership of the MDP for the climate that led to "counterrevolution." In this spirit, it accused the "Rákosi-Gerő clique" of preventing "the broadening of the democratization of party and social life; it crudely damaged socialist legality. It forced an economic policy on the people that ignored the economic potential of the country and prevented an increase in the living standards of the workers." From 1953 onward, "the sectarian policy of the former party leadership created a broad, democratic movement." While it praised those participants in this movement who remained "loyal to socialism," it condemned those around Nagy for taking their criticism "onto the streets, by which reactionary elements could join it."[19]

This ideological formula created the basis for the party leadership to plug the gaping hole in the construction of its own legitimacy that the 1956 Revolution had revealed—that industrial workers had taken to the streets in huge numbers against the socialist regime. Yet, in order to even attempt to rebuild this legitimacy, the state had to place material flesh on these ideological bones. The party leadership understood this as attempting to return to a point in 1948–49, before "the construction of the democratic state was deformed."[20] This required attempting to breathe life into the trade unions as "the old, traditional representatives of the working class" and to give them greater independence from the party and management. It also involved, in the short term, recognizing the workers' councils once they had been purged "of the remnants of foreign and enemy political influence."[21] As part of this turn to the "working class," the hegemonic wage systems and the tight production norms of the Rákosi years were scrapped, to be replaced with more decentralized forms of remuneration, which in many workplaces, especially those populated by the skilled male elite, were more in line with dominant moral economies.[22] While managements and the regime reintroduced labor competition in its collective, brigade-based form, they did so carefully, to ensure that memories of Stakhanovite mobilization were not awakened.[23] Conciliatory policies within the realm of work were combined with a sustained attempt to address the huge material discontent among industrial workers. The government proclaimed that "the basic mistake of our economic policy over recent years . . . was that the goal of the plan was not to improve the living and working conditions of the workers, but its basic goal was to expand the productive capacity of the economy through industrialization."[24] A continuous rise in workers' real incomes was placed at the heart of economic policy: the wage increases mandated as part of attempts to break the strike were confirmed, family allowances (*családi pótlék*) were hiked to help large families, a minimum wage in industry was introduced, and the value of pensions was increased. A major multifamily housing construction program was launched, along with improvements to public transport, major investment in public health services, and greater cultural opportunities for youth.[25]

By the end of 1957, the politics of conciliation had brought substantial material improvement, especially for urban workers. As a result of the combination of wage increases and other measures, the average income of a working family in Budapest was 18 percent higher than it had been a year previously.[26] This improvement provided the basis for the generation of a brittle and conditional legitimacy for the regime among urban workers. This legitimacy became increasingly visible during 1958, and it revived in a new context what had existed during 1948 and 1949. It was, however, far shallower in that it was based in large part on the degree to which Kádár had successfully differentiated his regime from the practice of Rákosi's; indeed, the acceptance and relative popularity of Kádár among urban workers coexisted with the fear of a return to the policies of the early 1950s.[27] Yet, as with earlier constructions of the socialist state's legitimacy, it was circumscribed politically. Among the rural population, the religious and political conservatives, the generation of brittle legitimacy among left-wing, urban workers was experienced as a consolidation of the defeat of the revolution, and such populations responded by retreating into the domestic sphere.[28]

The emergence of brittle legitimacy was highly protracted in Újpest, where it coexisted with a strong culture of underground protest that represented an afterlife of the 1956 Revolution in the district's factories until 1958. In southern Zala, attitudes toward the new regime were marked more by a reluctant acceptance of its assumption of power. Consequently, many oil workers, like the rest of the rural population, experienced the consolidation of Kádár's rule as a traumatic process of defeat, which prepared the way for the final, successful collectivization campaign in the region at the very end of the 1950s. Brittle legitimacy was established most successfully and completely in Tatabánya, despite the bitterness of the protracted and sometimes violent attempts to break the strike in the city's mines during the dying days of 1956. Established cultures of work, as well as class, made the urban population especially receptive to Kádár's workerist measures, while class tension directed toward professionals allowed the local variant of the myth of "counterrevolution" to win a degree of acceptance. Improvements in living standards eased material frustration, giving credibility to the regime's promises of a solution to the city's most persistent social problems, especially its housing shortage.

## The Gains of Defeat in Tatabánya

During his trial for "participation in a movement that aimed at the overthrow of the peoples' democratic order" in September 1957, Imre Kovács, who had led the anti-Communist workers' council in the Tatabánya Coal Mining Trust's machine plant during the strike that followed Soviet intervention in November 1956, defended himself in part by denying his anti-Soviet stance. He also did so by arguing that the demands of revolutionary bodies in Tatabánya he had supported had "been largely met by the Kádár government" since the revolution.[29] In making this defense, Kovács put his finger on the split opinion of many urban Tatabánya residents of the government that the Red Army had brought to power; they believed, on the one hand, that many of their material aspirations had been met, though they continued to be fearful and mistrustful of the regime that ruled them. At the end of 1957, party activists who went door to door in the city were "surprised" at their apparent popularity there.[30] The Kádár government's policies of social and economic conciliation generated what seemed to the city party committee to be "trust in the party and the government."³¹ Behind this startling recovery in the status of the regime after the low point it had reached after the crushing of the revolution lay deeper unease and insecurity. Workers found it difficult to negotiate the boundaries the regime had set around discussion of 1956; in discussions with party activists, as miners began referring to 1956 as the "counterrevolution," they often slipped into describing it as "a revolution." Defending their ideological clumsiness, most expressed opinions consistent with a conditional acceptance of the legitimacy of the regime: "You should give us an honest wage. I'm not bothered by the rest."³²

This turnaround was remarkable, given the bitter struggles that surrounded the Soviet intervention and the creation of the Kádár regime. When the news of the overthrow of the Nagy government was broadcast over the radio on the morning of 4 November, it met with a muted reaction in the city as the moderate majority on the Tatabánya Workers' and Soldiers' Council sought to restrain those who wished to fight. Placed under pressure by thirty radicals who "demanded weapons" because "Soviet troops are here and we've not done anything," the council leadership placated them by supplying empty gasoline cans for their attempted defense.³³ While the radicals prepared to fight, the moderate majority of the council met with the local Soviet command that had set itself up in the neighboring town of Tata, in order to ensure that the entry of Soviet troops into Tatabánya did not lead to bloodshed. The following day, they reoccupied the major public buildings in the city; while they met no armed resistance, their arrival was greeted with fury.³⁴ In one incident on the Wednesday evening following the arrival of the Soviets, outside one pub in new Tatabánya stood a "huge electricity pole, a telegraph pole, with three loudspeakers on it for broadcasting the news from the miners' radio, and on that night . . . it was announced that the city's Soviet commander was speaking to the city's population. The crowd toppled the pole with the strength of their bare hands, and they stamped all over, trampled all over the loudspeakers on the ground."³⁵ Miners refused to go to work in protest, and attempts to persuade them to end their strike were met with blunt refusal.³⁶ Anger combined with shock: "Everyone was just stunned that our independence was over, our neutrality. Neutrality—that was what the people were most happy about. You see, there was an example, Austria . . . the Russians left, they became neutral."³⁷

Despite the strike, the local supporters of socialist dictatorship had never disappeared from Tatabánya completely; Soviet intervention allowed them to counterattack. A restored county and city leadership demanded that anyone who thought of armed resistance must lay down their arms. The local MSzMP was uninterested in compromise; its cooperation with the Revolutionary Workers' and Soldiers' Council through a joint operational committee lasted all of four days. It maintained that, as the council "cannot secure order, . . . it has today become necessary that the legal authorities, the councils, and the armed defenders-of-order take back power."³⁸ Mistrustful of an army, state security agency officers, and police, who had capitulated in the face of the initial revolutionary demonstrations, the local MSzMP determined to form its own paramilitary unit, made up of its most trustworthy left-wing activists. It was organized under the leadership of János Beer, a hard-line Communist activist who worked as a pit deputy.[39] The Beer group, as it became known, was notorious for its poor relations with other security organs, its left-wing militancy, its poor discipline, and arbitrary and often violent behavior toward those who stood in its way—a product of its irregular nature and the lack of any form of legal supervision or control over its activities.[40]

Their activities were directed against the workers' councils in the city's mines and factories, where radical anti-Communists were entrenched. In Pit No. XI, the local workers' council, with the support of those miners who turned up, refused to produce any coal on the grounds that "they did not recognize the Kádár government, only Imre Nagy."[41] During the ten days following the second Soviet intervention, the government became increasingly desperate to end the strike; the situation in Tatabánya remained tense, with fewer than a third of miners turning up for work, problems of crime against property, and increasing shortages of basic foodstuffs.[42] They attempted persuasion, sending Teofild Sándor, banned from the city for his opposition to the district leadership of the MKP nine years previously and who had since worked as a government official, to persuade local workers' councils to end their support for the strike. In the machine shop, Sándor met with blunt refusal from the workers' council: "We do not recognize the Kádár government, it does not lead us; we have had enough of the Communist system, of twelve years of theft. Make sure you understand that we will not work for as long as Kádár and the Communists remain in the government."[43]

Futile attempts to persuade radicals in the workers' councils to endorse a return to work were matched by a policy of social and economic concessions made by the government. These were intended to appeal to the more moderate revolutionary activists and, going over the heads of the workers' councils entirely, to ordinary miners. On 10 November, the government hiked miners' wages by 12 percent, introducing special premiums for those who had reported for work during the previous week, while three days later they promised the workers' councils in the mines legal recognition.[44] Between the micropolitics of persuasion and the macropolitics of conciliation, the Tatabánya Coal Mining Trust called the unions, the party, and the factory-level workers' councils together to organize a return to work.[45] This meeting resulted in the election of a workers' council, which was led by a smaller executive committee that covered the whole coal trust. While this council was prepared to cooperate to end the strike and restart coal production, it made clear that it did not accept the legitimacy of the regime. To this end, it established contact with the Central Greater Budapest Workers' Council and stated that "with our full strength we wish to build our homeland and we trust that as a result of our work and struggle an independent and free Hungary will be born."[46] Given the tense political climate and continued anger, the return to work in the mines was partial and the recovery in production levels, slow and uneven. Other workers stayed home, saying that, "if the miners finally go back to work, we will join them."[47]

A frustrated local party leadership and its own paramilitaries, organized in the Beer group, further destabilized the situation by acting directly against activists in the plant-level workers' councils and by attempting to break strikes.[48] Their violent harassment of workers' council members escalated, as many were rounded up and taken to the Beer group's barracks for "a little chat," during which many were beaten.[49] The behavior of the group undermined the national government's attempts to break the strike by meeting the economic demands of miners. While the workers' council had on 23 November withdrawn its support for an all-out strike, only 50 percent of the workforce reported for work during the last week of the month. Of those who did, most were angry and believed that the government's promises were worthless, as a consequence of the local party's hard-line stance: "the workers are discontented with the government's measures, there are no concrete steps; their demands have not been met."[50] This growing sense of discontent and anger crystallized in a demand that Kádár himself come to Tatabánya. When he did so on 30 November, he laid the basis for his appeal to workers locally. On the one hand, he argued that he was defending the workers against "counterrevolutionary forces," yet he made clear that, in the workplace, "the leadership of production is not a task for the party. The workers' representative body, the workers' council, has both serious rights and serious obligations." He maintained that he would "ask for the support of the workers" by promising to raise living standards, while insisting that, although "the government had abolished the ÁVH," it required loyal security services.[51] This echoed promises made to the miners by the county's newspaper a few days previously: "the workers' councils have been given responsibility for the economic life of the country." Furthermore, "certain old privileges" of miners, like "the annual coal entitlement, rent-free accommodation, and lighting," would be restored.[52]

Further increases in wages and other measures following Kádár's visit eroded support for the strike, as sufficient numbers of miners returned to work to operate two shifts, believing "their economic demands" were being met.[53] Sensing a strengthening of its position, the government moved against workers' councils in mining nationwide, arresting pro-revolution officials in the Ministry of Mining and Heavy Industry. In protest and in the face of a growing atmosphere of intimidation coordinated by the local Soviet high command, miners began a strike to seek the disbanding of the Beer group. The work stoppage rapidly turned into demonstrations.[54] The following day—7 December—the workers' council organized a demonstration in front of the county party committee headquarters to press its demands.[55] As the party agreed to allow representatives from the demonstration into the building for talks, the ranks of the protesters swelled, joined by those anxious to voice disapproval about the events of the past month. The crowd shouted,

"Hungarians, don't work! All patriots are on strike! It is time we were liberated from Communist subjection! Russians go home!"[56] As the crowd grew more threatening, it was surrounded by Soviet tanks; some of the building's defenders fired into the air, as did the Russians, to force the crowd to disperse. Shots were fired into the crowd, allegedly by members of the Beer group, injuring several.[57]

The security forces were not content with dispersing the demonstrators but determined to round up those members of workers' councils they regarded as "troublemakers" in order to prevent further open protests.[58] As the news of arrests spread, generating panic across the city, residents in one tightly knit community of miners—those living on Site VI of the mining colony—resolved to use force to prevent any representatives of the state from arresting local residents. After 4 November, in order to avoid reprisals, young miners had hidden their weapons in a local "wood." On the evening of 7 December, they retrieved the arms under cover of darkness so "that everyone received a weapon."[59] From the next evening onward, whenever any motor vehicle identified as belonging to the security agencies approached the site, it was fired on. Two nights later, the security agents returned in force to clear the site of the armed group; three were injured, and a young female resident was killed after being shot in the head by the security forces.[60]

Despite solid support for the renewal of strike action in the mines, given the fury that members of the Beer group continued to serve among the state security forces, support from workers' councils countywide for Tatabánya's demands, and the calling of a national general strike for 11 and 12 December by the Central Greater Budapest Workers' Council, the explosion of violence in the city had the coal trust's workers' council convinced of the wisdom of a moderate course. They withdrew their support for the strike, calling for a return to work on 10 December.[61] Although the behavior of the security forces had generated outrage, behind this anger the workers' will to resist was crumbling. This was a product not only of a sense that Kádár was immovable but also of the worsening economic situation generated by coal shortages, themselves a product of the strike. By mid-December, "there was nothing like any meat [available], just bread, bread and fat. There weren't any cigarettes. You had to queue everywhere."[62] Given the collapse of the economy, coal was the only currency that local authorities could use to stock the city's shops, though given the state of production in the mines, the amount of coal produced was insufficient even to supply the power plants.[63] As growing numbers returned to work, conflict grew between returnees and those who wanted to hold out, given that "many didn't work and still picked up their wage packets as if they had."[64] With the regime insisting that wages be paid only for performance, the mid-December payment of wages that had many workers receiving tiny amounts of money as a result of staying off work further eroded support for the strike.[65]

By the end of 1956, the revolution was defeated in the city, and the leaders of the workers' councils were behind bars.[66] The regime's situation was far from stable, though it began to consolidate its authority. Following the wave of protest during mid-December, the authorities took measures to restrain the Beer group, whose violence toward the local population risked provoking further social explosion, by integrating them tightly into the formal structures of command in the army and police.[67] Some of the group's less well trained, more militant members were sidelined by being placed in the Workers' Guard—the party's volunteer paramilitary organization. Even there, some of their "undisciplined" behavior generated outrage, forcing the authorities to act throughout 1957. One member was expelled from the guard for firing his gun while drunk in front of the block of flats where he lived, while another threatened a woman with his weapon if she resisted his attempts to sexually assault her in a local pub. Behind these particularly shocking incidents, their general contempt for "ordinary, honest people" provoked constant complaint.[68]

The process of pacification involved the national authorities restraining a city party that they believed was too militant in its attitude toward the "counterrevolution" and those who had supported it. The city party committee in turn confronted factory and mine-based cells made up of those who had opposed the revolution during October 1956 and were determined to have their revenge on those who had participated. It reported that "we had to stand up to sectarian excesses in terms of the judgment of the counterrevolution" and the "issue of the removal of counterrevolutionaries."[69] Even as the situation calmed, many members were doubtful of the wisdom of conciliation and continued to support "the mistaken policy of the past," even though, as the control of party officials strengthened, they "did not express their opinion openly."[70] The extent to which the party consisted of the most left-wing types was demonstrated by the fact that, by August 1957, only 39 percent of those who had been members of the MDP at the outbreak of the revolution had joined the MSzMP. Of these, 62.8 percent were workers, while a further 30 percent were those of working-class origin promoted off the shop floor into management and administrative positions.[71] Restraint was necessary because of the social and political gap that existed between the MSzMP's grassroots membership and urban workers in the city. Months after the end of the revolution, in summer 1957, urban workers were prepared to argue with agitators that Soviet "intervention was not necessary." They maintained that "Imre Nagy was well intentioned," for "neutral countries always live in peace and are rich." They responded bluntly to some of the cruder propaganda surrounding the "counterrevolution" with the retort that "here nobody was strung up, nobody was murdered."[72]

Immediately after the revolution's final defeat at the very beginning of 1957, the situation in the factories and mines was profoundly tense. The new year had been greeted with rumors of a "ten-day strike" in the mines. Behind this rumor was discontent at the shortage of cigarettes, the threat of unemployment, and the restoration of the pre-October management.[73] As a consequence of the strike, the physical condition of the mines had deteriorated, creating severe obstacles to a speedy recovery of production.[74] The disappearance of many younger, hostel-dwelling commuters either to their home villages or to Austria left the mines with a serious labor shortage.[75] This shortage was exacerbated by the wave of retributive firings that formed part of the regime's drive to consolidate its authority after the breaking of the strike; during the first quarter of 1957, 1,435 of 9,151 employed by the coal trust lost their jobs for this reason. Labor shortages eased quickly as 3,217 workers were hired after they applied at the gate during the first six months of the year, while renewed labor recruitment campaigns in the poor, rural eastern counties yielded a further 585. By the end of September, the coal trust employed 10,000 workers.[76] From the spring onward, the mines "could not speak of serious labor shortage," as the workers' hostels, empty in the immediate aftermath of the revolution, filled again.[77]

Easing the tense climate that existed in the mines in January 1957 required pursuit of a policy of conciliation in the workplace. As coal production increased steadily throughout the year, management accommodated itself to the work cultures of skilled coal-face workers by adapting its production regimen; in order to secure the consent of workers, the authorities placed distance between the mechanisms of mobilization, introduced during 1957, and practice prior to October 1956. As the regime insisted on the reintroduction of labor competition, workers and activists were careful to stress that the perceived injustices of the prerevolutionary period would not be reproduced. As far as Károly Kilián, a coal hewer in Pit No. VI, was concerned, "at the point at which the competition is introduced it has to break with the old forms of organization, evaluation, and reward for competition. It shouldn't just point to and reward the same hewers all the time, but it should be a competition in which all miners can participate and emulate."[78] As the party launched a national campaign to resume labor competition to celebrate May Day in 1957, miners demanded "rewards" as a condition for participation, while many refused to join on the grounds that they would legitimize a revival of "Stakhanovism" by which "certain brigades will be promoted [and] others just left to their own devices."[79] In the face of such opposition, managers implemented the competition on paper, refusing to publicize the results of individual workers in the mines themselves. Consequently, while competition continued in 1957 as a part of political ritual and became an occasion for the payment of production bonuses to the workforce, it lost any meaningful presence in production itself.[80]

Equally fundamental to the politics of conciliation in the mines were the changes to the wage system for mineworkers. As workers returned to work at the beginning of 1957, management publicized the abolition of production norms. "The norms," it argued, "were based on the production of those who performed above the average; they had the consequence that an absolutely tiny group could earn for themselves a really high income, while the great mass of the workers suffered from low wages." It replaced this system with one of fees for work completed, in which all coal-face workers would be paid on the basis of the number of carts of coal they sent back from the face, with special premiums paid for working underground and for exceeding targets. Rather than being a fee for production, it was designed to reflect fairly the amount of work, for unlike the previous system rules, responsibility for setting the target lay with a mining engineer who had the discretion to take into account the conditions of production at a given place on the coal face.[81] Despite the sense, especially among coal-face workers, that the new system was "more just than the norms," in the climate immediately following the strike many greeted its introduction with "opposition" and demanded to be shown that it was "possible to earn" under the new system.[82] Of the elite workers producing coal at the face, earnings per shift increased from 67.62 forints per worker in January 1957 to 72.65 forints by the end of the year; average monthly earnings of all workers in the coal trust stood at 2,019 forints in December 1957, 18.27 percent higher than the average monthly income during 1956.[83]

The Kádár government's politics of workplace and economic conciliation rein-forced the hegemony of the male underground coal-face workers within estab-lished cultures of industrial labor in the city. In the coal trust, while workers in the pits themselves earned between 2,007 and 2,346 forints per month in October 1957, those in the various aboveground units took home between 1,282 and 1,847 forints.[84] Other male skilled workers were relatively privileged objects of official policies of consolidation yet complained of what they saw as the privileges of coal miners; in the Mine Machine Shop the presumed material privileges of those who worked underground in terms of "coal allowances, preferential flat distribution, . . . loyalty premiums, and other benefits" generated an undercurrent of resentment.[85] Plants like the Cement Factory, outside the privileged heavy industrial sector, were in an even less favorable position. Continued production problems generated by raw material shortages had plagued the plant throughout 1957, while the average monthly wage of its workers during the year, at 1,396 forints, was low relative to that of the mines and was only 12.25 percent above its 1956 level.[86] The gendered dimen-sions of workplace conciliation in the city were reinforced by the lack of employ-ment opportunities deemed suitable for women and exacerbated by the layoffs of women from the mines during early 1957, as part of an attempt to ensure sufficient jobs were available for men.[87] Furthermore, those aspects of its policies of social and economic conciliation directed at female workers revealed sharply gendered attitudes; in the Cement Factory, the company determined to ease the situation of its women workers by buying two washing machines to be placed on loan to them in order to "ease the burden of housework on working women."[88]

The consolidation of Kádár's authority in Tatabánya that was visible by summer 1957 rested on a growing sense of its accommodation with the culture of urban workers in the city. This acted as the base of a brittle legitimacy for the regime. In part, it rested on the considerable material improvement that had occurred since the end of the strike, which led many to maintain that, though "I don't understand politics, I can see that we are living ever better."[89] This improvement, however, was relative, visible in the ways in which the abolition of compulsory deliveries and easing of the pressure on agriculture following the revolution had led to an improved supply of foodstuffs to the city. Despite the government's stress on a consumerist model of socialism and the fact that its claims were more credible than those made in 1956 due to the postrevolutionary wage increases and improvements in goods supply, the supply of consumer materials remained limited. Sought-after goods like washing machines or status-based items, such as motorcycles, especially popular among high-earning young workers, were in short supply. Televisions, which had just come onto the market, were of poor quality.[90] Although material improvement was considerable, so too was frustration, especially with the high prices of food at the city market, the endemic housing shortage, and the "filthy state" of much of the city.[91] The material improvement since the revolution, however, made promises of further improvement, including accelerated construction of multifamily housing, credible. By the end of 1957, this had generated considerable personal popularity for Kádár, shaped by the perception that, in contrast to Rákosi, he was highly focused on improving the lot of workers.[92]

The patterns of the regime's accommodation to urban workers were visible in the ways in which the local party shaped its adaptation of the "counterrevolution" myth to the circumstances of Tatabánya. Despite the almost solid support for the strike during 1956 from all of those urban workers, except the minority who remained committed supporters of the regime, urban workers were notable in official representations of the "counterrevolution" by their absence. In explaining the scale of the demonstrations that toppled the regime locally on 26 October 1956, agitators maintained that they were made up of "hooligans" who "had come here from various parts of the country, or were made up of those freed from the prisons," rather than from the ranks of "old, core miners."[93] While such views echoed the stereotypical views that "older" miners had held of new recruits during the early 1950s, it also played to the more recent complaint among older workers, as the hostels refilled, that new recruits were undisciplined and that only a tiny percentage of them had grown up locally and therefore understood or were a legitimate part of the community.[94] The official propaganda's focus on the role local professionals elected to the Tatabánya Workers' and Soldiers' Council had played in apparently "misleading" the workers during 1956 was designed to appeal to the class resentment directed at local professionals, especially those who staffed health services. Such individuals had generated fury by their practice of demanding under-the-counter payments for medical treatment that was supposed to be free.[95]

Given the abolition of compulsory deliveries and the rapid improvement of the situation in agriculture, class resentment directed against agricultural smallholders was strong among urban workers. Where the two groups lived together in the city, in the former villages of Alsógalla and Bánhida, urban workers "blame them for the high agricultural prices. . . . The peasants live really well, and we pay the price!"[96] This antismallholder feeling would form the basis of support in urban areas when the Kádár regime, under pressure from Moscow and its socialist neighbors, began to prepare the ground for renewed collectivization during 1958.[97] Yet this resentment did not extend to the substantial number of local worker-peasant commuters who had jobs in Tatabánya's mines and its factories. These were "half peasants, half workers, who have between 1 and 3 holds of land, and work for wages. . . . Family members, sometimes more than one family member, work in one factory or another. . . . Their little farm provides them with the basic necessities."[98] Having benefited from a combination of wage increases in the factories and the abolition of compulsory deliveries, they regarded themselves as beneficiaries of the revolution. At the same time, however, they feared that the government at any moment would return to the practices of the pre-1956 era. As agricultural collectivization moved up the political agenda during 1958, they sought to defend their position, telling local party officials that "we agree with socialism, but without agricultural producer cooperatives."[99]

## Consolidation as a Culture of Defeat in Southern Zala

Two years after the revolution had led to attacks on the council and the local agricultural producer cooperatives in Becsehely, the party prepared its final collectivization drive. Agrarian society in the village was typical of many communities in the oil fields; three cooperatives operated on 16.1 percent of the village's agricultural land, and the membership consisted almost exclusively of the families of the former rural poor who had received land in 1945 in the aftermath of World War II. The marginality of collective agriculture in Becsehely was demonstrated by the fact that, while 3,456 people among 705 families lived in the village, the council registered the existence of 671 individual landholdings. A majority of these plots were small—58.1 percent were less than five and a half holds in size. Embedded within this culture of small-scale individual landholding was a worker-peasant ethos; of the households that owned farms smaller than five and a half holds, 19.2 percent contained a family member working in industry, and of those farms smaller than one hold, this percentage rose to 38.6. Most were employed at the drilling sites—the most significant source of nonagricultural local employment.[100]

At the point the regime embarked on its final collectivization drive, cultures of agricultural and industrial work were as fused in the oil fields as they had been in 1945. In April 1959, as the collectivization campaign raged through surrounding villages, 51.4 percent of workers at Lovászi had begun their careers working in agriculture, while party investigators estimated that as many as 55 percent of them lived in a household with agricultural land.[101] Because of this, the adjustments made in rural communities to deal with the defeat of the revolution proved as important as the post-November struggles for hegemony in the factories were to the consolidation of the Kádár government. Given the decentralized nature of the revolution in southern Zala's oil fields, resistance was more muted than in Tatabánya, though the long task of breaking the strike and persuading oil workers to return to work lasted almost a month. As in the rest of the country, news of the Soviet intervention on the morning of 4 November was greeted by an immediate strike on the part of oil workers. At Bázakerettye, one group of workers took arms from the plant and headed for the woods in order to resist the invaders. They returned the next day and handed back their weapons, convinced resistance was futile, as the Red Army took over the plant.[102] Aware of the damage that a long-term production stoppage could do to the oil fields, the workers' councils called for a return to work after a few days; however, poor transport conditions, strikes in other sectors, and the continued fury among many of the commuting workforce, which interacted with the fear, based on memories of 1945, that they would be rounded up and deported by Soviet troops, meant that the actual end of the strike was a discontinuous, uneven process drawn out over several weeks.[103] The damage done to production both by the strike among oil workers and the effect of stoppages in other sectors was considerable, and the heaviest blow fell disproportionately on the Nagylengyel field, which produced the bulk of Zala's oil. As late as January 1957, with all its workforce present, its output was only 30 percent of the planned target. This was in part a consequence of the emerging effects of overexploitation of the field during the previous two years.[104] It was also a product of the disorganization of the refineries and the railways as a consequence of strike action, which forced the plant to limit its production.[105]

The battle for control over the workers' councils of southern Zala in late 1956, just as in Tatabánya, was bitter. The councils threw their support behind the political position of the Greater Budapest Workers' Council by refusing to recognize the Kádár government yet making political, social, and economic demands of it. These demands were given added urgency by the climate of rumor regarding the threat of deportation, which led them to demand that those "innocent people who have been locked up" should be "freed."[106] Although there was no generalized strike when the leaders of the Greater Budapest Workers' Council were arrested, some workers attempted to persuade others to stop work. At Nagylengyel, one worker attempted to spark such a stoppage by arguing that "for as long as Soviet tanks remain in Hungary, we will not transport any oil."[107] From January 1957, with the defeat of the workers' councils as a potential locus of political opposition to the government, the party organizations in the plants asserted their control by insisting that the councils work under their supervision and by removing those members who actively opposed them.[108] Some members of the workers' councils accepted the bargain offered them by the Kádár government through which the councils were to relinquish their political demands in exchange for rights to govern the internal affairs of their enterprises. Lajos Horváth, who had been elected president of the Nagylengyel Workers' Council during an angry, anti-Communist mass meeting in October 1956, maintained in January 1957 that, if "the trust of the government and the MSzMP strengthens, the support and help of higher bodies increase . . . our electors will not be disappointed in us. The Workers' Council directs the production of the enterprise; from the social standpoint, things will be different and better than was the case when the company was run in the old way before last October."[109] Others were not prepared to compromise with the MSzMP in the way that Horváth was; at Bázakerettye, some had left Hungary to avoid arrest, while other members stayed away from meetings as a silent protest at the way in which the workers' councils had been incorporated into the power structures of the reemergent state.[110] The collapse of workers' councils as political organs was underpinned by the climate of fear that accompanied a reduction in staffing levels during early 1957. Factory-level party organs used some of these layoffs to target those who had been "troublemakers" during 1956.[111]

As the workers' councils were incorporated into state structures, the atmosphere in the villages was characterized by the process of retribution against those who had led local revolution, as leading demonstrators and members of revolutionary councils were detained in periodic raids by local state security forces.[112] This process of retribution led to marked tension within villages, which spilled over into the oil drilling plants via worker-peasants. This anxiety manifested itself in a culture of anti-Communist rumor; many county residents believed that Pál Maléter, the minister of defense in Imre Nagy's government, was holed up in the Bakony hills and engaged in a rearguard partisan action against the government, although he was actually in Soviet custody.[113] While some maintained that armed resistance to the Kádár government had not been vanquished, others argued that the revolution had spread to Hungary's neighbors. In one village it was believed that "new waves of Soviet troops have occupied Hungary, they are in the north, and have closed the Czechoslovak border; no one can go to Czechoslovakia, because there is also a revolution there."[114]

As it became ever clearer that the revolution had been defeated and consolidation was aided by economic concessions to propertied smallholders through the abolition of compulsory deliveries and favorable tax changes, tension was replaced with sullen and reluctant accommodation. The conservative political culture in the villages meant that southern Zala residents could not accept the Kádár government as legitimate, but, at the same time, they were forced to accept its reality. They coped with this by developing a culture of passive resistance to any state attempts to repoliticize everyday life. In April 1958, when the regime commemorated the thirteenth anniversary of Hungary's "liberation" in southern Zala's villages, its events were attended only by schoolchildren and teachers, as all of the adults stayed away and the propertied worked deliberately in their fields.[115] The attempts of the regime to argue that it stood "for peace" were met with the statement that "there is not going to be peace any more, like that of the 'good, old peaceful times.' Since the Second World War, the situation has been permanently tense, there won't be the sort of quiet in the country that we used to have."[116] This willingness to engage in infrapolitical forms of demonstration against the legitimacy of the socialist state underpinned increases in church attendance. Officials noted that the "influence" of the Catholic Church among the population, including workers, "had increased since the counterrevolution" but noted that this did not represent a deep commitment to religion. "They only go because of their wives, and mothers-in-law," commented one party activist on the churchgoing of male workers.[117] Passive resistance mixed with a feeling of resignation regarding the future of agriculture, for despite the relaxation of pressure on the sector, the young deserted the villages for industry, while the "elderly who remained at home were just not able to replace the loss of the young."[118]

As with the less far-reaching policy relaxation in June 1953, the abolition of compulsory deliveries did not affect the agricultural population evenly. While the average income of the agricultural population in the county increased by around 15 percent, smaller landholders and members of agricultural cooperatives found that their incomes increased by substantially less than this amount. On the other hand, those with larger properties who could take produce to market, especially those who produced fruit and wine in substantial quantities, saw their incomes rise disproportionately.[119] As the incomes and conspicuous consumption of some of the propertied rose in the south of the county, one party activist at Bázakerettye commented that "the middle peasant counts as the skilled worker in agriculture, just like the skilled worker here in industry, because they are much more developed than the little peasant, and it shows, for they gain much better results from their land."[120] Just as after 1953, the other group that benefited comprised those households that contained wage earners, who gained from both the increases in wages in industry and the reduction of pressure on agriculture. The incomes that flowed into the households of Zala's forty-two thousand small-scale landowners from industrial employment were fundamental to their economic strategies. All except the very poorest were able to begin building or renovating homes.[121] Perceptions of the relative wealth of worker-peasants generated jealousy among landless urban workers, who complained that such workers were taking jobs away from others when their means of existence were already secure, when others "have low wages, several kids, and the wife can't get a job."[122]

The generational dynamics of worker-peasant employment and the material benefits of a more consumerist socialism loosened young people's ties to the agricultural household. As the county party committee prepared the ground for a renewed collectivization drive from late 1957 onward, an increasing number of the younger people began to see their future as not being linked to the smallholding of their parents. In some villages, even in those close to the oil fields, it was "almost impossible to find a young person," given the number who sought to move away to the towns. The unpopularity of agricultural work among the young meant that "a greater part of the fields" in some villages, "as well as vineyards, are left derelict and uncared for." This situation pointed to a general problem among young workers of rural origin, both worker-peasants and long-distance commuters alike, who were profoundly alienated from agricultural labor, which they regarded as physically hard and a source of little reward.[123] The way in which the gradual consolidation of a worker-peasant existence broke the ties that bound the rural young to the land, thus preparing the ground for collectivization, was demonstrated in a party-led survey of commuters in one Zalaegerszeg factory in 1958. "It was interesting," they commented, "that they already don't deal with the land, none of them really work at home." For many, the money from the factory wages offered them the opportunity to benefit from the more consumerist model of socialism promoted by the regime.[124]

At the same time, worker-peasants in the oil fields exhibited the same attitudes that had been visible at the drilling sites before October 1956. The fact that worker-peasants, the young especially, were not "materially dependent on the factory" gave them a degree of countervailing power against management that allowed this culture to consolidate itself.[125] In the immediate aftermath of the revolution, when the authority of the regime was at an especially low ebb and managerial control was weak, young rural workers were able to exploit the situation. An endemic problem of drunkenness on the job among such workers existed at Bázakerettye during the first months of 1957.[126] At Nagylengyel, endemic drunkenness could not be wiped out through disciplinary measures alone; it was only through the implementation of wage increases that the problem was beaten back. Even then, the culture of alcohol consumption among the young, rural workforce could not be eliminated entirely, as some of the truck drivers still drank "the odd white wine spritzer" during working hours.[127] The subordination of wage labor at the drilling plant to the economic needs of worker-peasant households led to the reemergence of an endemic culture of theft focusing on those materials that could be sold in a shadow economy that revolved around rural private house building.[128] Among those who did manage their own farms, patterns of "indiscipline" emerged that were familiar to those who had managed production prior to 1956, for, "during the harvest, . . . one sees the most incidents of people sleeping on the job on the night shift."[129] At Lovászi, worker-peasants were believed to devote their time at key periods, such as harvest time, to the family farm, creating problems of worker fatigue in the plant and increasing absenteeism.[130]

The ways in which this highly conditional attitude became embedded in production relations at the drilling sites was in part a product of the ways in which the process of consolidation after 1956 necessitated substantial concessions to the workforce. The substantial wage increases and the introduction of significant profit-sharing bonuses paid to the workers for the good performance of their enterprises under the new, looser planning regime were fundamental to this process of consolidation; experiments with indicative planning in companies like Újpest's Danube Shoe Factory in 1956 were generalized in 1957 after the defeat of the revolution.[131] At the same time, the pressure to produce, especially in sections of the plants like the machine shops, where workers were paid according to individual work targets, was relaxed, and work intensity fell. This change contributed to decreases in the level of productivity; at Bázakerettye, workers produced only 76.1 percent on average of what they had a year previously in May 1957, and at Lovászi, the corresponding figure was only 68.1 percent.[132] As the party concentrated on an extension of its political control, at the drilling sites it was prepared to concede ground to workers, especially as their pace and conditions of work were concerned, given the party's awareness of its own political weakness and its anxiousness to avoid an explosion of open protest. Party activists at Bázakerettye were prepared to relaunch the labor competition on paper but displayed considerable reluctance to challenge workers to increase their productivity.[133] Likewise, at Lovászi, the authority of the trade union was "minimal" as far as mobilization was concerned.[134] In part, this was due to the considerable opposition that resulted, fueled as it was by the suspicion that practices of labor mobilization characteristic of the pre-1956 period were being reintroduced. When the "best workers in production" were decorated for their participation in labor competition during 1957 and 1958, their material rewards were referred to as "Judas money" by fellow workers, and they were stigmatized as "traitors to the working class."[135]

Managers and engineers faced a protracted struggle to restore their authority in production, which became a focus for the generation of class resentment that united all workers at the sites. At Bázakerettye, engineers and production managers resorted to a strict imposition of the disciplinary code, prosecuting workers for the slightest infringements during 1957. This crackdown led workers to accuse the engineers of behaving in a dictatorial manner and to demand, through the party, that they be stopped from using the disciplinary code for minor infractions.[136] Managers' rapid recourse to disciplinary measures was a symptom, however, of their actual lack of control over workers. Workers were prepared to cooperate to protect themselves from supervisors. When a lower-level manager entered the fitters' shop at Bázakerettye in spring 1957, "one worker" close to the door "cried out, 'watch out, it's an inspection!'"[137] This, together with the attitude of a factory-level party anxious to appease workers in the interests of avoiding open protest, effectively limited managerial authority. With little managerial support, the most difficult of the shifts to control—the night shift—frequently had neither a foreman nor a work group leader on duty.[138]

By early 1958, it had become clear that the dynamics of political consolidation in the absence of legitimacy forced the regime to concede to the workforce extensive micro-level control over production. At Lovászi, "the foremen don't even check when the workers come back from getting raw materials," complained one. The desire of lower-level management to defuse discontent through appeasement was visible in wage determination: "there are some people who have been disciplined by being given higher wages!"[139] The tacit acceptance of on-the-job bargaining over the pace of work, conditions, and remuneration ensured a crystallization of hierarchies. At Lovászi, the majority of workers employed in 1959—730 of 1,167—had worked at the plant continuously for at least eight years, as had 235 of the 298 employed in the highest-paid skilled positions.[140] Despite an undercurrent of jealousy among the landless with regard to their worker-peasant colleagues, the culture of individual landholding was so entrenched among workers—in Bázakerettye village in 1958, every household contained at least one oil worker, irrespective of whether they owned property—that there were no meaningful cultural distinctions between the two groups.[141] The work culture on the sites was profoundly masculine; at Lovászi, 129 women worked in manual positions in 1959, and of those only 4 were skilled workers. The ways in which gendered expectations were embedded in the moral economy of the site was revealed in the ways in which female workers were assumed to be secondary wage earners. This presumption hit the minority of single women with children especially hard, because they had to support children from a wage that was well below the factory average.[142] The hegemonic work culture at the plants valued seniority and loyalty to the company and displayed a marked hostility to "outsiders." In 1957, when a school for apprentices was established to train new skilled workers at Bázakerettye, workers demanded that it "only enroll the sons of workers at the company."[143]

Although the culture of defeat in southern Zala had secured acceptance of the existence of the Kádár government, it possessed little real legitimacy in the region. The party and management had been forced to accommodate and accept the hegemonic work cultures in the oil fields to a far greater extent than before October 1956. This was further reinforced by the impending drive to complete the collectivization of agriculture during the late 1950s. While the party in the factories remained as committed to eliminating the *kétlaki* lifestyle as they had been in the early 1950s, the methods by which they sought to do so had changed. The worker-peasants were seen as a potential tool for persuading family members: "if the families of those who work here can be persuaded to join agricultural cooperatives, that would be tremendous progress." Given the shift in policy in which, in contrast to the practice of the early 1950s, the state would invest to mechanize the cooperatives to boost the earning power of those within it, worker-peasants would see "that it would be possible to earn as much in agriculture as in the factory."[144] While such aspirations would be proved unrealistic, they were revealing of the way that, by the end of the 1950s, even in a region where the regime was weak, party activists believed their rule was consolidated in the factories and that they could use them as a base from which "socialist construction" could be taken to the villages.

## The Dynamic of Protest and Consolidation in Újpest

If accommodation to the culture of urban workers generated a degree of brittle legitimacy for the regime in Tatabánya, while concessions to workers at the drilling sites was necessitated by its lack in southern Zala, in Újpest the development of a brittle legitimacy coexisted with the slow and uneven retreat of stubborn protest. This situation was at its most visible in the ways in which the revolution was commemorated illegally in the United Incandescent Lamp and Electrical Factory, where the workers' council had been more than simply an instrument of anti-Communist protest but had represented the aspirations of skilled workers for a thorough democratization of the enterprise. Throughout 1957, the party was aware that "the enemy has not conceded the struggle."[145] This statement reflected the stubborn resistance among some elite skilled workers to the growing union and party presence on the shop floor.[146] On anniversaries of the revolution, an undercurrent of political protest rose to the surface in the plant, taking the form of small and covert acts of sabotage. On 23 October 1957, a year to the day after the student demonstration that launched the revolution, persons unknown cut the wiring that provided the electricity that lit the red star on the factory's roof, ensuring that it did not function for the following week.[147] In the days leading up to commemorations of the anniversary of Hungary's "liberation" in April 1958, the factory was hit by a wave of discontent over wages and profit-related premium payments. Voices among skilled workers attacked the regime by pointing to the "benefits" that had been brought to the plant by the workers' council in 1956.[148]

While the undercurrent of political protest was the result of production problems in the plant and the limits it placed on the material pacification of workers, the atmosphere of protest was also a product of both the role the factory's workers' council had taken in coordinating political opposition to the Kádár government after the collapse of the Újpest Revolutionary Committee and its rootedness in the aspirations of the skilled male elite of the factory's workforce. On the morning of 4 November 1956, when the Red Army intervened, the Újpest Revolutionary Committee had been divided between moderates and radicals on the wisdom of organizing armed resistance to Soviet tanks when they attempted to occupy Újpest. The armed defense of the city was a poorly organized affair in which groups of radical volunteers dug in to resist the entrance of Soviet tanks at several strategic points along the edges of the district. On 8 November, as Soviet tanks entered the city center, the largely ineffective armed resistance quickly collapsed.[149] Faced with the return of the MSzMP and the local council, which reoccupied rooms in the city hall, the Újpest Revolutionary Committee was left directionless. A strategy came from outside, as radicals within the Writers' Union sought to link to surviving revolutionary councils in the factories and districts to rally opposition to Kádár.[150] The student activists who went to meet with the Újpest committee on behalf of the Writers' Union persuaded the group to rename itself the Újpest Workers' Council and to assume the task of organizing a Central Workers' Council to act as a focus for the various revolutionary bodies, initially in Budapest but also nationwide.[151] The meeting, scheduled for 13 November at the Újpest city hall, never took place. In a preemptive move, the authorities arrested the members of the Újpest Revolutionary Committee, and Soviet tanks surrounded the city hall to prevent the meeting from taking place. Outraged at the tactics used by the Red Army and the government, the United Incandescent Lamp and Electrical Factory Workers' Council hosted the meeting the next day, allowing representatives of revolutionary bodies across the city to found the Central Greater Budapest Workers' Council on the factory site.[152]

The willingness of the United Incandescent Lamp and Electrical Factory Workers' Council to cooperate with radicals against the state, given their antagonism to them during late October, was a product of the anger generated by the second Soviet intervention. Across the district, this anger created an almost unanimous "feeling behind the strike" for the first week after 4 November, whereby workers' councils locked the factory gates in order to prevent Communists or Soviet troops from gaining entrance to restart production.[153] As the Kádár government and the Central Greater Budapest Workers' Council began negotiations for a political settlement, workers began to return to work fourteen days after 4 November, though this end to the strike was incomplete and uneven and disturbed by persistent rumor, which workers' councils had to defuse.[154] Another disruption was the impact of the strike on the rest of the economy. Coal shortages led to power outages, which meant that those who reported for work at the United Incandescent Lamp and Electrical Factory were unable to work through mid-November. In the HPS, many of the spinning masters were commuters, and they could not reach the factory in the absence of public transport, thus leaving the machines in the shop, and the operators who turned up, standing idle.[155] The political atmosphere remained tense because of the struggle between anti-Communist workers' councils, created by the purges instituted by the Újpest Revolutionary Committee at the end of October, and the MSzMP as it sought to reorganize in the factories. In the HPS, the workers' councils organized a secret ballot to give democratic legitimacy to its stance that the MSzMP should be banned from creating a cell in the factory. The secretary of the MSzMP was threatened with violence, while across the district, those interested in joining the party were threatened with dismissal.[156]

Given the desperate economic situation, divisions opened up between moderates and radicals among the workers and sometimes between the workers and the workers' councils. The conflict came to a head when the Central Greater Budapest Workers' Council called for a forty-eight-hour strike to run 11 and 12 December, sparked by the breakdown of relations between it and the government. As the government outlawed the body, the United Incandescent Lamp and Electrical Factory's workers' council resolved to continue to work. Its decision was overturned in a mass meeting of fifteen hundred of the plant's workers, who backed the strike. In order to avoid violent confrontations with radicals at the factory gate, the decision was made to close the factory to all workers for the duration of the strike.[157] Workers in the Magyar Pamutipar turned up for work on the morning of 11 December, but they laid down their tools as lunchtime approached, and one worker, who had attended a demonstration organized by strikers and violently broken up by the police, showed workmates injuries she said she had received as a result of being beaten.[158] Yet, by locking out those workers who wanted to work, radicals discredited strike action, given that the state and management refused to pay the striking workforce for the two days, in contrast to the situation from late October to mid-November, when they had received full pay.[159] On returning to work, workers "condemned the workers' councils particularly because they hadn't mentioned that they wouldn't be paid while on strike."[160]

The change of mood in the factories was visible as early as 13 December. Many of the female workers on the assembly lines in the radio components shops in the United Incandescent Lamp and Electrical Factory had a "truly condemnatory attitude toward the strike of the past forty-eight hours."[161] This was not merely about the nonpayment of wages for the strike. Energy shortages and the dire state of the economy had begun to have a direct impact on workers. Because of the frequent production stoppages, rather than lay off workers, the United Incandescent Lamp and Electrical Factory introduced a four-shift system. It warned, however, that it could not pay full wages if production stopped due to power outages.[162] Similar measures taken by managements across Újpest concentrated minds on the worsening economic situation and raised the specter of mass layoffs.[163] While most workers remained distrustful of the government, it exploited the window of opportunity opened by the debacle of the strike to attack the workers' councils. National radio accused the United Incandescent Lamp and Electrical Factory Workers' Council of bringing the plant to the brink of financial ruin by spending millions of forints on supporting strikes, to which the council issued loud denials.[164] As attacks from the party intensified and the workers' councils in the city became conscious of their unpopularity because of the strike, they attempted to rally the workers with a leaflet that called on them "not to allow us to be labeled as fascists."[165] During the last weeks of December, three of the seventy-one members of the workers' council of the United Incandescent Lamp and Electrical Factory left for the West; the president resigned from the factory, only to return after "thinking things over."[166]

While the workers' councils were defeated politically, the climate among ordinary workers in the factories remained tense, and protest could be sparked by material concerns. The government's announcement of a "rationalization" drive through which it would trim factory staffs provoked an explosion of protest throughout the capital in January 1957. Given the fears of unemployment raised by energy shortages and the introduction of reduced work shifts, this announcement reignited debate over the revolution, as many argued that, "had the revolution won," rationalization would not have been necessary, for "the West would have helped out."[167] Growing anger at layoffs alongside the impact of discontinuous production on workers' take-home pay produced widespread protest across the capital, leading to strikes, protests, and the mass resignations of workers' councils. In Újpest, the turmoil produced an unofficial strike in some workshops of the United Incandescent Lamp and Electrical Factory.[168] While the MSzMP persuaded the factory's workers' council not to attempt to dissolve itself, it warned that it was not prepared "to give up, or negotiate about the justified national and socialist demands of our people" and that it saw its mandate "as only existing for as long as the true interests of the workers dictate."[169]

Despite the defeat of the revolution, in order to preserve peace in the factories the regime had to demonstrate to workers continued material improvement. This set the stage for the substantial reforms to wage systems and the management of work that were introduced during early 1957. These were a consequence of more generalized reforms to the planning system designed to stabilize the economy after the shock of the revolution and to correct structural difficulties identified by reform-minded economists during the New Course period. However, given the post-1956 political climate, many of their recommendations could be implemented only in heavily diluted form. The number of plan targets was cut, and enterprises were given a greater degree of autonomy, while administratively determined prices were given a greater role to create a set of indirect incentives for enterprises.[170] Before the government made its decision to abolish them in late 1957, politically neutered workers' councils were envisaged as having a supervisory role.[171] Controls were loosened on the ways enterprises paid wages, as they were only measured by the center against the average wage of workers in their company. This decentralization was used as an opportunity to reintroduce payment-by-results wage systems in principle, while in practice conceding ground to the determination of workers not to return to the systems of payment in force before the revolution. To this end, wage systems that encouraged unlimited performance were criticized savagely, and centralized prescription was scrapped. Enterprises were encouraged to choose wage systems that fit their needs for production of both the correct quantity and quality. The reintroduction of piece-rate wages was discouraged heavily; they were only "justified in a substantially smaller number of cases than has been true to date."[172] The remodeling of labor competition reflected a similar balance of priorities, as competitions were shaped to fit the needs of enterprises. Workers were mobilized to produce by a biannual profit-share premium that was payable to workers of enterprises that met or exceeded their financial targets, which was supposed to generate a sense among workers that they were co-owners of their enterprise and therefore interested in its performance.[173]

As enterprises remolded their wage systems, workers' incomes in many factories fell slightly, generating a wave of temporary discontent at poor earnings possibilities and the high prices charged for foodstuffs by traders at local markets.[174] Yet such discontent was restricted to a climate of complaint. This was because wage levels still remained far higher than a year earlier, and they were supplemented throughout the second half of 1957 by the profit-share premiums, which, although largely symbolic, represented the equivalent of one week's wages.[175] The premiums also reinforced a sense that the government was interested in the material conditions of workers.[176] Furthermore, at the shop-floor level, reforms to the mechanisms for the management of production and remuneration were implemented through a process of compromise, especially with the male skilled elite in the heavy industrial plants. Often the wage systems that emerged resembled those that had existed prior to the beginnings of Rákosi's "revolution in production" in 1949. For the skilled workers of the Duclos Mining Machinery Factory, plant management proceeded carefully in reforming wage systems, directing a tortuous process of shop-by-shop compromise. In March 1958, 63.2 percent of the plant's workers were paid according to fixed hourly rates. Among the rest, the wage systems that resulted granted considerable informal power to workers on the job, with the payment systems often involving premiums that were calculated not according to the performance of individual workers but on the basis of the work group to which they belonged. The attempts of workers to limit their production were formalized, as in most shops the enterprise refused to pay for any production beyond 120 percent of the work target.[177]

The cumulative effect of wage decentralization implemented through shop-floor compromise was the formalization of patterns of hierarchy based on gender, skill, sector, and generation that had characterized shop-floor relations in the city during the early 1950s. In the United Incandescent Lamp and Electrical Factory, in the privileged heavy engineering sector, skilled workers' hourly wages of 8.32 forints were the highest for manual workers in the district in summer 1958. While 61.6 percent of the factory's manual workers were women, only 2.39 percent of skilled workers were female. To the financial advantages of masculinity was added a culture based on seniority among the skilled, for while 21.35 percent of their number had worked continuously in the plant for ten years or more, this was true of only 11.4 percent of the plant's manual workers as a whole.[178] Similar patterns that linked skill to hierarchies of gender and generation shaped wage relations that were similar in nature in light industrial plants, like the Danube Shoe Factory.[179] Yet the wages in those facilities were markedly lower—by more than 200 forints monthly—than those of experienced skilled workers in heavy engineering. This led many skilled workers in the factory to complain that their earnings failed to reflect "the greater command of their skill that they have gained over decades."[180]

This complaint reflected the traditionally lower wages paid in light industry when compared to heavy industry, for both semiskilled and unskilled positions. In textile plants like the Magyar Pamutipar, average wages for machine operators in the spinning and weaving shops, at 1,170 forints per month on average in summer 1958, remained lower than for those of similar skill even in nontextile light industrial factories.[181] Despite the relatively unfavorable position of the machine operators, most of whom were female, they also benefited from a politics of workplace conciliation in the aftermath of the revolution. Management agreed to a reduction in work targets of 25 percent to reduce work intensity and raise wages, while it abolished the Saturday night shift—a long-standing demand of the predominantly female machine operators.[182] Despite an average wage increase of 16.4 percent, labor turnover during 1957 stood at 46 percent of the total workforce, a product of relatively low wages and poor conditions.[183] Low earnings were made tolerable by the fact that most machine operators' earnings were a secondary source of income in the household in which they lived; in Spinning Shop No. II, only 18.3 percent subsisted from their work in the factory alone, though even in dual income households, families with three children or more struggled.[184] It was the unmarried population among whom labor turnover was concentrated; much like prior to 1956, these single workers consisted largely of young women from rural households who sought to escape laboring on the land by working in the city. Faced with high costs and poor housing in Budapest, they were the ones most likely to quit.[185]

While persistent labor turnover among the young semiskilled workforce in textile plants disrupted production, it did not affect the stability and legitimacy of the regime, which was more interested in the male skilled workers, who they saw as the base of their power. By early 1958, as in Tatabánya, the combination of conciliation in the workplace with increases in the general standard of living had bought the regime a degree of brittle legitimacy; the regime would be viewed as legitimate based on its ability to meet the material aspirations of urban workers. At the point when János Kádár relinquished the post of prime minister in favor of Ferenc Münnich so as to concentrate on leading the MSzMP in January 1958, many workers were of the view "that although it's all the same to them, who the prime minister is, and who's the party secretary, we want living standards to stay, and in the future to keep going up, and then it'll be all right."[186] Acceptance of the legitimacy of the regime was, however, politically circumscribed and was concentrated among the most highly paid of the relatively left-wing majority of urban workers in Újpest. Support for the government seemed to be marked among the older generation, too, with job security and relatively good employment prospects for younger family members being contrasted with the situation in the interwar years. Despite this, however, party activists noted that among those with "anti-Soviet" or "nationalist" views, many complained that "the government had not improved the situation of workers sufficiently," thus echoing earlier patterns of political polarization.[187]

Acceptance of the regime's claim to rule was not only circumscribed politically but also highly brittle and conditional. Temporary decreases in living standards could lead to outbursts of angry political protest from those otherwise well disposed toward the regime. This was apparent when, in March 1958, the United Lighting and Electrical Factory failed to make a profit and thus was unable to pay a semiannual profit-share premium to its workers. The wave of fury that resulted took the form of an open attack on the government and was made considerably worse by the approach of the thirteenth anniversary of Hungary's "liberation" on 4 April. Graffiti appeared on the factory walls, inciting workers to refuse to join the party's parade to commemorate the event, while informers for the state security agencies reported to their superiors that "on the trams they are discussing a strike if the plant doesn't pay a profit-share premium."[188] While such manifestations of protest revealed the nature of the tacit bargain on which brittle legitimacy rested—that urban workers accepted the legitimacy of the Kádár regime only in so far as it delivered material improvement—it did not reveal one crucial dimension of the construction of brittle legitimacy. This critical element related to the ways in which the regime had successfully used its combination of material measures and the politics of conciliation to differentiate itself from Rákosi's and Gerő's politics. Only two years after the revolution, such restrictive measures provoked explosive reactions because workers feared they represented a return to the politics of the recent past. Party investigators commenting on the elements that influenced the political climate on factory floors in the district commented in July 1958 that "the impact of old, bad experiences strongly lives on in people; fluctuations in earnings, the slightest decreases in wages . . . create problems, discontent, and distrust among the workers."[189] The shadow of the immediate past lay heavily on the nature of the legitimacy the socialist state had constructed for itself among Újpest's workers after 1956. Just as they saw the new regime as different from Rákosi's, many saw the material measures as gains of the "counterrevolution," believing that, had they not taken to the streets in 1956, none of the material improvement of 1957 and 1958 would have occurred.[190] The consolidation of the socialist order among industrial workers was closely linked to the 1956 Revolution, as well as the circumstances and aftermath of its defeat. The shadow of 1956 would shape fundamentally the relations between the Kádár regime and Hungary's industrial workers for the remainder of its existence.

# Conclusion

ON THE EARLY morning of 16 June 1958, the state executed Imre Nagy and two of his fellow defendants following a secret political trial for conspiracy to "overthrow the people's democratic state order."[1] As the news was made public, it caused shock among workers in the capital and, among some, revived political opposition toward the regime; "Imre Nagy died a freedom fighter," "if there had been an open trial, then Imre Nagy's supporters would have prevented the execution," and "there will be international condemnation of this" were among the opinions expressed in reaction.[2] These reactions revealed the limits of Kádár's consolidation, for brittle legitimacy was based on an enforced forgetting of the revolution and its political demands in exchange for the fulfillment of many of its social and economic ones.[3] Nagy's execution also represented a turning point of sorts in that it led to no real open protest. Thus, it paradoxically also revealed the strength of the tacit social contract on which brittle legitimacy rested. After the upheaval and instability of the thirteen years since 1945, the regime remained stable, yet constrained by the post-1956 settlement, for the following three decades. Thus, the revolution and its defeat had exposed the crisis of Hungary's socialist project, yet it was also strangely central to the consolidation of that effort.

Those who have examined socialist state formation in Hungary through a focus on its political institutions have told the story in a way very different relative to the account that has been presented here. While historians differ on the opportunity presented by the watershed of 1945 for the independent development of the country, they maintain that the immediate postwar period was a transitional phase quite distinct from that of the dictatorship. Despotism grew until state power and control reached their maximum extents between 1948 and 1953, when Rákosi and his allies, bolstered by Stalin in Moscow, forced through state-directed social revolution, emasculating all opposition. What followed was a halting period of retreat punctuated by the reversal of March 1955, the suppression of the revolution at the end of 1956, and Kádárist repression until 1963. Nevertheless, the post-Rákosi era was one of a progressive, albeit slow, decline in the influence of the socialist project. The dictatorship softened, for the state retreated gradually from the social and economic realms, breathing life into the forces that eventually brought about its collapse.

These other historical accounts have failed to interrogate critically the nature of socialist state power, assuming that despotism and repression were sufficient conditions for the accumulation of the material sinews of authority. This volume has argued that this approach to the power of the state is fatally undermined by its one-sidedness, as well as its failure to contextualize and historicize the emergent state and its use of violence. States exist in a dual sense—first as a collection of separate institutions that work in complementary and contradictory ways. In a second sense, these institutions clothe themselves in the myth of being a singular, coherent institution that is the legitimate source of primary authority over society. This myth of state unity and legitimacy is central to the state's acquisition of infrastructural power—in other words, the ability to operate across the territory it governs and secure its authority at the level of everyday life. This is because, to rule on a day-to-day basis, a state requires the active cooperation of those who staff its police, military institutions, tax collection authorities, and other bureaucracies. And for these institutions to operate, those who populate them require that a sufficient number of the ruled—by no means always a majority—are prepared to cooperate with them, on the grounds that they represent a legitimate authority. Therefore, a state needs to construct sufficient legitimacy for itself—it needs to be able to tell enough of the population a credible story as to why it should rule. This is especially true in cases like that of postwar Hungary, where the institutions of the state were shattered by the experience of defeat and occupation and then reconstructed after 1945 by a political project that aimed to give the state a new purpose and claim to rule. Especially in such an uncertain situation, in order to ensure a sufficient degree of acceptance, state institutions—especially those involved in the deployment of its monopoly of violence—must act in concert with their state's construction of its own legitimacy, for if they act outside of those constraints, they risk the collapse of the state's infrastructural power.

For this reason, an analysis of socialist state formation requires taking the ideology of the regimes, both within and beyond Hungary, seriously, rather than seeing them, as has so often been the case, as simply a cloak for their leaders' unbridled accumulation of their own power. Fulfilling this requirement mirrors the insistence in much of the recent historiography of mid-twentieth-century regimes of the extreme Right that the programs of fascist movements be taken seriously on their own terms.[4] While the mid-century European far Right claimed to rule on the basis of the undivided community of the nation, those of the Bolshevik Left rested on the revolutionary transformation of preexisting states into political communities based on the collective identities of those who worked. The party-states brought to power were, in terms of their own self-presentation, the vanguard of the "Communist working class," which was the collective subject of the socialist society that they would build. This claim rested on the realization of a social program that was, at one and the same time, one of both creation and destruction. Regimes were forced to forge the collective subjects of socialist transformation in Central and Eastern Europe—the "new working class" and the "working peasantry" that was allied to it—from the existing industrial workers and agricultural laborers. At the same time, they saw themselves as destroying the power of any workers and agricultural laborers who resisted identification with these new collective subjects, as well as banishing former "ruling classes" and their allies from the social realm entirely. Within this construction, legitimacy and repression were closely linked, for in seeing themselves as agents of social transformation, and building the future against the past, the region's socialist regimes in their early phases were kinds of "civil war" states that were able to consign those they perceived as enemies of their project to a "state of exception" beyond the boundaries of "normal" legality.[5] As this model of political practice was introduced within the borders of the region's nation-states in the immediate aftermath of World War II, it had to be adapted to both local and temporal circumstances. First, in 1945, the Soviet Union did not envisage, in territories like Hungary that it occupied, the immediate construction of socialist dictatorship, and it insisted that local Communists lay the foundations for future social transformation within the context of polities constructed according to "popular-front" principles. Second, those who shaped "new" states confronted national civil societies in which political and social actors had very different conceptions of the creation of the postwar state, sustained by political cultures that were sometimes profoundly antagonistic toward the Communist project. Third, and most important, industrial workers and the rural poor in each of the states had their own cultures and mentalities serving as the basis for aspirations for the future that sometimes intersected with but at other times opposed those of the Communists.

Much recent literature that deals with the early phase of postwar state formation in Central and Eastern Europe has highlighted the considerable differences between national civil societies and the distinct roads that Communist parties were forced to follow in order to acquire power by the end of the 1940s. The conclusions of this historiography suggest that, rather than concentrating on sovietization as simply the imposition of an alien model of political development on the region, the construction of socialist dictatorships are placed firmly in their domestic, national contexts. Yet none of the nation-states of the region was homogeneous in its political attitudes and cultures. Hungary emerged from World War II a deeply divided society; those who awaited left-wing transformation on the morrow of defeat were a distinct minority and faced a more conservative majority. The restricted social base of the state that the MKP sought to build in Hungary under Soviet patronage constrained its room for maneuver. The illusion that a transition to socialism could be engineered through the formula of a "popular front" of all antifascist parties, legitimated through democratic elections, foundered on the majority's suspicion of the Soviet Union and the Left. A socialist state in postwar Hungary could, therefore, only be a dictatorship constructed in circumstances of political polarization. Thus, the early socialist state in Hungary was a "civil war" state on two levels, both at the level of the dialectic of the destruction and re-creation of the social realm envisaged by its program of transformation and at the level of the actual process of its own creation when its state-building project confronted existing political cultures. The interaction of these processes is fundamental to grasping the nature of the early socialist state in Hungary.

These processes were visible in the character of repression instituted by the early socialist state, which borrowed from the Stalinist Soviet Union and adapted its political practice to the circumstances of postwar Hungary. The political trial and, from 1948 onward, the "show trial" became fundamental manifestations of the interface between repression and the regime's construction of its legitimacy. The "show trial" was designed to act as a public demonstration of the ubiquity of the "enemy," a manufactured process designed to show that opponents of the state conspired with nefarious external forces to destroy the socialist state. The "opponents"—whether senior members of the Catholic hierarchy like Cardinal Mindszenty, or József Grósz, archbishop of Kalocsa, tried in 1951 on similar charges, or managers of foreign-owned companies like Simon Papp, chief geologist of MAORT, or even those like László Rajk, tried and executed as an attempt to demonstrate that the regime's "enemies" could strike from within as well as from outside the labor movement—were chosen to symbolize deeper social and political conflicts. The clearest of example of this linking was the wave of trials of former members of the MSzDP in spring 1950, beginning with Hungary's president, Árpad Szakasits, which coincided with the regime's attempts to transform the workplace in the face of considerable unrest, which they termed the work of "right-wing social democrats."[6] It was visible in everyday practice outside the courtroom; for example, the

Hungarian regime borrowed the category of kulak from Soviet Stalinism to stig-matize those it regarded as its enemies within village society yet at the same time constructed that identity on the basis of class stereotypes widely current within everyday rural cultural practice.[7]

While practices of repression signaled the ways in which the regime attempt-ed to destroy those parts of the social and political realm that stood in the way of socialist construction, its relations with workers indicated the ways in which it sought to build legitimacy based on the creation of new subjectivities and the problems it confronted as a result. In recent years, research into the histories of industrial workers globally has abandoned a heroic meta-narrative of the working class as a product of early capitalism and potential collective agent of revolutionary transformation in favor of a more fractured view of the social and political role of workers. While some of this work has almost entirely abandoned notions of class, most has qualified it, especially in so far as the political role of workers' protest and collective action is concerned.[8] Research on the relationship between class and collective action suggests a theoretical break with assumptions in which individual industrial workers are automatically identified with the collective subject of the working class. Instead, the latter has been regarded as an "imagined community" of workers with which they actually came to identify only if certain context-specific circumstances were met.[9] This insight is of crucial importance for interrogating the role that industrial workers played in the regime's attempts to construct its legiti-macy, because—as part of the labor movement—it sought to argue that it repre-sented and led a "working class" as a heroic collective subjectivity, which was not entirely unlike that often envisaged and used as a critical tool by those who have studied workers in capitalist contexts.

As has been shown here, from 1945 onward, the various institutional incarna-tions of the Communist political tradition implicated in Hungary's state-building project saw the "working class" as the agent of its transformation, the object of its leadership, and the subject of its rule. While in the late 1940s Communists con-ceived of members of the "working class" as disciplined soldiers of reconstruction and guardians of the nation against "reaction," as the "construction of socialism" began at the end of the decade, workers were expected to become "a new Commu-nist working class." This entailed a transformation in attitudes toward work; with the abolition of capitalism, class-consciousness was redefined as the development of an awareness that, because the material basis of old antagonisms had vanished, the duty of the worker was to produce for the future. Class-consciousness entailed furthermore an outright abandonment of hierarchical gradations between workers on grounds of generation and gender. For persons from rural areas, this meant that those with land would have to relinquish it and embrace a future of industrial labor alone in exchange for a recognition of equality with their urban colleagues. The fun-damental problem with this new subjectivity was one of workers' identification with it. This problem of identification existed on two levels—a product of the fact that class in Hungary, as in the case globally, was "both an ongoing social reality, and an active part of the social imaginary."[10] At the level of the social imaginary, dominant discourses of the "working class" privileged the older, male, urban skilled worker, whose engagement in labor movement activism to defend their independence, control within the labor process, and skill, was combined with political activism. While at times visions of the "new Communist working class" and established notions of a "working class" that existed at the level of the social imaginary overlapped, especially during the political struggles of the late 1940s, at other points, especially from the early 1950s, they clashed profoundly. At the level of everyday social reality, the identification of industrial workers with any class-based collectivity was highly uneven and ambiguous. The identities, attitudes, and practices of individual industrial workers were shaped at points of intersection between discourses of class, gender, generation, of urban versus rural, religious versus secular, of occupation, of locality, and those rooted within political culture.

Capturing the contours of legitimacy as a contested process in early socialist Hungary requires untangling the complex interactions between the creation of a "new working class" as political project, notions of a working class as an active part of the Hungarian social imaginary, and the process through which individual workers' subjectivities were shaped. This process of untangling can be attempted only through a focus on the interaction between state formation and everyday practice within industrial communities. By selecting three specific industrial communities—Újpest, Tatabánya, and the oil fields of southern Zala, which were representative of the different kinds of industrial community in the country at the beginning of the socialist state-building processes—patterns of unity and diversity in worker responses to socialist state building have been interrogated. Notions of locality, the organization of space, the structures of the local economies, and the radical divergence in political cultures determined the differences between worker responses in each place. The experience of the dual class location of oil workers in the drilling plants and in agriculture, the ways in which state policies shaped this experience, and its combination with a conservative, antisocialist political culture produced a local working-class culture in southern Zala that was distinct from those of the cities. The geographically closed culture of urban workers in Tatabánya—dominated by poor housing, a masculine work culture shaped by the nature of local employment in mines, power plants, and heavy industrial factories, combined with the lack of employment opportunities for women, and a powerful sense of class demarcation from both management and those who lived in the city's rural hinterland—also shaped particular practices among local workers. It made possible the political hegemony of communism in the region, as workers invested their hope of overcoming their marginality in a future socialist society based on work. After 1950, this closed culture shaped a climate of disillusion, exclusion, and anger, which, after 1956, the regime attempted to defuse through a revival of the promises of the late 1940s. Újpest was a more diverse industrial community. On the fringes of the capital, Hungary's industrial powerhouse, it had a highly differentiated industrial structure. While in heavy engineering plants a labor movement culture in the 1940s was dominant, underpinned by the masculine work culture of the skilled male elite, its textile factories were dominated by female workforces excluded from this culture and at best deeply ambivalent about it. These divisions, combined with the clash between the political cultures of the Left and Right, and divisions based on residence and religious belief, meant that Communist mobilization of workers was uneven during the late 1940s. While such divisions were masked by the sense of overriding antagonism toward the state after 1950, they reemerged as divisions between radicals and moderates in 1956. As the restored regime during the late 1950s appeased the social and economic demands of workers while closing the door firmly on their political demands, it negotiated these divisions.

While the diversity of experiences and identities among actual industrial workers was important, it would be wrong to ignore the common patterns in the way class functioned across all three industrial communities, as they shed considerable light on the uneven process of socialist state formation in Hungary. Class as a dynamic of power, as well as both a form of knowledge and experience linked to positions within the social division of labor, related relations of power, and economic exploitation, played a fundamental role in the processes by which the socialist state was built, de-composed, collapsed, and was later restored and consolidated. During the late 1940s, it infused workers' political identities, even those of the more conservative workers. Class and conservative political identities reinforced each other in southern Zala's oil fields, allowing anger at food shortages, poor housing, and declining wages relative to those in other sectors to be displaced onto the popular-front regime in Budapest, its official trade unions, and left-wing parties. Likewise, among the conservative women in Újpest's textile plants, it underpinned their criticism of left-wing officials, whom they believed lived well off their work. During the inflation and moments of economic deprivation, class underpinned the periodic revivals of anti-Semitism directed against shopkeepers and market vendors. More crucially, it underpinned hegemonic left-wing political identities, which drew much of their force from the powerful sense of anger at the way that Hungary's interwar and wartime regimes had excluded workers from the public sphere and legally bolstered their subordination in workplaces and communities, while embroiling them in a war in which they suffered considerably—both physically and materially. Attacks by the MKP and other left-wing parties on the "reaction" provided a powerful way of cementing workers' perceptions of class to left-wing political identities, which allowed the MKP to mobilize workers behind its drives to secure its hegemony within the popular-front government and generate for itself a degree of partial legitimacy.

This use of class did not allow Hungary's socialist state-builders to gain unconditional support or uncontested legitimacy, even from left-wing workers. The tensions between the expectations rooted in hegemonic left-wing political identities
and the local dimensions of the politics of class compromise the Left pursued
during the popular-front period generated frustration and protest, which acted as
the flip side of the MKP's mobilization drives. When state policies toward wages,
social benefits, and working conditions clashed with workers' aspirations, protest
also resulted. This situation could be seen most clearly in Tatabánya, where the
hegemony of popular communism coexisted with periodic explosions of popular
protest centered on the city's mines. Examples include strikes over coal allowances
in December 1946, the potato crisis of September 1947, and the citywide protests in
January and February 1948. However, although prior to the autumn of 1947 class
manifested itself in workers' attitudes as a form of material frustration, after this
date, with the explicit construction of socialist dictatorship and an economic order
based on central planning, this situation changed.

The parallel transformations of the political system and the economy that took
place between 1947 and 1949 established a set of state socialist "social-property relations" that reshaped the relationships through which class worked.[11] The offensive
against private property had in theory led to the socialization of the economy: "The
land belongs to those who work it. The mines, the factories, the banks have become
the property of the working people."[12] This socialized property was directed and
managed by the "popular state power."[13] That phrase signifies a centralized state
whose activities at all levels were directed and supervised by the ruling party, organized along democratic centralist principles. The second element of state socialist
"social-property relations" was that all citizens were required to work "according to
their ability." This requirement to work, which was embodied in both the constitution and the 1951 Labor Code, came to represent the legal foundations of a society
based on commodified labor underpinned by state compulsion, while the liquidation of small businesses and the attacks on individual landholding in agriculture
extended the compulsion to work for wages to groups that had previously felt little
impact by proletarianization. The labor was alienated, commodified, and fragmented. The notion of fragmented, scientifically measurable labor was embodied
in the practices of planning, the policies toward wages, and the organization of
production and labor competition that underpinned them, but it also influenced
the design of model factories, such as the Danube Shoe Factory. Third, while cash
wages were tied to performance, this income was supplemented, at least in theory,
by a social wage, which rested on egalitarian principles. In their attempts to provide
holiday places to workers and even apartments, on a highly limited scale, the notion
of egalitarian distribution was something to which the socialist state aspired, even
if, in the first years of central planning, it was flatly contradicted by a reality of
generalized privation.[14] As a consequence of both this reality of generalized pri-

vation and the impact of the centralized, bureaucratic coordination of economic activity that the introduction of economic planning—a further, fourth feature of the regime's "social-property relations"—entailed, small legal, semilegal, and illegal private sectors survived on the margins of the economy. Fifth, while the centralized, authoritarian state claimed to rule on behalf of its worker-citizens, its behavior was influenced profoundly by its nature as a "civil war" state, resorting to political repression against those who opposed its economic decisions internally. Equally, however, as would become clear with the onset of the cold war, the ways in which it made decisions were determined too by the position in which the Hungarian socialist state and its Soviet patron found themselves internationally.

The regime sought to bridge the contradictions that emerged as a consequence of these "social-property relations" by promoting industrial workers' identification with its vision of the "new Communist working class"—a collective that would recognize that work under the dictates of the plan and the apparatus it rested on was necessary for building a new society. Since 1945, the MKP and its allies had sought to reshape workers' subjectivities through its campaigns of mobilization on the production front. During the earliest labor competitions, like those organized to motivate skilled workers from heavy industrial plants who had been sent to repair Budapest's shattered bridges, officials and activists were focused on how the experience of participating in national reconstruction would forge "new" workers, ones who would have a postcapitalist attitude to their labor.[15] Recognizing that the mentalities of actual industrial workers would not naturally be transformed, labor competition campaigns introduced in 1948 were intended to convert workers to new forms of behavior. Propaganda designed to publicize the lives and achievements of those selected as Stakhanovites was structured around narratives of conversion. According to his official ghostwritten biography, Tatabánya Stakhanovite Barnabás Varga's conversion occurred while, when attempting to overcome physical exhaustion that resulted from his own attempts to raise his production, he learned of the methods of coal hewers in the Soviet Union.[16] At the level of everyday life, however, such processes of conversion almost never occurred in the way they were represented in propaganda. Instead, the clash between visions of a "new Communist working class" and the mentalities of workers was bridged through a politics of informal compromise on the job. In this context, the conditional legitimacy the regime had constructed was maintained, as was the necessary degree of compromise to maintain production, but at the price of escalating wage costs as workers demanded material improvement and informal control over remuneration, which resulted in inadequate productivity growth—a problem for central planners.

The regime sought to smash the micropolitics of compromise on the job, as the response of the Soviet Union to a deteriorating international climate led the party and regime in Budapest to prioritize armaments-based industrialization over the need to maintain the consent of most workers—a decision that destroyed its legitimacy. The regime clamped down in summer 1950. Workers experienced the shift toward restrictions through cuts in wages, sharp increases in work intensity, and widespread repression. Not only did the conditional legitimacy the regime enjoyed disappear, but the micropolitics of work shifted toward the discontinuous production generated by armaments-based industrialization. Bargaining around scarce work and for higher wages not only destroyed effective managerial control over the pace of work, labor turnover, and quality of output but also strengthened hierarchical relationships based on gender, generation, skill, and social origin between workers. This in turn frustrated the attempts by the state to expand the workforce and integrate large numbers of new recruits into factories, mines, and construction sites. The cumulative result was widespread though small-scale unrest that profoundly destabilized the environment in which production occurred.

The cumulative effect of these processes was that, by 1953, industrial communities were on the verge of a social explosion—an explosion that was defused temporarily by the wage increases and social measures introduced by Imre Nagy's first government, appointed that June. The situation remained serious for the regime, for the discontent and lack of legitimacy it enjoyed among industrial workers represented the root of a serious crisis of socialist state building, simply because it sharply contradicted the claims of Hungary's rulers to govern in the name of the "working class." Between 1953 and 1956, during the mounting disputes within the party and between intellectuals over the future of socialism, workers and the state of the regime's legitimacy in industrial communities were all but invisible. Consequently, industrial communities came to constitute an "evental site" within the regime's construction of its own legitimacy—namely a place where central contradictions normally hidden to those outside were laid bare to insiders. Yet the reality of workers' relations with the regime at the everyday level was invisible within the broader public realm outside of the factories and the industrial districts, especially to policy makers, intellectuals, and students. When, however, the socialist state crumbled during 1956, the reality of the relationship between workers and the state became progressively more visible within the broader public realm, thus feeding the process of collapse. During the revolution in October, the very fact of large numbers of workers taking to the streets, while none were prepared to defend the regime, led to the collapse of its authority, as the credibility of its claim to legitimacy evaporated.[17]

While the intervention of the Soviet Union enabled a restored socialist state to crush the political institutions of the revolution and thus occupy power and while its control over security forces was sufficient to detain revolutionary activists, the state could not depend on repressive means alone to generate stability. This was simply because the revolution had transformed the situation utterly by revealing the socialist state's lack of legitimacy among workers. Therefore, to survive, the state was forced to repair its relationship with workers, especially the urban skilled workers who, within the Hungarian social imaginary, spoke for the "working class." This was made especially difficult because the regime had to mask the fact that most workers had supported the central political goals of the revolution, particularly the withdrawal of Soviet troops, democratization of the state, and Hungarian neutrality. Given that the state could not even begin to address these political demands, and was unwilling to try, it constructed a brittle legitimacy through which it repaired its relationship to workers—or at least relatively left-wing urban workers—by formalizing tacit bargains in the workplace achieved through the informal micropolitics of production of the previous eight years and by boosting living standards. This brittle legitimacy was conditional on the state meeting the material demands of at least the "core" of the industrial workforce. It also necessitated the de facto abandonment of attempts to create a "new Communist working class." While the regime paid lip service to goals of improving cultural and educational provision for workers and creating a new attitude among workers toward work, in practice it accommodated itself to established working-class cultures, especially those of older, skilled, male urban workers. This "workerist" settlement that had emerged by summer 1958 was fundamental to the consolidation of the regime. As a strategy, this arrangement allowed the regime to weather the storm of renewed agricultural collectivization in the late 1950s and acted as a cornerstone of the construction of its legitimacy throughout the 1960s and 1970s.[18]

This book has been an exploration of the importance of industrial workers to the process of socialist state formation in postwar Hungary and has argued for the centrality of this social group to the dynamics through which the regime was created and consolidated in the country. Some of the patterns through which the consolidation of the regime in Hungary occurred suggest points of comparison with its Central and Eastern neighbors that are worthy of further investigation. While the focus of recent research on the creation of socialist regimes has suggested the distinctiveness of national roads to dictatorship during the late 1940s, the experience of cold war–era, armaments-based industrialization during the 1950s was a common one, even if precise periodization varied between states. The 1956 Revolution, furthermore, occurred not only in the context of an extended crisis of Hungary's socialist order that began in late spring 1953. It also unfolded against the backdrop of region-wide popular protest and political crisis, in which industrial workers frequently took to the streets, whether in Plžen in Czechoslovakia, across the German Democratic Republic in late spring 1953, Poznań in Poland in June 1956, or in Hungary in October and November. This widespread surge in political unrest exposed the emptiness of each local regime's claim to rule on behalf of workers.[19] In each of these countries, political crisis necessitated a reconstruction of the practice of socialist rule. Where successful consolidation occurred, it was accompanied by a form of workerist settlement in industrial workplaces. In the GDR, this took the form of a "tacit social contract" between workers and the regime that limited the state's room for maneuver in the fields of labor and economic policy and set the stage for the considerable informal negotiation of production at the workplace level.[20] In Czechoslovakia, regime workerism rested on a settlement that made considerable concessions to the egalitarian sentiments that underpinned dominant moral economies on factory floors and conceded to the skilled members of the workforce considerable informal control over production.[21]

Workerist bargains in both East Germany and Czechoslovakia were about placating workers who would otherwise have demanded extensive political reform. In Czechoslovakia, workers were profoundly suspicious of economic reforms introduced during the mid-1960s to combat economic stagnation that threatened egalitarian wage spreads, and they shifted their stance only when the promise of political reform during 1968 captured their imaginations.[22] When the GDR implemented economic reform at the same time, the assertion of managerial authority that resulted provoked a wave of demands for political reform. During the 1970s, after Walter Ulbricht was replaced at the helm of the ruling party by Erich Honecker, quiescence was restored through a reassertion of the workerist settlement in factories in the context of the regime's attempts to expand socialist consumerism and social policy.[23] While successful workerist settlements established during the late 1950s and early 1960s were challenged by economic reform at the end of the decade but proved durable well into the 1970s in the GDR and Czechoslovakia, Poland experienced a different trajectory. Widespread material frustration among workers countrywide during the 1960s regarding low wages and persistent shortages of basic foodstuffs pointed to the relative failure of the Polish regime to create a successful workerist settlement along the lines of those established by its neighbors; these problems provoked marked alienation from the socialist state, and this sentiment was politicized sharply. While the regime was able to manipulate class-based resentment toward students and intellectuals, as well as anti-Semitic sentiment, to rally workers behind it in the face of protest in March 1968, it paid for its long-term failure to develop a durable settlement with industrial workers in December 1970 as unrest broke out countrywide. The turmoil centered on the Baltic ports and was sparked by hikes in the price of meat prior to the Christmas holidays, triggering broader political upheaval. This set the scene for the periodic explosions of protest during the 1970s that culminated in the outright crisis of 1980–81.[24]

The trajectory of Hungary's own workerist settlement, which rested on the brittle legitimacy established in the two years that followed the suppression of the 1956 Revolution, resembled the settlements in the GDR and Czechoslovakia more than it did the situation in Poland. Workers' real incomes rose at a steady rate throughout the 1960s, even if the increase was less than the 8 percent per annum rise between 1956 and the end of the decade. The regime protected the incomes of those it saw as the "core" segments of the working class, privileging those who worked in traditional heavy industrial sectors that contained most of the skilled elite. While wages in mining, the most privileged of industrial sectors, had been 129.7 percent of the industrial average in 1955, they rose to 140.3 percent ten years later. Wages in electrical goods production, steel making, and machine manufacture were set above the industrial average throughout the 1960s; those in chemicals, light industry, and food processing, where the workforces conformed less to established notions of an urban, male working class, lagged behind that industrial average. The preferential position of the "core" of the "working class," as it existed in the Hungarian social imaginary and was conceptualized by the regime, was bolstered by the increases through the decade in social benefits, which were often explicitly tied to work in key industrial sectors.[25]

While this settlement reinforced hierarchies within the industrial workforce, disproportionately privileging older, male skilled workers in heavy industry, and further marginalized women, the young, and rural commuters, this settlement was challenged by a range of processes during the 1960s. Policies of conciliation toward agriculture following the completion of collectivization in 1961 led to increases in living standards for the rural population, allowing them to close the gap between them and their urban counterparts. At the same time, controls on the business activities of agricultural producer cooperatives were relaxed. The introduction in January 1968 of the New Economic Mechanism, which institutionalized a form of "market socialism" in order to improve Hungary's economic performance, coincided with managerial offensives to wrest control of production in heavy industrial sectors by breaking the patterns of workplace bargaining formalized after 1956. When the skilled urban elite sensed that they were being attacked, a wave of complaint resulted.[26] This combined with the growth of visible social differentiation to strain the postrevolutionary settlement, generating demands for political reform from the factory floor.[27] Faced with the specter of worker discontent and already under pressure in the aftermath of the Soviet intervention in Czechoslovakia and the end of the reform course in Prague, and harried by its own antireform wing domestically, the party leadership instituted a gradual and partial reversal of the reform measures.[28] Yet the early 1970s was the last time that the core of the workforce would be able to assert its power politically. The regime proved powerless to prevent growing social differentiation, largely based on quasimarket, semilegal economic activity that mushroomed during the decade. With blocked reform, Hungary stagnated economically during the 1970s amid the onset of the long downturn in the global economy, and increasing living standards were paid for through the accumulation of sovereign debt. This forced a turn to austerity beginning in late 1978 and renewed economic reform during the early 1980s. By this point, the countervailing power of the core of the workforce generated by the postrevolutionary settlement was all but gone. Positive images of the male skilled worker in heavy industrial employment disappeared from the realm of the Hungarian social imaginary, both among the population as a whole and in official representations during the 1980s. As workers' living standards stagnated, privatization spread inside factory gates (as a consequence of economic reform measures that extended the logic of supplementary work in the informal economy into socialist production), working hours increased, and unemployment reemerged, the notion that the regime rested on a claim to rule on behalf of the "working class" lost any credibility.[29] As this claim dissolved, so too did the socialist state. Its own viability as a political regime was linked to the credibility of its claim to rule on behalf of an industrial "working class." Indeed, the political trajectory of the socialist regime cannot be grasped without an examination of how the socialist state ruled on an everyday level in Hungary's industrial communities.

# Notes

## Abbreviations Used in Notes

| | |
|---|---|
| BFL | Budapest Főváros Levéltára (Budapest City Archive) |
| FML | Fejér Megyei Levéltár (Fejér County Archive) |
| Gy.MSMGy.L | Győr-Moson-Sopron Megye Győri Levéltára (Győr Archive of Győr-Moson-Sopron County) |
| KEMÖL | Komárom-Esztergom Megyei Önkormányzat Levéltára (Archive of the Local Authority of Komárom-Esztergom County) |
| MOIMA | Magyar Olajipari Múzuem Achiviuma (Archive of the Hungarian Oil Industry Museum) |
| MOL | Magyar Országos Levéltár (Hungarian National Archive) |
| OSzK Kt. | Országos Szechényi Könyvtár, Kézirattár (Szechényi National Library, Manuscript Collection) |
| PtSzL | Politikatörténeti és Szakszervezeti Levéltár (Archive of Political History and Trade Unions) |
| TMA | Tatabánya Múzeum Adattára (Collection of the Tatabánya Museum) |
| ZML | Zala Megyei Levéltár (Zala County Archive) |

**Introduction**

1. On Kósa's role in the revolution in Újpest during 1956, see János M. Rainer, "Helyi politikai szerveződés 1956-ban – az újpesti példa," in *Az ostromtól a forradalomig: adalékok Budapest múltjáról*, ed. Zsuzsanna Bencsík and Gábor Kresalek (Budapest: Budapest Főváros Levéltára, 1990), 101–12. For basic information on his trial and that of his fellow members of the Újpest Revolutionary Committee, see András B. Hegedűs, Péter Kende, György Litván, and János M. Rainer, eds., *1956 kézikönyve: megtorlás és emlékezés* (Budapest: 1956-os Intézet, 1996), 202–3.

2. Országos Szechényi Könyvtár, Kézirattár (Szechényi National Library, Manuscripts Collection, hereafter, OSzK Kt.), 1956-os gyűjtemény (1956 collections, hereafter, 1956-os gy.), Budapest Fővárosi Bíróság Népbirósági Tanácsanak anyaga (Papers of the Peoples' Court Council of the Budapest City Court, hereafter, Bp.NB), 4491/74;2d/3.; A Budapest Fővárosi Bíróság Népbirósági Tanácsa, T.NB.8017/1958/III sz. Jegyzőkönyv készült szervezkedés és egyéb büncselekmények miatt Kósa Pál és 29 társa ellen inditott bünügyben a Budapesti Fővárosi Bíróság Népbirósági Tanácsanak 1958 április 30.-án reggel 9 órára tüzött zárt tárgyalásáról, 2–3.

3. OSzK Kt., 1956-os gy., Bp.NB, 4491/74; 2d./8; 1. Kihallgatási jegyzőkönyv, Budapest, 1.

4. OSzK Kt., 1956-os gy., Bp.NB, 4491/74; 2d./3; A Budapest Fővárosi Bíróság Népbirósági Tanácsa, T.NB.8017/1958/III sz. Jegyzőkönyv készült szervezkedés és egyéb büncselekmények miatt Kósa Pál és 29 társa ellen inditott bünügyben a Budapesti Fővárosi Bíróság Népbirósági Tanácsanak 1958 április 30.-án reggel 9 órára tüzött zárt tárgyalásáról, 3–6.

5. Rainer, "Helyi politikai szerveződés 1956-ban," 110–11.

6. Budapest Főváros Levéltára (Budapest City Archive, hereafter, BFL), Az MSZMP Budapesti Bizottságának iratai (Papers of the Budapest Committee of the Hungarian Socialist Workers' Party, hereafter, XXXV.1f.)/1958/apparatus/42ő.e. (őrzési egység, or preservation unit), 242.

7. Magyar Országos Levéltár (Hungarian National Archive, hereafter, MOL), A Magyar Szocialista Munkáspárt Központi Bizottságának iratai (Papers of the Central Committee of the Hungarian Socialist Workers' Party, hereafter, M-KS-288f.) 5/23ő.e./1957.április 23., 92.

8. MOL, M-KS-288f.5/1958/96ő.e., 3.

9. "Az MSzMP Központi Bizottságának határozata a munkásosztállyal kapcsolatos egyes feladatokról (1958. október 16)," in *A Magyar Szocialista Munkáspárt határozatai és dokumentumai, 1956–1962*, ed. Henrik Vass and Ágnes Ságvári, 2d expanded ed. (Budapest: Kossuth Könyvkiadó, 1973), 272–77.

10. MOL, M-KS-288f.23/1957/34ő.e., 34; BFL, XXXV.1f.1958/42ő.e., 49–52.

11. MOL, M-KS-288f.21/1958/19ő.e., 334.

12. For my own review and critique of this literature, see Mark Pittaway, "Control and Consent in East Europe's Workers' States, 1945–1989: Some Reflections on Totalitarianism, Social Organization and Social Control," in *Social Control in Europe*, vol. 2, *1800–2000*, ed. Clive Emsley, Eric Johnson, and Pieter Sprierenburg (Columbus: Ohio State University Press, 2004), 343–67. For a sample of this work in the Hungarian context, see Elemér

Hankiss, *East European Alternatives* (Oxford: Clarendon Press, 1990); Sándor Szakács and Tibor Zinner, *A háború "megváltozott természete" – adatok és adalékok, tények és összefüggések – 1944–1948* (Budapest: Batthyány Társaság, 1997); Ákos Róna-Tas, *The Great Surprise of the Small Transformation: The Demise of Communism and the Rise of the Private Sector in Hungary* (Ann Arbor: University of Michigan Press, 1997); Gyula Belényi, and Lajos Sz. Varga, "Bevezetés," in *Munkások Magyarországon, 1948–1956: dokumentumok,* ed. Gyula Belényi and Lajos Sz. Varga (Budapest: Napvilág Kiadó, 2000), 13–52; Sándor Szakács, "From Land Reform to Collectivization (1945–1956)," in *Hungarian Agrarian Society from the Emancipation of the Serfs (1848) to the Re-privatization of the Land (1998),* ed. Péter Gunst, trans. Tünde Bodnár (Boulder, CO: East European Monographs, 1998), 257–98.

13. Richard Bessel and Ralph Jessen, eds., *Die Grenzen der Diktatur: Staat und Gesellschaft in der DDR* (Göttingen: Vandenhoeck & Ruprecht, 1996).

14. Phillip Abrams, "Notes on the Difficulty of Studying the State (1977)," *Journal of Historical Sociology* 1, no. 1 (1988): 58–89; Thomas Blom Hansen and Finn Stepputat, "Introduction: States of Imagination," in *States of Imagination: Ethnographic Explorations of the Postcolonial State,* ed. Thomas Blom Hansen and Finn Stepputat (Durham, NC: Duke University Press, 2001), 1–38; Christian Krohn-Hansen and Knut G. Nustad, introduction to *State Formation: Anthropological Perspectives,* ed. Christian Krohn-Hansen and Knut G. Nustad (London: Pluto Press, 2005), 3–26; Timothy Mitchell, "Society, Economy and the State Effect," in *State/Culture: State-Formation after the Cultural Turn,* ed. George Steinmetz (Ithaca, NY: Cornell University Press, 1999), 76–97.

15. Michael Mann, "The Autonomous Power of the State: Its Origins, Mechanism and Results," in *States, War and Capitalism: Studies in Political Sociology,* by Michael Mann (Oxford: Basil Blackwell, 1988), 5–9.

16. These criteria are adapted from David Beetham, *The Legitimation of Power* (Basingstoke, England: Macmillan, 1991), 16.

17. Martin Conway and Peter Romijn, "Introduction," *Contemporary European History* 13, no. 4 (2004): 382.

18. I owe a considerable debt to the theoretical discussion of the "problem of legitimacy" in John D. Hoffman, *Beyond the State: An Introductory Critique* (Cambridge and Oxford: Polity Press, 1995), 76–93.

19. Mátyás Rákosi, "Mi a magyar demokrácia?" in *Válogatott beszédek és cikkek,* by Mátyás Rákosi (Budapest: Szikra, 1950), 47.

20. Erzsébet Andics, *Fasizmus és reakció Magyarországon* (Budapest: Szikra kiadás, 1948); Tibor Hajdu, *Az 1918-as magyarországi polgári demokratikus forradalom* (Budapest: Kossuth Könyvkiadó, 1968); Tibor Hajdu, *A Magyarországi Tanácsköztársaság* (Budapest: Kossuth Könyvkiadó, 1969).

21. Imre Nagy, *Agrárpolitikai tanulmányok: előadások az Agrártudományi Egyetemen és a Mezőgazdasági Akadémián* (Budapest: Szikra, 1950), 253.

22. Ernő Gerő, "Beszéd az ideiglenes nemzetgyűlésben," in *Harcban a szocialista népgazdaságért: válogatott beszédek és cikkek, 1944–1950,* by Ernő Gerő (Budapest: Szikra, 1950), 19.

23. A good example of this assumption can be seen in János Horváth, "Veszprém

megye Parasztsága a Munkássággal Együtt Halad," in *A népi demokrácia útja: A Magyar Kommunista Párt Budapesten 1946 szeptember 28., 29., 30. és október 1. napján megtartott III. Kongresszusának jegyzőkönyve* (Budapest: Szikra Kiadás, 1946), 284–85.

24. Komárom-Esztergom Megyei Önkormányzat Levéltára (Archive of the Local Authority of Komárom-Esztergom County, hereafter, KEMÖL), Az MKP Tata Járási Bizottságának iratai (Papers of the Tata District Committee of the Hungarian Communist Party, hereafter, XXXV.24f.)1ő.e., 2.

25. Aladár Mód, "Az üzemi bizottságok és az újjáépítés," *Szakszervezeti Közlöny,* 1 June 1945, 4–5.

26. KEMÖL, XXXV.24f.1ő.e., 2.

27. István Kovács, "A Nagyüzemi kommunista pártszervezet munkájáról és feladatairól," *Pártmunka,* 15 August 1945, 108.

28. For a very revealing analysis of how MKP activists saw rural society at the end of the "popular-front" period, see András Sándor, *Övék a föld* (Budapest: Szikra Kiadás, 1948), 9–31.

29. Nagy, *Agrárpolitikai tanulmányok,* 254.

30. Mátyás Rákosi, "A dolgozó nép alkotmánya," in *Válogatott beszédek és cikkek,* by Mátyás Rákosi (Budapest: Szikra, 1950), 446.

31. Ernő Gerő, "A Magyar Népgazdaság Ötéves Terve," in *Harcban a szocialista népgazdaságért,* by Gerő, 525.

32. For an example, see "Öt magyar sztahánovista újévi üzenete: az elmúlt év tanulságairól, az új esztendő feladatairól," *Szabad Nép,* 1 January 1950, 5.

33. Quoted in *A szocializmus építésének útján: A Magyar Dolgozók Pártja II;. kongresszusának anyagából,* 2d ed. (Budapest: Szikra, 1956), 276.

34. "Új munkásosztály születik," *Szabad Nép,* 5 March 1950, 1.

35. *A munkásosztály felelőssége a szocializmus építésében* (Budapest: Kiadja a Magyar Dolgozók Pártja Központi Vezetősége Oktatási Osztály, 1950), 5.

36. *Kétlakiság* (Budapest: Szakszervezeti Ismeretterjesztő Előadások, Népszava, 1952).

37. Mark Pittaway, "Workers in Hungary," in *Power and the People: A Social History of Central European Politics, 1945–1956,* ed. Eleonore Breuning, Jill Lewis, and Gareth Pritchard (Manchester: Manchester University Press, 2005), 57–75.

38. MOL, A Magyar Dolgozók Pártja Központi Vezetőségének iratai (Papers of the Central Leadership of the Hungarian Workers' Party, hereafter, M-KS-276f.)94/831ő.e., 261.

39. On the various aspects of Soviet policy in Hungary during the immediate postwar period, see Peter Kenez, *Hungary from the Nazis to the Soviets: The Establishment of the Communist Regime in Hungary, 1944–1948* (Cambridge: Cambridge University Press, 2006), 35–80; László Borhi, *Hungary in the Cold War: Between the United States and the Soviet Union* (Budapest: Central European University Press, 2004), 52–75; Julien Papp, *La Hongrie libérée: état, pouvoirs et société après la défaite du nazisme (septembre 1944–septembre 1947)* (Rennes, France: Presses Universitaires de Rennes, 2006), 33–85; István Vida, "Orosz levéltári források az 1944 őszen moszkvai kormányalakítási tárgyalásokról, az Ideiglenes Nemzetgyűlés összehívásáról és az Ideiglenes Nemzeti Kormány megválasztásáról," in *Az Ideiglenes Nemzetgyűlés és az Ideiglenes Nemzeti Kormány, 1944–1945,* ed. István Feitl (Budapest: Politikatörténeti Alapítvány, 1995), 52–107; István Feitl, ed., *A magyarországi*

*Szövetséges Ellenőrző Bizottság ülésének jegyzőkönyvei, 1945–1947* (Budapest: Napvilág Kiadó, 2003); Sándor Balogh and Margit Földesi, eds., *A magyar jóvátétel, és ami mögötte van . . .* (Budapest: Napvilág Kiadó, 1998).

40. For this point, see Martin Mevius, *Agents of Moscow: The Hungarian Communist Party and the Origins of Socialist Patriotism, 1941–1953* (Oxford: Clarendon Press, 2005), 47–68; and Mark Pittaway, "The Politics of Legitimacy and Hungary's Postwar Transition," *Contemporary European History* 13, no. 4 (2004): 453–75. On the semiofficial violence itself, see Papp, *La Hongrie libérée,* 16–24; Krisztián Ungváry, *Battle for Budapest: 100 Days in World War II,* trans. Ladislaus Löb (London: I. B. Tauris, 2005), 279–310; Andrea Pető, "Memory and the Narrative of Rape in Budapest and Vienna in 1945," in *Life after Death: Approaches to a Cultural and Social History of Europe during the 1940s and 1950s,* ed. Richard Bessel and Dirk Schumann (Washington, DC: German Historical Institute; Cambridge: Cambridge University Press, 2003), 129–48; György Zielbauer, "Magyar polgári lakosok deportálása és hadifogsága (1945–1948)," *Történelmi Szemle* 34, no. 3–4 (1992): 270–91.

41. Kenez, *Hungary from the Nazis to the Soviets,* 81–106; Borhi, *Hungary in the Cold War,* 47–109; Papp, *La Hongrie libérée,* 35–41; Vida, "Orosz levéltári források az 1944 őszen moszkvai kormányalakítási tárgyalásokról"; Mária Palasik, *A jogállamiság megteremtésének kísérlete és kudarca Magyarországon 1944–1949* (Budapest: Napvilág Kiadó, 2000), 21–93; Mihály Korom, *Magyarország ideiglenes nemzeti kormánya és a fegyverszünet (1944–1945)* (Budapest: Akadémiai Kiadó, 1981), 308–453; László Szűcs, ed., *Dálnoki Miklós Béla kormányának (Ideiglenes Nemzeti Kormány) minisztertanácsi jegyzőkönyvei, 1944. december 23.–1945. november 15. A-B kötet* (Budapest: Magyar Országos Levéltár, 1997).

42. Borhi, *Hungary in the Cold War,* 60–68; Mevius, *Agents of Moscow,* 265.

43. Mevius, *Agents of Moscow,* 81–6; "A Magyar Kommunista Párt országos értekezletének határozata a politikai helyzetről és a párt feladatairól," reprinted in *A Magyar Kommunista Párt és a Szociáldemokrata Párt határozatai, 1944–1948,* ed. Sándor Rákosi and Bálint Szabó, 2d ed. (Budapest: Kossuth Könyvkiadó, 1974), 85; József Kiss, ed., *"A párt foglya voltam" Demény Pál élete* (Budapest: Medvetánc, 1988); Béla Gadanecz Éva Gadanecz, "A weisshausisták tevékenysége és üldöztetése 1945 után," *Múltunk* 40, no. 3 (1995): 3–72; Mária Palasik, "A gyömrői gyilkosságok és következményeik, 1945–1946," *Valóság* 4 (1995): 58–67.

44. Politikatörténeti és Szakszervezeti Levéltár (Archive of Political History and Trade Unions, hereafter, PtSzL), A Szakszervezeti Tanács iratai (Papers of the Trade Union Council, hereafter, XII.1f.)19d./1945; MOL, Iparügyi Minisztérium III/1. osztály. 1227/"M"- 1945. szám. Jelentés az országos üzemi bizottsági kongresszusról., 3.

45. Jenő Gergely, *Gömbös Gyula: politikai pályakép* (Budapest: Vince Kiadó, 2001), 195–305; Mária Ormos, *A gazdasági világválság magyar visszahangja* (Budapest: Eötvös Kiadó – PolgART Könyvkiadó, 2004); József Vonyó, ed., *Gömbös pártja: a Nemzeti Egység Pártja dokumentumai* (Budapest and Pécs: Dialóg Campus Kiadó, 1998); József Vonyó, *Gömbös Gyula és a jobboldali radikalizmus: tanulmányok* (Pécs: Pannónia Könyvek, 2001).

46. C. A. Macartney, *October Fifteenth: A History of Modern Hungary, 1929–1945,* 2 vols., 2d ed. (Edinburgh: Edinburgh University Press, 1961), vol. 1; Paul A. Hanebrink, *In Defense of Christian Hungary: Religion, Nationalism, and Antisemitism in Hungary, 1890–1944* (Ithaca, NY: Cornell University Press, 2006), 108–63; Margit Szöllösi-Janze,

*Die Pfeilkreuzlerbewegung in Ungarn: Historischer Kontext, Entwicklung und Herrschaft* (Munich: R. Oldenbourg Verlag, 1989), 101–250; Zoltán Paksy, ed., *Az antiszemitzmus alakváltozatai: tanulmányok* (Zalaegerszeg: Zala Megyei Levéltár, 2005); János Pelle, *A gyűlölet vetése: a zsidótörvények és a magyar közvélemény, 1938–1944* (Budapest: Európa Könyvkiadó, 2001); Miklós Zeidler, *A magyar irredenta kultusz a két világháború között* (Budapest: Teleki László Alapítvány, 2002).

47. The best overview of this process is provided by Macartney, *October Fifteenth*, 1:202–490; see also the relevant documents in György Ránki, Ervin Pamlényi, Loránt Tilkovszky, and Gyula Juhász, eds., *A Wilhelmstrasse és Magyarország: német diplomáciai iratok magyarországról, 1933–1944* (Budapest: Kossuth Könyvkiadó, 1968), 554–99; Miklós Szinai and László Szűcs, eds., *Horthy Miklós Titkos Iratai* (Budapest: Kossuth Könyvkiadó, 1965), 289–312.

48. The best military history of the conflict is Krisztián Ungváry, *A magyar honvédség a második világháborúban* (Budapest: Osiris Kiadó, 2004), 123–228.

49. "Komoly idők intelmei," *Mosonvármegye Magyaróvári Hírlap,* 27 January 1944, 1.

50. Macartney, *October Fifteenth*, 2:124–220; György Lengyel, ed., *Hungarian Economy and Society during World War II,* trans. Judit Pokoly (Boulder, CO: East European Monographs, 1993); Pelle, *A gyűlölet vetése,* 252–315; Loránd Dombrády, *A magyar hadigazdaság a második világháború idején* (Budapest: Petit Real Könyvkiadó, 2003); Gyula Erdmann, *Begyűjtés, beszolgáltatás Magyarországon, 1945–1956* (Gyula: Békés Megyei Levéltár, 1996), 7–14; Péter Sipos, *Legális és illegális munkásmozgalom (1919–1944)* (Budapest: Gondolat, 1988), 290–309.

51. Macartney, *October Fifteenth*, 2:242–443; János Sebők, *A Horthy-mítosz és a holokauszt* (Budapest: privately published, 2004); László Karsai and Judit Molnár, eds., *A magyar quisling-kormány: Sztójay döme és társai a népbíróság előtt* (Budapest: 1956-os KHT., 2004); Christian Gerlach and Götz Aly, *Das letzte Kapitel: Der Mord an den ungarischen Juden, 1944–1945* (Frankfurt: Fischer Taschenbuch Verlag, 2004), 91–343; Randolph L. Braham, *The Politics of Genocide: The Holocaust in Hungary,* condensed ed. (Detroit: Wayne State University Press, 2000), 99–152; Tim Cole, *Holocaust City: The Making of a Jewish Ghetto* (New York: Routledge, 2003).

52. Szöllösi-Janze, *Die Pfeilkreuzlerbewegung in Ungarn,* 283–432; Béla Vinceller, *Sötet árny magyarhon felett: szálasi uralma (1944. október – 1945. május)* (Budapest: Makkabi Kiadó, 2004); Elek Karsai and László Karsai, eds., *A Szálasi per* (Budapest: Reform, 1988); Braham, *Politics of Genocide,* 181–97; Gerlach and Aly, *Das letzte Kapitel,* 344–74. For the political attitudes among the population in Arrow Cross–ruled western Hungary in early 1945, see Győr-Moson-Sopron Megye Győri Levéltára (Győr Archive of Győr-Moson-Sopron County, hereafter, Gy.MSMGy.L), Győr-Moson-Pozsony k.e.e. vm. és Győr sz. kír. város főispánjá 1938–1945, Bizalmas iratok (Confidential Papers of the Lord-Lieutenant of Győr-Moson-Pozsony and the Royal Free City of Győr, hereafter, IVf.451a.)/2d.; A m.kir. rendőrség politikai rendészeti osztálya szombathelyi kirendeltsége. 7/1945 pol.rend.biz. Szigoruan bizalmas. Szombathely, 1945 január hó 31-én, 1–21.

53. PtSzL, A Magyar Kommunista Párt iratai (Papers of the Hungarian Communist Party, hereafter, I.274f.)16/130ő.e., 89.

54. I make this case in more detail in Pittaway, "Politics of Legitimacy."

55. See Pittaway, "Politics of Legitimacy," 473–75. For the 1947 elections, see Károly Szerencsés, *A kékcédulás hadművelet (választások Magyarországon 1947)* (Budapest: IKVA, 1993); for the creation of socialist dictatorship, see the essays in Éva Standeisky, Gyula Kozák, Gábor Pataki, and János M. Rainer, eds., *A fordulat évei: politika – képzőművészet – építészet* (Budapest: 1956-os Intézet, 1998).

56. György Gyarmati, ed., *Államvédelem a Rákosi-korszakban: tanulmányok és dokumentumok a politikai rendőrség második világháború utáni tevékenységéről* (Budapest: Történeti Hivatal, 2000); Tibor Zinner, ed., *Rajk László és társai a népbíróság előtt 40 év távlatából* (Budapest: Magyar Eszperantó Szövetség, 1989); Imre Okváth, ed., *Katonai perek a kommunista diktatúra időszakában, 1945–1958: tanulmányok a fegyveres testületek tagjai elleni megtorlásokról a hidegháború kezdeti időszakában* (Budapest: Történeti Hivatal, 2001); Mária Ormos et al., *Törvénytelen szocializmus: a tényfeltáró bizottság jelentése* (Budapest: Zrinyi Kiadó Új Magyarország, 1991), 64–68; Margit Balogh, *Mindszenty József (1892–1975)* (Budapest: Elektra Kiadóház, 2002), 206–55; Jenő Gergely, *A Katolikus egyház Magyarországon, 1944–1971* (Budapest: Kossuth Könyvkiadó, 1985), 9–145.

57. Nigel Swain, *Hungary: The Rise and Fall of Feasible Socialism* (London: Verso, 1992), 40–43; Iván Pető and Sándor Szakács, *A hazai gazdaság négy évtizedének története, 1945–1985. I. Az újjáépítés és a tervutasításos irányítás időszaka* (Budapest: Közgazdasági és Jogi Könyvkiadó, 1985), 95–103; Martha Lampland, *The Object of Labor: Commodification in Socialist Hungary* (Chicago: University of Chicago Press, 1995), 135–53; Sándor Orbán, *Két agrárforradalom Magyarországon: demokratikus és szocialista agrárátalakulás 1945–1961* (Budapest: Akadémiai Kiadó, 1972), 65–159; Pál Závada, *Kulákprés: család- és falutörténeti szociográfia. Tótkomlós 1945–1956* (Budapest: Szépirodalmi-Széphalom Könyvkiadó, 1991), 85–91.

58. Gy.MSMGy.L, Az MDP Győr-Moson-Sopron Megyei Bizottság, Mezőgazdasági Osztály iratai (Papers of the Agricultural Department of the Győr-Moson-Sopron County Committee of the Hungarian Workers' Party, hereafter, Xf.402/2/Mezőgazdaság)/8ő.e. M.D.P. Járási Bizottság Mosonmagyaróvár, Sallai Imre ut 3 sz, Jelentés. Mosonmagyaróvár, 1950. augusztus 9-én., 1.

59. Rákosi, "A dolgozó nép alkotmánya," 446.

60. Mark Pittaway, "Industrial Workers, Socialist Industrialization and the State, 1948–1958" (PhD thesis, University of Liverpool, 1998); Lampland, *Object of Labor,* 131–60.

61. János M. Rainer, *Nagy Imre: politikai életrajz; első kötet 1896–1953* (Budapest: 1956-os Intézet, 1996), 489–542; Miklós Vásárhelyi, "Az első meghiúsított reformkísérlet," *Medvetánc* no. 2–3 (1988): 149–205.

62. BFL, Az MDP Budapesti Bizottságának iratai (Papers of the Budapest Committee of the Hungarian Workers' Party, hereafter, XXXV.95f.)2/215ő.e., 139; BFL, XXXV.95f.4/62ő.e.

63. János M. Rainer, *Nagy Imre: politikai életrajz; második kötet 1953–1958* (Budapest: 1956-os Intézet, 1999), 9–202; János M. Rainer, *Az iró helye: viták a Magyar irodalmi sajtóban, 1953–1956* (Budapest: Magvető Kiadó, 1990).

64. István Márkus, "Somogyi összegezés," reprinted in *Az ismeretlen főszereplő: tanulmányok,* by István Márkus (Budapest: Szépirodalmi Könyvkiadó, 1991), 167–83; MOL, M-KS-276f.94/829ő.e., 90–92.

65. There is now a vast literature on the 1956 Revolution. For a sampling, see Charles

Gati, *Failed Illusions: Moscow, Washington, and the 1956 Hungarian Revolt* (Washington, DC: Woodrow Wilson Center; Stanford: Stanford University Press, 2006); Bill Lomax, *Hungary 1956* (London: Allison & Busby, 1976); György Litván et al., *The Hungarian Revolution of 1956: Reform, Revolt and Repression 1953–1963* (London: Longman, 1996); Johanna Granville, *The First Domino: International Decision Making during the Hungarian Crisis of 1956* (College Station: Texas A&M University Press, 2004); Attila Szakolczai, *Az 1956-os forradalom és szabadságharc* (Budapest: 1956-os Intézet, 2001); Csaba Békés, Malcolm Byrne, and János M. Rainer, eds., *The 1956 Hungarian Revolution: A History in Documents* (Budapest: Central European University Press, 2002).

66. *Ellenforradalmi erők a magyar októberi eseményekben: I–IV kötet* (Budapest: A Magyar Népköztársaság Minisztertanácsa Tájékoztatási Hivatala – Zrinyi Nyomda, 1957); *Nagy Imre és bűntársai ellenforradalmi összeskűvése* (Budapest: A Magyar Népköztársaság Minisztertanácsa Tájékoztatási Hivatala – Zrinyi Nyomda, 1958).

67. Fejér Megyei Levéltár (Fejér County Archive, hereafter, FML), Az MSzMP Fejér Megyei Bizottságának iratai (Papers of the Fejér County Committee of the Hungarian Socialist Workers' Party, hereafter, XXXV.19f.)/1957/14ő.e., 59; BFL, XXXV.1f./apparatus/1958/138ő.e., 289–95.

68. For Kádár's policies in rural communities, see Zsuzsanna Varga, *Politika, paraszti érdekérvényesítés és szövetkezetek Magyarországon, 1956–1967* (Budapest: Napvilág Kiadó, 2001); for urban Hungary, see Mark Pittaway, "Accommodation and the Limits of Economic Reform: Industrial Workers during the Making and Unmaking of Kádár's Hungary," in *Arbeiter im Staatsozialismus: Ideologischer Anspruch und soziale Wirklichkeit*, ed. Peter Hübner, Christoph Kleβmann, and Klaus Tenfelde (Cologne: Weimar; Vienna: Böhlau Verlag, 2005), 453–71; György Földes, "A Kádár-rendszer és a munkásság," *Eszmélet* no. 18–19 (1993): 57–73.

69. MOL, M-KS-288f.21/1958/19ő.e., 301.

70. "Az MSzMP Ideiglenes Központi Bizottságának 1956. decemberi határozata (1956. december 5.)," in *A Magyar Szocialista Munkáspárt határozatai és dokumentumai, 1956–1962*, ed. Vass and Ságvári, 13.

71. MOL, M-KS-288f.21/1958/20ő.e., 250.

72. MOL, M-KS-288f.21/1958/20ő.e., 253.

73. On the social history of trade unions and labor movement activism prior to socialism, see Gyula Rézler, *A magyar nagyipari munkásság kialakulása, 1867–1914* (Budapest: Rekord Könyvkiadó, 1938); the revealing essays on individual sectors in Gyula Rézler, ed., *Magyar gyári munkásság: szociális helyzetkép* (Budapest: Magyar Közgazdasági Társaság, 1940); and the later history of the presocialist organization of the Metalworkers' Union in Márton Buza, Tibor Hetés, Sándorné Gábor, János Kende, and Péter Sipos, *A Magyarországi Vas- és Fémmunkások Központi Szövetségének története* (Budapest: A Magyarországi Vas- és Fémmunkások Központi Szövetsége, 1990), 293–560. See also the analysis in András Tóth, "Civil társadalom és szakszervezetek" (Kandídátusi értekezés, Budapest, 1994). For a useful analysis of the nature and limits of support for labor movement activism in one textile plant during the interwar years, see Péter Hanák and Katalin Hanák, *A Magyar Pamutipar története, 1867–1962* (Budapest: A PNYV, Magyar Pamutipar 1 sz. Gyáregysége, 1964), 170–74.

74. Rézler, *A magyar nagyipari munkásság kialakulása*, 7–45; Gyula Rézler, "A magyar gyári munkásság," in *Magyar gyári munkásság*, ed. Rézler, 7–47; Miklós Lackó, *Ipari munkásságunk összetételének alakulása, 1867–1949* (Budapest: Kossuth Könyvkiadó, 1961); Gábor Gyáni, "Migráció és mobilitás: a városi munkásság szerkezete a két világháború között," in *Rendi társadalom – polgári társadalom 1*, ed. László A. Varga (Salgótarján: Nógrád Megyei Levéltár, 1987), 495–505.

75. For the characteristics of these kinds of communities and the establishments within them, see Lajos I. Illyefalvi, *A munkások szociális és gazdasági viszonyai Budapesten* (Budapest: Budapest Székesfőváros Statisztikai Hivatal, 1930); Gyula Rézler, *Egy magyar textilgyár munkástársadalma* (Budapest: Magyar Ipari Munkatudományi Intézet, 1943); László Gereblyés, *Így volt: szociográfiai jegyzetek a 30-as évekből* (Budapest: Magvető Könyvkiadó, 1959); András Kubinyi et al., *Csepel története* (Budapest: A Csepel Vas- és Fémművek Pártbizottsága, 1965); József Kiss, *Vázlat Csepel társadalomtörténetéhez, 1919–1945* (Budapest: Művelődési Minisztérium Marxizmus-Leninizmus Oktatási Főosztálya, 1984); Miklós Lackó, "Gépgyári munkások az 1930-as években," *Századok* 123, no. 1–2 (1989): 3–44.

76. The classic analysis of workers in northern Hungarian company towns in the interwar years is Zoltán Szabó, *Cifra nyomorúság: A Cserhát, Mátra, Bükk földje és népe* (Budapest: Cserépfalvi Kiadása, 1938), 122–67. For the best attempts to approach the social histories of such communities, see Iván T. Berend, ed., *Az Ózdi Kohászati Üzemek története* (Ózd: Ózdi Kohászati Üzemek, 1980); and László R. Réti, *A Rimamurány-Salgótarjáni Vasmű Részvénytársaság története, 1881–1919* (Budapest: Akadémiai Kiadó, 1977), 115–41.

77. György Kövér, *Iparosodás agrárországban: Magyarország gazdaságtörténete, 1848–1914* (Budapest: Gondolat, 1982); Vilmos Olti, "A fűrészipari munkásság," in *Magyar gyári munkásság*, ed. Rézler, 86–106; Lajos Jorkády, "Téglagyári munkások," in *Magyar munkásszociográfiák, 1888–1945*, ed. György Litván (Budapest: Kossuth Könyvkiadó, 1974), 338–42; Klára T. Merey, *Dél-Dunántúl iparának története a kapitalizmus idején* (Budapest: Akadémiai Kiadó, 1985).

78. For the operation of discourses of gender on hierarchies in a sector with a high concentration of female workers, see Rézler, *Egy magyar textilgyár munkástársadalma*, 14–20; and Hanák and Hanák, *A Magyar Pamutipar története*, 188–201; for one where the workforce was predominantly male, see László Hantos, "Nyomdászok," in *Magyar gyári munkásság*, ed. Rézler, 203–5; for revealing information on discourses of respectability among the skilled workers of greater Budapest, see the interviews in Péter Győri, "Telepek Újpesten," in *Újpest: tanulmánykötet*, ed. Mihály Andor (Budapest: Művelődéskutató Intézet, 1982), 9–15. Similar information can be inferred from Miklós Kassai-Végh, ed., *A salgótarjáni munkások műveltsége és művelődése: munkásportrék* (Budapest: MSZMP Központi Bizottsága Társadalomtudományi Intézete, 1977), 23–50.

79. For hierarchies of generation, see Lackó, "Gépgyári munkások az 1930-as években"; on the paternalistic nature of the culture of certain sectors, see János Urbán, "Az üveggyári munkásság," in *Magyar gyári munkásság*, ed. Rézler, 76–77.

80. András Tóth, "Munkanélküliség és falusi polgárosodás" (unpublished manuscript, 1992), 1–4; Imre Bán, "Szénbányászok," in *Magyar gyári munkásság*, ed. Rézler, 222–27; Dénes Vidos, *Zalai olajos történetek* (Zalaegerszeg: Magyar Olajipari Múzeum, 1990), 40–43.

81. Rézler, *A magyar nagyipari munkásság kialakulása*, 23–129; Lajos Varga et al., *A magyar szociáldemokrácia kézikönyve* (Budapest: Napvilág Kiadó, 1999), 19–80; István Schlett, *A szociáldemokrácia és a magyar társadalom 1914-ig* (Budapest: Gondolat Kiadó, 1982); Gábor Gyáni, "'Civil társadalom' kontra liberális állam a XIX. század végén," *Századvég*, no. 1 (1991): 145–56.

82. Sipos, *Legális és illegális munkásmozgalom*.

83. József Vonyó, "A Nemzeti Egység Pártjának társadalmi bázisa Baranya megyében (1933–1935)," in *Gömbös pártja*, ed. Vonyó, 107–10.

84. Szöllösi-Janze, *Die Pfeilkreuzlerbewegung in Ungarn*, 126–86; Miklós Lackó, *Nyilasok, nemzetiszocialisták, 1935–1944* (Budapest: Kossuth Könyvkiadó, 1966), 117–36; György Borsányi, "A budapesti munkások választási magatartása (1922–1945)," in *Magyarország társadalomtörténete, 1920–1944: szöveggyűjtemény*, ed. Gábor Gyáni, 2d ed. (Budapest: Nemzeti Tankönyvkiadó, 2000), 532–34.

85. Gyula Ugró, *Újpest 1831–1930: magyar városok monografia* (Budapest: A Magyar Városok Monografiája Kiadóhivatala, 1932), 170; András Sipos, "Bevezetés," in *Dokumentumok Újpest történetéhez, 1840–1949*, ed. András Sipos (Budapest: Budapest Főváros Levéltára, 2001), 19–30; András Kubinyi, "Újpest községe alakulása, 1831–1849," in *Újpest története*, ed. Ede Gerelyes (Budapest: Közgazdasági és Jogi Könyvkiadó, 1977), 23–42; György Berkovits, "A gyarmat: Újpest történeti szociográfiája, 1835–1868," *Valóság* 24, no. 8 (1981): 32–50.

86. For Újpest's industrialization, see Gyula Ugró, "Újpest," in *Pest-Pilis-Solt Vármegye II: Magyarország Vármegyei és Városai Magyarország monografiája*, ed. Samu Borovsky (Budapest: Országos Monográfia Társaság, 1910), 486–89; Imre Csabai, "Újpest: község – nagyközség – város," in *Újpest története*, ed. Gerelyes, 73–84; András Berényi et al., *Újpest: IV. kerület* (Budapest: Ceba Kiadó, 1998), 48–63; Hanák and Hanák, *A Magyar Pamutipar története*, 7–72; Károly Jeney, "A Tungsram Rt. története I. rész, 1896–1919," in *A Tungsram Rt. története, 1896–1945*, ed. László Surguta (Budapest: Tungsram Rt. Gyártörténeti Bizottsága, 1987), 5–25.

87. Ugró, *Újpest 1831–1930*, 171–73; Ella Kalmár, "Statisztikai adatok Újpest történetéhez," in *Dokumentumok Újpest történetéhez*, ed. Sipos, 388–402; Csabai, "Újpest: község – nagyközség – város," 81–112; Ugró, "Újpest," 486.

88. Péter Lang, "A polgári demokratikus forradalom és a Tanácsköztársaság," in *Újpest története*, ed. Gerelyes, 113–49; Sipos, "Bevezetés," 49–50; Ede Gerelyes, "Újpest a két világháború között," in *Újpest története*, ed. Gerelyes, 151–208; Ferenc Gáspár, "A Tungsram Rt. története II. rész, 1919–1945," in *A Tungsram Rt. története*, ed. Surguta, 94–107; Hanák and Hanák, *A Magyar Pamutipar története*, 134–44.

89. Berényi et al., *Újpest*, 51–2; Hanák and Hanák, *A Magyar Pamutipar története*, 144–47.

90. Központi Statisztikai Hivatal, *Az 1941. évi népszámlálás demografiai adatok községek szerint* (Budapest: Stephaneum Nyomda Részvénytársaság, 1947), 91; Központi Statisztikai Hivatal, *Az 1941. évi népszámlálás 1. foglalkozási adatok községek szerint* (Budapest: Központi Statisztikai Hivatal Könyvtár és Dokumentációs Szolgálat – Magyar Országos Levéltár, 1975), 500–501; György Földes, "Az újpesti munkásság életviszonyai az 1930-as években," *Történelmi Szemle* 20, no. 2 (1980): 309–18.

91. Központi Statisztikai Hivatal, *Az 1941. évi népszámlalás demografiai adatok* (1947), 588.

92. László Hubai, "Az országgyűlési választások Újpesten, 1920–1947," in *Dokumentumok Újpest történetéhez,* ed. Sipos, 422.

93. Gerelyes, "Újpest a két világháború között," 151–201; Sipos, "Bevezetés," 50–56; Péter Győri, "A Mátyás-téri házák," in *Újpest,* ed. Andor, 32–34.

94. Lajos Szende, "Tatabánya," in *Komárom Vármegye és Komárom Sz. Kir. Város: Magyarország Vármegyei és Városai Magyarország monografiája,* ed. Samu Borovsky (Budapest: Országos Monográfia Társaság, 1907), 244–56; András Orutay, "A bányatelep kialakulása: az ipar fejlődése 1896-tól 1918-ig," in *Tatabánya története: helytörténeti tanulmányok i. kötet,* ed. Gábor Gombkötö (Tatabánya: Tatabánya Városi Tanács, 1972), 69–86; Gyula Csics, Sándor Pataki, and Sándor Rozsnyói, eds., *A Tatabányai szénbányászat története* (Tatabánya: Tatabánya Szébányászati Tröszt, 1994), 55–76.

95. *A magyar általános kőszénbánya részvénytársulat 50 éve, 1891–1941: az igazgatóság külön jelentése az 1942.évi április hó 30-ra egybehivott ünnepi közgyűléshez* (Budapest: MÁK Rt., 1942), 11–12; Endre Haintz, "A népesség alakulása," in *Tatabánya története,* ed. Gombkötö et al., 59–60.

96. Ferenc Szántó, "A szénbányászat és a gyáripar fejlődése a két világháború között," in *Tatabánya története,* ed. Gombkötö et al., 165–78; Zoltán Magyary and István Kiss, *A közigazgatás és az emberek: ténymegállapító tanulmány a tatai járás közigazgatásáról* (Budapest: Pécsi Egyetemi Könyvkiadó és Nyomda Rt., 1939), 101; Bán, "Szénbányászok," 222–25; *Az 1941. évi népszámlalás demografiai adatok* (1947), 94–95.

97. On the workforce see Magyary and Kiss, *A közigazgatás és az emberek,* 101; on other industrial establishments, see Szántó, "A szénbányászat és a gyáripar fejlődése a két világháború között"; *Az 1941. évi népszámlalás 1. foglalkozási adatok kőzségek szerint* (1975), 574–75.

98. On the culture of the interwar mining "colony" in Tatabánya, see Magyary and Kiss, *A közigazgatás és az emberek,* 99–102; Anikó Molnár Fűrészné, "Lakáshelyzet, otthonkultúra az ipartelepeken," in *Tatabánya 45 éve város,* ed. Anikó Molnár Fűrészné (Tata: Komárom-Esztergom Megyei Önkormányzat Múzeumainak Igazgatósága, 1992), 87–98; Klára Kovács, *Szén volt az életük: portrék, riportok, tárcák, elbeszélések* (Tatabánya: Tatabánya Megyei Jogú Város Önkormányzata, 1999), 26.

99. Éva Ravasz, "A Tanácsköztársaság napjai Tatabányán," in *Tatabánya története,* ed. Gombkötö et al., 120–29; Éva Ravasz, "Az ellenforradalom hatalomra jutása. Bányászmegmozdulások a fehérterror kezdeti időszakában," in *Tatabánya története,* ed. Gombkötö et al., 133–46; Tatabánya Múzeum Adattára (Collection of the Tatabánya Museum, hereafter, TMA), Roznai Florián visszaemlékezése (hereafter, 15-76), 3; Ernő Gergely, *A magyarországi bányász munkásmozgalom története 1867–1944* (Budapest: Friedrich Ebert Alapítvány, 1994), 105–207; Ferenc Szántó, *A tizhetes tatabányai bányászsztrajk története. 1925 február 3 – április 4* (Tatabánya: Tatabánya Városi Tanács – Tatabányai Szénbányák, 1985).

100. Szöllösi-Janze, *Die Pfeilkreuzlerbewegung in Ungarn,* 173–83; József Szekeres, *A magyar bányamunkásság harcai (1933–1944)* (Budapest: Akadémiai Kiadó, Budapest, 1970), 161–202.

101. Róbert Páldy, "Dél Zala," *Kelet Népe* 4, no. 7 (1938): 24.

102. Tibor Bacsinszky, "A kőolaj- és földgáztermelés," in *Ötven éves a magyar kőolaj-*
*és földgázbányászat KFV 1937-1987,* ed. Ernő Buda and József Kovács (Nagykanizsa:
Kőolaj- és Földgázbányászati Vállalat, 1987), 15-24; Lajos Srágli, *Munkások a "fekete arany"*
*birodalmában: a munkásság és anyagi-szociális helyzete a magyarországi olajiparban (a*
*kezdetektől az államosításig)* (Zalaegerszeg: Magyar Olajipari Múzeum - MOL Bányász
Szakszervezet, 2004), 12-18.

103. Srágli, *Munkások a "fekete arany" birodalmában,* 26-29; Lajos Srágli, "Adatok
az olajiipari munkásság szociális helyzetének alakulásához, 1937-1944 (A MAORT
munkásjóléti intézkedés)," in *Közlemények Zala megye közgyűjteményeinek kutatásaiból,*
*1984-1985,* ed. Alajos Degré and Imre Halász (Zalaegerszeg: Zala Megyei Levéltár, 1985),
169-81; Mihály Ferencz, "Munkaerőhelyzet, szociális ellátás, a dolgozók szakmai fejlődése,"
in *Ötven éves a magyar kőolaj- és földgázbányászat,* ed. Buda and Kovács, 194-96.

104. MOL, A MAORT, Üzemi Bizottságának iratai (Papers of the MAORT Factory
Committee, hereafter, Z355)/1cs./26t., 2.

105. Srágli, *Munkások a "fekete arany" birodalmában*, appendix V, 1.

106. On everyday culture in a village—Lovászi—that was the site of a major drilling
plant, see Sándor Tóth and Lajos Srágli, *Lovászi* (Budapest: Száz Magyar Falu Könyvesháza, 2000); Srágli, *Munkások a "fekete arany" birodalmában,* appendix XVI, 13-18; Vidos,
*Zalai olajos történetek,* 40-43.

107. PtSzL, I.274f.16/44ő.e., 4.

## 1. The Limits of Liberation, March 1944-November 1945

1. PtSzL, XII.1f./107d./1945: Textilipari nagygyülések szept. 19 és 20. án. Hangulat
jelentés, 2.

2. "A textilmunkásnő az urnák elé járul," *Textilmunkás,* September 1945, 1; PtSzL, Az
MKP Budapesti Területi Bizottsága (Papers of the Budapest Regional Committee of the
MKP, hereafter, X.38f.)48ő.e., 5.

3. "Felejthetetlen ünnepséggel avatta fel Újpest népe az orosz hősi emlékművet,"
*Független Nemzet: Független Kisgazdapárti politikai hetilap,* 16 May 1947, 5.

4. KEMÖL, XXXV.24f.1ő.e., 2.

5. KEMÖL, XXXV.24f.15ő.e., 2.

6. Mihály Földes, *Pillanatképek az újpesti partizánharcokról: kollektiv riport* (Újpest:
Magyar Kommunista Párt Újpesti szervezete, 1945), 7.

7. "A Budapesti Népbíróság ítélete Hess Pál volt Újpesti polgármestere perében. Budapest, 1945. július 14.," in Sipos, ed., *Dokumentumok Újpest történetéhez,* 311-23; "Hess Pál
polgármester jelentése Endre László alispánnak a munkásotthon helyiségeinek lefogla-
lásáról és a Szociáldemokrata Párt beszüntetéséről," in ibid., 295-96.

8. Gerelyes, "Újpest a két világháború között," 206. On the NMK in 1944, see Rudolfné
Dósa, *A MOVE: egy jellegzetes magyar fasiszta szervezet, 1918-1944* (Budapest: Akadémiai
Kiadó, 1972), 209-10.

9. Dombrády, *A magyar hadigazdaság a második világháború idején,* 143-56; Iván
T. Berend and György Ránki, *Magyarország gyáripara a második világháború elött és a*
*háború időszakában, 1933-1944* (Budapest: Akadémiai Kiadó, 1958), 551-62.

10. "Az Egyesült Izzólámpa és Villamossági Rt. ügyvezető igazgatóságának feljegyzése a vállalat vezetőinek és munkásságának ellenállási mozgalmáról, valamint a kitelepítés és üzembénítás részbeni megakadályozásáról, Budapest, 1945. November," in Károly Jenei, ed., *A munkásság az üzemekért, a termelésért, 1944–1945: dokumentumgyűjtemény* (Budapest: Tánsics Könyvkiadó, 1970), 94; Berend and Ránki, *Magyarország gyáripara a második világháború elött és a háború időszakában*, 538–39.

11. "1944 április 7. A Belügyminisztérium bizalmas rendelete a zsidók gyűjtőtáborokba való szállításáról," in Ilona Benoschofsky and Elek Karsai, eds., *Vádirat a Nácizmus ellen: dokumentumok a magyarországi zsidóüldözés történetéhez. I. 1944 március 19 – 1944 május 15; a német megszállástól a deportálás megkezdéséig* (Budapest: Magyar Izraeliták Országos Képviselete Kiadása, 1958), 124–27.

12. "Szalay Sándor polgármester jelentése az Újpesti gettóról és a zsidók deportálásáról, Újpest, 1945. március 1.," in Sipos, ed., *Dokumentumok Újpest történetéhez*, 300–301; "Az Újpesti Stadion szebb lesz, mint volt!" *Független Nemzet: Független Kisgazdapárti politikai hetilap*, 19 July 1946, 2.

13. "Szalay Sándor polgármester jelentése az Újpesti gettóról és a zsidók deportálásáról," 301; "Epperjesy Wittich, a vegre hurokra került újpesti nyilás briganti bűnlajstroma: kik a még bujkáló nyilas bűnőzők?" *Független Nemzet: Független Kisgazdapárti politikai hetilap*, 23 March 1946, 1.

14. "1944 július 9. Kormányrendelet Budapest és környéke lakásügyi kormánybiztosa kinevezésének szükségességéről, hatásköréről," in Elek Karsai, ed., *Vádirat a Nácizmus ellen: dokumentumok a magyarországi zsidóüldözés történetéhez. I. 1944 március 19 – 1944 május 15; a német megszállástól a deportálás megkezdéséig* (Budapest: Magyar Izraeliták Országos Képviselete Kiadása, 1967), 121–24.

15. "Az Egyesült Izzólámpa és Villamossági Rt. ügyvezető igazgatóságának feljegyzése," 92–93.

16. "Az egyházak mindenben támogatják a demokrácia becsületes törekvéseit," *Független Nemzet: Független Kisgazdapárti politikai hetilap* 3 April 1947, 7.

17. PtSzL, XII.1f./113d./1945: T. Magyar Népjóléti Miniszter Úrnak, Debrecen. 1945. marc. 22, 3.

18. Szöllösi-Janze, *Die Pfeilkreuzlerbewegung in Ungarn*, 283–432; Ungváry, *Battle for Budapest*, 1–91; Gerlach and Aly, *Das letzte Kapitel*, 344–74; Ferenc Gáspár, "A magyar nagyipari munkásság harca az üzemek megmentéséért helyreállításáért és a termelés megindításáért, 1944–1945," in *A munkásság az üzemekért, a termelésért*, ed. Jenei, 5–31.

19. Vinceller, *Sötet Árny Magyarhon Felett*, 110–11; "Epperjesy Wittich, a verge hurokra került újpesti nyilás briganti bűnlajstroma," 1–2; "Ahol Eperjessy-Wittich hóhérmunkát végzett, ott most a magyar jövőt épitik," *Független Nemzet: Független Kisgazdapárti politikai hetilap*, 17 April 1946, 1–2; "Újpesti nyilasok a népbíróságon: halálraitélték Eperjessy-Wittich Zoltánt," *Független Nemzet: Független Kisgazdapárti politikai hetilap*, 2 November 1946, 2.

20. PtSzL, XII.1f.113d./1945: T. Magyar Népjóléti Miniszter Úrnak, Debrecen. 1945. márc. 22, 2; "Az Egyesült Izzólámpa és Villamossági Rt. ügyvezető igazgatóságának feljegyzése," 87–94.

21. Gerelyes, "Újpest a két világháború között," 206; "Az Egyesült Izzólámpa és Villa-

mossági Rt. ügyvezető igazgatóságának feljegyzése," 95–96; "Egy kis ellenállási tevékenység Újpesten," *Független Nemzet: Független Kisgazdapárti politikai hetilap*, 23 March 1946, 2.

22. Földes, *Pillanatképek az újpesti partizánharcokról*, 24.

23. Az 1956-os Magyar Forradalom Történetének Dokumentációs és Kutatóintézete, Oral History Archívium (Oral History Archive of the Institute for the Documentation of and Research of the 1956 Hungarian Revolution, hereafter, 1956-os Intézet, OHA) – Nagy Pál Jenő (hereafter, 177), 28.

24. PtSzL, Munkásmozgalmi Visszaemlékezések (Labor Movement Autobiographies Collection, hereafter, VI.867f.), Döbrentei Károly (hereafter, 1/d-50), 48.

25. Földes, *Pillanatképek az újpesti partizánharcokról*, 30–45; Gerelyes, "Újpest a két világháború között," 208.

26. "Egy épületbe kerül a járásbíróság és a rendőrség," *Független Nemzet: Független Kisgazdapárti politikai hetilap*, 1 April 1948, 1.

27. Földes, *Pillanatképek az újpesti partizánharcokról*, 48.

28. 1956-os Intézet, OHA 177, 27.

29. PtSzL, I.283f.15/32ő.e., 2–3.

30. MOL, Az Egyesült Izzólámpa és Villamossági Rt., Ügyvezető Igazgatóságának iratai (Papers of the Managing Director of the United Incandescent Lamp and Electrical Factory, hereafter, Z601)/10cs./93t., 3; MOL, A Magyar Pamutipar, Személyzeti Osztályának iratai (Papers of the Personnel Department of the Hungarian Cotton Industry Company, hereafter, Z693)/3cs./19t., 3.

31. "A légó-pince betegségei," *Szabad Újpest*, 14 July 1945, 3.

32. "Nincs tifuszjárvány Újpesten!" *Szabad Újpest*, 31 January 1945, 2.

33. PtSzL, VI.867f., 1/d-50, 3.

34. PtSzL, Vas-, Fém és Villamosipari Dolgozók Szakszervezete (Metalworkers' Union, hereafter, XII.47f.)28d./1945: Jegyzőkönyv felvétetett 1945 január 13.-án az Újpesti Kommunista Párt E.I.V.R.T.Rt. csoportjának helyiségében, 2.

35. Földes, *Pillanatképek az újpesti partizánharcokról*, 48

36. 1956-os Intézet, OHA Péterffy Miklós (hereafter, 181), 55.

37. James Mark, "Remembering Rape: Divided Social Memory and the Red Army in Hungary, 1944–1945," *Past and Present* 188 (2005): 133–61.

38. Pető, "Memory and the Narrative of Rape in Budapest and Vienna in 1945," 129–48.

39. 1956-os Intézet, OHA 181, 56.

40. "Azoknak a hadifoglyoknak a névsora akik 1945 július–augusztus havában Focsányiban (Románia) elosztótáborban voltak. Mindnyájan épségben, egészségben mentek ki Oroszországba," *Független Nemzet: Független Kisgazdapárti politikai hetilap*, 7 September 1946, 3.

41. Zielbauer, "Magyar polgári lakosok deportálása és hadifogsága."

42. PtSzL, XII.1f.113d./1945: T. Magyar Népjóléti Miniszter Úrnak, Debrecen. 1945. márc. 22, 3.

43. János Sztankovits, interview by author.

44. 1956-os Intézet, OHA 181, 57.

45. Ormos et al., *Törvénytelen szocializmus*, 15–42; Szakács and Zinner, *A háború "megváltozott természete,"* 214–18; László Karsai, "The People's Courts and Revolution-

ary Justice in Hungary, 1945–46," in *The Politics of Retribution in Europe: World War II and Its Aftermath*, ed. István Deák, Jan T. Gross, and Tony Judt (Princeton, NJ: Princeton University Press, 2000), 233.

46. "Internálótábor Újpesten," *Szabad Újpest*, 17 March 1945, 2.

47. PtSzL, XII.1f.60d./1945: Magyar Rendőrség Budapesti Főkapitánysága.

48. "Jegyzőkönyv 1945. évi január hó 18.-án 10 órától 15 óráig (majd január 19-én 10 órakor folytatott ülésről) Debrecenben a miniszterelnöki tanácsteremben," in Szűcs, ed., *Dálnoki Miklós Béla kormányának (Ideiglenes Nemzeti Kormány) minisztertanácsi jegyzőkönyvei A*, 137–39.

49. "Rendet a közmunkák téren!" *Szabad Újpest*, 24 February 1945, 2; "Megint a közmunka," *Szabad Újpest*, 17 March 1945, 2.

50. PtSzL, Az MKP Egyesült Izzólámpa és Villamossági Rt. Bizottságának iratai (Papers of the United Incandescent Lamp and Electrical Company Committee of the MKP, hereafter, X.77f.)1d., 86.

51. 1956-os Intézet, OHA 177, 27.

52. PtSzL, VI.867f., 1/d-50, 3.

53. "Az iparügyi minister 50 100/1945 IpM számú rendelete az üzemi bizottságok tárgyában (Debrecen, 1945 február 15.)," in Károly Jenei, Béla Rácz, and Erzsébet Strassenreiter, eds., *Az üzemi bizottságok a munkáshatalomért 1944–1948* (Budapest: Tánsics Könyvkiadó, 1966), 222–31.

54. PtSzL, XII.47f.28d./1945: Jegyzőkönyv felvétetett 1945 január 13.-án az Újpesti Kommunista Párt E.I.V.R.T.Rt. csoportjának helyiségében, 1–2; MOL, A Magyar Pamutipar, Üzemi Bizottságának iratai (Papers of the Factory Committee of the Magyar Pamutipar, hereafter, Z1204)/1cs./1t., 24–25; PtSzL, I.274f.20/31ő.e., 30–31; PtSzL, I.274f.20/31ő.e., 38.

55. Hanák and Hanák, *A Magyar Pamutipar története*, 280–81; PtSzL, VI.867f., 1/d-50, 4–5.

56. PtSzL, I.274f.20/32ő.e., 142–43; PtSzL, XII.47f.28d./1945: Jegyzőkönyv az EIVRT. Üzemi Bizottságának IB. ülésen, hivatali helyégében 1945. február 21-én, 2; PtSzL, X.77f.1d., 86.

57. PtSzL, XII.1f.71d./1945: Levél a Magyar Bőripari Munkások Országos Szabad Szakszervezete Fegyelmi Bizottságának, Újpest, K.F.-től, 1945.X.18, 2.

58. MOL, Z1204/1cs./1t., 27.

59. MOL, Z1204/1cs./1t., 26; PtSzL, XII.47f.29d./1945: Jelentés Lévai igazgató urnak, Újpest, 1945. augusztus 9.

60. "A magyar fegyverszüneti egyezmény," in Balogh and Földesi, eds., *A magyar jóvátétel*, 19–23.

61. Iván T. Berend, *Újjáépítés és a nagytőke elleni harc Magyarországon 1945–1948* (Budapest: Közgazdasági és Jogi Könyvkiadó, 1962), 29.

62. PtSzL, XII.1f.71d./1945: Magyar Bőripari Munkások Országos Szabad Szakszervezete, A Bőripari Munkások rendes mozgalmi-jelentése. 1945 ápr. 28; Központi Statitisztikai Hivatal Levéltára (Archive of the Central Statistical Office, hereafter, KSHL), Iparstatisztikai kerdőivek, 1945 (Industry statistics questionnaires 1945, hereafter, A.5.1)/132d: Környék, VII.156 Bőrgyártás és bőrfestés iparág, 1–5.

63. MOL, Z1204/1cs./1t., 26.

64. "A magyar fegyverszüneti egyezmény."

65. MOL, Z601/10cs./93t., 15–16.

66. PtSzL, XII.47f.28d./1945: Jegyzőkönyv felvétetett az EIV Rt. Üzemi Bizottságának 1945. május 7-én megtartott IB. ülésen, 1; MOL, Egyesült Izzó és Villámossági Rt., Személyzeti Osztály iratai (Papers of the Personnel Department of the United Incandescent Lamp and Electrical Company, hereafter, Z606)/4cs/9t., 5.

67. 1956-os Intézet, OHA 177, 40–41.

68. PtSzL, X.77f.1d., 86.

69. Pittaway, "Workers in Hungary," 62–65.

70. PtSzL, I.274f.20/31ő.e., 66–68; PtSzL, XII.1f.113d./1945: T. Magyar Népjóléti Miniszter Úrnak, Debrecen. 1945. márc. 22, 1–2.

71. "Az újjáépítés akadályai," Szabad Újpest, 9 June 1945, 1; MOL, Z1204/1cs./3t., 290.

72. See the questionnaires in KSHL, A.5.1, 132d.; PtSzL, XII.1f.44d./1945, Közgazdasági és Statisztikai Osztály. Tájékoztató, 1945. december hó., 2.

73. PtSzL, Az MKP Újpest Városi Bizottságának iratai (Papers of the Újpest City Committee of the MKP, hereafter, X.6of.)168d.; PtSzL, I.283f.17/85ő.e., 11.

74. "Beszél a rendőrtiszt," Független Nemzet: Független Kisgazdapárti politikai hetilap, 9 March 1946, 3; "Pusztán kedvtelésből loptam . . . razzia a faés széntolvajok ellen," Független Nemzet: Független Kisgazdapárti politikai hetilap, 16 March 1946, 2.

75. PtSzL, XII.1f.71d./1945, Levél a Magyar Bőripari Munkások Országos Szabad Szakszervezete Fegyelmi Bizottságának, Újpest, K.F.-től, 1945.X.18, 2.

76. Berend, Újjáépítés és a nagytőke elleni harc Magyarországon, 59–84; Pető and Szakács, A hazai gazdaság négy évtizedének története, 58–62.

77. "Hogyan alakulnak a piaci árak?" Szabad Újpest, 18 August 1945, 3.

78. "Bőripari nagygyűlés," Szabad Újpest, 9 June 1945, 2.

79. "Kenyér és piac," Szabad Újpest, 8 September 1945, 2.

80. For such attempts, see PtSzL, XII.1f.45d./1945, Szakszervezeti Tanács, Újjáépitési Bizottsága, Javaslat az Újjáépitési Verseny szervezésére, 1–6; PtSzL, XII.1f.49d./1945, Megjegyzések. Tárgy: akkordbérek bevezetése, 1–7; MOL, Z1204/1cs./3t., 7.

81. MOL, A Magyar Pamutipar, Ügyvezető Igazgatóságának iratai (Papers of the Managing Director of the Magyar Pamutipar, hereafter, Z691)/16cs./88t., 148; MOL, Z1204/1cs./3t., 306.

82. PtSzL, XII.1f.49d./1945, Országos Munkabérmegállapitó Bizottság, V. Szabadság tér 5–6.IV.410., Budapest, 1945.évi november hó 3.-án.

83. "Azokról a munkástársainkról is gondoskodni kell, akik nem tudnak csereárut adni," Szabad Újpest, 10 November 1945, 4.

84. "Munkássors," Szabad Újpest, 10 November 1945, 4.

85. PtSzL, XII.1f.111d./1945, Jegyzőkönyv 1945. december 15.-én megtartott rendkivüli összbizalmi értekezletről, 1.

86. "Éhező asszonyok tüntetése a piacon," Szabad Újpest, 3 November 1945, 3.

87. PtSzL, X.77f.1d., 15.

88. "'A dolgozók ma ugyanugy, vagy meg jobban éheznek,'" Szabad Újpest, 8 December 1945, 5.

89. PtSzL, X.77f.1d., 3.

90. KEMÖL, XXXV.24f.9ő.e., 3.

91. PtSzL, XII.1f.70d./1945, Másolat. Magyar Iparügyi Minisztériumnak, Budapest. Budapest, 1945. július hó 28., 5.

92. KEMÖL, XXXV.24f.9ő.e., 3–4.

93. Ferenc Szántó, "A bányamunkásság harcai a második világháború idején," in *Tatabánya története*, ed. Gombkötö et al., 230–44.

94. György Huszár, "Közvetítés a magyar munkás életéből . . . , " *Tatabánya Egyházközségi Értesitő*, April 1943, 4.

95. "Szent István-napi ünnepség a Népházban," *Tatabánya Egyházközségi Értesitő*, 4 September 1943, 3.

96. Szántó, "A bányamunkásság harcai a második világháború idején," 239–41.

97. *Az 1941. évi népszámlalás demografiai adatok* (1947), 558.

98. Braham, *Politics of Genocide*, 142n.

99. "Csendőrségi összefoglaló a dorogi és tatabányai bányamunkásság hangulatáról (1944. augusztus 16.)," in András Orutay, ed., *Komárom megyei helytörténeti olvasókönyv* (Tatabánya: Komárom Megyei Tanács VB. Művelődési Osztálya, 1988), 280.

100. Gáspár, "A magyar nagyipari munkásság harca az üzemek megmentéséért helyreállításáért és a termelés megindításáért," 21.

101. TMA, Az MKP Megalakulása és Tevékenységének Első Időszaka Komárom-Esztergom Vármegyében, 1945–1946 (hereafter, 347-78), 1–5.

102. Szántó, "A bányamunkásság harcai a második világháború idején," 245–47; "A tatabányai bányaigazgatóság körrendelete: statáriummal fenyegeti a munkahelyüket elhagyó bányászokat (Tatabánya, 1944. december 9.)," in Jenei, ed., *A munkásság az üzemekért, a termelésért*, 134–35.

103. Ungváry, *A magyar honvédség a második világháborúban*, 394–97; Miklós M. Szabó, *A Magyarországi felszabadító hadműveletek, 1944–1945* (Budapest: Kossuth Könyvkiadó, 1985), 92–110.

104. "A tatai m.kir. postafelügyelő jelentése Tata község kiürítéséről, az oroszok általi részleges megszállásról, valamint az életkörülményekről és veszteségekről (1945. január 20–25.)," in Éva Ravasz, ed., *Tatabánya a II: világháborúban; dokumentumok és tanulmányok* (Tatabánya: Tatabánya Megyei Jogú Város Levéltára, 2006), 146–52.

105. PtSzL, VI.867f., Droppa Samuel (hereafter, d.-129), 17.

106. Gy.MSMGy.L, IVf.451a./2d., A m.kir.rendőrség politikai rendészeti osztálya szombathelyi kirendeltsége. 7/1945 pol.rend.biz. Szigoruan bizalmas. Szombathely, 1945 január hó 31-én, 14–17.

107. Ibid., 13.

108. "A magyar urak nyugaton is urak. Egy nyugatról hazatért levente elbeszélése," *Komárom-Esztergom Vármegyei Dolgozók Lapja*, 13 July 1947, 2; Sztankovits interview.

109. "Öt népbirósági tárgyalás Felsőgallán," *Komárom-Esztergom Vármegyei Dolgozók Lapja*, 7 September 1947, 5.

110. Tamás Kakuk, "Tábori történetek: tatabányaiak a szovjet munkatáborokban," *Komárom-Esztergom Múzeumok Közleményei*, no. 4 (1991): 139–46.

111. PtSzL, VI.867f., Kobor Ferenc (hereafter, k.-306), 13.

112. TMA, Tatabányai Hőerőmű Vállalat Története (hereafter, 513-82), I.sz.telep története, 15; TMA, 513-82, II-es számu /bánhidai/ Hőerőmű története, 4.

113. "A Bánhidai Erőmű felszabadulása (1945. március 17–április 4.)," in Orutay, ed., *Komárom megyei helytörténeti olvasókönyv*, 288–89.

114. TMA, 347-78, 1–14.

115. Szántó, "A bányamunkásság harcai a második világháború idején," 247.

116. PtSzL, I.274f.16/109ő.e., 48.

117. PtSzL, I.274f.16/109ő.e., 182.

118. PtSzL, I.274f.16/109ő.e., 66.

119. PtSzL, I.274f.16/82ő.e., 23.

120. F. S., "Tudja meg mindenki," *Egység*, 26 May 1945, 3.

121. MOL, A Magyar Általános Kőszénbánya Rt., Ügyvezető Igazgatóságának iratai (Papers of the Managing Director of the Hungarian General Coal Mining Company, hereafter, Z992)/1cs./3t., 282.

122. PtSzL, I.274f.16/81ö.e., 9–10.

123. PtSzL, VI.867f., k.-306, 13.

124. MOL, Z992/1cs./3t., 115–17.

125. PtSzL, VI.867f., Szám Róbert (hereafter, sz.-245), 5.

126. PtSzL, VI.867f., k.-306, 13.

127. PtSzL, XII.1f.111d./1945, Emlékeztető Budapest székesfőváros villamosenergia-ellátásáról, 1–2.

128. "110 KW és a bánhidai MaDISZ," *Egység*, 2 June 1945, 2.

129. MOL, Z992/1cs./3t., 509.

130. MOL, Z992/1cs./3t., 505.

131. TMA, A bányavidék négy községe /Alsógálla, Bánhida, Felsőgalla, Tatabánya/ közellátásának alakulása a második világháboru idején és utána 1956-ig. (hereafter, TMA, 746-90), 2.

132. "Sváb volksbundisták lázadása Táton. Ki védje meg a betelepített magyarokat?" *Szabad Esztergom*, 2 September 1945, 3.

133. József Somorjai, "A földosztás története Komárom-Esztergom vármegyében I.," *Komárom-Esztergom Múzeumok Közleményei*, no. 4 (1991): 123–38.

134. MOL, A Magyar Általános Kőszénbánya Rt., Személyzeti Osztályának iratai (Papers of the Personnel Department of the Hungarian General Coal Mining Company, hereafter, Z254)/4cs./49t., 850.

135. KEMÖL, XXXV.24f.9ő.e., 3.

136. PtSzL, I.274f.16/109ő.e., 49.

137. PtSzL, I.274f.16/109ő.e., 66.

138. KEMÖL, XXXV.24f.4ő.e., 1.

139. KEMÖL, XXXV.24f.9ő.e., 3.

140. MOL, Z992/1cs./3t., 45–47; MOL, Z254/18cs./69t., 2–4.

141. MOL, Z992/1cs./3t., 152.

142. MOL, Z254/14cs./49t., 850.

143. MOL, Z992/1cs./3t., 153.

144. MOL, Z992/1cs./3t., 171.

145. MOL, Z992/1cs./3t., 169.

146. MOL, Z992/1cs./3t., 154.

147. MOL, Z992/1cs./3t., 155.

148. MOL, Z992/1cs./3t., 152-53.

149. PtSzL, I.274f.16/1096.e., 182.

150. PtSzL, I.274f.16/1096.e., 117.

151. PtSzL, I.274f.16/1096.e., 66.

152. "Nagykanizsa, 1945. április 8-10. A Magyar-Amerikai Olajipar Rt. üzemi bizottságának közleménye: újra megkezdődött a zalai olajmezők kitermelése és a nyersolaj szállítása," in Jenei, ed., *A munkásság az üzemekért, a termelésért*, 367-68.

153. On the surge in support for National Socialism in Zala, see "1937. január 7. A nyilasok szervezkedése Zalában. A zalaegerszegi rendőrkapitány jelentése a főispánnak a nyilaskeresztes mozgalomról (részletek)," in András Molnár, ed., *Zala megye történelmi olvasókönyve: helytörténeti szöveggyűjtemény* (Zalaegerszeg: Zala Megyei Levéltár, 1996), 296-97. On traditions of National Socialism in Zala, see Zoltán Paksy, "A nyilaskeresztes mozgalom tevékenysége és társadalmi bázisa a Dunántúlon 1932 és 1935 között," in *Az antiszemitzmus alakváltozatai*, ed. Paksy, 106-67.

154. Attila Kovács, *Földreform és kolonizáció a Lendva-vidéken a két világháború között* (Lendva: Magyar Nemzetiségi Művelődési Intézet, 2004); Enikő A. Sajti, *Impériumváltások, revízió, kisebbség: magyarok a délvidéken, 1918-1947* (Budapest: Napvilág Kiadó, 2004), 153-78.

155. "1943. január 5 - január 27. Zalai honvéd a Donnál. Részletek Németh József tizedes frontnaplójából," in Molnár, ed., *Zala megye történelmi olvasókönyve*, 307-8; Srágli, "Adatok az olajiipari munkásság szociális helyzetének alakulásához, 1937-1944," 169-80.

156. Lajos Srágli, *A MAORT: olaj - gazdaság - politika* (Budapest: Útmutató Kiadó, 1998), 55-63; József Kovács "Vállalattörténet," in *Ötven éves a magyar kőolaj és földgázbányászat*, ed. Buda and Kovács, 134; Simon Papp, *Életem*, 2d ed. (Zalaegerszeg: Magyar Olaipari Múzeum, 2000), 128-30.

157. Dombrády, *A magyar hadigazdaság a második világháború idején*, 166-71.

158. Srágli, "Adatok az olajiipari munkásság szociális helyzetének alakulásához, 1937-1944," 177-78.

159. "A Lovászi olajkutaknál dolgozó munkások tiltakozása a munkaszolgálatosok 'kedvező' elhelyezése ellen. 1942. augusztus 12.," in Csaba Katona et al., eds., *Emlékezz! Válogatott levéltári források a magyarországi zsidóság üldöztetésének történetéhez 1938-1945* (Budapest: Magyar Országos Levéltár, 2004), 65.

160. Dombrády, *A magyar hadigazdaság a második világháború idején*, 171-73.

161. "1944. Angolszász légitámadások. A Zalai Magyar Élet című lap beszámolója a beszámolója a bázakerettyei ipartelepet ért légitámadásról," in Molnár, ed., *Zala megye történelmi olvasókönyve*, 311-12; Géza Bencze, *Zala megye iparának története a felszabadulás után (1945-1975)* (Zalaegerszeg: Zala Megyei Tanács V.B. & az MTESZ Zala megyei szervezete, 1980), 6.

162. "1944. december 4. Fontos hadiüzemek termelésének biztosítása. A német Déli Hadseregcsoport parancsa a MAORT-üzemek folyamatos működtetéséről," in Molnár, ed., *Zala megye történelmi olvasókönyve*, 314-15; Srágli, *A MAORT*, 63.

163. "Nagykanizsa, 1945. május 2. Az újonnan kinevezett rendőr-főkapitány első intézkedései," in Csaba Káli and Zsuzsa Mikó, eds., *Dokumentumok Zala megye történetéből 1944–1947* (Zalaegerszeg: Zala Megyei Levéltár, 1995), 78–80.

164. "A nagykanizsai járás főszolgabírójának jelentése a főispánnak a közbiztonság és a vagyonbiztonság romlásáról," in Molnár, ed., *Zala megye történelmi olvasókönyve,* 326–27.

165. "Lenti, 1945. június 1. A lenti járás főjegyzőjének jelentése a főispánhoz az oroszoktól teherbe esett nők helyzetéről," in Káli and Mikó, ed., *Dokumentumok Zala megye történetéből 1944–1947,* 92.

166. On the long-term impact of postwar deportations and propaganda that was designed to deflect this impact, see "Hogy élnek a magyar hadifoglyok a Szovjet-Unióban?" *Új Zala,* 8 May 1946, 3.

167. PtSzL, I.274f.16/88ő.e., 44.

168. "Zalaegerszeg, 1945, július 11. Jelentés a Muraköz területén, magyar községek ellen elkövetett atrocitásokról," in Káli and Mikó, ed., *Dokumentumok Zala megye történetéből 1944–1947,* 107–8.

169. Bencze, *Zala megye iparának története a felszabadulás után,* 13–15; Srágli, *A MAORT,* 66–68.

170. MOL, Z355/1cs./26t., 2–3; MOL, A MAORT Rt., Titkárságának iratai (Papers of the Secretariat of MAORT Rt., hereafter, Z356)/11cs./101t., 956–59.

171. Magyar Olajipari Múzeum Archívuma (Archive of the Hungarian Oil Industry Museum, hereafter MOIMA), 21, Gyulay Zoltán iratai (Papers of Zoltán Gyulay, hereafter Gy.) 45. doboz (d. - box) XLV2ő.e. A Maort (Magyar-Amerikai Olajipari Rt.) munkásainak élelemellátása, 1–3.

172. "Zala megye aranya: az olaj . . . teljes erővel dolgozik a MAORT lovászi telep," *Új Zala,* 1 May 1946, 3; Bencze, *Zala megye iparának története a felszabadulás után,* 15.

173. MOL, Z356/11cs./101t., 961.

174. MOL, Z356/10cs./100t., 55.

175. MOIMA, MAORT Szakszervezetek és Üzemi Bizottság iratai (Papers of the MAORT Trade Unions and the Factory Committee, hereafter, MAORT XXVII), A Magyar-Amerikai Olajipari Rt. Központi Üzemi Bizottságának beszámolója 1946. évről, 11–12; Lajos Srágli, "Adatok a MAORT üzemi bizottságai működésének történetéhez (1945–1949)," in *Évkönyv 1986* (Zalaegerszeg: Kiadja az MSZMP Zala Megyei Bizottsága, Oktatási Igazgatósága, 1986), 65–78.

176. PtSzL, XII.1f.20d./1945: Jegyzőkönyv felvétetett Nagykanizsán a Szociáldemokrata Párt helységében 1945. augusztus hó 12-én d.u. 4 órakor; MOL, Z355/1cs./26t., 2–3.

177. MOL, Z355/2cs./54t., 2–3.

178. MOL, Z355/1cs./1t., 32–36; MOL, Z355/6cs./86t., 230.

179. PtSzL, I.274f.16/44ő.e., 7; Zala Megyei Levéltár (Zala County Archive, hereafter, ZML), Az MKP Zala Vármegyei Bizottságának iratai (Papers of the MKP Zala County Committee, hereafter, XXXV.38f.)1945/31ő.e., 16.

180. ZML, Az MKP Nagykanizsa Városi Bizottságának iratai (Papers of the MKP Nagykanizsa City Committee, hereafter, XXXV.44f.)1945/16ő.e., 3.

181. MOL, Z356/11cs./101t., 960. The figures were very similar in late 1946; see MOIMA, Gy. 45. d. XLV 2. ő.e., Kimutatás a MAORT alkalmazásban álló munkások és tisztviselők lakásviszonyairól, 1946. november 1-i állomány.

182. József Béli, *Az 1945-ös földreform végrehajtása Zala megyében* (Zalaegerszeg: Zala Megyei Levéltár, 1977), 204.

183. ZML, Az MSzMP Bázakerettye Olajüzemi Bizottságának iratai (Papers of the Bázakerettye Oil Plant Committee of the MSzMP, hereafter, XXXV.25f.)1957–1960/10ő.e., 10.

184. MOIMA, Gy. 45 d. XXVII 2. ő.e., Másolat. A Központi Üzemi Bizottság II. ülésének határozatai, 1; see also the documents in MOL, A MAORT Rt., Személyzeti és Munkaügyi Osztályának iratai (Papers of the Personnel and Labor Department of MAORT Rt., hereafter, Z905)/10cs./58t.

185. MOIMA, Gy. 45 d. XXVII 3. ő.e., Jegyzőkönyv felvétetett a nagykanizsai lakótelepi irodában, 1945. szeptember 2.-án d.u. 4 órakor, 2.

186. MOL, Z355/6cs./86t., 230.

187. MOIMA, Gy. 45 d. XXVII 3. ő.e., Jegyzőkönyv felvétetett a nagykanizsai lakótelepi irodában, 1945. szeptember 2.-án d.u. 4 órakor, 2; MOL, Z355/1cs./1t., 38.

188. "Zala megye aranya: az olaj . . . teljes erővel dolgozik A MAORT lovászi telep."

189. MOL, Z355/1cs./1t., 40; MOIMA, Gy. 45 d. XXVII 2. ő.e., Magyar Amerikai Olajipari Rézvénytársaság nagykanizsai irodától, Maort Üzemi Bizottságának, Nagykanizsa, 1945. november 6.

190. MOL, Z355/6cs./86t., 230.

191. MOL, Z355/1cs./1t., 39.

192. "Zala megye aranya: az olaj . . . teljes erővel dolgozik A MAORT lovászi telep."

## 2. Struggles for Legitimacy, November 1945–August 1947

1. Ernő Gerő, "A felelősség kérdése és a választások," in *Harcban a szocialista népgazdaságért*, by Gerő, 41.

2. László Hubai, "A Független Kisgazdapárt szavazóbázisának regionális változása, 1931–1947," in *Hatalom és társadalom a XX századi magyar történelemben*, ed. Tibor Valuch (Budapest: 1956-os Intézet – Osiris Kiadó, 1995), 439–41.

3. Pittaway, "Politics of Legitimacy," 466–68.

4. Balázs Sipos, "Adattár," in *A magyar szociáldemokrácia kézikönyve*, ed. Varga et al., 539.

5. Éva Szabó, "A Magyar Kommunista Párt," in *Legyőzhetetlen erő: a Magyar Kommunista mozgalom szervezeti fejlődésének 50 éve*, ed. Tibor Erényi and Sándor Rákosi, 2d ed. (Budapest: Kossuth Könyvkiadó, 1974), 175.

6. Mátyás Rákosi, "A népi demokrácia útja," in *Válogatott beszédek és cikkek*, by Rákosi, 150.

7. István Csicsery-Rónay and Géza Cserenyey, *Koncepciós pér: a Független Kisgazdapárt szétzúzására, 1947* (Budapest: 1956-os Intézet, 1998), 13–69.

8. PtSzL, I.274f.16/95ő.e., 14.

9. PtSzL, I.283f.17/85ő.e., 260.

10. Sándor Balogh, *Parlamenti és pártharcok magyarországon, 1945–1947* (Budapest: Kossuth Könyvkiadó, 1975), 105–65.

11. Tibor Kolossa, "A Szénbányák Államosítása," in *Tanulmányok a magyar népi demokrácia történetéből,* ed. Miklós Lackó (Budapest: Magyar Tudományos Akadémia Történettudományi Intézet, 1955), 423.

12. KEMÖL, XXXV.24f.9ő.e., 5.

13. PtSzL, I.274f.12/120ő.e., 4.

14. MOL, A Magyar Dunántúli Villámos Művek Rt. iratai (Papers of the Public Company of the Transdanubian Electrical Works, hereafter, Z595)/87d./58t., 339.

15. PtSzL, I.283f.17/176ő.e., 1.

16. Kolossa, "A szénbányák államosítása," 424.

17. See Sándor Nógrádi, "A szénbányák államosítása," *Társadalmi Szemle,* February 1946, 103; "A munkások ellatása helyett spekulációval foglalkoznak a bányatőkések," in Sándor Rákosi, Erzsébet Strassenreiter, Bálint Szabó, and Éva Szabó, eds., *A munkásosztály az újjáépítésért, 1945–1946* (Budapest: Kossuth Könyvkiadó, 1960), 179–80.

18. On the politics of mine nationalization, see Gyula Erdmann and Iván Pető, *A magyar szénbányászat a felszabadulástól a hároméves terv végéig* (Budapest: Akadémiai Kiadó, 1977), 37–70; and Kolossa, "A Szénbányák Államosítása," 426–32.

19. TMA, A tatabányai szénbányák államosítása (hereafter, 410-80), 18.

20. Kolossa, "A Szénbányák Államosítása," 427–28.

21. PtSzL, I.283f.17/55ő.e., 26.

22. Berend, *Újjáépítés és a nagytőke elleni harc Magyarországon,* 74.

23. "A tatabányai Üzemi Bizottságok 1946. évi müködésének főbb eredményei," *Komárom-Esztergom Vármegyei Dolgozók Lapja,* 25 December 1946, 4.

24. MOL, Z254/4cs./13t., 204–7.

25. "A Tatabánya-Újtelepi bányászok versenyre hívják az ország valamennyi bányászát," in Rákosi, Strassenreiter, Szabó, and Szabó, eds., *A munkásosztály az újjáépítésért, 1945–1946,* 188–89.

26. KEMÖL, XXXV.24f.10ő.e., 10.

27. KEMÖL, XXXV.24f.15ő.e., 24.

28. KEMÖL, XXXV.24f.10ő.e., 11.

29. PtSzL, I.274f.16/81ő.e., 42.

30. KEMÖL, XXXV.24f.9ő.e., 7.

31. KEMÖL, XXXV.24f.9ő.e., 7.

32. PtSzL, I.274f.16/81ő.e., 45.

33. "Vármegyénk szociálpolitikai helyzete," *Szabad Esztergom,* 21 April 1946, 2.

34. Erdmann and Pető, *A magyar szénbányászat a felszabadulástól a hároméves terv végéig,* 56–57.

35. PtSzL, Bányaipari Dolgozók Szakszervezete iratai (Papers of the Mineworkers' Union, hereafter, XII.30f.)/62d./1946, Tatabányai Bányamunkások Sz. Szakszervezet Ker. Titkárságától, Budapest, 1946. jan. 8.-án.

36. MOL, Z254/14cs./49t., 702.

37. PtSzL, XII.1f./16d./1945–6, Felsőgalla – Újtelep Bányamunkások Szabad

Szakszervezetétől, MÁK Központi Igazgatóságnak, Budapest, 1946. III, 5.

38. Erdmann and Pető, *A magyar szénbányászat a felszabadulástól a hároméves terv végéig*, 57.

39. PtSzL, I.274f.16/81ő.e., 44; MOL, Z595/87d./58t., 453.

40. MOL, A Tatabányai Szénbányák iratai (Papers of the Tatabánya Coal Mines, hereafter, XXIX-F-107)-m./91d., Kimutatás, 1946. június hó, Tatai bányászat, Összesítés 1945 december hó, Tatai bányászat.

41. MOL, A Magyar Állami Szénbányák Rt. iratai (Papers of the Hungarian State Coal Mining Company, hereafter, XXIX-F-32)/108d., Másolat. M.Á.Sz. Végrehajtó Bizottsága Bányászellátási Osztálynak minden hó 1.-én és 15-én 1 példányban, cim 1946 július 26-án kelt levele értelmében.

42. "A 'Szabad Nép' a széncsata eredményeiről," in Rákosi, Strassenreiter, Szabó, and Szabó, *A munkásosztály az újjáépítésért, 1945–1946*, 201.

43. "100%-al emelkedett a széntermelés Tatabányán az 1945-ös évhez viszonyítva," *Komárom-Esztergom Vármegyei Dolgozók Lapja*, 5 January 1947, 3.

44. PtSzL, I.274f.16/81ő.e., 45.

45. Erdmann and Pető, *A magyar szénbányászat a felszabadulástól a hároméves terv végéig*, 74–76.

46. PtSzL, I.274f.16/82ő.e., 12.

47. PtSzL, I.274f.16/81ő.e., 41.

48. Ágnes Tóth, *Migrationen in Ungarn, 1945–1948: Vertreibung der Ungarndeutschen, Binnenwanderungen und Slowakisch-Ungarischer Bevölkerungsaustausch*, trans. Rita Fejér (Munich: R. Oldenbourg Verlag, 2001).

49. PtSzL, I.274f.16/177ő.e., 16.

50. PtSzL, I.274f.16/81ő.e., 45.

51. PtSzL, I.274f.16/81ő.e., 55.

52. Pető and Szakács, *A hazai gazdaság négy évtizedének története*, 58–82.

53. PtSzL, I.274f.12/120ő.e., 67–68; PtSzL, I.274f.12/121ő.e., 33–34; PtSzL, I.274f.12/121ő.e., 76; PtSzL, XII.1f./106d./1946, Magyarázat a progressziv bérezésre, 2; PtSzL, XII.1f./1946, Vasipari bérezés.

54. PtSzL, XII.1f./82d./1946, I. sz. Függelék a Magyar Állami Szénbányák és a Magyar Bányaés Kohóvállalatok Egyesülete, másrészről a Magyar Bányamunkások Szabad Szakszervezete között 1946. augusztus 7.-én megkötött kollektiv szerződéshez; PtSzL, XII.1f./82d./1946, Kollektiv szerződés, Budapest, 1946. augusztus 7.; *Szakszervezeti Tanács Gazdasági és Statisztikai Közlönye* 1, no. 2 (1946): 4–16; *Szakszervezeti Tanács Gazdasági és Statisztikai Közlönye* 1, no. 10–11 (1947): 28–41; MOL, XXIX-F-32/165d., Magyar Állami Szénbányák R.T., Tatai bányakerület, Munkáskereset Kimutatás, 1946. aug – 1947 júl. F.gallai Karbidgyár; MOL, Z254/22cs./87t., 250, 253, 256, 259, 314.

55. "Az újjáépítés programjába a bányászlakótelepek átépítését is be kell illeszteni," *Komárom-Esztergom Vármegyei Dolgozók Lapja*, 1 December 1946, 3; László Benjámin, "Egy magyar járás egészségügye," *Fórum* 3, no. (5) (1948): 383; "Lakásinség, tömegnyomor, bacillusfészkek, a tatabányai lakótelepeken," *Komárom-Esztergom Vármegyei Dolgozók Lapja*, 22 June 1947, 3.

56. PtSzL, I.274f.16/82ő.e., 111.

57. "Több gondot kell fordítani a bányászlakótelepekre," *Komárom-Esztergom Vármegyei Dolgozók Lapja,* 24 November 1946, 5.

58. MOL, Z254/10cs./38t., 193.

59. PtSzL, XII.1f./23d./1946, Szakszervezeti Tanács Munkaközvetitő Osztálya, 1946. X.21.

60. MOL, XXIX-F-32/108d., Másolat. M.Á.Sz.Végrehajtó Bizottsága Bányászellátási Osztálynak minden hó 1.-én és 15.-én 1 példányban, Cim 1946. július 26-án kelt levele értelmében. 1946. szeptember 17.; MOL, Z595/87d./58t., 132–34.

61. PtSzL, XII.30f./106d./1947, Levél, Magyar Bányamunkások Szabad Szakszervezete Tatabányai Helyicsoporttól, Dr. Molnár Erik népjóléti miniszter úrnak, Tatabánya, 1947. május 7; MOL, Z254/10cs./38t., 738.

62. "Elfogták a felsőgállai üzletsor rémét, az alsógallai templom fosztogatóját," *Komárom-Esztergom Vármegyei Dolgozók Lapja,* 5 October 1946, 2.

63. MOL, XXIX-F-107-m./91d., Kimutatás, 1946. június hó, Tatai bányászat, Kimutatás, 1946. december hó, Tatai bányászat.

64. Erdmann and Pető, *A magyar szénbányászat a felszabadulástól a hároméves terv végéig,* 86–93.

65. MOL, XXIX-F-32/109d., Másolat. Magyar Állami Kőszénbányák Központi Végrehajtó Bizottsága. Racionaliázási és Gépészeti Főosztály. Tatabánya, 1946. augusztus 31-én.

66. "A Tatabányai Szénbányászat hároméves terve," *Komárom-Esztergom Vármegyei Dolgozók Lapja,* 26 January 1947, 3.

67. "Miért kevés és ingadozó a síkvölgyi akna termelése," *Komárom-Esztergom Vármegyei Dolgozók Lapja,* 8 December 1946, 3.

68. MOL, XXIX-F-32/109d., Összes mulasztott müszakok százalékos aránya.

69. PtSzL, XII.30f./62d./1946, Levél, a Magyar Bánya és Ipari Munkások Szabad Szaksz. Tatabányai Csoportjától, a Bányavezetőségének, Tatabánya, 1946. szeptember 6., 1.

70. "Bányászokat az igazgatóságba!" *Bányamunkás,* 20 March 1947, 1.

71. PtSzL, I.274f.16/81ő.e., 87.

72. PtSzL, I.274f.16/92ő.e., 49.

73. MOL, XXIX-F-32/166d., Levél, Magyar Állami Szénbányák Bányaigazgatósága. Tatabánya, 1947. augusztus 9., 1.

74. PtSzL, XII.30f./62d./1946, Levél, a Magyar Bánya és Ipari Munkások Szabad Szaksz. Tatabányai Csoportjától, a Bányavezetőségének, Tatabánya, 1946. szeptember 6., 1.

75. MOL, XXIX-F-32/164d., 1946. augusztus havi átlag vajárkeresetek /30%-kal együtt/, 2.

76. István Kubinyi, "Norma vagy szakmány," *Bányamunkás,* 7 May 1947, 3.

77. PtSzL, XII.30f./106d./1947, Levél, Magyar Bánya Munkások Országos Szabad Szakszervezete, Zgyerka János főtitkárnak, 1947. június 27.

78. MOL, XXIX-F-32/166d., Levél, Magyar Állami Szénbányák Bányaigazgatósága. Tatabánya, 1947. augusztus 9., 3.

79. MOL, Z254/6cs./15t., Jelentés a felsőgallai Ipari üzemeknél bérelszámolások ügyében megtartott vizsgálatról.

80. PtSzL, XII.30f./62d./1946, Levél, a Magyar Bánya és Ipari Munkások Szabad Szaksz. Tatabányai Csoportjától, a Bányavezetőségének, Tatabánya, 1946. szeptember 6., 1.

81. "Budapest, 1946 december 5. A MÁSZ jelentése a Budapesti Bányakapitányságnak a Tatabányai sztrajkról," in Gyula Erdmann and Iván Pető, eds., *Dokumentumok a magyar szénbányászat történetéből, 1945–1949. források a magyar népi demokrácia történetehez i. kötet* (Budapest: Kossuth Könyvkiadó – Új Magyar Központi Levéltár – Nehézipari Miniszterium, 1975), 273.

82. KEMÖL, XXXV.24f.13ő.e., 11–12, 15–17.

83. PtSzL, I.274f.16/92ő.e., 113; KEMÖL, XXXV.24f.13ő.e., 15–17; PtSzL, I.274f.16/82ő.e., 5–27; PtSzL, I.274f.16/95ő.e., 18.

84. PtSzL, I.274f.16/95ő.e., 14; "A tatai bányászok válasza a Kisgazdapárt paraszti-képviselőinek," *Bányamunkás,* 5 January 1947, 2.

85. PtSzL, I.274f.16/81ő.e., 66.

86. "A munkások sérelmeit és a megoldás útját tárta fel Rákosi Mátyás a szombati nagygyűlésen," *Komárom-Esztergom Vármegyei Dolgozók Lapja,* 5 October 1946, 1.

87. "6000 Forintot keres havonta Réhling Konrád, míg a dolgozók nyomorognak!" *Komárom-Esztergom Vármegyei Dolgozók Lapja,* 5 October 1946, 3.

88. PtSzL, I.283f.16/237ő.e., 104; PtSzL, XII.30f./105d./1947, 9/40, Tatabánya, 1.

89. KEMÖL, Az MKP Komárom-Esztergom Vármegyei Bizottságának iratai (Papers of the MKP Komárom-Esztergom county committee, hereafter, XXXV.23f.)21ő.e., 8.

90. PtSzL, I.283f.17/85ő.e., 126.

91. PtSzL, I.283f.17/85ő.e., 1–7.

92. PtSzL, I.283f.17/85ő.e., 26; PtSzL, I.283f.17/54ő.e., 42; PtSzL, I.283f.17/54ő.e., 34–5; PtSzL, I.283f.17/54ő.e., 31–32.

93. "A Magyar Kommunista Párt központi vezetőségének határozata az országgyűlési választások eredményeiről és a párt előtt álló feladatokról, 1945. december 1," reprinted in Rákosi and Szabó, eds., *A Magyar Kommunista Párt és a Szociáldemokrata Párt határozatai,* 174.

94. "A Magyar Kommunista Párt Nagy-Budapesti pártértekezletének, 1946. január 5–6," reprinted in Rákosi and Szabó, eds., *A Magyar Kommunista Párt és a Szociáldemokrata Párt határozatai,* 198.

95. PtSzL, Az MKP Nagy-Budapesti Bizottságának iratai (Papers of the MKP Greater Budapest Committee, hereafter, X.39f.)62ő.e., 9; PtSzL, I.274f.16/130ő.e., 38.

96. PtSzL, I.283f.17/85ő.e., 17.

97. PtSzL, X.39f.63ő.e., 58.

98. PtSzL, XII.47f.77d./1946, Jegyzőkönyv, felvétetett 1946.jan.9-én. az Üveggyári értekezleten, 1.

99. PtSzL, X.39f.63ő.e., 33.

100. László Elek, "Tisztitsák meg a piacot a zugárosoktól," *Szabad Újpest,* 11 May 1946, 3; MOL, Z606/13cs./43t., 478; PtSzL., XII.47f.77d./1946, Kalóriaértekezlet 1946 maj. 16-án; Ernő Kovács, "Hogyan él a bőrgyárak városának bőripari dolgozója," *Szabad Újpest,* 13 April 1946, 3.

101. MOL, Z1204/1cs./2t., 36.

102. PtSzL, XII.47f.77d./1946, Jegyzőkönyv 1946. április 15.-én megtartott összbizalmi értekezletről, Emlékeztető az EIVRT-ben 1946.VI.13.-án végrehajtott bérkiegyenlitéssel kapcsolatban.

103. PtSzL, Textilipari Dolgozók Szakszervezete iratai (Papers of the Textile Workers' Union, hereafter, XII.46f.)/14d./1945–1948, Levél a Hazai Pamut-Szövő munkásai és Üzemi Bizottságától, a Szakszervezeti Tanács Titkárságának, 1946. III.21.

104. "Emberhús, macskahús az Újpesti piacon?" *Független Nemzet: Független Kisgazdapárti politikai hetilap,* 30 March 1946, 1.

105. Elek, "Tisztitsák meg a piacot a zugárosoktól," 3.

106. PtSzL, XII.47f.78d./1946, Jegyzőkönyv felvétetett 1946 . . . az Üzemi Bizottság II. számu fegyelmibizottság előtt T.J. gépműhelyi csoportvezető lopás ügyében.

107. "Különös bőrspekuláció, melyből munkáselbocsátás születik," *Szabad Újpest,* 8 June 1946, 5; "Tizezer pár cipő anyagát titkolta el a sváb Schmidt Mátyás, aki nem ismeri el az üzemi bizalmi," *Szabad Újpest,* 26 January 1946, 3.

108. "Válságban a kisipar," *Jövő: a Szociáldemokrata Párt Újpesti Szervezetének társadalomtudományi és politikai hetilapja,* 1 May 1946, 10.

109. PtSzL, XII.47f.78d./1946, Jelentés. Gépjavitóban Dolgozó T. I.köszörüszt 1946. VI.27-én a kapunál tettenérték..

110. PtSzL, I.283f.17/85ő.e., 27.

111. "Látogatás az Egyesült Izzóban," *Jövő: a Szociáldemokrata Párt Újpesti Szervezetének társadalomtudományi és politikai hetilapja,* 13 May 1946, 6.

112. PtSzL, I.283f.17/85ő.e., 30.

113. "Szabotáló nyilasokat tartóztattak le a Magyar Pamutiparnál," *Szabad Újpest,* 4 May 1946, 3.

114. PtSzL, I.283f.17/85ő.e., 30.

115. "Képek az Újpesti piacról," *Szabad Újpest,* 10 August 1946, 5.

116. MOL, Z606/4cs./7t., 108; PtSzL, I.274f.16/130ő.e., 230; László Solt, "Nagyarányu feketézést leplezett a gazdasági rendőrség," *Szabad Újpest,* 15 February 1947, 3.

117. PtSzL, X.39f.65ő.e., 87.

118. "Segédmunkások lenagyobb gyárainkban," *Szabad Újpest,* 9 November 1946, 3.

119. Anna Süle, "Újpest Szégyenfoltja a Baross-utca 77. szám alatti barakktelep," *Független Nemzet: Független Kisgazdapárti politikai hetilap,* 20 February 1947, 1.

120. "Több mint 100 lakó egy házban – még sincs egyetlen WC," *Szabad Újpest,* 2 August 1947, 5; "Segitség! . . . kiáltanak a város vezetőihez a barakktelep lakói," *Független Nemzet: Független Kisgazdapárti politikai hetilap,* 28 August 1947, 3.

121. MOL, A Magyar Pamutipar, Könyvelőségének iratai (Papers of the Accountancy Department of the Magyar Pamutipar, hereafter, Z694)/3cs./20t., 12–124; MOL, Z606/4cs./9t., 14–18; PtSzL, I.283f.17/85ő.e., 43; "Élelmiszer főelosztókat jelölt ki, a menekültek és munkanélküliek kérdéséről tárgyalt a Nemzeti Bizottság ülése," *Független Nemzet: Független Kisgazdapárti politikai hetilap,* 19 October 1946, 2.

122. PtSzL, I.274f.16/130ő.e., 231.

123. Sándor Jakab, *A magyar szakszervezeti mozgalom, 1944–1950: fordulópontok a szakszervezeti mozgalomban* (Budapest: Kossuth Könykiadó, 1985), 17; PtSzL, I.283f.17/85ő.e., 43.

124. PtSzL, XII.47f./185d./1947, Fegyelmi jegyzőkönyv. Felvétetett T.J.-né napközi otthonbeli beosztott és Zs. S.-né Audion mérésbeli mérőnő ügyében, Újpest, 1947 május 10.

125. PtSzL, I.283f.17/85ő.e., 73.

126. PtSzL, I.283f.17/85ő.e., 75; PtSzL, I.283f.17/85ő.e., 155.

127. Hanák and Hanák, *A Magyar Pamutipar története*, 304–5; PtSzL, I.274f.16/131ő.e., 75; PtSzL, I.283f.17/113ő.e., 170–72; PtSzL. I.274f.16/131ő.e., 102; PtSzL, I.274f.16/131ő.e., 108.

128. PtSzL, XII.47f./185d./1947, Jegyzőkönyv mely felvétetett Újpesten az Egyesült Izzólámpa és Villomásági RT. telepén lévő 10 számu szobában 1947. febr.13-án T.J. fegyelmi ügyében.

129. PtSzL, X.39f.66ő.e., 122–24.

130. PtSzL, X.39f.64ő.e., 91.

131. PtSzL, X.39f.65ő.e., 238; PtSzL, X.39f.62ő.e., 108.

132. PtSzL, X.39f.64ő.e., 144.

133. PtSzL, I.274f.16/131ő.e., 82.

134. PtSzL, X.39f.62ő.e., 107.

135. "Futószalagok, zakatoló gépek között a Magyar Pamutipar Újpesti gyártelepen," *Újpest Figyelő*, 28 November 1946, 3; PtSzL, I.283f.17/85ő.e, 82.

136. PtSzL, VI.867f., Kiss József (hereafter, k.-290), 3.

137. BFL, A BÁMERT iratai (Papers of BÁMERT, hereafter, XI.103f.)7d., Magyar Vasművek és Gépgyárak Országos Egyesülete, Fizikai munkavállalók munkaidő és bérkimutatása.

138. MOL, Z1204/1cs./3t., 229.

139. Domokos Varga, *Kiszlinger József Sztahanovista esztergályos élete és munkamódszere* (Budapest: A Munka Hősei, Népszava, 1951), 20–21.

140. MOIMA, Gy.XLV.3, Bérezés kérdése. Budapest, 1947. június 3., 1.

141. PtSzL, I.274f.16/239ő.e., 135.

142. PtSzL, I.274f.16/44ő.e., 4.

143. PtSzL, I.274f.16/44ő.e., 6; PtSzL, I.274f.16/44ő.e., 7.

144. ZML, Az MKP MAORT Központi Titkárságának iratai (Papers of the Central Secretariat of the MAORT MKP, hereafter, XXXV.52f.)4ö.e., 2; ZML, XXXV.38f.1945/31ő.e., 36.

145. PtSzL, I.274f.16/90ő.e., 33; PtSzL, I.283f.16/347ő.e., 61–63.

146. "Zala megye aranya: az olaj . . . teljes erővel dolgozik a MAORT lovászi telep."

147. Srágli, *Munkások a "fekete arany" birodalmában*, 88–91; "Mit jelent a MAORT-dolgozó Nagykanizsa gazdasági életében," *Zala*, 28 July 1946, 2.

148. "Zala megye aranya: az olaj . . . teljes erővel dolgozik a MAORT lovászi telep."

149. Srágli, *Munkások a "fekete arany" birodalmában*, 91.

150. PtSzL, I.274f.16/237ő.e. 142.

151. PtSzL, I.274f.16/89ő.e., 79.

152. PtSzL, I.274f.16/90ő.e., 33.

153. MOIMA, MAORT XXVII, A Magyar-Amerikai Olajipari Rt. Központi Üzemi Bizottságának beszámolója 1946. évről, 33–34.

154. Srágli, *A MAORT: olaj – gazdaság – politika*, 84–87.

155. MOL, Z355/1cs./1t., 95.

156. MOL, Z356/10cs./100t., 86.

157. MOL, Z355/1cs./1t., 89.

158. MOL, Z355/1cs./1t., 94.

159. MOIMA, MAORT XXVII, A Magyar-Amerikai Olajipari Rt. Központi Üzemi Bizottságának beszámolója 1946. évről, 46; MOIMA, Gy. XLV.3, Levél Gaál Antaltól Mr. Paul Ruedemannak, Budapest, 1947. május 27., 4.

160. MOL, Z905/11cs./64t., 219.

161. MOIMA, Gy.XLV.3, Bérezés kérdése. Budapest, 1947. június 3., 2; MOIMA, Gy.XXVII.1, C. melléklet a MAORT üzemi kollektiv szerződéséhez. Budapest, 1946. szeptember 7.; MOIMA, MAORT XXVII, A Magyar-Amerikai Olajipari Rt. Központi Üzemi Bizottságának beszámolója 1946. évről, 18; MOL, A MAORT Rt., Szakszervezeti Bizottságának iratai (Papers of the Trade Union Committee of MAORT Rt., hereafter, Z909)/1cs./2t., 106.

162. MOL, Z905/11cs./64t., 219–20; MOIMA, Gy.XXVII.3, Jegyzőkönyv, felvétetett 1947. július 4.-én a Szakszervezeti Tanács helyiségében.

163. MOL, Z905/11cs./64t., 75.

164. MOIMA, MAORT XXVII, A Magyar-Amerikai Olajipari Rt. Központi Üzemi Bizottságának beszámolója 1947. évről, 8.

165. PtSzL, I.274f.16/44ő.e., 23.

166. PtSzL, I.274f.16/239ő.e., 135.

167. MOIMA, MAORT XXVII, A Magyar-Amerikai Olajipari Rt. Központi Üzemi Bizottságának beszámolója 1947. évről, 32; PtSzL, I.274f.16/44ő.e., 23; "Nagykereskedők spekulációi a Zalai falvakban," Új Zala, 27 June 1947, 3.

168. PtSzL, I.274f.16/44ő.e., 23.

169. PtSzL, I.274f.16/238ő.e., 22.

170. MOL, Z905/17cs./114t., 8.

171. PtSzL, I.274f.16/94ő.e., 41; PtSzL, I.274f.16/239ő.e., 101–2.

172. PtSzL, I.274f.16/44ő.e., 7; "Mi az igazság a MAORT fizikai és szellemi dolgozóinak kirobbant vitájában," Zala, 29 August 1946, 3.

173. ZML, XXXV.38f.1946–1948/27ő.e., Jelentés a Maort üzemi pártszervezet szervezési ügyeiről.

174. PtSzL, I.274f.16/93ő.e., 10.

175. PtSzL, I.274f.16/44ő.e., 19.

176. "Olaj – A magyar olajipart is megmenti az MKP hároméves terve," Új Zala, 26 February 1947, 3.

177. Lajos Srágli, "A dunántúli olajbányászat hároméves terve (adatok a MAORT történetéhez, 1947–1949)," Zalai Gyűjteménye, no. 25 (1986): 295–99; Srágli, A MAORT: olaj – gazdaság – politika, 92–98.

178. MOIMA, Gy.XXVII.3, Memorandum. Budapest, 1947. július 3, Jegyzőkönyvkivonat a MAORT. Központi Üzemi Bizottságának 1947.júl.3.-án tartott üléséről, 1–2.

## 3. The Social Roots of Dictatorship, August 1947–August 1949

1. BFL, XXXV.95f.3/55ő.e., 15.

2. BFL, XXXV.95f.3/55ő.e., 15.

3. Pető and Szakács, A hazai gazdaság négy évtizedének története, 95–103.

4. Mátyás Rákosi, "Építjük a nép országát," in *Építjük a nép országát,* by Mátyás Rákosi (Budapest: Szikra Kiadás, 1949), 150–51.

5. Tibor Garai, *A kultúrtényező jelentősége a versenyszellem kialakításában* (Budapest: Munkatudományi és Racionalizálási Intézet, 1948), 8.

6. "Vésztő, 1946. szeptember 2. A vésztői Balodali Blokk végrehajtó Bizottságának felterjesztése a földművelésügyi miniszterhez: visszautasítja a vésztői községi földigénylő bizottság elleni támadásokat," in Magda M. Somlyai, ed., *Földreform 1945, tanulmány és dokumentumgyűjtemény* (Budapest: Kossuth Könyvkiadó, 1965), 519–21.

7. Ernő Gerő, "A Magyar Dolgozók Pártjának agrárpolitikája a szocializmus építése idején," in *Harcban a szocialista népgazdaságért,* by Gerő, 404.

8. Balogh, *Mindszenty József,* 167–82.

9. Ormos et al., *Törvénytelen szocializmus,* 64–68.

10. Zoltán Ripp, "Példaképből ellenség: a magyar kommunisták viszonya Jugoszláviához, 1947–1948," in *A fordulat évei,* ed. Standeisky, Kozák, Pataki, and Rainer, 45–62.

11. "A Politikai Bizottság Határozata a tagfelvételi és tagjelöltfelvételi zárlatról, a párttagság felülvizsgálatáról (1948 szeptember)," in *A Magyar Dolgozók Pártja központi vezetőségének, politikai bizottságának és szervező bizottságának fontosabb határozatai* (Budapest: Szikra, 1951), 5–6; Sándor Rákosi, "A Magyar Dolgozók Pártja," in *Legyőzhetetlen erő,* ed. Erényi and Rákosi, 197.

12. László Gács, "A dolgozók tömegeit kell a szocializmus öntudatos építővé nevelnünk," *Népszava,* 1 January 1949, 3.

13. See, for example, György Marosán, *A tanúk még élnek 1956* (Budapest: Hírlapkiadó Vállalat, 1989), 144–45. See also his contributions to one discussion in the provisional leadership body of the MSZMP in late 1956: "Az MSzMP Ideiglenes Központi Bizottsága 1956. december 2–3-i ülésének jegyzőkönyve," reprinted in Karola Vágyi Némethné and Levente Sipos, eds., *A Magyar Szocialista munkáspárt ideiglenes vezető testületeinek jegyzőkönyvei. I. kötet. 1956. november 11–1957. január 14.* (Budapest: Intera Rt., 1993), 154–55.

14. PtSzL, Szakszervezetek Országos Tanácsa iratai (Papers of the National Council of Trade Unions, hereafter, XII.2f.)10/49d./1949, Az egész gyáripar adatai ./élelmezés és épitőipar nélkül, Budapest, 1950 január 27., 7; "A Központi Vezetőség határozata az ötéves tervről," in Miklós Habuda, Sándor Rákosi, Gábor Székely, and György T. Varga, eds., *A Magyar Dolgozók Pártja határozatai, 1948–1956* (Budapest: Napvilág Kiadó, 1997), 57.

15. Mark Pittaway, "The Social Limits of State Control: Time, the Industrial Wage Relation and Social Identity in Stalinist Hungary, 1948–1953," *Journal of Historical Sociology* 12, no. 3 (1999): 273–78; PtSzL, I.274f.20/23ő.e., 73–76.

16. "Megváltozott a szellem a MAORT-nál. Indul a szocialista munkaverseny," *Új Zala,* 1 March 1949, 3.

17. "Kérdései Lovásziban," *MAORT Üzemi Híradó: A MAORT Dolgozók Hetilapja,* 1 October 1949, 20.

18. ZML, XXXV.52f./36ő.e., 10; ZML, IV.403f., 1d., Jegyzőkönyv Letenyei járásban a választás eredményéről, kelt Letenye, 1947. évi szeptember hó 1. napján.

19. PtSzL., I.274f.16/96ő.e., 208.

20. Palasik, *A jogállamiság megteremtésének kísérlete és kudarca Magyarországon,*

261–66; Erzsébet Strassenreiter, "A Szociáldemokrata Párt a központi és a helyi hatalom szerveiben (1944–1948)," in *A magyar szociáldemokrácia kézikönyve*, ed. Varga et al., 158.

21. PtSzL, I.274f.16/97ő.e., 32.

22. ZML, XXXV.52f./36ő.e., 11.

23. ZML, XXXV.52f./3ő.e., 13.

24. PtSzL, I.274f.16/100ő.e., 11.

25. PtSzL, I.274f.16/240ő.e., 145.

26. PtSzL, I.274f.16/97ő.e., 52; PtSzL, I.274f.16/116ő.e., 48.

27. László Sors, *A mutatószámos teljesítménybérezés elméleti és gyakorlati alapjai* (Budapest: Munkatudományi és Racionalizálási Intézet, 1948), 8–10.

28. MOL, Z905/11cs./64t., 32.

29. MOL, Z905/11cs./64t., 54–55; MOIMA, MAORT XXVII, A Magyar-Amerikai Olajipari Rt. Központi Üzemi Bizottságának beszámolója 1947. évről, 47; ZML, XXXV.38f.1946–1948/57ö.e., 53.

30. ZML, XXXV.52f./36ő.e., 17.

31. "A Szociáldemokrata Párt XXVI. Kongresszusának Határozata (1948. március 6–8)," in Rákosi and Szabó, eds., *A Magyar Kommunista Párt és a Szociáldemokrata Párt határozatai*, 550–52; PtSzL, I.274f.16/44ő.e., 38–41.

32. Aladárné Mód, "Munkaverseny Magyarországon," *Társadalmi Szemle* 3, no. 4 (April–May 1948): 299–315; Aladárné Mód, "Az első magyar munkaverseny mérlege – új jelenségek a magyar munkásmozgalomban," *Társadalmi Szemle* 3, no. 8–9 (August–September 1948): 513–36; PtSzL, I.274f.20/23ő.e., 73–76.

33. "Jó kommunista – jó munkaerő," *Új Zala*, 1 May 1948, 3.

34. ZML, XXXV.52f./28ő.e., 137.

35. MOL, Z355/3cs./39t., 5.

36. ZML, Az MDP Letenye Járási Bizottságának iratai (Papers of the Letenye District Committee of the MDP, hereafter, XXXV.61f.)3/1/1–2ő.e., Jegyzőkönyv felvétetett 1948. december 23-án, a bázakerettyei pártszervezet vezetőségi üléséről, 2.

37. ZML, Az MDP Zala Megyei Bizottságának iratai (Papers of the Zala County Committee of the MDP, hereafter, XXXV.57f.)1/70ő.e., 27.

38. PtSzL, I.274f.16/103ő.e., 36; "A főispán jelentése a belügyminiszternek az iskolák államosítása kapcsán tartott járási tiszti értekezletekről," in Csaba Káli, ed., *Dokumentumok Zala megye történetéből 1947–1956* (Zalaegerszeg: Zala Megyei Levéltár, 1999), 60–67.

39. ZML, XXXV.57f.1/70ő.e., 19.

40. ZML, XXXV.57f.2/Olajipar/1ő.e., 11.

41. The abbreviation *kh*, meaning *katasztrális hold*, is a Hungarian land measurement, with one unit equal to 0.58 hectares (1.43 acres), and is hereafter rendered as a hold.

42. Központi Statisztikai Hivatal, *1949. évi népszámlálás 8. foglalkozási statisztika részletes eredményei* (Budapest: Állami Nyomda, 1950), 470–73.

43. Erdmann, *Begyűjtés, beszolgáltatás Magyarországon*, 67–98.

44. ZML, XXXV.57f.1/70ő.e., 20.

45. ZML, XXXV.57f.1/75ő.e., 11.

46. János Sallai, *Az államhatárok* (Budapest: Press Publica, 2004), 114; Miklós Horváth, *1956 hadikrónikája* (Budapest: Akadémiai Kiadó, 2003), 470.

47. MOL, Belügyminisztérium iratai (Papers of the Interior Ministry, hereafter, XIX-B-1)-j/45d., Kimutatás a deli és a nyugati határövezetbe tartozó városokról és községekről, 6.

48. ZML, XXXV.57f.1/71ő.e., 34.

49. Lajos Srágli, "A MAORT-per és háttere," Üzemtörténeti Értesítő (1990): 23–38.

50. ZML, XXXV.57f.1/70ő.e., 26.

51. Lajos Srágli, "A magyarországi szénhidrogénbányászat első ötéves tervéhez – adatok a Zalai olajbányászatról, 1950–1954," Zalai Gyűjteménye, no. 26 (1987): 223–24.

52. ZML, XXXV.57f.1/73ő.e., 60.

53. ZML, XXXV.57f.2/Olajipar/20ő.e., 7.

54. ZML, XXXV.61f.3/1/1–2ő.e., Jegyzőkönyv felvétetett 1948. december 23-án, a bázakerettyei pártszervezet vezetőségi üléséről, 2; ZML, XXXV.57f.2/PTO/37ő.e., 42/1948. Jelentés 1948. október hóról.

55. ZML, XXXV.57f.2/Olajipar/20ő.e., 5.

56. ZML, XXXV.61f.4/1/3ő.e., MAORT MDP Lovászi Üzemi Szervezete. november havi jelentés, 1.

57. Lajos Sz. Varga, Szakszervezetek a diktatúrában: a Magyar Dolgozók Pártja és a szakszervezetek (1948–1953) (Pécs: Pannónia Könyvek, 1995), 77–94.

58. MOL, Z355/1cs./12t., 29–31; ZML, XXXV.61f.4/1/13ő.e., Szakszervezetek Országos Tanácsa, Zalamegyei Titkárságától, az MDP MAORT Üzemi pártszervezetének, Zalaegerszeg, 1949. január 11.

59. MOIMA, MAORT XXVII, MAORT üzemi kollektív szerződés 1949 évre.

60. This capping of oil workers' wage rates had been a state intention since 1948. See Ferenc Zala, "A bérpolitika iparági sajátságai," in Szakszervezetek bérpolitikája (Budapest: Népszava, 1948), 60–69.

61. ZML, XXXV.61f.4/3/PTO/19ő.e., Jegyzőkönyv felvétetett Lovászi, 1949. január 3, 1–4.

62. ZML, XXXV.57f.2/PTO/37ő.e., MDP. Lovászi üzemi pártszervezet titkársága. Hangulatjelenés 1949. január hónapról, 1.

63. ZML, XXXV.57f.1/60ő.e., 18.

64. ZML, XXXV.57f.2/Olajipar/18ő.e., Magyar Amerikai Olajipar Rt., 1949.IV.havi versenyjelentése.

65. ZML, XXXV.57f.1/71ő.e., 5–7.

66. ZML, XXXV.57f.1/73ő.e., 26.

67. ZML, XXXV.57f.1/75ő.e., 60.

68. ZML, XXXV.57f.1/71ő.e., 6.

69. ZML, XXXV.57f.1/75ő.e., 17.

70. ZML, XXXV.57f.1/75ő.e., 26.

71. ZML, XXXV.57f.2/Olajipar/1ő.e., Magyar Dolgozók Pártja Zalamegyei Pártbizottság jelentés a MDP. Közpönti Vezetőség Szervezési Osztálynak, Zalaegerszeg 1949. február 15.

72. PtSzL, X.39f.66ő.e., 177.

73. PtSzL, I.283f.17/85ő.e., 143; PtSzL, X.39f.66ő.e., 193; PtSzL, I.274f.16/132ő.e., 183–84; PtSzL, X.39f.62ő.e., 9.

74. PtSzL, I.283f.17/85ő.e., 163.

75. "Somlai László," in Imre Cserhalmi, ed., Történelmi kulcsátvétel: interjúk államo-sító igazgatókkal (Budapest: Kossuth Könyvkiadó, 1983), 140–51; PtSzL, X.77f.1ő.e., 181–83;

PtSzL, XII.47f.353d./1948, Jegyzőkönyv felvétetett az Egyesült Izzólámpa és villamossági R.T. Üzemi Bizottságának 1948. március 26.-án megtartott üléséről, 1.

76. PtSzL, X.39f.62ő.e., 253; "A jobbodali szociáldemokraták a nép ellenségei és a külföld ügynökei a munkások soraiban," *Textilmunkás,* 10 April 1948, 2; PtSzL, XII.47f.353d./1948, Egyesült Izzó gyárértekezlet 1948.február 26.-án, 1.

77. PtSzL, I.283f.17/85ő.e., 153.

78. PtSzL, I.283f.17/85ő.e., 172.

79. PtSzL, X.39f.62ő.e., 253.

80. PtSzL, XII.47f.353d./1948, Egyesült Izzó gyárértekezlet 1948.február 26-án, 5.

81. BFL, Az MDP Egyesült Izzó Bizottságának iratai (Papers of the United Incandescent Lamp and Electrical Factory Committee of the MDP, hereafter, XXXV.134f.)3ő.e., 24.

82. BFL, XXXV.134f.4ő.e., 104.

83. "Normarendezés a Pannoniában," *Szabad Munkás: A Pannonia Báránybőrnemesítő és Kereskedei Vállalat Üzemi Híradója,* 19 February 1949, 4.

84. BFL, XXXV.95f.4/75ő.e., 151.

85. BFL, XXXV.134f.3ő.e., 10.

86. BFL, XXXV.134f.3ő.e., 22.

87. BFL, XXXV.95f.3/299ő.e., 199.

88. BFL, XXXV.134f.3ő.e., 22.

89. BFL, XXXV.95f.3/299ő.e., 166; "Megyeri gondok," *Jövő: a Szociáldemokrata Párt Újpesti Szervezetének társadalomtudományi és politikai hetilapja,* 15 October 1947, 7; "A tavalyi rossz termés ellenére kiváló eredményt értek el a megyeri újbirtokosok," *Szabad Újpest,* 15 February 1947, 2.

90. BFL, XXXV.134f.3ő.e., 22.

91. BFL, XXXV.95f.3/299ő.e., 175; "Letartóztatták Márk Lajos megyeri plébánost," *Észak Pestkörnyék,* 15 January 1949, 3.

92. BFL, XXXV.95f.3/299ő.e., 173.

93. BFL, XXXV.95f.2/177ő.e., 142.

94. BFL, XXXV.95f.3/55ő.e., 47; BFL, XXXV.95f.2/293ő.e., 7.

95. "Újpest város vezetősége és a népi szervek együtt tárgyalták a város ötéves tervét," *Észak Pestkörnyék,* 2 April 1949, 1.

96. BFL, XXXV.95f.3/55ő.e., 47.

97. MOL, M-KS-276f.115/86ő.e., 128–31, 165, 213; MOL, M-KS-276f.115/85ő.e., 8–13.

98. BFL, XXXV.95f.3/55ő.e., 47.

99. "Mentsük meg a gyermekeket," *Szabad Újpest,* 20 September 1947, 3; "Akik az utcán keresik kenyerüket," *Szabad Újpest,* 25 October 1947, 3.

100. BFL, Az MDP Magyar Pamutipar Bizottságának iratai (Papers of the Magyar Pamutipar Committee of the MDP, hereafter, XXXV.143f.)2ő.e., 109–16; "Álkoldusok visszaéléseit leplezték le," *Észak Pestkörnyék,* 23 April 1949, 3; "Megoldják Rákospalotán a cigánykérdést," *Észak Pestkörnyék,* 9 July 1949, 9.

101. "Új városrész épül a Szent László téren," *Észak Pestkörnyék,* 23 April 1949, 3; "Újpest város vezetősége és a népi szervek együtt tárgyalták a város ötéves tervét"; Ferenc Sebestyén, "Agitációs feladatok Nagybudapest megvalósításával kapcsolatban," *Pártmunkás,* 10 January 1950, 18.

102. BFL, XXXV.134f.3ő.e., 91.

103. MOL, Z1204/1cs./3t., 229.

104. "Termelési verseny kiirása a fonodában," *Pamutipari Értesítő*, 4 October 1947, 3.

105. "Beszámoló az Erkel-utcai fonoda hathetes munkaversenyéről," *Pamutipari Értesítő*, 16 December 1947, 6.

106. MOL, Z1204/3cs./15t., 305–6; "Szövödei munkaverseny a HPS-ben," *Pamutipari Értesítő*, 16 December 1947, 7.

107. László Alpar, "Munkaverseny: új ember kovácsa," *Textilmunkás*, 10 April 1948, 1.

108. PtSzL, XII.47f.307d./1948, Az Újpest Vasas Titkárság jelentése a brigádmozgalomról, 1948 december 10-én.

109. Mód, "Munkaverseny Magyarországon"; *Az első országos Élmunkás Kongresszus határozata* (Budapest: Szakszervezetek Országos Tanácsa, 1948), 2–3; "A munkaverseny mérlege," *Tungsram Híradó*, 10 August 1948, 5; "Csatlálkoztunk az új munkaversenyhez," *Tungsram Híradó*, 10 September 1948, 7.

110. BFL, XXXV.134f.3ő.e., 64–65; "Dolgoznak a brigádok," *Tungsram Híradó*, 15 November 1948, 5.

111. PtSzL, XII.46f.12d./1945–1948, Textilipari versényhirek, Budapest. 1948. július 13.; MOL, Z691/17cs./123t., 141.

112. PtSzL, X.39f.81ő.e., 20.

113. BFL, XXXV.134f.3ő.e., 24.

114. PtSzL, XII.46f.13d./1945–1948, Levél a Budavidéki és Újpesti Gyapjúfonó-Szövögyár Versenybizottságától a Textilipari Munkások Szabad Szakszervezevete Versenybizottság Titkárságanak, Újpest, 1948. május 8.

115. MOL, Z1204/1cs.6t., 341–43; PtSzL, XII.46f.13d./1945–1948, Magyar Pamutipar Újpest, Erkel u. 30., Versenytitkárság. Jelentés. Újpest, 1948.V.5., 3.

116. PtSzL, XII.46f.13d./1945–1948, Magyar Pamutipar Újpest, Erkel u. 30., Versenytitkárság. Jelentés. Újpest, 1948.V.5., 3.

117. BFL, XXXV.134f.3ő.e., 80.

118. MOL, Z1204/1cs./6t., 373; BFL, XXXV.95f.4/59ő.e., 3–4.

119. PtSzL, XII.46f.12d./1945–1948, A textilipari verseny tapasztalatai, 4.

120. MOL, M-KS-276f.115/88ő.e., 15–17.

121. BFL, XXXV.95f.4/119ő.e., 12–15.

122. BFL, XXXV.95f.4/119ő.e., 32–34.

123. MOL, XXXIX-F-107-m/91d., Tatai bányászat. Összesítés, 1948 szeptember hó, 2–3; Tatai bányászat. Összesítés, 1949 március hó.

124. PtSzL, XII.30f.298d./1949, Brigád jelentés, Tatabánya, 1949. április 11.

125. KEMÖL, Az MDP Komárom Megyei Bizottságának iratai (Papers of the Komárom County Committee of the MDP, hereafter, XXXV.32f.)4/18ő.e., 213; PtSzL, Szakszervezetek Komárom Megyei Tanácsa (Komárom County Trade Union Council, hereafter, XII.20f.)12d./1948, Jelentés Práth Károly elvtársnak, 2.

126. MOL, XXXIX-F-107-m/91d., Tatai bányászat. Összesítés, 1949 június hó; KEMÖL, XXXV.32f.4/18ő.e., 214; MOL, XXXIX-F-107-m/91d., Tatai bányászat. Összesítés, 1949 június hó.

127. PtSzL, XII.30f.358d./1949, Jegyzőkönyv felvétetett 1949 jún.13-án az Újtelepi bányász Szakszervezet helységében tartandó propaganda értekezeletről, 4.

128. "Munkások, újgazdák beszélnek a választásokról," *Komárom-Esztergom Vármegyei Dolgozók Lapja*, 7 September 1947, 5.

129. Ferencné Horváth, "Eltünt a burgonya," *Komárom-Esztergom Vármegyei Dolgozók Lapja*, 28 September 1947, 2.

130. "Bányászok a tárnák mélyén: az új kormány feladatairól beszélnek," *Komárom-Esztergom Vármegyei Dolgozók Lapja*, 28 September 1947, 3.

131. MOL, XXIX-F-32/185d., Jegyzőkönyv, felvétetett 1947. október 11-én Tatabányán.

132. PtSzL, I.274f.16/83ő.e., 104.

133. PtSzL, I.274f.16/97ő.e., 29; PtSzL, I.274f.16/97ő.e., 48.

134. PtSzL, I.274f.16/98ő.e., 30.

135. PtSzL, XII.30f.162d./1948, Jegyzőkönyv, felvétetett 1948, február 3.-án a Tatabány-Újtelep Bányamunkás Szakszervezet nagytermében, 3.

136. MOL, Z252/32cs./166t., 13; Sándor Rákosi, "Normarendezések 1948–1950-ben," in *Tanulmányok a magyar népi demokrácia negyven évéről*, ed. János Molnár, Sándor Orbán, and Károly Urbán (Budapest: Kossuth Könyvkiadó, 1985), 202–3.

137. PtSzL, I.274f.16/99ő.e., 34.

138. KEMÖL, Az MKP Tatabánya Városi Titkárságának iratai (Papers of the MKP Tatabánya City Secretariat, hereafter, XXXV.28f.)2ő.e., 1.

139. PtSzL, I.283f.16/288ő.e., 100; KEMÖL, XXXV.28f.1ő.e., 3.

140. KEMÖL, XXXV.28f.2ő.e., 1.

141. KEMÖL, XXXV.28f.2ő.e., 1.

142. PtSzL, I.283f.16/288ő.e., 100.

143. KEMÖL, XXXV.28f.2ő.e., 2.

144. KEMÖL, XXXV.28f.2ő.e., 3.

145. KEMÖL, XXXV.23f.49ő.e., 7.

146. KEMÖL, XXXV.28f.1ő.e., 2–6.

147. KEMÖL, XXXV.23f.49ö.e., 4.

148. TMA, A tatabányai üzemek államositása (hereafter, 413-80).

149. "A város és kerületei," *Komárom-Esztergom Vármegyei Dolgozók Lapja,* 28 September 1947, 5.

150. PtSzL, XII.20f.15d./1948, Jegyzőkönyv felvétett Tatabányán 1949. február hó 9.-én a villamos erőmü rendkivüli üzemi értekezletéről, 1–2.

151. PtSzL, XII.30f.298d./1949, Vállalatvezetői beszámoló az 1949. év első negyedévről.

152. Központi Statisztikai Hivatal, *1949. évi népszámlalás 9. demográfiai eredmények* (Budapest: Állami Nyomda, 1950), 210; Központi Statisztikai Hivatal, *1949. évi népszámlalás 8. foglalkozási statisztika részletes eredményei*, 342.

153. "Közép-Európa legmodernebb munkáslakasai épülnek fel Tatabányán a szakértők véleménye szerint," *Komárom-Esztergom Vármegyei Dolgozók Lapja*, 14 September 1947, 8.

154. PtSzL, XII.20f.15d./1948, Jegyzőkönyv felvétett Tatabányán 1949. február hó 9.-én a villamos erőmü rendkivüli üzemi értekezletéről, 4.

155. KEMÖL, XXXV.28f.2ő.e., 9.

156. Ibid.

157. Központi Statisztikai Hivatal, *1949. évi népszámlálás 3. részletes mezőgazdasági eredmények*, 326–27.

158. Központi Statisztikai Hivatal, *1949. évi népszámlálás 8. foglalkozási statisztika részletes eredményei*, 338–39.

159. Központi Statisztikai Hivatal, *1949. évi népszámlálás 3. részletes mezőgazdasági eredmények*, 326–27.

160. PtSzL, XII.20f.36d./1949, Jegyzőkönyv felvétett 1949.május 4.-én az Újtelepi Szakszervezetben megtartott instruktori beszámolóról, 2.

161. MOL, Z252/32cs./166t., 8–9.

162. PtSzL, XII.20f.15d./1948, Jegyzőkönyv felvéve Tatabánya-Aluminiumkohó N.V. II.7sz. Aktiva Értekezletén, 5.

163. PtSzL, XII.20f.19d./1949, Havi jelentés, Tatabánya, 1949.III.1.

164. "3 munkabrigád: Normaszigorítás az 'Aluban' – Megváltozott a munkarendszer – változzon a norma is," *Komárom-Esztergommegyei Dolgozók Lapja*, 9 January 1949, 3; PtSzL, XII.20f.22d./1949, Termelési felelős jelentés 1949 március hóról, Tatabánya, 1949.ápr. hó 5-én, 2.

165. MOL, M-KS-276f.115/86ő.e., 114.

166. MOL, XXIX-F-107-m/113d., Vajárok egy müszakra eső alapkeresetének és bérpotlékainak alakulása, 1948 június hó; Földalatti munkások egy müszakra eső alapkeresetének és bérpotlékainak alakulása, 1948 június hó; Külszini munkások egy müszakra eső alapkeresetének és bérpotlékainak alakulása, 1948 június hó; Földalatti munkások egy müszakra eső teljes keresete, 1949. február hó; Külszini munkások egy müszakra eső teljes keresete, 1949. február hó.

167. MOL, M-KS-276f.115/20ő.e., 14.

168. MOL, XXIX-F-32/4d, Jelentés a tatai bérkülönbözetek ellenőrzésének részleteiről (1948.III.10–13).

169. MOL, XXIX-F-32/4d, Jelentés az 1948.október 20–23.-iki tatabányai kiküldetésről, 1.

170. PtSzL, XII.30f.254d./1949, Tatabányai Szénbányák N.V. I. körzet. XII akna versenyterve 1949.I.1-től 1949.XII.31-ig.

171. PtSzL, XII.30f.298d./1949, Jegyzőkönyv készült Tatabányán a XI.sz.akna üzemvezetői irodájában 1949. január 18-án 14-h-kor megtartott versenybizottsági ülésen, 1; "Megjavultak a munkavizsonyok, a normáknak is meg kell változniuk," *Komárom-Esztergommegyei Dolgozók Lapja*, 23 January 1949, 3.

172. "Munkaverseny XIV-es akna 202. csapat," *Komárom-Esztergom Vármegyei Dolgozók Lapja* 2 May 1948, 5; "Száz mázsás teljesítmény a XIV. aknában," *Komárom-Esztergom Vármegyei Dolgozók Lapja*, 16 May 1948, 1; György Ember, *Varga Barnabás Kossuth-Díjás vájár* (Budapest: A Munka Hősei, Népszava, 1951), 38.

173. PtSzL, XII.30f.163d./1948, Jelentés. Tárgy: tatai kerület munkaverseny jutalmazásának kivizgálása.

174. PtSzL, XII.30f.163d./1948, Jegyzőkönyv felvétetett Tatabányán 1948. évi október hó 27-én a Mentőállomás nagy termében a brigád-mozgalom megszervezése tárgyában, 2.

175. PtSzL, XII.30f.163d./1948, Jegyzőkönyv készült Tatabányán a mentőállomás nagytermében kerületi ifjúság vezetői értekezleten 1948.X.16-án, 2.

176. "Tatabánya ifjúsága munkaversennyel készül a Világ Ifjúságának Találkozójára," *Komárom-Esztergommegyei Dolgozók Lapja,* 17 July 1949, 3.

## 4. Revolution in Production, August 1949–January 1951

1. BFL, Az MDP Budapest IV. Kerületi Bizottságának iratai (Papers of the Budapest IV. District Committee of the MDP, hereafter, XXXV.176f.)2/190/10ő.e., 43.

2. Pető and Szakács, *A hazai gazdaság négy évtizedének története,* 112–14; Iván T. Berend, *Gazdaságpolitika az első ötéves terv megindulásakor 1948–1950* (Budapest: Közgazdasági és Jogi Könyvkiadó, 1964), 17–19.

3. "22 nappal a kitűzött határidő előtt elkészült a 302-es tűző-és aljazókör: hatalmas lendülettel folyik a munka az ötéves terv első évének kitűzött celjaiért," *Duna Híradó,* 10 June 1950, 3.

4. BFL, A Duna Cipőgyár iratai (Papers of the Danube Shoe Factory, hereafter, XXIX/551f.)1d., Duna Cipőgyár N.V. Munkaerőgazdálkodótól a Könnyűipari Minisztérium X. Főosztály, Üzemgazdasági osztályának levél, 1950 május 23.

5. "Hatalmas fejlődést biztosít az ötéves terv üzemünkben," *Futószalag,* 25 September 1952, 1.

6. The conceptualization of classical central planning presented here is adapted from the analysis presented in Jacques Sapir, *Logik der sowjetischen Ökonomie oder die permanente Kriegswirtschaft* (Münster: Lit Verlag, 1993).

7. *A dolgozó nép alkotmánya: a Magyar Népköztársaság alkotmánya* (Budapest: Szikra, 1949), 37–39.

8. Quoted in Ferenc Mikos, László Nagy, and Andor Weltner, eds., *A munka törvénykönyve és végrehajtási szabályai* (Budapest: Közgazdasági és Jogi Könyvkiadó, 1955), 31.

9. "Eredmények és hibák az új munkakönyvek bevezetése téren," *Munkaerőtartálék* 1, no. 1 (15 December 1950): 24–27.

10. Pittaway, "Social Limits of State Control," 273–82.

11. P. Balázs Nagy, "Tervfelbontás, tervfegyelem," *Tungsram Híradó,* 8 March 1951, 4.

12. "A Magyar Dolgozók Pártja központi vezetőségének határozata a szocialista munkaverseny eredményeinek megszilárdításáról és továbbfejlesztéséről," in *A Magyar Dolgozók Pártja központi vezetőségének, politikai bizottságának és szervező bizottságának fontosabb határozatai,* 87–95.

13. János Kornai, "A Magyar Sztahánov-mozgalom időszerű kérdései (Sztálin elvtársnak a sztahánovisták tanácskozásán mondott beszéde 15. évfordulójára)," *Társadalmi Szemle* 5, no. 12 (December 1950): 948–58.

14. Sándor Dekán, *Darrabérrendzerrel a szocialista bérezés megvalósitása felé* (Budapest: Népszava, 1950), 7; PtSzL, XII.2f.10/3d./1949, Tervezet a Darrabérendszere Való Áttéres Előkészitésére.

15. László Somogyi, "A műszaki időnormákról," *Bér és Norma* 1, no. 1 (December 1950): 16–21.

16. For the concept of a "factory regime," see Michael Burawoy, *The Politics of Produc-*

tion: *Factory Regimes under Capitalism and Socialism* (London: Verso, 1985); Michael Burawoy and János Lukács, *The Radiant Past: Ideology and Reality in Hungary's Road to Capitalism* (Chicago: University of Chicago Press, 1992).

17. MOL M-KS-276f.116/18ő.e., 34.

18. István Birta, "A szocialista iparositási politika néhány kérdése az első ötéves terv időszakában," *Párttörténeti Közlemények* 16, no. 3 (1970): 113–51.

19. MOL M-KS-276f.116/19ő.e., 129–30.

20. Pittaway, "Social Limits of State Control," 282–86.

21. BFL, Az Újpesti Cipőgyár iratai (Papers of the Újpest Shoe Factory, hereafter, XXIX.553f.)1d., Jegyzőkönyv mely felvétetett az Ujpesti Cipőgyár Rt. Újpest, Tavasz u. 77/79.sz. alatti telephelyén a vállalatvezető irodahelységben 1950. április 7.-én., 1

22. BFL, XXIX.553f.1d., Jegyzőkönyv, felvétetett az Ujpesti Cipőgyár Vizsgázó Bizottság ülésen 1950. V. 13.

23. BFL, XXIX.553f.1d., Kijelentés.

24. "Munkaverseny az Izzóban," *Tungsram Híradó*, 8 September 1949, 5.

25. BFL, XXXV.143f.2ő.e., 131.

26. BFL, XXXV.134f.5/aő.e., 94–95.

27. BFL, XXXV.134f.8/aő.e., 60–61.

28. BFL, XXXV.134f./8/aő.e., 10–13.

29. "Munkaverseny az Izzóban," 5.

30. Varga, *Kiszlinger József Sztahanovista esztergályos élete és munkamódszere*, 24.

31. "2216 Százalék! Kimagasló eredmények születnek a 3 éves terv utolsó hónapjában, a sztálini felajánlások során – Akik egy nap alatt 2–3 hét munkáját teljesítik. – Magyar sztahanovisták az Izzóban," *Tungsram Híradó*, 5 December 1949, 1.

32. "Munkaverseny az Izzóban," 5.

33. BFL, XXXV.134f.5/aő.e., 55.

34. BFL, XXXV.134f./8/aő.e., 6.

35. BFL, XXXV.134f./8/aő.e., 4.

36. BFL, XXXV.134f./8/aő.e., 19.

37. BFL, XXXV.95f.4/147ő.e., 55.

38. BFL, XXXV.134f./5/aő.e., 8.

39. Sztankovits interview.

40. Zoltán Halázs, *Sztankovits János sztahanovista marós élete és munkamódszere* (Budapest: A Munka Hősei, Népszava, 1951), 3.

41. BFL, XXXV.95f.4/147ő.e., 55.

42. Vilmos Zolnay, *Pióker Ignác az ország legjobb gyalusa* (Budapest: A Munka Hősei, Népszava, 1951), 9.

43. Ibid., 15.

44. BFL, XXXV.134f.5/aő.e., 243.

45. BFL, XXXV.95f.4/147ő.e., 55.

46. Hanák and Hanák, *A Magyar Pamutipar története*, 312; Központi Statisztikai Hivatal, *A magyar könnyüipar statisztikai adatgyűjteménye* (Budapest: Központi Statisztikai Hivatal, 1962), 371–74.

47. BFL, XXXV.95f.4/59ő.e., 43–47.

48. Sándor Nagy, "Hat nappal előbb fejezzük be a hároméves tervet," *Pamut Újság,* 15 September 1949, 2; PtSzL, XII.46f.130d./1949, Jelentés a Magyar Pamutipar HPS-ben tartott ellenőrzésről, 1–3.

49. "Több termelés, több kereset," *Pamut Újság,* 15 November 1949, 3.

50. Mária Zsigmondi, *Makár Jánosné Sztahanovista szövőnő élete és munkamódszere* (Budapest: A Munka Hősei, Népszava, 1951), 22.

51. BFL XXXV.143f./3ő.e., 67; BFL, XXXV.143f./3ő.e., 68; PtSzL, XII.46f.107d./1949–1955, Jelentés a terv időelőtti teljesitésének állásáról, 2.

52. *Pamutipari sztahanovisták élete és munkamódszere* (Budapest: Könnyüipari Könyvkiadó, 1951), 24.

53. Gyula Hevesi, *Sztahánov útján: a magyar újító mozgalom fejlődése és feladatai* (Budapest: Athenaeum Könyvkiadó, 1949), 85–103.

54. PtSzL, XII.46f.130d./1949, Jelentés, 1949 december 2, A Magyar Pamutiparból/ Újpest Erkel u./, 3.

55. BFL, XXXV.143f.4ő.e., 2, 40; MOL, Z693/8cs./63t., 14–15.

56. "Sztálini műszak a 'HPS'-ben," *Pamut Újság,* 1 January 1950, 6; MOL, Z693/8cs./52t., 5.

57. "Fellendült az egyéni verseny – nincs többé szűk keresztmetszet," *Észak Pest-környék,* 3 December, 1949, 5; BFL, XXXV.95f.4/77ő.e, 6–10.

58. "Kitűnő eredményeket hozott a sztálini műszak," *Tungsram Híradó,* 5 January 1950, 1.

59. BFL, XXXV.95f.4/65ő.e., 26.

60. BFL, XXXV.134f.12ő.e., 95.

61. BFL, XXXV.95f.4/59ő.e., 84.

62. BFL, A Wolfner Gyula és Társa iratai (Papers of Gyula Wolfner and Associ- ates, hereafter, XXIX/554f.)2d., Jegyzőkönyv felvétetett 1949.december 2-án a Wolfner bőrgyár vállalatvezetői szobájában osztályvezetők, osztályvezető helyettesek, mesterek és müvezetők részére megtartott értekezletről.

63. BFL, XXXV.95f.3/273ő.e., 27.

64. MOL, Z693/8cs./54t., 50.

65. BFL, XXXV.95f.4/65ő.e., 31.

66. BFL, Az Egyesült Izzólámpa és Villamossági Rt. Iratai (Papers of the Incandescent Lamp and Electrical Public Limited Company, hereafter, XXIX.321f.)9d., Levél az Egyesült Izzólámpa és Villamossági Részvénytársáság Előkalkulációtól, T. S. elvtársnak, 1950. június 1.

67. BFL, A Pannónia Szörmearúgyár iratai (Papers of the Pannónia Fur Factory, hereafter, XXIX.555f.)2d., Műszak elszámolások.

68. BFL, A Chinoin Gyógyszer és Vegyeszeti Gyár iratai (Papers of the Chinoin Pharmaceuticals and Chemical Factory, hereafter, XXIX.403f.)63d., Jegyzőkönyv készült a Chinoin gyógyszer és vegyészeti termékek gyára r.t. Újpest Tó u. 1–3. sz. alatti telepén megtartott kibővitett üzemi-háromszög értekezleten; BFL, XXIX/403f.64d., Levél, 1950 július 4; BFL, XXXV.95f.4/115ő.e., 2.

69. "Csoportnormák felbontása," *Pamut Újság,* 1 January 1950, 4.

70. BFL, XXXV.95f.4/115ő.e., 7.

71. "Az első darabbérkifizetés," *Pamut Újság,* 9 May 1950, 4.

72. Dekán, *Darabbérrendzerrel a szocialista bérezés megvalósitása felé*, 7; PtSzL, XII.2f.10/3d./1949, Tervezet a Darabbérendszere Való Áttéres Előkészitésére.

73. BFL, XXXV.134f.15a/ő.e., 33.

74. BFL, XXXV.95f.3/55ő.e., 117.

75. BFL, XXXV.95f.4/114ő.e., 40.

76. BFL, XXXV.95f.4/56ő.e., 40.

77. "Kiméleltlen harc a normacsalások ellen," *Pamut Újság*, 16 May 1950, 2.

78. MOL M-KS-276f.116/18ő.e., 34.

79. MOL M-KS-276f.116/19ő.e., 220–23.

80. BFL, XXXV.95f.4/32ő.e., 20.

81. BFL, XXXV.134f.12ő.e., 353.

82. BFL, XXXV.134f.19ő.e., 64.

83. BFL, XXXV.95f.2/301ő.e., 78.

84. BFL, XXXV.95f.2/301ő.e., 102.

85. BFL, XXXV.95f.2/301ő.e., 79.

86. BFL, XXIX/321f.11d., Sztahanovisták átlagteljesitménye 35–44 hétig, Egyesült Izzólámpa és Villamossági Részvénytársaság.

87. BFL, XXXV.95f.4/120ő.e., 193.

88. MOL, M-KS-276f.116/40ő.e., 79.

89. MOL, M-KS-276f.116/40ő.e., 74.

90. BFL, XXXV.95f.4/120ő.e., 252.

91. MOL, M-KS-276f.116/40ő.e., 110.

92. BFL, XXXV.95f.4/36ő.e., 35.

93. "A nagy eredemény részesei," *Tungsram Híradó*, 21 August 1950, 1–2.

94. "Akadályok az új norma teljesítésében," *Tungsram Híradó*, 10 September 1950, 4.

95. BFL, XXXV.95f.4/36ő.e., 31.

96. BFL, XXXV.134f.12ő.e., 455.

97. TMA, A tatabányai XII számú Bányaüzem 1950 évi bányaszerencsétlensége (hereafter, 791-95), 1.

98. "Győzelemre visszük az ügyet amelyért bányásztestvéreink életüket adták," *Komárommegyei Dolgozók Lapja*, 7 January 1951, 1–2; TMA, 795-91, 17.

99. TMA, 791-95, 2.

100. MOL, M-KS-276f.65/261ő.e.

101. "A budapesti államügyésztől. Megyei Biróság Elnökének, Budapest, 1951.áü. 001190/2.sz. vádirat," reprinted in Erzsébet Bircher, ed., *Kor-Kép: dokumentumok és tanulmányok a magyar bányászat 1945 és 1958 közötti történetéből* (Sopron: Központi Bányászati Múzeum Alapítvány, 2002), 161.

102. PtSzL, XII.20f./43d./1950, Jelentés a tervfelbontó értekezletekről, Tatabánya, 1950. dec. 30-án, 2.

103. KEMÖL, XXXV.32f.4/17ő.e., 143.

104. PtSzL, XII.2f.16/23d./1951, Kereskedelmi és Pénzügyi Dolgozók Szakszervezete, Hangulatjelentés a tatabányai bányarobbanással kapcsolatban. Budapest, 1951, január 6.

105. PtSzL, XII.20f./25d./1949, Jegyzőkönyv, felvétetett Tatabányán, 1949. augusztus hó 31.-én a Tatabányai Erőmű N.V. rendkivüli üzemi értekezletéről, 8–10.

106. PtSzL, XII.20f./36d./1949, Jelentés a Tatabánya-i-bányaüzemek munkájának kiértékelése a Tatabánya-i termelési értekezletek óta.

107. PtSzL, XII.30f./298d./1949, Tatabánya Szénbányák N.V., Az Üzem Termelési Felelősének Havi Mozgalmi Jelentése. Tatabánya, 1949 december hó.

108. "Sztahanov nyomán – a IX-es aknában. Felszínre kerül a 'rejtett tartalék,'" Komárom-Esztergommegyei Dolgozók Lapja, 16 October 1949, 3.

109. PtSzL, XII.30f./360d./1949, Jegyzőkönyv felvéve 1949. augusztus 11-én 11 órai kezdettel a Tatabányai Szénbányák N.V. igazgatósági tanácstermében, 8; KEMÖL, XXXV.32f.4/17ő.e., 217.

110. KEMÖL, XXXV.32f.4/17ő.e., 211.

111. József Horváth, "A bányamunka, a munkahelyi széntermelése gépesítése (1946–1958)," in Kor-Kép, ed. Bircher, 79–112.

112. KEMÖL, XXXV.32f.4/17ő.e., 203.

113. András Csuha, "Bányászati bérezésünkről," Bér és Norma 2, no. 7 (July 1951): 23.

114. KEMÖL, XXXV.32f.4/17ő.e., 217.

115. KEMÖL, XXXV.32f.4/2ő.e., 146.

116. On the role of SzIT nationally, see Miklós Habuda, ed., A SZIT: a szakszervezeti ifjúmunkásés tanoncmozgalom, 1945–1950 (Budapest: Kossuth Könyvkiadó, 1985), 243–345; Harc a másodpercekért: kézikönyv az országos termelési versenyhez (Budapest: Szakszervezeti Ifjúmunkás és Tanoncmogalom, 1948).

117. "A 'Zsigri' csapat érdeme," Komárom-Esztergommegyei Dolgozók Lapja, 14 August 1949, 3.

118. János Varga, "Elmondom hogyan lettem sztahánovista," Komárom-Esztergommegyei Dolgozók Lapja, 1 January 1950, 5.

119. KEMÖL, XXXV.32f.4/17ő.e., 217.

120. "A nagy ünnep napján – Sztálini műszakokon," Komárom-Esztergommegyei Dolgozók Lapja, 21 December 1949, 3.

121. PtSzL, XII.30f./361d./1949, Jegyzőkönyv, felvétetett Tatabányán, 1949. augusztus 31-én az Újtelepi volt Munkáskaszinó helyiségében megtartott termelési értekezletről, 3.

122. Ember, Varga Barnabás Kossuth-Díjás vájár, 48–49.

123. "Varga Barnabás elvtárs felkészült a sztahanovista tanácskozásra," Komárom-Esztergommegyei Dolgozók Lapja, 26 February 1950, 5.

124. Ember, Varga Barnabás Kossuth-Díjás vájár, 49–51.

125. Quoted in Sándor Horváth, "A lakás és a fürdő: a munkásés szociálpolitika prototípusai az ötvenes években," Múltunk 52, no. 2 (2007): 35–36.

126. PtSzL, XII.30f./210d./1949, Csapatkereseti kimutatás a XV.sz. aknáról, 1949 december hóban.

127. KEMÖL, XXXV.32f.4/17ő.e., 216.

128. Kovács, Szén volt az életük, 53; KEMÖL, XXXV.32f.4/3ő.e., 22.

129. KEMÖL, XXXV.32f.4/17ő.e., 213; PtSzL, XII.20f./61d./1950, Jelentés a bányász falvakról.

130. KEMÖL, XXXV.32f.4/23ő.e., 2.

131. KEMÖL, XXXV.32f.4/17ő.e., 215.

132. PtSzL, XII.20f./59d./1950, Építők Szakszervezete Komárommegyei Bizottsága, Tatabánya, Tóth-Bucsoki út 187. Havijelentés, Tatabánya, 1950.XII.7-én, 2.

133. KEMÖL, XXXV.32f.4/17ő.e., 217.

134. "Harci képek a Bánhidai Erőműből a széntakarékosság frontjáról," *Komárom-Esztergommegyei Dolgozók Lapja*, 4 June 1950, 3.

135. Péter Kollok, "Magasépítkezésünk féléve," *Komárommegyei Dolgozók Lapja*, 30 July 1950, 3.

136. KEMÖL, XXXV.32f.4/17ő.e., 211.

137. KEMÖL, XXXV.32f.4/17ő.e., 210.

138. PtSzL, XII.20f./42d./1950, Szakszervezetek Országos Tanácsa, Esztergom-Komárom Megye Bizottság, Tatabánya. Jelentés, 441/1950., 3.

139. KEMÖL, Az MDP Tatabánya Városi Bizottságának iratai (Papers of the Tatabánya City Committee of the MDP, hereafter, XXXV.36f.)3/23ő.e., 9–10.

140. PtSzL, XII.20f./42d./1950, Szakszervezetek Országos Tanácsa, Esztergom-Komárom Megye Bizottság, Tatabánya. Jelentés, 441/1950., 2.

141. KEMÖL, XXXV.36f.3/24ő.e., 16.

142. PtSzL, XII.20f./49d./1950, Propaganda Felelős Havijelentése. 1950 február hóról., 1.

143. "Az ellenség keze a tatabányai állami áruház építkezéseinél," *Komárommegyei Dolgozók Lapja*, 30 April 1950, 5.

144. PtSzL, XII.20f./60d./1950, Építők Szakszervezete Komárommegyei Bizottsága, Tatabánya, Tóth-Bucsoki út 187. Jelentés a Tatabányai Cement és Mészműveknél folyó hó 22.-én újabb szabotázs történt.

145. PtSzL, XII.20f./43d./1950, Összesitő jelentés az alapbéremelés és normarendezés tapasztalatairól, 1.

146. PtSzL, XII.2f.10/31d./1950, A szakmányos keresetek megközelitő értékkel történő összehasonlitása, augusztus 1–15-ig terjedő időre vonatkozólag. Budapest, 1950. augusztus 21.

147. PtSzL, XII.20f./43d./1950, Szakszervezetek Országos Tanácsa. Esztergom-Komárom Megye Bizottság, Tatabánya. Hangulatjelentés, Tatabánya, 1950. aug 3-án, 1.

148. PtSzL, XII.20f./43d./1950, Szakszervezetek Országos Tanácsa. Esztergom-Komárom Megye Bizottság, Tatabánya. Hangulatjelentés, Tatabánya, 1950 július hó 21-én.

149. Tatabánya Megyei Jogú Város Levéltára (Archive of the County Borough of Tatabánya, hereafter, TMJVL), Tatabánya Városi Tanács V.B. Jegyzőkönyvek (Minutes of the Implementation Committee of Tatabánya City Council, hereafter, V.B. Jegyzőkönyvek), V.B. ülés, 1950 szeptember 29, 4. napirendi pont, 3.

150. PtSzL, XII.20f./42d./1950, Titkári jelentés 1950 év november hóról, 1; TMJVL, V.B. Jegyzőkönyvek, V.B. ülés, 1950 november 24-én, 4. napirendi pont, 2.

151. PtSzL, XII.20f./61d./1950, Magyar Bányamunkások Szakszervezetének Kerületi Titkársága. Hangulatjelentés. Tatabánya, 1950. IX.19.

152. PtSzL, XII.20f./61d./1950, Összesitett jelentés, Tatabánya, 1950.IX.30.

153. *Kétlakiság*, 3–7.

154. Mátyás Rákosi, *Visszaemlékezések, 1940–1956, II. kötet* (Budapest: Napvilág Kiadó, 1997), 845.

155. PtSzL, XII.2of./59d./1950, Építők Szakszervezete Komárommegyei Bizottsága, Tatabánya, Tóth-Bucsoki út 187. Havijelentés, Tatabánya, 1950.XII.7-én, 2.

156. PtSzL, Szakszervezetek Zala Megyei Tanácsa (Zala County Council of Trade Unions, hereafter, XII.29f.)/31–32d./1949, 9. dec 1, 1082/1949 sz./V., Üzemi Bizottságank, Bázakerretye, 1.

157. ZML, XXXV.61f.3/3/Ipar/7ő.e., Kimutatás a bázakerettyei üzemeben dolgozó munkavállalók vagyoni helyzetéről.

158. Béla Fazekas, *A mezőgazdasági termelőszövetkezeti mozgalom Magyarországon* (Budapest: Kossuth Könyvkiadó, 1976), 57–58.

159. "Zalaegerszeg, 1950. január 26. Az MDP Zala Megyei Bizottságának jelentése a KV Szervezési Osztályának, a zalai termelőszövetkezeti csoportok, állami gazdaságok és gépállomások helyzetéről," in Káli, ed., *Dokumentumok Zala megye történetéből 1947–1956*, 132.

160. Zsuzsanna Varga, "A falusi társadalom feszültséggócai az 1950-es évek közepén," *Múltunk* 51, no. 4 (2006): 232–33.

161. "Letenye, 1950. szeptember 7. Az MDP letenyei járási titkárának levele a megyei pártbizottsághoz, a helyi gépállomáson tett vizgálatról," in Káli, ed., *Dokumentumok Zala megye történetéből 1947–1956*, 174–76.

162. ZML, XXXV.57f.2/Agitprop/9ő.e., Magyar Dolgozók Pártja, Járási Pártbizottság, Tapolca. Tapolca, 1950 jan. 25, Hangulatjelentés, 1.

163. ZML, XXXV.57f.2/Agitprop/9ő.e., Magyar Dolgozók Pártja Járási Pártbizottsága, Zalaegerszeg. Zalaegerszeg, 1950. feb 24.-én. Hangulatjelentés, 1.

164. ZML, XXXV.57f.2/Agitprop/9ő.e., o. augusztus. 31, MDP Központi Vezetősége Agit.prop.osztály. Budapest, Hangulat jelentés, 2.

165. ZML, XXXV.57f.2/Agitprop/9ő.e., o. június 1., MDP Központi Vezetősége Agit. prop.osztály. Budapest, Hangulat jelentés május hóról, 4.

166. ZML, XXXV.57f.1/77ő.e., 6.

167. "A politikai bizottság határozata a részleges tagosítási kampányról," in Habuda, Rákosi, Székely, and Varga, eds., *A Magyar Dolgozók Pártja határozatai, 1948–1956*, 78–82.

168. "Nagykanizsa, 1949. szeptember 7. Az MDP Nagykanizsai Járási Bizottságának hangulatjelentése a megyei pártbizottsághoz, a részleges tagosítással és a termelőszövetkezeti csoportok alakításával kapcsolatban," in Káli, ed., *Dokumentumok Zala megye történetéből 1947–1956*, 104.

169. ZML, XXXV.57f.1/78ő.e., 34.

170. ZML, XXXV.57f.2/Agitprop/9ő.e., Magyar Dolgozók Pártja, Nagykanizsai Városi Bizottság. Nagykanizsa, 1950. január 3. Hangulatjelentés /1949.XII.27–1950.I.2-ig/, 1.

171. ZML, XXXV.57f.1/71ő.e., 34.

172. Melissa K. Bokovoy, *Peasants and Communists: Politics and Ideology in the Yugoslav Countryside, 1941–1953* (Pittsburgh: University of Pittsburgh Press, 1998), 116–20.

173. ZML, XXXV.57f.2/Agitprop/9ő.e., 50.jan.31., MDP Központi Vezetősége Agit.prop. osztály. Budapest, Hangulat jelentés január hóra, 1.

174. ZML, XXXV.57f.2/Agitprop/9ő.e., Maort üzemekben a hangulat.

175. ZML, XXXV.57f.2/Agitprop/9ő.e., o.feb.28., MDP Központi Vezetősége Agit.prop. osztály. Budapest, Hangulat jelentés február hóra, 5.

176. "Budapest, 1950. június 22. A Nehézipari Minisztérium Ásványolaj Főosztálya

vezetőjének feljegyzése Zsofinyecz Mihály minister részére, a jugoszlav határ mentén létesített olajkutató fúrásokról," in Káli, ed., *Dokumentumok Zala megye történeteből 1947–1956*, 151–52.

177. Csaba Borsodi, "A szerzetesek kitelepítései 1950 nyarán," *Jel* 12, no. 6 (2000): 12–16.

178. ZML, XXXV.57f.2/Agitprop/9ő.e., MDP Városi Bizottság, Nagykanizsa. Nkanizsa, 1950.jun.13, Magyar Dolgozók Pártja Központi Vezetősége, Agitációs Osztály. Budapest, 1.

179. "Zalaegerszeg, 1950 június 23. Az MDP Zala Megyei Bizottságának jelentése a Központi Vezetőségének, a határsávból történt kitelepítésekről," in Káli, ed., *Dokumentumok Zala megye történeteből 1947–1956*, 153.

180. ZML, XXXV.57f.1/77ő.e., 41–43.

181. ZML, XXXV.57f.1/77ő.e., 36.

182. ZML, XXXV.57f.1/73ő.e., 85.

183. ZML, XXXV.57f.1/73ő.e., 59–64.

184. ZML, XXXV.57f.1/73ő.e., 87.

185. Srágli, "A magyarországi szénhidrogénbányászat első ötéves tervéhez," 224.

186. György Faluvégi, "Helyzetjelentése az új szocialista munkaverseny megindulásáról Lovásziban," *MAORT Üzemi Híradó: A MAORT Dolgozók Hetilapja*, 15 March 1949, 5.

187. János Csörgits, "A békénk megvédéséhez az 5 éves terv sikeréhez, mi a fúrólyukak lemélyítésének meggyorsításával járulhatunk hozzá," *Olajmunkás*, 1 May 1950, 6.

188. PtSzL, XII.29f./31–32d./1949, MAORT. Bázakerettyei üzeme. Üzemi Bizottság. Bázakerettye, 1949. december 22., Jelentés a bázakerettyei termelő üzem dolgozóinak a "Sztalin"-i müszak alkamával elért eredményeiről, 1.

189. Bencze, *Zala megye iparának története a felszabadulás után*, 35–36.

190. PtSzL, XII.29f./40–41d./1950, Jelentés Furási üzemek április 4-I felajánlásairól és annak teljesitéséről.

191. Srágli, "A magyarországi szénhidrogénbányászat első ötéves tervéhez," 226; ZML, XXXV.57f.1/77ő.e., 1–4.

192. ZML, XXXV.57f.1/77ő.e., 9.

193. ZML, XXXV.57f.2/Ipar/37ő.e., Jelentés az alapbéremelésről és normarendezésről, 0. július 29, 2.

194. PtSzL, XII.29f./47d./1950, Jelentés. Bázakerettye, 1950. október. 16, 1.

## 5. Expanding Workforces, Reproducing Traditions, January 1951–June 1953

1. Központi Statisztikai Hivatal Könyvtára (Library of the Central Statistical Office, hereafter, KSHK), KSH Jelentés ÁLT 8, 1954.VIII.9, "A Magyar Munkásosztály Fejlődése," 14.

2. "1949. évi XXV. törvény a Magyar Népköztársaság első ötéves népgazdasági tervéről, az 1950. január 1-től az 1954. december 31-ig terjedő időszakra," reprinted in Sándor Balogh, ed., *Nehéz esztendők krónikája, 1949–1953* (Budapest: Gondolat Könyvkiadó, 1986), 165; *A szocializmus építésének útján*, 217.

3. Mikos, Nagy, and Weltner, eds., *A munka törvénykönyve és végrehajtási szabályai*, 21–22.

4. Gézáné Kelemen, "A nők bevonása a termelő munkába," *Munkaerőtartálék* 2, no. 3 (Mar. 1951): 98.

5. PtSzL, XII.2f.10/17d./1950, Munkaerőtartalékok Hivatala, Budapest.V., József Attila-u., Munkaerőközvetitő tevékenység 1950.január havában, Budapest, 1950. február 25.

6. Mark Pittaway, "The Reproduction of Hierarchy: Skill, Working-Class Culture and the State in Early Socialist Hungary," *Journal of Modern History* 74, no. 4 (2002): 743–44.

7. Péter Darvas, "Oktatás és tervgazdálkodás," *Medvetánc*, no. 4 (1983): 59–75.

8. MOL, Az Országos Tervhivatal iratai (Papers of the National Planning Office, hereafter, XIX-A-16)-b, 248d., Országos Tervhivatal. Előterjesztés a Népgazdasági Tanácshoz. Tárgy: A szakmunkásképzés szabályozása. Budapest, 1951.XI.23.

9. MOL, M-KS-276f.116/43ő.e., 11–18.

10. "A minisztertanács határozata a munkaerőtoborzásról," *Munkaerőtartálék* 2, no. 2 (Feb. 1951): 33–34.

11. András Kürti, "A bányászok közötti politikai munka néhány kérdése," *Társadalmi Szemle* 9, no. 8 (Aug. 1953): 1024–25.

12. Columbia University Libraries (hereafter, CUL), Rare Book & Manuscript Library, Bakhmeteff Archive (hereafter, RBML, BAR), Hungarian Refugees Project Manuscripts (hereafter, CURPH), Interview No. 54-M, p. IX/28.

13. CUL, RBML, BAR, CURPH, Interview No. 59-M, p. XI/3.

14. PtSzL, XII.2f.16/9d./1951, Kereskedelmi és Pénzügyi Dolgozók Szakszervezete, Jelentés a jegyrendszer megszüntetésével és a fizetésemeléssel kapcsolatos hangulatról. Budapest, 1951 december 3.

15. KSHK, KSH Jelentés ÁLT 8, 1955.VII.22, "A lakosság anyagi helyzete: reálbérek – reáljövedelmek, 1949–1954," 6.

16. PtSzL, XII.2f.16/22d./1952, A 1952 II.negyedév kiskereskedelmi forgalomról, 5.

17. KSHK, KSH Jelentés ÁLT 8, 1954.VIII.9, "A Magyar Munkásosztály Fejlődése," 12.

18. MOL, XIX-A-16-b, 250d., Országos Tervhivatal, Igazságügyminisztéium. Előterjesztés a Népgazdasági Tanácshoz. Tárgy: Letartóztatottak termelőmunkában foglalkoztatásának egységes megszervezése. Budapest, 1951. november hó 15.

19. MOL, XIX-A-16-b, 403d., A munkafegyelem kérdése.

20. MOL, M-KS-276f.94/596ő.e., 362–64.

21. Pittaway, "Social Limits of State Control," 282–26.

22. Pittaway, "Reproduction of Hierarchy," 751–53.

23. KSHK, KSH Jelentés ÁLT 8, 1954.VIII.9, "A Magyar Munkásosztály Fejlődése," 15.

24. Pittaway, "Reproduction of Hierarchy," 753–69.

25. "A minisztertanács határozata a munkaerőtoborzásról," 33.

26. MOL, M-KS-276f.116/4ő.e., 3–4.

27. Doris Wastl-Walter, Mónika Váradi, and Károly Kocsis, "Leben im Dorf an der Grenze," in *Bruchlinie Eiserner Vorhang: Regionalentwicklung im österreich-ungarischen Grenzraum (Südburgenland/Oststeiermark-Westungarn)*, ed. Martin Seger and Pál Beluszky (Vienna, Cologne, and Graz: Böhlau Verlag, 1993), 240–46.

28. ZML, XXXV.57f.2/Ipar/33ő.e., Szakszervezet Zalamegyei Tanácsa, Zalaegerszeg. 392/II levélre. Munkaerőtoborzásról. Zalaegerszeg, 1951 március 2., 1.

29. ZML, XXXV.57f.2/Ipar/33ő.e., Jelentés a munkaerőtoborzás eddigi eredményeiről., Zalaegerszeg, 1951 február 27-én.

30. MOL, M-KS-276f.116/4ő.e., 20.

31. MOL, M-KS-276f.116/4ő.e., 122.

32. ZML, XXXV.57f.2/Agitprop/10ő.e., 1951. január 2. du. 4.30, Nagykanizsai városi pártbizottság.

33. ZML, XXXV.57f.2/Agitprop/10ő.e., Magyar Dolgozók Pártja Járási Pártbizottsága, Zalaegerszeg. MDP Megyei Pártbizottságának, Zalaegerszeg, 1951. febr. 20, 1.

34. ZML, XXXV.61f.1/47ő.e., Letenyei járás.

35. ZML, XXXV.61f.2/Agitprop/7ő.e., 2. jún.18, MDP Megyebizottság, Zalaegerszeg. Hangulat jelentés.

36. ZML, XXXV.61f.4/4/4/3ő.e., Jegyzőkönyv készült Lovászi, 1952.XI.25-én a gazolin-telepi alapszervezet vezetőségi ülésen., 1.

37. ZML, XXXV.61f.4/2/32ő.e., MDP. Lovászi Pártszervezet, Jelentés. Lovászi, 1951. július 10.

38. Open Society Archives (hereafter, OSA), Records of Radio Free Europe/Radio Liberty Research Institute, Hungarian Unit, 1949–1995 (hereafter, 300/40)/4/22, Item No. 8027/55, 2.

39. OSA, 300/40/4/22, Item No. 4154/55, 2–3.

40. OSA, 300/40/4/22, Item No. 7957/55, 9.

41. MOL, M-KS-276f.65/300ő.e., 7.

42. "Zalaegerszeg, 1952 július 12. A Zala Megyei Tanács V.B. Begyűtési Osztálya vezetőjének jelentése az MDP megyei bizottságának a kulákok számáról, földterületéről, beadási kötelezettségéről," in Káli, ed., Dokumentumok Zala megye történetéből 1947–1956, 270.

43. OSA, 300/40/4/22, Item No. 4154/55, 3.

44. "Zalaegerszeg, 1951. december 30. Az MDP Zala Megyei Bizottságának ülésére készült jelentés a zalai termelőszövetkezeti csoportok helyzetéről (részlet)," in Káli, ed., Dokumentumok Zala megye történetéből 1947–1956, 243–44.

45. ZML, XXXV.57f.2/Agitprop/11ő.e., M.D.P. Üzemi Pártszervezet, Bázakerettye. Hangulatjelentés, Bázakerettye, 1951. június 18., 1.

46. "Lenti, 1952. augusztus 21. Tszcs-szervezők jelentése a Baglad községben tapasztal-takról," in Káli, ed., Dokumentumok Zala megye történetéből 1947–1956, 273.

47. ZML, XXXV.57f.1/79ő.e., 71.

48. OSA, 300/40/4/22, Item No. 4154/55, 10.

49. KSHK, KSH Jelentés ÁLT 5, 1956.VIII.1, "A Lakósság Fogyasztása és a Reálbérek, Reáljövedelmek Alakulása 1955-ben, és a 1949–1955 időszakban," 14.

50. OSA, 300/40/4/22, Item No. 4154/55, 6.

51. OSA, 300/40/4/22, Item No. 4154/55, 4.

52. OSA, 300/40/4/22, Item No. 8503/55, 1–2.

53. OSA, 300/40/4/22, Item No. 4154/55, 9.

54. "Zalaegerszeg, 1951. május 16. Az MDP Zala Megyei Bizottságának kibővített ülésére készített jelentés a megyében folyó munkástoborzás eredményeiről és hiá-nyosságairól," in Káli, ed., Dokumentumok Zala megye történetéből 1947–1956, 211.

55. Bencze, Zala megye iparának története a felszabadulás után, 37–67.

56. MOL, M-KS-288f.21/1958/23ő.e., 494.

57. OSA, 300/40/4/22, Item No. 4154/55, 7.

58. Bencze, *Zala megye iparának története a felszabadulás után*, 40–47.

59. ZML, XXXV.61f.3/3/Ipar/1ő.e., Feljegyzés a Dunántúli Ásványolajtermelő Vállalat bázakerettyei üzemének, illetve a Budafai Kőolajtermelő Vállalat 1951. évi munkaerőgazdálkodással kapcsolatos kérdeseiről, Bázakerettye, 1951. évi november hó 27-én.

60. ZML, XXXV.57f.2/Olajipar/20ő.e., Feljegyzés a furás nehézségeiről, Nagykanizsa, 1951. június 28., 1.

61. ZML, XXXV.57f.2/Olajipar/11ő.e., Az Ásványolajkutató és Mélyfuró Vállalat állománycsoportok létszámának aránya az összlétszámhoz viszonyitva; Az Ásványolajkutató és Mélyfuró Vállalat 26 éven aluliak létszámának alakulása 1951.I-VIII.hóig.

62. ZML, XXXV.57f.2/Olajipar/25ő.e., Kimutatás a Budafai Furási Üzem kétlaki dolgozóiról; Kimutatás az Ásványolajkutató és Mélyfuró V. Lovászi üzemében dolgozó kétlaki munkavállalókról; Kimutatás az Ásványolajkutató és Mélyfuró V. Újfalusi üzemében dolgozó kétlaki munkavállalókról.

63. ZML, XXXV.57f.2/Olajipar/25ő.e., Kimutatás az Ásványolajkutató és Mélyfuró V. nagylengyeli üzemében dolgozó kétlaki munkavállalókról.

64. ZML, XXV.61f.3/2/22ő.e., Bázakerettye, 1952. február 11., 1; ZML, XXXV.61f.3/3/Agitprop/3ő.e., MDP. Üzemi Pártbizottság, Bázakerettye. 10 napos jelentés. Bázakerettye, 1952. június 24-én.

65. MOL, M-KS-276f.116/7ő.e., 94.

66. "Így dolgozik az ellenség az olajmezőkön. Példás fegyelmi büntetések," *Olajmunkás*, 15 July 1951, 8.

67. ZML, XXXV.57f.2/Olajipar/5ő.e., 2 szeptember 10. 37/0–114. 2 P.J./H.E. Jelentés, 1–2.

68. ZML, XXXV.61f.4/2/8ő.e., Jegyzőkönyv készült, 1952.III.24-én, a Pártbizottság ülésen, 4.

69. ZML, XXXV.61f.2/Agitprop/20ő.e., Hangulat jelentés: 1951 október 8-án; Hangulat jelentés: 1951. szept. 29.

70. See the documents in MOL, A Magyar-Szovjet Olajipari Részvénytársaság iratai (Papers of the Hungarian-Soviet Public Limited Oil Company, hereafter, XXIX-F-40)-a, 48d.

71. MOL, XXIX-F-40/43d., «MASZOLAJ» Magyar-Szovjet Olaj Rt., Budafai Kőolajtermelő Vállalat. 2360/1953. Bázakerettye, 1953. július 13., Tárgy: Müszaki normákra vonatkozó adatszolgáltatás, 1–2.

72. ZML, XXXV.61f.3/2/6ő.e., Jegyzőkönyv felvétetett Bázakerettyén, 1951.október 11-én tartott kibővített Pártszervezet vezetőségi ülésről a pártirodában, 1.

73. ZML, XXXV.61f.3/2/9ő.e., MDP. Üzemi Pártbizottság, Bázakerettye. Jegyzőkönyv, felvétetett 1952. november 24-én tartott Pártbizottsági ülésen, 8.

74. MOL, A Lovászi Kőolajtermelő Vállalat iratai (Papers of the Lovászi Oil Production Enterprise, hereafter, XXIX-F-135)/8d., Gazolin 139/1952. Lovászi, 1952. október 9. Tárgy: Béralaptullépés.

75. ZML, XXXV.61f.4/3/PTO/22ő.e., Feljegyzés. Lovászi, 1953. január 28.

76. ZML, XXXV.57f.2/Olajipar/11ő.e., Az Ásványolajkutató és Mélyfuró Vállalat állománycsoportok létszámának aránya az összlétszámhoz viszonyita; Női munkavállalók megoszlása.

77. ZML, XXXV.57f.2/Agitprop/14ő.e., Hangulatjelentés, Lovászi, 1952. I.24.

78. ZML, XXXV.61f.3/3/PTO/8ő.e., MDP. Üzemi Pártbizottság, Bázakerettye. Bázakerettye, 1953. márc. 6, 1.

79. ZML, XXXV.57f.2/Agitprop/13ő.e., Jelentés Rákosi elvtárs nov.30-i beszédével kapcsolatban, Lovászi, 1951. december 3.

80. ZML, XXXV.61f.4/2/7ő.e., Jegyzőkönyv készült, 1951.XII.6-án a Pártbizottság vezetőségi értekezletén, 3–6.

81. ZML, XXXV.57f.2/Agitprop/15ő.e., MDP. Járási Pártbizottság Letenye, Jelentés, 1953.V.2, 3.

82. ZML, XXXV.57f.1/Agitprop/15ő.e., MDP. Járási Bizottsága Lenti, Jelentés, 1953.IV.28, 2.

83. ZML, XXXV.61f.2/Ipar/2ő.e., Jelentés, Letenye, 1953.II.27.

84. ZML, XXXV.57f.1/79ő.e., 102.

85. MOL, A Határőrség Országos Parancsnokság iratai (Papers of the National Border Guard Command, hereafter, XIX-B-10)-1953/6d., Ksz.: 0292/Pk.-1953.sz., Jelentés a B.M. Határőrség helyzetéről, 2.

86. OSA, 300/40/4/12, Item No. 3656/54, 1–5.

87. OSA, 300/40/4/12, Item No. 11727/53, 8.

88. PtSzL, XII.30f./422d./1950, Kimutatás Tatabánya kerületről a minisztertanács jan. 8.-i határozata sempontjából lehetséges munkaerő átcsoportositásokról; KEMÖL, XXXV.32f.4/15ő.e., 66–68.

89. PtSzL, XII.2f.16/16d./1952, Feljegyzés a Komárom megyei lakásépitkezésekről, Tatabánya-újváros, Oroszlány, és Eterniti épitkezések ellenőrzése alapján, 1.

90. KEMÖL, XXXV.32f.4/12ő.e., 6.

91. Pál Germuska, Indusztria bűvöletében: fejlesztéspolitika és a szocialista városok (Budapest: 1956-os Intézet, 2004), 110–15.

92. Miklós Visontai, "Tatabánya," in Sztálinváros-Miskolc-Tatabánya, városépítésünk fejlődése, ed. Aladár Sós, Kálman Faragó, Géza Hermány, and György Korompay (Budapest: Műszaki Könyvkiadó, 1959), 143–91.

93. KEMÖL, XXXV.32f.4/15ő.e., 32.

94. KEMÖL, XXXV.32f.4/15ő.e., 17.

95. MOL, M-KS-276f.88/252ő.e., 19.

96. MOL, M-KS-276f.88/254ő.e., 5–6.

97. PtSzL, XII.2f.10/31d /1953, Bérproblémák az Építőés Épitőanyagipar területén, 1; PtSzL, XII.20f.85d./1951, Jegyzőkönyv, felvételett Tatabánya Mémosz Megyebizottságon megyebizottsági ülésen 1951.V.26, 4.

98. MOL, M-KS-276f.88/297ő.e., 5–7; PtSzL, XII.20f.86d./1951, Építő-, Fa és Építőipari Dolgozók Szakszervezete Komárommegyei Bizottsága, Jelentés, 1951.IX.5.

99. PtSzL, XII.20f.85d./1951, Jegyzőkönyv, felvételett Tatabánya Mémosz Megyebizottságon megyebizottsági ülésen 1951.V.26, 4.

100. PtSzL, XII.20f.84d./1951, Jegyzőkönyv, felvételett Tatabánya Mémosz Megyebizottságon megyebizottsági ülésen 1951.III.31, 2.

101. MOL, M-KS-276f.88/297ő.e., 9; "Miért nem teljesíti tervét a Cementgyár?" Tatabányai Cement: A Tatabányai Cementés Mészművek Dolgozóinak Lapja, 15 July 1951, 2.

102. Gyula Kulcsár, "Üzemeink közötti sovinizmusról," *Tatabányai Cement: A Tatabányai Cementés Mészművek Dolgozóinak Lapja*, 26 May 1951, 2; MOL, A Cementés Mészművek Igazgatóságának iratai (Papers of the Cement Works' and Lime-Kilns' Directorate, hereafter, XXIX-D-22-d), 65d., Munkások átlagos állományi létszám vállalatonként, 1951.

103. KEMÖL, XXXV.32f.2/68ő.e., 114.

104. "Üzemlátogatáson: az ó-mészüzemben," *Tatabányai Cement: A Tatabányai Cementés Mészművek Dolgozóinak Lapja*, 13 February 1953, 4.

105. Gyula Verbó, "Hozzászólás a 'Jobban foglalkozzanak üzemeinkben az új felvételesekkel' cimű cíkkhez," *Tatabányai Cement: A Tatabányai Cementés Mészművek Dolgozóinak Lapja*, 21 March 1952, 2.

106. Iván T. Berend and György Ránki, "A magyar iparfejlődés a felszabadulás után: az ipar növekedési ütemének kérdéséhez," in *Húsz év. tanulmányok a szocialista Magyarország történetéből*, ed. Miklós Lackó and Bálint Szabó (Budapest: Kossuth Könyvkiadó, 1964), 35; Sándor Rozsnyói, "A város nagyüzemei," in *Tatabánya története: helytörténeti tanulmányok ii. kötet*, ed. Gábor Gombkötö et al. (Tatabánya: Tatabánya Városi Tanács VB, 1972), 87.

107. TMA, A szocialista építőmunka néhány kérdése a Magyar Dolgozók Pártja helyi szerveinek irányító tevékenységben 1948–1956 (hereafter, 149-76), 12–13.

108. MOL, XXIX-F-107-m/52d., Törzskönyvi (Állományi) Létszámkimutatások a Tatabányai Felső N.V.-ről az 1951-es évre; MOL, XXIX-F-107-m/51d., Törzskönyvi (Állományi) Létszámkimutatások a Tatabányai Szénbányák és a Tatabányai Alsó N.V.-ról az 1951-es évre.

109. KEMÖL, XXXV.32f.4/3ő.e., 82.

110. Mark Pittaway, "Workers, Management and the State in Socialist Hungary: Shaping and Re-shaping the Socialist Factory Regime in Újpest and Tatabánya, 1950–1956," in *Sozialgeschichtliche Kommunismusforschung: Tscechoslowakei, Polen, Ungarn und DDR, 1948–1968*, ed. Christiane Brenner and Peter Heumos (Munich: R. Oldenbourg Verlag, 2005), 105–31.

111. MOL, XXIX-F-107-m/51d., Beszámolási időszak 1951. december hónap. Számjel, 0110025640169. II. Munkások (Az átképzősökkel és az építőipari jellegű termelésben foglalkoztatott munkásokkal együtt).

112. MOL, XXIX-F-107-m/51d., Bánya és Energiaügyi Minisztérium. Vállalat néve: Tb. Alsó Szénbányák. IV.a. Létszámadatok 1951. december hóról; Bánya és Energiaügyi Minisztérium. Vállalat néve: Tb. Alsó Szénbányák. IV.a. Létszámadatok 1951. november hóról; Bánya és Energiaügyi Minisztérium. Vállalat néve: Tb. Alsó Szénbányák. IV.a. Létszámadatok 1951. október hóról; Bánya és Energiaügyi Minisztérium. Vállalat néve: Tb. Alsó Szénbányák. IV.a. Létszámadatok 1951. szeptember hóról; Bánya és Energiaügyi Minisztérium. Vállalat néve: Tb. Alsó Szénbányák. IV.a. Létszámadatok 1951. augusztus hóról.

113. OSA, 300/40/4/12, Item No. 11727/53, 7.

114. OSA, 300/40/4/12, Item No. 8083/54, 6.

115. Kovács, *Szén volt az életük*, 53–57.

116. PtSzL, XII.20f.96d./1951, Jegyzőkönyv felvéve: 1951. augusztus 18-án a Bányász Szakszervezet Komárom m. Területi Bizottságán megtartott munkaértekezleten, 2.

117. KEMÖL, XXXV.32f.4/15ő.e., 26.

118. "Feladataink," *Harc a Szénért: Tatabánya Város Pártbizottságának Lapja*, 22 November, 1951, 1.

119. KEMÖL, XXXV.32f.4/18ő.e., 60.

120. PtSzL, XII.20f.95d./1951, Jegyzőkönyv, felvéve: 1951. április 17-én a Bányaipari Dolgozók Szakszervezte Komárom m. területi bizottságán megtartott felelős harmadbizottsági és körzeti üzemi bizottság tagjai részére megtartott értekezleten, 10.

121. OSA, 300/40/4/12, Item No. 11727/53, 8.

122. "Azt hallotuk," *Harc a Szénért: Tatabánya Város Pártbizottságának Lapja*, 22 November 1951, 4.

123. PtSzL, XII.20f.95d./1951, Jegyzőkönyv, felvéve: 1951. április 17-én a Bányaipari Dolgozók Szakszervezte Komárom m. területi bizottságán megtartott felelős harmadbizottsági és körzeti üzemi bizottság tagjai részére megtartott értekezleten, 6.

124. The law is outlined in *A munkafegyelem megszilárdítása és a munkakönyvrendszer* (Budapest: Jogi és Államigazgatási Könyvés Folyóiratkiadó, 1954), 35–39; on its application in Tatabánya, see "Szilárd munka és terv fegyelem előbbre viszi a termelést," *Harc a Szénért: Tatabánya Város Pártbizottságának Lapja*, 22 November 1951, 2.

125. "Azt hallotuk," *Harc a Szénért: Tatabánya Város Pártbizottságának Lapja*, 20 December 1951, 40. See also Kovács, *Szén volt az életük*, 53–57.

126. KEMÖL, XXXV.32f.1/17ő.e., 213; MOL, M-KS-276f.88/249ő.e., 13; "Miért hagyják el Tatabányát az új dolgozók?" *Harc a Szénért: Tatabánya Város Pártbizottságának Lapja*, 18 April 1952, 3.

127. KEMÖL, XXXV.32f.4/18ő.e., 90.

128. KEMÖL, XXXV.32f.4/24ő.e., 45–47.

129. Tamás Gyekiczky, *A munkafegyelem jogi szabályozásának társadalmi háttere az 1952-es év Magyarországon* (Budapest: Művelődési Minisztérium Marxizmus-Leninizmus Oktatási Főosztálya, Budapest, 1986); MOL, M-KS-276f.116/7ő.e., 103.

130. KEMÖL, XXXV.36f.3/13ő.e., 92–94; KEMÖL, XXXV.32f.4/42ő.e., 29–31.

131. MOL, XXIX-F-107-o/51d., Mérlegbeszámoló 1953 II.évnegyedről, 24–30.

132. TMA, Adatok a tatabányai VIII és XIV aknák történetéhez (hereafter, 728-89), 10–11.

133. MOL, XXIX-F-107-e/34d., Körrendelet szénbányászati trösztök, vállalatok és a bányarendészeti felügyelőségek részére; MOL, XXIX-F-107-o/51d., Mérlegbeszámoló 1953 II.évnegyedről, 1–3.

134. OSA, 300/40/4/6, Item No.10040/55, 5.

135. OSA, 300/40/4/12, Item No. 6094/53, 3.

136. MOL, XXIX-F-107-j/116d., Belügyminisztérium VII. Főosztály, Gál István elvtársnak, Budapest, 1953. április 1.

137. KEMÖL, XXXV.32f.4/32ő.e., 122; KEMÖL, XXXV.32f.4/24ő.e., 91.

138. PtSzL, XII.20f.108d./1952, Jelentés üzemeinkben folyó normaszigorítás, Tatabánya, 1952. május 12, 2.

139. PtSzL, XII.20f.79d./1951, 1.XI.19. Válasz az 1951. XVI P.E. jelzésű levélre, 1.

140. PtSzL, XII.2f.16/21d./1952, Szénszállitó és Szólgáltató Vállalat Szakszervezeti Bizottsága, Tatabánya. Jegyzőkönyv Társadalmi ellenőrök részére megtartott értekezeltről, 4.

141. MOL, M-KS-276f.53/145ő.e., Tájékoztató az üzemi dolgozók és az üzemi vezetők által felvetett szociális és kultúrális problémákról, 40.

142. PtSzL, XII.2f.16/9d./1951, Kereskedelmi és Pénzügyi Dolgozók Szakszervezete. Jelentés a vidék közellátási helyzetéről, Budapest, 1951 december 19., 3.

143. PtSzL, XII.2f.16/15d./1953, Tatabánya, VIII.akna. 1953. február 9., 2.

144. MOL, XXIX-F-107-e/3d., Jegyzőkönyv készült Tatabányán az 1953.évi szeptember hó 14-én a Tatabányai Szénbányászati Tröszt kollektiv szerződésének 1953.II.negyedévi beszámoló értekezletéről, 5.

145. PtSzL, XII.2f.16/9d./1951, Feljegyzés Tatabánya Alsó és Felső bányászdolgozóinak ellátási helyzetéről, 4–5; "Boldog emberek az Újvárosban," *Tatabányai Cement: A Tatabányai Cementés Mészművek Dolgozóinak Lapja,* 19 September 1952, 3.

146. András Preizler, "Az Újvárosban is akad javítani való!" *Harc a Szénért: Tatabánya Város Pártbizottságának Lapja,* 10 July 1953, 4.

147. "Mi épül 1953-ban Újpesten," *Esti Budapest,* 20 March 1953, 3.

148. PtSzL, XII.2f.16/12d./1951, Bőripari Dolgozók Szakszervezetének Társadalombizotsitási és Üdülési Osztálya. Javaslat. Budapest, 1951.V.22.

149. Tibor Dessewffy and András Szántó, *"Kitörő éberséggel": A budapesti kitelepítések hiteles története* (Budapest: Lapés Könyvkiadó, 1989), 102–3.

150. PtSzL, XII.2f.16/12d./1951, Jelentés a kitelepítési akcióval megüresedő lakások felosztásról az üzemi dolgozók részére, illetve azok beköltőzéséről.

151. OSA, 300/40/4/17, Item No. 6911/54, 1.

152. PtSzL, XII.2f.16/19d./1953, Jegyzőkönyv készült 1953.október 29.-én a SZOT munkásellátási osztálya által egyes üzemek részére tartott megbeszélesről, 4–6.

153. "Elkészült az Ország Legkorszerűbb Áruháza: ma délután nyílik meg az újpesti Állami Áruház," *Esti Budapest,* 11 October 1952, 1.

154. MOL, M-KS-288f.21/1958/20ő.e., 272.

155. PtSzL, XII.2f.16/4d./1953, Kedves elvtársak! Üzemi levél.

156. Erzsébet Percze, "Vitás cipők amelyekről érdemes beszélni," *Esti Budapest,* 30 October 1952, 5.

157. "A 'Duna Híradó' fényszórója az üzemrészeken: a minőség megjavításával véget kell vetni a selejtgyártásnak a 303-as körön," *Duna Híradó,* May 1951, 2.

158. BFL, XXXV.176f.2/190/2ő.e., 79–89.

159. BFL, XXXV.176f.2/190/2ö.e., 90; BFL, XXXV.176f.2/190/6ő.e., 18.

160. BFL, XXXV.176f.2/190/6ő.e., 242; BFL, XXXV.176f.2/279/6ő.e., 64; BFL, XXXV.176f.2/279/8ő.e., 88.

161. BFL, XXXV.176f.2/190/6ő.e., 16–31.

162. BFL, XXXV.176f.2/190/7ő.e., 73–86.

163. MOL, M-KS-276f.65/246ő.e., 60, 63.

164. CUL, RBML, BAR, CURPH, Interview No. 455, 2.

165. OSA, 300/40/4/14, Item No. 3677/56, 2.

166. CUL, RBML, BAR, CURPH, Interview No. 455, 3.

167. Pittaway, "Reproduction of Hierarchy," 750.

168. CUL, RBML, BAR, CURPH, Interview No. 455, 6.

169. BFL, XXXV.176f.2/190/7ő.e., 73–86.

170. BFL, XXXV.176f.2/190/7ő.e., 244.

171. BFL, XXXV.176f.2/194/5ő.e., 161.

172. BFL, XXXV.176f.2/194/19ő.e., 13.

173. József Diószegi, "Anyagellátás hiányában nem tudjuk teljesíteni vállalásunkat," *Izzó*, 4 September 1952, 3.

174. BFL, XXXV.176f.2/191/8ő.e., 71.

175. BFL, XXXV.95f.4/65ő.e., 43, 30.

176. "Munkafolyamatosság a szereldében," *Kaparó*, 20 February 1952, 3; BFL, XXXV.176f.2/191/4ő.e., 83.

177. BFL, XXXV.176f.2/191/5ő.e., 126–28; BFL, XXXV.176f.2/191/8ő.e., 53–71.

178. BFL, XXXV.176f.2/184/4ő.e., 181; BFL, XXXV.176f.2/184/5ő.e., 108.

179. BFL, XXIX/403f., 63d., Feljegyzés a Chinoin gyár 1951. évi termelési tervének akadályairól, 3.

180. BFL, XXIX/403f., 64d., Feljegyzés Kőszegi vezérigazgató részere, Budapest, 1952. október 10.

181. BFL, XXXV.176f.2/184/5ő.e., 108–27.

182. BFL, XXXV.95f.4/56ő.e., 86.

183. BFL, XXXV.176f.2/236/3ő.e., 19.

184. BFL, XXXV.176f.2/190/6ő.e., 16, 29; BFL, XXXV.176f.2/212/11ő.e., 35, 49; BFL, XXXV.176f.2/236/10ő.e., 8, 25; BFL, XXXV.176f.2/256/3ő.e., 20, 32; BFL, XXXV.176f.2/279/8ő.e., 73, 88.

185. PtSzL, XII.2f.10/30 d./1953, Könnyűipari és Mezőgazdasági osztály Jelentés, 1.

186. "Meg kell szüntetni a munkaerővándorlást, amely akadályozza tervteljesítésünket," *Pamut Újság*, 2 August 1951, 5.

187. BFL, XXXV.176f.2/190/2ő.e., 79; BFL, XXXV.176f.2/190/6ő.e., 16; BFL, XXXV.176f.2/212/2ő.e., 42; BFL, XXXV.176f.2/212/11ő.e., 35; BFL, XXXV.176f.2/236/1ő.e., 5; BFL, XXXV.176f.2/236/10ő.e., 8; BFL, XXXV.176f.2/256/1ő.e., 69; BFL, XXXV.176f.2/256/3ő.e., 20; BFL, XXXV.176f.2/279/6ő.e., 25; BFL, XXXV.176f.2/279/8ő.e., 73.

188. CUL, RBML, BAR, CURPH, Interview No.154, 15.

189. BFL, XXXV.134f.21ő.e., 94.

190. BFL, XXXV.134f.22ő.e., 172; BFL, XXXV.176f.2/194/19ő.e., 16.

191. "Az ellenség aknamunkája a gépműhely fiatal dolgozói között," *Izzó*, 16 January 1953, 3.

192. BFL, XXIX/321f.1d., Jegyzőkönyv, felvétetett 1951, december hó 15-én reggel 6 órakor a II. Alapszerv szakszervezeti helyiségben megtartandó termelési értekezlet, 3.

193. "Nagyobb türelemmel tanítsuk az újonnan belépő dolgozókat," *Izzó*, 17 January 1952, 3.

194. BFL, XXIX/321f.4d., Levél a Vacumntechnikai Gépgyár Gyáregységvezetőtől a T.P. Nagy Balázs elvtársnak, 1953.V.6.

195. CUL, RBML, BAR, CURPH, Interview No. 154, 20–21.

196. "A műhely gazdái? . . . ," *Kaparó,* 20 November 1952, 4.

197. BFL, XXXV.176f.2/191/4ő.e., 138–39.

198. BFL, XXXV.176f.2/194/19ő.e., 13.

199. BFL, XXXV.176f.2/236/1ő.e., 14; BFL, XXXV.176f.2/236/10ő.e., 8.

200. BFL, XXXV.95f.3/345ő.e., 8; BFL, XXXV.176f.2/236/4ő.e., 268.

201. "A tervvel lemaradni szégyen," *Pamut Újság*, 31 January 1952, 3.

202. BFL, XXXV.143f.14ő.e., 222.

203. PtSzL, XII.46f.140d./1949–1955, Magyar Pamutipar. Jegyzőkönyv amely készült 1951. nov 10-én az olvasó teremben megtartott Ü.B. értekezeleten, 2.

204. "A munkafegyelem megbontói elnyerík méltó bűntetésűket," *Pamut Újság*, 25 April 1952, 5.

205. Mária Balogh, "Nyilt level a munkafegyelem megbontóihoz," *Pamut Újság*, 17 October 1952, 5.

206. CUL, RBML, BAR, CURPH, Interview No. 154, 19, 22.

207. Mark Pittaway, "The Education of Dissent: The Reception of the Voice of Free Hungary, 1951–1956," *Cold War History* 4, no. 1 (2003): 97–116.

208. BFL, XXXV.95f.2/215ő.e., 54–55.

## 6. Dynamics of Reform and Retreat, June 1953–February 1956

1. "Jegyzőkönyv a szovjet és a magyar partés állami vezetők tárgyalásairól (1953. június 13–16)," reprinted in *Múltunk* 37, no. 2–3 (1992): 234–69.

2. "A Magyar Dolgozók Pártja Központi Vezetőségének Határozata a Párt Politikai Irányvonalában és Gyakorlati Munkájában elkövetett hibákról és az ezek kijávitásával kapcsolatos feladatokról, 1953. június 28," reprinted in Balogh, ed., *Nehéz esztendők krónikája*, 497–510.

3. Imre Nagy, "A kormány prográmmja az Országgyűlés előtt," in *Egy évtized: válogatott beszédek és írások (1948–1954) II*, by Imre Nagy (Budapest: Szikra, 1954), 353.

4. Miklós Habuda, "A Magyar Dolgozók Pártja munkáspolitikájának néhány kérdése a Központi Vezetőség 1953. júniusi határozata után," *Párttörténeti Közlemények* 26, no. 1 (1980): 23–38.

5. BFL, XXXV.95f.4/62ő.e., 22–24.

6. For a revealing analysis of this issue in general terms, see Edwin Horlings and Bart van Ark, "Benchmark Comparisons of Manufacturing Productivity in Eastern Europe, 1937–1989," in *Historical Benchmark Comparison of Output and Productivity,* ed. Bart van Ark, Erik Buyst, and Jan Luiten van Zanden (Seville: Secretariado de Publicaciones de la Universidad de Sevilla, 1998), 107–22. For its specific manifestations in Hungary, see KSHK, KSH Jelentés ÁLT II, 1953.VIII.6., "Központi Statisztikai Hivatal Jelentése Munkaügyi Adatok, 1953 II.n.év," 9.

7. MOL, M-KS-276f.94/739ő.e., 230–33.

8. Pető and Szakács, *A hazai gazdaság négy évtizedének története*, 271.

9. 1956-os Intézet, OHA 99, 157.

10. Orbán, *Két agrárforradalom Magyarországon*, 131.

11. Gy.MSMGy.L, X.fond402/2/Mezőgazdaság/19ő.e., Jelentés, Sopron, 1953. szeptember 5.

12. MOL, M-KS-276f.65/251ő.e., 147.

13. MOL, M-KS-276f.94/739ő.e., 195.

14. Rainer, *Nagy Imre: politikai életrajz; második kötet 1953–1958*, 110–24.

15. Ibid., 23–26.

16. Rainer, *Az iró helye*, 160–221.

17. Varga, *Politika, paraszti érdek, szövetkezet Magyarországon*, 18; István Márkus, "Somogyi összegezés," in *Az ismeretlen főszereplő*, by Márkus, 167–83.

18. MOL, M-KS-276f.94/831ő.e., 125–26, 151, 186.

19. BFL, XXXV.95f.2/77ő.e., 32; "A lakosság fogyasztása és a reálbérek, reáljövedelmek alakulása 1955-ben, és a 1949–1955 időszakban," 22; MOL, M-KS-276f.65/36ő.e., 34–52.

20. "Tegyenek eleget a dolgozók egyszerű kérésenek," *Tatabányai Cement: A Tatabányai Cementés Mészművek Dolgozóinak Lapja*, 14 July 1953, 3.

21. MOL XXIX-F-107-e/3d., 953.III.n.é. beszámoló hozzászólások, 1–5.

22. MOL, M-KS-276f.88/249ő.e., 158.

23. OSA, 300/40/4/12, Item No. 11727/53, 6.

24. MOL, M-KS-276f.88/249ő.e., 37; MOL, XXIX-F-107-o/51d., Mérlegbeszámoló jelentés 1953 III. Évnegyedről, 2.

25. MOL, M-KS-276f.88/249ő.e., 157; MOL, M-KS-276f.94/743ő.e., 58–59.

26. MOL, XXXIX-F-107-o/51d., Mérlegbeszámoló jelentés az 1953. évről és 1953. IV. évnegyedről, 3.

27. PtSzL, XII.2f.10/28d./1953, A Bizottság vizsgálatai során bér-és normakérdésekben az alábbiakat tapasztalta, 8–10.

28. *Mit adott a népi demokrácia a dolgozóknak?* (Budapest: Kiadja a Magyar Dolgozók Pártja Központi Vezetősége Agitációs és Propaganda Osztály, 1953), 12–13.

29. Habuda, "A Magyar Dolgozók Pártja munkáspolitikájának néhány kérdése," 26–27.

30. "Boldogan vásárolnak dolgozóink az árleszállítás után," *Harc a Szénért: Tatabánya Város Pártbizottságának Lapja*, 11 September 1953, 2.

31. *Komárom megye fontosabb statisztikai adatai, 1952–1955* (Tatabánya: KSH Komárommegyei Igazgatósága, 1956), 120–46.

32. László István Bárdos, *Egy bányászváros a szocialista fejlődés útján: Tatabánya 1945–1960* (Tatabánya: Tatabánya Városi Tanács, 1960), 81; MOL, M-KS-276f.88/249ő.e., 13.

33. "A sajátház – a boldog, békés életünk ajándéka," *Harc a Szénért: Tatabánya Város Pártbizottságának Lapja*, 26 June 1953, 4.

34. PtSzL, XII.2f.16/16d./1952, Feljegyzés Bányász lakásakció helyzetéről, 1–2; "Egy toborzott dolgozó házat épít," *Harc a Szénért: Tatabánya Város Pártbizottságának Lapja*, 28 August 1953, 2.

35. Éva Ravasz, *Gál István, 1917–1979: egy bányaigazgató portréja* (Tatabánya: Tatabányai Bányász Hagyományokért Alapítvány, 2004), 35.

36. "A családiház építéséről," *Tatabányai Cement: A Tatabányai Cementés Mészművek Dolgozóinak Lapja*, 2 February 1954, 3.

37. KEMÖL, XXXV.32f.4/12ő.e., 33.

38. Preizler, "Az Újvárosban is akad javítani való!"

39. OSA, 300/40/4/12, Item No. 3656/54, 4.

40. "Néhány probléma a Kertvárosból," *Harc a Szénért: Tatabánya Város Pártbizottságának Lapja*, 13 November 1953, 3.

41. OSA, 300/40/4/12, Item No. 3656/54, 4.

42. "A saját házban," *Harc a Szénért: Tatabánya Város Pártbizottságának Lapja,* 13 May 1954, 4.

43. "A családiház építéséről," 3.

44. Mark Pittaway, "Stalinism, Working-Class Housing and Individual Autonomy: The Encouragement of Private House Building in Hungary's Mining Areas," in *Style and Socialism: Modernity and Material Culture in Post-War Eastern Europe,* ed. Susan E. Reid and David Crowley (Oxford: Berg, 2000), 49–64.

45. PtSzL, XII.20f.163d./1955, Komárommegye közellátásának helyzete, 2.

46. MOL, M-KS-276f.65/251ő.e., 178–82; KEMÖL, XXXV.32f.4/53ő.e., 10–11.

47. Visontai, "Tatabánya," 149.

48. *Komárom megye legfontosabb statisztikai adatai, 1956* (Tatabánya: KSH Komárommegyei Igazgatósága, 1957), 69.

49. PtSzL, XII.20f.163d./1955, Komárommegye közellátásának helyzete, 1.

50. "Ne kifogásokat tegyen, hanem árut bizotsítson kereskedelmünk," *Harc a Szénért: Tatabánya Város Pártbizottságának Lapja,* 18 December 1953, 4.

51. "Több bútort – nagyobb választékot a bányászoknak," *Harc a Szénért: Tatabánya Város Pártbizottságának Lapja,* 16 October 1953, 4.

52. PtSzL, XII.30f.745d./1954, A Tatabányai szénbányászati trösztbizottság II. negyedévi jelentése, Tatabánya, 1954. július 8., 2.

53. OSA, 300/40/4/12, Item No.8083/54, 12.

54. PtSzL, XII.20f.151d./1954, Építő és Faipari Dolgozók Szakszervezete Komárommegyei Bizottsága. Beszámoló Jelentés a III ¼ eves szakszervezeti munkáról, 3.

55. PtSzL, XII.20f.151d./1954, Jegyzőkönyv, felvették Tatabánya-Újvárosban a Megyei Tanács tanácstermében 1954.VII.2.-án a Szakszervezet által tartott műszaki, gazdasági és adminisztrativ értekezletről, 6.

56. *Komárom megye legfontosabb statisztikai adatai, 1956,* 81.

57. Ibid., 69–72.

58. PtSzL, XII.20f.146d./1954, Jelentés a Tatabányai-Dorogi bányaipari dolgozók keresetének alakulásáról, 1.

59. PtSzL, VI.867f., Becker Ferenc (hereafter, 1/b-448), 8.

60. PtSzL, XII.20f.146d./1954, Jelentés a Tatabányai-Dorogi bányaipari dolgozók keresetének alakulásáról, 4.

61. MOL, XXIX-F-107-j/116d., Tatabányai Szénbányászati Tröszt, Bérés Normaosztály. Vizsgálati jelentés, 1954. november 8–10 és 11-én.

62. PtSzL, XII.30f.755d./1954, Jelentés a Tatabányai kiszállásomról, 1954.jan.hó 24–27-ig, 1.

63. KEMÖL, XXXV.36f.3/10ő.e., 156.

64. PtSzL, XII.30f.769d./1954, Jegyzőkönyv felvétett: 1954. XII.10.-én a Trösztbizottság helységében megtartott elnökségi ülésről, 3.

65. PtSzL, XII.30f.745d./1954, A Tatabányai szénbányászati trösztbizottság II. negyedévi jelentése, Tatabánya, 1954. július 8., 3.

66. MOL, M-KS-276f.94/745ő.e., 104.

67. MOL, XXIX-F-107-e/3d., Tatabányai Jogi Titkárság, Helyben, 1953. november 4.

68. MOL, XXIX-F-107-j/116d., 101/1954.szám. Körrendelet.

69. PtSzL, XII.30f.806d./1954, Feljegyzés Zentai Elvtársnak: A Szénbányászat Jelenlegi Helyzetéről, 1.

70. PtSzL, XII.30f.806d./1954, Statisztikai csoport. Feljegyzés a halálos balesetekről a szénbányászatban.

71. PtSzL, XII.20f.165d./1955, Jelentés a bérezés egyszerűsítésének, és összevonásának levitele, annak eredményei és hibái, 1–2.

72. MOL, M-KS-276f.94/829ő.e., 213, 271.

73. MOL, M-KS-276f.94/831ő.e., 125–31.

74. KEMÖL, XXXV.32f.4/29ő.e., 48.

75. PtSzL, XII.30f.923d./1955, Jegyzőkönyv felvéve: 1955. október 8.-án a trösztbizottság helyiségében megtartott elnökségi ülésen, 3.

76. ZML, Az MDP Zalaegerszeg Járási Bizottságának iratai (Papers of the MDP Zalaegerszeg District Committee, hereafter, XXXV.58f.)3/16ő.e., Jegyzőkönyv, készült Nagylengyelben 1955 október 5-én a Kőolajtermelő Vállalat tanácstermében tartott müszaki értekezleten, 1.

77. ZML, XXXV.61f.4/2/110.e., Hozzászólások a lovászi Társadalombiztosítási Tanács beszámolójához, 9.

78. ZML, XXXV.57f.1/80ő.e., 58–59.

79. ZML, XXXV.57f.1/80ő.e., 63.

80. ZML, XXXV.57f.1/80ő.e., 73.

81. ZML, XXXV.57f.1/80ő.e., 56.

82. "Zalaegerszeg, 1954. március 10. A Zala Megyei Tanács V.B. Mezőgazdasági Osztályának jelentése a zalai termelőszövetkezetek és termelőcsoportok helyzetéről 1951-től terjedően," in Káli, ed., Dokumentumok Zala megye történetéből 1947–1956, 355.

83. "A bázakerettyei pártszervezetek harca a munkafegyelem megszilárdításáért," Olajmunkás, 30 August 1953, 2.

84. Quoted in Rainer, Nagy Imre: politikai életrajz; második kötet 1953–1958, 11.

85. "Zalaegerszeg, 1953. szeptember 17. Az MDP Zala Megyei Bizottságának levele a KV Mezőgazdasági Osztályához, a zalai tsz-ek és a tszcs-k helyzetéről," in Káli, ed., Dokumentumok Zala megye történetéből 1947–1956, 338–39; "(Zalaegerszeg), 1953. augusztus 7. Az MDP Zala Megyei Bizottságának levele a földművelésügyi miniszternek, a mezőgazdasági érintő új intézkedések hatására kialakult helyzetről," in ibid., 319–20.

86. "A bázakerettyei pártszervezetek harca a munkafegyelem megszilárdításáért," 2.

87. "Zalaegerszeg, 1953. július 13. Az ÁVH Zala Megyei Osztályának jelentése az MDP megyei bizottságának a lakosság hangulatáról, Rákosi Mátyásnak a budapesti pártaktíván elmondott beszéde után," in Káli, ed., Dokumentumok Zala megye történetéből 1947–1956, 313.

88. ZML, XXXV.57f.1/73ő.e., 117–20. The official account of the match recorded the draw but was silent on the circumstances in which it occurred; see "Sport," Olajmunkás, 30 August 1953, 4.

89. ZML, XXXV.61f.4/2/13ő.e., Jegyzőkönyv, felvéve Lovásziban, 1954. július 29.-én az MDP Üzemi Pártbizottság, Végrehajtóbizottságának vezetőségi ülésén, 7.

90. ZML, XXXV.61f.3/2/2ő.e., MDP. Üzemi Pártbizottság, Bázakerettye. Az üzemi párt-bizottság beszámolója a központi vezetőségének határozata értelmében, part szervezetünk és szervünk helyzetének kapcsolatában, 1–7.

91. Sándor Szalai, "A tervteljesítés az életszinvonal további emelkedésének az alapja," *Olajmunkás,* 15 October 1953, 1.

92. "A dolgozók panaszolják . . . ," *Olajmunkás,* 30 September 1953, 3.

93. ZML, XXXV.57f.2/Ipar/10ő.e., Feljegyzés vállalataink bér, szociális, kulturális, munkavédelmi és egyéb meglévő problémáiról, Zalaegerszeg, 1953. október 3., 1.

94. ZML, XXXV.61f.3/2/11ő.e., Jelentés a KV határozatából a part népnevelő munkájának megjavitására vonatkozólag, 1.

95. ZML, XXXV.61f.3/2/16ő.e., Jegyzőkönyv felvétetett Bázakerettyén 1955. január 31.-én az étterem nagytermében megtartott összevont taggyülésen, 1.

96. ZML, Az MSZMP Zala Megyei Bizottság Archiviuma, Vegyes Iratok, 3360D/KSH Jelentések, Központi Statisztikai Hivatal, Zala Megyei Igazgatósága. Táblázatok a megye gazdasági helyzetéről. 1955.I.félév, 38–40.

97. Erdmann, *Begyűjtés, beszolgáltatás Magyarországon,* 182–236.

98. "A lakosság fogyasztása és a reálbérek, reáljövedelmek alakulása 1955-ben, és a 1949–1955 időszakban," 12.

99. OSA, 300/40/4/22, Item No. 4154/55, 6.

100. "A Lakosság Fogyasztása és a Reálbérek, Reáljövedelmek Alakulása 1955-ben, és a 1949–1955 időszakban," 46.

101. ZML, XXXV.57f.2/Ipar/63ő.e., Kimutatás a Zalamegyében engedélyezett építési kölcsönről, Zalaegerszeg, 1954. június 25.

102. ZML, XXXV.57f.2/Ipar/66ő.e., 37/9–633sz. Levél, 3.aug.4.

103. ZML, Az MSZMP Zala Megyei Bizottság Archiviuma, Vegyes Iratok, 3360D/KSH Jelentések, Központi Statisztikai Hivatal, Zala Megyei Igazgatósága. Táblázatok a megye gazdasági helyzetéről. 1955.I.félév, 40.

104. ZML, XXXV.61f.3/4/5/2ő.e., Jegyzőkönyv készült 1954. szeptember 22-én a csőszerelő alapszervezet taggyülésen. Hozzászólások, 1–2.

105. ZML, Az MDP Zalaegerszeg Városi Bizottságának iratai (Papers of the MDP Zalaegerszeg City Committee, hereafter, XXXV.63f.)3/2/2ő.e., Jegyzőkönyv készült a Zalai Ásványolajipari Vállalat MDP helyiségében 1954. november 17-én megtatott taggyülés alkalmával, 3.

106. ZML, XXXV.61f.4/2/16ő.e., címtelen beszámoló, 3.

107. ZML, XXXV.63f.3/2/2ő.e., Jegyzőkönyv készült a Zalai Kőolajipari Vállalat hivata-los helyiségében 1955 június 29-én, 1–2.

108. ZML, XXXV.58f.3/16ő.e., Munkafegyelem. Nagylengyel, 1955. június 8.

109. ZML, XXXV.58f.3/32ő.e., Jegyzőkönyv készült Nagylengyelben, 1954. március 10.-én 17 órakor, a "MASZOLAJ" Kőolajtermelő Vállalat üzemi pártszervezetének pártvezetőség ujjáválasztó taggyülésen, 2–3.

110. ZML, Dunántúli Kőolajtermelő Vállalat Gellénháza (Gellénháza Branch of the Transdanubian Oil Production Enterprise, hereafter, XXIX.8f.)1d., 55.sz., 3–4.

111. Az MSZMP Zala Megyei Bizottság Archiviuma, Vegyes Iratok, 3360D/KSH

Jelentések, Központi Statisztikai Hivatal, Zala Megyei Igazgatósága. Táblázatok a megye gazdasági helyzetéről. 1955.I.félév, 20, 24. See also ZML, XXXV.61f.3/2/3ő.e., Beszámoló vállalatunk I. félévi munkájáról.

112. ZML, XXXV.61f.3/2/18ő.e., Jelentés üzemünkben az állami fegyelemről, 3–4.

113. ZML, XXXV.58f.3/2ő.e., címtelen beszámoló, 4.

114. Zsuzsanna Varga, "Érdek, érdekeltség, érdekérvényesítés a termelőszövetkezetekben, különös tekintettel a zalai szövetkezetekre," in *Zalai történeti tanulmányok*, ed. Káli, 363–64.

115. ZML, XXXV.61f.2/27ő.e., 371F-/1–201. Letenye, 1955. szept.15, 1.

116. BFL, XXXV.176f.2/194/26ő.e., 196.

117. BFL, XXXV.176f.2/194/26ő.e., 197.

118. BFL, XXXV.176f.2/194/24ő.e., 100.

119. BFL, XXXV.176f.2/194/24ő.e., 219.

120. Pető and Szakács, *A hazai gazdaság négy évtizedének története*, 195–96.

121. Dezső Csikvári, "Látogatás az újpesti Állami Áruház elektromos osztályán," *Izzó*, 12 March 1954, 3.

122. "Látogatás az újpesti Állami Áruház cipőosztályán: tavaszi cipővásárlás és problémái," *Futószalag*, 13 March 1954, 3.

123. Ferenc Schrődl, "Új minőségi bérezés bevezetése," *Futószalag*, 15 August 1953, 3.

124. BFL, XXXV.176f.2/190/10ő.e., 7.

125. BFL, XXXV.95f.4/62ő.e., 21–24.

126. BFL, XXXV.95f.4/62ő.e., 10.

127. BFL, XXXV.95f.2/77ő.e., 35.

128. BFL, XXXV.176f.2/190/10ő.e., 85.

129. MOL, M-KS-276f.65/251ő.e., 169.

130. Erzsébet Őrszigethy, *Asszonyok férfisorban* (Budapest: Szépirodalmi Könyvkiadó, 1986), 99–158.

131. OSA, 300/40/4/43. Item No. 7095/54, 6.

132. "Vidám hangulat az 'Izzó-buszon,'" *Izzó*, 5 March 1954, 3.

133. BFL, XXXV.176f.2/212/13ő.e., 61.

134. BFL, XXXV.95f.2/77ő.e., 32.

135. BFL, XXIX/321f.3d., Feljegyzés.

136. CUL, RBML, BAR, CURPH, Interview No. 455, 8.

137. MOL, M-KS-288f.25/1957/6ő.e., 112; MOL, M-KS-276f.65/251ő.e., 174.

138. BFL, XXXV.176f.2/190/10ő.e., 11.

139. BFL, XXXV.95f.4/57ő.e., 127.

140. BFL, XXXV.176f.2/212/19ő.e., 29.

141. "Keresztesi Ilona ifjúmunkás jó munkájával a választási békeműszak sikeréért harcol," *Pamut Újság*, 23 April 1953, 1; BFL, XXXV.176f.2/236/17ő.e., 38.

142. BFL, XXXV.176f.2/236/17ő.e., 41.

143. BFL, XXXV.176f.2/236/17ő.e., 37.

144. "Amiről sok igazolatlan hiányzó elfeledkezett …," *Pamut Újság*, 3 September 1953, 1.

145. BFL, XXXV.95f.4/57ő.e., 65.

146. BFL, XXXV.176f.2/212/19ő.e., 242–43.

147. "Szövödénkben romlott a minőségi munka – ezzel is növekszik az önköltség," *Pamut Újság*, 12 August 1954, 3.

148. "Tűrhetetlen körülmények között dolgoznak a vigonyfonoda tépő dolgozói," *Pamut Újság*, 9 July 1953, 3.

149. BFL, XXXV.176f.2/212/19ő.e., 243.

150. BFL, XXXV.176f.2/236/17ő.e., 44.

151. Ernő Gerő, "Magasabb termelékenységgel, alacsonyabb önköltséggel a népjólétért," in *A Magyar Dolgozók Pártja III: kongresszusának rövidített jegyzőkönyve*, 2d ed. (Budapest: Szikra, 1954), 163.

152. Illés Esztán, "Harcoljunk gyártmányainak jobb minőségéért," *Futószalag*, 1 August 1953) 3.

153. "Javítsák meg a gépkarbantartást," *Futószalag*, 1 August 1953, 3.

154. "Hetven darab fogaskerék gyászjelentése," *Izzó*, 16 October 1954, 3.

155. CUL, RBML, BAR, CURPH, Interview No. 153, 7.

156. BFL, XXXV.176f.2/194/25ő.e., 154.

157. BFL, XXXV.176f.2/191/11ő.e., 111.

158. BFL, XXXV.176f.2/194/27ő.e., 293.

159. BFL, XXXV.176f.2/191/9ő.e., 27–28.

160. Pető and Szakács, *A hazai gazdaság négy évtizedének története*, 196.

161. György Földes, "Egyszerűsítés, mechanizmus és iparirányítás, 1953–1956," *Párttörténeti Közlemények* 30, no. 2 (1984): 72–108; László Szamuely, ed., *A magyar közgazdasági gondolat fejlődése 1954–1978: a szocialista gazdaság mechanizmusának kutatása* (Budapest: Közgazdasági és Jogi Könyvkiadó, 1986), 57–153; BFL, XXXV.95f.4/110ő.e., 78.

162. OSA, 300/40/4/14, Item No. 673/57, 1.

163. BFL, XXXV.176f.2/194/26ő.e., 192–94.

164. OSA, 300/40/4/14, Item No. 6519/56, 5.

165. BFL, XXXV.176f.2/194/26ő.e., 202.

166. OSA, 300/40/4/14, Item No. 6519/56, 5.

## 7. The Process of Revolution, February–November 1956

1. FML, Az MDP Dunai Vasmű épitkezés és Dunapentele / Sztálinváros / Városi Bizottságának iratai (Papers of the Danube Steel Works and Dunapentele-Sztálinváros City Committee, hereafter, XXXV.17f.)2/8ő.e., A rendikivüli taggyülésen felvetett kérdések, 1–10.

2. Zoltán Ripp, "Jugoszlávia," in *Evolúció és revolúció: Magyarország és a nemzetközi politika 1956-ban,* ed. Csaba Békés (Budapest: 1956-os Intézet – Gondolat Kiadó, 2007), 55–82.

3. BFL, XXXV.176f.2/154ő.e., 274.

4. András B. Hegedűs and János M. Rainer, eds., *A Petőfi Kör vitai hiteles jegyzőkönyvek alapján: IV. Partizántalálkozó-sajtóvita* (Budapest: Múszák Kiadó -1956-os Intézet, 1991); Gábor Gyáni, "A forradalom társadalomtörténeti paradoxonjai," in *Ezerkilencszázötvenhat az újabb történeti irodalomban: tanulmányok,* ed. Gábor Gyáni and János M. Rainer (Budapest: 1956-os Intézet, 2007), 94–95.

5. MOL, M-KS-276f.66/23ő.e., 63; quoted in Lomax, *Hungary 1956*, 45.

6. For two provincial examples, see Erzsébet Csomor, *1956 Zalaegerszegen* (Zalaegerszeg: Millecentenárium Közalapítvány, 2001), 25–33; and "Győr-Sopron megyei Ügyészség, 1957 Tük. 0019 szám. Feljegyzés," in József Bana, ed., *Győr 1956 III: Munkástanácsvezetők per a Győri Megyei Bíróság előtt, 1957–1958* (Győr: Győr Megyei Jogú Város Önkormányzata, 2002), 5–6.

7. For one example, see ZML, Zala Megyei Bíróság Büntetőperes iratai (Papers of Criminal Trials held at the Zala County Court, hereafter, XXV.19.ZMB.) B.322/1957 – Gáti József, Zalamegyei Ügyészség Zalaegerszeg. 1957. Bül.59/3 szám. Izgatás büntette miatt Gáti József.

8. Frigyes Kahler et al., eds., *Sortűzek 1956,* 2d ed. (Budapest and Lakitelek: Igazságügyi Minisztérium – Antológia Kiadó, 1993).

9. Adapted from "Halottak – Mosonmagyaróvár Anyakönyvi Hivatal," reprinted in Kahler et al., eds., *Sortűzek 1956,* 61–66.

10. George Paloczi-Horváth, *The Undefeated* (London: Eland, 1993), 294.

11. Zoltán Ripp, "A pártvezetés végnapjai," in *Ötvenhat októbere és a hatalom: a Magyar Dolgozók Pártja vezető testületeinek dokumentumai 1956 október 24–október 28,* ed. Julianna Horváth and Zoltán Ripp (Budapest: Napvilág Kiadó, 1997), 219–57.

12. "Magyarok, munkások, polgártársak: magyar nemzeti bizotmány," reprinted in Lajos Izsák, József Szabó, and Róbert Szabó, eds., *1956 plakátjai és röplapjai: október 22–november 5* (Budapest: Zrínyi Kiadó, 1991), 268.

13. Sándor Horváth, "Kollektív erőszak és városi térhasználat 1956-ban," *Múltunk* 51, no. 4 (2006): 268–89.

14. "The 'Sixteen Points' Prepared by Hungarian Students, October 22–23, 1956," in Békés, Byrne, and Rainer, eds., *1956 Hungarian Revolution,* 188–90; BFL, Az MSzMP Budapest IV. Kerületi Bizottságának iratai (Papers of the 4th District of Budapest Committee of the Hungarian Socialist Workers' Party, hereafter, XXXV.9f.)1957/15ő.e., 102.

15. OSzK Kt., 1956-os gy., Bp.NB, 4491/74, 1d./6, Budapesti Rendőrfőkapitányság Politikai Nyomozó Osztály, Vizsgálati Alosztály. Jegyzőkönyv Lészai/Lothringer/Béla őrizetes kihallgatásáról. Budapest, 1957. augusztus 23., 1.

16. 1956-os Intézet, OHA 449, 5.

17. OSzK Kt., 1956-os gy., Bp.NB, 4491/74, 1d./6, Budapesti Rendőrfőkapitányság Politikai Nyomozó Osztály, Vizsgálati Alosztály. Jegyzőkönyv Lészai/Lothringer/Béla őrizetes kihallgatásáról. Budapest, 1957. augusztus 23., 1.

18. OSA, 300/40/4/14, Item No. 6519/56, 5.

19. BFL, XXXV.176f.2/158ő.e., 32.

20. BFL, XXXV.176f.2/154ő.e., 65.

21. BFL, XXXV.176f.2/147ő.e., 16.

22. BFL, XXXV.176f.2/154ő.e., 191.

23. Hegedüs and Rainer, eds., *A Petőfi Kör vitai hiteles jegyzőkönyvek alapján: IV. Partizántalálkozó-sajtóvita.*

24. BFL, XXXV.176f.2/154ő.e., 188.

25. BFL, XXXV.176f.2/154ő.e., 274.

26. BFL, XXXV.176f.2/151ő.e., 305.

27. Iván Pető, "Ellentmondásos kiútkeresés: az 1956-ban elfogadott második ötéves terv koncepciójához," in *Válság és megújulás: gazdaság, társadalom és politika Magyarországon; az MSzMP 25 éve*, ed. Henrik Vass (Budapest: Kossuth Könyvkiadó, 1982), 35–50.

28. "Levelek a második ötéves terv irányelveiről," *Izzó*, 5 May 1956, 1.

29. BFL, XXXV.176f.2/149ő.e., 100.

30. BFL, XXXV.176f.2/147ő.e., 352–53.

31. BFL, XXXV.176f.2/147ő.e., 350.

32. László Revitz, "Új tervezési rendszer – vállalatunknál," *Futószalag*, 5 May 1956, 3.

33. "A marxista politikai gazdaságtan időszerű kérdéseiről és a második ötéves terv irányelveiről," in András B. Hegedűs and János M. Rainer, eds., *A Petőfi Kör vitai hiteles jegyzőkönyvek alapján: I. Két közgazdasági vita* (Budapest: Kelenföld Kiadó-ELTE, 1989), 37–102.

34. "A Központi Vezetősége Határozata: Pártegységgel a Szocialista Demokráciaért," in Habuda, Rákosi, Székely, and Varga, eds., *A Magyar Dolgozók Pártja határozatai*, 446; PtSzL, XII.20f./71d./1956, Javaslatok az üzemi szakszervezeti szervek önállóságának, hatáskörének növelésére.

35. "Régi harcos szemmel látom," *Futószalag*, 22 September 1956, 3.

36. BFL, XXXV.176f.2/149ő.e., 4.

37. Ifj. László Kronstein, "Így látom én – vita az önállóságról," *Izzó*, 6 October 1956, 3.

38. MOL, M-KS-276f.66/23ő.e., 42–43.

39. BFL, XXXV.176f.2/149ő.e., 7–8.

40. 1956-os Intézet, OHA 449, 5.

41. OSzK Kt., 1956-os gy., Bp.NB, 4491/74, 3d./4, Budapest Rendőrfőkapitányság Politikai Nyomozó Osztály, Vizsgálati Osztály. Jegyzőkönyv Kollár József kihallgatásáról. Budapest, 1957. augusztus 1, 1.

42. BFL, XXXV.9f.1957/15ő.e., 102.

43. 1956-os Intézet, OHA 449, 9.

44. OSzK Kt., 1956-os gy., Bp.NB, 4491/74, 1d./8, Bp.Főkap.Pol.Nyom.Osztály Vizsg. alo.57 nov. 6, Bp., 1–2.

45. BFL, XXXV.9f.1957/15ő.e., 102.

46. OSzK Kt., 1956-os gy., Bp.NB, 4491/74, 2d./6, Budapesti Rendőrfőkapitányság Politikai Nyomozó Osztály VI/7 csop. Jegyzőkönyv Bpest, 1957.VI.24. Tóth Gábor gyanusitott kihallgatásáról, 2.

47. OSzK Kt., 1956-os gy., Bp.NB, 4491/74, 2d./3, A Budapesti Fővárosi Bíróság Népbírósági Tanácsa. T.NB.8017/1958/III Jegyzőkönyv készült a szervezkedés és egyéb büncselekmények miatt Kósa Pál és 32 társa ellenindított büntető ügyben a Budapesti Fővárosi Biróság Népbírósági Tanácsánál 1958. április 30-án megtartott zárt tárgyalásról, 4.

48. OSzK Kt., 1956-os gy., Bp.NB, 4491/74, 2d/3., A Budapest Fővárosi Biróság Népbírósági Tanácsa, T.NB.8017/1958/III sz. Jegyzőkönyv készült szervezkedés és egyéb büncselekmények miatt Kósa Pál és 29 társa ellen inditott bünügyben a Budapesti Fővárosi Biróság Népbírósági Tanácsanak 1958 április 30.-án reggel 9 órára tüzött zárt tárgyalásáról, 4–6.

49. BFL, XXXV.9f.1957/15ő.e., 102.

50. PtSzL, Az 1956-os gyűjtemény (1956 Collection, hereafter, IX.290f.)37ő.e., 57.

51. For the deeds of the workers' council in its first three days of operation, see Dobricia Cosic, *7 nap Budapesten 1956: október 23–30* (Budapest: Bethlen Gábor Könyvkiadó, 1989), 80–82; Bill Lomax, ed., *Workers' Councils in 1956,* trans. Bill Lomax and Julian Schöpflin (New York: Columbia University Press, 1990), 15–17.

52. PtSzL, IX.29of.39ő.e., 1–2.

53. János Kenedi and László Varga, eds., *A forradalom hangja: Magyarországi rádióadások 1956. október 23–november 9* (Budapest: Századvég Kiadó-Nyilvánosság Klub, 1989), 174; PtSzL, IX.29of.37ő.e., 95, 107.

54. OSzK Kt. 1956-os gy., Bp.NB, 4491/74, 3d./8, Budapesti Fővárosi Biróság Népbirósági Tanácsa NB.II.8017/1958.szám. L. Jegyzőkönyv készült a szervezkedés és egyéb bűncselekmények miatt Kósa Pál és 29 társa ellenindított büntető ügyben a Budapesti Fővárosi Biróság Népbirósági Tanácsánál 1958. október 13-án megtartott zárt tárgyalásról, 11; OSzK Kt., 1956-os gy., Bp.NB, 4491/74, 2d./6, B.M. Budapesti Rendőrfőkapitányság Pol.Nyom. Oszt.Vizsg.Alosztálya. Jegyzőkönyv Sohonyai János gyanusitott kihallgatásáról. Budapest, 1957. augusztus 15-én, 4.

55. OSzK Kt. 1956-os gy., Bp.NB, 4491/74, 3d./5, Budapesti Rendőrfőkapitányság Politikai Nyomozó Alosztály Vizsgálati Alosztály. Jegyzőkönyv, Budapest, 1957. június 10-én, 3.

56. PtSzL, IX.29of.39ő.e., 1–11.

57. PtSzL, IX.29of.52ő.e., 5–20.

58. OSzK Kt., 1956-os gy., Bp.NB, 4491/74, 3d./8, Budapest Fővárosi Biróság Népbirósági Tanácsa NB.II.8017/1958. LXXXVIII Jegyzőkönyv készült a szervezkedés és egyéb bűncselekmények miatt Kósa Pál és 32 társa ellenindított büntető ügyben a Budapesti Fővárosi Biróság Népbirósági Tanácsánál 1959. február 9-én megtartott zárt tárgyalásról, 3.

59. Ibid., 3–4.

60. OSzK Kt., 1956-os gy., Bp.NB, 4491/74, 3d./8, Budapest Fővárosi Biróság Népbirósági Tanácsa NB.II.8017/1958. LXXXI Jegyzőkönyv készült a szervezkedés és egyéb bűncselekmények miatt Kósa Pál és 32 társa ellenindított büntető ügyben a Budapesti Fővárosi Biróság Népbirósági Tanácsánál 1959. január 2-án megtartott zárt tárgyalásról, 2.

61. KEMÖL, Az MSzMP Tatabánya Városi Bizottságának iratai (Papers of the Tatabánya City Committee of the Hungarian Socialist Workers' Party, hereafter, XXXV.2f.)3/1957/14ő.e., 9.

62. OSzK Kt., 1956-os gy., Komárom-Esztergom megye (Komárom-Esztergom County, hereafter, 412.VIIf.), 1d., Az Esztergom Megyei Biróság Elnökétől. 1958. El.IX.22.szám. 1958. évi áprilitis havi jelentés az Igazságügyminiszter Elvtársnak, 2.

63. KEMÖL, XXXV.2f.3/1957/14ő.e., 9.

64. OSzK Kt., 1956-os gy., 412.VIIf.7d., Városi Tanács VB. Elnökétől, Oroszlány. 775/1957. Tárgy: Az ellenforradalmi események leirása, 1.

65. OSzK Kt., 1956-os gy., 412.VIIf.7d., 4991/1957. Tatabánya Városi Tanács Végrehajtóbizottsága. Az 1956.okt.23.-i és ezt követő ellenforradalmi események leirása, 1.

66. 1956-os Intézet, OHA Asztalos János (hereafter, 484), 44.

67. KEMÖL, XXXV.32f.4/16ő.e., 114–19.

68. MOL, XXIX-F-107-m/54d., Kimutatás az 1957. október 1-i állapotnak megfelelő adatokról.

69. KEMÖL, Az MSZMP Komárom Megyei Bizottságának iratai (Papers of the Komárom County Committee of the Hungarian Socialist Workers' Party, hereafter, XXXV.1f.)2/1958/5ő.e., 63.

70. OSA, 300/40/4/12, Item No. 06687/53, 3–6.

71. "Az Újvárosban lakó dolgozóink is akarnak szórakozni," *Tatabányai Cement: A Tatabányai Cementés Mészművek Dolgozóinak Lapja*, 5 September 1956, 2.

72. PtSzL, XII.20f.168d./1956, Jelentés a falusi osztályharc helyzetéről.

73. "A Tatabányai Szénbányászati Tröszt ötéves tervjavaslata," *Harc a Szénért: Tatabánya Város Pártbizottságának Lapja*, 18 May 1956, 1.

74. PtSzL, XII.20f.171d./1956, Feljegyzés az ü.b. önállóságának növeléséhez, 3.

75. "Kik kaphatnak 'kiváló dolgozó' címet, oklevélet és jelvényt?" *Tatabányai Cement: A Tatabányai Cementés Mészművek Dolgozóinak Lapja*, 18 April 1956, 2.

76. "A cementgyári sztahanovista feltétel meghatározása a III-ik negyedévre," *Tatabányai Cement: A Tatabányai Cementés Mészművek Dolgozóinak Lapja*, 18 July 1956, 3.

77. "Megindult a '100 000 Tonnás Nagyverseny!'" *Harc a Szénért: Tatabánya Város Pártbizottságának Lapja*, 10 August 1956, 1.

78. KEMÖL, XXXV.32f.4/22ő.e., 61.

79. MOL, XXIX-F-107-m/53d., Munkások és alkalmazottak létszámának megoszlása 1956. június havi keresetük szerint, 1915/1956.

80. József Bertalan, "Létesítsünk Tatabányán edényvagy szövőgyárat," *Harc a Szénért: Tatabánya Város Pártbizottságának Lapja*, 22 June 1956, 4.

81. "'Vásárló' szemmel . . . ," *Harc a Szénért: Tatabánya Város Pártbizottságának Lapja*, 27 July 1956, 4.

82. Antal Eichhardt, "Vannak, akik ebből is megélnek. . . ," *Tatabányai Cement: A Tatabányai Cementés Mészművek Dolgozóinak Lapja*, 8 August 1956, 3.

83. Sándor Torjai, "Minden pletyka ellen! A Graf-ügy – avagy egy bányászcsalád furcsa története," *Harc a Szénért: Tatabánya Város Pártbizottságának Lapja*, 22 June 1956, 2.

84. OSzK Kt., 1956-os gy., Győri Megyei Bíróság Népbírósági Tanácsanak anyaga (Papers of the People's Court Council of the Győr County Court, hereafter, Gy.NB), Klébert Márton és társai (Márton Klébert and codefendants, hereafter, 1127/1957), 2d., B.M. Komárom Megyei Rendőrfőkapitányság Politikai Osztály, Vizsgálati Alosztály. Jegyzőkönyv, Dr. Klébert Márton kihallgatásáról, Ttbánya, 1957. június 4., 1–2.

85. "Megyeszerte zavartalan a termelés," *Komárom Megyei Dolgozók Lapja*, 25 October 1956, 2.

86. "Megvédjük a nép hatalmát," *Komárom Megyei Dolgozók Lapja*, 25 October 1956, 1.

87. "Látogatás a MÁVAUT dolgozóinál," *Harc a Szénért: Tatabánya Város Pártbizottságának Lapja*, 10 February 1956, 4.

88. KEMÖL, XXXV.2f.3/1958/23ő.e., 4.

89. "Hogyan történt? Az ellenforradalom tatabányai napjaiból," *Komárom Megyei Hírlap*, 26 January 1957, 4.

90. OSzK Kt., 1956-os gy., Gy.NB, 1127/1957, 3d., B.M. Komárom Megyei Rendőrfőkapitányság Politikai Osztály, Vizsgálati Alosztály. Jegyzőkönyv, Dr. Timea Endre kihallgatásáról, Ttbánya, 1957. jún. 14., 4.

91. OSzK Kt., 1956-os gy., Gy.NB, 1127/1957, 2d., B.M. Komárom Megyei Rendőrfőkapitányság Politikai Osztály, Vizsgálati Alosztály. Jegyzőkönyv, Dr. Klébert Márton kihallgatásáról, Ttbánya, 1957. június 4., 5.

92. László Gyüszi, "A forradalom forgószele egy vidéki szerkesztőségben (emlékezet és napló)," in László Gyüszi, Tatabánya 1956 (Tatabánya: A Kultsár István Társadalomtudományi és Kiadói Alapítvány, 1994), 90.

93. OSzK Kt., 1956-os gy., 412.VIIf.3d., Esztergom Megyei Biróság 457/1957, A rendőrség Tatabánya Városi kapitánysága. Szám:381/1957. Gyanúsított kihallgatásáról jegyzőkönyv készült Tatabánya 1957 évi július hónap 20 napján 16 órakor Izgatás büntettével gyanúsított Farbinger Teréz kihallgatása alkalmával, 27.

94. OSzK Kt., 1956-os gy., 412.VIIf.4d., Komárommegyei Ügyészség Esztergom. 1957. Tük.Bfü.09.szám. Határozat, Esztergom, 1957 augusztus 23.

95. 1956-os Intézet, OHA 417, 17; OSzK Kt., 1956-os gy., 412.VIIf.1d., Az Esztergom Megyei Biróság Elnökétől. 1958.El.IX.B.27.sz. Tárgy: 1958. évi május havi jelentés. Hiv.sz.: 334/1957.I.M.I/1., 2–3.

96. 1956-os Intézet, OHA 417, 20; "Hogyan történt? Az ellenforradalom tatabányai napjaiból," Komárom Megyei Hírlap, 26 January 1957, 4.

97. Pál Germuska, "Komárom Megye," in A vidék forradalma 1956, II. kötet, ed. Attila Szakolczai (Budapest: 1956-os Intézet-Budapest Főváros Levéltára, 2006), 223–24.

98. Quoted in Kenedi and Varga, eds., A forradalom hangja, 44.

99. OSzK Kt., 1956-os gy., Gy.NB, 1127/1957, 5d., B.M. Komárom Megyei Rendőrfőkapitányság Politikai Osztály, Vizsgálati Alosztály. Jegyzőkönyv, Horváth János kihallgatásáról, Tatabánya, 1957.máj.20., 1–5.

100. OSzK Kt., 1956-os gy., Gy.NB, 1127/1957, 2d., Tatabánya dolgozó népéhez!

101. OSzK Kt., 1956-os gy., Gy.NB, 1127/1957, 1d., Győr megyei biróság népbirósági tanácsa Nb.1122/1957.3sz. Jegyzőkönyv, készült a népi demokratikus államrend megdöntésére irányuló szervezkedés vezetésének büntette miatt Dr. Klébert Mátron és társa ellen inditott bünügyben a győri megyei biróság népbirósági tanácsa előtt 1957. október 26-napján megtartott nyilvános tárgyalásról, 3.

102. OSzK Kt., 1956-os gy., Gy.NB, 1127/1957, 2d., B.M. Komárom Megyei Rendőrfőkapitányság Politikai Osztály, Vizsgálati Alosztály. Jegyzőkönyv, Dr. Klébert Márton kihallgatásáról, Ttbánya, 1957. június 4., 2–4.

103. Quoted in Gyüszi, Tatabánya 1956, 33.

104. OSzK Kt., 1956-os gy., Gy.NB, 1127/1957, 6d., B.M. Komárom Megyei Rendőrfőkapitányság Politikai Osztály, Vizsgálati Alosztály. Jegyzőkönyv, Szerdahelyi Pál tanu kihallgatásáról, Tatabánya, 1957. július 4-én., 1–4.

105. OSzK Kt., 1956-os gy., Gy.NB, 1127/1957, 1d., Győr megyei biróság népbirósági tanácsa Nb.1122/1957.3sz. Jegyzőkönyv, készült a népi demokratikus államrend megdöntésére irányuló szervezkedés vezetésének büntette miatt Dr. Klébert Mátron és társa ellen inditott bünügyben a győri megyei biróság népbirósági tanácsa előtt 1957. október 26-napján megtartott nyilvános tárgyalásról, 4; OSzK Kt., 1956-os gy., Gy.NB, 1127/1957, 1d., Győr megyei biróság népbirósági tanácsa Nb.1122/1957.3sz. Jegyzőkönyv, készült a népi demokratikus államrend megdöntésére irányuló szervezkedés vezetésének büntette miatt

Dr. Klébert Mátron és társa ellen inditott bünügyben a győri megyei biróság népbirósági tanácsa előtt 1957. október 30 napján megtartott nyilvános folytalagos tárgyalásról, 1.

106. OSzK Kt., 1956-os gy., 412.VIIf.5d., Komárom Megyei Egyeztető Bizottság, 6275/2/VI/1957. Jegyzőkönyv felvéve: 1957.VIII.26-án.

107. "Hogyan dolgozzék a munkástanács?" in Izsák, Szabó, and Szabó, eds., *1956 plakátjai és röplapjai*, 445.

108. OSzK Kt., 1956-os gy., 412.VIIf.4d., Győri Népbiróság B.0027/1957/16, Mazalin György és társai. A Magyar Népköztársaság Legfelsőbb Birósága népbirósági tanácsa. Nbf.I.5198/1958/31.szám, 5–9.

109. OSzK Kt., 1956-os gy., 412.VIIf.2d.-Esztergom Megyei Biróság-429/1957-Kovács Imre és társai; B.429/1957/5 szám. Jegyzőkönyv készült a Nép.d.áll.rend.megdönt.ir.mozg. való részv.btte. miatt Kovács Imre és társai ellen inditott bűnügyben az Esztergomi Megyei Biróság Tatabány-án biróságnál 1957 szeptember hó 2 napján tartott zárt tárgyalásról, 3; OSzK Kt., 1956-os gy., 412.VIIf., 1d., Az Esztergom Megyei Biróság Elnökétől. 1958.El.IX.22. szám. 1958. évi április havi jelentés az Igazságügyminiszter Elvtársnak, 2.

110. "Tatabánya dolgozó népe követeli," *Komárommegyei Figyelő: A Komárom megyei Forradalmi Munkás és Katona Tanács lapja*, 1 November 1956, 1.

111. OSzK Kt., 1956-os gy., Gy.NB, 1127/1957, 1d., Biztositják az Erőmüvek üzemeltetését, a korházak fütést a tatabányai bányászok, Tatabánya, 1956 október 29.

112. OSzK Kt., 1956-os gy., Gy.NB, 1127/1957, 1d., Megindult az élet Tatabányán. Tatabánya, 1956 november 3.

113. OSzK Kt., 1956-os gy., 412.VIIf.4d., Komárom Megyei Ügyészség, I-XV 1957, 1957. Ig.III-1/I. Tájékoztató jelentés a tatabányai városi ügyészség első negyedévi munkájáról, 2.

114. OSzK Kt., 1956-os gy., Gy.NB, 1127/1957, 1d., Megindult az élet Tatabányán. Tatabánya, 1956 november 3., 1.

115. "Újra az élen! Ismét elsők a tatabányai XI-es aknaiak," *Komárom Megyei Hírlap*, 26 January 1957, 3; KEMÖL, XXXV.1f.3/1957/18ő.e., 261–62.

116. OSzK Kt., 1956-os gy., 412.VIIf.7d., Komárom Megyei Tanács, Titkárság, Várgesztes községi Tanács V.B. Az 1956. évi október 23.-utáni események megörökitése, 1–7.

117. OSzK Kt., 1956-os gy., 412.VIIf.7d., Komárom Megyei Tanács, Titkárság; Vértesszőllős községi tanács V.B.től. 572/1957.szám. Tárgy: 1957.október 23-i és azt követő ellenforradalmi cselekmény leirása, 1.

118. ZML, XXV.19.ZMB.B.695/1958 – Villányi József és társai. Zalamegyei Ügyészség Zalaegerszeg. B.10.050/1958.3.szám. Vádirat, 1–2.

119. "Éjszakai jelentés Kanizsáról," *Zala: Rendkívüli kiadás*, 26 October 1956, 1.

120. "Nagykanizsa város," in Erzsébet Csomor and Imre Kapiller, eds., *'56 Zala megyei kronológiája és személyi adattára I.* (Zalaegerszeg: Zala Megyei Levéltár, 2004), 157.

121. ZML, XXV.19.ZMB.B.322/1957 – Gáti József, Zalamegyei Ügyészség Zalaegerszeg. 1957. Bül.59/3 szám. Vádirat.

122. ZML, XXV.19.Tb.1/1958 – Majerszky Béla és társai, 2d., Másolat! Feljegyzés, Zalaegerszeg, 1957. október 9, 1.

123. ZML, XXV.19.Tb.1/1958 – Majerszky Béla és társai, 2d., Másolat! Önvallomás, Várkony Rezső, 1957. november 1., 1.

124. ZML, XXV.19.Tb.1/1958 – Majerszky Béla és társai, 2d., Másolat! Feljegyzés, Zalaegerszeg, 1957. október 9, 1.

125. ZML, XXV.19.B.781/157 – Papp Imre és társai, Zalamegyei Ügyészség Zalaegerszeg. 1957. Bül.189.szám. Vádirat, 4.

126. OSzK Kt., 1956-os gy., Zala megye (Zala County, hereafter, XI.f.)7/19d., 1956-évi októberi események alatt történt szélsőséges magatartásokról jelentés, Várfölde, 1957 június 20-án.

127. Varga, "Érdek, érdekeltség, érdekérvényesítés a termelőszövetkezetekben," 363–64.

128. "Zalaegerszeg, 1956. július 16. A Megyei Begyűjtési Hivatal kimutatása a begyűjtésben hátralékot felhalmozók számáról, az 1955-ös és 1956-os év első félévére vonatkozóan," in Káli, ed., Dokumentumok Zala megye történetéből 1947–1956, 432.

129. ZML, XXXV.57f.2/Agitprop/16ő.e., Magyar Dolgozók Pártja, Járási Végrehajtóbizottsága Zalaszentgrót. Jelentés, Zalaszentgrót, 1956 július 12-én, 1.

130. ZML, XXXV.61f.3/2/13ő.e., Feljegyzés a termelő brigádok bérezésével kapcsolatban. Bázakerettye, 1956. március hó 14.-én.

131. ZML, XXXV.61f.3/2/13ő.e., Jegyzőkönyv készült: Bázakerettyén 1956. április 12.-én megtartott VB. ülésen., 1.

132. ZML, XXXV.58f.3/16ő.e., Termelékenységi mutatók 1956.I. félévről.

133. ZML, XXXV.61f.3/2/13ő.e., Feljegyzés a termelő brigádok bérezésével kapcsolatban. Bázakerettye, 1956. március hó 14.-én.

134. ZML, XXXV.63f.2/Agitprop/7ő.e., M.D.P. Megyei Párt-VB, Agit.Prop. Osztálya. Jelentés, Rákosi elvtárs budapesti aktiva ülésen elhangzott beszámolója utáni hangulatról. 6. május 23.

135. Ripp, "Jugoszlávia," 62.

136. "Budapest, 1956. április 19. Az MDP KV Adminisztratív Osztályánál levele a part megyei első titkárához, a határsáv megszüntetésével kapcsolatos egyes kérdésekről," in Káli, ed., Dokumentumok Zala megye történetéből 1947–1956, 422.

137. MOL, XIX-B-10–1956/11d., 01316. BM. Határőrség Parancsnokság /Szolgálati Osztály/ Tárgy: Javaslat felterjesztése.

138. ZML, XXXV.61f.3/4/3/3ő.e., Jegyzőkönyv felvétetett 1956. március 30-án a gazolintelep megtartott taggyülésen, 2.

139. ZML, XXXV.61f.1/42ő.e., Nagyaktiva ülésen készült feljegyzések, 1956.VIII.7-én, 1.

140. ZML, XXXV.61f.4/2/17ő.e., 1956. július 1-i bérrendezés.

141. ZML, XXXV.61f.1/42ő.e., Nagyaktiva ülésen készült feljegyzések, 1956.VIII.7-én, 2–3.

142. ZML, XXXV.61f.4/2/17ő.e., Jegyzőkönyv, felvétetett: 1956. augusztus 9.-én megtartott part végrehajtóbizottság ülésen, 6–8; ZML, XXXV.61f.1/42ő.e., Magyar Dolgozók Pártja Letenyei Párt Végrehajtó Bizottság, Letenye, 1956.VIII.21, 1.

143. "Lovászi," in Csomor and Kapiller, eds., '56 Zala megyei kronológiája és személyi adattára I., 115.

144. ZML, XXV.19.Tb.1/1958 – Majerszky Béla és társai, 1d., A zalaegerszegi megyei bíróság. Tb.1/1958/37/szám. Itélet, 13–14; "Lovásziban megalakult a munkástanács – a termelés zavartalanul folyik," Új Zala: A Zala Megyei Munkástanács Lapja, 28 October 1956, 1.

145. ZML, XXV.19.Tb.1/1958 – Majerszky Béla és társai, 1d., A zalaegerszegi megyei biróság. Tb.1/1958/37/szám. Itéletet, 14.

146. ZML, XXV.19.B.676/1958 – Vörös Zoltán és társai, Jegyzőkönyv készült 1956. okt.27-én a Furási Üzem hivatalos helyiségében.

147. ZML, XXV.19.Tb.1/1958 – Majerszky Béla és társai, 4d., Jegyzőkönyv felvétetett 1956. október 31-én megtartott Munkás-Tanács értekezleten, 1; "Bázakerettye," in Csomor and Kapiller, eds., '56 Zala megyei kronológiája és személyi adattára I., 87.

148. Lajos Srágli, "Munkások a forradalomban – a Zalai olajipar 1956-ban," in Erzsébet Csomor and Imre Kapiller, eds., '56 Zalában: a forradalom eseményeinek Zala megyei dokumentumai, 1956–1958 (Zalaegerszeg: Zala Megyei Levéltár, 1996), 33.

149. ZML, XXV.19.Tb.1/1958 – Majerszky Béla és társai, 2d., Másolat! Önvallomás, Várkony Rezső, 1957. november 1., 2 3.

150. ZML, XXV.19.Tb.1/1958 – Majerszky Béla és társai, 4d., 217; Jegyzőkönyv felvétetett 1956. október 31-én megtartott Munkás-Tanács értekezleten, 1–2.

151. ZML, XXV.19.Tb.1/1958 – Majerszky Béla és társai, 2d., Másolat! Önvallomás, Várkony Rezső, 1957. november 1., 3.

152. ZML, XXV.19.Tb.1/1958 – Majerszky Béla és társai, 4d., Az olajipari dolgozók egyesült Munkástanácsának határozata Zala megye Nemzeti Tanácsának, Bázakerettye, 1956.október 31.

153. "Nagylengyel," in Erzsébet Csomor and Imre Kapiller, eds., '56 Zala megyei kronológiája és személyi adattára II. (Zalaegerszeg: Zala Megyei Levéltár, 2004), 155.

154. Csomor, 1956 Zalaegerszegen, 25–33.

155. OSzK Kt., 1956-os gy., XIf.7/10d., A zalaegerszegi megyei biróság. B.541/1957/8.szám. Itéletet, 3.

156. ZML, XXV.19.B.833/1957 – Mecséri József, A zalaegerszegi megyei biróság. B.833/1957/6.szám. Itéletet, 1.

157. ZML, XXV.19.B.833/1957 – Mecséri József, A zalaegerszegi megyei biróság. B.833/1957.6.szám. Jegyzőkönyv, készült a népi demokratikus államrend megdöntésére irányuló szervezkedés és egyéb büntette miatt Mecséri József ellen inditott bünügyben a zalaegerszegi megyei biróságnál Zalaegerszegen 1958. január 14-én nyilvános tárgyalásról, 2, 5–6.

158. "Nagylengyel, 1956. október 27. A Nagylengyel Kőolajtermelő Vállalat Munkástanácsának jegyzőkönyve," in Csomor and Kapiller, eds., '56 Zalában, 73–79.

159. ZML, XXV.19.B.541/1957 – Simon Lajos és társai, A zalaegerszegi megyei biróság. B.541/1957/9.szám. Itéletet, 3.

160. ZML, XXV.19.B.1003/1957 – Varga Sándor és társai, Zalamegyei Ügyészség Zalae-gerszeg. 1957.Bül. 207 szám. Vádirat, 1–2.

161. ZML, XXV.19.B.780/1957 – Rácz István és társai, Zalamegyei Ügyészség Zalae-gerszeg. 1957.Bül. 188 szám. Vádirat, 3.

162. "Becsehely," in Csomor and Kapiller, eds., '56 Zala megyei kronológiája és személyi adattára I., 96.

## 8. The Foundations of Consolidation, November 1956–June 1958

1. Granville, *First Domino*, 79–85; Gati, *Failed Illusions*, 186–94.

2. István Vida, ed., *1956 és a politikai pártok: politikai pártok az 1956-os forradalomban; 1956. október 23.–november 4.* (Budapest: MTA Jelenkor-kutató Bizottság, 1998).

3. Kenedi and Varga, eds., *A forradalom hangja*, 361.

4. László Eörsi, *Köztársaság tér 1956* (Budapest: 1956-os Intézet, 2006).

5. Granville, *First Domino*, 85–92.

6. András B. Hegedüs, Péter Kende, György Litván, and János M. Rainer, eds., *1956 kézikönyve: megtorlás és emlékezés* (Budapest: 1956-os Intézet, 1996), 303–5.

7. Sándor Horváth, "A Központi Munkástanács története," *Első század* 1, no. 1 (1998): 113–209.

8. BFL, XXXV.1f.1957/42ő.e., 163; OSA, 300/40/4/18, Item No. 1643/57, 2; MOL, M-KS-288f.21/1958/20ő.e., 40; BFL, XXXV.1f.1957/42ő.e., 121; Erzsébet Kajári, ed., *Rendőrségi napi jelentések, 1956. október 23.–december 12: első kötet* (Budapest: A Belügyminisztérium és az 1956-os Magyar Forradalom Történetének Dokumentációs és Kutató Intézete Közalapít-ványa, 1996), 42.

9. BFL, XXXV.1f.1956–7/41ő.e., 110; Erzsébet Kajári, ed., *Rendőrségi napi jelentések, 1956. december 13–december 31: második kötet* (Budapest: A Belügyminisztérium és az 1956-os Magyar Forradalom Történetének Dokumentációs és Kutató Intézete Közalapítványa, 1997), 43–81.

10. MOL, M-KS-288f.25/1957/7ő.e., 135.

11. Hegedűs, Kende, Litván, and Rainer, eds., *1956 kézikönyve: megtorlás és emlékezés*, 310–11; Ibolya Murber, "Ungarnflüchtlinge in Österreich 1956," in *Die Ungarische Revolution und Österreich 1956*, ed. Ibolya Murber and Zoltán Fónagy (Vienna: Czernin Verlag, 2006), 373–76.

12. Balázs Schuller, "Példaképek lázadása? A magyar bányásztársadalom 1956-ban," in *Bányászok és bányászvárosok forradalma, 1956: tanulmányok az 1956-os forradalom és szabadságharc tiszteletére*, ed. Erzsébet Bircher and Balázs Schuller (Sopron: Központi Bányászati Múzeum, 2006), 276–78.

13. BFL, XXXV.1f.1956–7/41ő.e., 23; Kajári, ed., *Rendőrségi napi jelentések, 1956. október 23.–december 12: első kötet*, 476–511.

14. Iván Szenes, *A Kommunista Párt újjászervezése Magyarországon, 1956–1957* (Budapest: Kossuth Könyvkiadó, 1976), 74–109.

15. BFL, XXXV.1f.1958/41ő.e., 38–39.

16. MOL, M-KS-288f.5/96ő.e., 11–12; BFL, XXXV.1f.1958/44ő.e., 20–22; BFL, XXXV.1f.1958/45ő.e., 291–94.

17. See *Ellenforradalmi erők a magyar októberi eseményekben: I–IV kötet;* and *Nagy Imre és bűntársai ellenforradalmi összeesküvése*.

18. László Eörsi, *The Hungarian Revolution of 1956: Myths and Realities*, trans. Mario D. Fenyo (Boulder, CO: Social Science Monographs; Wayne, NJ: Center for Hungarian Studies and Publications, 2006), x; Alajos Dornbach, "A pártállam igazságszolgáltatása és a Nagy Imre-per," in *A per: Nagy Imre és társai, 1958, 1989*, ed. Alajos Dornbach, László Győri,

Notes to Pages 233–236

Péter Kende, János M. Rainer, and Katalin Somlai (Budapest: 1956-os Intézet – Nagy Imre Alapítvány, 2008), 22–27.

19. "Az MSzMP Ideiglenes Központi Bizottságának 1956. decemberi határozata (1956. December 5)," in Vass and Ságvári, eds., *A Magyar Szocialista Munkáspárt határozatai és dokumentumai, 1956–1962*, 13–14.

20. "Az MSZMP Ideiglenes Központi Bizottsága 1956. december 2–3-i ülésének jegyzőkönyve," in Némethné and Sipos, eds., *A Magyar Szocialista munkáspárt ideiglenes vezető testületeinek jegyzőkönyvei. I. kötet. 1956. november 11–1957. január 14*, 171.

21. "Az MSzMP Ideiglenes Központi Bizottságának 1957. februári határozata az időszerű kérdésekről és feladatokról (1957. február 26.)," in Vass and Ságvári, eds., *A Magyar Szocialista Munkáspárt határozatai és dokumentumai, 1956–1962*, 41–42.

22. MOL, M-KS-288f.23/1957/29ő.e., 6–9.

23. MOL, M-KS-288f.25/1957/8ő.e., 112–17.

24. MOL, M-KS-288f.23/1957/29ő.e., 35.

25. MOL, M-KS-288f.23/1957/29ő.e., 36–37.

26. MOL, M-KS-288f.23/1957/34ő.e., 34.

27. BFL, XXXV.1f.1958/42ő.e., 111; BFL, XXXV.1f.1958/43ő.e., 162.

28. BFL, XXXV.1f.1958/138ő.e., 289–95.

29. OSzK Kt., 1956-os gy., 412.VIIf.2d.-Esztergom Megyei Biróság-429/1957-Kovács Imre és társai; B.429/1957/5 szám. Jegyzőkönyv készült a Nép.d.áll.rend.megdönt.ir.mozg. való részv.btte miatt Kovács Imre és társai ellen inditott bűnügyben a Esztergomi Megyei Biróság Tatabány-án biróságnál 1957 évi szeptember hó 2 napján tartott zárt tárgyalásról, 3.

30. KEMÖL, XXXV.2f.2/1957/2ő.e., 28.

31. KEMÖL, XXXV.2f.3/1958/17ő.e., 2.

32. KEMÖL, XXXV.1f.3/1957/23ő.e., 4–5.

33. OSzK Kt., 1956-os gy., Gy.NB, 1127/1957, 2d., B.M. Komárom Megyei Rendőrfőkapitányság Politikai Osztály, Vizsgálati Alosztály. Jegyzőkönyv, Dr. Klébert Márton kihallgatásáról, Ttbánya, 1957.aug.3, 2.

34. Pál Germuska, "Komárom megye bányászai az 1956-os forradalomban," in *Bányászok és bányászvárosok forradalma, 1956*, ed. Bircher and Schuller, 88–90.

35. 1956-os Intézet, OHA 484, 44.

36. Kajári, ed., *Rendőrségi napi jelentések, 1956. október 23.–december 12: első kötet*, 31.

37. 1956-os Intézet, OHA 449, 21.

38. Tihamér Takács, "A város dolgozóinak harca a munkáshatalomért, a szocialista vivmányok védelméért," in *Tatabánya története: helytörténeti tanulmányok ii. kötet*, ed. Gombkötö et al., 65.

39. Pál Germuska, "A forradalom Tatabányán, kronológiai vázlat," in *Az 1956-os magyar forradalom történetének dokumentációs és kutatóintézete évkönyv III. 1994*, ed. János Bak, András B. Hegedűs, György Litván, János M. Rainer, and Katalin S. Varga (Budapest: 1956-os Intézet, 1994), 209.

40. "Kik és miért félnek a tatabányai karhatalomtól?" *Komárom Megyei Hírlap*, 22 December 1956, 3; Germuska, "Komárom megye," 242–43.

41. OSzK Kt., 1956-os gy., 412.VIIf.,1d., Az Esztergom Megyei Biróság Elnökétől. 1958. El.IX.22.szám.1958. évi április havi jelentés az Igazságügyminiszter Elvtársnak, 2.

42. Kajári, ed., *Rendőrségi napi jelentések, 1956. október 23.–december 12: első kötet*, 56–57.

43. OSzK Kt., 1956-os gy., 412.VIIf.2d.-Esztergom Megyei Biróság-429/1957-Kovács Imre és társai; B.429/1957/5 szám., Komárom Megyei Ügyészség Esztergom, 1957. Tük.Bül.317/2. sz. Vádirat, 2.

44. Schuller, "Példaképek lázadása? A magyar bányásztársadalom 1956-ban," 277.

45. OSzK Kt., 1956-os gy., 412.VIIf.3d.-Esztergom Megyei Biróság-664/1957-Solymos Mihály és társai; Az Ideiglenes Munkástanács kiküldöttek és a Trösztigazgatóság 1956. november 13-i értekezletéről szóló jegyzőkönyv.

46. OSzK Kt., 1956-os gy., 412.VIIf.3d.-Esztergom Megyei Biróság-664/1957-Solymos Mihály és társai, Felhivás., Tatabánya, 1956.november 23.

47. Kajári, ed., *Rendőrségi napi jelentések, 1956. október 23.–december 12: első kötet*, 204.

48. Germuska, "Komárom megye bányászai az 1956-os forradalomban," 93.

49. 1956-os Intézet, OHA 449, 24.

50. Kajári, ed., *Rendőrségi napi jelentések, 1956. október 23.–december 12: első kötet*, 232.

51. "Tájékoztató a Központi Munkástanácsnak Kádár János Miniszterelnökkel 1956. November 30-án folytatott Tárgyalásairól," reprinted in Pál Germuska, "Kádár János Tatabányán 1956. november 30-án." *Beszélő*, ser. 3, vol. 1, no. 7 (1996): 77–85.

52. "A bányászok nehéz munkájukhoz méltó bért kapnak," *Komárom Megyei Hírlap*, 27 November 1956, 1.

53. Kajári, ed., *Rendőrségi napi jelentések, 1956. október 23.–december 12: első kötet*, 343.

54. "Hogyan történt? Az ellenforradalom tatabányai napjaiból – Esztó Zoltán a bíróság előtt," *Komárom Megyei Hírlap*, 16 April 1957, 2.

55. PtSzL, IX.290f.31ő.e., 173.

56. OSzK Kt., 1956-os gy., 412.VIIf.3d., Esztergom Megyei Ügyészség, Esztergom. 1957. Bül.248.sz. Vádirat, 1.

57. Kajári, ed., *Rendőrségi napi jelentések, 1956. október 23.–december 12: első kötet*, 415.

58. "Senkit sem tartanak indokolatlanul letartóztatásban: a karhatalmi parancsnokság nyilatkozata," *Komárom Megyei Hírlap*, 15 December 1956, 1.

59. 1956-os Intézet, OHA 449, 28.

60. Kajári, ed., *Rendőrségi napi jelentések, 1956. október 23.–december 12: első kötet*, 479; "A tatabányai karhatalom vezetőinek nyilatkozata," *Komárom Megyei Hírlap*, 19 December 1956, 1.

61. Kajári, ed., *Rendőrségi napi jelentések, 1956. október 23.–december 12: első kötet*, 432; OSzK Kt., 1956-os gy., 412.VIIf.3d.-Esztergom Megyei Biróság-664/1957-Solymos Mihály és társai, Felhivás, Tatabánya, 1956. december 9.

62. 1956-os Intézet, OHA 449, 28.

63. OSzK, KT., 1956-os gy., 412.VIIf.6d., Jegyzőkönyv, készült a Komárom Megyei Tanács Végrehajtó Bizottságának 1956.évi december hó 4-én megtartott rendes ülése alkalmával, 2.

64. "Ha nincs szén – veszélyben Tatabánya élelmiszerellátása," *Komárom Megyei Hírlap*, 15 December 1956, 1.

65. Kajári, ed., *Rendőrségi 1956. december 13–december 31., második kötet*, 75.

66. Germuska, "A forradalom Tatabányán," 219.

67. Germuska, "Komárom megye," 252.

68. KEMÖL, XXXV.2f.2/1957/2ő.e., 29.

69. KEMÖL, XXXV.1f.3/1957/30ő.e., 8.

70. KEMÖL, XXXV.1f.3/1957/24ő.e., 15.

71. KEMÖL, XXXV.2f.3/1957/7ő.e., 8.

72. KEMÖL, XXXV.1f.3/1957/23ő.e., 5.

73. "A tatabányai bányászok válasz: a sztrájkra, a munkanélküliségre," *Komárom Megyei Hírlap*, 6 January 1957, 3.

74. "A teljesítmény, az önköltségről, az új bérekről számolt be Gál István, a tatabányai munkástanácselnökeinek értekezletén," *Komárom Megyei Hírlap*, 16 February 1957, 1.

75. "Újra az Élen!" Ismét elsők a tatabányai XI-es aknaiak," *Komárom Megyei Hírlap*, 26 January 1957, 3.

76. MOL, XXIX-F-107-m/70d., Szénbányászati Műszaki-Gazdasági Jelentés 1957, 17–18.

77. KEMÖL, XXXV.2f.3/1957/15ő.e., 16; KEMÖL, XXXV.2f.3/1957/13ő.e., 15–16.

78. "Május elsejére készülnek bányáink dolgozói: munkaversennyel ünnepelünk, *Komárom Megyei Hírlap*, 10 April 1957, 1.

79. KEMÖL, XXXV.1f.3/1957/11ő.e., 10.

80. KEMÖL, XXXV.1f.3/1957/17ő.e., 4.

81. István Jancsák, "A szakmánybérezésről," *Komárom Megyei Hírlap*, 6 January 1957, 2.

82. "A szakmánybérezés jó – lehet vele keresni," *Komárom Megyei Hírlap*, 12 January 1957, 2.

83. MOL, XXIX-F-107-m/70d., Szénbányászati Műszaki-Gazdasági Jelentés 1957, 23; *Komárom megye legfontosabb statisztikai adatai, 1956*, 69.

84. MOL, XXIX-F-107-m/89d., Tatabányai Szénbányászati Tröszt. Kimutatás 1957. október havi tulórapótlék, tulmüszak és az egy főre eső átlagkereset alakulásáról.

85. KEMÖL, XXXV.2f.3/1958/27ő.e., 10.

86. KEMÖL, XXXV.2f.3/1958/20ő.e., 7; *Komárom megye legfontosabb statisztikai adatai, 1956*, 69.

87. KEMÖL, XXXV.2f.3/1958/17ő.e., 13.

88. KEMÖL, XXXV.2f.3/1958/20ő.e., 12.

89. KEMÖL, XXXV.2f.3/1958/17ő.e., 8.

90. KEMÖL, XXXV.2f.3/1957/13ő.e., 20.

91. KEMÖL, XXXV.2f.3/1958/17ő.e., 10–14.

92. KEMÖL, XXXV.2f.2/1957/2ő.e., 28.

93. KEMÖL, XXXV.2f.3/1958/33ő.e., 9.

94. KEMÖL, XXXV.1f.2/1958/5ő.e., 58.

95. "Hogyan történt? Az ellenforradalom tatabányai napjaiból," *Komárom Megyei Hírlap*, 6 February 1957, 2; KEMÖL, XXXV.2f.3/1958/24ő.e., 13.

96. KEMÖL, XXXV.2f.3/1958/17ő.e., 9.

97. Varga, *Politika, paraszti érdekérvényesítés és szövetkezetek Magyarországon*, 58–59.

98. KEMÖL, XXXV.1f.2/1958/4ő.e., 10.

99. KEMÖL, XXXV.1f.2/1958/4ő.e., 3.

100. ZML, Az MSzMP Letenye Járási Bizottságának iratai (Papers of the Letenye District Committee of the Hungarian Socialist Workers' Party, hereafter, XXXV.5f.)1958/5ő.e., 39–40.

101. ZML, Az MSzMP Lovászi Olajüzemi Bizottságának iratai (Papers of the Lovászi Oil Factory Committee of the Hungarian Socialist Workers' Party, hereafter, XXXV.26f.)1957–1960/8ő.e., 14–15.

102. "Bázakerettye," in Csomor and Kapiller, eds., '56 Zala megyei kronológiája és személyi adattára I., 87.

103. Srágli, "Munkások a forradalomban," 36.

104. ZML, Az MSzMP Zala Megyei Bizottságának iratai (Papers of the Zala County Committee of the Hungarian Socialist Workers' Party, hereafter, XXXV.1f.)1957/25ő.e., Jelentés Zalamegye olajiparának helyzetéről, 5–6.

105. "Olajat! Olajat!" Zalai Hírlap, 1 January 1957, 3.

106. ZML, XXV.19.Tb.1/1958 – Majerszky Béla és társai, 4d., A zalai kőolajipari vállalatok összevont Munkástanácsa a f.évi XI.hó 19.-én tartott együttes ülésen az alábbi határozatokat hozta.

107. ZML, XXV.19.B.833/1957 – Mecséri József, Zalamegyei Ügyészség Zalaegerszeg. 1957. Bül.187.szám. Vádirat, 1.

108. ZML, XXXV.5f.1957/2ő.e., 27–29.

109. Lajos Horváth, "Mit tett eddig a nagylengyeli munkástanács?" Zalai Hírlap, 27 January 1957, 7.

110. ZML, XXV.19.Tb.1/1958 – Majerszky Béla és társai, 4d., Jegyzőkönyv készült Bázakerettyén 1957. február hó 28-án megtartott Munkás Tanács ülésről, 1.

111. ZML, XXXV.25f.1957–1960/B.-Asz./1ő.e., 7.

112. Katalin Béres, "Egy zalai kisfalu a forradalom idején – ozmánbük 1956," in Csomor and Kapiller, eds., '56 Zalában, 14–15.

113. ZML, XXXV.1f.1957/9ő.e., Hangulat-jelentés.

114. ZML, XXXV.1f.1957/9ő.e., MSzMP. Nagykanizsa Járási Pártbizottság, Nagykanizsa. Jelentés, 1957 július 13, 1.

115. ZML, XXXV.5f.1958/7ő.e., 18.

116. ZML, XXXV.26f.1957–1960/6ő.e., 20.

117. ZML, XXXV.1f.1957/24ő.e., Néhány megjegyzés a Jelentés az ateista és antiklerikális propaganda helyzetéről és a Tézisek a vallással kapcsolatos tömegnevelő munka cimü anyagokhoz, 1.

118. ZML, Az MSzMP Zalaegerszeg Járási Bizottságának iratai (Papers of the Zalaegerszeg District Committee of Hungarian Socialist Workers' Party, XXXV.2f.)1957/10ő.e., 29.

119. ZML, XXXV.1f.1958/1ő.e., Jelentés a pártbizottság számára a falusi pártpolitikai munka megjavitására, 2.

120. ZML, XXXV.25f.1957–1960/B.-Asz./2ő.e., 33–34.

121. ZML, XXXV.1f.1958/1ő.e., Jelentés a pártbizottság számára a falusi pártpolitikai munka megjavitására, 4.

122. ZML, Az MSzMP Nagykanizsa Városi Bizottságának iratai (Papers of the Nagykanizsa City Committee of the Hungarian Socialist Workers' Party, hereafter, XXXV.8f.)1958/1ő.e., 56.

123. Varga, "Érdek, érdekeltség, érdekérvényesítés a termelőszövetkezetekben," 397–99; ZML, XXXV.25f.1957–1960/B.-Asz./5ő.e., 46; ZML, XXXV.1f.1958/1ő.e., Jegyzőkönyv,

készült: Zalaegerszegen 1958. június 7-én megtartott pártbizottsági ülésen a Megyeháza Nagytermében, 2.

124. ZML, XXXV.1f.1958/12ő.e., 30.

125. ZML, XXXV.25f.1957–1960/3ő.e., 129.

126. ZML, XXXV.25f.1957–1960/B.-Asz./3ő.e., 6.

127. ZML, XXXV.2f.1958/12ő.e., 2–3.

128. ZML, XXXV.25f.1957–1960/B.-Asz./2ő.e., 37.

129. ZML, XXXV.25f.1957–1960/3ő.e., 129.

130. ZML, XXXV.26f.1957–1960/B.-Asz./2ő.e., 53.

131. Iván T. Berend, *Gazdasági útkeresés, 1956–1965: a szocialista gazdaság magyarországi modelljének történetéhez* (Budapest: Magvető Könyvkiadó, 1983), 17–122; ZML, XXXV.26f.1957–1960/8ő.e., 8.

132. ZML, XXXV.1f.1957/27ő.e., Jelentés a termelés és munkaverseny tapasztalatairól, 2.

133. ZML, XXXV.25f.1957–1960/14ő.e., 13.

134. ZML, XXXV.26f.1957–1960/15ő.e., 23.

135. ZML, XXXV.26f.1957–1960/15ő.e., 21.

136. ZML, XXXV.25f.1957–1960/3ő.e., 127.

137. ZML, XXXV.25f.1957–1960/B.-Asz./3ő.e., 9.

138. ZML, XXXV.25f.1957–1960/B.-Asz./3ő.e., 6.

139. ZML, XXXV.26f.1957–1960/3ő.e., 129.

140. ZML, XXXV.26f.1957–1960/8ő.e., 14–15.

141. ZML, XXXV.25f.1957–1960/10ő.e., 10.

142. ZML, XXXV.26f.1957–1960/8ő.e., 17.

143. ZML, XXXV.25f.1957–1960/B.-Asz./3ő.e., 8.

144. ZML, XXXV.25f.1957–1960/B.-Asz./5ő.e., 45.

145. "Kik lehetnek az MSZMP tagjai?" *Izzó*, 30 April 1957, 2.

146. BFL, XXXV.1f.1958/135ő.e., 341–47.

147. BFL, XXXV.1f.1957/46ő.e., 30.

148. BFL, XXXV.1f.1958/44ő.e., 44.

149. OSzK Kt., 1956-os gy., Bp.NB, 4491/74, 1d./4, Budapest Rendőrfőkapitányság Politikai Nyomozó Osztály, Vizsgálati Osztály. Jegyzőkönyv Roik János gyanusitott kihallgatásáról. Budapest, 1957. július 12-én.

150. Éva Standeisky, *Az írók és a hatalom, 1956–1963* (Budapest: 1956-os Intézet, 1996), 121–24.

151. Miklós Krassó, "Hungary 1956: An Interview," in *Eyewitness in Hungary: The Soviet Invasion of 1956*, ed. Bill Lomax (Nottingham, England: Spokesman Press, 1980), 162; Lomax, ed., *Workers' Councils in 1956*, 93.

152. László Varga, *Az elhagyott tömeg: tanulmányok 1950–1956-ról* (Budapest: Cserépfalvi-Budapest Főváros Levéltára, 1994), 211–16.

153. BFL, XXXV.9f.1957/15ő.e., 104.

154. PtSzL, IX.290f.38ő.e., 10

155. BFL, XXXV.1f.1956–57/41ő.e., 81.

156. BFL, XXXV.1f.1956–57/41ő.e., 135.

157. PtSzL, IX.290f.38ő.e., 69.

158. BFL, XXXV.1f.1956–57/41ő.e., 160.
159. PtSzL, IX.290f.38ő.e., 77.
160. BFL, XXXV.1f.1956–57/41ő.e., 176.
161. PtSzL, IX.290f.38ő.e., 87.
162. PtSzL, IX.290f.39ő.e. 12.
163. BFL, XXXV.1f.1956–57/41ő.e., 176.
164. PtSzL, IX.290f.39ő.e., 14.
165. BFL, XXXV.1f.1956–57/41ő.e., 170.
166. BFL, XXXV.1f.1957/42ő.e., 1–2.
167. BFL, XXXV.1f.1957/42ő.e, 87.
168. BFL, XXXV.1f.1957/42ő.e., 104.
169. PtSzL, IX.290f.39ő.e., 21–22.
170. Berend, *Gazdasági útkeresés, 1956–1965*, 108–22.
171. MOL, M-KS-288f.23/1957/15ő.e., 1–8
172. MOL, M-KS-288f.23/1957/29ő.e., 7.
173. MOL, M-KS-288f.23/1957/8ő.e., 117.
174. BFL, XXXV.1f.1957/45ő.e., 144.
175. BFL, XXXV.1f.1957/60ő.e., 97.
176. BFL, XXXV.1f.1957/45ő.e., 215–17.
177. BFL, XXXV.9f.1958/14ő.e., 90.
178. BFL, XXXV.9f.1958/7ő.e., 108–9.
179. BFL, XXXV.9f.1958/7ő.e., 4.
180. MOL, M-KS-288f.21/1958/20ő.e., 249, 253.
181. MOL, M-KS-288f.21/1958/20ő.e., 249.
182. BFL, XXXV.9f.1958/41ő.e., 129.
183. BFL, XXXV.9f.1958/41ő.e., 13.
184. BFL, XXXV.9f.1958/7ő.e., 20.
185. BFL, XXXV.1f.1958/134ő.e., 48–53.
186. BFL, XXXV.1f.1958/42ő.e., 49.
187. MOL, M-KS-288f.21/1958/20ő.e., 253–54.
188. BFL, XXXV.1f.1958/44ő.e., 99.
189. MOL, M-KS-288f.21/1958/20ő.e., 250.
190. MOL, M-KS-288f.20/1958/20ő.e., 251.

## Conclusion

1. Dornbach, Győri, Kende, Rainer, and Somlai, eds., *A per: Nagy Imre és társai, 1958, 1989*, 223–24.
2. BFL, XXXV.1f.1958/46ő.e., 44.
3. Péter György, *Néma hagyomány: kollektív felejtés és a kései múltértelmezés 1956 1989-ben* (Budapest: Magvető, 2000), 19–26.
4. See especially Robert O. Paxton, *The Anatomy of Fascism* (London: Penguin Books, 2004), 2–23; Ruth Ben-Ghiat, *Fascist Modernities: Italy, 1922–1945* (Berkeley and Los Angeles: University of California Press, 2001); Jeffrey Herf, *Reactionary Modernism: Technology,*

*Culture and Politics in Weimar and the Third Reich* (Cambridge: Cambridge University Press, 1984).

5. Giorgio Agamben, *State of Exception,* trans. Kevin Atell (Chicago: Chicago University Press, 2005). [*Editor's note:* The term "civil war state" is striking but, I think, deliberate. It was a phrase Mark also used in an unpublished article written not long before his death.—*Nigel Swain*]

6. Zsuzsanna Kádár, "A magyarországi szociáldemokrata perek története," *Múltunk* 41, no. 2 (1996): 3–49.

7. Dániel Bolgár, "A kulak érthető arca: fogalomtörténeti vázlat," in *Mindennapok Rákosi és Kádár korában: új utak a szocialista korszak kutatásában,* ed. Sándor Horváth (Budapest: Nyitott Könyvműhely, 2008), 50–93.

8. For a useful survey of these developments, see Geoff Eley and Keith Nield, *The Future of Class in History: What's Left of the Social?* (Ann Arbor: University of Michigan Press, 2007). See also Miguel A. Cabrera, *Postsocial History: An Introduction,* trans. Marie McMahon (Lanham, MD: Lexington Books, 2004); Geoff Eley, *A Crooked Line: From Cultural History to the History of Society* (Ann Arbor: University of Michigan Press, 2005); William H. Sewell Jr., *Logics of History: Social Theory and Social Transformation* (Chicago: University of Chicago Press, 2005).

9. John Urry, "Rethinking Class," in *Social Movements and Social Classes,* ed. Louis Maheu (London: Sage Publications, 1995), 169–81.

10. Fredric Jameson, "Marx's Purloined Letter," in *Ghostly Demarcations: A Symposium on Derrida's Specters of Marx,* ed. Michael Sprinker (London: Verso, 2008), 48.

11. The concept of "social-property relations" is adapted from Robert Brenner, "Property and Progress: Where Adam Smith Went Wrong," in *Marxist History-Writing for the Twenty-First Century,* ed. Chris Wickham (Oxford: Oxford University Press, 2007), 49–71.

12. *A munkásosztály felelőssége a szocializmus építésében,* 3.

13. *A dolgozó nép alkotmánya a Magyar Népköztársaság alkotmánya,* 37.

14. Horváth, "A lakás és a fürdő."

15. Erzsébet Severini, *Munkaverseny és a magyar munkás lelkisége (MÁVAG és a csepeli WM Müvek), munkalélektani tanulmány mühelyben a termelésről* (Budapest: Athenaeum, 1946), 7–18.

16. Ember, *Varga Barnabás Kossuth-Díjás vájár,* 39–41.

17. The concept of an "evental site" is adapted from Alain Badiou, *Being and Event,* trans. Oliver Feltham (London: Continuum, 2006), 173–77.

18. This case is made in more depth in Pittaway, "Accommodation and the Limits of Economic Reform."

19. Johann Smula, "The Party and the Proletariat: Škoda, 1948–53," *Cold War History* 6, no. 2 (2006): 153–75; Manfred Hagen, *DDR – Juni '53: Die erste Volkserhebung im Stalinismus* (Stuttgart: Franz Steiner Verlag, 1992); Andrew I. Port, *Conflict and Stability in the German Democratic Republic* (Cambridge: Cambridge University Press, 2007), 70–94; Johanna Granville, "Poland and Hungary, 1956: A Comparative Essay Based on New Archival Findings," in *Revolution and Resistance in Eastern Europe: Challenges to Communist Rule,* ed. Kevin McDermott and Matthew Stibbe (Oxford: Berg Publishers, 2006), 57–77.

20. Jeffrey Kopstein, *The Politics of Economic Decline in East Germany, 1945–1989* (Chapel Hill: University of North Carolina Press, 1997); Peter Hübner, *Konsens, Konflikt und Kompromiß: Soziale Arbeiterinteressen und Sozialpolitik in der SBZ/DDR, 1945–1971* (Berlin: Akademie Verlag, 1995).

21. Peter Heumos, "'Wenn sie sieben Turbinen schaffen, kommt die Musik' Sozialistische Arbeitsinitiativen und egalitarische Defensive in tschechoslowakischen Industriebetrieben und Bergwerkern, 1945–1965," in *Sozialgeschichtliche Kommunismusforschung,* ed. Brenner and Heumos, 133–77.

22. Peter Heumos, "Betriebsräte, Betriebsausschüsse der Einheitsgewerkschaft und Werktätigenräte: Zur Frage der Partizipation in der tschechoslowakischen Industrie vor und im Jahr 1968," in *1968 und die Arbeiter: Studien zum "proletarischen Mai" in Europa,* ed. Bernd Gehrke and Gerd-Rainer Horn (Hamburg: VSA-Verlag, 2007), 131–59.

23. Anikó Eszter Bartha, "Alienating Labor: Workers on the Road from Socialism to Capitalism in East Germany and Hungary" (PhD diss., Central European University, 2007), 179–303.

24. Marcin Zaremba, "Am Rande der Rebellion: Polnische Arbeiter am Vorabend des Arbeiteraufstandes im Dezember 1970," in *1968 und die Arbeiter,* ed. Gehrke and Horn, 210–28.

25. *Az életszínvonal alakulása Magyarországon* (Budapest: A Munkaerő és Életszínvonal Távlati Bizottság, 1970), 23–34; Eszter Zsófia Tóth, "A munkáspolitika hosszú évtízede, 1956–1970," in *Budapest az 1960-as években,* ed. István Feitl (Budapest: Napvilág Kiadó, 2009), 81–94.

26. Pittaway, "Accommodation and the Limits of Economic Reform."

27. Eszter Bartha, "Would You Call Back the Capitalists? Workers and the Beginnings of Market Socialism in Hungary," *Social History* 34, no. 2 (2009): 123–44.

28. Károly Attila Soós, "Béralku és 'sérelmi politika': Adalékok a mechanizmusreform 1969. évi első megtorpanásának magyarázatához," in *Magyar gazdaság és szociológia a 80-as években,* ed. Tamás Miklós (Budapest: Medvetánc, 1988), 91–99.

29. Mark Pittaway, "Workers, Industrial Conflict and the State in Socialist Hungary, 1948–1989" (unpublished), 35–45; Anikó Eszter Bartha, "The Disloyal 'Ruling Class'": The Conflict between Ideology and Experience in Hungary," in *Arbeiter im Staatsozialismus,* ed. Hübner, Kleßmann, and Tenfelde, 227–47.

# Selected Bibliography

## Archival Sources

Az 1956-os Magyar Forradalom Történetének Dokumentációs és Kutatóintézete, Oral History Archívium (1956-os Intézet, OHA), Budapest
    99, Borovszky Ambrus
    177, Nagy Pál Jenő
    181, Péterffy Miklós
    417, Hűvös Oszkár
    449, Homola István
    484, Asztalos János
Budapest Főváros Levéltára (BFL), Budapest
    XI.103f. A BÁMERT iratai
    XXIX.321f. Az Egyesült Izzólámpa és Villamossági Rt. iratai
    XXIX.403f. A Chinoin Gyógyszer és Vegyeszeti Gyár iratai
    XXIX.551f. A Duna Cipőgyár iratai
    XXIX.553f. Az Újpesti Cipőgyár iratai

XXIX.554f. A Wolfner Gyula és Társa iratai

XXIX.555f. A Pannónia Szörmearúgyár iratai

XXXV.1f. Az MSzMP Budapesti Bizottságának iratai

XXXV.9f. Az MSzMP Budapest IV. Kerületi Bizottságának iratai

XXXV.95f. Az MDP Budapesti Bizottságának iratai

XXXV.134f. Az MDP Egyesült Izzó Bizottságának iratai

XXXV.143f. Az MDP Magyar Pamutipar Bizottságának iratai

XXXV.176f. Az MDP Budapest IV. Kerületi Bizottságának iratai

Columbia University Libraries, Rare Book & Manuscript Library, Bakhmeteff Archive
(CUL, RBML, BAR), New York City

    CURPH      Hungarian Refugees Project Manuscripts

Fejér Megyei Levéltár (FML), Székesfehérvár

XXXV.17f. Az MDP Dunai Vasmű épitkezés és Dunapentele / Sztálinváros / Városi
Bizottságának iratai

XXXV.19f. Az MSzMP Fejér Megyei Bizottságának iratai

Győr-Moson-Sopron Megye Győri Levéltára (GyMSMGy.L), Győr

IVf.451a. Győr-Moson-Pozsony k.e.e. vm. és Győr sz. kír. város főispánjá 1938–1945,
Bizalmas iratok

Xf.402 Az MDP Győr-Moson-Sopron Megyei Bizottságának iratai

Komárom-Esztergom Megyei Önkormányzat Levéltára (KEMÖL), Esztergom

XXXV.1f. Az MSzMP Komárom Megyei Bizottságának iratai

XXXV.2f. Az MSzMP Tatabánya Városi Bizottságának iratai

XXXV.23f. Az MKP Komárom-Esztergom Vármegyei Bizottságának iratai

XXXV.24f. Az MKP Tata Járási Bizottságának iratai

XXXV.28f. Az MKP Tatabánya Városi Titkárságának iratai

XXXV.32f. Az MDP Komárom Megyei Bizottságának iratai

XXXV.36f. Az MDP Tatabánya Városi Bizottságának iratai

Központi Statitisztikai Hivatal Könyvtára (KSHK), Budapest

KSH Jelentés ÁLT II, 1953.VIII.6., "Központi Statisztikai Hivatal Jelentése Munkaügyi
Adatok, 1953 II.n.év"

KSH Jelentés ÁLT 8, 1954.VIII.9, "A Magyar Munkásosztály Fejlődése"

KSH Jelentés ÁLT 8, 1955.VII.22, "A lakosság anyagi helyzete: reálbérek – reáljövedelmek, 1949–1954"

KSH Jelentés ÁLT 5, 1956.VIII.1, "A Lakósság Fogyasztása és a Reálbérek, Reáljövedelmek Alakulása 1955-ben, és a 1949–1955 időszakban"

Központi Statisztikai Hivatal Levéltára (KSHL), Budapest

A.5.1. Iparstatisztikai kerdőivek, 1945

Magyar Olajipari Múzeum Archívuma (MOIMA), Zalaegerszeg

45 doboz. Gyulay Zoltán iratai

XXVI. MAORT iratai

XXVII. MAORT Szakszervezetek és Üzemi Bizottság iratai

Magyar Országos Levéltár (MOL), Budapest

M-KS-276f. A Magyar Dolgozók Pártja Központi Vezetőségének iratai

M-KS-288f. A Magyar Szocialista Munkáspárt Központi Bizottságának iratai

XIX-A-16 Az Országos Tervhivatal iratai

XIX-B-1 A Belügyminisztérium iratai

XIX-B-10 A Határőrség Országos Parancsnokság iratai

XXIX-D-22 A Cement- és Mészmüvek Igazgatóságának iratai

XXIX-F-32 A Magyar Állami Szénbányák Rt. iratai

XXIX-F-40 A Magyar-Szovjet Olajipari Részvénytársaság iratai

XXIX-F-107 A Tatabányai Szénbányák Rt. iratai

XXIX-F-135 A Lovászi Kőolajtermelő Vállalat iratai

Z252 A Magyar Általános Kőszénbánya Rt., Titkárságának iratai

Z254 A Magyar Általános Kőszénbánya Rt., Személyzeti Osztályának iratai

Z355 A MAORT Rt., Üzemi Bizottságának iratai

Z356 A MAORT Rt., Titkárságának iratai

Z595 A Magyar Dunántúli Villámos Művek Rt. iratai

Z601 Az Egyesült Izzólámpa és Villamossági Rt., Ügyvezető Igazgatóságának iratai

Z606 Az Egyesült Izzólámpa és Villamossági Rt., Személyzeti Osztályának iratai

Z691 A Magyar Pamutipar, Ügyvezető Igazgatóságának iratai

Z693 A Magyar Pamutipar, Személyzeti Osztályának iratai

Z694 A Magyar Pamutipar, Könyvelőségének iratai

Z905 A MAORT Rt., Személyzeti és Munkaügyi Osztályának iratai

Z909 A MAORT Rt., Szakszervezeti Bizottságának iratai

Z992 A Magyar Általános Kőszénbánya Rt., Ügyvezető Igazgatóságának iratai

Z1204 A Magyar Pamutipar, Üzemi Bizottságának iratai

Open Society Archives (OSA), Budapest

OSA 300/40 Records of the Radio Free Europe/Radio Liberty Research Institute, Hungarian Unit

Országos Szechényi Könyvtár, Kézirattár (OSzK Kt.), Budapest

1956-os gy. 412.VIIf. 1956-os gyűjtemény, Komárom-Esztergom megye

1956-os gy. 412.XIf. 1956-os gyűjtemény, Zala megye

1956-os gy. Bp.NB 1956-os gyűjtemény, Budapest Fővárosi Biróság Népbirósági Tanácsának anyaga

1956-os gy. Gy.NB 1956-os gyűjtemény, Győri Megyei Biróság Népbirósági Tanácsanak anyaga

Politikatörténeti és Szakszervezeti Levéltár (PtSzL), Budapest

I.274f. A Magyar Kommunista Párt iratai

I.283f. A Magyarországi Szociáldemokrata Párt iratai

VI.867f. Munkásmozgalmi Visszaemlékezések

IX.290f. Az 1956-os gyűjtemény

X.38f. Az MKP Budapesti Területi Bizottsága

X.39f. Az MKP Nagy-Budapesti Bizottsága

X.60f. Az MKP Újpest Városi Bizottságának iratai

X.77f. Az MKP Egyesült Izzólámpa és Villamossági Rt. Bizottságának iratai

XII.1f. Szakszervezeti Tanács iratai

XII.2f. Szakszervezetek Országos Tanácsa iratai

XII.20f. Szakszervezetek Komárom Megyei Tanácsa

XII.29f. Szakszervezetek Zala Megyei Tanácsa

XII.30f. Bányaipari Dolgozók Szakszervezete

XII.46f. Textilipari Dolgozók Szakszervezete

XII.47f. Vas-, Fém és Villamosipari Dolgozók Szakszervezete

Tatabánya Megyei Jogú Város Levéltára (TMJVL), Tatabánya

Tatabánya Városi Tanács V.B. Jegyzőkönyvek

Tatabánya Múzeum Adattára (TMA), Tatabánya

15-76 Roznai Florián visszaemlékezése

149-76 A szocialista építőmunka néhány kérdése a Magyar Dolgozók Pártja helyi szerveinek irányító tevékenységben 1948–1956

347-78 Az MKP Megalakulása és Tevékenységének Első Időszaka Komárom-Esztergom Vármegyében, 1945–1946

410-80 A tatabányai szénbányák államosítása

413-80 A tatabányai üzemek államosítása

513-82 Tatabányai Hőerőmű Vállalat Története

746-90 A bányavidék négy községe /Alsógálla, Bánhida, Felsőgalla, Tatabánya/ közel-látásának alakulása a második világháboru idején és utána 1956-ig

728-89 Adatok a tatabányai VIII és XIV aknák történetéhez

791-95 A tatabányai XII számú Bányaüzem 1950 évi bányaszerencsétlensége

Zala Megyei Levéltár (ZML), Zalaegerszeg

IV.403f. Zala Vármegye Törvényhatósági Bizottsága Központi Választmányanak iratai

XXV.19. Zala Megyei Bíróság Büntetőperes iratai

XXIX.8f. Dunántúli Kőolajtermelő Vállalat Gellénháza

XXXV.1f. Az MSzMP Zala Megyei Bizottságának iratai

XXXV.2f. Az MSzMP Zalaegerszeg Járási Bizottságának iratai

XXXV.5f. Az MSzMP Letenye Járási Bizottságának iratai

XXXV.8f. Az MSzMP Nagykanizsa Városi Bizottságának iratai

XXXV.25f. Az MSzMP Bazakerettye Olajüzemi Bizottságának iratai

XXXV.26f. Az MSzMP Lovászi Olajüzemi Bizottságának iratai

XXXV.38f. Az MKP Zala Vármegyei Bizottságának iratai

XXXV.44f. Az MKP Nagykanizsa Városi Bizottságának iratai

XXXV.52f. Az MKP MAORT Központi Titkárságának iratai

XXXV.57f. Az MDP Zala Megyei Bizottságának iratai

XXXV.58f. Az MDP Zalaegerszeg Járási Bizottságának iratai

XXXV.61f. Az MDP Letenye Járási Bizottságának iratai

XXXV.63f. Az MDP Zalaegerszeg Városi Bizottságának iratai

Uncatalogued. Az MSzMP Zala Megyei Bizottság Archiviuma, Vegyes Iratok, 3360D/ KSH Jelentések

## Published Primary Sources

Andics, Erzsébet. *Fasizmus és reakció Magyarországon.* Budapest: Szikra kiadás, 1948.

Balogh, Sándor, ed. *Nehéz esztendők krónikája, 1949–1953.* Budapest: Gondolat Könyvkiadó, 1986.

———, and Margit Földesi, eds. *A magyar jóvátétel, és ami mögötte van. . . .* Budapest: Napvilág Kiadó, 1998.

Bana, József, ed. *Győr 1956 III: Munkástanács-vezetők per a győri megyei biróság előtt, 1957–1958.* Győr: Győr Megyei Jogú Város Önkormányzata, 2002.

Békés, Csaba, Malcolm Byrne, and János M. Rainer, eds. *The 1956 Hungarian Revolution: A History in Documents.* Budapest: Central European University Press, 2002.

Belényi, Gyula, and Lajos Sz. Varga, eds. *Munkások Magyarországon, 1948–1956: dokumentumok.* Budapest: Napvilág Kiadó, 2000.

Benoschofsky, Ilona, and Elek Karsai, eds. *Vádirat a Nácizmus ellen: dokumentumok a magyarországi zsidóüldözés történetéhez. I. 1944 március 19 – 1944 május 15; a német megszállástól a deportálás megkezdéséig.* Budapest: Magyar Izraeliták Országos Képviselete Kiadása, 1958.

Bircher, Erzsébet, ed. *Kor-Kép: dokumentumok és tanulmányok a magyar bányászat 1945 és 1958 közötti történetéből.* Sopron: Központi Bányászati Múzeum Alapítvány, 2002.

Borovsky, Samu, ed. *Komárom Vármegye és Komárom Sz. Kir. Város: Magyarország Vármegyei és Városai Magyarország monografiája.* Budapest: Országos Monográfia Társaság, 1907.

———, ed. *Pest-Pilis-Solt Vármegye II: Magyarország Vármegyei és Városai Magyarország monografiája.* Budapest: Országos Monográfia Társaság, 1910.

Cosic, Dobricia. *7 nap Budapesten 1956: október 23–30.* Budapest: Bethlen Gábor Könyvkiadó, 1989.

Cserhalmi, Imre, ed. *Történelmi kulcsátvétel: interjúk államosító igazgatókkal.* Budapest: Kossuth Könyvkiadó, 1983.

Csomor, Erzsébet, and Imre Kapiller, eds. *'56 Zalában: a forradalom eseményeinek Zala megyei dokumentumai, 1956–1958.* Zalaegerszeg: Zala Megyei Levéltár, 1996.

Dekán, Sándor. *Darrabérrendzerrel a szocialista bérezés megvalósitása felé.* Budapest: Népszava, 1950.

*A dolgozó nép alkotmánya: a Magyar Népköztársaság alkotmánya.* Budapest: Szikra, 1949.

*Az életszínvonal alakulása Magyarországon.* Budapest: A Munkaerő és Életszínvonal Távlati Bizottság, 1970.

*Ellenforradalmi erők a magyar októberi eseményekben. I–IV kötet.* Budapest: A Magyar Népköztársaság Minisztertanácsa Tájékoztatási Hivatala – Zrinyi Nyomda, 1957.

*Az első országos Élmunkás Kongresszus határozata.* Budapest: Szakszervezetek Országos Tanácsa, 1948.

Ember, György. *Varga Barnabás Kossuth-Díjás vájár.* Budapest: A Munka Hősei, Népszava, 1951.

Erdmann, Gyula, and Iván Pető, eds. *Dokumentumok a magyar szénbányászat történetéből, 1945–1949: források a magyar népi demokrácia történetehez I. kötet.* Budapest: Kossuth Könyvkiadó – Új Magyar Központi Levéltár – Nehézipari Minisztérium, 1975.

Feitl, István, ed. *A magyarországi Szövetséges Ellenőrző Bizottság ülésének jegyzőkönyvei, 1945–1947.* Budapest: Napvilág Kiadó, 2003.

Földes, Mihály. *Pillanatképek az újpesti partizánharcokról: kollektiv riport.* Újpest: Magyar Kommunista Párt Újpesti szervezete, 1945.

Garai, Tibor. *A kultúrtényező jelentősége a versenyszellem kialakításában.* Budapest: Munkatudományi és Racionalizálási Intézet, 1948.

Gereblyés, László. *Így volt: szociográfiai jegyzetek a 30-as évekből.* Budapest: Magvető Könyvkiadó, 1959.

Gerő, Ernő. *Harcban a szocialista népgazdaságért: válogatott beszédek és cikkek, 1944–1950.* Budapest: Szikra, 1950.

Habuda, Miklós, ed. *A SZIT: a szakszervezeti ifjúmunkás- és tanoncmozgalom, 1945–1950.* Budapest: Kossuth Könyvkiadó, 1985.

Habuda, Miklós, Sándor Rákosi, Gábor Székely, and György T. Varga, eds. *A Magyar Dolgozók Pártja határozatai, 1948–1956.* Budapest: Napvilág Kiadó, 1997.

Halázs, Zoltán. *Sztankovits János sztahanovista marós élete és munkamódszere.* Budapest: A Munka Hősei, Népszava, 1951.

*Harc a másodpercekért: kézikönyv az országos termelési versenyhez.* Budapest: Szakszervezeti Ifjúmunkás és Tanoncmogalom, 1948.

Hegedűs, András B., and János M. Rainer, eds. *A Petőfi Kör vitai hiteles jegyzőkönyvek alapján: I. Két közgazdasági vita.* Budapest: Kelenföld Kiadó-ELTE, 1989.

———. *A Petőfi Kör vitai hiteles jegyzőkönyvek alapján: IV. Partizántalálkozó-sajtóvita.* Budapest: Múszák Kiadó – 1956-os Intézet, 1991.

Hevesi, Gyula. *Sztahánov útján: a magyar újító mozgalom fejlődése és feladatai.* Budapest: Athenaeum Könyvkiadó, 1949.

Horváth, Julianna, and Zoltán Ripp, eds. *Ötvenhat októbere és a hatalom: a Magyar Dolgozók Pártja vezető testületeinek dokumentumai 1956 október 24–október 28.* Budapest: Napvilág Kiadó, 1997.

Illyefalvi, Lajos I. *A munkások szociális és gazdasági viszonyai Budapesten.* Budapest: Budapest Székesfőváros Statisztikai Hivatal, 1930.

Izsák, Lajos, József Szabó, and Róbert Szabó, eds. *1956 plakátjai és röplapjai: október 22–november 5.* Budapest: Zrínyi Kiadó, 1991.

"Jegyzőkönyv a szovjet és a magyar part- és állami vezetők tárgyalásairól (1953. június 13–16)." Reprinted in *Múltunk* 37, no. 2–3 (1992): 234–69.

Jenei, Károly, ed. *A munkásság az üzemekért, a termelésért, 1944–1945: dokumentumgyűjtemény.* Budapest: Tánsics Könyvkiadó, 1970.

———, Béla Rácz, and Erzsébet Strassenreiter, eds. *Az üzemi bizottságok a munkáshatalomért 1944–1948.* Budapest: Tánsics Könyvkiadó, 1966.

Kahler, Frigyes, et al., eds. *Sortüzek 1956.* 2d ed. Budapest and Lakitelek: Igazságügyi Minisztérium – Antológia Kiadó, 1993.

Kajári, Erzsébet, ed. *Rendőrségi napi jelentések, 1956. október 23.–december 12., első kötet.* Budapest: A Belügyminisztérium és az 1956-os Magyar Forradalom Történetének Dokumentációs és Kutató Intézete Közalapítványa, 1996.

———. *Rendőrségi napi jelentések, 1956. december 13–december 31., második kötet.* Budapest:

A Belügyminisztérium és az 1956-os Magyar Forradalom Történetének Dokumentációs és Kutató Intézete Közalapítványa, 1997.

Káli, Csaba, ed. *Dokumentumok Zala megye történetéből 1947–1956.* Zalaegerszeg: Zala Megyei Levéltár, 1999.

——, and Zsuzsa Mikó, eds. *Dokumentumok Zala megye történetéből 1944–1947.* Zalaegerszeg: Zala Megyei Levéltár, 1995.

Karsai, Elek, ed. *Vádirat a Nácizmus ellen: dokumentumok a magyarországi zsidóüldözés történetéhez, 3. 1944 május 16–1944 október 15; a Budapesti zsidóság deportálásának felfüggesztése.* Budapest: Magyar Izraeliták Országos Képviselete Kiadása, 1967.

——, and László Karsai, eds. *A Szálasi per.* Budapest: Reform, 1988.

Karsai, László, and Judit Molnár, eds. *A magyar quisling-kormány: Sztójay döme és társai a népbíróság előtt.* Budapest: 1956-os KHT., 2004.

Kassai-Végh, Miklós, ed. *A salgótarjáni munkások műveltsége és művelődése: munkásportrék.* Budapest: MSzMP Központi Bizottsága Társadalomtudományi Intézete, 1977.

Katona, Csaba, et al., eds. *Emlékezz! Válogatott levéltári források a magyarországi zsidóság üldöztetésének történetéhez 1938–1945.* Budapest: Magyar Országos Levéltár, 2004.

*Kétlakiság.* Budapest: Szakszervezeti Ismeretterjesztő Előadások, Népszava, 1952.

Kenedi, János, and László Varga, eds. *A forradalom hangja: magyarországi rádióadások 1956; október 23–november 9.* Budapest: Századvég Kiadó-Nyilvánosság Klub, 1989.

*Komárom megye fontosabb statisztikai adatai, 1952–1955.* Tatabánya: KSH Komárommegyei Igazgatósága, 1956.

*Komárom megye legfontosabb statisztikai adatai, 1956.* Tatabánya: KSH Komárommegyei Igazgatósága, 1957.

Kovács, Klára. *Szén volt az életük: portrék, riportok, tárcák, elbeszélések.* Tatabánya: Tatabánya Megyei Jogú Város Önkormányzata, 1999.

Központi Statisztikai Hivatal. *Az 1941. évi népszámlálás demografiai adatok kőzségek szerint.* Budapest: Stephaneum Nyomda Részvénytársaság, 1947.

——. *Az 1941. évi népszámlálás 1: foglalkozási adatok kőzségek szerint.* Budapest: Központi Statisztikai Hivatal Könyvtár és Dokumentációs Szolgálat – Magyar Országos Levéltár, 1975.

——. *1949. évi népszámlálás 3: részletes mezőgazdasági eredmények.* Budapest: Állami Nyomda, 1950.

——. *1949. évi népszámlálás 8: foglalkozási statisztika részletes eredményei.* Budapest: Állami Nyomda, 1950.

——. *1949. évi népszámlálás 9: demográfiai eredmények.* Budapest: Állami Nyomda, 1950.

——. *A magyar könnyüipar statisztikai adatgyűjteménye.* Budapest: Központi Statisztikai Hivatal, 1962.

——. *Statisztikai évkönyv 1950.* Budapest: Központi Statisztikai Hivatal, 1951.

——. *Statisztikai évkönyv 1951.* Budapest: Központi Statisztikai Hivatal, 1952.

——. *Statisztikai évkönyv 1952.* Budapest: Központi Statisztikai Hivatal, 1953.

——. *Statisztikai évkönyv 1953.* Budapest: Központi Statisztikai Hivatal, 1954.

Litván, György, ed. *Magyar munkásszociográfiák, 1888–1945.* Budapest: Kossuth Könyvkiadó, 1974.

Lomax, Bill, ed. *Eyewitness in Hungary: The Soviet Invasion of 1956.* Nottingham, England: Spokesman Press, 1980.

———, ed. *Workers' Councils in 1956.* Translated by Bill Lomax and Julian Schöpflin. New York: Columbia University Press, 1990.

*A magyar általános kőszénbánya részvénytársulat 50 éve, 1891–1941: az igazgatóság külön jelentése az 1942.évi április hó 30-ra egybehivott ünnepi közgyűléshez.* Budapest: MÁK Rt., 1942.

*A Magyar Dolgozók Pártja III: kongresszusának rövidített jegyzőkönyve.* 2d ed. Budapest: Szikra, 1954.

*A Magyar Dolgozók Pártja központi vezetőségének, politikai bizottságának és szervező bizottságának fontosabb határozatai.* Budapest: Szikra, 1951.

Magyary, Zoltán, and István Kiss. *A közigazgatás és az emberek: ténymegállapító tanulmány a tatai járás közigazgatásáról.* Budapest: Pécsi Egyetemi Könyvkiadó és Nyomda Rt., 1939.

Márkus, István. *Az ismeretlen főszereplő: tanulmányok.* Budapest: Szépirodalmi Könyvkiadó, 1991.

Marosán, György. *A tanúk még élnek 1956.* Budapest: Hírlapkiadó Vállalat, 1989.

Mikos, Ferenc, László Nagy, and Andor Weltner, eds. *A munka törvénykönyve és végrehajtási szabályai.* Budapest: Közgazdasági és Jogi Könyvkiadó, 1955.

*Mit adott a népi demokrácia a dolgozóknak?* Budapest: Kiadja a Magyar Dolgozók Pártja Közpönti Vezetősége Agitációs és Propaganda Osztály, 1953.

Molnár, András, ed. *Zala megye történelmi olvasókönyve: helytörténeti szöveggyűjtemény.* Zalaegerszeg: Zala Megyei Levéltár, 1996.

*A munkafegyelem megszilárdítása és a munkakönyvrendszer.* Budapest: Jogi és Államigazgatási Könyv- és Folyóiratkiadó, 1954.

*A munkásosztály felelőssége a szocializmus építésében.* Budapest: Kiadja a Magyar Dolgozók Pártja Központi Vezetősége Oktatási Osztály, 1950.

Nagy, Imre. *Agrárpolitikai tanulmányok: előadások az Agrártudományi Egyetemen és a Mezőgazdasági Akadémián.* Budapest: Szikra, 1950.

———. *Egy évtized: válogatott beszédek és írások (1948–1954) II.* Budapest: Szikra, 1954.

*Nagy Imre és bűntársai ellenforradalmi összesküvése.* Budapest: A Magyar Népköztársaság Minisztertanácsa Tájékoztatási Hivatala – Zrinyi Nyomda, 1958.

*A népi demokrácia útja: A Magyar Kommunista Párt Budapesten 1946 szeptember 28., 29., 30. és október 1. napján megtartott III. Kongresszusának jegyzőkönyve.* Budapest: Szikra Kiadás, 1946.

Orutay, András. *Komárom megyei helytörténeti olvasókönyv.* Tatabánya: Komárom Megyei Tanács VB. Művelődési Osztálya, 1988.

Paloczi-Horváth, George. *The Undefeated.* London: Eland, 1993.

*Pamutipari sztahanovisták élete és munkamódszere.* Budapest: Könnyüipari Könyvkiadó, 1951.

Papp, Simon. *Életem.* 2d ed. Zalaegerszeg: Magyar Olaipari Múzeum, 2000.

Rákosi, Mátyás. *Építjük a nép országát.* Budapest: Szikra Kiadás, 1949.

———. *Válogatott beszédek és cikkek.* Budapest: Szikra, 1950.

———. *Visszaemlékezések, 1940–1956, II. kötet.* Budapest: Napvilág Kiadó, 1997.

Rákosi, Sándor, Erzsébet Strassenreiter, Bálint Szabó, and Éva Szabó, eds. *A munkásosztály az újjáépítésért, 1945–1946.* Budapest: Kossuth Könyvkiadó, 1960.

Rákosi, Sándor, and Bálint Szabó, eds. *A Magyar Kommunista Párt és a Szociáldemokrata Párt határozatai, 1944–1948.* 2d ed. Budapest: Kossuth Könyvkiadó, 1974.

Ránki, György, Ervin Pamlényi, Loránt Tilkovszky, and Gyula Juhász, eds. *A Wilhelmstrasse és Magyarország: német diplomáciai iratok magyarországról, 1933–1944.* Budapest: Kossuth Könyvkiadó, 1968.

Ravasz, Éva, ed. *Tatabánya a II: világháborúban; dokumentumok és tanulmányok.* Tatabánya: Tatabánya Megyei Jogú Város Levéltára, 2006.

Rézler, Gyula. *Egy magyar textilgyár munkástársadalma.* Budapest: Magyar Ipari Munkatudományi Intézet, 1943.

———, ed. *Magyar gyári munkásság: szociális helyzetkép.* Budapest: Magyar Közgazdasági Társaság, 1940.

Sándor, András. *Övék a föld.* Budapest: Szikra Kiadás, 1948.

Severini, Erzsébet. *Munkaverseny és a magyar munkás lelkisége (MÁVAG és a csepeli WM Müvek), munkalélektani tanulmány mühelyben a termelésről.* Budapest: Athenaeum, 1946.

Sipos, András, ed. *Dokumentumok Újpest történetéhez, 1840–1949.* Budapest: Budapest Főváros Levéltára, 2001.

Somlyai, Magda M., ed. *Földreform 1945, tanulmány és dokumentumgyűjtemény.* Budapest: Kossuth Könyvkiadó, 1965.

Sors, László. *A mutatószámos teljesítménybérezés elméleti és gyakorlati alapjai.* Budapest: Munkatudományi és Racionalizálási Intézet, 1948.

Sós, Aladár, Kálman Faragó, Géza Hermány, György Korompay, eds. *Sztálinváros-Miskolc-Tatabánya, városépítésünk fejlődése.* Budapest: Műszaki Könyvkiadó, 1959.

Szabó, Zoltán. *Cifra nyomorúság: a Cserhát, Mátra, Bükk földje és népe.* Budapest: Cserépfalvi Kiadása, 1938.

*Szakszervezetek bérpolitikája.* Budapest: Népszava, 1948.

Szamuely, László, ed. *A magyar közgazdasági gondolat fejlődése 1954–1978: a szocialista gazdaság mechanizmusának kutatása.* Budapest: Közgazdasági és Jogi Könyvkiadó, 1986.

Szinai, Miklós, and László Szűcs, eds. *Horthy Miklós titkos iratai.* Budapest: Kossuth Könyvkiadó, 1965.

*A szocializmus építésének útján: a Magyar Dolgozók Pártja II; kongresszusának anyagából.* 2d ed. Budapest: Szikra, 1956.

Szűcs, László, ed. *Dálnoki Miklós Béla kormányának (Ideiglenes Nemzeti Kormány) minisztertanácsi jegyzőkönyvei, 1944. december 23.–1945. november 15. A-B kötet.* Budapest: Magyar Országos Levéltár, 1997.

"Tájékoztató a Központi Munkástanácsnak Kádár János Miniszterelnökkel 1956. November 30-án folytatott Tárgyalásairól." Reprinted in Pál Germuska, "Kádár János Tatabányán 1956. november 30-án." *Beszélő,* ser. 3, vol. 1, no. 7 (1996): 77–85.

Ugró, Gyula. *Újpest 1831–1930: magyar városok monografia.* Budapest: A Magyar Városok Monografiája Kiadóhivatala, 1932.

Vágyi Némethné, Karola, and Levente Sipos, eds. *A Magyar Szocialista Munkáspárt ideiglenes vezető testületeinek jegyzőkönyvei. I. kötet. 1956. november 11.–1957. január 14.* Budapest: Intera Rt., 1993.

Varga, Domokos. *Kiszlinger József Sztahanovista esztergályos élete és munkamódszere.* Budapest: A Munka Hősei, Népszava, 1951.

Vass, Henrik, and Ágnes Ságvári, eds. *A Magyar Szocialista Munkáspárt határozatai és dokumentumai, 1956–1962.* 2d expanded ed. Budapest: Kossuth Könyvkiadó, 1973.

Vida, István, ed. *1956 és a politikai pártok: politikai pártok az 1956-os forradalomban; 1956. október 23.–november 4.* Budapest: MTA Jelenkor-kutató Bizottság, 1998.

Vidos, Dénes. *Zalai olajos történetek.* Zalaegerszeg: Magyar Olajipari Múzeum, 1990.

Vonyó, József, ed. *Gömbös pártja: a Nemzeti Egység Pártja dokumentumai.* Budapest and Pécs: Dialóg Campus Kiadó, 1998.

Zolnay, Vilmos. *Pióker Ignác az ország legjobb gyalusa.* Budapest: A Munka Hősei, Népszava, Budapest, 1951.

Zsigmondi, Mária. *Makár Jánosné Sztahanovista szövőnő élete és munkamódszere.* Budapest: A Munka Hősei, Népszava, Budapest, 1951.

## Secondary Sources

Abrams, Bradley F. *The Struggle for the Soul of the Nation: Czech Culture and the Rise of Communism.* Lanham, MD: Rowman & Littlefield, 2004.

Agamben, Giorgio. *State of Exception.* Translated by Kevin Atell. Chicago: University of Chicago Press, 2005.

Andor, Mihály, ed. *Újpest: tanulmánykötet.* Budapest: Művelődéskutató Intézet, 1982.

Ark, Bart van, Erik Buyst, and Jan Luiten van Zanden, eds. *Historical Benchmark Comparison of Output and Productivity.* Seville: Secretariado de Publicaciones de la Universidad de Sevilla, 1998.

Badiou, Alain. *Being and Event.* Translated by Oliver Feltham. London: Continuum, 2006.

Bak, János, András B. Hegedűs, György Litván, János M. Rainer, and Katalin S. Varga, eds. *Az 1956-os magyar forradalom történetének dokumentációs és kutatóintézete évkönyv III. 1994.* Budapest: 1956-os Intézet, 1994.

Balogh, Margit. *Mindszenty József (1892–1975).* Budapest: Elektra Kiadóház, 2002.

Balogh, Sándor. *Parlamenti és pártharcok magyarországon, 1945–1947.* Budapest: Kossuth Könyvkiadó, 1975.

———. *Választások Magyarországon 1945: a fővárosi törvényhatósági és nemzetgyűlési Választások.* Budapest: Kossuth Könyvkiadó, 1984.

Bárdos, László István. *Egy bányászváros a szocialista fejlődés útján: Tatabánya 1945–1960.* Tatabánya: Tatabánya Városi Tanács, 1960.

Bartha, Anikó Eszter. "Alienating Labor: Workers on the Road from Socialism to Capitalism in East Germany and Hungary." PhD dissertation, Central European University, 2007.

———. "Would You Call Back the Capitalists? Workers and the Beginnings of Market Socialism in Hungary." *Social History* 34, no. 2 (2009): 123–44.

Beetham, David. *The Legitimation of Power*. Basingstoke, England: Macmillan, 1991.

Békés, Csaba, ed. *Evolúció és revolúció: Magyarország és a nemzetközi politika 1956-ban*. Budapest: 1956-os Intézet – Gondolat Kiadó, 2007.

Béli, József. *Az 1945-ös földreform végrehajtása Zala megyében*. Zalaegerszeg: Zala Megyei Levéltár, 1977.

Bencsík, Zsuzsanna, and Gábor Kresalek, eds. *Az ostromtól a forradalomig: adalékok Budapest múltjáról*. Budapest: Budapest Főváros Levéltára, 1990.

Bencze, Géza. *Zala megye iparának története a felszabadulás után (1945–1975)*. Zalaegerszeg: Zala Megyei Tanács V.B. & az MTESZ Zala megyei szervezete, 1980.

Ben-Ghiat, Ruth. *Fascist Modernities: Italy, 1922–1945*. Berkeley and Los Angeles: University of California Press, 2001.

Berend, Iván T. *Gazdaságpolitika az első ötéves terv megindulásakor 1948–1950*. Budapest: Közgazdasági és Jogi Könyvkiadó, 1964.

———. *Gazdasági útkeresés, 1956–1965: a szocialista gazdaság magyarországi modelljének történetéhez*. Budapest: Magvető Könyvkiadó, 1983.

———, ed. *Az Ózdi Kohászati Üzemek története*. Ózd: Ózdi Kohászati Üzemek, 1980.

———. *Újjáépítés és a nagytőke elleni harc Magyarországon 1945–1948*. Budapest: Közgazdasági és Jogi Könyvkiadó, 1962.

Berend, Iván T., and György Ránki. *Magyarország gyáripara a második világháború elött és a háború időszakában, 1933–1944*. Budapest: Akadémiai Kiadó, 1958.

Berényi, András, et al. *Újpest: IV. kerület*. Budapest: Ceba Kiadó, 1998.

Berkovits, György. "A gyarmat: Újpest történeti szociográfiája, 1835–1868." *Valóság* 24, no. 8 (1981): 32–50.

Bessel, Richard, and Ralph Jessen, eds. *Die Grenzen der Diktatur: Staat und Gesellschaft in der DDR*. Göttingen: Vandenhoeck & Ruprecht, 1996.

———, and Dirk Schumann, eds. *Life after Death: Approaches to a Cultural and Social History of Europe during the 1940s and 1950s*. Washington, DC: German Historical Institute; Cambridge: Cambridge University Press, 2003.

Bircher, Erzsébet, and Balázs Schuller, eds. *Bányászok és bányászvárosok forradalma, 1956: tanulmányok az 1956-os forradalom és szabadságharc tiszteletére*. Sopron: Központi Bányászati Múzeum, 2006.

Birta, István. "A szocialista iparositási politika néhány kérdése az első ötéves terv időszakában." *Párttörténeti Közlemények* 16, no. 3 (1970): 113–51.

Bokovoy, Melissa K. *Peasants and Communists: Politics and Ideology in the Yugoslav Countryside, 1941–1953*. Pittsburgh: University of Pittsburgh Press, 1998.

Borhi, László. *Hungary in the Cold War 1945–1956: Between the United States and the Soviet Union*. Budapest: Central European University Press, 2004.

Borsodi, Csaba. "A szerzetesek kitelepítései 1950 nyarán." *Jel* 12, no. 6 (2000): 12–16.

Braham, Randolph L. *The Politics of Genocide: The Holocaust in Hungary*. Condensed ed. Detroit: Wayne State University Press, 2000.

Brenner, Christiane, and Peter Heumos, eds. *Sozialgeschichtliche Kommunismusforschung: Tscechoslowakei, Polen, Ungarn und DDR, 1948–1968*. Munich: R.Oldenbourg Verlag, 2005.

Breuning, Eleonore, Jill Lewis, and Gareth Pritchard, eds. *Power and the People: A Social History of Central European Politics, 1945–1956*. Manchester: Manchester University Press, 2005.

Brzezinski, Zbigniew K. *The Soviet Bloc: Unity and Conflict*. Rev. ed. Cambridge, MA: Harvard University Press, 1967.

Buda, Ernő, and József Kovács, eds. *Ötven éves a magyar kőolaj- és földgázbányászat KFV 1937–1987*. Nagykanizsa: Kőolaj- és Földgázbányászati Vállalat, 1987.

Burawoy, Michael. *The Politics of Production: Factory Regimes under Capitalism and Socialism*. London: Verso, 1985.

———, and János Lukács. *The Radiant Past: Ideology and Reality in Hungary's Road to Capitalism*. Chicago: University of Chicago Press, 1992.

Buza, Márton, Tibor Hetés, Sándorné Gábor, János Kende, and Péter Sipos. *A Magyarországi Vas- és Fémmunkások Központi Szövetségének története*. Budapest: A Magyarországi Vas- és Fémmunkások Központi Szövetsége, 1990.

Cabrera, Miguel A. *Postsocial History: An Introduction*. Translated by Marie McMahon. Lanham, MD: Lexington Books, 2004.

Cole, Tim. *Holocaust City: The Making of a Jewish Ghetto*. New York and London: Routledge, 2003.

Connelly, John. *Captive University: The Sovietization of East German, Czech, and Polish Higher Education*. Chapel Hill: University of North Carolina Press, 2000.

Conway, Martin, and Peter Romijn. "Introduction." *Contemporary European History* 13, no. 4 (2004): 377–88.

Csics, Gyula, Sándor Pataki, and Sándor Rozsnyói, eds. *A Tatabányai szénbányászat története*. Tatabánya: Tatabánya Szébányászati Tröszt, 1994.

Csicsery-Rónay, István, and Géza Cserenyey. *Koncepciós pér: a Független Kisgazdapárt szétzúzására, 1947*. Budapest: 1956-os Intézet, 1998.

Csomor, Erzsébet. *1956 Zalaegerszegen*. Zalaegerszeg: Millecentenárium Közalapítvány, 2001.

———, and Imre Kapiller, eds. *'56 Zala megyei kronológiája és személyi adattára I.–II. kötet*. Zalaegerszeg: Zala Megyei Levéltár, 2004.

Darvas, Péter. "Oktatás és tervgazdálkodás." *Medvetánc*, no. 4 (1983): 59–75.

Deák, István, Jan T. Gross, and Tony Judt, eds. *The Politics of Retribution in Europe: World War II and Its Aftermath*. Princeton NJ: Princeton University Press, 2000.

Degré, Alajos, and Imre Halász, eds. *Közlemények Zala megye közgyűjteményeinek kutatásaiból, 1984–1985*. Zalaegerszeg: Zala Megyei Levéltár, 1985.

Dessewffy, Tibor, and András Szántó. *"Kitörő éberséggel": A budapesti kitelepítések hiteles története*. Budapest: Lap-és Könyvkiadó, 1989.

Dimitrov, Vesselin. *Stalin's Cold War: Soviet Foreign Policy, Democracy and Communism in Bulgaria, 1941–48*. Basingstoke, England: Palgrave Macmillan, 2008.

Dombrády, Loránd. *A magyar hadigazdaság a második világháború idején*. Budapest: Petit Real Könyvkiadó, 2003.

Dornbach, Alajos, László Győri, Péter Kende, János M. Rainer, and Katalin Somlai, eds. *A per: Nagy Imre és társai, 1958, 1989*. Budapest: 1956-os Intézet – Nagy Imre Alapítvány, 2008.

Dósa, Rudolfné. *A MOVE: egy jellegzetes magyar fasiszta szervezet, 1918–1944*. Budapest: Akadémiai Kiadó, 1972.

Eley, Geoff. *A Crooked Line: From Cultural History to the History of Society*. Ann Arbor: University of Michigan Press, 2005.

———, and Keith Nield. *The Future of Class in History: What's Left of the Social?* Ann Arbor: University of Michigan Press, 2007.

Emsley, Clive, Eric Johnson, and Pieter Sprierenburg, eds. *Social Control in Europe*. Volume 2, *1800–2000*. Columbus: Ohio State University Press, 2004.

Eörsi, László. *The Hungarian Revolution of 1956: Myths and Realities*. Translated by Mario D. Fenyo. Boulder, CO: Social Science Monographs; Wayne, NJ: Center for Hungarian Studies and Publications, 2006.

———. *Köztársaság tér 1956*. Budapest: 1956-os Intézet, 2006.

Erdmann, Gyula. *Begyűjtés, beszolgáltatás Magyarországon, 1945–1956*. Gyula: Békés Megyei Levéltár, 1996.

———, and Iván Pető. *A magyar szénbányászat a felszabadulástól a hároméves terv végéig*. Budapest: Akadémiai Kiadó, 1977.

Erényi, Tibor, and Sándor Rákosi, eds. *Legyőzhetetlen erő: a magyar kommunista mozgalom szervezeti fejlődésének 50 éve*. 2d ed. Budapest: Kossuth Könyvkiadó, 1974.

Fazekas, Béla. *A mezőgazdasági termelőszövetkezeti mozgalom Magyarországon*. Budapest: Kossuth Könyvkiadó, 1976.

Feitl, István, ed. *Az Ideiglenes Nemzetgyűlés és az Ideiglenes Nemzeti Kormány, 1944–1945*. Budapest: Politikatörténeti Alapítvány, 1995.

———, ed. *Budapest az 1960-as években*. Budapest: Napvilág Kiadó, 2009.

Földes, György. "Egyszerűsítés, mechanizmus és iparirányítás, 1953–1956." *Párttörténeti Közlemények* 30, no. 2 (1984): 72–108.

———. "A Kádár-rendszer és a munkásság." *Eszmélet*, no. 18–19 (1993): 57–73.

———. "Az újpesti munkásság életviszonyai az 1930-as években." *Történelmi Szemle* 20, no. 2 (1980): 309–18.

Frommer, Benjamin. *National Cleansing: Retribution against Nazi Collaborators in Postwar Czechoslovakia*. Cambridge: Cambridge University Press, 2004.

Fűrészné Molnár, Anikó, ed. *Tatabánya 45 éve város*. Tata: Komárom-Esztergom Megyei Önkormányzat Múzeumainak Igazgatósága, 1992.

Gadanecz, Béla, and Éva Gadanecz. "A weisshausisták tevékenysége és üldöztetése 1945 után." *Múltunk* 40, no. 3 (1995): 3–72.

Gati, Charles. *Failed Illusions: Moscow, Washington, and the 1956 Hungarian Revolt*. Washington, DC: Woodrow Wilson Center; Stanford: Stanford University Press, 2006.

Gehrke, Bernd, and Gerd-Rainer Horn, eds. *1968 und die Arbeiter: Studien zum "proletarischen Mai" in Europa*. Hamburg: VSA-Verlag, 2007.

Gerelyes, Ede, ed. *Újpest története*. Budapest: Közgazdasági és Jogi Könyvkiadó, 1977.

Gergely, Ernő. *A magyarországi bányász munkásmozgalom története 1867–1944*. Budapest: Friedrich Ebert Alapítvány, 1994.

Gergely, Jenő. *A Katolikus egyház Magyarországon, 1944–1971*. Budapest: Kossuth Könyvkiadó, 1985.

———. *Gömbös Gyula: politikai pályakép*. Budapest: Vince Kiadó, 2001.

Gerlach, Christian, and Götz Aly. *Das letzte Kapitel: Der Mord an den ungarischen Juden, 1944–1945*. Frankfurt: Fischer Taschenbuch Verlag, 2004.

Germuska, Pál. *Indusztria bűvöletében: fejlesztéspolitika és a szocialista városok*. Budapest: 1956-os Intézet, 2004.

Gombkötö, Gábor, et al., eds. *Tatabánya története: helytörténeti tanulmányok I.–II. kötet*. Tatabánya: Tatabánya Városi Tanács, 1972.

Granville, Johanna. *The First Domino: International Decision Making during the Hungarian Crisis of 1956*. College Station: Texas A&M University Press, 2004.

Gunst, Péter, ed. *Hungarian Agrarian Society from the Emancipation of the Serfs (1848) to the Re-privatization of the Land (1998)*. Translated by Tünde Bodnár. Boulder, CO: East European Monographs, 1998.

Gyáni, Gábor. "'Civil társadalom' kontra liberális állam a XIX. század végén." *Századvég*, no. 1 (1991): 145–56.

———, ed. *Magyarország társadalomtörténete, 1920–1944: szöveggyűjtemény*. 2d ed. Budapest: Nemzeti Tankönyvkiadó, 2000.

———, and János M. Rainer, eds. *Ezerkilencszázötvenhat az újabb történeti irodalomban: tanulmányok*. Budapest: 1956-os Intézet, 2007.

Gyarmati, György, ed. *Államvédelem a Rákosi-korszakban: tanulmányok és dokumentumok a politikai rendőrség második világháború utáni tevékenységéről*. Budapest: Történeti Hivatal, 2000.

Gyekiczky, Tamás. *A munkafegyelem jogi szabályozásának társadalmi háttere az 1952-es év Magyarországon*. Budapest: Művelődési Minisztérium Marxizmus-Leninizmus Oktatási Főosztálya, Budapest, 1986.

György, Péter. *Néma hagyomány: kollektív felejtés és a kései múltértelmezés 1956 1989-ben*. Budapest: Magvető, 2000.

Gyüszi, László. *Tatabánya 1956*. Tatabánya: A Kultsár István Társadalomtudományi és Kiadói Alapítvány, 1994.

Habuda, Miklós. "A Magyar Dolgozók Pártja munkáspolitikájának néhány kérdése a Központi Vezetőség 1953. júniusi határozata után." *Párttörténeti Közlemények* 26, no. 1 (1980): 23–38.

Hagen, Manfred. *DDR – Juni '53: Die erste Volkserhebung im Stalinismus*. Stuttgart: Franz Steiner Verlag, 1992.

Hajdu, Tibor. *Az 1918-as magyarországi polgári demokratikus forradalom*. Budapest: Kossuth Könyvkiadó, 1968.

———. *A Magyarországi Tanácsköztársaság*. Budapest: Kossuth Könyvkiadó, 1969.

Hanák, Péter, and Katalin Hanák. *A Magyar Pamutipar története, 1867–1962*. Budapest: A PNYV, Magyar Pamutipar 1 sz. Gyáregysége, 1964.

Hanebrink, Paul A. *In Defense of Christian Hungary: Religion, Nationalism, and Antisemitism in Hungary, 1890–1944*. Ithaca, NY: Cornell University Press, 2006.

Hankiss, Elemér. *East European Alternatives*. Oxford: Clarendon Press, 1990.

Hegedüs, András B., Péter Kende, György Litván, and János M. Rainer, eds. *1956 kézikönyve: megtorlás és emlékezés*. Budapest: 1956-os Intézet, 1996.

Herf, Jeffrey. *Reactionary Modernism: Technology, Culture, and Politics in Weimar and the Third Reich*. Cambridge: Cambridge University Press, 1984.

Hoffman, John D. *Beyond the State: An Introductory Critique.* Cambridge and Oxford: Polity Press, 1995.

Horváth, Miklós. *1956 hadikrónikája.* Budapest: Akadémiai Kiadó, 2003.

Horváth, Sándor. "Kollektív erőszak és városi térhasználat 1956-ban." *Múltunk* 51, no. 4 (2006): 268–89.

———. "A Központi Munkástanács története." *Első század* 1, no. 1 (1998): 113–209.

———. "A lakás és a fürdő: a munkás- és szociálpolitika prototípusai az ötvenes években." *Múltunk* 52, no. 2 (2007): 31–49.

———, ed. *Mindennapok Rákosi és Kádár korában: új utak a szocialista korszak kutatásában.* Budapest: Nyitott Könyvműhely, 2008.

Hübner, Peter. *Konsens, Konflikt und Kompromiß: Soziale Arbeiterinteressen und Sozialpolitik in der SBZ/DDR, 1945–1971.* Berlin: Akademie Verlag, 1995.

———, Christoph Kleßmann, and Klau Tenfelde, eds. *Arbeiter im Staatsozialismus: Ideologischer Anspruch und soziale Wirklichkeit.* Cologne: Weimar; Vienna: Böhlau Verlag, 2005.

Jakab, Sándor. *A magyar szakszervezeti mozgalom, 1944–1950: fordulópontok a szakszervezeti mozgalomban.* Budapest: Kossuth Könykiadó, 1985.

Kádár, Zsuzsanna. "A magyarországi szociáldemokrata perek története." *Múltunk* 41, no. 2 (1996): 3–49.

Kakuk, Tamás. "Tábori történetek. Tatabányaiak a szovjet munkatáborokban." *Komárom-Esztergom Múzeumok Közleményei,* no. 4 (1991): 139–46.

Káli, Csaba, ed. *Zalai történeti tanulmányok.* Zalaegerszeg: Zala Megyei Levéltár, 1997.

Kenez, Peter. *Hungary from the Nazis to the Soviets: The Establishment of the Communist Regime in Hungary, 1944–1948.* Cambridge: Cambridge University Press, 2006.

Kenney, Padraic. *Rebuilding Poland: Workers and Communists, 1945–1950.* Ithaca, NY: Cornell University Press, 1997.

Kiss, József, ed. *"A párt foglya voltam" Demény Pál élete.* Budapest: Medvetánc, 1988.

———. *Vázlat csepel társadalomtörténetéhez, 1919–1945.* Budapest: Művelődési Minisztérium Marxizmus-Leninizmus Oktatási Főosztálya, 1984.

Kopstein, Jeffrey. *The Politics of Economic Decline in East Germany, 1945–1989.* Chapel Hill: University of North Carolina Press, 1997.

Korom, Mihály. *Magyarország ideiglenes nemzeti kormánya és a fegyverszünet (1944–1945).* Budapest: Akadémiai Kiadó, 1981.

Kovács, Attila. *Földreform és kolonizáció a Lendva-vidéken a két világháború között.* Lendva: Magyar Nemzetiségi Művelődési Intézet, 2004.

Kövér, György. *Iparosodás agrárországban: Magyarország gazdaságtörténete, 1848–1914.* Budapest: Gondolat, 1982.

Kovrig, Bennett. *Communism in Hungary: From Kun to Kádár.* Stanford, CA: Hoover Institution Press, 1979.

Kubinyi, András, et al. *Csepel története.* Budapest: A Csepel Vas- és Fémművek pártbizottsága, 1965.

Lackó, Miklós. "Gépgyári munkások az 1930-as években." *Századok* 123, no. 1–2 (1989): 3–44.

———. *Ipari munkásságunk összetételének alakulása, 1867–1949.* Budapest: Kossuth Könyvkiadó, 1961.

——. *Nyilasok, nemzetiszocialisták, 1935–1944*. Budapest: Kossuth Könyvkiadó, 1966.

——, ed. *Tanulmányok a magyar népi demokrácia to̊rténetéből*. Budapest: Magyar Tudományos Akadémia Történettudományi Intézet, 1955.

——, and Bálint Szabó, eds. *Húsz év: tanulmányok a szocialista Magyarország történetéből*. Budapest: Kossuth Könyvkiadó, 1964.

Lampland, Martha. *The Object of Labor: Commodification in Socialist Hungary*. Chicago: University of Chicago Press, 1995.

Lengyel, György, ed. *Hungarian Economy and Society during World War II*. Translated by Judit Pokoly. Boulder, CO: East European Monographs, 1993.

Lilly, Carol S. *Power and Persuasion: Ideology and Rhetoric in Communist Yugoslavia, 1944–1953*. Boulder, CO: Westview Press, 2001.

Litván, György, et al. *The Hungarian Revolution of 1956: Reform, Revolt and Repression 1953–1963*. London: Longman, 1996.

Lomax, Bill. *Hungary 1956*. London: Allison & Busby, 1976.

Macartney, C. A. *October Fifteenth: A History of Modern Hungary, 1929–1945*. 2 vols. 2d ed. Edinburgh: Edinburgh University Press, 1961.

Maheu, Louis, ed. *Social Movements and Social Classes*. London: Sage Publications, 1995.

Mann, Michael. *States, War and Capitalism: Studies in Political Sociology*. Oxford: Basil Blackwell, 1988.

Mark, James. "Remembering Rape: Divided Social Memory and the Red Army in Hungary, 1944–1945." *Past and Present* 188 (2005): 133–61.

McCauley, Martin, ed. *Communist Power in Europe, 1944–1949*. London and Basingstoke, England: Macmillan, in association with the School of Slavonic and East European Studies, 1977.

McDermott, Kevin, and Matthew Stibbe, eds. *Revolution and Resistance in Eastern Europe: Challenges to Communist Rule*. Oxford: Berg Publishers, 2006.

Merey, Klára T. *Dél-Dunántúl iparának története a kapitalizmus idején*. Budapest: Akadémiai Kiadó, 1985.

Mevius, Martin. *Agents of Moscow: The Hungarian Communist Party and the Origins of Socialist Patriotism, 1941–1953*. Oxford: Clarendon Press, 2005.

Migdal, Joel S., Atul Kohli, and Vivienne Shue, eds. *State Power and Social Forces: Domination and Transformation in the Third World*. Cambridge: Cambridge University Press, 1994.

Miklós, Tamás, ed. *Magyar gazdaság és szociológia a 80-as években*. Budapest: Medvetánc, 1988.

Molnár, János, Sándor Orbán, and Károly Urbán. *Tanulmányok a magyar népi demokrácia negyven évéről*. Budapest: Kossuth Könyvkiadó, 1985.

Murber, Ibolya, and Zoltán Fónagy, eds. *Die Ungarische Revolution und Österreich 1956*. Vienna: Czernin Verlag, 2006.

Naimark, Norman. *The Russians in Germany: A History of the Soviet Zone of Occupation, 1945–1949*. Cambridge, MA: Harvard University Press, 1997.

Okváth, Imre, ed. *Katonai perek a kommunista diktatúra időszakában, 1945–1958: tanulmányok a fegyveres testületek tagjai elleni megtorlásokról a hidegháború kezdeti időszakában*. Budapest: Történeti Hivatal, 2001.

Orbán, Sándor. *Két agrárforradalom Magyarországon: demokratikus és szocialista agrárátalakulás 1945–1961.* Budapest: Akadémiai Kiadó, 1972.

Ormos, Mária. *A gazdasági világválság magyar visszahangja.* Budapest: Eötvös Kiadó – PolgART Könyvkiadó, 2004.

———, et al. *Törvénytelen szocializmus: a tényfeltáró bizottság jelentése.* Budapest: Zrinyi Kiadó - Új Magyarország, 1991.

Őrszigethy, Erzsébet. *Asszonyok férfisorban.* Budapest: Szépirodalmi Könyvkiadó, 1986.

Paksy, Zoltán, ed. *Az antiszemitzmus alakváltozatai: tanulmányok.* Zalaegerszeg: Zala Megyei Levéltár, 2005.

Palasik, Mária. "A gyömrői gyilkosságok és következményeik, 1945–1946." *Válóság* 4 (1995): 58–67.

———. *A jogállamiság megteremtésének kísérlete és kudarca Magyarországon, 1944–1949.* Budapest: Napvilág Kiadó, 2000.

Paxton, Robert O. *The Anatomy of Fascism.* London: Penguin Books, 2004.

Pelle, János. *A gyűlölet vetése: a zsidótörvények és a magyar közvélemény, 1938–1944.* Budapest: Európa Könyvkiadó, 2001.

Pető, Iván, and Sándor Szakács. *A hazai gazdaság négy évtizedének története, 1945–1985. I. Az újjáépítés és a tervutasításos irányítás időszaka.* Budapest: Közgazdasági és Jogi Könyvkiadó, 1985.

Pittaway, Mark, "The Education of Dissent: The Reception of the Voice of Free Hungary, 1951–1956." *Cold War History* 4, no. 1 (2003): 97–116.

———. "Industrial Workers, Socialist Industrialization and the State, 1948–1958." PhD thesis, University of Liverpool, 1998.

———. "The Politics of Legitimacy and Hungary's Postwar Transition." *Contemporary European History* 13, no. 4 (2004): 453–75.

———. "The Reproduction of Hierarchy: Skill, Working-Class Culture and the State in Early Socialist Hungary." *Journal of Modern History* 74, no. 4 (2002): 737–69.

———. "The Social Limits of State Control: Time, the Industrial Wage Relation and Social Identity in Stalinist Hungary, 1948–1953." *Journal of Historical Sociology* 12, no. 3 (1999): 271–301.

———. "Workers, Industrial Conflict and the State in Socialist Hungary, 1948–1989." Unpublished manuscript, 2003.

Port, Andrew I. *Conflict and Stability in the German Democratic Republic.* Cambridge: Cambridge University Press, 2007.

Postone, Moishe. *Time, Labor, and Social Domination: A Reinterpretation of Marx's Critical Theory.* Cambridge: Cambridge University Press, 2003.

Pritchard, Gareth. *The Making of the GDR 1945–53: From Antifascism to Stalinism.* Manchester: Manchester University Press, 2000.

Rainer, János M. *Az iró helye: viták a Magyar irodalmi sajtóban, 1953–1956.* Budapest: Magvető Kiadó, 1990.

———. *Nagy Imre: politikai életrajz; első kötet 1896–1953.* Budapest: 1956-os Intézet, 1996.

———. *Nagy Imre: politikai életrajz; második kötet 1953–1958.* Budapest: 1956-os Intézet, 1999.

Ravasz, Éva. *Gál István, 1917–1979: egy bányaigazgató portréja.* Tatabánya: Tatabányai Bányász Hagyományokért Alapítvány, 2004.

Reid, Susan E., and David Crowley, eds. *Style and Socialism: Modernity and Material Culture in Post-War Eastern Europe.* Oxford: Berg, 2000.

Réti, László R. *A Rimamurány-Salgótarjáni Vasmű Részvénytársaság története, 1881–1919.* Budapest: Akadémiai Kiadó, 1977.

Rézler, Gyula. *A magyar nagyipari munkásság kialakulása, 1867–1914.* Budapest: Rekord Könyvkiadó, 1938.

Roman, Eric. *Hungary and the Victor Powers, 1945–1950.* Basingstoke, England, and London: Macmillan, 1996.

Róna-Tas, Ákos. *The Great Surprise of the Small Transformation: The Demise of Communism and the Rise of the Private Sector in Hungary.* Ann Arbor: University of Michigan Press, 1997.

Sajti, Enikő A. *Impériumváltások, revízió, kisebbség: magyarok a délvidéken, 1918–1947.* Budapest: Napvilág Kiadó, 2004.

Sallai, János. *Az államhatárok.* Budapest: Press Publica, 2004.

Sapir, Jacques. *Logik der sowjetischen Ökonomie oder die permanente Kriegswirtschaft.* Münster: Lit Verlag, 1993.

Schlett, István. *A szociáldemokrácia és a magyar társadalom 1914-ig.* Budapest: Gondolat Kiadó, 1982.

Sebők, János. *A Horthy-mítosz és a holokauszt.* Budapest: privately published, 2004.

Seger, Martin, and Pál Beluszky, eds. *Bruchlinie Eiserner Vorhang: Regionalentwicklung im österreich-ungarischen Grenzraum (Südburgenland/Oststeiermark-Westungarn).* Vienna, Cologne, and Graz: Böhlau Verlag, 1993.

Sewell, William H., Jr. *Logics of History: Social Theory and Social Transformation.* Chicago: University of Chicago Press, 2005.

Sipos, Péter. *Legális és illegális munkásmozgalom (1919–1944).* Budapest: Gondolat, 1988.

Smula, Johann. "The Party and the Proletariat: Škoda, 1948–53." *Cold War History* 6, no. 2 (2006): 153–75.

Somorjai, József. "A földosztás története Komárom-Esztergom vármegyében I." *Komárom-Esztergom Múzeumok Közleményei,* no. 4 (1991): 123–38.

Sprinker, Michael, ed. *Ghostly Demarcations: A Symposium on Derrida's Specters of Marx.* London: Verso, 2008.

Srágli, Lajos. "Adatok a MAORT üzemi bizottságai működésének történetéhez (1945–1949)." In *Évkönyv 1986,* 65–78. Zalaegerszeg: Kiadja az MSzMP Zala Megyei Bizottsága, Oktatási Igazgatósága, 1986.

———. "A Dunántúli Olajbányászat Hároméves Terve (Adatok a MAORT történetéhez, 1947–1949)." *Zalai Gyűjteménye,* no. 25 (1986): 295–307.

———. "A Magyarországi Szénhidrogénbányászat első ötéves tervéhez – adatok a zalai olajbányászatról, 1950–1954." *Zalai Gyűjteménye,* no. 26 (1987): 223–36.

———. *A MAORT: olaj – gazdaság – politika.* Budapest: Útmutató Kiadó, 1998.

———. "A MAORT-per és háttere." *Üzemtörténeti Értesítő* 9, no. 9 (1990): 23–38.

———. *Munkások a "fekete arany" birodalmában: A munkásság és anyagi-szociális helyzete a magyarországi olajiparban (a kezdetektől az államosításig).* Zalaegerszeg: Magyar Olajipari Múzeum – MOL Bányász Szakszervezet, 2004.

Standeisky, Éva. *Az irók és a hatalom, 1956–1963.* Budapest: 1956-os Intézet, 1996.

——, Gyula Kozák, Gábor Pataki, and János Rainer, eds. *A fordulat évei: politika –
képzőművészet – építészet.* Budapest: 1956-os Intézet, 1998.

Surguta, László, ed. *A Tungsram Rt. története, 1896–1945.* Budapest: Tungsram Rt. Gyártörténeti Bizottsága, 1987.

Swain, Nigel. *Hungary: The Rise and Fall of Feasible Socialism.* London: Verso, 1992.

Szabó, Miklós M. *A Magyarországi felszabadító hadműveletek, 1944–1945.* Budapest: Kossuth Könyvkiadó, 1985.

Szakács, Sándor, and Tibor Zinner. *A háború "megváltozott természete": adatok és
adalékok, tények és összefüggések – 1944–1948.* Budapest: Batthyány Társaság, 1997.

Szakolczai, Attila. *Az 1956-os forradalom és szabadságharc.* Budapest: 1956-os Intézet, 2001.

——, ed. *A vidék forradalma 1956, II. kötet.* Budapest: 1956-os Intézet-Budapest Főváros
Levéltára, 2006.

Szántó, Ferenc. *A tizhetes tatabányai bányászsztrajk története. 1925 február 3 – április 4.*
Tatabánya: Tatabánya Városi Tanács – Tatabányai Szénbányák, 1985.

Szekeres, József. *A magyar bányamunkásság harcai (1933–1944).* Budapest: Akadémiai
Kiadó, Budapest, 1970.

Szenes, Iván. *A Kommunista Párt újjászervezése Magyarországon, 1956–1957.* Budapest:
Kossuth Könyvkiadó, 1976.

Szerencsés, Károly. *A kékcédulás hadművelet (választások Magyarországon 1947).* Budapest:
IKVA, 1993.

Szöllősi-Janze, Margit. *Die Pfeilkreuzlerbewegung in Ungarn: Historischer Kontext, Entwicklung und Herrschaft.* Munich: R. Oldenbourg Verlag, 1989.

Tóth, Ágnes. *Migrationen in Ungarn, 1945–1948. Vertreibung der Ungarndeutschen, Binnenwanderungen und Slowakisch-Ungarischer Bevölkerungsaustausch.* Translated by
Rita Fejér. Munich: R. Oldenbourg Verlag, 2001.

Tóth, András. "Civil társadalom és szakszervezetek." Kandídátusi értekezés, Budapest, 1994.

——. "Munkanélküliség és falusi polgárosodás." Unpublished manuscript, 1992.

Tóth, Sándor, and Lajos Srágli. *Lovászi.* Budapest: Száz Magyar Falu Könyvesháza, 2000.

Ungváry, Krisztián. *A magyar honvédség a második világháborúban.* Budapest: Osiris
Kiadó, 2004.

——. *Battle for Budapest: 100 Days in World War II.* Translated by Ladislaus Löb. London:
I. B. Tauris, 2005.

Valuch, Tibor, ed. *Hatalom és társadalom a XX századi magyar történelemben.* Budapest:
1956-os Intézet – Osiris Kiadó, 1995.

Varga, Lajos, et al., eds. *A magyar szociáldemokrácia kézikönyve.* Budapest: Napvilág
Kiadó, 1999.

Varga, Lajos Sz. *Szakszervezetek a diktatúrában: a Magyar Dolgozók Pártja és a szakszervezetek (1948–1953).* Pécs: Pannónia Könyvek, 1995.

Varga, László. *Az elhagyott töme: tanulmányok 1950–1956-ról.* Budapest: Cserépfalvi-Budapest Főváros Levéltára, 1994.

Varga, László A. *Rendi társadalom – polgári társadalom 1.* Salgótarján: Nógrád Megyei
Levéltár, 1987.

Varga, Zsuzsanna. "A falusi társadalom feszültséggócai az 1950-es évek közepén." *Múltunk* 51, no. 4 (2006): 223–39.

———. *Politika, paraszti érdekérvényesítés és szövetkezetek Magyarországon, 1956–1967.* Budapest: Napvilág Kiadó, 2001.

Vass, Henrik, ed. *Válság és megújulás: gazdaság, társadalom és politika Magyarországon; az MSzMP 25 éve.* Budapest: Kossuth Könyvkiadó, 1982.

Vinceller, Béla. *Sötet árny magyarhon felett: szálasi uralma (1944. október – 1945. május).* Budapest: Makkabi Kiadó, 2004.

Vonyó, József. *Gömbös Gyula és a jobboldali radikalizmus: tanulmányok.* Pécs: Pannónia Könyvek, 2001.

Závada, Pál. *Kulákprés: család- és falutörténeti szociográfia; Tótkomlós 1945–1956.* Budapest: Szépirodalmi-Széphalom Könyvkiadó, 1991.

Zeidler, Miklós. *A magyar irredenta kultusz a két vilaghaboru között.* Budapest: Teleki László Alapítvány, 2002.

Zielbauer, György. "Magyar polgári lakosok deportálása és hadifogsága (1945–1948)." *Történelmi Szemle* 34, no. 3–4 (1992): 270–91.

Zinner, Tibor, ed. *Rajk László és társai a népbíróság előtt 40 év távlatából.* Budapest: Magyar Eszperantó Szövetség, 1989.

# Index

absenteeism, 7, 162; causes of, 44–45, 198; by coal miners, 65, 162, 184; by oil workers, 50, 156; as protest of material conditions, 148; state cracking down on, 148, 162–63; to work smallholds, 43–45, 50, 135, 156, 172–73

accidents: in coal mines, 130, 163, 178, 182–83, 185; in oil fields, 97

Ács, István, 24–25, 75

Aczél, Tamás, 203

agrarian policies, 86; conciliatory, 176, 242, 269; effects of, 150–52; New Course's, 177, 179, 186, 190; relaxation of, 184, 186, 190, 222. *See also* collectivization

agricultural cooperatives, 138–39, 196; dissolution of, 187–88, 229; formation of, 176–77, 224; opposition to, 151, 229, 243; state investment in, 249–50; withdrawals from, 175–76

agricultural taxation, 81, 91, 94, 111, 139, 147, 150, 223

agriculture, 44, 118, 140, 181, 247; absenteeism to tend, 43, 135, 156, 158; compulsory deliveries of, 12; compulsory deliveries of produce from, 12, 79, 81, 94, 137, 139, 150, 152, 190, 223–24, 242; damage to, 8, 43; income from, 151–52, 181–82, 196, 242–43, 246; industry and, 50–51, 138, 243–44; landownership in Zala County, 95; in oil field communities, 20, 49–50, 79, 81, 243–44; recruitment of workers from, 149, 150; supplying cities with food, 137, 196; by women, 20, 64. *See also* agricultural cooperatives; collectivization; land reform

Alsógalla. *See* Tatabánya

aluminum smelter, in Tatabánya, 18, 40, 111–12, 179, 183

tensions in, 136, 239–40, 242–43; transformation of, 157–58; worker discontent
in, 67, 76, 143; workers leaving due to
housing conditions in, 106, 132, 152. *See
also* coal miners; coal mines
Tatabánya Workers' and Soldiers' Council,
221, 235–36, 242
taxes, 81, 91, 94, 111, 139, 147, 150, 190, 223
territorial revision, 9, 16, 46, 232
textile industry, 17, 76, 152–53; labor
competitions in, 103–4; as undesirable
work, 197–98, 255; work intensity in, 77,
123–26, 129. *See also* Magyar Pamutipar
cotton factory
Textile Workers' Union, 24, 75, 104
three-year plan (1947), 65, 80, 118, 123
Tildy, Zoltán, 25–26
Tito, Marshal, 203
trade unions, 9, 37, 38, 74, 88, 106–7, 120,
159, 233; coal miners', 108–9, 161; MKP
control over, 59, 96, 98; oil workers',
223, 248; workers' increased involvement in, 208–9
Trade Union Young Workers' and Apprentices' Movement (SzIT), 133
transportation, public, 19, 48–49, 233, 251;
bus drivers' role in revolution, 205, 218;
in Tatabánya, 164, 221
Treaty of Trianon, 16, 46
trials: Nagy's, 257; for participation in
revolution, 1–2, 232, 234; show, 11, 96,
176, 225, 260

Újpest, 32, 72, 196; Communists in, 31, 33;
demographics of, 17, 101; diversified
economy of, 17, 72, 194, 263; effects of
WWII in, 28, 31; elections in, 25, 53,
68–70; expansion of, 164–65; experiments with decentralization in, 207–9;
"final solution" for Jews in, 29–30; food
availability in, 71, 73, 165–66; industrial
hierarchies in, 148, 177; industry in,
16–17, 123, 166–69, 263; labor competitions in, 103–5, 119, 120–21; labor shortages in, 197–200; legitimacy of Kádár
government in, 234, 250; low-priority
light industry in, 169–70; material

conditions in, 71, 98, 173; memorial to
Soviet soldier in, 25–26; MKP in, 56,
74–75, 98; norm revisions in, 100, 105–6,
136, 193; obstacles to production in, 166,
169; politics in, 28, 39, 56, 100, 205–6,
209, 251; poor housing in, 73–74, 102;
poor quality products from factories,
194–95; protests in, 100, 105–6, 193, 250;
revolution in, 205–7, 209–12, 250–51;
shoe production in, 115–16; socialist
regime and, 89, 99, 120, 201, 214, 255–56;
Stalin shifts in, 124–26; strikes in, 212,
251–52; workers' anger in, 36–37, 71–72,
98, 143. *See also* industrial workers;
industry
Újpest Leather Factory, 165
Újpest Revolutionary Committee, 1–2, 213,
231, 250
Újpest Shoe Factory, 119–20
Újpest Workers' Council, 251
unemployment, 74, 88, 118, 231; in coal mining communities, 64; levels of, 57, 102;
in southern Zala, 79–80, 90–91
United Incandescent Lamp and Electrical
Company, 17, 29; anti-Communist
stance by workers of, 101; factory
party officials in, 211–12; hierarchies
at, 172, 199–200; labor competitions
at, 103–5; MKP *vs.* MSzDP in, 70–71,
74; MSzDP strength in, 98, 100; poor
quality products from, 194–95, 200; as
preferred employer, 168, 197; production norms at, 123, 128, 193; revolution
and, 206, 209–10, 210–11, 231, 250;
Soviets taking plant for reparations, 35;
Stakhanovites at, 121–22, 129–30; Stalin
shifts in, 124–25; strikes at, 37, 210–11;
training for skilled positions in, 170–71;
wages at, 31, 127, 254; workers' council
at, 212–13, 251–52; workplace culture at,
77, 120–21
urban workers. *See* industrial workers

Varga, Barnabás, 107, 133–34, 265
Varga, János, 133
Varró, János, 165
Vas, Zoltán, 142
Vienna, 18